Modern American Prose

Fifteen Writers

Modern American Prose

Second Edition

Fifteen Writers

John Clifford
University of North Carolina, Wilmington

Robert DiYanni
Pace University, Pleasantville

McGraw-Hill Publishing Company

New York St. Louis San Francisco Auckland Bogotá
Caracas Hamburg Lisbon London Madrid Mexico
Milan Montreal New Delhi Oklahoma City Paris San Juan
São Paulo Singapore Sydney Tokyo Toronto

Second Edition

98765

MODERN AMERICAN PROSE

Copyright © 1987, 1983 by McGraw-Hill, Inc.

Library of Congress Cataloging-in-Publication Data

Modern American prose.

   1. College readers. 2. English language—Rhetoric. 3. American prose
literature—20th century. I. Clifford, John. II. DiYanni, Robert.
PE1417.M57 1986   808'.0427   86–6590
ISBN 07–554789-9

Copyrights and acknowledgments appear on pages 557–565.

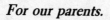

For our parents.

Preface

Modern American Prose: Fifteen Writers is based upon our conviction that reading and writing are reciprocal acts that should be integrated rather than separated. Because reading and writing stimulate and reinforce one another, we believe that the best way to go about either is to ally it with the other. Associated with this belief in the reciprocity of reading and writing is another: that in addition to their own writing, students can profit most as readers and writers from reading essays that are accessible, engaging, thought-provoking, and, above all, well crafted. In saying this we do not mean to deny that students learn to write primarily by writing, but rather to suggest that in learning to read and respond critically to their own writing and to the writing of others—both amateurs and professionals alike—students mature as writers themselves.

The essayists whose works we anthologize are among the best of contemporary American writers. Taken together they have produced a diversified and substantial body of outstanding nonfictional prose. Ranging widely in subject, style, structure, and tone, their prose includes autobiographical and polemical essays, observations and speculations, reminiscences and sketches, meditations and expostulations, celebrations and attacks. Overall, our selections from their works offer a balance of the flamboyant and innovative with the restrained and classically lucid.

This second edition of *Modern American Prose* follows the principles that guided the first: to select as models for student writing contemporary American essays from among our best prose stylists; to offer multiple selections from the work of each writer. The changes we have made in this edition increase the range and scope of the text. While we have dropped one writer, Edward Hoagland, we have added four others —Stephen Jay Gould, Richard Selzer, Barbara Tuchman, and Alice Walker—so that *Modern American Prose* now includes the work of fifteen writers. In addition, thirty-one essays are new to this edition while forty-four have been retained from the first edition.

Our aim in choosing selections for *Modern American Prose* has been to collect between the covers of one book some of the most distinctive nonfiction of the last forty years, written by American writers who have something to say and know how to say it powerfully. It has been our experience that nonfictional prose in general and the essay in particular have been underrated as literature. Traditionally accorded secondary status behind the major genres of fiction, poetry, and drama, the essay has consistently been relegated to a literary limbo. But this has recently begun to change. Nonfictional prose has benefited from the revitalization of studies in rhetoric and composition as well as from the upsurge of scholarly work in linguistics and style. Also contributing to the belated recognition of the literary stature of nonfictional prose has been the rise of the new journalism. New journalistic experiments with the novel-as-history and with the nonfiction novel along with a general elevation in the significance of brute fact and sharply observed details of social and personal history have all contributed to the acceptability of the essay as a flexible instrument for recording reality and expressing the self.

By restricting ourselves to fifteen writers, we have been able to include at least four essays by each. We have done this because we believe students can come closer to an understanding of an author's ideas, style, and tone by encountering more than one example of his or her work. Within the selections from a particular writer we have tried to offer variety of subject, purpose, tone, and length of essay. And we have included, for the most part, either complete essays, complete chapters, or self-contained sections of books. In addition, we have tried to show each writer working in the four rhetorical modes: narration, description, exposition, and argumentation. Sometimes these modes are kept fairly pure. Far more often, however, they are mixed in complex and interesting ways, as in Joan Didion's essay "On Going Home," which is reprinted along with an extended commentary in the Introduction.

To help students simultaneously become more critical readers and more confident writers, we have provided a thorough discussion of how to read and respond to essays (the Introduction). In addition, following each essay selection is an extensive set of questions designed to guide students through a careful reading—or rereading—of the pieces, and to assist them in analyzing their style, structure, and meaning. The group of questions headed "Ideas" is meant to serve as a set of probes, a series of ways into the author's main point or central idea. The questions on "Organization," "Sentences," and "Words" invite students to look closely at the writer's craft. Our "Suggestions for Writing" invite students to learn to write by writing, with the essayists as exemplars and fellow writers. Some of these writing suggestions ask for short, informal opinions, often as reactions to an author's ideas. Other assignments ask for more considered assessments of style, form, and meaning. Still others ask students to imitate effective patterns of language and form, in phrase, sentence, paragraph, essay. For a few essays we have avoided categorizing our questions because we wanted to focus less on aspects of style than on what the writers have to say about writing as craft and vocation.

Beyond these aids to reading and writing we have written, for each writer, a headnote that subordinates biographical and bibliographical information to focus on how and why each writes. In these introductory headnotes we have explored different facets of the writer's world: his or her writing habits, reasons for writing, methods of composition, conceptions of intention, purpose, and design. And in each we have commented briefly on the essays in that section.

Throughout *Modern American Prose* our intent has been to help students read, understand, and imitate good writing in the belief that, by providing students with guided practice in reading and writing, we will help them increase both their competence and their confidence. Through repeated acts of attention to their own writing and to the writing of others, we expect students to acquire a sense of the original meaning of "essay": a foray into thought, an attempt to discover an idea, work out its implications, and share it with others. And we hope further that our students will come to see the essay as a way of both enriching their experience and discovering effective ways to communicate it.

John Clifford
Robert DiYanni

Editors' Acknowledgments

For assistance of varying kinds at different stages of our work we would like to thank our friends and colleagues who inspired, criticized, and sustained by listening carefully and giving good advice. Appreciation and thanks to Linnea Aycock, Cynthia Bathurst, Lil Brannon, Janis Forman, Dennis Jarrett, Kathleen Kelly, Robert Lyons, Bill Naufftus, Steve Schmidt, Sally Sullivan, Karen Thomas, Myron Tuman, and Dick Veit. Special appreciation to Richard Garretson and Christine Pellicano, who believed in the book early on and gave support in abundance. Thanks also to our reviewers Victoria Casana, Fred Crews, Richard Hootman, Paula Johnson, Dick Larson, and Don McQuade.

We have been fortunate in working with a knowledgeable and exacting professional staff. We would like to thank especially Fred Burns, David Follmer, Steve Pensinger, June Smith, and Cynthia Ward, and also Carol Barnes and Pat Kolonosky, both of Kansas State University; Teresa M. Brown, University of Florida; Pat Hoy, United States Military Academy; Robert Lorenzi, Camden County College; Edward McCarthy, Harrisburg Area Community College; Robert G. Noreen, California State University at Northridge; David Schaafsma, Grand Valley State College; and Robert Seufert, MacMurray College.

Finally, we would like to thank our wives, Joan and Mary, who helped us in less academic but no less enduring ways.

Contents

Thematic Table of Contents

History and Politics

Science and Technology

Race, Culture, and Society

The Natural World

Work And Play

Relationships

Personal Values

Writing And Language

Ignorance And Insight

Rhetorical Table of Contents

Description

Narration

Modern American Prose

Fifteen Writers

ONE

Introduction

1: READING ESSAYS

Common sense can often lead us astray. Most readers, for example, assume that the meaning of a story or essay is there, in the text. But that is only partially true. A writer certainly does have a theme in mind as he or she composes an essay, but equally important is what a competent reader brings to the work. The author's intention is only one of the three important ingredients in literary nonfiction. In a complete reading, the writer, the reader, and the text must all play their parts.

Critical reading, therefore, is a creative process, requiring active minds. The black marks on the white page have potential meaning, but they remain inert until readers bring the words to life in the reading process. That's not an exaggeration or a metaphor. Critical reading is not simply decoding from printed symbol to sound to meaning. It is, rather, an interaction or a transaction. What a particular reader gets from the page is a blend of that reader's experiences, ideas, and attitudes and the experiences, ideas, and attitudes the writer put in the text. Readers do not simply discover what is already there, like solving a puzzle. Instead, engaged readers use their familiarity with the conventions of writing as tools to make meaning. As readers, our previous experiences in the world, our present preoccupations and biases, our familiarity with the conventions of nonfiction, our knowledge of vocabulary, syntax, and organization join with a writer's intention at the crossroads of meaning. Although the road has already been paved by the writer, only an active reader can give the journey significance.

An active response to a written text has long been considered an important dimension of the reading of literary texts, especially fictional ones. And although most college students think of essays as merely the packages that information comes in, we want to suggest that nonfiction texts, especially essays, require a similar kind of attentiveness and an equal degree of critical response. Even when the author's primary pur-

3

pose is to convey information, as it is in many essays, the reader's contribution is also crucial. Reading involves two minds—the mind of the writer and the mind of the reader. And even though the writer isn't there to respond to your questions and criticisms or to your expressions of approval and disapproval, a real conversation can occur, as long as you respond honestly and fully.

Although some writing—the scientific prose in your biology text, for example—does try to minimize creative contributions, it still demands your participation. Whereas literature asks that you be an active reader, technical prose tries to keep you passively receptive to its purely informational or directional goal. Some scientific writers strive to be objective and detached through techniques such as omitting the use of "I," letting the subject of the sentence receive the action (via verbs in the passive voice), avoiding highly connotative words, and appealing primarily to logic. In technical writing, snappy, personal anecdotes, wide swings of feeling, and literary language are inappropriate.

Even so, if your background is inadequate on a particular subject, you will not make much sense of sophisticated scientific prose, regardless of how clearly and objectively it is written. Try reading a bridge or chess column without any practical experiences of those games: you will know the words, but because you do not bring enough background with you, you will not be able to read for meaning. If you can't bring the relevant knowledge to the reading, the content will be opaque. Of course, this need for background information is not limited just to reading. We all know people who think quality rock bands like Bruce Springsteen and the E Street Band and Pink Floyd all sound alike—noisy; while others think Bach, Mozart, and Beethoven all sound alike—classical. They can't "read" or hear the differences because they don't have the necessary knowledge and experience of the kind of music in question. The result is a blurring of distinctions, an oversimplifying and stereotyping of complex, individual forms of expression. Discrimination comes with experience. You rarely find what you don't even know exists: you see more when you know what to look for.

Although some of the essays in this collection deal with technical matters, they cannot be considered scientific writing. This may sound odd, but it isn't. The content of the essays is not the deciding factor. More telling is the way the ideas are presented. In distinguishing literary from scientific prose, an author's style, attitude, purpose, and organizational pattern are all more important than the essay's content, its facts. Lewis Thomas, for example, writes about DNA, symbiants, rhizobial bacteria, and death, with emotion and grace, in the most natural language. Perhaps Thomas's audience is crucial. He is not writing to fellow scientists, reporting on his latest research; he is writing to a much wider lay audience (of which you are a part). At times he tries to explain his deepest feelings about life and death, cells and computers; at times he tries to change your mind about the nature of man, hoping to share with you his awe at the complexity and wonder of our world. And he does all this with imagination and style. His aim is not exclusively to tell you particular factual information; he wants instead to engage your intellect and imagination; he wants you to bring your own experiences to his essay so that reader and writer are both present, ready for an active conversation, an intellectual transaction. All the writers in this book are offering an invitation to enter this kind of creative dialog, one that can lead to a literary experience. Because this conversation between reader and writer adds such an energizing dimension to the life of the mind, it is central to a vigorous university education.

In fact, many of the essays in this book *are* literature, and should be read as such. Although students generally know that poems, drama, and fiction are literature, they often assume that nonfiction is not. They figure that since literature involves the imaginative and the fanciful, nonfiction, especially essays, do not qualify as serious literature. This attitude, we believe, denies status to undeniably great works of imagination and literary art—works like Boswell's *Life of Samuel Johnson,* Gibbon's *Decline and Fall of the Roman Empire,* essays such as Swift's "A Modest Proposal" and Lamb's "A Dissertation on Roast Pig." Because these works don't fall under the canonized literary categories of poetry, drama, or fiction, they are accorded an inferior place as literary or belletristic works, but not literature.

Without pursuing the complex issue of just how "literature" ought to be defined, we want to suggest that works of nonfiction such as the essays included in this collection should be accorded the same status, granted the same respect, and read with the same care as a poem by Robert Frost or a story by Ernest Hemingway. Like a Frost poem or a Hemingway story, many of the essays in this volume will reward repeated readings. They invite and gratify a considered and deliberate reading primarily because the authors gave as much attention to diction, voice, image, form, and theme as they gave to information.

The distinction between fiction and nonfiction raises one other problem: the puzzle of what is real, of what a fact is. Norman Mailer's book *The Executioner's Song* and some of his earlier work, including

Miami and the Siege of Chicago and *The Armies of the Night,* are based on fact, on historical events, on real people. But they are also novelistic in technique. His books oscillate uneasily between fact and fiction, history and novel, objective reality and subjective response. As a result, there is considerable confusion about how to read them and what to label them.

The traditional division between factual and fictional discourse creates more problems than it solves. The notion that nonfiction mirrors reality while literature creates its own reality is oversimplified. Joan Didion has a relevant comment in her essay "On Keeping a Notebook": "Not only have I always had trouble distinguishing what happened and what merely might have happened, but I remain unconvinced that the distinction, for my purposes, matters." The essays in this anthology use language in such a way that they help readers give birth to a new creation. They are nonfiction, but they are also literature.

And literature, as we have said, demands more than your attention: it demands your active participation as well. Without you, these essays are merely texts; with your imaginative participation they become something more: literary experiences. And to do your part you don't have to be a highly skilled reader, knowledgeable about esoteric writing techniques and about a wide range of topics. Yet, there is no denying that these essays were written to be read by good readers. We expect that you are one of these good readers, or that in working through the essays, you will become one.

II: READING TECHNIQUES

To emphasize our point that literature requires active readers, we said that scientific writing tries to discourage imagination, to make the words point to specific objects in the world. That is true, in a way. It would be better, however, to think of prose as a continuum with imaginative literature on one end and pure scientific discourse on the other. The essays in this book would lie somewhere in between. Strangely enough, much will depend on your attitude and on the special reading you give each essay. One thing to observe as you read essays is how much the language differs from conventional practice. Poetry, for example, consciously calls attention to its language. Technical language, on the other hand, tries for anonymity, with attention focused only on the message. When you are trying to read instructions for defusing a bomb, for example, you want the language to be as clear as a pane of glass. Essays generally fall between the density and resonance of poetry and the clarity and directness of a set of directions, often containing something of each.

To get the most out of reading the nonfiction in this book, then, you will need to read each piece more than once. You will want to focus primarily on ideas the first time and then on organization and style, keeping in mind, however, that content and form are ultimately inseparable.

There are, nonetheless, different ways to read. You can, if you want, read the most lyrical of poems for information; or you can read a physics text for its syntax and structure. Here, we are asking for a synthesis, for a balanced reading, attending first to ideas, then to structure and syntax. To get a full reading, you will be called on to use your imagination and your analytical ability, or in the current formulation, to integrate the right and left sides of your brain, to blend intuition with logic.

Reading literature is not a one-shot event; it is a process that involves repetition and reflection. Meaning emerges out of the fog only after you read, reflect, reread, and reflect again. As with writing, few people get it right the first time, or even the second. If, as Thoreau noted, books should be read with the same care and deliberation with which they were written, then your investment of time in repeated readings of these essays will be essential for real understanding. This kind of investment of time and effort will also be a necessary first step toward literary competence and confidence. To gain that competence and to acquire that confidence, we suggest the following reading sequence:

1. Read the essay through in one sitting. When you finish, jot down some notes indicating what the piece was about, if only in a literal sense. This simple notemaking about the essay's subject and ideas should help you clarify what the piece is about. Be sure to notice your personal reactions, your subjective responses, to the events and the ideas of the essay. These seemingly random associations are part of the unique baggage each of us brings to reading. In reading an essay about death, for example, we can't ignore our preconceptions about suicide, nor can we forget our biases against disco when reading an article about popular music. Meaning exists, Kenneth Burke suggests, in the "margin of overlap between the writer's experience and the reader's." Don't try to deny that you are a person whose experiences and ideas are relevant. Since the writer of the essay certainly didn't, neither should you.

The easiest way to bring these valuable associations to the surface is to write quickly for a few minutes, sketching your immediate feelings and thoughts in any order that occurs to you. Concentrate on getting down an honest, detailed response: if you were bored or confused, say so. But try to locate the source of the boredom or confusion. Finally, write one or two sentences about your impression of the author's point in this piece, that is, the theme or generalization that might cover or bind together most of the information the essay presents. Remember: depending on your experiences and attitudes, or even on your present mood, you will probably have different notions about what this general statement might be, especially after one reading.

2. Do your second reading, remembering that it will probably be different from the first: no two readings can be the same, especially since you will be integrating the memory of the first reading experience with this more informed second reading. This is the excitement and surprise of reading literary exposition: each encounter is unique, each reading unfolds new insights and new possibilities. As you read, try to fill in the gaps, to creatively participate in the literary experience. After this reading, jot down your reaction. Has the writer's focus now become clearer to you? What minor points are developed?

This is also the time to begin seeing how the parts of the essay work together. A crucial question in this regard is the relation between the theme (or the purpose) and the material the author presents to support it. What is the relationship between the general and the specific, the abstract and the concrete? Another important consideration is whether the writer presents the main point in the introduction and then supports it in the body, or whether he or she builds up to the point, arranging facts, anecdotes, events, and arguments in such a way that the point is made forcefully in the conclusion. Ask yourself also about the major parts, and whether there are natural "blocks of discourse," that is, paragraphs that go together, that develop the same idea. Although it may sound strange to you, the purpose of taking an essay apart like this is to better understand how it was put together. An active reader first analyzes, then synthesizes.

3. At the end of your second reading, take note of the voice, the personality, you hear. It may be forceful and direct; it may be effacing and oblique. Sometimes you'll hear the same writer being alternately sarcastic and tender. Each time we write we need to decide anew what mask—or persona—will work best. Of course, the writer's ideas are important in determining tone, but equally crucial is how they are

stated. Read groups of sentences out loud, slowly. Try to see how close the writing is to the rhythms of speech. Some writers, like Didion and Thomas, will seem clear and natural; others, like Baldwin and Eiseley, will seem elaborate, formal, and complex. Try to explain to yourself why this is so.

4. You are now ready for the third and best reading of all, the one that should clarify your impressions of the author's theme, persona, and arguments. You will also be more aware of why you are responding to certain ideas and images. If you focus primarily on one thing, and another reader focuses on something else, it doesn't mean one of you is wrong. Perhaps you are both responding openly to the rich possibilities of literature. If in discussing your responses and in analyzing the craft of expository writing you find yourself differing from others in the class, you should look to the text to see if you can support your reading. If you think the text validates your minority view, it might be because your experiences, your attitudes, or your expectations differ from those of your classmates. Fine. Literary critics have been arguing for hundreds of years over Hamlet's madness and Macbeth's motives. As a dissenter, you are in the best of company. What is important is that you learn to engage intelligently in the process of analytical reading.

We will try to illustrate some ideas by looking at the following essay by Joan Didion. One editor of this book, John Clifford, then presents his response to the essay in order to illustrate one possible approach, one reading among many he might have chosen, depending on his audience and his purposes. A psychologist's first reaction would be quite different, as would that of a teenage reader from China, or an elderly woman from Italy. All readers are different simply because people are. That notion should give you confidence in responding. You shouldn't be looking for what the teacher wants or what critics see. Your ideas and experiences and your training as a reader will enable you to feel, think, and read with your own personal style. That's just as it should be in a university setting that encourages critical and speculative discussion.

Reading well, then, means reading on several levels. One teacher, Robert Scholes from Brown University, has a useful set of definitions about how to do this, how to give more dimension to your responses.

In *Reading*, suggests Professor Scholes, we decode and paraphrase, attempting a literal translation of the text. In the average college classroom there will be a rough agreement about what happens in most of the nonfiction in this text. There will be a general consensus, in such classrooms, about the subject of the essays and their general purpose. In *Interpretation* we move beyond "what's there" to what it means, to generalizations about society or human nature, to looking at events or details as standing for something else, something representative. In moving from reading to interpretation, there will be more differences of opinion, more individual responses. The more homogeneous the class, the more consensus. The more diverse the class, the less agreement about meaning. In *Criticism* we reach outside the text to the world. We take issue with the writer's ideas, his or her vision of right and wrong; we compare the social issues in the story or essay with the world we know; we may be angered by a character's racism or sexism; we may accuse the writer of oversimplifying leftist politics, or of unfairly stereo-typing the military.

According to Scholes's formulation, in *reading* we create a text within a text; in *interpreting* we produce a text upon a text; and in *criticism* we generate a text against a text. If you were reading directions for assembling a computer, *reading* would be primary. In reading a lyric poem, you might highlight *interpretation,* whereas in a realistic novel, *criticism* might be more important. Of course, all three are to be considered in reading most literature.

In the following essay, the *reading* is fairly simple, but the literary nature of Didion's piece encourages a range of *interpretations* and *criticism.* In the scientific essays of Lewis Thomas and Stephen Jay Gould, the *reading* is more difficult, but they still require some *interpretation* and *criticism.* See if you can unravel these three aspects of response in the notes that follow Didion's classic essay, "On Going Home."

On Going Home

---

1   I am home for my daughter's first birthday. By "home" I do not mean the house in Los Angeles where my husband and I and the baby live, but the place where my family is, in the Central Valley of California. It is a vital although troublesome distinction. My husband likes my family but is uneasy in their house, because once there I fall into their ways, which are difficult, oblique, deliberately inarticulate, not my husband's ways. We live in dusty houses ("D-U-S-T," he once wrote

with his finger on surfaces all over the house, but no one noticed it) filled with mementos quite without value to him (what could the Canton dessert plates mean to him? how could he have known about the assay scales, why should he care if he did know?), and we appear to talk exclusively about people we know who have been committed to mental hospitals, about people we know who have been booked on drunk-driving charges, and about property, particularly about property, land, price per acre and C-2 zoning and assessments and freeway access. My brother does not understand my husband's inability to perceive the advantage in the rather common real-estate transaction known as "sale-leaseback," and my husband in turn does not understand why so many of the people he hears about in my father's house have recently been committed to mental hospitals or booked on drunk-driving charges. Nor does he understand that when we talk about sale-leasebacks and right-of-way condemnations we are talking in code about the things we like best, the yellow fields and the cottonwoods and the rivers rising and falling and the mountain roads closing when the heavy snow comes in. We miss each other's points, have another drink and regard the fire. My brother refers to my husband, in his presence, as "Joan's husband." Marriage is the classic betrayal.

2   Or perhaps it is not any more. Sometimes I think that those of us who are now in our thirties were born into the last generation to carry the burden of "home," to find in family life the source of all tension and drama. I had by all objective accounts a "normal" and a "happy" family situation, and yet I was almost thirty years old before I could talk to my family on the telephone without crying after I had hung up. We did not fight. Nothing was wrong. And yet some nameless anxiety colored the emotional charges between me and the place that I came from. The question of whether or not you could go home again was a very real part of the sentimental and largely literary baggage with which we left home in the fifties; I suspect that it is irrelevant to the children born of the fragmentation after World War II. A few weeks ago in a San Francisco bar I saw a pretty young girl on crystal take off her clothes and dance for the cash prize in an "amateur-topless" contest. There was no particular sense of moment about this, none of the effect of romantic degradation, of "dark journey," for which my generation strived so assiduously. What sense could that girl possibly make of, say, *Long Day's Journey into Night?* Who is beside the point?

3   That I am trapped in this particular irrelevancy is never more apparent to me than when I am home. Paralyzed by the neurotic

lassitude engendered by meeting one's past at every turn, around every corner, inside every cupboard, I go aimlessly from room to room. I decide to meet it head-on and clean out a drawer, and I spread the contents on the bed. A bathing suit I wore the summer I was seventeen. A letter of rejection from The Nation, an aerial photograph of the site for a shopping center my father did not build in 1954. Three teacups hand-painted with cabbage roses and signed "E.M.," my grandmother's initials. There is no final solution for letters of rejection from The Nation and teacups hand-painted in 1900. Nor is there any answer to snapshots of one's grandfather as a young man on skis, surveying around Donner Pass in the year 1910. I smooth out the snapshot and look into his face, and do and do not see my own. I close the drawer, and have another cup of coffee with my mother. We get along very well, veterans of a guerrilla war we never understood.

4   Days pass. I see no one. I come to dread my husband's evening call, not only because he is full of news of what by now seems to me our remote life in Los Angeles, people he has seen, letters which require attention, but because he asks what I have been doing, suggests uneasily that I get out, drive to San Francisco or Berkeley. Instead I drive across the river to a family graveyard. It has been vandalized since my last visit and the monuments are broken, overturned in the dry grass. Because I once saw a rattlesnake in the grass I stay in the car and listen to a country-and-Western station. Later I drive with my father to a ranch he has in the foothills. The man who runs his cattle on it asks us to the roundup, a week from Sunday, and although I know that I will be in Los Angeles I say, in the oblique way my family talks, that I will come. Once home I mention the broken monuments in the graveyard. My mother shrugs.

5   I go to visit my great-aunts. A few of them think now that I am my cousin, or their daughter who died young. We recall an anecdote about a relative last seen in 1948, and they ask if I still like living in New York City. I have lived in Los Angeles for three years, but I say that I do. The baby is offered a horehound drop, and I am slipped a dollar bill "to buy a treat." Questions trail off, answers are abandoned, the baby plays with the dust motes in a shaft of afternoon sun.

6   It is time for the baby's birthday party: a white cake, strawberry-marshmallow ice cream, a bottle of champagne saved from another party. In the evening, after she has gone to sleep, I kneel beside the crib and touch her face, where it is pressed against the slats, with mine. She is an open and trusting child, unprepared for and unaccustomed to the

ambushes of family life, and perhaps it is just as well that I can offer her little of that life. I would like to give her more. I would like to promise her that she will grow up with a sense of her cousins and of rivers and of her great-grandmother's teacups, would like to pledge her a picnic on a river with fried chicken and her hair uncombed, would like to give her *home* for her birthday, but we live differently now and I can promise her nothing like that. I give her a xylophone and a sundress from Madeira, and promise to tell her a funny story.

III: A PERSONAL RESPONSE

1. Didion returns to her home in the Central Valley of California with her husband for her daughter's first birthday. Her husband's discomfort with her family makes Didion think marriage is a betrayal of family bonds. But then she wonders if young people today worry about "the burden of home" in the same way she did.

She wanders around her old home, poking into drawers, finding old clothes, letters, and snapshots. Her present home in Los Angeles now seems far away as she drives to family graves and visits great aunts who barely remember her. After the baby's party, she watches her child sleep and realizes that she will grow up with a different sense of home.

The following are my slightly edited notes written in response to "On Going Home," and in general accord with the sequence described earlier; they are not meant as a formal essay, merely the kind of notes you might write as you read. In a sense, they are writer-based, prepared not for readers but to help me understand my response to Didion's essay. I would have to do lots of rearranging and cutting to make these notes into a reader-based essay. Because I am trying to illustrate a technique I have tried to be detailed. Perhaps you will not want to do as much. And because I have different goals and a different reading background from you, you should not compare yours to mine, except to see how each of us follows the suggested steps.

The essay seems to be about the difference between Didion's sense of home now—as a grown woman—and her sense of it when she was a child. Is she talking about home as a place or as a point in time? Somehow I think she means both. I am wondering why she stayed for so long; her visits are probably infrequent. Her husband was uncomfortable in her house. I can understand that. Families seem to develop their own idiosyncratic ways of doing things, of relating to each other. I can understand his uneasiness: he couldn't bear all that real estate talk; neither could I.

I'm not sure what she means by marriage as the "classic betrayal." Perhaps she thinks her family felt rejected when she left home. But she takes that idea away in the second paragraph: "Perhaps it is not any more." I can see that time will be important here. This is probably an essay that comes to a resolution at the end. Didion is giving me a record of her thinking; she is showing me how she arrived at her conclusion about the possibility of going home. Going home surely has a wider meaning than just physically returning. She says hers is the last generation to carry the burden of home. "Burden" is a strong word.

She claims she was normal but then talks about crying and about a nameless anxiety. Then she says it is different for those born of the "fragmentation after World War II." I guess that is the key to her concept of home. She seems to be focusing on the differences between the extended and the nuclear family. That's interesting for me, since I grew up in the forties and fifties during the break-up of the traditional family structure. My grandparents lived around the corner from me, and their nine children and their families all lived within ten city blocks. Their house was the center around which our lives revolved. Gradually, however, my aunts and uncles drifted off, first to the edges of the city and then to the growing suburbs of Long Island and New Jersey. And now, some thirty years later, we are scattered throughout the East, with a few grandchildren testing the exotic climes of Los Angeles and San Diego.

My grandmother's house was also a moral and cultural center. At holiday parties we had to ask her permission to play American music instead of traditional Irish ballads and dance music. So I can understand the poignancy of Didion's feeling that she was "beside the point," of feeling irrelevant. She had to struggle, as I did, to break away from the established moral and cultural traditions of an extended family. The topless girl, of course, never had those rules to begin with. And as I read this essay, I am thinking that my daughters, thousands of miles from my childhood neighborhood and decades from the conformity and pressure of a religious upbringing, will also never experience Didion's "dark journey." Their sense of morality will be mostly their own construction; they will have themselves to answer to, not to scores of relatives and to a tradition many centuries old.

As Didion walks through her former home, I also sense her mixed feelings of nostalgia and distance. I read the last sentence of the third paragraph several times: I'm not sure why she says "guerrilla war"; isn't that a contradiction of normal and happy? Perhaps not. But her not understanding makes sense. I don't think I ever understood the reasons for the disagreement, the points missed, the tension. I am surprised that she dreads her husband's evening call. I would have thought she would be anticipating it, as an escape. Maybe her old ways are taking over again. When she visits her old aunts, I could not help but remember my last visit to my grandmother, then ninety-five: she thought I was several people, never me. And questions trailed off, answers were abandoned. Her description here seems very real.

In her conclusion she paints a vivid picture, one I've experienced many times: staring at my sleeping children, wondering about their future, their "possibilities," my hopes and dreams for them, and my fears about the world they will have to cope with. Will it be easier or harder? Didion's thoughts are clear: she wants for her daughter the myth of the happy extended family, a sense of roots and shared values, a connection to a rich cultural heritage, a sense of community, of belonging somewhere with people who accept and support your efforts. But realistically, she promises what she can: a xylophone, a sundress, and a story. I like that. She seems to be coming to grips with her break with the home she can never go back to. Instead of depression or anger, she thinks positively. She seems to be saying: "OK, things are not what they were or what they could be, but given the way I live now, this is the best I can do."

I am still wondering if she thinks her "home" in the Central Valley of California is worth going back to—back in the sense of becoming a part of an extended family, adopting its values, its idiosyncratic customs—or if she wants to go back in time to a simpler America, one with common purposes and dreams. Looking back to the first paragraph, I notice her description of her family's ways: "difficult, oblique, deliberately inarticulate." Then I remember the "nameless anxiety" of the second paragraph and the "guerrilla war" and "my mother shrugs." Finally, I looked at the third sentence in the last paragraph, especially the phrase "unprepared for and unaccustomed to the ambushes of family life, and perhaps it is just as well that I can offer her little of that life." All this certainly sounds negative, as if her daughter is better off without that home in the Central Valley. I am wondering why she didn't put a "Yet" before the next sentence: "I would like to give her more." More of what? Of the comforts and benefits of community? Surely Didion realizes that the positive feelings of belonging cannot be separated from the disadvantages of conformity.

2. After my second reading the focus does seem clearer. I think she is talking about accepting the present without attempting to recapture the past, a past that had a good many problems anyhow. I think she realizes that America has changed, that the old center—the extended family rooted for generations in the same place—is no more. New ways are replacing the old. But even if things fall apart, even if we cannot go home again, I do not sense pessimism or despair here. I sense rather a need to confront reality, to see what's possible. She is a realist; she does not offer false hope for a world that isn't (and perhaps wasn't).

Didion is not afraid to admit that her moral concerns are, in the modern world, irrelevant. She is not afraid to admit that she has ambiguous, contradictory feelings about her home: she longs for and flees from the "picnic on a river with fried chicken." After all, if the "young girl on crystal" taking off her clothes is the result of the atomization of modern life, then perhaps an alternative is to be hoped for. Somehow winning an amateur topless contest strung out on acid in front of tipsy strangers doesn't seem like much of a victory for freedom.

As I turn my attention to the organization, I notice that there are only six paragraphs. Didion begins concretely, with lots of specific details (dust, plates, real estate talk, people committed to mental hospitals) to suggest what she means by the first three sentences. This place is different from her home in Los Angeles. She is surely making this point, but indirectly. She lets her details do the work—or rather she invites you to make the connections, to work out the implications. She respects the reader's ability to do just that. I respond to that challenge positively; I know it will pay off.

The second paragraph picks up the last sentence of the first. Here, however, she is both more explicit and more abstract. She is, in a sense, thinking out loud about the links between her generation (those born in the 1930s) and their childhood homes. Her opening sentence clearly states the idea she wants to explore: she left a clearly defined home, and the young girl in the bar never had one. I assume she wants us to imagine that she's making a point about different generations, not just one or two people. She seems to be setting herself up as typical, as representative. This universality is, in fact, one of the touches of art that makes this essay literature. So she makes her point again by ending with a concrete and provocative image. Her concluding question is at this point rhetorical, since today she would have little of the old morality to rebel against. Again she weaves this last sentence into the pattern of the next paragraph. And again she supports this abstract topic sentence by poignantly detailing specific items from her past, a past that makes little sense to the present generation.

The next paragraph, however, is loosely tied to the previous one. The first three paragraphs form a block; the last three, another. She picks up the abandoned narrative again. She tells us about the dread and then gives us the details of her drive to the graveyard. Is this incident meant to suggest the present generation's lack of respect for death, for the past and its traditional values? I think so.

The fifth paragraph focuses on a specific visit to the edges of her family. The details here are rich and telling. It is clear that this is only a ritual visit: no real contact is made. Didion seems comfortable with specific details; she seems to shy away from the announced theme, the explicit point. That is one of the things I like about her work: I'm included; I'm asked to see the relation between the abandoned answers and her inability to go "home."

And finally her snapshot of the party. We have come back now to the essay's opening sentence. The details here are sharply drawn: crisp and appropriate. The final statement, the wrap-up, is, typically, given in concrete form. She cannot bear to say "this is what I meant." No, that would break the cooperative bond with the reader. She wants more; she wants creative involvement, a partner in her art. Perhaps I am going beyond what she calls for, but I think Didion is saying that we can give our children culture, style, grace and love, or whatever else the presents suggest to our imagination. These can create a new definition of home.

IV: CONCLUSION

The traditional essays usually written in college bear little resemblance to "On Going Home," at least when the editors of this anthology were in college in the sixties. We were usually asked, instead, to begin with an explicit thesis statement (or to lead up to it, placing it dramatically as the last sentence of the first paragraph). We were then asked to support that generalization with three paragraphs all beginning with clear topic sentences and providing detailed evidence for our thematic assertion. It is clear that Didion chose not to follow that mode; yet, we suspect that she wrote many of these traditional deductive essays at Berkeley in the fifties. Her choice, however, was not arbitrary; she selected a structure that would best fit her meaning. If a traditional five-paragraph theme were appropriate, she would not hesitate to use it.

Organization is not neutral. It suggests a writer's attitude toward his or her readers and material. If Didion had begun, as is typical in academic articles, with a strong thematic statement, such as "After World War II, the American family was transformed from a closely knit community to a mobile nuclear unit," she would then have developed and supported this thesis with evidence from sociology. She would have been the authority telling us something she knows. Didion, however, chose to begin with a specific incident from her own experience, which she hedges on throughout. She is suggesting that her abstract thinking is firmly rooted in her own experiences. She does not begin with a strong thesis because she doesn't feel that secure about it. She is exploring and wondering. She is also presenting us with a tentative persona, one who is willing to look at the topic with us. Only after she has illustrated her experiences of going home does she make her point about "we live differently now." And even then it is couched in concrete details, not in the usual abstractions that often refer only vaguely to a world the reader knows.

Didion's honest voice is reinforced by her unadorned style. There is little flowery or pompous diction here. Look at the opening sentences of each paragraph: simple, clear, declarative sentences. Notice how she varies the rhythm and length of her sentences in the first paragraph, ending with a crisp and powerful expression of her thought. Her vivid, stark prose suggests that she is trying not to delude herself or us with uncalled-for optimism or self-defeating pessimism. She is just trying to see clearly, to understand. Cluttered sentences would fog that understanding. That seems a realistic alternative to the sometimes artificial authority of the deductive essay.

There is, of course, no doubt that the generalization-support pattern is useful and necessary. You will find some fine examples of that form in this anthology. But Didion's essay demonstrates that a writer can also be forceful, focused, and informative by developing a structure that parallels her intention. Writers usually try to let their content and purpose determine their organization, not the other way around. This discussion of Didion's essay, and the questions in the text, are intended to turn your attention to two things: the essay as a finished product and crafted work, and the essay as an action and a process.

Fortunately, by being such an alert reader, you are also preparing yourself to be an attentive writer. It is no secret that one effective way to become a better writer is to read frequently. Since other writers are the most fertile resource for topics, forms, styles, and ideas, it makes sense to read them often. Professional writers regularly read other practitioners because they know it enriches their own prose. Consciously or not, writers imitate each other, modifying and experimenting as they borrow. It follows that your writing is more likely to improve if you read with a writer's eye, noting voice, style, and language, and studying the development of ideas, the movement between the general and the specific that informs all good writing.

Of course, the most obvious way to become a stronger writer is to write frequently. That's why we have questions and suggestions for writing after each piece in this anthology: so that you will blend your reading with regular writing. They do, after all, have a good deal in common. Both are processes, not static activities; both are ways to make meaning. Reading and writing are also recursive; we move forward but we are always going back to see what we've read or written so we can clarify, rearrange, reformulate, and reinterpret. We only gradually come to understand what we read or what we want to write. This essential act of revision is at the heart of both; without it your reading and writing run the risk of superficiality. By writing about your reading you not only clarify and discover what you think, you also learn how to control your own composing habits. And when your instructor, classmates, or friends read and comment on these responses, you become part of a literate environment where writers can flourish.

TWO

James Baldwin
(1924–   )

James Baldwin was born in Harlem, the son of funda-mentalist religious parents. Baldwin followed his father's voca-tion and became, at fourteen, a preacher. At seventeen he abandoned the ministry and devoted himself to the craft of writing. He had been writing all along, from early childhood, but this writing had been discouraged by his family in favor of the religion that overshadowed it.

Baldwin received institutional support in the form of fellowships to help sustain him while he wrote and published his first two novels: *Go Tell It on the Mountain* (1953) and *Giovanni's Room* (1956), both of which were written abroad. Sandwiched between these works was a collection of essays, *Notes of a Native Son* (1955), which many readers consider his finest work. More fiction and essays followed: *Nobody Knows My Name* (essays, 1961), *Another Country* (a novel, 1962), *The Fire Next Time* (a polemical essay, 1963), *Going to Meet the Man* (stories, 1965)—and more.

In his early essays, for which he has received considerable praise, Baldwin struggled to define himself—as an American, as a writer, and as a black. (And for Baldwin the three are inextricably intertwined.) In coming to terms with what was, for him, the most difficult thing in his life—the fact that he was born a Negro, "and was forced, therefore, to effect some kind of truce with this reality"—Baldwin revealed himself to be a passionate and eloquent writer. His most frequent subject has been the relations between the races, about which he notes sardonically, "the color of my skin makes me, automatically, an expert."

Baldwin has written of pain, of rage and bitterness, of persecution and paranoia, of identity and responsibility, of the relations between fathers and sons, and of the search for

21

equanimity, understanding, and love. Regardless of title, occasion, and place of composition, his essays revolve around these subjects and often stress the importance of accepting and understanding one another, whatever our differences of race, sex, culture, religion, or intellectual disposition.

In "Autobiographical Notes" Baldwin explores the meaning and purpose of his vocation, which he describes simply as to be "a good writer," to get his work done. But the essay explores something more: the fact of Baldwin's blackness and its effect on both his life and his writing. Another essay that explores Baldwin's identity as a writer and as a black is "The Discovery of What It Means to Be an American," an essay whose title reveals a third dimension of Baldwin's identity—his American-ness. This last element of his identity Baldwin examines with thoroughness and acuity by developing a set of contrasts between the social and cultural contexts available to a writer in Europe and in America.

"Fifth Avenue Uptown: A Letter from Harlem" and "Notes of a Native Son" are devoted more specifically and more fully to the problem of race relations in America. In "Fifth Avenue" Baldwin works largely by description and comparison, providing commentary after he takes us on a "tour" of Harlem. His purpose is to help us understand the despair and hopelessness of the black ghetto. In "Notes of a Native Son" Baldwin is more strictly autobiographical than in any of his other essays. This piece combines a reminiscence of his father with an account of the day of his father's funeral. And it includes as well a narrative of an unpleasant incident that brought home to Baldwin a painful social fact concerning his race and an important and even more painful personal revelation of his feelings toward white people. As one of Baldwin's most impressive attempts to explore problematic social issues through personal experience, "Notes of a Native Son" fulfills what Baldwin sees as one of the most important obligations of the writer: "to examine attitudes, to go beneath the surface, to tap the source."

In the prefatory essay to the collection *Notes of a Native Son*, Baldwin stressed the absolute priority of his personal experience for his writing. He put it this way: "One writes out of one thing only—one's own experience. . . . Everything depends on how relentlessly one forces from this experience the last drop, sweet or bitter, it can possibly give." That Baldwin's experience was bitter helped his writing as much as it may have hindered it. For he himself noted that "any writer . . . finds that the things which hurt him and the things which helped him cannot be divorced from each other." Baldwin's anguished experience thus was essential for his acute understanding of the hatred and bitterness in his own heart and of the bitter hatred at the heart of the racial antagonisms existing between many Americans.

Although Baldwin may have resigned from his religious ministry at seventeen, his writing, nonetheless, is strongly influenced by the style of pulpit oratory. It possesses the same strong emotional cast, a similar quality of exhortation, and a common vision of apocalypse. In its rhythm, in its imagery, and in its ethical imperatives, Baldwin's style reveals the influence of both the King James Bible and the storefront church—the two influences he specifically mentions as formative.

Preacher, polemicist, social critic, autobiographer, essayist—Baldwin brings together repeatedly, in deeply affecting ways, public issues and private agonies with relentless candor and inexorable logic. On the success of his best essays rest his fame and fate as a writer, on what he himself claims is the only real concern of the artist: "to recreate out of the disorder of life that order which is art."

Autobiographical Notes

---

1   I was born in Harlem thirty-one years ago. I began plotting novels at about the time I learned to read. The story of my childhood is the usual bleak fantasy and we can dismiss it with the restrained observation that I certainly would not consider living it again. In those days my mother was given to the exasperating and mysterious habit of having babies. As they were born, I took them over with one hand and held a book with the other. The children probably suffered, though they have since been kind enough to deny it, and in this way I read *Uncle Tom's Cabin* and *A Tale of Two Cities* over and over and over again; in this way, in fact, I read just about everything I could get my hands on—except the Bible, probably because it was the only book I was encouraged to read. I must also confess that I wrote—a great deal—and my first professional triumph, in any case, the first effort of mine to be

seen in print, occurred at the age of twelve or thereabouts, when a short story I had written about the Spanish revolution won some sort of prize in an extremely short-lived church newspaper. I remember the story was censored by the lady editor, though I don't remember why, and I was outraged.

2   Also wrote plays, and songs, for one of which I received a letter of congratulations from Mayor La Guardia, and poetry, about which the less said, the better. My mother was delighted by all these goings-on, but my father wasn't; he wanted me to be a preacher. When I was fourteen I became a preacher, and when I was seventeen I stopped. Very shortly thereafter I left home. For God knows how long I struggled with the world of commerce and industry—I guess they would say they struggled with *me*—and when I was about twenty-one I had enough done of a novel to get a Saxton Fellowship. When I was twenty-two the fellowship was over, the novel turned out to be unsalable, and I started waiting on tables in a Village restaurant and writing book reviews—mostly, as it turned out, about the Negro problem, concerning which the color of my skin made me automatically an expert. Did another book, in company with photographer Theodore Pelatowski, about the store-front churches in Harlem. This book met exactly the same fate as my first—fellowship, but no sale. (It was a Rosenwald Fellowship.) By the time I was twenty-four I had decided to stop reviewing books about the Negro problem—which, by this time, was only slightly less horrible in print than it was in life—and I packed my bags and went to France, where I finished, God knows how, *Go Tell It on the Mountain*.

3   Any writer, I suppose, feels that the world into which he was born is nothing less than a conspiracy against the cultivation of his talent—which attitude certainly has a great deal to support it. On the other hand, it is only because the world looks on his talent with such a frightening indifference that the artist is compelled to make his talent important. So that any writer, looking back over even so short a span of time as I am here forced to assess, finds that the things which hurt him and the things which helped him cannot be divorced from each other; he could be helped in a certain way only because he was hurt in a certain way; and his help is simply to be enabled to move from one conundrum to the next—one is tempted to say that he moves from one disaster to the next. When one begins looking for influences one finds them by the score. I haven't thought much about my own, not enough anyway; I hazard that the King James Bible, the rhetoric of the store-front church, something ironic and violent and perpetually understated

in Negro speech—and something of Dickens' love for bravura—have something to do with me today; but I wouldn't stake my life on it. Likewise, innumerable people have helped me in many ways; but finally, I suppose, the most difficult (and most rewarding) thing in my life has been the fact that I was born a Negro and was forced, therefore, to effect some kind of truce with this reality. (Truce, by the way, is the best one can hope for.)

4   One of the difficulties about being a Negro writer (and this is not special pleading, since I don't mean to suggest that he has it worse than anybody else) is that the Negro problem is written about so widely. The bookshelves groan under the weight of information, and everyone therefore considers himself informed. And this information, furthermore, operates usually (generally, popularly) to reinforce traditional attitudes. Of traditional attitudes there are only two—For or Against—and I, personally, find it difficult to say which attitude has caused me the most pain. I am speaking as a writer; from a social point of view I am perfectly aware that the change from ill-will to good-will, however motivated, however imperfect, however expressed, is better than no change at all.

5   But it is part of the business of the writer—as I see it—to examine attitudes, to go beneath the surface, to tap the source. From this point of view the Negro problem is nearly inaccessible. It is not only written about so widely; it is written about so badly. It is quite possible to say that the price a Negro pays for becoming articulate is to find himself, at length, with nothing to be articulate about. ("You taught me language," says Caliban to Prospero, "and my profit on't is I know how to curse.") Consider: the tremendous social activity that this problem generates imposes on whites and Negroes alike the necessity of looking forward, of working to bring about a better day. This is fine, it keeps the waters troubled; it is all, indeed, that has made possible the Negro's progress. Nevertheless, social affairs are not generally speaking the writer's prime concern, whether they ought to be or not; it is absolutely necessary that he establish between himself and these affairs a distance which will allow, at least, for clarity, so that before he can look forward in any meaningful sense, he must first be allowed to take a long look back. In the context of the Negro problem neither whites nor blacks, for excellent reasons of their own, have the faintest desire to look back; but I think that the past is all that makes the present coherent, and further, that the past will remain horrible for exactly as long as we refuse to assess it honestly.

6   I know, in any case, that the most crucial time in my own develop-

ment came when I was forced to recognize that I was a kind of bastard of the West; when I followed the line of my past I did not find myself in Europe but in Africa. And this meant that in some subtle way, in a really profound way, I brought to Shakespeare, Bach, Rembrandt, to the stones of Paris, to the cathedral at Chartres, and to the Empire State Building, a special attitude. These were not really my creations, they did not contain my history; I might search in them in vain forever for any reflection of myself. I was an interloper; this was not my heritage. At the same time I had no other heritage which I could possibly hope to use—I had certainly been unfitted for the jungle or the tribe. I would have to appropriate these white centuries, I would have to make them mine—I would have to accept my special attitude, my special place in this scheme—otherwise I would have no place in *any* scheme. What was the most difficult was the fact that I was forced to admit something I had always hidden from myself, which the American Negro has had to hide from himself as the price of his public progress; that I hated and feared white people. This did not mean that I loved black people; on the contrary, I despised them, possibly because they failed to produce Rembrandt. In effect, I hated and feared the world. And this meant, not only that I thus gave the world an altogether murderous power over me, but also that in such a self-destroying limbo I could never hope to write.

7   One writes out of one thing only—one's own experience. Everything depends on how relentlessly one forces from this experience the last drop, sweet or bitter, it can possibly give. This is the only real concern of the artist, to recreate out of the disorder of life that order which is art. The difficulty then, for me, of being a Negro writer was the fact that I was, in effect, prohibited from examining my own experience too closely by the tremendous demands and the very real dangers of my social situation.

8   I don't think the dilemma outlined above is uncommon. I do think, since writers work in the disastrously explicit medium of language, that it goes a little way towards explaining why, out of the enormous resources of Negro speech and life, and despite the example of Negro music, prose written by Negroes has been generally speaking so pallid and so harsh. I have not written about being a Negro at such length because I expect that to be my only subject, but only because it was the gate I had to unlock before I could hope to write about anything else. I don't think that the Negro problem in America can be even discussed coherently without bearing in mind its context; its context being the history, traditions, customs, the moral assumptions and preoccupations

of the country; in short, the general social fabric. Appearances to the contrary, no one in America escapes its effects and everyone in America bears some responsibility for it. I believe this the more firmly because it is the overwhelming tendency to speak of this problem as though it were a thing apart. But in the work of Faulkner, in the general attitude and certain specific passages in Robert Penn Warren, and, most significantly, in the advent of Ralph Ellison, one sees the beginnings—at least —of a more genuinely penetrating search. Mr. Ellison, by the way, is the first Negro novelist I have ever read to utilize in language, and brilliantly, some of the ambiguity and irony of Negro life.

9   About my interests: I don't know if I have any, unless the morbid desire to own a sixteen-millimeter camera and make experimental movies can be so classified. Otherwise, I love to eat and drink—it's my melancholy conviction that I've scarcely ever had enough to eat (this is because it's *impossible* to eat enough if you're worried about the next meal)—and I love to argue with people who do not disagree with me too profoundly, and I love to laugh. I do *not* like bohemia, or bohemians, I do not like people whose principal aim is pleasure, and I do not like people who are *earnest* about anything. I don't like people who like me because I'm a Negro; neither do I like people who find in the same accident grounds for contempt. I love America more than any other country in the world, and, exactly for this reason, I insist on the right to criticize her perpetually. I think all theories are suspect, that the finest principles may have to be modified, or may even be pulverized by the demands of life, and that one must find, therefore, one's own moral center and move through the world hoping that this center will guide one aright. I consider that I have many responsibilities, but none greater than this: to last, as Hemingway says, and get my work done.

10   I want to be an honest man and a good writer.

QUESTIONS

1.   Baldwin, like many writers, says he read voraciously as a child. And he says also that he wrote a lot as well. Do you think there is any connection between these two facts? What is the relationship between reading and writing?

2.   Does Baldwin seem honest in this brief overview of his life as a writer? Does he seem boastful? Modest? Paranoid? Cite specific sentences where you sense strongly his tone.

3. In paragraph 3 Baldwin discusses the effect of circumstance on a writer's talent. How, specifically, does he apply that point to his own situation? What is the single most important fact of his life—the fact that conditions, influences, and affects all others?

4. How do you explain this remark of Baldwin's: "I suppose the most difficult (and most rewarding) thing in my life has been the fact that I was born a Negro and was forced, therefore, to come to some kind of truce with reality. (Truce, by the way, is the best one can hope for.)" How does this statement tie in with his earlier statement that a writer "finds that the things which hurt him and the things which helped him cannot be divorced from each other"?

5. In paragraph 4 Baldwin makes a distinction between how the changes in the civil status of blacks affect him as a man and how they affect him as a writer. Why is or isn't this a valid and useful distinction?

6. What does Baldwin see as the business of the writer? Should a writer be more concerned with art and craft or with ideas and values, perhaps even with social change? Does Baldwin seem to stress one or the other? (See paragraphs 5 and 7.)

7. Baldwin states that "the past is all that makes the present coherent." From what you have learned about Baldwin in reading this essay, and perhaps others, how has this been true for him? Is it true for you? How?

8. Baldwin makes two complex and important points in paragraph 6. One concerns his attitude toward the cultural monuments of Western civilization. What is this point? Can it be extended to others besides blacks?

9. The second important point of paragraph 6 comes at the end, where Baldwin says he hated both white and black people. Why is this an important aspect of his experience?

10. In paragraph 8 Baldwin remarks: "I have not written about being a Negro at such length because I expect that to be my only subject, but only because it was the gate I had to unlock before I could write about anything else." Explain.

11. The last long paragraph of the essay (paragraph 9) contains a miscellany of things Baldwin does and does not like. Which do you think is the most important? Is there any relationship between this point and the final sentence of the essay: "I want to be an honest man and a good writer"?

12. Reread the first sentence of each paragraph. What do these opening sentences reveal about the organization of "Autobiographical Notes"?

Suggestions for Writing

A. Write your own "Autobiographical Notes," perhaps focusing on one central fact of your life such as your race, religion, ethnic background, special talents, place of birth. You could, if you wish, structure your essay as Baldwin structures his: facts in the opening and closing paragraphs, longer speculations and explanations in the middle.

B. Write an essay discussing, exploring, examining one of the ideas raised in Baldwin's essay—perhaps hatred, the white world, or blackness.

The Discovery of What It Means to Be an American

---

1   "It is a complex fate to be an American," Henry James observed, and the principal discovery an American writer makes in Europe is just how complex this fate is. America's history, her aspirations, her peculiar triumphs, her even more peculiar defeats, and her position in the world—yesterday and today—are all so profoundly and stubbornly unique that the very word "America" remains a new almost completely undefined and extremely controversial proper noun. No one in the world seems to know exactly what it describes, not even we motley millions who call ourselves Americans.

2   I left America because I doubted my ability to survive the fury of the color problem here. (Sometimes I still do.) I wanted to prevent myself from becoming *merely* a Negro; or, even, merely a Negro writer. I wanted to find out in what way the *specialness* of my experience could be made to connect me with other people instead of dividing me from them. (I was as isolated from Negroes as I was from whites, which is what happens when a Negro begins, at bottom, to believe what white people say about him.)

3   In my necessity to find the terms on which my experience could be related to that of others, Negroes and whites, writers and non-writers, I proved, to my astonishment, to be as American as any Texas G.I. And I found my experience was shared by every American writer I knew in Paris. Like me, they had been divorced from their origins, and it turned out to make very little difference that the origins of white Americans were European and mine were African—they were no more at home in Europe than I was.

4   The fact that I was the son of a slave and they were the sons of free men meant less, by the time we confronted each other on European

soil, than the fact that we were both searching for our separate identities. When we had found these, we seemed to be saying, why, then, we would no longer need to cling to the shame and bitterness which had divided us so long.

5   It became terribly clear in Europe, as it never had been here, that we knew more about each other than any European ever could. And it also became clear that, no matter where our fathers had been born, or what they had endured, the fact of Europe had formed us both was part of our identity and part of our inheritance.

6   I had been in Paris a couple of years before any of this became clear to me. When it did, I, like many a writer before me upon the discovery that his props have all been knocked out from under him, suffered a species of breakdown and was carried off to the mountains of Switzerland. There, in that absolutely alabaster landscape, armed with two Bessie Smith records and a typewriter, I began to try to recreate the life that I had first known as a child and from which I had spent so many years in flight.

7   It was Bessie Smith, through her tone and her cadence, who helped me to dig back to the way I myself must have spoken when I was a pickaninny, and to remember the things I had heard and seen and felt. I had buried them very deep. I had never listened to Bessie Smith in America (in the same way that, for years, I would not touch water-melon), but in Europe she helped to reconcile me to being a "nigger."

8   I do not think that I could have made this reconciliation here. Once I was able to accept my role—as distinguished, I must say, from my "place"—in the extraordinary drama which is America, I was released from the illusion that I hated America.

9   The story of what can happen to an American Negro writer in Europe simply illustrates, in some relief, what can happen to any American writer there. It is not meant, of course, to imply that it happens to them all, for Europe can be very crippling, too; and, anyway, a writer, when he has made his first breakthrough, has simply won a crucial skirmish in a dangerous, unending and unpredictable battle. Still, the breakthrough is important, and the point is that an American writer, in order to achieve it, very often has to leave this country.

10   The American writer, in Europe, is released, first of all, from the necessity of apologizing for himself. It is not until he *is* released from the habit of flexing his muscles and proving that he is just a "regular guy" that he realizes how crippling this habit has been. It is not necessary for him, there, to pretend to be something he is not, for the artist does not

encounter in Europe the same suspicion he encounters here. Whatever the Europeans may actually think of artists, they have killed enough of them off by now to know that they are as real—and as persistent—as rain, snow, taxes or businessmen.

11   Of course, the reason for Europe's comparative clarity concerning the different functions of men in society is that European society has always been divided into classes in a way that American society never has been. A European writer considers himself to be part of an old and honorable tradition—of intellectual activity, of letters—and his choice of a vocation does not cause him any uneasy wonder as to whether or not it will cost him all his friends. But this tradition does not exist in America.

12   On the contrary, we have a very deep-seated distrust of real intellectual effort (probably because we suspect that it will destroy, as I hope it does, that myth of America to which we cling so desperately). An American writer fights his way to one of the lowest rungs on the American social ladder by means of pure bull-headedness and an indescribable series of odd jobs. He probably *has* been a "regular fellow" for much of his adult life, and it is not easy for him to step out of that lukewarm bath.

13   We must, however, consider a rather serious paradox: though American society is more mobile than Europe's, it is easier to cut across social and occupational lines there than it is here. This has something to do, I think, with the problem of status in American life. Where everyone has status, it is also perfectly possible, after all, that no one has. It seems inevitable, in any case, that a man may become uneasy as to just what his status is.

14   But Europeans have lived with the idea of status for a long time. A man can be as proud of being a good waiter as of being a good actor, and, in neither case, feel threatened. And this means that the actor and the waiter can have a freer and more genuinely friendly relationship in Europe than they are likely to have here. The waiter does not feel, with obscure resentment, that the actor has "made it," and the actor is not tormented by the fear that he may find himself, tomorrow, once again a waiter.

15   This lack of what may roughly be called social paranoia causes the American writer in Europe to feel—almost certainly for the first time in his life—that he can reach out to everyone, that he is accessible to everyone and open to everything. This is an extraordinary feeling. He feels, so to speak, his own weight, his own value.

16   It is as though he suddenly came out of a dark tunnel and found

himself beneath the open sky. And, in fact, in Paris, I began to see the sky for what seemed to be the first time. It was borne in on me—and it did not make me feel melancholy—that this sky had been there before I was born and would be there when I was dead. And it was up to me, therefore, to make of my brief opportunity the most that could be made.

17   I was born in New York, but have lived only in pockets of it. In Paris, I lived in all parts of the city—on the Right Bank and the Left, among the bourgeoisie and among *les misérables,* and knew all kinds of people, from pimps and prostitutes in Pigalle to Egyptian bankers in Neuilly. This may sound extremely unprincipled or even obscurely immoral: I found it healthy. I love to talk to people, all kinds of people, and almost everyone, as I hope we still know, loves a man who loves to listen.

18   This perceptual dealing with people very different from myself caused a shattering in me of preconceptions I scarcely knew I held. The writer is meeting in Europe people who are not American, whose sense of reality is entirely different from his own. They may love or hate or admire or fear or envy this country—they see it, in any case, from another point of view, and this forces the writer to reconsider many things he had always taken for granted. This reassessment, which can be very painful, is also very valuable.

19   This freedom, like all freedom, has its dangers and its responsibilities. One day it begins to be borne in on the writer, and with great force, that he is living in Europe as an American. If he were living there as a European, he would be living on a different and far less attractive continent.

20   This crucial day may be the day on which an Algerian taxi-driver tells him how it feels to be an Algerian in Paris. It may be the day on which he passes a café terrace and catches a glimpse of the tense, intelligent and troubled face of Albert Camus. Or it may be the day on which someone asks him to explain Little Rock and he begins to feel that it would be simpler—and, corny as the words may sound, more honorable—to *go* to Little Rock than sit in Europe, on an American passport, trying to explain it.

21   This is a personal day, a terrible day, the day to which his entire sojourn has been tending. It is the day he realizes that there are no untroubled countries in this fearfully troubled world; that if he has been preparing himself for anything in Europe, he has been preparing himself —for America. In short, the freedom that the American writer finds in

Europe brings him, full circle, back to himself, with the responsibility for his development where it always was: in his own hands.

22 Even the most incorrigible maverick has to be born somewhere. He may leave the group that produced him—he may be forced to—but nothing will efface his origins, the marks of which he carries with him everywhere. I think it is important to know this and even find it a matter for rejoicing, as the strongest people do, regardless of their station. On this acceptance, literally, the life of a writer depends.

23 The charge has often been made against American writers that they do not describe society, and have no interest in it. They only describe individuals in opposition to it, or isolated from it. Of course, what the American writer is describing is his own situation. But what is *Anna Karenina* describing if not the tragic fate of the isolated individual, at odds with her time and place?

24 The real difference is that Tolstoy was describing an old and dense society in which everything seemed—to the people in it, though not to Tolstoy—to be fixed forever. And the book is a masterpiece because Tolstoy was able to fathom, and make us see, the hidden laws which really governed this society and made Anna's doom inevitable.

25 American writers do not have a fixed society to describe. The only society they know is one in which nothing is fixed and in which the individual must fight for his identity. This is a rich confusion, indeed, and it creates for the American writer unprecedented opportunities.

26 That the tensions of American life, as well as the possibilities, are tremendous is certainly not even a question. But these are dealt with in contemporary literature mainly compulsively; that is, the book is more likely to be a symptom of our tension than an examination of it. The time has come, God knows, for us to examine ourselves, but we can only do this if we are willing to free ourselves of the myth of America and try to find out what is really happening here.

27 Every society is really governed by hidden laws, by unspoken but profound assumptions on the part of the people, and ours is no exception. It is up to the American writer to find out what these laws and assumptions are. In a society much given to smashing taboos without thereby managing to be liberated from them, it will be no easy matter.

28 It is no wonder, in the meantime, that the American writer keeps running off to Europe. He needs sustenance for his journey and the best models he can find. Europe has what we do not have yet, a sense of the mysterious and inexorable limits of life, a sense, in a word, of tragedy. And we have what they sorely need: a new sense of life's possibilities.

29   In this endeavor to wed the vision of the Old World with that of
the New, it is the writer, not the statesman, who is our strongest arm.
Though we do not wholly believe it yet, the interior life is a real life,
and the intangible dreams of people have a tangible effect on the world.

QUESTIONS

Ideas

1. Why is to be an American a "complex fate"? Why, particularly, was it a
   complex fate for Baldwin?
2. What does Baldwin suggest about origins—about what and where a person
   is born and how he is raised? Why does he mention Bessie Smith?
3. Throughout the second and third parts of this essay, Baldwin contrasts
   Europe with America. What differences does he emphasize? And what are
   the reasons for and the focus of his contrasts?
4. How can living in another country help a writer—or any artist? (See
   especially paragraph 18.)

Organization

5. Why is the essay divided into three sections? What are the focus and
   emphasis of each?
6. How does Baldwin achieve coherence and continuity in this essay? Look
   closely at the first sentence of each paragraph of section two, for example.
   What words and phrases link the thought of each opening sentence to the
   idea of the paragraph before it? Look also at paragraph 20. Notice how
   Baldwin begins each sentence in that paragraph:

   This crucial day may be the day on which . . .
   It may be the day on which . . .
   Or it may be the day on which . . .

   And then paragraph 21:

   This is a personal day, a terrible day, the day to which . . .
   It is the day . . .

   Are these repetitions necessary? Helpful? Monotonous? Explain.

Sentences

7. Read paragraphs 11–15, noting particularly the length of Baldwin's sentences. In that five-paragraph stretch, do you find any consistency in the
   kind of sentence Baldwin uses or in how he begins and ends his paragraphs?

8. Baldwin uses balance and parallelism of syntax throughout the essay. Here are two brief examples:

> This reassessment, which can be very painful,
> is also   very valuable.

> This freedom, like all freedom, has its dangers
>   and its responsibilities.

In both of these simple sentences Baldwin interrupts the direct flow of syntax with interpolated phrases or clauses. These interruptions change the rhythm of the sentences, making them more emphatic. Analyze the repetitions, balances, and interruptions of the following two sequential sentences from paragraph 5:

> It became terribly clear in Europe,
>   as it never had been here,
>   that we knew more about each other than any
>   European ever could.

> And it also became   clear   that,
>   no matter where our fathers had been born,
> or   what   they   had endured,
>   the fact of Europe had formed us both,
>   was part of our identity
>   and   part of our inheritance.

9. Baldwin varies the rhythm of his sentences and achieves emphasis and expansiveness by careful use of punctuation. Consider, for example, the commas in paragraphs 16–19. Read the sentences aloud, noting the pauses and the pacing. Try reading the same paragraphs as if the commas had been omitted.

10. Baldwin interrupts his sentences with the dash as well as with the comma. Consider the dashes in the following paragraphs: 1, 8, 10, 11, 15, 16, and 17. What kind of information is interpolated between the dashes? Can we remove the words between dashes, thus eliminating the internal punctuation of those sentences? In reading the sentences aloud, what tone of voice would you use and why?

11. In paragraphs 2 and 7, Baldwin could have used dashes or commas instead of parentheses. Try reading the sentences aloud, testing in turn parentheses, dashes, commas. What differences do you hear?

Words

12. Many words in the essay convey the meaning of division or separation. Reread paragraphs 2–12, marking off these words as well as those suggesting an opposite idea, that of unity or reconciliation.

13. In paragraph 9, Baldwin uses a central metaphor—that for the writer life is a battle. What specific words and phrases carry the comparison between life and war? What is the point of the paragraph overall, and how do the comparisons help to convey it?

14. How would you describe Baldwin's language in this essay? Is it formal, informal, serious, casual, heavy, or light? How, for example, would you classify the language of the following phrases: "the mysterious and inexorable limits of life" (28), "incorrigible maverick" (22), "obscure resentment" (14)? Is the essay written primarily in this style of language? In another?

15. Why does Baldwin use quotation marks around the following words: "nigger" (7), "place" (8), "regular guy" (10), "made it" (14)?

Suggestions for Writing

A. Write an essay explaining what it means to be an American, especially what it means to be a particular kind of American, such as a Jewish or Chinese American or an American traveling abroad. Try to focus on your identity as this particular kind of American—or upon the reactions of other people to you as a particular kind of American. Has it been a complex fate for you to be an American? Explain.

B. Write an essay in which you identify and define yourself as belonging to a particular social group or as being one of a particular type of people. You might explain what it means, for example, for you to be a musician, an athlete, a feminist, a science fiction fan, or a moviegoer.

C. In the last section of "The Discovery of What It Means to Be an American," and especially in paragraphs 22–27, Baldwin comments on the American writer and his relation to American society. Apply any one of Baldwin's remarks on this subject to a writer whose work you know (perhaps Baldwin) and develop an essay either confirming or refuting Baldwin's assertion. You might take, for example, one of the following comments:

> The charge has often been made against American writers that they do not describe society, and have no interest in it. They only describe individuals in opposition to it, or isolated from it. (23)

> American writers do not have a fixed society to describe. The only society they know is one in which nothing is fixed and in which the individual must fight for his identity. (25)

> [The tensions of American life] are dealt with in contemporary literature mainly compulsively; that is, the book is more likely to be a symptom of our tension than an examination of it. (26)

If Black English Isn't a Language, Then Tell Me, What Is?

1   Sᴛ. PAUL DE VENCE, France—The argument concerning the use, or the status, or the reality, of black English is rooted in American history and has absolutely nothing to do with the question the argument supposes itself to be posing. The argument has nothing to do with language itself but with the *role* of language. Language, incontestably, reveals the speaker. Language, also, far more dubiously, is meant to define the other—and, in this case, the other is refusing to be defined by a language that has never been able to recognize him.

2   People evolve a language in order to describe and thus control their circumstances, or in order not to be submerged by a reality that they cannot articulate. (And, if they cannot articulate it, they *are* submerged.) A Frenchman living in Paris speaks a subtly and crucially different language from that of the man living in Marseilles; neither sounds very much like a man living in Quebec; and they would all have great difficulty in apprehending what the man from Guadeloupe, or Martinique, is saying, to say nothing of the man from Senegal—although the "common" language of all these areas is French. But each has paid, and is paying, a different price for this "common" language, in which, as it turns out, they are not saying, and cannot be saying, the same things: They each have very different realities to articulate, or control.

3   What joins all languages, and all men, is the necessity to confront life, in order, not inconceivably, to outwit death: The price for this is the acceptance, and achievement, of one's temporal identity. So that, for example, though it is not taught in the schools (and this has the potential of becoming a political issue) the south of France still clings to its ancient and musical Provençal, which resists being described as a "dialect." And much of the tension in the Basque countries, and in Wales, is due to the Basque and Welsh determination not to allow their languages to be destroyed. This determination also feeds the flames in Ireland for among the many indignities the Irish have

been forced to undergo at English hands is the English contempt for
their language.

4   It goes without saying, then, that language is also a political instrument, means, and proof of power. It is the most vivid and crucial key
to identity: It reveals the private identity, and connects one with, or
divorces one from, the larger, public, or communal identity. There have
been, and are, times, and places, when to speak a certain language could
be dangerous, even fatal. Or, one may speak the same language, but in
such a way that one's antecedents are revealed, or (one hopes) hidden.
This is true in France, and is absolutely true in England: The range (and
reign) of accents on that damp little island make England coherent for
the English and totally incomprehensible for everyone else. To open
your mouth in England is (if I may use black English) to "put your
business in the street": You have confessed your parents, your youth,
your school, your salary, your self-esteem, and, alas, your future.

5   Now, I do not know what white Americans would sound like if
there had never been any black people in the United States, but they
would not sound the way they sound. *Jazz,* for example, is a very specific
sexual term, as in *jazz me, baby,* but white people purified it into the Jazz
Age. *Sock it to me,* which means, roughly, the same thing, has been
adopted by Nathaniel Hawthorne's descendants with no qualms or hesi-
tations at all, along with *let it all hang out* and *right on! Beat to his socks,*
which was once the black's most total and despairing image of poverty,
was transformed into a thing called the Beat Generation, which phenomenon was, largely, composed of *uptight,* middle-class white people, imitating poverty, trying to *get down,* to get *with it,* doing their *thing,* doing
their despairing best to be *funky,* which we, the blacks, never dreamed of
doing—we *were* funky, baby, like *funk* was going out of style.

6   Now, no one can eat his cake, and have it, too, and it is late in
the day to attempt to penalize black people for having created a language
that permits the nation its only glimpse of reality, a language without
which the nation would be even more *whipped* than it is.

7   I say that this present skirmish is rooted in American history, and
it is. Black English is the creation of the black diaspora. Blacks came to
the United States chained to each other, but from different tribes:
Neither could speak the other's language. If two black people, at that
bitter hour of the world's history, had been able to speak to each other,
the institution of chattel slavery could never have lasted as long as it did.
Subsequently, the slave was given, under the eye, and the gun, of his
master, Congo Square, and the Bible—or, in other words, and under

these conditions, the slave began the formation of the black church, and it is within this unprecedented tabernacle that black English began to be formed. This was not, merely, as in the European example, the adoption of a foreign tongue, but an alchemy that transformed ancient elements into a new language: *A language comes into existence by means of brutal necessity, and the rules of the language are dictated by what the language must convey.*

8   There was a moment, in time, and in this place, when my brother, or my mother, or my father, or my sister, had to convey to me, for example, the danger in which I was standing from the white man standing just behind me, and to convey this with a speed, and in a language, that the white man could not possibly understand, and that, indeed, he cannot understand, until today. He cannot afford to understand it. This understanding would reveal to him too much about himself, and smash that mirror before which he has been frozen for so long.

9   Now, if this passion, this skill, this (to quote Toni Morrison) "sheer intelligence," this incredible music, the mighty achievement of having brought a people utterly unknown to, or despised by "history" —to have brought this people to their present, troubled, troubling, and unassailable and unanswerable place—if this absolutely unprecedented journey does not indicate that black English is a language, I am curious to know what definition of language is to be trusted.

10   A people at the center of the Western world, and in the midst of so hostile a population, has not endured and transcended by means of what is patronizingly called a "dialect." We, the blacks, are in trouble, certainly, but we are not doomed, and we are not inarticulate because we are not compelled to defend a morality that we know to be a lie.

11   The brutal truth is that the bulk of the white people in America never had any interest in educating black people, except as this could serve white purposes. It is not the black child's language that is in question, it is not his language that is despised: It is his experience. A child cannot be taught by anyone who despises him, and a child cannot afford to be fooled. A child cannot be taught by anyone whose demand, essentially, is that the child repudiate his experience, and all that gives him sustenance, and enter a limbo in which he will no longer be black, and in which he knows that he can never become white. Black people have lost too many black children that way.

12   And, after all, finally, in a country with standards so untrustworthy, a country that makes heroes of so many criminal mediocrities, a country unable to face why so many of the non-white are in prison,

or on the needle, or standing, futureless, in the streets—it may very well
be that both the child, and his elder, have concluded that they have
nothing whatever to learn from the people of a country that has
managed to learn so little.

QUESTIONS

Ideas

1. What are the essential attributes or characteristics of a language (as opposed to a dialect) as Baldwin describes them? What, according to Baldwin, is the relation between language and reality?
2. What, according to Baldwin, are the functions of language? What does
   a language *do* for its speakers?
3. What are the purpose and point of the essay? Who is the intended or
   implied audience?

Organization

4. Baldwin begins with a reference to a previously articulated position—or at
   least a counterview—to the one he wishes to argue. He enters the debate
   in the middle of things rather than at the beginning. What does this
   approach suggest about the audience for whom Baldwin originally wrote
   this essay?
5. Outline the structure of the essay—its movement of thought from one
   paragraph to another. State in a single sentence the main thrust of each
   paragraph and examine the relationship of each paragraph to the ones
   before and after it.

Sentences

6. Single out two sentences you consider particularly effective and explain
   why they are effective.
7. Examine the sentences in which Baldwin expresses his ideas by punctuat-
   ing with a colon. For each sentence explain the relationship between the
   information on the right and left sides of the colon. Consider a revision
   of each sentence to eliminate the colon and decide which version you
   prefer, and why.

Words

8. Examine the italicized words and phrases in paragraphs 5 and 6. What
   does Baldwin illustrate with these examples?

9. Consider the following adverbs from paragraphs 1–4. What would be gained or lost if each were omitted?

    absolutely, incontestably, dubiously (1);
    subtly, crucially, very (2);
    inconceivably (3);
    absolutely, totally (4).

Suggestions for Writing

A. Explain and illustrate from your own experience or from your reading how language, as Baldwin says in paragraph 4, "is a political instrument, means, and proof of power."

B. Discuss Baldwin's idea that language is a key to identity—both personal identity and social identity.

C. Agree or disagree with Baldwin's comment that to open your mouth and speak in England is to confess "your parents, your youth, your school, your salary, your self-esteem, and alas, your future."

Fifth Avenue, Uptown:
A Letter from Harlem

---

1   There is a housing project standing now where the house in which we grew up once stood, and one of those stunted city trees is snarling where our doorway used to be. This is on the rehabilitated side of the avenue. The other side of the avenue—for progress takes time— has not been rehabilitated yet and it looks exactly as it looked in the days when we sat with our noses pressed against the windowpane, longing to be allowed to go "across the street." The grocery store which gave us credit is still there, and there can be no doubt that it is still giving credit. The people in the project certainly need it—far more, indeed, than they ever needed the project. The last time I passed by, the Jewish proprietor was still standing among his shelves, looking sadder and heavier but scarcely any older. Farther down the block stands the shoe-repair store in which our shoes were repaired until reparation became impossible and in which, then, we bought all our "new" ones. The Negro proprietor is still in the window, head down, working at the leather.

2   These two, I imagine, could tell a long tale if they would (perhaps they would be glad to if they could), having watched so many, for so long, struggling in the fishhooks, the barbed wire, of this avenue.

3   The avenue is elsewhere the renowned and elegant Fifth. The area I am describing, which, in today's gang parlance, would be called "the turf," is bounded by Lenox Avenue on the west, the Harlem River on the east, 135th Street on the north, and 130th Street on the south. We never lived beyond these boundaries; this is where we grew up. Walking along 145th Street—for example—familiar as it is, and similar, does not have the same impact because I do not know any of the people on the block. But when I turn east on 131st Street and Lenox Avenue, there is first a soda-pop joint, then a shoeshine "parlor," then a grocery store, then a dry cleaners', then the houses. All along the street there are people who watched me grow up, people who grew up with me, people I watched grow up along with my brothers and sisters; and, sometimes in my arms, sometimes underfoot, sometimes at my shoulder—or on it —their children, a riot, a forest of children, who include my nieces and nephews.

4   When we reach the end of this long block, we find ourselves on wide, filthy, hostile Fifth Avenue, facing that project which hangs over the avenue like a monument to the folly, and the cowardice, of good intentions. All along the block, for anyone who knows it, are immense human gaps, like craters. These gaps are not created merely by those who have moved away, inevitably into some other ghetto; or by those who have risen, almost always into a greater capacity for self-loathing and self-delusion; or yet by those who, by whatever means—World War II, the Korean war, a policeman's gun or billy, a gang war, a brawl, madness, an overdose of heroin, or, simply, unnatural exhaustion—are dead. I am talking about those who are left, and I am talking principally about the young. What are they doing? Well, some, a minority, are fanatical churchgoers, members of the more extreme of the Holy Roller sects. Many, many more are "moslems," by affiliation or sympathy, that is to say that they are united by nothing more—and nothing less—than a hatred of the white world and all its works. They are present, for example, at every Buy Black street-corner meeting—meetings in which the speaker urges his hearers to cease trading with white men and establish a separate economy. Neither the speaker nor his hearers can possibly do this, of course, since Negroes do not own General Motors or RCA or the A & P, nor, indeed, do they own more than a wholly insufficient fraction of anything else in Harlem (those who *do* own

anything are more interested in their profits than in their fellows). But these meetings nevertheless keep alive in the participators a certain pride of bitterness without which, however futile this bitterness may be, they could scarcely remain alive at all. Many have given up. They stay home and watch the TV screen, living on the earnings of their parents, cousins, brothers, or uncles, and only leave the house to go to the movies or to the nearest bar. "How're you making it?" one may ask, running into them along the block, or in the bar. "Oh, I'm TV-ing it"; with the saddest, sweetest, most shamefaced of smiles, and from a great distance. This distance one is compelled to respect; anyone who has traveled so far will not easily be dragged again into the world. There are further retreats, of course, than the TV screen or the bar. There are those who are simply sitting on their stoops, "stoned," animated for a moment only, and hideously, by the approach of someone who may lend them the money for a "fix." Or by the approach of someone from whom they can purchase it, one of the shrewd ones, on the way to prison or just coming out.

5   And the others, who have avoided all of these deaths, get up in the morning and go downtown to meet "the man." They work in the white man's world all day and come home in the evening to this fetid block. They struggle to instill in their children some private sense of honor or dignity which will help the child to survive. This means, of course, that they must struggle, stolidly, incessantly, to keep this sense alive in themselves, in spite of the insults, the indifference, and the cruelty they are certain to encounter in their working day. They patiently browbeat the landlord into fixing the heat, the plaster, the plumbing; this demands prodigious patience; nor is patience usually enough. In trying to make their hovels habitable, they are perpetually throwing good money after bad. Such frustration, so long endured, is driving many strong, admirable men and women whose only crime is color to the very gates of paranoia.

6   One remembers them from another time—playing handball in the playground, going to church, wondering if they were going to be promoted at school. One remembers them going off to war—gladly, to escape this block. One remembers their return. Perhaps one remembers their wedding day. And one sees where the girl is now—vainly looking for salvation from some other embittered, trussed, and struggling boy— and sees the all-but-abandoned children in the streets.

7   Now I am perfectly aware that there are other slums in which white men are fighting for their lives, and mainly losing. I know that

blood is also flowing through those streets and that the human damage there is incalculable. People are continually pointing out to me the wretchedness of white people in order to console me for the wretchedness of blacks. But an itemized account of the American failure does not console me and it should not console anyone else. That hundreds of thousands of white people are living, in effect, no better than the "niggers" is not a fact to be regarded with complacency. The social and moral bankruptcy suggested by this fact is of the bitterest, most terrifying kind.

8   The people, however, who believe that this democratic anguish has some consoling value are always pointing out that So-and-So, white, and So-and-So, black, rose from the slums into the big time. The existence—the public existence—of, say, Frank Sinatra and Sammy Davis, Jr. proves to them that America is still the land of opportunity and that inequalities vanish before the determined will. It proves nothing of the sort. The determined will is rare—at the moment, in this country, it is unspeakably rare—and the inequalities suffered by the many are in no way justified by the rise of a few. A few have always risen—in every country, every era, and in the teeth of regimes which can by no stretch of the imagination be thought of as free. Not all of these people, it is worth remembering, left the world better than they found it. The determined will is rare, but it is not invariably benevolent. Furthermore, the American equation of success with the big times reveals an awful disrespect for human life and human achievement. This equation has placed our cities among the most dangerous in the world and has placed our youth among the most empty and most bewildered. The situation of our youth is not mysterious. Children have never been very good at listening to their elders, but they have never failed to imitate them. They must, they have no other models. That is exactly what our children are doing. They are imitating our immorality, our disrespect for the pain of others.

9   All other slum dwellers, when the bank account permits it, can move out of the slum and vanish altogether from the eye of persecution. No Negro in this country has ever made that much money and it will be a long time before any Negro does. The Negroes in Harlem, who have no money, spend what they have on such gimcracks as they are sold. These include "wider" TV screens, more "faithful" hi-fi sets, more "powerful" cars, all of which, of course, are obsolete long before they are paid for. Anyone who has ever struggled with poverty knows how extremely expensive it is to be poor; and if one is a member of a captive

population, economically speaking, one's feet have simply been placed on the treadmill forever. One is victimized, economically, in a thousand ways—rent, for example, or car insurance. Go shopping one day in Harlem—for anything—and compare Harlem prices and quality with those downtown.

10   The people who have managed to get off this block have only got as far as a more respectable ghetto. This respectable ghetto does not even have the advantages of the disreputable one—friends, neighbors, a familiar church, and friendly tradesmen; and it is not, moreover, in the nature of any ghetto to remain respectable long. Every Sunday, people who have left the block take the lonely ride back, dragging their increasingly discontented children with them. They spend the day talking, not always with words, about the trouble they've seen and the trouble—one must watch their eyes as they watch their children—they are only too likely to see. For children do not like ghettos. It takes them nearly no time to discover exactly why they are there.

11   The projects in Harlem are hated. They are hated almost as much as policemen, and this is saying a great deal. And they are hated for the same reason: both reveal, unbearably, the real attitude of the white world, no matter how many liberal speeches are made, no matter how many lofty editorials are written, no matter how many civil-rights commissions are set up.

12   The projects are hideous, of course, there being a law, apparently respected throughout the world, that popular housing shall be as cheerless as a prison. They are lumped all over Harlem, colorless, bleak, high, and revolting. The wide windows look out on Harlem's invincible and indescribable squalor: the Park Avenue railroad tracks, around which, about forty years ago, the present dark community began; the unrehabilitated houses, bowed down, it would seem, under the great weight of frustration and bitterness they contain; the dark, the ominous schoolhouses from which the child may emerge maimed, blinded, hooked, or enraged for life; and the churches, churches, block upon block of churches, niched in the walls like cannon in the walls of a fortress. Even if the administration of the projects were not so insanely humiliating (for example: one must report raises in salary to the management, which will then eat up the profit by raising one's rent; the management has the right to know who is staying in your apartment; the management can ask you to leave, at their discretion), the projects would still be hated because they are an insult to the meanest intelligence.

13   Harlem got its first private project, Riverton*—which is now, naturally, a slum—about twelve years ago because at that time Negroes were not allowed to live in Stuyvesant Town. Harlem watched Riverton go up, therefore, in the most violent bitterness of spirit, and hated it long before the builders arrived. They began hating it at about the time people began moving out of their condemned houses to make room for this additional proof of how thoroughly the white world despised them. And they had scarcely moved in, naturally, before they began smashing windows, defacing walls, urinating in the elevators, and fornicating in the playgrounds. Liberals, both white and black, were appalled at the spectacle. I was appalled by the liberal innocence—or cynicism, which comes out in practice as much the same thing. Other people were delighted to be able to point to proof positive that nothing could be done to better the lot of the colored people. They were, and are, right in one respect: that nothing can be done as long as they are treated like colored people. The people in Harlem know they are living there because white people do not think they are good enough to live anywhere else. No amount of "improvement" can sweeten this fact. Whatever money is now being earmarked to improve this, or any other ghetto, might as well be burnt. A ghetto can be improved in one way only: out of existence.

14   Similarly, the only way to police a ghetto is to be oppressive. None of the Police Commissioner's men, even with the best will in the world, have any way of understanding the lives led by the people they swagger about in twos and threes controlling. Their very presence is an insult, and it would be, even if they spent their entire day feeding gumdrops to children. They represent the force of the white world, and that world's real intentions are, simply, for that world's criminal profit and ease, to keep the black man corraled up here, in his place. The badge, the gun in the holster, and the swinging club make vivid what will happen should his rebellion become overt. Rare, indeed, is the Harlem citizen, from the most circumspect church member to the most shiftless adolescent, who does not have a long tale to tell of police incompetence,

---

*The inhabitants of Riverton were much embittered by this description; they have, apparently, forgotten how their project came into being; and have repeatedly informed me that I cannot possibly be referring to Riverton, but to another housing project which is directly across the street. It is quite clear, I think, that I have no interest in accusing any individuals or families of the depredations herein described: but neither can I deny the evidence of my own eyes. Nor do I blame anyone in Harlem for making the best of a dreadful bargain. But anyone who lives in Harlem and imagines that he has *not* struck this bargain, or that what he takes to be his status (in whose eyes?) protects him against the common pain, demoralization, and danger, is simply self deluded.

injustice, or brutality. I myself have witnessed and endured it more than once. The businessmen and racketeers also have a story. And so do the prostitutes. (And this is not, perhaps, the place to discuss Harlem's very complex attitude toward black policemen, nor the reasons, according to Harlem, that they are nearly all downtown.)

15   It is hard, on the other hand, to blame the policeman, blank, good-natured, thoughtless, and insuperably innocent, for being such a perfect representative of the people he serves. He, too, believes in good intentions and is astounded and offended when they are not taken for the deed. He has never, himself, done anything for which to be hated —which of us has?—and yet he is facing, daily and nightly, people who would gladly see him dead, and he knows it. There is no way for him not to know it: there are few things under heaven more unnerving than the silent, accumulating contempt and hatred of a people. He moves through Harlem, therefore, like an occupying soldier in a bitterly hostile country; which is precisely what, and where, he is, and is the reason he walks in twos and threes. And he is not the only one who knows why he is always in company: the people who are watching him know why, too. Any street meeting, sacred or secular, which he and his colleagues uneasily cover has as its explicit or implicit burden the cruelty and injustice of the white domination. And these days, of course, in terms increasingly vivid and jubilant, it speaks of the end of that domination. The white policeman standing on a Harlem street corner finds himself at the very center of the revolution now occurring in the world. He is not prepared for it—naturally, nobody is—and, what is possibly much more to the point, he is exposed, as few white people are, to the anguish of the black people around him. Even if he is gifted with the merest mustard grain of imagination, something must seep in. He cannot avoid observing that some of the children, in spite of their color, remind him of children he has known and loved, perhaps even of his own children. He knows that he certainly does not want *his* children living this way. He can retreat from his uneasiness in only one direction: into a callousness which very shortly becomes second nature. He becomes more callous, the population becomes more hostile, the situation grows more tense, and the police force is increased. One day, to everyone's astonishment, someone drops a match in the powder keg and everything blows up. Before the dust has settled or the blood congealed, editorials, speeches, and civil-rights commissions are loud in the land, demanding to know what happened. What happened is that Negroes want to be treated like men.

16   *Negroes want to be treated like men:* a perfectly straightforward

statement, containing only seven words. People who have mastered
Kant, Hegel, Shakespeare, Marx, Freud, and the Bible find this statement utterly impenetrable. The idea seems to threaten profound, barely
conscious assumptions. A kind of panic paralyzes their features, as
though they found themselves trapped on the edge of a steep place. I
once tried to describe to a very well-known American intellectual the
conditions among Negroes in the South. My recital disturbed him and
made him indignant; and he asked me in perfect innocence, "Why
don't all the Negroes in the South move North?" I tried to explain what
has happened, unfailingly, whenever a significant body of Negroes move
North. They do not escape Jim Crow: they merely encounter another,
not-less-deadly variety. They do not move to Chicago, they move to the
South Side; they do not move to New York, they move to Harlem. The
pressure within the ghetto causes the ghetto walls to expand, and this
expansion is always violent. White people hold the line as long as they
can, and in as many ways as they can, from verbal intimidation to
physical violence. But inevitably the border which has divided the
ghetto from the rest of the world falls into the hands of the ghetto. The
white people fall back bitterly before the black horde; the landlords
make a tidy profit by raising the rent, chopping up the rooms, and all
but dispensing with the upkeep; and what has once been a neighborhood
turns into a "turf." This is precisely what happened when the Puerto
Ricans arrived in their thousands—and the bitterness thus caused is, as
I write, being fought out all up and down those streets.

17   Northerners indulge in an extremely dangerous luxury. They seem
to feel that because they fought on the right side during the Civil War,
and won, they have earned the right merely to deplore what is going on in
the South, without taking any responsibility for it; and that they can
ignore what is happening in Northern cities because what is happening in
Little Rock or Birmingham is worse. Well, in the first place, it is not
possible for anyone who has not endured both to know which is "worse." I
know Negroes who prefer the South and white Southerners, because "At
least there, you haven't got to play any guessing games!" The guessing
games referred to have driven more than one Negro into the narcotics
ward, the madhouse, or the river. I know another Negro, a man very dear
to me, who says, with conviction and with truth, "The spirit of the South
is the spirit of America." He was born in the North and did his military
training in the South. He did not, as far as I can gather, find the South
"worse"; he found it, if anything, all too familiar. In the second place,
though, even if Birmingham *is* worse, no doubt Johannesburg, South

Africa, beats it by several miles, and Buchenwald was one of the worst things that ever happened in the entire history of the world. The world has never lacked for horrifying examples; but I do not believe that these examples are meant to be used as justification for our own crimes. This perpetual justification empties the heart of all human feeling. The emptier our hearts become, the greater will be our crimes. Thirdly, the South is not merely an embarrassingly backward region, but a part of this country, and what happens there concerns every one of us.

18   As far as the color problem is concerned, there is but one great difference between the Southern white and the Northerner: the Southerner remembers, historically and in his own psyche, a kind of Eden in which he loved black people and they loved him. Historically, the flaming sword laid across this Eden is the Civil War. Personally, it is the Southerner's sexual coming of age, when, without any warning, unbreakable taboos are set up between himself and his past. Everything, thereafter, is permitted him except the love he remembers and has never ceased to need. The resulting, indescribable torment affects every Southern mind and is the basis of the Southern hysteria.

19   None of this is true for the Northerner. Negroes represent nothing to him personally, except, perhaps, the dangers of carnality. He never sees Negroes. Southerners see them all the time. Northerners never think about them whereas Southerners are never really thinking of anything else. Negroes are, therefore, ignored in the North and are under surveillance in the South, and suffer hideously in both places. Neither the Southerner nor the Northerner is able to look on the Negro simply as a man. It seems to be indispensable to the national self-esteem that the Negro be considered either as a kind of ward (in which case we are told how many Negroes, comparatively, bought Cadillacs last year and how few, comparatively, were lynched), or as a victim (in which case we are promised that he will never vote in our assemblies or go to school with our kids). They are two sides of the same coin and the South will not change—*cannot* change—until the North changes. The country will not change until it re-examines itself and discovers what it really means by freedom. In the meantime, generations keep being born, bitterness is increased by incompetence, pride, and folly, and the world shrinks around us.

20   It is a terrible, an inexorable, law that one cannot deny the humanity of another without diminishing one's own: in the face of one's victim, one sees oneself. Walk through the streets of Harlem and see what we, this nation, have become.

QUESTIONS

Ideas

1. What is implied by the title of the essay? Consider individually three elements of the title: Fifth Avenue, Harlem, Letter.

2. What is Baldwin's purpose in writing this essay, this letter from Harlem? Who is his implied audience? What is his major point?

3. In paragraph 4 Baldwin suggests that the projects are "a monument to the folly, and the cowardice, of good intentions." What does he mean? And whose "folly," "cowardice," and "good intentions" is he referring to?

4. In describing Harlem, or at least in describing the section he knows well, Baldwin contrasts what he remembers from his childhood with what he sees later as an adult. What does he remember, what does he see, and what is the significance of the difference?

5. Twice in "Fifth Avenue" Baldwin considers counterarguments, alternate explanations for why slums exist (paragraphs 8 and 13). What are Baldwin's views about this problem, and what are the counterviews? Which do you find more persuasive and why?

6. Children are mentioned five times in the essay—in paragraphs 3, 5, 6, 10, and 15. What common thread ties together the references to children? What point does Baldwin make when he mentions them?

7. What does Baldwin say about the relationship between the police and the people of Harlem? Reread paragraph 15, then outline the pattern of cause and effect that Baldwin provides as an explanation for why riots occur.

8. Why does Baldwin discuss the South? Why does he bring South Africa and Buchenwald into the argument? What justification for crime does he offer? Is it persuasive? Is it valid? Why or why not?

9. The final paragraph of the essay makes one of Baldwin's most important points: that in diminishing other people we diminish ourselves. Explain how this is or is not true.

Organization

10. One way of looking at the structure of "Fifth Avenue" is to see it as composed of two major parts: paragraphs 1–10 and paragraphs 11–20. Provide a title for each part and explain how the two parts are related.

11. Another way of looking at the organization of the essay is to see it as oscillating between description and argumentation. How are the descriptive sections related to the polemical sections?

12. Baldwin structures part of the essay as a walk through Harlem. Where does the tour begin and end? How does Baldwin lead into and slide out of this section?

Sentences

13. Paragraph 2 is only a single sentence. Why? Would this sentence be better attached to paragraph 1 or 3? Explain.

14. The last sentence of paragraph 5 packs in many details. Why does Baldwin cram them into one sentence? Would these details be more effectively presented in a series of short sentences? How are the length, shape, and style of the sentence as Baldwin wrote it related to the point he makes in it?

15. The end of paragraph 15 and the beginning of paragraph 16 contain the same sentence—or part of the same sentence. What does Baldwin gain by repeating it this way?

16. Read the final sentences of the following paragraphs: 7–13, 15, 19–20. What do you notice about how Baldwin concludes his paragraphs?

Words

17. What is the tone of the opening paragraphs? Consider especially the word "rehabilitated" (paragraphs 2 and 3) and the clause "for progress takes time" (paragraph 1).

18. Paragraphs 4–6 contain highly charged, emotional language. Which words carry especially strong connotations? Of these, which have positive and which negative connotations? What point does Baldwin make with this strongly connotative language?

19. Throughout the essay Baldwin places many words in quotation marks. Explain the tone of each word, especially the following: "the turf" (3), "moslems" (4), "the man" (5), "powerful" (9), and "improvement" (13). Explain also the tone and point of the sentences quoted in paragraphs 4, 16, and 17.

Suggestions for Writing

A. Write a polemical essay about a social problem, using a place as the central focus. Try to mix description of the location of the problem with an analysis of how it got that way. Decide whether you want primarily to persuade readers to do something about the problem or whether you want simply to enable them to better understand it. Decide on the relative proportions

of description, explanation, and analysis—but only after you write a couple
of rough drafts.

B. Argue with or support Baldwin. Choose one of the following statements
from "Fifth Avenue" and write an essay confirming or refuting Baldwin's
idea.

Negroes want to be treated like men. (15, 16)

It is a terrible, an inexorable, law that one cannot deny the humanity
of another without diminishing one's own: in the face of one's victim,
one sees oneself. (20)

Children have never been very good at listening to their elders, but they
have never failed to imitate them. (8)

Notes of a Native Son

I

1   On the 29th of July, in 1943, my father died. On the same
day, a few hours later, his last child was born. Over a month before this,
while all our energies were concentrated in waiting for these events,
there had been, in Detroit, one of the bloodiest race riots of the century.
A few hours after my father's funeral, while he lay in state in the
undertaker's chapel, a race riot broke out in Harlem. On the morning
of the 3rd of August, we drove my father to the graveyard through a
wilderness of smashed plate glass.

2   The day of my father's funeral had also been my nineteenth
birthday. As we drove him to the graveyard, the spoils of injustice,
anarchy, discontent, and hatred were all around us. It seemed to me that
God himself had devised, to mark my father's end, the most sustained
and brutally dissonant of codas. And it seemed to me, too, that the
violence which rose all about us as my father left the world had been
devised as a corrective for the pride of his eldest son. I had declined to
believe in that apocalypse which had been central to my father's vision;
very well, life seemed to be saying, here is something that will certainly
pass for an apocalypse until the real thing comes along. I had inclined
to be contemptuous of my father for the conditions of his life, for the

conditions of our lives. When his life had ended I began to wonder about that life and also, in a new way, to be apprehensive about my own.

3   I had not known my father very well. We had got on badly, partly because we shared, in our different fashions, the vice of stubborn pride. When he was dead I realized that I had hardly ever spoken to him. When he had been dead a long time I began to wish I had. It seems to be typical of life in America, where opportunities, real and fancied, are thicker than anywhere else on the globe, that the second generation has no time to talk to the first. No one, including my father, seems to have known exactly how old he was, but his mother had been born during slavery. He was of the first generation of free men. He, along with thousands of other Negroes, came North after 1919 and I was part of that generation which had never seen the landscape of what Negroes sometimes call the Old Country.

4   He had been born in New Orleans and had been a quite young man there during the time that Louis Armstrong, a boy, was running errands for the dives and honky-tonks of what was always presented to me as one of the most wicked of cities—to this day, whenever I think of New Orleans, I also helplessly think of Sodom and Gomorrah. My father never mentioned Louis Armstrong, except to forbid us to play his records; but there was a picture of him on our wall for a long time. One of my father's strong-willed female relatives had placed it there and forbade my father to take it down. He never did, but he eventually maneuvered her out of the house and when, some years later, she was in trouble and near death, he refused to do anything to help her.

5   He was, I think, very handsome. I gather this from photographs and from my own memories of him, dressed in his Sunday best and on his way to preach a sermon somewhere, when I was little. Handsome, proud, and ingrown, "like a toe-nail," somebody said. But he looked to me, as I grew older, like pictures I had seen of African tribal chieftains: he really should have been naked, with war-paint on and barbaric mementos, standing among spears. He could be chilling in the pulpit and indescribably cruel in his personal life and he was certainly the most bitter man I have ever met; yet it must be said that there was something else in him, buried in him, which lent him his tremendous power and, even, a rather crushing charm. It had something to do with his blackness, I think—he was very black—with his blackness and his beauty, and with the fact that he knew that he was black but did not know that he was beautiful. He claimed to be proud of his blackness but it had also been the cause of much humiliation and it had fixed bleak boundaries

to his life. He was not a young man when we were growing up and he had already suffered many kinds of ruin; in his outrageously demanding and protective way he loved his children, who were black like him and menaced, like him; and all these things sometimes showed in his face when he tried, never to my knowledge with any success, to establish contact with any of us. When he took one of his children on his knee to play, the child always became fretful and began to cry; when he tried to help one of us with our homework the absolutely unabating tension which emanated from him caused our minds and our tongues to become paralyzed, so that he, scarcely knowing why, flew into a rage and the child, not knowing why, was punished. If it ever entered his head to bring a surprise home for his children, it was, almost unfailingly, the wrong surprise and even the big watermelons he often brought home on his back in the summertime led to the most appalling scenes. I do not remember, in all those years, that one of his children was ever glad to see him come home. From what I was able to gather of his early life, it seemed that this inability to establish contact with other people had always marked him and had been one of the things which had driven him out of New Orleans. There was something in him, therefore, grop-ing and tentative, which was never expressed and which was buried with him. One saw it most clearly when he was facing new people and hoping to impress them. But he never did, not for long. We went from church to smaller and more improbable church, he found himself in less and less demand as a minister, and by the time he died none of his friends had come to see him for a long time. He had lived and died in an intolerable bitterness of spirit and it frightened me, as we drove him to the graveyard through those unquiet, ruined streets, to see how powerful and overflowing this bitterness could be and to realize that this bitter-ness now was mine.

6   When he died I had been away from home for a little over a year. In that year I had had time to become aware of the meaning of all my father's bitter warnings, had discovered the secret of his proudly pursed lips and rigid carriage: I had discovered the weight of white people in the world. I saw that this had been for my ancestors and now would be for me an awful thing to live with and that the bitterness which had helped to kill my father could also kill me.

7   He had been ill a long time—in the mind, as we now realized, reliving instances of his fantastic intransigence in the new light of his affliction and endeavoring to feel a sorrow for him which never, quite, came true. We had not known that he was being eaten up by paranoia,

and the discovery that his cruelty, to our bodies and our minds, had been one of the symptoms of his illness was not, then, enough to enable us to forgive him. The younger children felt, quite simply, relief that he would not be coming home anymore. My mother's observation that it was he, after all, who had kept them alive all these years meant nothing because the problems of keeping children alive are not real for children. The older children felt, with my father gone, that they could invite their friends to the house without fear that their friends would be insulted or, as had sometimes happened with me, being told that their friends were in league with the devil and intended to rob our family of everything we owned. (I didn't fail to wonder, and it made me hate him, what on earth we owned that anybody else would want.)

8   His illness was beyond all hope of healing before anyone realized that he was ill. He had always been so strange and had lived, like a prophet, in such unimaginably close communion with the Lord that his long silences which were punctuated by moans and hallelujahs and snatches of old songs while he sat at the living-room window never seemed odd to us. It was not until he refused to eat because, he said, his family was trying to poison him that my mother was forced to accept as a fact what had, until then, been only an unwilling suspicion. When he was committed, it was discovered that he had tuberculosis and, as it turned out, the disease of his mind allowed the disease of his body to destroy him. For the doctors could not force him to eat, either, and, though he was fed intravenously, it was clear from the beginning that there was no hope for him.

9   In my mind's eye I could see him, sitting at the window, locked up in his terrors; hating and fearing every living soul including his children who had betrayed him, too, by reaching towards the world which had despised him. There were nine of us. I began to wonder what it could have felt like for such a man to have had nine children whom he could barely feed. He used to make little jokes about our poverty, which never, of course, seemed very funny to us; they could not have seemed very funny to him, either, or else our all too feeble response to them would never have caused such rages. He spent great energy and achieved, to our chagrin, no small amount of success in keeping us away from the people who surrounded us, people who had all-night rent parties to which we listened when we should have been sleeping, people who cursed and drank and flashed razor blades on Lenox Avenue. He could not understand why, if they had so much energy to spare, they could not use it to make their lives better. He treated almost everybody

on our block with a most uncharitable asperity and neither they, nor, of course, their children were slow to reciprocate.

10   The only white people who came to our house were welfare workers and bill collectors. It was almost always my mother who dealt with them, for my father's temper, which was at the mercy of his pride, was never to be trusted. It was clear that he felt their very presence in his home to be a violation: this was conveyed by his carriage, almost ludicrously stiff, and by his voice, harsh and vindictively polite. When I was around nine or ten I wrote a play which was directed by a young, white schoolteacher, a woman, who then took an interest in me, and gave me books to read and, in order to corroborate my theatrical bent, decided to take me to see what she somewhat tactlessly referred to as "real" plays. Theatergoing was forbidden in our house, but, with the really cruel intuitiveness of a child, I suspected that the color of this woman's skin would carry the day for me. When, at school, she suggested taking me to the theater, I did not, as I might have done if she had been a Negro, find a way of discouraging her, but agreed that she should pick me up at my house one evening. I then, very cleverly, left all the rest to my mother, who suggested to my father, as I knew she would, that it would not be very nice to let such a kind woman make the trip for nothing. Also, since it was a schoolteacher, I imagine that my mother countered the idea of sin with the idea of "education," which word, even with my father, carried a kind of bitter weight.

11   Before the teacher came my father took me aside to ask *why* she was coming, what *interest* she could possibly have in our house, in a boy like me. I said I didn't know but I, too, suggested that it had something to do with education. And I understood that my father was waiting for me to say something—I didn't quite know what; perhaps that I wanted his protection against this teacher and her "education." I said none of these things and the teacher came and we went out. It was clear, during the brief interview in our living room, that my father was agreeing very much against his will and that he would have refused permission if he had dared. The fact that he did not dare caused me to despise him: I had no way of knowing that he was facing in that living room a wholly unprecedented and frightening situation.

12   Later, when my father had been laid off from his job, this woman became very important to us. She was really a very sweet and generous woman and went to a great deal of trouble to be of help to us, particularly during one awful winter. My mother called her by the highest name she knew. She said she was a "christian." My father could scarcely

disagree but during the four or five years of our relatively close association he never trusted her and was always trying to surprise in her open, Midwestern face the genuine, cunningly hidden, and hideous motivation. In later years, particularly when it began to be clear that this "education" of mine was going to lead me to perdition, he became more explicit and warned me that my white friends in high school were not really my friends and that I would see, when I was older, how white people would do anything to keep a Negro down. Some of them could be nice, he admitted, but none of them were to be trusted and most of them were not even nice. The best thing was to have as little to do with them as possible. I did not feel this way and I was certain, in my innocence, that I never would.

13   But the year which preceded my father's death had made a great change in my life. I had been living in New Jersey, working in defense plants, working and living among southerners, white and black. I knew about the south, of course, and about how southerners treated Negroes and how they expected them to behave, but it had never entered my mind that anyone would look at me and expect *me* to behave that way. I learned in New Jersey that to be a Negro meant, precisely, that one was never looked at but was simply at the mercy of the reflexes the color of one's skin caused in other people. I acted in New Jersey as I had always acted, that is as though I thought a great deal of myself—I had to *act* that way—with results that were, simply, unbelievable. I had scarcely arrived before I had earned the enmity, which was extraordinarily ingenious, of all my superiors and nearly all my co-workers. In the beginning, to make matters worse, I simply did not know what was happening. I did not know what I had done, and I shortly began to wonder what *anyone* could possibly do, to bring about such unanimous, active, and unbearably vocal hostility. I knew about jim-crow but I had never experienced it. I went to the same self-service restaurant three times and stood with all the Princeton boys before the counter, waiting for a hamburger and coffee; it was always an extraordinarily long time before anything was set before me; but it was not until the fourth visit that I learned that, in fact, nothing had ever been set before me: I had simply picked something up. Negroes were not served there, I was told, and they had been waiting for me to realize that I was always the only Negro present. Once I was told this, I determined to go there all the time. But now they were ready for me and, though some dreadful scenes were subsequently enacted in that restaurant, I never ate there again.

14   It was the same story all over New Jersey, in bars, bowling alleys,

diners, places to live. I was always being forced to leave, silently, or with mutual imprecations. I very shortly became notorious and children giggled behind me when I passed and their elders whispered or shouted— they really believed that I was mad. And it did begin to work on my mind, of course; I began to be afraid to go anywhere and to compensate for this I went places to which I really should not have gone and where, God knows, I had no desire to be. My reputation in town naturally enhanced my reputation at work and my working day became one long series of acrobatics designed to keep me out of trouble. I cannot say that these acrobatics succeeded. It began to seem that the machinery of the organization I worked for was turning over, day and night, with but one aim: to eject me. I was fired once, and contrived, with the aid of a friend from New York, to get back on the payroll; was fired again, and bounced back again. It took a while to fire me for the third time, but the third time took. There were no loopholes anywhere. There was not even any way of getting back inside the gates.

15   That year in New Jersey lives in my mind as though it were the year during which, having an unsuspected predilection for it, I first contracted some dread, chronic disease, the unfailing symptom of which is a kind of blind fever, a pounding in the skull and fire in the bowels. Once this disease is contracted, one can never be really carefree again, for the fever, without an instant's warning, can recur at any moment. It can wreck more important things than race relations. There is not a Negro alive who does not have this rage in his blood—one has the choice, merely, of living with it consciously or surrendering to it. As for me, this fever has recurred in me, and does, and will until the day I die.

16   My last night in New Jersey, a white friend from New York took me to the nearest big town, Trenton, to go to the movies and have a few drinks. As it turned out, he also saved me from, at the very least, a violent whipping. Almost every detail of that night stands out very clearly in my memory. I even remember the name of the movie we saw because its title impressed me as being so patly ironical. It was a movie about the German occupation of France, starring Maureen O'Hara and Charles Laughton and called *This Land Is Mine.* I remember the name of the diner we walked into when the movie ended: it was the "American Diner." When we walked in the counterman asked what we wanted and I remember answering with the casual sharpness which had become my habit: "We want a hamburger and a cup of coffee, what do you think we want?" I do not know why, after a year of such rebuffs, I so completely failed to anticipate his answer, which was, of course, "We don't

serve Negroes here." This reply failed to discompose me, at least for the moment. I made some sardonic comment about the name of the diner and we walked out into the streets.

17   This was the time of what was called the "brown-out," when the lights in all American cities were very dim. When we re-entered the streets something happened to me which had the force of an optical illusion, or a nightmare. The streets were very crowded and I was facing north. People were moving in every direction but it seemed to me, in that instant, that all of the people I could see, and many more than that, were moving toward me, against me, and that everyone was white. I remember how their faces gleamed. And I felt, like a physical sensation, a *click* at the nape of my neck as though some interior string connecting my head to my body had been cut. I began to walk. I heard my friend call after me, but I ignored him. Heaven only knows what was going on in his mind, but he had the good sense not to touch me—I don't know what would have happened if he had—and to keep me in sight. I don't know what was going on in my mind, either; I certainly had no conscious plan. I wanted to do something to crush these white faces, which were crushing me. I walked for perhaps a block or two until I came to an enormous, glittering, and fashionable restaurant in which I knew not even the intercession of the Virgin would cause me to be served. I pushed through the doors and took the first vacant seat I saw, at a table for two, and waited.

18   I do not know how long I waited and I rather wonder, until today, what I could possibly have looked like. Whatever I looked like, I frightened the waitress who shortly appeared, and the moment she appeared all of my fury flowed towards her. I hated her for her white face, and for her great, astounded, frightened eyes. I felt that if she found a black man so frightening I would make her fright worth-while.

19   She did not ask me what I wanted, but repeated, as though she had learned it somewhere, "We don't serve Negroes here." She did not say it with the blunt, derisive hostility to which I had grown so accustomed, but, rather, with a note of apology in her voice, and fear. This made me colder and more murderous than ever. I felt I had to do something with my hands. I wanted her to come close enough for me to get her neck between my hands.

20   So I pretended not to have understood her, hoping to draw her closer. And she did step a very short step closer, with her pencil poised incongruously over her pad, and repeated the formula: ". . . don't serve Negroes here."

21   Somehow, with the repetition of that phrase, which was already ringing in my head like a thousand bells of a nightmare, I realized that she would never come any closer and that I would have to strike from a distance. There was nothing on the table but an ordinary water-mug half full of water, and I picked this up and hurled it with all my strength at her. She ducked and it missed her and shattered against the mirror behind the bar. And, with that sound, my frozen blood abruptly thawed, I returned from wherever I had been, I *saw,* for the first time, the restaurant, the people with their mouths open, already, as it seemed to me, rising as one man, and I realized what I had done, and where I was, and I was frightened. I rose and began running for the door. A round, potbellied man grabbed me by the nape of the neck just as I reached the doors and began to beat me about the face. I kicked him and got loose and ran into the streets. My friend whispered, *"Run!"* and I ran.

22   My friend stayed outside the restaurant long enough to misdirect my pursuers and the police, who arrived, he told me, at once. I do not know what I said to him when he came to my room that night. I could not have said much. I felt, in the oddest, most awful way, that I had somehow betrayed him. I lived it over and over and over again, the way one relives an automobile accident after it has happened and one finds oneself alone and safe. I could not get over two facts, both equally difficult for the imagination to grasp, and one was that I could have been murdered. But the other was that I had been ready to commit murder. I saw nothing very clearly but I did see this: that my life, my *real* life, was in danger, and not from anything other people might do but from the hatred I carried in my own heart.

II

23   I had returned home around the second week in June—in great haste because it seemed that my father's death and my mother's confinement were both but a matter of hours. In the case of my mother, it soon became clear that she had simply made a miscalculation. This had always been her tendency and I don't believe that a single one of us arrived in the world, or has since arrived anywhere else, on time. But none of us dawdled so intolerably about the business of being born as did my baby sister. We sometimes amused ourselves, during those endless, stifling weeks, by picturing the baby sitting within in the safe, warm dark, bitterly regretting the necessity of becoming a part of our chaos and

stubbornly putting it off as long as possible. I understood her perfectly and congratulated her on showing such good sense so soon. Death, however, sat as purposefully at my father's bedside as life stirred within my mother's womb and it was harder to understand why he so lingered in that long shadow. It seemed that he had bent, and for a long time, too, all of his energies towards dying. Now death was ready for him but my father held back.

24   All of Harlem, indeed, seemed to be infected by waiting. I had never before known it to be so violently still. Racial tensions throughout this country were exacerbated during the early years of the war, partly because the labor market brought together hundreds of thousands of ill-prepared people and partly because Negro soldiers, regardless of where they were born, received their military training in the south. What happened in defense plants and army camps had repercussions, naturally, in every Negro ghetto. The situation in Harlem had grown bad enough for clergymen, policemen, educators, politicians, and social workers to assert in one breath that there was no "crime wave" and to offer, in the very next breath, suggestions as to how to combat it. These suggestions always seemed to involve playgrounds, despite the fact that racial skirmishes were occurring in the playgrounds, too. Playground or not, crime wave or not, the Harlem police force had been augmented in March, and the unrest grew—perhaps, in fact, partly as a result of the ghetto's instinctive hatred of policemen. Perhaps the most revealing news item, out of the steady parade of reports of muggings, stabbings, shootings, assaults, gang wars, and accusations of police brutality is the item concerning six Negro girls who set upon a white girl in the subway because, as they all too accurately put it, she was stepping on their toes. Indeed she was, all over the nation.

25   I had never before been so aware of policemen, on foot, on horseback, on corners, everywhere, always two by two. Nor had I ever been so aware of small knots of people. They were on stoops and on corners and in doorways, and what was striking about them, I think, was that they did not seem to be talking. Never, when I passed these groups, did the usual sound of a curse or a laugh ring out and neither did there seem to be any hum of gossip. There was certainly, on the other hand, occurring between them communication extraordinarily intense. Another thing that was striking was the unexpected diversity of the people who made up these groups. Usually, for example, one would see a group of sharpies standing on the street corner, jiving the passing chicks; or a group of older men, usually, for some reason, in the vicinity of a barber

shop, discussing baseball scores, or the numbers or making rather chilling observations about women they had known. Women, in a general way, tended to be seen less often together—unless they were church women, or very young girls, or prostitutes met together for an unprofessional instant. But that summer I saw the strangest combinations: large, respectable, churchly matrons standing on the stoops or the corners with their hair tied up, together with a girl in sleazy satin whose face bore the marks of gin and the razor, or heavy-set, abrupt, no-nonsense older men, in company with the most disreputable and fanatical "race" men, or these same "race" men with the sharpies, or these sharpies with the churchly women. Seventh Day Adventists and Methodists and Spiritualists seemed to be hobnobbing with Holyrollers and they were all, alike, entangled with the most flagrant disbelievers; something heavy in their stance seemed to indicate that they had all, incredibly, seen a common vision, and on each face there seemed to be the same strange, bitter shadow.

26   The churchly women and the matter-of-fact, no-nonsense men had children in the Army. The sleazy girls they talked to had lovers there, the sharpies and the "race" men had friends and brothers there. It would have demanded an unquestioning patriotism, happily as uncommon in this country as it is undesirable, for these people not to have been disturbed by the bitter letters they received, by the newspaper stories they read, not to have been enraged by the posters, then to be found all over New York, which described the Japanese as "yellow-bellied Japs." It was only the "race" men, to be sure, who spoke ceaselessly of being revenged—how this vengeance was to be exacted was not clear—for the indignities and dangers suffered by Negro boys in uniform; but everybody felt a directionless, hopeless bitterness, as well as that panic which can scarcely be suppressed when one knows that a human being one loves is beyond one's reach, and in danger. This helplessness and this gnawing uneasiness does something, at length, to even the toughest mind. Perhaps the best way to sum all this up is to say that the people I knew felt, mainly, a peculiar kind of relief when they knew that their boys were being shipped out of the south, to do battle overseas. It was, perhaps, like feeling that the most dangerous part of a dangerous journey had been passed and that now, even if death should come, it would come with honor and without the complicity of their countrymen. Such a death would be, in short, a fact with which one could hope to live.

27   It was on the 28th of July, which I believe was a Wednesday, that

I visited my father for the first time during his illness and for the last time in his life. The moment I saw him I knew why I had put off this visit so long. I had told my mother that I did not want to see him because I hated him. But this was not true. It was only that I *had* hated him and I wanted to hold on to this hatred. I did not want to look on him as a ruin: it was not a ruin I had hated. I imagine that one of the reasons people cling to their hates so stubbornly is because they sense, once hate is gone, that they will be forced to deal with pain.

28   We traveled out to him, his older sister and myself, to what seemed to be the very end of a very Long Island. It was hot and dusty and we wrangled, my aunt and I, all the way out, over the fact that I had recently begun to smoke and, as she said, to give myself airs. But I knew that she wrangled with me because she could not bear to face the fact of her brother's dying. Neither could I endure the reality of her despair, her unstated bafflement as to what had happened to her brother's life, and her own. So we wrangled and I smoked and from time to time she fell into a heavy reverie. Covertly, I watched her face, which was the face of an old woman; it had fallen in, the eyes were sunken and lightless; soon she would be dying, too.

29   In my childhood—it had not been so long ago—I had thought her beautiful. She had been quick-witted and quick-moving and very generous with all the children and each of her visits had been an event. At one time one of my brothers and myself had thought of running away to live with her. Now she could no longer produce out of her handbag some unexpected and yet familiar delight. She made me feel pity and revulsion and fear. It was awful to realize that she no longer caused me to feel affection. The closer we came to the hospital the more querulous she became and at the same time, naturally, grew more dependent on me. Between pity and guilt and fear I began to feel that there was another me trapped in my skull like a jack-in-the-box who might escape my control at any moment and fill the air with screaming.

30   She began to cry the moment we entered the room and she saw him lying there, all shriveled and still, like a little black monkey. The great, gleaming apparatus which fed him and would have compelled him to be still even if he had been able to move brought to mind, not beneficence, but torture; the tubes entering his arm made me think of pictures I had seen when a child, of Gulliver, tied down by the pygmies on that island. My aunt wept and wept, there was a whistling sound in my father's throat; nothing was said; he could not speak. I wanted to take his hand, to say something. But I do not know what I could have

said, even if he could have heard me. He was not really in that room with us, he had at last really embarked on his journey; and though my aunt told me that he said he was going to meet Jesus, I did not hear anything except that whistling in his throat. The doctor came back and we left, into that unbearable train again, and home. In the morning came the telegram saying that he was dead. Then the house was suddenly full of relatives, friends, hysteria, and confusion and I quickly left my mother and the children to the care of those impressive women, who, in Negro communities at least, automatically appear at times of bereavement armed with lotions, proverbs, and patience, and an ability to cook. I went downtown. By the time I returned, later the same day, my mother had been carried to the hospital and the baby had been born.

III

31   For my father's funeral I had nothing black to wear and this posed a nagging problem all day long. It was one of those problems, simple, or impossible of solution, to which the mind insanely clings in order to avoid the mind's real trouble. I spent most of that day at the downtown apartment of a girl I knew, celebrating my birthday with whiskey and wondering what to wear that night. When planning a birthday celebration one naturally does not expect that it will be up against competition from a funeral and this girl had anticipated taking me out that night, for a big dinner and a night club afterwards. Sometime during the course of that long day we decided that we would go out anyway, when my father's funeral service was over. I imagine *I* decided it, since, as the funeral hour approached, it became clearer and clearer to me that I would not know what to do with myself when it was over. The girl, stifling her very lively concern as to the possible effects of the whiskey on one of my father's chief mourners, concentrated on being conciliatory and practically helpful. She found a black shirt for me somewhere and ironed it and, dressed in the darkest pants and jacket I owned, and slightly drunk, I made my way to my father's funeral.

32   The chapel was full, but not packed, and very quiet. There were, mainly, my father's relatives, and his children, and here and there I saw faces I had not seen since childhood, the faces of my father's one-time friends. They were very dark and solemn now, seeming somehow to suggest that they had known all along that something like this would happen. Chief among the mourners was my aunt, who had quarreled

with my father all his life; by which I do not mean to suggest that her mourning was insincere or that she had not loved him. I suppose that she was one of the few people in the world who had, and their incessant quarreling proved precisely the strength of the tie that bound them. The only other person in the world, as far as I knew, whose relationship to my father rivaled my aunt's in depth was my mother, who was not there.

33   It seemed to me, of course, that it was a very long funeral. But it was, if anything, a rather shorter funeral than most, nor, since there were no overwhelming, uncontrollable expressions of grief, could it be called—if I dare to use the word—successful. The minister who preached my father's funeral sermon was one of the few my father had still been seeing as he neared his end. He presented to us in his sermon a man whom none of us had ever seen—a man thoughtful, patient, and forbearing, a Christian inspiration to all who knew him, and a model for his children. And no doubt the children, in their disturbed and guilty state, were almost ready to believe this; he had been remote enough to be anything and, anyway, the shock of the incontrovertible, that it was really our father lying up there in that casket, prepared the mind for anything. His sister moaned and this grief-stricken moaning was taken as corroboration. The other faces held a dark, non-committal thoughtfulness. This was not the man they had known, but they had scarcely expected to be confronted with *him;* this was, in a sense deeper than questions of fact, the man they had not known, and the man they had not known may have been the real one. The real man, whoever he had been, had suffered and now he was dead: this was all that was sure and all that mattered now. Every man in the chapel hoped that when his hour came he, too, would be eulogized, which is to say forgiven, and that all of his lapses, greeds, errors, and strayings from the truth would be invested with coherence and looked upon with charity. This was perhaps the last thing human beings could give each other and it was what they demanded, after all, of the Lord. Only the Lord saw the midnight tears, only He was present when one of His children, moaning and wringing hands, paced up and down the room. When one slapped one's child in anger the recoil in the heart reverberated through heaven and became part of the pain of the universe. And when the children were hungry and sullen and distrustful and one watched them, daily, growing wilder, and further away, and running headlong into danger, it was the Lord who knew what the charged heart endured as the strap was laid to the backside; the Lord alone who knew what one *would* have said if one had had, like the Lord, the gift of the living word. It was the Lord who knew

of the impossibility every parent in that room faced: how to prepare the child for the day when the child would be despised and how to *create* in the child—by what means?—a stronger antidote to this poison than one had found for oneself. The avenues, side streets, bars, billiard halls, hospitals, police stations, and even the playgrounds of Harlem—not to mention the houses of correction, the jails, and the morgue—testified to the potency of the poison while remaining silent as to the efficacy of whatever antidote, irresistibly raising the question of whether or not such an antidote existed; raising, which was worse, the question of whether or not an antidote was desirable; perhaps poison should be fought with poison. With these several schisms in the mind and with more terrors in the heart than could be named, it was better not to judge the man who had gone down under an impossible burden. It was better to remember: *Thou knowest this man's fall; but thou knowest not his wrassling.*

34   While the preacher talked and I watched the children—years of changing their diapers, scrubbing them, slapping them, taking them to school, and scolding them had had the perhaps inevitable result of making me love them, though I am not sure I knew this then—my mind was busily breaking out with a rash of disconnected impressions. Snatches of popular songs, indecent jokes, bits of books I had read, movie sequences, faces, voices, political issues—I thought I was going mad; all these impressions suspended, as it were, in the solution of the faint nausea produced in me by the heat and liquor. For a moment I had the impression that my alcoholic breath, inefficiently disguised with chewing gum, filled the entire chapel. Then someone began singing one of my father's favorite songs and, abruptly, I was with him, sitting on his knee, in the hot, enormous, crowded church which was the first church we attended. It was the Abyssinia Baptist Church on 138th Street. We had not gone there long. With this image, a host of others came. I had forgotten, in the rage of my growing up, how proud my father had been of me when I was little. Apparently, I had had a voice and my father had liked to show me off before the members of the church. I had forgotten what he had looked like when he was pleased but now I remembered that he had always been grinning with pleasure when my solos ended. I even remembered certain expressions on his face when he teased my mother—had he loved her? I would never know. And when had it all begun to change? For now it seemed that he had not always been cruel. I remembered being taken for a haircut and scraping my knee on the footrest of the barber's chair and I remembered my father's

face as he soothed my crying and applied the stinging iodine. Then I remembered our fights, fights which had been of the worst possible kind because my technique had been silence.

35 I remembered the one time in all our life together when we had really spoken to each other.

36 It was on a Sunday and it must have been shortly before I left home. We were walking, just the two of us, in our usual silence, to or from church. I was in high school and had been doing a lot of writing and I was, at about this time, the editor of the high school magazine. But I had also been a Young Minister and had been preaching from the pulpit. Lately, I had been taking fewer engagements and preached as rarely as possible. It was said in the church, quite truthfully, that I was "cooling off."

37 My father asked me abruptly, "You'd rather write than preach, wouldn't you?"

38 I was astonished at his question—because it was a real question. I answered, "Yes."

39 That was all we said. It was awful to remember that that was all we had *ever* said.

40 The casket now was opened and the mourners were being led up the aisle to look for the last time on the deceased. The assumption was that the family was too overcome with grief to be allowed to make this journey alone and I watched while my aunt was led to the casket and, muffled in black, and shaking, led back to her seat. I disapproved of forcing the children to look on their dead father, considering that the shock of his death, or, more truthfully, the shock of death as a reality, was already a little more than a child could bear, but my judgment in this matter had been overruled and there they were, bewildered and frightened and very small, being led, one by one, to the casket. But there is also something very gallant about children at such moments. It has something to do with their silence and gravity and with the fact that one cannot help them. Their legs, somehow, seem *exposed*, so that it is at once incredible and terribly clear that their legs are all they have to hold them up.

41 I had not wanted to go to the casket myself and I certainly had not wished to be led there, but there was no way of avoiding either of these forms. One of the deacons led me up and I looked on my father's face. I cannot say that it looked like him at all. His blackness had been equivocated by powder and there was no suggestion in that casket of what his power had or could have been. He was simply an old man dead,

and it was hard to believe that he had ever given anyone either joy or pain. Yet, his life filled that room. Further up the avenue his wife was holding his newborn child. Life and death so close together, and love and hatred, and right and wrong, said something to me which I did not want to hear concerning man, concerning the life of man.

42   After the funeral, while I was downtown desperately celebrating my birthday, a Negro soldier, in the lobby of the Hotel Braddock, got into a fight with a white policeman over a Negro girl. Negro girls, white policemen, in or out of uniform, and Negro males—in or out of uniform —were part of the furniture of the lobby of the Hotel Braddock and this was certainly not the first time such an incident had occurred. It was destined, however, to receive an unprecedented publicity, for the fight between the policeman and the soldier ended with the shooting of the soldier. Rumor, flowing immediately to the streets outside, stated that the soldier had been shot in the back, an instantaneous and revealing invention, and that the soldier had died protecting a Negro woman. The facts were somewhat different—for example, the soldier had not been shot in the back, and was not dead, and the girl seems to have been as dubious a symbol of womanhood as her white counterpart in Georgia usually is, but no one was interested in the facts. They preferred the invention because this invention expressed and corroborated their hates and fears so perfectly. It is just as well to remember that people are always doing this. Perhaps many of those legends, including Christianity, to which the world clings began their conquest of the world with just some such concerted surrender to distortion. The effect, in Harlem, of this particular legend was like the effect of a lit match in a tin of gasoline. The mob gathered before the doors of the Hotel Braddock simply began to swell and to spread in every direction, and Harlem exploded.

43   The mob did not cross the ghetto lines. It would have been easy, for example, to have gone over Morningside Park on the west side or to have crossed the Grand Central railroad tracks at 125th Street on the east side, to wreak havoc in white neighborhoods. The mob seems to have been mainly interested in something more potent and real than the white face, that is, in white power, and the principal damage done during the riot of the summer of 1943 was to white business establishments in Harlem. It might have been a far bloodier story, of course, if, at the hour the riot began, these establishments had still been open. From the Hotel Braddock the mob fanned out, east and west along 125th Street, and for the entire length of Lenox, Seventh, and Eighth

avenues. Along each of these avenues, and along each major side street
—116th, 125th, 135th, and so on—bars, stores, pawnshops, restaurants,
even little luncheonettes had been smashed open and entered and looted
—looted, it might be added, with more haste than efficiency. The
shelves really looked as though a bomb had struck them. Cans of beans
and soup and dog food, along with toilet paper, corn flakes, sardines and
milk tumbled every which way, and abandoned cash registers and cases
of beer leaned crazily out of the splintered windows and were strewn
along the avenues. Sheets, blankets, and clothing of every description
formed a kind of path, as though people had dropped them while
running. I truly had not realized that Harlem *had* so many stores until
I saw them all smashed open; the first time the word *wealth* ever entered
my mind in relation to Harlem was when I saw it scattered in the streets.
But one's first, incongruous impression of plenty was countered immediately by an impression of waste. None of this was doing anybody any
good. It would have been better to have left the plate glass as it had been
and the goods lying in the stores.

44   It would have been better, but it would also have been intolerable,
for Harlem had needed something to smash. To smash something is the
ghetto's chronic need. Most of the time it is the members of the ghetto
who smash each other, and themselves. But as long as the ghetto walls
are standing there will always come a moment when these outlets do not
work. That summer, for example, it was not enough to get into a fight
on Lenox Avenue, or curse out one's cronies in the barber shops. If ever,
indeed, the violence which fills Harlem's churches, pool halls, and bars
erupts outward in a more direct fashion, Harlem and its citizens are
likely to vanish in an apocalyptic flood. That this is not likely to happen
is due to a great many reasons, most hidden and powerful among them
the Negro's real relation to the white American. This relation prohibits,
simply, anything as uncomplicated and satisfactory as pure hatred. In
order really to hate white people, one has to blot so much out of the
mind—and the heart—that this hatred itself becomes an exhausting and
self-destructive pose. But this does not mean, on the other hand, that
love comes easily: the white world is too powerful, too complacent, too
ready with gratuitous humiliation, and, above all, too ignorant and too
innocent for that. One is absolutely forced to make perpetual qualifica-
tions and one's own reactions are always canceling each other out. It is
this, really, which has driven so many people mad, both white and black.
One is always in the position of having to decide between amputation
and gangrene. Amputation is swift but time may prove that the amputa-

tion was not necessary—or one may delay the amputation too long. Gangrene is slow, but it is impossible to be sure that one is reading one's symptoms right. The idea of going through life as a cripple is more than one can bear, and equally unbearable is the risk of swelling up slowly, in agony, with poison. And the trouble, finally, is that the risks are real even if the choices do not exist.

45   "But as for me and my house," my father had said, "we will serve the Lord." I wondered, as we drove him to his resting place, what this line had meant for him. I had heard him preach it many times. I had preached it once myself, proudly giving it an interpretation different from my father's. Now the whole thing came back to me, as though my father and I were on our way to Sunday school and I were memorizing the golden text: *And if it seem evil unto you to serve the Lord, choose you this day whom you will serve; whether the gods which your fathers served that were on the other side of the flood, or the gods of the Amorites, in whose land ye dwell: but as for me and my house, we will serve the Lord.* I suspected in these familiar lines a meaning which had never been there for me before. All of my father's texts and songs, which I had decided were meaningless, were arranged before me at his death like empty bottles, waiting to hold the meaning which life would give them for me. This was his legacy: nothing is ever escaped. That bleakly memorable morning I hated the unbelievable streets and the Negroes and whites who had, equally, made them that way. But I knew that it was folly, as my father would have said, this bitterness was folly. It was necessary to hold on to the things that mattered. The dead man mattered, the new life mattered; blackness and whiteness did not matter; to believe that they did was to acquiesce in one's own destruction. Hatred, which could destroy so much, never failed to destroy the man who hated and this was an immutable law.

46   It began to seem that one would have to hold in the mind forever two ideas which seemed to be in opposition. The first idea was acceptance, the acceptance, totally without rancor, of life as it is, and men as they are: in the light of this idea, it goes without saying that injustice is a commonplace. But this did not mean that one could be complacent, for the second idea was of equal power: that one must never, in one's own life, accept these injustices as commonplace but must fight them with all one's strength. This fight begins, however, in the heart and it now had been laid to my charge to keep my own heart free of hatred and despair. This intimation made my heart heavy and, now that my father was irrecoverable, I wished that he had been beside me so that

I could have searched his face for the answers which only the future would give me now.

QUESTIONS

Ideas

1. In section I Baldwin describes his father and characterizes him. Where does this begin and end? What does Baldwin say about his father? What observations about his father does Baldwin make in section III, and how do they echo his observations and descriptions of section I?

2. In the descriptions of his father, Baldwin also reveals things about himself, particularly, of course, about his relationship with his father. What kind of relationship was it? What is Baldwin's final assessment of his father—of his life and character?

3. We might say that Baldwin uses description and narration throughout the essay in the service of argumentation. What point does Baldwin make in narrating the restaurant incident? What point is made by the description of Harlem as he rides through in a car on the day of his father's funeral?

4. In the second paragraph of section II, Baldwin moves out in thought. Up to that point—in section I and in the first paragraph of section II—he has been describing his family. What new considerations are introduced, and how are they related to the facts and actions presented in section I?

5. Trace the sequence of ideas—and the pattern of cause and effect—through paragraphs 24, 25, and 26. What is Baldwin's point here?

6. What ironies of circumstance does Baldwin indicate in the first paragraph of section III? What other ironies do you detect in the essay?

7. What is the point of mentioning who attended the funeral? What does Baldwin mean when he suggests that his aunt was one of the few people in the world who had loved his father, and yet "their incessant quarreling proved precisely the strength of their tie"?

8. In paragraph 45 Baldwin brings together the personal and the social, the private and public, his father and Harlem. What conclusions does he draw about his relationship to his father and about the hatred and rage and bitterness that sparked the riots? Explain the final sentence of the paragraph: "Hatred, which could destroy so much, never failed to destroy the man who hated and this was an immutable law."

9. "Notes of a Native Son" ends with a pair of contradictory impulses, with two irreconcilable ideas. What are they, and how does Baldwin both emphasize them and tie them in with what has gone before?

Organization

10. The essay is divided into three major sections. Provide a title for each, explain the main point of each, and comment on the relationship among the three sections.

11. Take any one of the three sections and examine its structure. Explain how it begins, where it goes, and how it ends. Explain how each of its parts fits into the whole section and into the entire essay.

12. As you reread the first paragraph of section II, think back or look back to the opening of section I. What connections do you notice? Why does Baldwin begin section II this way? How does this opening tie in to the essay as a whole?

13. The third paragraph of section III (33) splits in half. In the first part Baldwin mentions that his father was eulogized, that the preacher's description of the man he and his brothers and sisters had known was strikingly different from the reality. Yet Baldwin finds comfort and meaning in this discrepancy. Why? In the second part of this paragraph Baldwin himself eulogizes his father—but not only his father. He presents an imaginative and sympathetic account of how his father and other men under similar pressures of prejudice, fear, insecurity, and bitterness must have felt and why they must be forgiven this bitter hatred. Find the place where Baldwin shifts from one concern to the other. How, specifically, does he accomplish the shift?

14. How does Baldwin manage the shift from the preacher's sermon to happier memories of his childhood? (Consider paragraph 34.) Paragraphs 35–39 form a unit. What is the point of this highly condensed segment, and why is it so brief?

Sentences

15. Baldwin ends many of his paragraphs with emphatic, vivid sentences. Read through the final sentences of all the paragraphs in section I in sequence. What do you notice?

16. What balances and parallels does Baldwin include in his opening sentences? How do the rhythm and the word order of the third and fourth sentences continue the rhythm and structure established in the first and second sentences? What is the effect of this structural and rhythmic patterning? For convenience, here are the first four sentences of the essay:

> On the 29th of July, in 1943, my father died. On the same day, a few hours later, his last child was born. Over a month before this, while all our energies were concentrated in waiting for these events, there had been, in Detroit, one of the bloodiest race riots of the century. A few hours after my father's funeral, while he lay in state in the undertaker's chapel, a race riot broke out in Harlem. On the morning of the 3rd of

August, we drove my father to the graveyard through a wilderness of smashed plate glass.

17. In paragraph 2 of section I Baldwin again uses parallel sentences. Look especially at sentences 3 and 4 and at sentences 5 through 7. Read the sentences aloud, noting pacing and pauses.

18. Reread one of Baldwin's paragraphs, mentally deleting all material between commas. What happens to the sound and the weight of the sentences?

19. Here is one of Baldwin's paragraphs without punctuation. Punctuate it, then compare your version with those of other students and with Baldwin's punctuation. What differences in tone, rhythm, and emphasis do you notice?

> My friend stayed outside the restaurant long enough to misdirect my pursuers and the police who arrived he told me at once I do not know what I said to him when he came to my room that night I could not have said much I felt in the oddest most awful way that I had somehow betrayed him I lived it over and over and over again the way one relives an automobile accident after it has happened and one finds oneself alone and safe I could not get over two facts both equally difficult for the imagination to grasp and one was that I could have been murdered but the other was that I had been ready to commit murder I saw nothing very clearly but I did see this that my life my real life was in danger and not from anything other people might do but from the hatred I carried in my own heart.

20. In the third paragraph from the end of the essay, Baldwin uses two unusual sentence patterns: a sentence beginning with an infinitive; another sentence beginning with a nominalization:

> *infinitive:* To smash something is the ghetto's chronic need.
> *nominalization:* That this is not likely to happen is due to a great many reasons, most hidden and powerful among them the Negro's real relation to the white American.

In this paragraph also, Baldwin mixes and varies his sentences in length, form, and opening phrasing. Examine the paragraph from these standpoints.

21. The final paragraph of the essay achieves coherence, continuity, and emphasis, mainly by careful repetition of words and phrases. Circle or underline the words and phrases that establish this coherence and continuity.

Words

22. There are two vocabularies in "Notes of a Native Son": simple, common words; more formal and unusual longer words, usually of Latin derivation.

Read paragraphs 2 and 3, marking off words of each type. Then find a passage of five or six sentences where Baldwin blends the two kinds of diction. What is the effect of the mixture?

23. In the narrative portions of the essay, especially in paragraphs 17, 21, and 22, Baldwin employs comparisons. What is the point of each?

24. Explain how Baldwin uses imagery—especially comparisons—to make his point in paragraphs 28, 29, 30, and 45.

25. Read the following passage, noting especially its sound effects of assonance, consonance, rhyme, and alliteration:

> He could be chilling in the pulpit and indescribably cruel in his personal life and he was certainly the most bitter man I have ever met; yet it must be said that there was something else in him, buried in him, which lent him his tremendous power and, even, a rather crushing charm. It had something to do with his blackness, I think—he was very black—with his blackness and beauty, and with the fact that he knew that he was black but did not know that he was beautiful. He claimed to be proud of his blackness but it had also been the cause of much humiliation and it had fixed bleak boundaries to his life.

26. In paragraph 43 Baldwin describes the effects of the looting. What comparisons does he use and how effective are they? In the next paragraph (44) he uses the language of disease to express the consequences for blacks of race relations in the United States. What psychological difference is Baldwin suggesting by means of describing the physical differences between gangrene and amputation?

Suggestions for Writing

A. Baldwin ends section I with a narrative account of an episode at a New Jersey restaurant. He begins this account with an idea and he ends it with one. Write an essay in which you describe something that happened to you, something that made you aware of yourself, or something that made you aware of a social, political, religious, or racial situation. Begin and end your account, as Baldwin does, with an idea.

B. Write your own "Notes of a Native Son or Daughter." Try to come to terms with your ethnic or racial heritage and with your place in relation to the society of which you are a part.

C. Describe one of your parents or relatives, examining your relationship with that person. Or compare your parents or two of your other relatives.

D. Reread the last paragraph of section I and of section III. Discuss the ideas in an essay.

E. Write imitations of the sentences discussed in questions 15–21.

F. Discuss the following poem by Stephen Crane in relation to what Baldwin says about himself in the final paragraph of section I.

A MAN FEARED

A man feared that he might find an assassin;
Another that he might find a victim.
One was more wise than the other.

THREE

Joan Didion

(1934–   )

Joan Didion writes to understand herself and her culture. For her writing is a tool, a way to overcome the randomness of life and to create order and clarity. Writing can do that. It can help us give shape to experience. In fact, one cognitive skill that separates us from primitive cultures is our ability to create an identity, a special voice for ourself by writing down what we think about things.

If you lived in a traditional culture, your identity would be given to you. You would not think of shaping and interpreting your experience, and you would not even imagine that you could create new and important ways of looking at the world. In highly literate societies, however, writers do just that. Didion is often striving for greater self-knowledge through her essays. She does not accept what is given to her by the media, her parents, or school. She is exploring and searching for her own understanding of the world through language. In advanced societies, like ours, writing can be a powerful tool for knowing.

But Didion goes even further than that. She begins one of her essays, "The White Album" (after the famous 1968 Beatles double album), with this provocative sentence: "We tell ourselves stories in order to live." Isn't she implying that giving shape and meaning to our lives through writing is necessary and vital? When we see and read about events, we can impose a structure and significance on them through writing. As a result, we really begin to know them. This is what E. M. Forster meant when he said, "How do I know what I think until I see what I say?" Our experiences and ideas exist as shapeless, half-articulated thoughts and impressions until we impose order on them through writing. Didion continues: "We interpret what we see, select the most workable of the multiple choices. We live entirely, especially if we are writers, by the imposition of a narrative line upon disparate images, by the 'ideas' with which we have learned to freeze the shifting phantasmagoria which is our actual experience."

That sounds positive and encouraging. Writing, unlike speech, freezes our experiences and our ideas and helps us to see, to understand, to contemplate what we have written. Then we can look back and revise; we can get to the center of things, the heart of the matter. And in doing so, Didion refines and strengthens her voice and her sense of self.

Although Didion is a reporter, she is not strictly a journalist. In *The White Album,* for example, she gives us vivid and representative snapshots of life in the 1960s. But these are subjective reports, usually offered without commentary. She does not tie things together in neat bundles, and she is clearly not trying to be objective. She wants readers to fit the pieces together to form their own pictures, their own understanding, their own theme. She is a witness to important truths about our culture, but she does not usually present her findings explicitly. In "Salvador" and "Marrying Absurd" she makes her points by carefully selecting details and placing them in precisely the right place. The reader must do the rest.

Didion's prose style is also understated, almost indirect. She gives the impression of being in control, of withholding strong emotion. And she can be direct "without being trivial or colloquial." The following two sentences from "Goodbye to All That" are typical of her spare, elegant prose: "All I know is that it was very bad when I was twenty-eight. Everything that was said to me I seemed to have heard before, and I could no longer listen." The directness of these lines makes a promise to the reader. Didion is not hiding behind elaborately complex sentences or difficult vocabulary. Such clear, strong writing does not come naturally to anyone. Didion had to work at it, long and hard. Like all writers, regardless of ability or success, Didion worries about her ability to "get it right." Her solution is both simple and rigorous: revise, cut, rearrange, rework—again and again. The hard work pays off in the bite and authority of her exact prose.

Some of this concern for stylistic precision she learned as a student, from reading Hemingway:

I learned a lot about how sentences worked. How a short sentence worked. How they worked in a paragraph. Where the commas worked. How every word had to matter. It made me excited about words.

. . . When I was fifteen or sixteen I would type out his stories . . . I
mean they're perfect sentences. Very direct sentences, smooth rivers,
clear water over granite, no sinkholes.

After she graduated from the University of California, Berkeley, in 1956 with a degree in English, she wrote for such
national magazines as *Mademoiselle, Saturday Evening Post,*
and *Life.* Early in her career she worked on *Vogue's* editorial
staff. Later, she commented that she learned how verbs work
from a senior editor there: "Every day I would go into her office
with eight lines of copy or a caption or something. She would
sit there and mark it up with a pencil and get very angry about
extra words, about verbs not working. . . . In an eight-line
caption everything had to work, every word, every comma."
   She went on to publish a novel, *Run River,* in 1963.
Then, after having spent about eight years in New York, she
moved back to California, where she still lives with her husband, the novelist John Gregory Dunne. She wrote about the
move: "We took an afternoon flight back to Los Angeles, and
on the way home from the airport that night I could see the
moon on the Pacific and smell jasmine all around and we both
knew that there was no longer any point in keeping the apartment we still kept in New York." Although she continues to
write interesting novels *(Play It As It Lays, The Book of Common Prayer,* and *Democracy),* she has received the most acclaim for her essay collections, *Slouching Towards Bethlehem*
(1968) and *The White Album* (1979), and most recently for
Salvador (1983), a journalistic chronicle of the two weeks that
she and her husband spent amidst the confusion of war-torn El
Salvador in 1982. Supporters of the government did not like it.
It has been praised as "a withering indictment of American
foreign policy." Most, however, agree that in this "surrealist
docudrama" Didion is able to achieve what she seldom does in
her fiction: "a consummate political artwork."
   Probably because her family has lived in Sacramento for
generations, Didion is concerned with traditional values in
conflict with modern life-styles, with what we've lost and what
we still have in America. She is afraid that "the children of the
aerospace engineers" who "have never met a great-aunt" will
"have lost the real past and gained a manufactured one, and
there will be no way for them to know, no way at all." But even
this nostalgia cannot withstand her passion for a deeper, more
personal truth. She continues: "But perhaps it is presumptuous

of me to assume that they will be missing something. Perhaps in retrospect this has been a story not about Sacramento at all, but about the things we lose and the promises we break as we grow older; perhaps I have been playing out unawares the Margaret in the poem:

Margaret, are you grieving
Over Goldengrove unleaving? . . .
It is the blight man was born for,
It is Margaret you mourn for.

There is no doubt that Didion often despairs about the fragmentation and banality of contemporary American life, but the clarity and energy of her writing suggest that she has found an antidote to inconclusiveness and plastic values.

Marrying Absurd

1   To be married in Las Vegas, Clark County, Nevada, a bride must swear that she is eighteen or has parental permission and a bridegroom that he is twenty-one or has parental permission. Someone must put up five dollars for the license. (On Sundays and holidays, fifteen dollars. The Clark County Courthouse issues marriage licenses at any time of the day or night except between noon and one in the afternoon, between eight and nine in the evening, and between four and five in the morning.) Nothing else is required. The State of Nevada, alone among these United States, demands neither a premarital blood test nor a waiting period before or after the issuance of a marriage license. Driving in across the Mojave from Los Angeles, one sees the signs way out on the desert, looming up from that moonscape of rattlesnakes and mesquite, even before the Las Vegas lights appear like a mirage on the horizon: "GETTING MARRIED? Free License Information First Strip Exit." Perhaps the Las Vegas wedding industry achieved its peak operational efficiency between 9:00 p.m. and midnight of August 26, 1965, an otherwise unremarkable Thursday which happened to be, by Presidential order, the last day on which anyone could improve his draft status merely by getting married. One hundred and seventy-one couples were pronounced man and wife in the name of Clark County and the

State of Nevada that night, sixty-seven of them by a single justice of the peace, Mr. James A. Brennan. Mr. Brennan did one wedding at the Dunes and the other sixty-six in his office, and charged each couple eight dollars. One bride lent her veil to six others. "I got it down from five to three minutes," Mr. Brennan said later of his feat. "I could've married them *en masse*, but they're people, not cattle. People expect more when they get married."

2   What people who get married in Las Vegas actually do expect— what, in the largest sense, their "expectations" are—strikes one as a curious and self-contradictory business. Las Vegas is the most extreme and allegorical of American settlements, bizarre and beautiful in its venality and in its devotion to immediate gratification, a place the tone of which is set by mobsters and call girls and ladies' room attendants with amyl nitrite poppers in their uniform pockets. Almost everyone notes that there is no "time" in Las Vegas, no night and no day and no past and no future (no Las Vegas casino, however, has taken the obliteration of the ordinary time sense quite so far as Harold's Club in Reno, which for a while issued, at odd intervals in the day and night, mimeographed "bulletins" carrying news from the world outside); neither is there any logical sense of where one is. One is standing on a highway in the middle of a vast hostile desert looking at an eighty-foot sign which blinks "STARDUST" or "CAESAR'S PALACE." Yes, but what does that explain? This geographical implausibility reinforces the sense that what happens there has no connection with "real" life; Nevada cities like Reno and Carson are ranch towns, Western towns, places behind which there is some historical imperative. But Las Vegas seems to exist only in the eye of the beholder. All of which makes it an extraordinarily stimulating and interesting place, but an odd one in which to want to wear a candlelight satin Priscilla of Boston wedding dress with Chantilly lace insets, tapered sleeves and a detachable modified train.

3   And yet the Las Vegas wedding business seems to appeal to precisely that impulse. "Sincere and Dignified Since 1954," one wedding chapel advertises. There are nineteen such wedding chapels in Las Vegas, intensely competitive, each offering better, faster, and, by implication, more sincere services than the next: Our Photos Best Anywhere, Your Wedding on A Phonograph Record, Candlelight with Your Ceremony, Honeymoon Accommodations, Free Transportation from Your Motel to Courthouse to Chapel and Return to Motel, Religious or Civil Ceremonies, Dressing Rooms, Flowers, Rings, Announcements, Witnesses Available, and Ample Parking. All of these services, like most

others in Las Vegas (sauna baths, payroll-check cashing, chinchilla coats for sale or rent) are offered twenty-four hours a day, seven days a week, presumably on the premise that marriage, like craps, is a game to be played when the table seems hot.

4   But what strikes one most about the Strip chapels, with their wishing wells and stained-glass paper windows and their artificial bouvardia, is that so much of their business is by no means a matter of simple convenience, of late-night liaisons between show girls and baby Crosbys. Of course there is some of that. (One night about eleven o'clock in Las Vegas I watched a bride in an orange minidress and masses of flame-colored hair stumble from a Strip chapel on the arm of her bridegroom, who looked the part of the expendable nephew in movies like *Miami Syndicate.* "I gotta get the kids," the bride whimpered. "I gotta pick up the sitter, I gotta get to the midnight show." "What you gotta get," the bridegroom said, opening the door of a Cadillac Coupe de Ville and watching her crumple on the seat, "is sober.") But Las Vegas seems to offer something other than "convenience"; it is merchandising "niceness," the facsimile of proper ritual, to children who do not know how else to find it, how to make the arrangements, how to do it "right." All day and evening long on the Strip, one sees actual wedding parties, waiting under the harsh lights at a crosswalk, standing uneasily in the parking lot of the Frontier while the photographer hired by The Little Church of the West ("Wedding Place of the Stars") certifies the occasion, takes the picture: the bride in a veil and white satin pumps, the bridegroom usually in a white dinner jacket, and even an attendant or two, a sister or a best friend in hot-pink *peau de soie,* a flirtation veil, a carnation nosegay. "When I Fall in Love It Will Be Forever," the organist plays, and then a few bars of Lohengrin. The mother cries; the stepfather, awkward in his role, invites the chapel hostess to join them for a drink at the Sands. The hostess declines with a professional smile; she has already transferred her interest to the group waiting outside. One bride out, another in, and again the sign goes up on the chapel door: "One moment please—Wedding."

5   I sat next to one such wedding party in a Strip restaurant the last time I was in Las Vegas. The marriage had just taken place; the bride still wore her dress, the mother her corsage. A bored waiter poured out a few swallows of pink champagne ("on the house") for everyone but the bride, who was too young to be served. "You'll need something with more kick than that," the bride's father said with heavy jocularity to his new son-in-law; the ritual jokes about the wedding night had a certain

Panglossian character, since the bride was clearly several months pregnant. Another round of pink champagne, this time not on the house, and the bride began to cry. "It was just as nice," she sobbed, "as I hoped and dreamed it would be."

QUESTIONS

Ideas

1. Didion jumps into this essay without the usual introductory announcement of the theme. Does she, in fact, give us one later on? What is it, in your own words?

2. What contrast does Didion hope the reader will see between the "candlelight satin . . . wedding dress" and the Las Vegas chapels? Just what does Las Vegas have to offer these young people? Is it false or real? Does that matter to them? To Didion? To you? You need to consider the implications of the title, of course.

3. What is Didion's purpose in the essay? To entertain? To persuade? To ridicule? What is she suggesting about Las Vegas marriages and about the cast of characters involved in them? On a more general level, what does the contrast between the traditional "Norman Rockwell" wedding and the chapels in Las Vegas suggest about America? Is this the same theme Didion develops in "On Going Home"?

4. Are we meant to laugh at the scene in the last paragraph?

5. On a more abstract level, what is the function of ritual in our lives? Can we do without it? Should we?

Organization

6. Didion organized this piece as a blend of description, narration, and exposition. She provides the essay with a narrative frame: we begin with Mr. Brennan, then comes the show girl section, and then the final paragraph. How effective is this structure? Could Didion have organized the essay differently? How?

7. Notice the connecting devices between each of the paragraphs. What is the connection between the first and last sentences of paragraph 2? Between the first sentence of paragraph 2 and the last sentence of paragraph 1?

8. Paragraph 2 has a different function than paragraphs 1 and 3. And it contains a different kind of information. How does that information help us to understand the details of the first and third paragraphs?

Sentences

9. Didion makes extensive use of direct quotation in this essay. Three paragraphs, in fact, end with a direct statement (1, 4, and 5). What is the effect of these quotations?

10. Do the sentences in the second paragraph seem more complicated than those in either the first or last? What might be the reason for this?

Words

11. When Didion uses a simile in comparing marriage in Las Vegas to playing craps (paragraph 3), what does the use of that device suggest about her attitude toward the Strip chapels? What other comparisons does she use, and what is she implying by the comparisons?

12. Is the title effective? Can you think of an alternate title? How about "Marriage in Las Vegas"? Is Didion's title better? Why or why not?

13. Irony is often conveyed by writing one thing but meaning another. We are not, it seems, meant to be impressed by Mr. Brennan's concern for the individual just because he doesn't marry people en masse. Didion uses irony throughout her essay for a variety of purposes. What are some other examples of Didion's use of irony? Look especially at the last paragraph. What effect is she trying to achieve? Does she assume you will agree with her view of the people in Las Vegas? Do you? Would the bride of the last paragraph agree with the thesis of this essay? Why does she cry? Does the last sentence surprise you?

Suggestions for Writing

A. Try rewriting one or two quotations (from paragraphs 1, 4, or 5), converting the direct speech into an indirectly reported statement without quotation marks. Which do you prefer? What is different about them?

B. Write an essay combining narration and description about a place you have a strong feeling about. Try to let the details indicate what your attitude is, i.e., avoid stating an explicit theme while still communicating a central impression.

C. Write an essay about something you are critical of—violent sports, TV game shows, political conventions, shopping centers, fast-food eateries, commercials, whatever. Try to describe your subject without explicitly stating your viewpoint and attitude. Carefully select specific details to convey your point by implication. When you read your essay to a friend, ask him or her to state your attitude. See how close it comes to your intentions. Perhaps you will want to select new details or add to those you have after receiving this feedback.

On Self-Respect

1   Once, in a dry season, I wrote in large letters across two pages of a notebook that innocence ends when one is stripped of the delusion that one likes oneself. Although now, some years later, I marvel that a mind on the outs with itself should have nonetheless made painstaking record of its every tremor, I recall with embarrassing clarity the flavor of those particular ashes. It was a matter of misplaced self-respect.

2   I had not been elected to Phi Beta Kappa. This failure could scarcely have been more predictable or less ambiguous (I simply did not have the grades), but I was unnerved by it; I had somehow thought myself a kind of academic Raskolnikov, curiously exempt from the cause-effect relationships which hampered others. Although even the humorless nineteen-year-old that I was must have recognized that the situation lacked real tragic stature, the day that I did not make Phi Beta Kappa nonetheless marked the end of something, and innocence may well be the word for it. I lost the conviction that lights would always turn green for me, the pleasant certainty that those rather passive virtues which had won me approval as a child automatically guaranteed me not only Phi Beta Kappa keys but happiness, honor, and the love of a good man; lost a certain touching faith in the totem power of good manners, clean hair, and proven competence on the Stanford-Binet scale. To such doubtful amulets had my self-respect been pinned, and I faced myself that day with the nonplused apprehension of someone who has come across a vampire and has no crucifix at hand.

3   Although to be driven back upon oneself is an uneasy affair at best, rather like trying to cross a border with borrowed credentials, it seems to me now the one condition necessary to the beginnings of real self-respect. Most of our platitudes notwithstanding, self-deception remains the most difficult deception. The tricks that work on others count for nothing in that very well-lit back alley where one keeps assignations with oneself: no winning smiles will do here, no prettily drawn lists of good intentions. One shuffles flashily but in vain through one's marked cards —the kindness done for the wrong reason, the apparent triumph which involved no real effort, the seemingly heroic act into which one had been shamed. The dismal fact is that self-respect has nothing to do with the approval of others—who are, after all, deceived easily enough; has noth-

ing to do with reputation, which, as Rhett Butler told Scarlett O'Hara, is something people with courage can do without.

4   To do without self-respect, on the other hand, is to be an unwilling audience of one to an interminable documentary that details one's failings, both real and imagined, with fresh footage spliced in for every screening. *There's the glass you broke in anger, there's the hurt on X's face; watch now, this next scene, the night Y came back from Houston, see how you muff this one.* To live without self-respect is to lie awake some night, beyond the reach of warm milk, phenobarbital, and the sleeping hand on the coverlet, counting up the sins of commission and omission, the trusts betrayed, the promises subtly broken, the gifts irrevocably wasted through sloth or cowardice or carelessness. However long we postpone it, we eventually lie down alone in that notoriously uncomfortable bed, the one we make ourselves. Whether or not we sleep in it depends, of course, on whether or not we respect ourselves.

5   To protest that some fairly improbable people, some people who *could not possibly respect themselves,* seem to sleep easily enough is to miss the point entirely, as surely as those people miss it who think that self-respect has necessarily to do with not having safety pins in one's underwear. There is a common superstition that "self-respect" is a kind of charm against snakes, something that keeps those who have it locked in some unblighted Eden, out of strange beds, ambivalent conversations, and trouble in general. It does not at all. It has nothing to do with the face of things, but concerns instead a separate peace, a private reconciliation. Although the careless, suicidal Julian English in *Appointment in Samarra* and the careless, incurably dishonest Jordan Baker in *The Great Gatsby* seem equally improbable candidates for self-respect, Jordan Baker had it, Julian English did not. With that genius for accommodation more often seen in women than in men, Jordan took her own measure, made her own peace, avoided threats to that peace: "I hate careless people," she told Nick Carraway. "It takes two to make an accident."

6   Like Jordan Baker, people with self-respect have the courage of their mistakes. They know the price of things. If they choose to commit adultery, they do not then go running, in an access of bad conscience, to receive absolution from the wronged parties; nor do they complain unduly of the unfairness, the undeserved embarrassment, of being named co-respondent. In brief, people with self-respect exhibit a certain toughness, a kind of moral nerve; they display what was once called *character,* a quality which, although approved in the abstract, sometimes

loses ground to other, more instantly negotiable virtues. The measure of its slipping prestige is that one tends to think of it only in connection with homely children and United States senators who have been defeated, preferably in the primary, for reelection. Nonetheless, character —the willingness to accept responsibility for one's own life—is the source from which self-respect springs.

7   Self-respect is something that our grandparents, whether or not they had it, knew all about. They had instilled in them, young, a certain discipline, the sense that one lives by doing things one does not particularly want to do, by putting fears and doubts to one side, by weighing immediate comforts against the possibility of larger, even intangible, comforts. It seemed to the nineteenth century admirable, but not remarkable, that Chinese Gordon put on a clean white suit and held Khartoum against the Mahdi; it did not seem unjust that the way to free land in California involved death and difficulty and dirt. In a diary kept during the winter of 1846, an emigrating twelve-year-old named Narcissa Cornwall noted coolly: "Father was busy reading and did not notice that the house was being filled with strange Indians until Mother spoke about it." Even lacking any clue as to what Mother said, one can scarcely fail to be impressed by the entire incident: the father reading, the Indians filing in, the mother choosing the words that would not alarm, the child duly recording the event and noting further that those particular Indians were not, "fortunately for us," hostile. Indians were simply part of the *donnée*.

8   In one guise or another, Indians always are. Again, it is a question of recognizing that anything worth having has its price. People who respect themselves are willing to accept the risk that the Indians will be hostile, that the venture will go bankrupt, that the liaison may not turn out to be one in which *every day is a holiday because you're married to me*. They are willing to invest something of themselves; they may not play at all, but when they do play, they know the odds.

9   That kind of self-respect is a discipline, a habit of mind that can never be faked but can be developed, trained, coaxed forth. It was once suggested to me that, as an antidote to crying, I put my head in a paper bag. As it happens, there is a sound physiological reason, something to do with oxygen, for doing exactly that, but the psychological effect alone is incalculable: it is difficult in the extreme to continue fancying oneself Cathy in *Wuthering Heights* with one's head in a Food Fair bag. There

is a similar case for all the small disciplines, unimportant in themselves; imagine maintaining any kind of swoon, commiserative or carnal, in a cold shower.

10   But those small disciplines are valuable only insofar as they represent larger ones. To say that Waterloo was won on the playing fields of Eton is not to say that Napoleon might have been saved by a crash program in cricket; to give formal dinners in the rain forest would be pointless did not the candlelight flickering on the liana call forth deeper, stronger disciplines, values instilled long before. It is a kind of ritual, helping us to remember who and what we are. In order to remember it, one must have known it.

11   To have that sense of one's intrinsic worth which constitutes self-respect is potentially to have everything: the ability to discriminate, to love and to remain indifferent. To lack it is to be locked within oneself, paradoxically incapable of either love or indifference. If we do not respect ourselves, we are on the one hand forced to despise those who have so few resources as to consort with us, so little perception as to remain blind to our fatal weaknesses. On the other, we are peculiarly in thrall to everyone we see, curiously determined to live out —since our self-image is untenable—their false notions of us. We flatter ourselves by thinking this compulsion to please others an attractive trait: a gist for imaginative empathy, evidence of our willingness to give. *Of course* I will play Francesca to your Paolo, Helen Keller to anyone's Annie Sullivan: no expectation is too misplaced, no role too ludicrous. At the mercy of those we cannot but hold in contempt, we play roles doomed to failure before they are begun, each defeat generating fresh despair at the urgency of divining and meeting the next demand made upon us.

12   It is the phenomenon sometimes called "alienation from self." In its advanced stages, we no longer answer the telephone, because someone might want something; that we could say *no* without drowning in self-reproach is an idea alien to this game. Every encounter demands too much, tears the nerves, drains the will, and the specter of something as small as an unanswered letter arouses such disproportionate guilt that answering it becomes out of the question. To assign unanswered letters their proper weight, to free us from the expectations of others, to give us back to ourselves—there lies the great, the singular power of self-respect. Without it, one eventually discovers the final turn of the screw: one runs away to find oneself, and finds no one at home.

QUESTIONS

Ideas

1. Essentially, this essay works toward a definition, an extended personal definition of self-respect. What are the essential characteristics of self-respect in Didion's view? Did she leave anything out? Is any one of these elements of her definition more important than the others? Which one? Why?

2. Do you like Didion's definition? Did it surprise you? Is it too subjective, embedded as it is in her own emotional life, or does it seem objective enough to apply to many people?

3. Can you underline a generalization, a broad statement that might serve as the theme or thesis of the essay? Then try to state, in your words, the central idea of the essay.

4. Why, according to Didion, is self-respect so important? Do you agree?

Organization

5. Take another look at how this piece is put together. Does it have a clear plan?

6. Why does Didion begin so personally? Where does the essay become more objective? How did you decide this?

7. Why are there three divisions in the essay? What is the purpose of each section? What is the relationship of each part to the other two?

8. Look at paragraph 6. What device does Didion use to provide a transition (a bridge) from paragraph 5? How does she link the following pairs of paragraphs: 7–8, 8–9, 9–10, and 11–12? Can you think of a general rule or guideline that would cover these five cases?

9. According to a writing theorist, there are five grammatical markers for the relationships that exist between sentences: "and," "but," "for," "so," and the colon. How do the sentences in paragraphs 6 and 10 conform to this observation?

10. How does Didion support her ideas about self-respect? Make a brief list of the specifics she uses, the concrete details, the illustrations, the facts.

11. One kind of detail Didion uses in this essay is the allusion (a reference to a person, place, or thing, often historical or literary). Didion alludes to Raskolnikov, Scarlett O'Hara, Jordan Baker, and others. Why? Are these allusions helpful, or do they confuse you? What do such allusions suggest about the audience Didion assumes she is writing for?

Sentences

12. Didion's sentences seem disciplined and controlled. They are varied and resilient. Read the first paragraph slowly, noting the blend of long and short sentences and the way each begins differently. Look also at the words that are placed between commas at the beginning of the first and second sentences. We might call these phrases "interrupters" because they break the straightforward movement of the sentence. Try reading the sentences without their interrupters. What is different about the sentences this way?

13. What are the threads running through and binding together the sentences in paragraph 11?

14. Count the number of words in each sentence in paragraphs 5 and 7. Is there a pattern? How many sentences in paragraph 5 follow the basic subject-verb-object pattern? Which sentences are simple, compound, complex? Which use subordination? Why does Didion choose to subordinate one part of a sentence to another? Is this just arbitrary; could you reverse what she does and subordinate differently?

15. Look at how the colon is used in paragraphs 3, 7, 11, and 12. What functions does it perform? Find the semicolons in paragraphs 2, 3, and 6. Based on the use of the semicolon here, what general rule might you write about it?

16. The final sentence of paragraph 6 uses the double dash. What information is embedded between the dashes? How is it related to the rest of the information in the sentence? What would be lost without the central part of the sentence—the part within the dashes?

Words

17. The essay makes extensive use of imagery, metaphors, and similes—often in a rapidly shifting sequence. Consider, for example, paragraphs 3 and 4. What are the one or two major images used in each paragraph? How is each extended and developed? What does each image contribute to Didion's meaning?

18. Didion's vocabulary in this essay, as in her others, is varied. It often surprises. What are the meaning and effect of the following words and phrases: "the totem power of good manners" (2); "doubtful amulets" (2); "private reconciliation" (5); "imaginative empathy" (11); "alienation from self" (12). What are some other unusual words or phrases? Why does she choose these rather than other, more usual terms?

Suggestions for Writing

A. Write a short sentence about the purpose of each of the twelve paragraphs.

B. Look at the way the sentences begin in paragraphs 4 and 5. Consider especially the sentences starting with infinitive phrases ("To live," "To protest that," "To do without self-respect is . . ."). Try to write two sentences that begin this way.

C. Try to imitate the general organizational pattern of this essay, at least by starting with a personal anecdote and moving to a more objective definition; try for concrete, specific details to illustrate what your abstraction is and is not. Some possibilities: success, failure, morality, self-fulfillment, deception, wisdom, charisma, masculinity, femininity, courage, soul, friendship.

D. Think about some quality, virtue, or personal characteristic that is important to you, perhaps something you possess. But it might be something you wish you had, maybe something you are trying hard to achieve or acquire. Write an essay exploring its characteristics and explaining its importance.

Bureaucrats

---

1   The closed door upstairs at 120 South Spring Street in downtown Los Angeles is marked OPERATIONS CENTER. In the windowless room beyond the closed door a reverential hush prevails. From six A.M. until seven P.M. in this windowless room men sit at consoles watching a huge board flash colored lights. "There's the heart attack," someone will murmur, or "we're getting the gawk effect." 120 South Spring is the Los Angeles office of Caltrans, or the California Department of Transportation, and the Operations Center is where Caltrans engineers monitor what they call "the 42-Mile Loop." The 42-Mile Loop is simply the rough triangle formed by the intersections of the Santa Monica, the San Diego and the Harbor freeways, and 42 miles represents less than ten percent of freeway mileage in Los Angeles County alone, but these particular 42 miles are regarded around 120 South Spring with a special veneration. The Loop is a "demonstration system," a phrase much favored by everyone at Caltrans, and is part of a "pilot project," another two words carrying totemic weight on South Spring.

2   The Loop has electronic sensors embedded every half-mile out there in the pavement itself, each sensor counting the crossing cars every twenty seconds. The Loop has its own mind, a Xerox Sigma V computer which prints out, all day and night, twenty-second readings on what is and is not moving in each of the Loop's eight lanes. It is the Xerox Sigma

V that makes the big board flash red when traffic out there drops below fifteen miles an hour. It is the Xerox Sigma V that tells the Operations crew when they have an "incident" out there. An "incident" is the heart attack on the San Diego, the jackknifed truck on the Harbor, the Camaro just now tearing out the Cyclone fence on the Santa Monica. "Out there" is where incidents happen. The windowless room at 120 South Spring is where incidents get "verified." "Incident verification" is turning on the closed-circuit TV on the console and watching the traffic slow down to see (this is "the gawk effect") where the Camaro tore out the fence.

3   As a matter of fact there is a certain closed-circuit aspect to the entire mood of the Operations Center. "Verifying" the incident does not after all "prevent" the incident, which lends the enterprise a kind of tranced distance, and on the day recently when I visited 120 South Spring it took considerable effort to remember what I had come to talk about, which was that particular part of the Loop called the Santa Monica Freeway. The Santa Monica Freeway is 16.2 miles long, runs from the Pacific Ocean to downtown Los Angeles through what is referred to at Caltrans as "the East-West Corridor," carries more traffic every day than any other freeway in California, has what connoisseurs of freeways concede to be the most beautiful access ramps in the world, and appeared to have been transformed by Caltrans, during the several weeks before I went downtown to talk about it, into a 16.2-mile parking lot.

4   The problem seemed to be another Caltrans "demonstration," or "pilot," a foray into bureaucratic terrorism they were calling "The Diamond Lane" in their promotional literature and "The Project" among themselves. That the promotional literature consisted largely of schedules for buses (or "Diamond Lane Expresses") and invitations to join a car pool via computer ("Commuter Computer") made clear not only the putative point of The Project, which was to encourage travel by car pool and bus, but also the actual point, which was to eradicate a central Southern California illusion, that of individual mobility, without anyone really noticing. This had not exactly worked out. "FREE-WAY FIASCO," the *Los Angeles Times* was headlining page-one stories. "THE DIAMOND LANE: ANOTHER BUST BY CAL-TRANS." "CALTRANS PILOT EFFORT ANOTHER IN LONG LIST OF FAILURES." "OFFICIAL DIAMOND LANE STANCE: LET THEM HOWL."

5   All "The Diamond Lane" theoretically involved was reserving the fast inside lanes on the Santa Monica for vehicles carrying three or more

people, but in practice this meant that 25 per cent of the freeway was reserved for 3 per cent of the cars, and there were other odd wrinkles here and there suggesting that Caltrans had dedicated itself to making all movement around Los Angeles as arduous as possible. There was for example the matter of surface streets. A "surface street" is anything around Los Angeles that is not a freeway ("going surface" from one part of town to another is generally regarded as idiosyncratic), and surface streets do not fall directly within the Caltrans domain, but now the engineer in charge of surface streets was accusing Caltrans of threatening and intimidating him. It appeared that Caltrans wanted him to create a "confused and congested situation" on his surface streets, so as to force drivers back to the freeway, where they would meet a still more confused and congested situation and decide to stay home, or take a bus. "We are beginning a process of deliberately making it harder for drivers to use freeways," a Caltrans director had in fact said at a transit conference some months before. "We are prepared to endure considerable public outcry in order to pry John Q. Public out of his car. . . . I would emphasize that this is a political decision, and one that can be reversed if the public gets sufficiently enraged to throw us rascals out."

6   Of course this political decision was in the name of the greater good, was in the interests of "environmental improvement" and "conservation of resources," but even there the figures had about them a certain Caltrans opacity. The Santa Monica normally carried 240,000 cars and trucks every day. These 240,000 cars and trucks normally carried 260,000 people. What Caltrans described as its ultimate goal on the Santa Monica was to carry the same 260,000 people, "but in 7,800 fewer, or 232,200 vehicles." The figure "232,200" had a visionary precision to it that did not automatically create confidence, especially since the only effect so far had been to disrupt traffic throughout the Los Angeles basin, triple the number of daily accidents on the Santa Monica, prompt the initiation of two lawsuits against Caltrans, and cause large numbers of Los Angeles County residents to behave, most uncharacteristically, as an ignited and conscious proletariat. Citizen guerrillas splashed paint and scattered nails in the Diamond Lanes. Diamond Lane maintenance crews expressed fear of hurled objects. Down at 120 South Spring the architects of the Diamond Lane had taken to regarding "the media" as the architects of their embarrassment, and Caltrans statements in the press had been cryptic and contradictory, reminiscent only of old communiqués out of Vietnam.

7   To understand what was going on it is perhaps necessary to have participated in the freeway experience, which is the only secular commu-

nion Los Angeles has. Mere driving on the freeway is in no way the same as participating in it. Anyone can "drive" on the freeway, and many people with no vocation for it do, hesitating here and resisting there, losing the rhythm of the lane change, thinking about where they came from and where they are going. Actual participants think only about where they are. Actual participation requires a total surrender, a concentration so intense as to seem a kind of narcosis, a rapture-of-the-freeway. The mind goes clean. The rhythm takes over. A distortion of time occurs, the same distortion that characterizes the instant before an accident. It takes only a few seconds to get off the Santa Monica Freeway at National-Overland, which is a difficult exit requiring the driver to cross two new lanes of traffic streamed in from the San Diego Freeway, but those few seconds always seem to me the longest part of the trip. The moment is dangerous. The exhilaration is in doing it. "As you acquire the special skills involved," Reyner Banham observed in an extraordinary chapter about the freeways in his 1971 *Los Angeles: The Architecture of Four Ecologies,* "the freeways become a special way of being alive . . . the extreme concentration required in Los Angeles seems to bring on a state of heightened awareness that some locals find mystical."

8   Indeed some locals do, and some nonlocals too. Reducing the number of lone souls careening around the East-West Corridor in a state of mechanized rapture may or may not have seemed socially desirable, but what it was definitely not going to seem was easy. "We're only seeing an initial period of unfamiliarity," I was assured the day I visited Caltrans. I was talking to a woman named Eleanor Wood and she was thoroughly and professionally grounded in the diction of "planning" and it did not seem likely that I could interest her in considering the freeway as regional mystery. "Any time you try to rearrange people's daily habits, they're apt to react impetuously. All this project requires is a certain rearrangement of people's daily planning. That's really all we want."

9   It occurred to me that a certain rearrangement of people's daily planning might seem, in less rarefied air than is breathed at 120 South Spring, rather a great deal to want, but so impenetrable was the sense of higher social purpose there in the Operations Center that I did not express this reservation. Instead I changed the subject, mentioned an earlier "pilot project" on the Santa Monica: the big electronic message boards that Caltrans had installed a year or two before. The idea was that traffic information transmitted from the Santa Monica to the Xerox Sigma V could be translated, here in the Operations Center, into suggestions to the driver, and flashed right back out to the Santa Monica. This operation, in that it involved telling drivers electronically what they

already knew empirically, had the rather spectral circularity that seemed to mark a great many Caltrans schemes, and I was interested in how Caltrans thought it worked.

10   "Actually the message boards were part of a larger pilot project," Mrs. Wood said. "An ongoing project in incident management. With the message boards we hoped to learn if motorists would modify their behavior according to what we told them on the boards."

11   I asked if the motorists had.

12   "Actually no," Mrs. Wood said finally. "They didn't react to the signs exactly as we'd hypothesized they would, no. *But.* If we'd *known* what the motorist would do . . . then we wouldn't have needed a pilot project in the first place, would we."

13   The circle seemed intact. Mrs. Wood and I smiled, and shook hands. I watched the big board until all lights turned green on the Santa Monica and then I left and drove home on it, all 16.2 miles of it. All the way I remembered that I was watched by the Xerox Sigma V. All the way the message boards gave me the number to call for CAR POOL INFO. As I left the freeway it occurred to me that they might have their own rapture down at 120 South Spring, and it could be called Perpetuating the Department. Today the California Highway Patrol reported that, during the first six weeks of the Diamond Lane, accidents on the Santa Monica, which normally range between 49 and 72 during a six-week period, totaled 204. Yesterday plans were announced to extend the Diamond Lane to other freeways at a cost of $42,500,000.

QUESTIONS

Ideas

1. Why do you think Didion chose such a broad title?

2. Even though Didion appears to be objective in the opening paragraphs, what clues to her attitude about Caltrans does she provide?

3. How does she prevent the impression that she is merely a crank? That is, how does she establish authority?

4. In the last paragraph, what does Didion mean by "the circle seemed intact" and "Perpetuating the Department"?

Organization

5. Describe Didion's strategy for arranging her evidence against Caltrans. Why doesn't she begin with an explicit generalization explaining her point?

6. Writers sometimes fully develop an idea in a single paragraph but rely on groups of paragraphs for further elaboration. With this in mind, how can this essay be divided?

Sentences

7. After a couple of silent readings, read paragraphs 1 and 7 out loud, with expression. What differences do you notice? What is Didion's purpose in each? How are style and meaning related here?

Words

8. Why are so many words and phrases in quotes? What kinds of words are they?
9. Why is "windowless" repeated in the first two sentences? What is the tone of "reverential," "veneration," and "totemic" in this first paragraph?
10. In paragraph 7 what words and phrases does Didion use to reinforce her "freeway as communion" metaphor?

Suggestions for Writing

A. Write an explicit introduction and conclusion; let the last sentence in the introduction be the thesis sentence.
B. Write an essay criticizing some organization—your high school, the post office, a branch of the government, etc. However, instead of stating your opinions directly, let a sequence of concrete incidents make your point. Let your evidence do the work of abstractions.

Goodbye To All That

How many miles to Babylon?
Three score miles and ten—
Can I get there by candlelight?
Yes, and back again—
If your feet are nimble and light
You can get there by candlelight.

1   It is easy to see the beginnings of things, and harder to see the ends. I can remember now, with a clarity that makes the nerves in the back of my neck constrict, when New York began for me, but I cannot lay my finger upon the moment it ended, can never cut through the ambiguities and second starts and broken resolves to the exact place on the page where the heroine is no longer as optimistic as she once was. When I first saw New York I was twenty, and it was summertime, and I got off a DC-7 at the old Idlewild temporary terminal in a new dress which had seemed very smart in Sacramento but seemed less smart already, even in the old Idlewild temporary terminal, and the warm air smelled of mildew and some instinct, programmed by all the movies I had ever seen and all the songs I had ever heard sung and all the stories I had ever read about New York, informed me that it would never be quite the same again. In fact it never was. Some time later there was a song on all the jukeboxes on the upper East Side that went "but where is the schoolgirl who used to be me," and if it was late enough at night I used to wonder that. I know now that almost everyone wonders something like that, sooner or later and no matter what he or she is doing, but one of the mixed blessings of being twenty and twenty-one and even twenty-three is the conviction that nothing like this, all evidence to the contrary notwithstanding, has ever happened to anyone before.

2   Of course it might have been some other city, had circumstances been different and the time been different and had I been different, might have been Paris or Chicago or even San Francisco, but because I am talking about myself I am talking here about New York. That first night I opened my window on the bus into town and watched for the skyline, but all I could see were the wastes of Queens and the big signs that said MIDTOWN TUNNEL THIS LANE and then a flood of summer rain (even that seemed remarkable and exotic, for I had come out of the West where there was no summer rain), and for the next three days I sat wrapped in blankets in a hotel room air-conditioned to 35° and tried to get over a bad cold and a high fever. It did not occur to me to call a doctor, because I knew none, and although it did occur to me to call the desk and ask that the air conditioner be turned off, I never called, because I did not know how much to tip whoever might come—was anyone ever so young? I am here to tell you that someone was. All I could do during those three days was talk long-distance to the boy I already knew I would never marry in the spring. I would stay in New York, I told him, just six months, and I could see the Brooklyn Bridge from my

window. As it turned out the bridge was the Triborough, and I stayed eight years.

3   In retrospect it seems to me that those days before I knew the names of all the bridges were happier than the ones that came later, but perhaps you will see that as we go along. Part of what I want to tell you is what it is like to be young in New York, how six months can become eight years with the deceptive ease of a film dissolve, for that is how those years appear to me now, in a long sequence of sentimental dissolves and old-fashioned trick shots—the Seagram Building fountains dissolve into snowflakes, I enter a revolving door at twenty and come out a good deal older, and on a different street. But most particularly I want to explain to you, and in the process perhaps to myself, why I no longer live in New York. It is often said that New York is a city for only the very rich and the very poor. It is less often said that New York is also, at least for those of us who came there from somewhere else, a city for only the very young.

4   I remember once, one cold bright December evening in New York, suggesting to a friend who complained of having been around too long that he come with me to a party where there would be, I assured him with the bright resourcefulness of twenty-three, "new faces." He laughed literally until he choked, and I had to roll down the taxi window and hit him on the back. "New faces," he said finally, "don't tell me about *new faces.*" It seemed that the last time he had gone to a party where he had been promised "new faces," there had been fifteen people in the room, and he had already slept with five of the women and owed money to all but two of the men. I laughed with him, but the first snow had just begun to fall and the big Christmas trees glittered yellow and white as far as I could see up Park Avenue and I had a new dress and it would be a long while before I would come to understand the particular moral of the story.

5   It would be a long while because, quite simply, I was in love with New York. I do not mean "love" in any colloquial way, I mean that I was in love with the city, the way you love the first person who ever touches you and never love anyone quite that way again. I remember walking across Sixty-second Street one twilight that first spring, or the second spring, they were all alike for a while. I was late to meet someone but I stopped at Lexington Avenue and bought a peach and stood on the corner eating it and knew that I had come out

of the West and reached the mirage. I could taste the peach and feel
the soft air blowing from a subway grating on my legs and I could
smell lilac and garbage and expensive perfume and I knew that it
would cost something sooner or later—because I did not belong there,
did not come from there—but when you are twenty-two or twenty-
three, you figure that later you will have a high emotional balance, and
be able to pay whatever it costs. I still believed in possibilities then,
still had the sense, so peculiar to New York, that something extraordinary would happen any minute, any day, any month. I was making
only $65 or $70 a week then ("Put yourself in Hattie Carnegie's
hands," I was advised without the slightest trace of irony by an editor
of the magazine for which I worked), so little money that some weeks
I had to charge food at Bloomingdale's gourmet shop in order to eat,
a fact which went unmentioned in the letters I wrote to California. I
never told my father that I needed money because then he would have
sent it, and I would never know if I could do it by myself. At that time
making a living seemed a game to me, with arbitrary but quite inflexi-
ble rules. And except on a certain kind of winter evening—six-thirty in
the Seventies, say, already dark and bitter with a wind off the river,
when I would be walking very fast toward a bus and would look in the
bright windows of brownstones and see cooks working in clean kitch-
ens and imagine women lighting candles on the floor above and beautiful children being bathed on the floor above that—except on nights
like those, I never felt poor; I had the feeling that if I needed money
I could always get it. I could write a syndicated column for teenagers
under the name "Debbi Lynn" or I could smuggle gold into India or
I could become a $100 call girl, and none of it would matter.

6   Nothing was irrevocable; everything was within reach. Just
around every corner lay something curious and interesting, something
I had never before seen or done or known about. I could go to a party
and meet someone who called himself Mr. Emotional Appeal and ran
The Emotional Appeal Institute or Tina Onassis Blandford or a
Florida cracker who was then a regular on what he called "the Big C,"
the Southampton–El Morocco circuit ("I'm well-connected on the Big
C, honey," he would tell me over collard greens on his vast borrowed
terrace), or the widow of the celery king of the Harlem market or a
piano salesman from Bonne Terre, Missouri, or someone who had already made and lost two fortunes in Midland, Texas. I could make
promises to myself and to other people and there would be all the time

in the world to keep them. I could stay up all night and make mistakes, and none of it would count.

7   You see I was in a curious position in New York: it never occurred to me that I was living a real life there. In my imagination I was always there for just another few months, just until Christmas or Easter or the first warm day in May. For that reason I was most comfortable in the company of Southerners. They seemed to be in New York as I was, on some indefinitely extended leave from wherever they belonged, disinclined to consider the future, temporary exiles who always knew when the flights left for New Orleans or Memphis or Richmond or, in my case, California. Someone who lives always with a plane schedule in the drawer lives on a slightly different calendar. Christmas, for example, was a difficult season. Other people could take it in stride, going to Stowe or going abroad or going for the day to their mothers' places in Connecticut; those of us who believed that we lived somewhere else would spend it making and canceling airline reservations, waiting for weather-bound flights as if for the last plane out of Lisbon in 1940, and finally comforting one another, those of us who were left, with the oranges and mementos and smoked-oyster stuffings of childhood, gathering close, colonials in a far country.

8   Which is precisely what we were. I am not sure that it is possible for anyone brought up in the East to appreciate entirely what New York, the idea of New York, means to those of us who came out of the West and the South. To an Eastern child, particularly a child who has always had an uncle on Wall Street and who has spent several hundred Saturdays first at F. A. O. Schwarz and being fitted for shoes at Best's and then waiting under the Biltmore clock and dancing to Lester Lanin, New York is just a city, albeit *the* city, a plausible place for people to live. But to those of us who came from places where no one had heard of Lester Lanin and Grand Central Station was a Saturday radio program, where Wall Street and Fifth Avenue and Madison Avenue were not places at all but abstractions ("Money," and "High Fashion," and "The Hucksters"), New York was no mere city. It was instead an infinitely romantic notion, the mysterious nexus of all love and money and power, the shining and perishable dream itself. To think of "living" there was to reduce the miraculous to the mundane; one does not "live" at Xanadu.

9   In fact it was difficult in the extreme for me to understand those young women for whom New York was not simply an ephemeral Estoril but a real place, girls who bought toasters and installed new cabi-

nets in their apartments and committed themselves to some reasonable future. I never bought any furniture in New York. For a year or so I lived in other people's apartments; after that I lived in the Nineties in an apartment furnished entirely with things taken from storage by a friend whose wife had moved away. And when I left the apartment in the Nineties (that was when I was leaving everything, when it was all breaking up) I left everything in it, even my winter clothes and the map of Sacramento County I had hung on the bedroom wall to remind me who I was, and I moved into a monastic four-room floor-through on Seventy-fifth Street. "Monastic" is perhaps misleading here, implying some chic severity; until after I was married and my husband moved some furniture in, there was nothing at all in those four rooms except a cheap double mattress and box springs, ordered by telephone the day I decided to move, and two French garden chairs lent me by a friend who imported them. (It strikes me now that the people I knew in New York all had curious and self-defeating sidelines. They imported garden chairs which did not sell very well at Hammacher Schlemmer or they tried to market hair straighteners in Harlem or they ghosted exposés of Murder Incorporated for Sunday supplements. I think that perhaps none of us was very serious, *engagé* only about our most private lives.)

10   All I ever did to that apartment was hang fifty yards of yellow theatrical silk across the bedroom windows, because I had some idea that the gold light would make me feel better, but I did not bother to weight the curtains correctly and all that summer the long panels of transparent golden silk would blow out the windows and get tangled and drenched in the afternoon thunderstorms. That was the year, my twenty-eighth, when I was discovering that not all of the promises would be kept, that some things are in fact irrevocable and that it had counted after all, every evasion and every procrastination, every mistake, every word, all of it.

11   That is what it was all about, wasn't it? Promises? Now when New York comes back to me it comes in hallucinatory flashes, so clinically detailed that I sometimes wish that memory would effect the distortion with which it is commonly credited. For a lot of the time I was in New York I used a perfume called *Fleurs de Rocaille*, and then *L'Air du Temps*, and now the slightest trace of either can short-circuit my connections for the rest of the day. Nor can I smell Henri Bendel jasmine soap without falling back into the past, or the particular mixture of spices used for boiling crabs. There were barrels of crab boil in a Czech place

in the Eighties where I once shopped. Smells, of course, are notorious memory stimuli, but there are other things which affect me the same way. Blue-and-white striped sheets. Vermouth cassis. Some faded night-gowns which were new in 1959 or 1960, and some chiffon scarves I bought about the same time.

12   I suppose that a lot of us who have been young in New York have the same scenes on our home screens. I remember sitting in a lot of apartments with a slight headache about five o'clock in the morning. I had a friend who could not sleep, and he knew a few other people who had the same trouble, and we would watch the sky lighten and have a last drink with no ice and then go home in the early morning light, when the streets were clean and wet (had it rained in the night? we never knew) and the few cruising taxis still had their headlights on and the only color was the red and green of traffic signals. The White Rose bars opened very early in the morning; I recall waiting in one of them to watch an astronaut go into space, waiting so long that at the moment it actually happened I had my eyes not on the television screen but on a cockroach on the tile floor. I liked the bleak branches above Washington Square at dawn, and the monochromatic flatness of Second Avenue, the fire escapes and the grilled storefronts peculiar and empty in their perspective.

13   It is relatively hard to fight at six-thirty or seven in the morning, without any sleep, which was perhaps one reason we stayed up all night, and it seemed to me a pleasant time of day. The windows were shuttered in that apartment in the Nineties and I could sleep a few hours and then go to work. I could work then on two or three hours' sleep and a container of coffee from Chock Full O' Nuts. I liked going to work, liked the soothing and satisfactory rhythm of getting out a magazine, liked the orderly progression of four-color closings and two-color closings and black-and-white closings and then The Product, no abstraction but something which looked effortlessly glossy and could be picked up on a newsstand and weighed in the hand. I liked all the minutiae of proofs and layouts, liked working late on the nights the magazine went to press, sitting and reading *Variety* and waiting for the copy desk to call. From my office I could look across town to the weather signal on the Mutual of New York Building and the lights that alternately spelled out TIME and LIFE above Rockefeller Plaza; that pleased me obscurely, and so did walking uptown in the mauve eight o'clocks of early summer evenings and looking at things, Lowestoft tureens in Fifty-seventh Street windows, people in evening clothes trying to get taxis, the trees just coming

into full leaf, the lambent air, all the sweet promises of money and summer.

14   Some years passed, but I still did not lose that sense of wonder about New York. I began to cherish the loneliness of it, the sense that at any given time no one need know where I was or what I was doing. I liked walking, from the East River over to the Hudson and back on brisk days, down around the Village on warm days. A friend would leave me the key to her apartment in the West Village when she was out of town, and sometimes I would just move down there, because by that time the telephone was beginning to bother me (the canker, you see, was already in the rose) and not many people had that number. I remember one day when someone who did have the West Village number came to pick me up for lunch there, and we both had hangovers, and I cut my finger opening him a beer and burst into tears, and we walked to a Spanish restaurant and drank Bloody Marys and *gazpacho* until we felt better. I was not then guilt-ridden about spending afternoons that way, because I still had all the afternoons in the world.

15   And even that late in the game I still liked going to parties, all parties, bad parties, Saturday-afternoon parties given by recently married couples who lived in Stuyvesant Town, West Side parties given by unpublished or failed writers who served cheap red wine and talked about going to Guadalajara, Village parties where all the guests worked for advertising agencies and voted for Reform Democrats, press parties at Sardi's, the worst kinds of parties. You will have perceived by now that I was not one to profit by the experience of others, that it was a very long time indeed before I stopped believing in new faces and began to understand the lesson in that story, which was that it is distinctly possible to stay too long at the Fair.

16   I could not tell you when I began to understand that. All I know is that it was very bad when I was twenty-eight. Everything that was said to me I seemed to have heard before, and I could no longer listen. I could no longer sit in little bars near Grand Central and listen to someone complaining of his wife's inability to cope with the help while he missed another train to Connecticut. I no longer had any interest in hearing about the advances other people had received from their publishers, about plays which were having second-act trouble in Philadelphia, or about people I would like very much if only I would come out and meet them. I had already met them, always. There were certain parts of the city which I had to avoid. I could not bear upper Madison Avenue on

weekday mornings (this was a particularly inconvenient aversion, since I then lived just fifty or sixty feet east of Madison), because I would see women walking Yorkshire terriers and shopping at Gristede's, and some Veblenesque gorge would rise in my throat. I could not go to Times Square in the afternoon, or to the New York Public Library for any reason whatsoever. One day I could not go into a Schrafft's; the next day it would be Bonwit Teller.

17   I hurt the people I cared about, and insulted those I did not. I cut myself off from the one person who was closer to me than any other. I cried until I was not even aware when I was crying and when I was not, cried in elevators and in taxis and in Chinese laundries, and when I went to the doctor he said only that I seemed to be depressed, and should see a "specialist." He wrote down a psychiatrist's name and address for me, but I did not go.

18   Instead I got married, which as it turned out was a very good thing to do but badly timed, since I still could not walk on upper Madison Avenue in the mornings and still could not talk to people and still cried in Chinese laundries. I had never before understood what "despair" meant, and I am not sure that I understand now, but I understood that year. Of course I could not work. I could not even get dinner with any degree of certainty, and I would sit in the apartment on Seventy-fifth Street paralyzed until my husband would call from his office and say gently that I did not have to get dinner, that I could meet him at Michael's Pub or at Toots Shor's or at Sardi's East. And then one morning in April (we had been married in January) he called and told me that he wanted to get out of New York for a while, that he would take a six-month leave of absence, that we would go somewhere.

19   It was three years ago that he told me that, and we have lived in Los Angeles since. Many of the people we knew in New York think this a curious aberration, and in fact tell us so. There is no possible, no adequate answer to that, and so we give certain stock answers, the answers everyone gives. I talk about how difficult it would be for us to "afford" to live in New York right now, about how much "space" we need. All I mean is that I was very young in New York, and that at some point the golden rhythm was broken, and I am not that young any more. The last time I was in New York was in a cold January, and everyone was ill and tired. Many of the people I used to know there had moved to Dallas or had gone on Antabuse or had bought a farm in New Hampshire. We stayed ten days, and then we took an afternoon flight

back to Los Angeles, and on the way home from the airport that night I could see the moon on the Pacific and smell jasmine all around and we both knew that there was no longer any point in keeping the apartment we still kept in New York. There were years when I called Los Angeles "the Coast," but they seem a long time ago.

QUESTIONS

Ideas

1. Didion says her purpose is to explain why she no longer lives in New York. What other impulses seem to animate her essay?

2. What image of New York does Didion present? What is her attitude toward the city? Why does she think and feel the way she does? Consider the implications of the final sentence in paragraph 3 and the whole of paragraphs 16–19.

3. What is Didion's central point about herself as she was in her early twenties? What contrasting perspectives does she offer on her experience? What general ideas can be drawn from Didion's experience as a woman in her twenties coming to live in a new and glamorous place?

Organization

4. Divide the essay into an introduction, body, and conclusion, and then comment on the effectiveness of each.

5. Once you have identified the essay's introductory and concluding sections, focus on its large mid-section or body. Divide this section into smaller parts, explain how the parts are related and how Didion moves from one aspect of her subject to another. Consider, for example, the relationship and method of transition between paragraphs 7 and 8, 8 and 9, 14 and 15, 15 and 16, 16 and 17.

6. What principle of selection governs Didion's description of the city? What aspects of New York does she neglect? Why?

Sentences

7. Didion writes many balanced sentences. Some of these she punctuates with the colon, others with the semicolon, still others with the comma. Consider the following examples and comment on the effectiveness of each sentence and the appropriateness of its punctuation.

Nothing was irrevocable; everything was within reach. (7)

To think of "living" there was to reduce the miraculous to the mundane; one does not "live" at Xanadu. (8)

You see I was in a curious position in New York: it never occurred to me that I was living a real life there. (7)

One day I could not go into a Schrafft's; the next day it would be Bonwit Teller. (16)

I hurt the people I cared about, and insulted those I did not. (17)

It is easy to see the beginnings of things, and harder to see the ends. (1)

8. Read through the first two paragraphs noting the blend of long and short sentences. Comment on the effect of the short sentences in both paragraphs.

9. The three sentences that end paragraph 3 achieve emphasis by means of repetition and parallelism. They also illustrate how a writer can control the rhythm of a sentence while qualifying an idea. Identify the repeated elements and the qualifying words and phrases.

> But most particularly I want to explain to you,
>   and in the process perhaps   to myself,
>   why I no longer live in New York.
>
>   It is often said that New York is a city for only the very rich
>   and the very poor.
>   It is less often said that New York is also, at least for those of us who
> came from somewhere else, a city only for the very young.

10. Comment on Didion's use of questions in paragraphs 2, 11, and 12 and on her sentence fragment in paragraph 8. Would any of the questions benefit from being recast as a statement? Should the fragment be rewritten as a grammatically complete sentence? Why or why not?

Words

11. Identify and comment on the effect of the specific details Didion includes in paragraphs 3, 5, and 11, especially the peach, the subway grating, and the revolving door.

12. Occasionally Didion italicizes words or puts quotation marks around them. Explain the point of these uses for the words thus affected in the following paragraphs: 4, 5, 8, 9, 17, 18, and 19.

Suggestions for Writing

A. Write imitations of the sentences mentioned in questions 9 and 11.

B. Write an imitation of any paragraph, concentrating on varying the length of your sentences.

C. Discuss what you think Didion means by saying the early twenties is a time of mixed blessings.

D. Write an essay about the importance of a place in your life. It might be a place that you needed to leave or it might be a place that you have always enjoyed living in. You may decide to compare two different places and why you feel about them as you do.

Salvador

1   During the week before I flew down to El Salvador a Salvadoran woman who works for my husband and me in Los Angeles gave me repeated instructions about what we must and must not do. We must not go out at night. We must stay off the street whenever possible. We must never ride in buses or taxis, never leave the capital, never imagine that our passports would protect us. We must not even consider the hotel a safe place: people were killed in hotels. She spoke with considerable vehemence, because two of her brothers had been killed in Salvador in August of 1981, in their beds. The throats of both brothers had been slashed. Her father had been cut but stayed alive. Her mother had been beaten. Twelve of her other relatives, aunts and uncles and cousins, had been taken from their houses one night the same August, and their bodies had been found some time later, in a ditch. I assured her that we would remember, we would be careful, we would in fact be so careful that we would probably (trying for a light touch) spend all our time in church.

2   She became still more agitated, and I realized that I had spoken as a *norteamericana:* churches had not been to this woman the neutral ground they had been to me. I must remember: Archbishop Romero killed saying mass in the chapel of the Divine Providence Hospital in San Salvador. I must remember: more than thirty people killed at Archbishop Romero's funeral in the Metropolitan Cathedral in San Salvador.

I must remember: more than twenty people killed before that on the steps of the Metropolitan Cathedral. CBS had filmed it. It had been on television, the bodies jerking, those still alive crawling over the dead as they tried to get out of range. I must understand: the Church was dangerous.

3   I told her that I understood, that I knew all that, and I did, abstractly, but the specific meaning of the Church she knew eluded me until I was actually there, at the Metropolitan Cathedral in San Salvador, one afternoon when rain sluiced down its corrugated plastic windows and puddled around the supports of the Sony and Phillips billboards near the steps. The effect of the Metropolitan Cathedral is immediate, and entirely literary. This is the cathedral that the late Archbishop Oscar Arnulfo Romero refused to finish, on the premise that the work of the Church took precedence over its display, and the high walls of raw concrete bristle with structural rods, rusting now, staining the concrete, sticking out at wrenched and violent angles. The wiring is exposed. Fluorescent tubes hang askew. The great high altar is backed by warped plyboard. The cross on the altar is of bare incandescent bulbs, but the bulbs, that afternoon, were unlit: there was in fact no light at all on the main altar, no light on the cross, no light on the globe of the world that showed the northern American continent in gray and the southern in white; no light on the dove above the globe, *Salvador del Mundo.* In this vast brutalist space that was the cathedral, the unlit altar seemed to offer a single ineluctable message: at this time and in this place the light of the world could be construed as out, off, extinguished.

4   In many ways the Metropolitan Cathedral is an authentic piece of political art, a statement for El Salvador as *Guernica* was for Spain. It is quite devoid of sentimental relief. There are no decorative or architectural references to familiar parables, in fact no stories at all, not even the Stations of the Cross. On the afternoon I was there the flowers laid on the altar were dead. There were no traces of normal parish activity. The doors were open to the barricaded main steps, and down the steps there was a spill of red paint, lest anyone forget the blood shed there. Here and there on the cheap linoleum inside the cathedral there was what seemed to be actual blood, dried in spots, the kind of spots dropped by a slow hemorrhage, or by a woman who does not know or does not care that she is menstruating.

5   There were several women in the cathedral during the hour or so I spent there, a young woman with a baby, an older woman in house slippers, a few others, all in black. One of the women walked the aisles

as if by compulsion, up and down, across and back, crooning loudly as she walked. Another knelt without moving at the tomb of Archbishop Romero in the right transept. "Loor a Monsenor Romero," the crude needlepoint tapestry by the tomb read, "Praise to Monsignor Romero from the Mothers of the Imprisoned, the Disappeared, and the Murdered," the *Comité de Madres y Familiares de Presos, Desaparecidos, y Asesinados Politicos de El Salvador.*

6 The tomb itself was covered with offerings and petitions, notes decorated with motifs cut from greeting cards and cartoons. I recall one with figures cut from a Bugs Bunny strip, and another with a pencil drawing of a baby in a crib. The baby in this drawing seemed to be receiving medication or fluid or blood intravenously, through the IV line shown on its wrist. I studied the notes for a while and then went back and looked again at the unlit altar, and at the red paint on the main steps, from which it was possible to see the guardsmen on the balcony of the National Palace hunching back to avoid the rain. Many Salvadorans are offended by the Metropolitan Cathedral, which is as it should be, because the place remains perhaps the only unambiguous political statement in El Salvador, a metaphorical bomb in the ultimate power station. . . .

7 ". . . I had nothing more to do in San Salvador. I had given a lecture on the topic that had occurred to me on the train to Tapachula: Little-known Books by Famous American Authors— *Pudd'nhead Wilson, The Devil's Dictionary, The Wild Palms.* I had looked at the university; and no one could explain why there was a mural of Marx, Engels, and Lenin in the university of this right-wing dictatorship."

—Paul Theroux, *The Old Patagonian Express.*

8 The university Paul Theroux visited in San Salvador was the National University of El Salvador. This visit (and, given the context, this extraordinary lecture) took place in the late seventies, a period when the National University was actually open. In 1972 the Molina government had closed it, forcibly, with tanks and artillery and planes, and had kept it closed until 1974. In 1980 the Duarte government again moved troops onto the campus, which then had an enrollment of about 30,000, leaving fifty dead and offices and laboratories systematically smashed. By the time I visited El Salvador a few classes were being held in storefronts

around San Salvador, but no one other than an occasional reporter had been allowed to enter the campus since the day the troops came in. Those reporters allowed to look had described walls still splashed with the spray-painted slogans left by the students, floors littered with tangled computer tape and with copies of what the National Guardsmen in charge characterized as *subversivo* pamphlets, for example a reprint of an article on inherited enzyme deficiency from *The New England Journal of Medicine.*

9   In some ways the closing of the National University seemed another of those Salvadoran situations in which no one came out well, and everyone was made to bleed a little, not excluding the National Guardsmen left behind to have their ignorance exposed by *gringo* reporters. The Jesuit university, UCA, or La Universidad Centroamericana José Simeón Cañas, had emerged as the most important intellectual force in the country, but the Jesuits had been so widely identified with the left that some local scholars would not attend lectures or seminars held on the UCA campus. (Those Jesuits still in El Salvador had in fact been under a categorical threat of death from the White Warriors Union since 1977. The Carter administration forced President Romero to protect the Jesuits, and on the day the killing was to have begun, July 22, 1977, the National Police are said to have sat outside the Jesuit residence in San Salvador on their motorcycles, with UZIs.) In any case UCA could manage an enrollment of only about 5,000. The scientific disciplines, which never had a particularly tenacious hold locally, had largely vanished from local life.

10   Meanwhile many people spoke of the National University in the present tense, as if it still existed, or as if its closing were a routine event on some long-term academic calendar. I recall talking one day to a former member of the faculty at the National University, a woman who had not seen her office since the morning she noticed the troops massing outside and left it. She lost her books and her research and the uncompleted manuscript of the book she was then writing, but she described this serenely, and seemed to find no immediate contradiction in losing her work to the Ministry of Defense and the work she did later with the Ministry of Education. The campus of the National University is said to be growing over, which is one way contradictions get erased in the tropics.

11   I was invited one morning to a gathering of Salvadoran writers, a kind of informal coffee hour arranged by the American embassy. For some days there had been a question about where to hold this *café*

literario, since there seemed to be no single location that was not considered off-limits by at least one of the guests, and at one point the ambassador's residence was put forth as the most neutral setting. On the day before the event it was finally decided that UCA was the more appropriate place ("and just never mind," as one of the embassy people put it, that some people would not go to UCA), and at ten the next morning we gathered there in a large conference room and drank coffee and talked, at first in platitudes, and then more urgently.

12 These are some of the sentences spoken to me that morning: *It's not possible to speak of intellectual life in El Salvador. Every day we lose more. We are regressing constantly. Intellectual life is drying up. You are looking at the intellectual life of El Salvador. Here. In this room. We are the only survivors. Some of the others are out of the country, others are not writing because they are engaged in political activity. Some have been disappeared, many of the teachers have been disappeared. Teaching is very dangerous, if a student misinterprets what a teacher says, then the teacher may be arrested. Some are in exile, the rest are dead. Los muertos, you know? We are the only ones left. There is no one after us, no young ones. It is all over, you know?* At noon there was an exchange of books and *curricula vitae.* The cultural attaché from the embassy said that she, for one, would like to see this *café literario* close on a hopeful note, and someone provided one: it was a hopeful note that *norteamericanos* and *centroamericanos* could have such a meeting. This is what passed for a hopeful note in San Salvador in the summer of 1982.

QUESTIONS

Ideas

1. If someone told you about the events described in the first two paragraphs, would you still travel there as a journalist?

2. Although Didion describes the Cathedral's actual appearance, much of what she says about it is interpretation. What, for example, are possible reasons for Salvadorans being offended by Metropolitan Cathedral? What reason does Didion offer? How does this support the first sentence of paragraph 4?

3. In the last two or three sentences of paragraph 3 Didion seems to be "reading" the cathedral as a critic would read a poem, finding meaning in little details. What does she "find"? Is this fair to do?

4. Didion often makes her point indirectly, by selecting particular details for certain effects. What response is she after with the journal example in the last sentence of paragraph 8?

5. What tone do you detect in the last sentence? What is the effect of the phrase "what passed for"?

6. Based on these observations from Didion, what is your impression of life in El Salvador? Do you think our State Department is influenced by writers like Didion?

Organization

7. In the first sentence of paragraphs 2–6 and 8–12, underline the words or phrase that serves as a link to the previous paragraph. Comment on these transitions. Are they forced? Do they work? Are there different types?

8. How do the opening paragraphs of Didion's portrait of the Salvadorean church and university (or the spirit and the mind) set the mood for her concluding thoughts in each section?

Sentences

9. In the first two paragraphs Didion repeats two sentence patterns for rhetorical effect. Which series of sentences do you find more effective? Why?

10. Didion uses the colon a good deal in this essay. Examine half a dozen examples. Describe her method. If you were writing a rule for its use based on this essay, what would it be? Give an original example.

Words

11. What is the effect of using the three words at the end of paragraph 3?

12. Make a list of words or phrases that you think Didion means to be taken ironically? Compare your list with those of your classmates. Is this a matter of interpretation? Is irony in the mind of the reader?

Suggestions for Writing

A. Find an interesting place that you can describe in some detail, perhaps a church, a section of a mall, a deserted house, or a wooded area. Write about it, noting its specific details and, most importantly, interpreting its meaning.

B. Find a reproduction of *Guernica* (paragraph 5) in an art history text. What do you think Didion meant by her comparison between that painting and the Metropolitan Cathedral?

Why I Write

1      $\mathbf{O}$f course I stole the title for this talk, from George Orwell. One reason I stole it was that I like the sound of the words: *Why I Write.* There you have three short unambiguous words that share a sound, and the sound they share is this:

I

I

I

2   In many ways writing is the act of saying *I*, of imposing oneself upon other people, of saying *listen to me, see it my way, change your mind.* It's an aggressive, even a hostile act. You can disguise its aggressiveness all you want with veils of subordinate clauses and qualifiers and tentative subjunctives, with ellipses and evasions—with the whole manner of intimating rather than claiming, of alluding rather than stating —but there's no getting around the fact that setting words on paper is the tactic of a secret bully, an invasion, an imposition of the writer's sensibility on the reader's most private space.

3   I stole the title not only because the words sounded right but because they seemed to sum up, in a no-nonsense way, all I have to tell you. Like many writers I have only this one "subject," this one "area": the act of writing. I can bring you no reports from any other front. I may have other interests: I am "interested," for example, in marine biology, but I don't flatter myself that you would come out to hear me talk about it. I am not a scholar. I am not in the least an intellectual, which is not to say that when I hear the word "intellectual" I reach for my gun, but only to say that I do not think in abstracts. During the years when I was an undergraduate at Berkeley I tried, with a kind of hopeless late-adolescent energy, to buy some temporary visa into the world of ideas, to forge for myself a mind that could deal with the abstract.

4   In short I tried to think. I failed. My attention veered inexorably back to the specific, to the tangible, to what was generally considered, by everyone I knew then and for that matter have known since, the peripheral. I would try to contemplate the Hegelian dialectic and would find myself concentrating instead on a flowering pear tree outside my window and the particular way the petals fell on my floor. I would try

to read linguistic theory and would find myself wondering instead if the lights were on in the bevatron up the hill. When I say that I was wondering if the lights were on in the bevatron you might immediately suspect, if you deal in ideas at all, that I was registering the bevatron as a political symbol, thinking in shorthand about the military-industrial complex and its role in the university community, but you would be wrong. I was only wondering if the lights were on in the bevatron, and how they looked. A physical fact.

5   I had trouble graduating from Berkeley, not because of this inability to deal with ideas—I was majoring in English, and I could locate the house-and-garden imagery in "The Portrait of a Lady" as well as the next person, "imagery" being by definition the kind of specific that got my attention—but simply because I had neglected to take a course in Milton. For reasons which now sound baroque I needed a degree by the end of that summer, and the English department finally agreed, if I would come down from Sacramento every Friday and talk about the cosmology of "Paradise Lost," to certify me proficient in Milton. I did this. Some Fridays I took the Greyhound bus, other Fridays I caught the Southern Pacific's City of San Francisco on the last leg of its transcontinental trip. I can no longer tell you whether Milton put the sun or the earth at the center of his universe in "Paradise Lost," the central question of at least one century and a topic about which I wrote 10,000 words that summer, but I can still recall the exact rancidity of the butter in the City of San Francisco's dining car, and the way the tinted windows on the Greyhound bus cast the oil refineries around Carquinez Straits into a grayed and obscurely sinister light. In short my attention was always on the periphery, on what I could see and taste and touch, on the butter, and the Greyhound bus. During those years I was traveling on what I knew to be a very shaky passport, forged papers: I knew that I was no legitimate resident in any world of ideas. I knew I couldn't think. All I knew then was what I couldn't do. All I knew then was what I wasn't, and it took me some years to discover what I was.

6   Which was a writer.

7   By which I mean not a "good" writer or a "bad" writer but simply a writer, a person whose most absorbed and passionate hours are spent arranging words on pieces of paper. Had my credentials been in order I would never have become a writer. Had I been blessed with even limited access to my own mind there would have been no reason to write. I write entirely to find out what I'm thinking, what I'm looking at, what I see and what it means. What I want and what I fear. Why

did the oil refineries around Carquinez Straits seem sinister to me in the summer of 1956? Why have the night lights in the bevatron burned in my mind for twenty years? *What is going on in these pictures in my mind?*

8   When I talk about pictures in my mind I am talking, quite specifically, about images that shimmer around the edges. There used to be an illustration in every elementary psychology book showing a cat drawn by a patient in varying stages of schizophrenia. This cat had a shimmer around it. You could see the molecular structure breaking down at the very edges of the cat: the cat became the background and the background the cat, everything interacting, exchanging ions. People on hallucinogens describe the same perception of objects. I'm not a schizophrenic, nor do I take hallucinogens, but certain images do shimmer for me. Look hard enough, and you can't miss the shimmer. It's there. You can't think too much about these pictures that shimmer. You just lie low and let them develop. You stay quiet. You don't talk to many people and you keep your nervous system from shorting out and you try to locate the cat in the shimmer, the grammar in the picture.

9   Just as I meant "shimmer" literally I mean "grammar" literally. Grammar is a piano I play by ear, since I seem to have been out of school the year the rules were mentioned. All I know about grammar is its infinite power. To shift the structure of a sentence alters the meaning of that sentence, as definitely and inflexibly as the position of a camera alters the meaning of the object photographed. Many people know about camera angles now, but not so many know about sentences. The arrangement of the words matters, and the arrangement you want can be found in the picture in your mind. The picture dictates the arrangement. The picture dictates whether this will be a sentence with or without clauses, a sentence that ends hard or a dying-fall sentence, long or short, active or passive. The picture tells you how to arrange the words and the arrangement of the words tells you, or tells me, what's going on in the picture. *Nota bene:*

10   It tells you.

11   You don't tell it.

12   Let me show you what I mean by pictures in the mind. I began "Play It As It Lays" just as I have begun each of my novels, with no notion of "character" or "plot" or even "incident." I had only two pictures in my mind, more about which later, and a technical intention, which was to write a novel so elliptical and fast that it would be over before you noticed it, a novel so fast that it would scarcely exist on the

page at all. About the pictures: the first was of white space. Empty space. This was clearly the picture that dictated the narrative intention of the book—a book in which anything that happened would happen off the page, a "white" book to which the reader would have to bring his or her own bad dreams—and yet this picture told me no "story," suggested no situation. The second picture did. This second picture was of something actually witnessed. A young woman with long hair and a short white halter dress walks through the casino at the Riviera in Las Vegas at one in the morning. She crosses the casino alone and picks up a house telephone. I watch her because I have heard her paged, and recognize her name: she is a minor actress I see around Los Angeles from time to time, in places like Jax and once in a gynecologist's office in the Beverly Hills Clinic, but have never met. I know nothing about her. Who is paging her? Why is she here to be paged? How exactly did she come to this? It was precisely this moment in Las Vegas that made "Play It As It Lays" begin to tell itself to me, but the moment appears in the novel only obliquely, in a chapter which begins:

13   "Maria made a list of things she would never do. She would never: walk through the Sands or Caesar's alone after midnight. She would never: ball at a party, do S-M unless she wanted to, borrow furs from Abe Lipsey, deal. She would never: carry a Yorkshire in Beverly Hills."

14   That is the beginning of the chapter and that is also the end of the chapter, which may suggest what I meant by "white space."

15   I recall having a number of pictures in my mind when I began the novel I just finished, "A Book of Common Prayer." As a matter of fact one of these pictures was of that bevatron I mentioned, although I would be hard put to tell you a story in which nuclear energy figured. Another was a newspaper photograph of a hijacked 707 burning on the desert in the Middle East. Another was the night view from a room in which I once spent a week with paratyphoid, a hotel room on the Colombian coast. My husband and I seemed to be on the Colombian coast representing the United States of America at a film festival (I recall invoking the name "Jack Valenti" a lot, as if its reiteration could make me well), and it was a bad place to have fever, not only because my indisposition offended our hosts but because every night in this hotel the generator failed. The lights went out. The elevator stopped. My husband would go to the event of the evening and make excuses for me and I would stay alone in this hotel room, in the dark. I remember standing at the window trying to call Bogotá (the telephone seemed to work on the same principle as the generator) and watching the night wind come up and

wondering what I was doing eleven degrees off the equator with a fever of 103. The view from that window definitely figures in "A Book of Common Prayer," as does the burning 707, and yet none of these pictures told me the story I needed.

16   The picture that did, the picture that shimmered and made these other images coalesce, was the Panama airport at 6 A.M. I was in this airport only once, on a plane to Bogotá that stopped for an hour to refuel, but the way it looked that morning remained superimposed on everything I saw until the day I finished "A Book of Common Prayer." I lived in that airport for several years. I can still feel the hot air when I step off the plane, can see the heat already rising off the tarmac at 6 A.M. I can feel my skirt damp and wrinkled on my legs. I can feel the asphalt stick to my sandals. I remember the big tail of a Pan American plane floating motionless down at the end of the tarmac. I remember the sound of a slot machine in the waiting room. I could tell you that I remember a particular woman in the airport, an American woman, a *norteamericana,* a thin *norteamericana* about 40 who wore a big square emerald in lieu of a wedding ring, but there was no such woman there.

17   I put this woman in the airport later. I made this woman up, just as I later made up a country to put the airport in, and a family to run the country. This woman in the airport is neither catching a plane nor meeting one. She is ordering tea in the airport coffee shop. In fact she is not simply "ordering" tea but insisting that the water be boiled, in front of her, for twenty minutes. Why is this woman in this airport? Why is she going nowhere, where has she been? Where did she get that big emerald? What derangement, or disassociation, makes her believe that her will to see the water boiled can possibly prevail?

18   "She had been going to one airport or another for four months, one could see it, looking at the visas on her passport. All those airports where Charlotte Douglas's passport had been stamped would have looked alike. Sometimes the sign on the tower would say 'Bienvenidos' and sometimes the sign on the tower would say 'Bienvenue,' some places were wet and hot and others dry and hot, but at each of these airports the pastel concrete walls would rust and stain and the swamp off the runway would be littered with the fuselages of cannibalized Fairchild F-227's and the water would need boiling.

19   "I knew why Charlotte went to the airport even if Victor did not.

20   "I knew about airports."

21   These lines appear about halfway through "A Book of Common Prayer," but I wrote them during the second week I worked on the book,

long before I had any idea where Charlotte Douglas had been or why she went to airports. Until I wrote these lines I had no character called "Victor" in mind: the necessity for mentioning a name, and the name "Victor," occurred to me as I wrote the sentence. *I knew why Charlotte went to the airport* sounded incomplete. *I knew why Charlotte went to the airport even if Victor did not* carried a little more narrative drive. Most important of all, until I wrote these lines I did not know who "I" was, who was telling the story. I had intended until that moment that the "I" be no more than the voice of the author, a 19th-century omniscient narrator. But there it was:

22   "I knew why Charlotte went to the airport even if Victor did not.
23   "I knew about airports."

24   This "I" was the voice of no author in my house. This "I" was someone who not only knew why Charlotte went to the airport but also knew someone called "Victor." Who was Victor? Who was this narrator? Why was this narrator telling me this story? Let me tell you one thing about why writers write: had I known the answer to any of these questions I would never have needed to write a novel.

QUESTIONS

1.   Why does Didion write? Do her reasons make sense to you? What reason for writing is suggested in the last paragraph? How does that reason tie in with the ones given in paragraph 7?

2.   How does Didion begin the process of writing? What does she start with and from? What do you think of her method? Of her compulsion? Are there any advantages to starting this way? Any disadvantages?

3.   Didion says she stole her title from George Orwell. Is her theft legitimate? Can one writer steal from another? How far can any writer, including you, legitimately go in this kind of stealing?

4.   Didion likes her title because she says it's no-nonsense. What does she mean? Are her first three paragraphs also no-nonsense paragraphs?

5.   In the second paragraph Didion says writers are bullies, and in the first paragraph she suggests that they are egocentric. Is she convincing here? Do you feel this way? Compare this with what E. B. White says about writers in "The Essayist."

6.   In paragraphs 4 and 5 Didion makes a lot of her alleged inability to think —abstractly and generally. Reread these paragraphs carefully and make a list of the general ideas she includes and of the specific details she sets up as counters to them and illustrations of them.

7. What does Didion mean when she says: "To shift the structure of a sentence alters the meaning of that sentence." Can you provide an example either by altering the structure of one of Didion's sentences or by altering one of your own? How does the analogy that follows this statement help to clarify her meaning: "as the position of a camera alters the meaning of the object photographed"?

Suggestions for Writing

A. Explain, in an essay, why you write. Has writing helped you to see or to think in ways you wouldn't without writing? Has it hindered or hurt you in any way? You might describe your own composing process—that is, exactly what you do from the time you first sit down to write until you turn your essay in. Or you might write an essay about why you don't write, and how and why you avoid it.

B. In another essay, "On Keeping a Notebook," Didion says that "the point of my keeping a notebook has never been, nor is it now, to have an accurate factual record of what I have been doing or thinking." Her instinct, as she explains it, is neither for reality nor for history. It is rather, she insists, a personal impulse—a desire to remember who she was at different points in her life, an urge to recall how things felt, what they seemed like then. "It is a good idea, then," she continues, "to keep in touch, and I suppose that keeping in touch is what notebooks are all about." Try for a week, a month, or longer if you like, to keep some kind of notebook or journal of responses to things you do, see, hear, encounter. Avoid making it either a diary so private you'd want no one to read it, or simply a record of trivial and uninteresting actions ("I got up, ate, and went to work"). Instead, make it a re-acting notebook, literally a book of notes on your thoughts and feelings, your ideas and attitudes about any and every thing.

On Keeping a Notebook

---

1   " 'THAT WOMAN ESTELLE,' " the note reads, " 'is partly the reason why George Sharp and I are separated today.' *Dirty crepe-de-Chine wrapper, hotel bar, Wilmington RR, 9:45 a.m. August Monday morning.* "

2   Since the note is in my notebook, it presumably has some meaning to me. I study it for a long while. At first I have only the most general notion of what I was doing on an August Monday morning in the bar

of the hotel across from the Pennsylvania Railroad station in Wilmington, Delaware (waiting for a train? missing one? 1960? 1961? why Wilmington?), but I do remember being there. The woman in the dirty crepe-de-Chine wrapper had come down from her room for a beer, and the bartender had heard before the reason why George Sharp and she were separated today. "Sure," he said, and went on mopping the floor. "You told me." At the other end of the bar is a girl. She is talking, pointedly, not to the man beside her but to a cat lying in the triangle of sunlight cast through the open door. She is wearing a plaid silk dress from Peck & Peck, and the hem is coming down.

3   Here is what it is: the girl has been on the Eastern Shore, and now she is going back to the city, leaving the man beside her, and all she can see ahead are the viscous summer sidewalks and the 3 a.m. long-distance calls that will make her lie awake and then sleep drugged through all the steaming mornings left in August (1960? 1961?). Because she must go directly from the train to lunch in New York, she wishes that she had a safety pin for the hem of the plaid silk dress, and she also wishes that she could forget about the hem and the lunch and stay in the cool bar that smells of disinfectant and malt and make friends with the woman in the crepe-de-Chine wrapper. She is afflicted by a little self-pity, and she wants to compare Estelles. That is what that was all about.

4   Why did I write it down? In order to remember, of course, but exactly what was it I wanted to remember? How much of it actually happened? Did any of it? Why do I keep a notebook at all? It is easy to deceive oneself on all those scores. The impulse to write things down is a peculiarly compulsive one, inexplicable to those who do not share it, useful only accidentally, only secondarily, in the way that any compulsion tries to justify itself. I suppose that it begins or does not begin in the cradle. Although I have felt compelled to write things down since I was five years old, I doubt that my daughter ever will, for she is a singularly blessed and accepting child, delighted with life exactly as life presents itself to her, unafraid to go to sleep and unafraid to wake up. Keepers of private notebooks are a different breed altogether, lonely and resistant rearrangers of things, anxious malcontents, children afflicted apparently at birth with some presentiment of loss.

5   My first notebook was a Big Five tablet, given to me by my mother with the sensible suggestion that I stop whining and learn to amuse myself by writing down my thoughts. She returned the tablet to me a few years ago; the first entry is an account of a woman who believed herself to be freezing to death in the Arctic night, only to find, when

day broke, that she had stumbled onto the Sahara Desert, where she would die of the heat before lunch. I have no idea what turn of a five-year-old's mind could have prompted so insistently "ironic" and exotic a story, but it does reveal a certain predilection for the extreme which has dogged me into adult life; perhaps if I were analytically inclined I would find it a truer story than any I might have told about Donald Johnson's birthday party or the day my cousin Brenda put Kitty Litter in the aquarium.

6 So the point of my keeping a notebook has never been, nor is it now, to have an accurate factual record of what I have been doing or thinking. That would be a different impulse entirely, an instinct for reality which I sometimes envy but do not possess. At no point have I ever been able successfully to keep a diary; my approach to daily life ranges from the grossly negligent to the merely absent, and on those few occasions when I have tried dutifully to record a day's events, boredom has so overcome me that the results are mysterious at best. What is this business about "shopping, typing piece, dinner with E, depressed"? Shopping for what? Typing what piece? Who is E? Was this "E" depressed, or was I depressed? Who cares?

7 In fact I have abandoned altogether that kind of pointless entry; instead I tell what some would call lies. "That's simply not true," the members of my family frequently tell me when they come up against my memory of a shared event. "The party was *not* for you, the spider was *not* a black widow, *it wasn't that way at all.*" Very likely they are right, for not only have I always had trouble distinguishing between what happened and what merely might have happened, but I remain unconvinced that the distinction, for my purposes, matters. The cracked crab that I recall having for lunch the day my father came home from Detroit in 1945 must certainly be embroidery, worked into the day's pattern to lend verisimilitude; I was ten years old and would not now remember the cracked crab. The day's events did not turn on cracked crab. And yet it is precisely that fictitious crab that makes me see the afternoon all over again, a home movie run all too often, the father bearing gifts, the child weeping, an exercise in family love and guilt. Or that is what it was to me. Similarly, perhaps it never did snow that August in Vermont; perhaps there never were flurries in the night wind, and maybe no one else felt the ground hardening and summer already dead even as we pretended to bask in it, but that was how it felt to me, and it might as well have snowed, could have snowed, did snow.

8   *How it felt to me:* that is getting closer to the truth about a notebook. I sometimes delude myself about why I keep a notebook, imagine that some thrifty virtue derives from preserving everything observed. See enough and write it down, I tell myself, and then some morning when the world seems drained of wonder, some day when I am only going through the motions of doing what I am supposed to do, which is write—on that bankrupt morning I will simply open my notebook and there it will all be, a forgotten account with accumulated interest, paid passage back to the world out there: dialogue overheard in hotels and elevators and at the hat-check counter in Pavillon (one middle-aged man shows his hat check to another and says, "That's my old football number"); impressions of Bettina Aptheker and Benjamin Sonnenberg and Teddy ("Mr. Acapulco") Stauffer; careful *aperçus* about tennis bums and failed fashion models and Greek shipping heiresses, one of whom taught me a significant lesson (a lesson I could have learned from F. Scott Fitzgerald, but perhaps we all must meet the very rich for ourselves) by asking, when I arrived to interview her in her orchid-filled sitting room on the second day of a paralyzing New York blizzard, whether it was snowing outside.

9   I imagine, in other words, that the notebook is about other people. But of course it is not. I have no real business with what one stranger said to another at the hat-check counter in Pavillon; in fact I suspect that the line "That's my old football number" touched not my own imagination at all, but merely some memory of something once read, probably "The Eighty-Yard Run." Nor is my concern with a woman in a dirty crepe-de-Chine wrapper in a Wilmington bar. My stake is always, of course, in the unmentioned girl in the plaid silk dress. *Remember what it was to be me:* that is always the point.

10   It is a difficult point to admit. We are brought up in the ethic that others, any others, all others, are by definition more interesting than ourselves; taught to be diffident, just this side of self-effacing. ("You're the least important person in the room and don't forget it," Jessica Mitford's governess would hiss in her ear on the advent of any social occasion; I copied that into my notebook because it is only recently that I have been able to enter a room without hearing some such phrase in my inner ear.) Only the very young and the very old may recount their dreams at breakfast, dwell upon self, interrupt with memories of beach picnics and favorite Liberty lawn dresses and the rainbow trout in a creek near Colorado Springs. The rest of us are expected, rightly, to affect absorption in other people's favorite dresses, other people's trout.

11   And so we do. But our notebooks give us away, for however dutifully we record what we see around us, the common denominator of all we see is always, transparently, shamelessly, the implacable "I." We are not talking here about the kind of notebook that is patently for public consumption, a structural conceit for binding together a series of graceful *pensées;* we are talking about something private, about bits of the mind's string too short to use, an indiscriminate and erratic assemblage with meaning only for its maker.

12   And sometimes even the maker has difficulty with the meaning. There does not seem to be, for example, any point in my knowing for the rest of my life that, during 1964, 720 tons of soot fell on every square mile of New York City, yet there it is in my notebook, labeled "FACT." Nor do I really need to remember that Ambrose Bierce liked to spell Leland Stanford's name "£eland $tanford" or that "smart women almost always wear black in Cuba," a fashion hint without much potential for practical application. And does not the relevance of these notes seem marginal at best?:

> In the basement museum of the Inyo County Courthouse in Independence, California, sign pinned to a mandarin coat: "This MANDARIN COAT was often worn by Mrs. Minnie S. Brooks when giving lectures on her TEAPOT COLLECTION."
> Redhead getting out of car in front of Beverly Wilshire Hotel, chinchilla stole, Vuitton bags with tags reading:
>
> MRS LOU FOX
> HOTEL SAHARA
> VEGAS

13   Well, perhaps not entirely marginal. As a matter of fact, Mrs. Minnie S. Brooks and her MANDARIN COAT pull me back into my own childhood, for although I never knew Mrs. Brooks and did not visit Inyo County until I was thirty, I grew up in just such a world, in houses cluttered with Indian relics and bits of gold ore and ambergris and the souvenirs my Aunt Mercy Farnsworth brought back from the Orient. It is a long way from that world to Mrs. Lou Fox's world, where we all live now, and is it not just as well to remember that? Might not Mrs. Minnie S. Brooks help me to remember what I am? Might not Mrs. Lou Fox help me to remember what I am not?

14   But sometimes the point is harder to discern. What exactly did I have in mind when I noted down that it cost the father of someone

I know $650 a month to light the place on the Hudson in which he lived
before the Crash? What use was I planning to make of this line by
Jimmy Hoffa: "I may have my faults, but being wrong ain't one of
them"? And although I think it interesting to know where the girls who
travel with the Syndicate have their hair done when they find themselves
on the West Coast, will I ever make suitable use of it? Might I not be
better off just passing it on to John O'Hara? What is a recipe for
sauerkraut doing in my notebook? What kind of magpie keeps this
notebook? *"He was born the night the Titanic went down."* That seems
a nice enough line, and I even recall who said it, but is it not really a
better line in life than it could ever be in fiction?

15   But of course that is exactly it: not that I should ever use the line,
but that I should remember the woman who said it and the afternoon
I heard it. We were on her terrace by the sea, and we were finishing the
wine left from lunch, trying to get what sun there was, a California
winter sun. The woman whose husband was born the night the *Titanic*
went down wanted to rent her house, wanted to go back to her children
in Paris. I remember wishing that I could afford the house, which cost
$1,000 a month. "Someday you will," she said lazily. "Someday it all
comes." There in the sun on her terrace it seemed easy to believe in
someday, but later I had a low-grade afternoon hangover and ran over
a black snake on the way to the supermarket and was flooded with
inexplicable fear when I heard the checkout clerk explaining to the man
ahead of me why she was finally divorcing her husband. "He left me no
choice," she said over and over as she punched the register. "He has a
little seven-month-old baby by her, he left me no choice." I would like
to believe that my dread then was for the human condition, but of
course it was for me, because I wanted a baby and did not then have
one and because I wanted to own the house that cost $1,000 a month
to rent and because I had a hangover.

16   It all comes back. Perhaps it is difficult to see the value in having
one's self back in that kind of mood, but I do see it; I think we are well
advised to keep on nodding terms with the people we used to be,
whether we find them attractive company or not. Otherwise they turn
up unannounced and surprise us, come hammering on the mind's door
at 4 a.m. of a bad night and demand to know who deserted them, who
betrayed them, who is going to make amends. We forget all too soon
the things we thought we could never forget. We forget the loves and
the betrayals alike, forget what we whispered and what we screamed,
forget who we were. I have already lost touch with a couple of people

I used to be; one of them, a seventeen-year-old, presents little threat, although it would be of some interest to me to know again what it feels like to sit on a river levee drinking vodka-and-orange-juice and listening to Les Paul and Mary Ford and their echoes sing "How High the Moon" on the car radio. (You see I still have the scenes, but I no longer perceive myself among those present, no longer could even improvise the dialogue.) The other one, a twenty-three-year-old, bothers me more. She was always a good deal of trouble, and I suspect she will reappear when I least want to see her, skirts too long, shy to the point of aggravation, always the injured party, full of recriminations and little hurts and stories I do not want to hear again, at once saddening me and angering me with her vulnerability and ignorance, an apparition all the more insistent for being so long banished.

17   It is a good idea, then, to keep in touch, and I suppose that keeping in touch is what notebooks are all about. And we are all on our own when it comes to keeping those lines open to ourselves: your notebook will never help me, nor mine you. *"So what's new in the whiskey business?"* What could that possibly mean to you? To me it means a blonde in a Pucci bathing suit sitting with a couple of fat men by the pool at the Beverly Hills Hotel. Another man approaches, and they all regard one another in silence for a while. "So what's new in the whiskey business?" one of the fat men finally says by way of welcome, and the blonde stands up, arches one foot and dips it in the pool, looking all the while at the cabaña where Baby Pignatari is talking on the telephone. That is all there is to that, except that several years later I saw the blonde coming out of Saks Fifth Avenue in New York with her California complexion and a voluminous mink coat. In the harsh wind that day she looked old and irrevocably tired to me, and even the skins in the mink coat were not worked the way they were doing them that year, not the way she would have wanted them done, and there is the point of the story. For a while after that I did not like to look in the mirror, and my eyes would skim the newspapers and pick out only the deaths, the cancer victims, the premature coronaries, the suicides, and I stopped riding the Lexington Avenue IRT because I noticed for the first time that all the strangers I had seen for years—the man with the seeing-eye dog, the spinster who read the classified pages every day, the fat girl who always got off with me at Grand Central—looked older than they once had.

18   It all comes back. Even that recipe for sauerkraut: even that brings it back. I was on Fire Island when I first made that sauerkraut, and it was raining, and we drank a lot of bourbon and ate the sauerkraut and

went to bed at ten, and I listened to the rain and the Atlantic and felt safe. I made the sauerkraut again last night and it did not make me feel any safer, but that is, as they say, another story.

QUESTIONS

Ideas

1. Didion seems to be working toward an understanding of her own motives in this piece, admitting that she sometimes deludes herself about why she keeps a notebook. What, finally, do you think her purpose is in keeping a notebook?

2. Do you agree with Didion's opening statement in paragraph 17 that it is a good idea to keep in touch with former selves? Why?

3. What do you think Didion means in the first sentence of paragraph 4 when she claims that she tells what "some would call lies"?

4. As a college student what advantages do you see in keeping a notebook? What do you make of Didion's rather negative interpretation of notebook-keepers in the last sentence of paragraph 4?

Organization

5. List several stages in Didion's thinking, beginning with "it presumably has some meaning to me" in paragraph 2.

6. Look at the opening sentences in paragraphs 10 through 15. Describe the techniques Didion uses to link one group of thoughts to another.

7. There are four major sections here, indicated by a space after paragraphs 5, 9, and 13. What would be an appropriate title for each?

Sentences

8. Revise Didion's long third sentence in paragraph 8. First try for several shorter sentences, then try to change the sequence.

9. Where does Didion's conclusion begin? Describe what she does in her conclusion.

Words

10. What do the following words mean? "viscous" (paragraph 3); "*aperçus*" (paragraph 8); "presentiment" (paragraph 4); "predilection" (paragraph

5); *"pensées"* (paragraph 11); "apparition" (paragraph 16). Can you suggest more appropriate synonyms?

Suggestions for Writing

A. Using one of the following statements from Didion's essay as your focus, write a personal essay:

> We forget all too soon the things we thought we could never forget. (paragraph 16)

> The rest of us are expected, rightly, to affect absorption in other people's favorite dresses, other people's trout. (paragraph 10).

B. In paragraph 16 Didion says it would be of some interest to her to know again what it feels like to sit on a river levee drinking vodka-and-orange-juice. Try to remember some comparable situation from your past and write a paragraph about how it felt.

FOUR

Annie Dillard
(1945–   )

Annie Dillard's writing is rooted in an impassioned awe of the natural world. In prose by turns taut and expansive she reveals both the delights of this world and its terrors. Something of a visionary with a mystical strain, Dillard writes prose that often reads more like poetry or fiction than like nonfiction prose. The range of her published writing testifies to her imaginative sensibility as her books include a collection of poems, *Tickets for a Prayer Wheel* (1974); works of philosophical speculation, *Holy the Firm* (1977), and literary theory, *Living by Fiction* (1979); and most recently, a collection of essays, *Teaching a Stone to Talk* (1982).

Her first book, *Pilgrim at Tinker Creek* (1974), was a best seller, and won a Pulitzer Prize. In this work Dillard describes what she saw while patiently observing nature at Tinker Creek in the Roanoke Valley in Virginia. Throughout the book, Dillard moves from a careful exploration of the natural world to the largest philosophical and theological questions, questions about the design and purpose of the universe and of man's place in it; questions about pain, cruelty, suffering, and death —unanswerable yet inescapable questions all.

Meaning and design are central not only as subjects of Dillard's writing, but also as dimensions of its substance and form as well. Her essays, that is, are attempts to explore and explain the meanings hidden in nature; however, Dillard's essays also raise questions about the meaning of life and the purpose of nature. Moreover, just as Dillard seeks to discover patterns of form and structure in nature, in her chance encounters with mystery, so too do her essays both reveal and conceal intricacies of structure and form. (Perhaps we ought to read Dillard with the same attention and deliberation she lavishes on nature.)

What is apparent from even a casual reading of her work is its intensity, its seriousness. There's nothing chatty about her tone, nothing superficial about her subjects or her ideas. In "Jest and Earnest," an excerpt from the first chapter of *Pilgrim at Tinker Creek,* Dillard describes a shocking event: a frog being drained of its internal organs, reduced to juice by a powerful enzyme of the giant water bug. This event stirs Dillard, provoking her to ask a series of questions about God, nature, beauty, and terror. The writing, highly charged with feeling, relies heavily on an accumulation of verbs in the descriptive section and on a pile-up of questions in the speculative part. This is typical of the way Dillard arranges her essays. She often starts with a close description of something she has seen or heard about—a frog, a bird, a fire, a dream, an airplane accident. From description she moves out through a series of questions and provisional answers into speculation and argument.

Her concern throughout *Pilgrim* is with seeing. Her interest, however, is less in what we see than in how we see; less in what we know than in how we come to know. Chapter Two, entitled "Seeing," is an investigation of what it means to really see something; it is an exploration of the different ways of seeing, knowing, and understanding available to us. In another book, *Holy the Firm* (1977), Dillard raises other questions. "God's Tooth," an excerpt from that book, explores the meaning of suffering, particularly the seemingly senseless suffering of children. The essay is casual in structure, angry in tone, and passionate in its agonized quest for meaning in a chance tragic event.

One of the things Dillard seeks to understand is nature, especially the relationship between human and animal life. She explores this subject in "Living like Weasels," in which she describes her own stunning encounter with a weasel, and in which she explores the questions the encounter gave rise to. In "Transfiguration" she describes the death of a moth by incineration, seeing in its burning brightness an image of the writer. Dillard has described herself as "an explorer" and "a stalker"—both of the natural world and of the meanings locked within it. Both naturalist and symbolist, Dillard searches in and through nature for transcendent truths. Her intense scrutiny of nature is fueled by a passionate search for meaning. And the risks she takes in describing the marvelous steep her writing in wonder and make it a continual blend of insight and vision.

Seeing

1   It is still the first week in January, and I've got great plans. I've been thinking about seeing. There are lots of things to see, unwrapped gifts and free surprises. The world is fairly studded and strewn with pennies cast broadside from a generous hand. But—and this is the point—who gets excited by a mere penny? If you follow one arrow, if you crouch motionless on a bank to watch a tremulous ripple thrill on the water and are rewarded by the sight of a muskrat kit paddling from its den, will you count that sight a chip of copper only, and go your rueful way? It is dire poverty indeed when a man is so malnourished and fatigued that he won't stoop to pick up a penny. But if you cultivate a healthy poverty and simplicity, so that finding a penny will literally make your day, then, since the world is in fact planted in pennies, you have with your poverty bought a lifetime of days. It is that simple. What you see is what you get.

2   I used to be able to see flying insects in the air. I'd look ahead and see, not the row of hemlocks across the road, but the air in front of it. My eyes would focus along that column of air, picking out flying insects. But I lost interest, I guess, for I dropped the habit. Now I can see birds. Probably some people can look at the grass at their feet and discover all the crawling creatures. I would like to know grasses and sedges—and care. Then my least journey into the world would be a field trip, a series of happy recognitions. Thoreau, in an expansive mood, exulted, "What a rich book might be made about buds, including, perhaps, sprouts!" It would be nice to think so. I cherish mental images I have of three perfectly happy people. One collects stones. Another—an Englishman, say—watches clouds. The third lives on a coast and collects drops of seawater which he examines microscopically and mounts. But I don't see what the specialist sees, and so I cut myself off, not only from the total picture, but from the various forms of happiness.

3   Unfortunately, nature is very much a now-you-see-it, now-you-don't affair. A fish flashes, then dissolves in the water before my eyes like

so much salt. Deer apparently ascend bodily into heaven; the brightest
oriole fades into leaves. These disappearances stun me into stillness and
concentration; they say of nature that it conceals with a grand nonchalance, and they say of vision that it is a deliberate gift, the revelation
of a dancer who for my eyes only flings away her seven veils. For nature
does reveal as well as conceal: now-you-don't-see-it, now-you-do. For a
week last September migrating red-winged blackbirds were feeding
heavily down by the creek at the back of the house. One day I went out
to investigate the racket; I walked up to a tree, an Osage orange, and
a hundred birds flew away. They simply materialized out of the tree. I
saw a tree, then a whisk of color, then a tree again. I walked closer and
another hundred blackbirds took flight. Not a branch, not a twig
budged: the birds were apparently weightless as well as invisible. Or, it
was as if the leaves of the Osage orange had been freed from a spell in
the form of red-winged blackbirds; they flew from the tree, caught my
eye in the sky, and vanished. When I looked again at the tree the leaves
had reassembled as if nothing had happened. Finally I walked directly
to the trunk of the tree and a final hundred, the real diehards, appeared,
spread, and vanished. How could so many hide in the tree without my
seeing them? The Osage orange, unruffled, looked just as it had looked
from the house, when three hundred red-winged blackbirds cried from
its crown. I looked downstream where they flew, and they were gone.
Searching, I couldn't spot one. I wandered downstream to force them
to play their hand, but they'd crossed the creek and scattered. One show
to a customer. These appearances catch at my throat; they are the free
gifts, the bright coppers at the roots of trees.

4   It's all a matter of keeping my eyes open. Nature is like one of
those line drawings of a tree that are puzzles for children: Can you find
hidden in the leaves a duck, a house, a boy, a bucket, a zebra, and a boot?
Specialists can find the most incredibly well-hidden things. A book I
read when I was young recommended an easy way to find caterpillars
to rear: you simply find some fresh caterpillar droppings, look up, and
there's your caterpillar. More recently an author advised me to set my
mind at ease about those piles of cut stems on the ground in grassy fields.
Field mice make them; they cut the grass down by degrees to reach the
seeds at the head. It seems that when the grass is tightly packed, as in
a field of ripe grain, the blade won't topple at a single cut through the
stem; instead, the cut stem simply drops vertically, held in the crush of
grain. The mouse severs the bottom again and again, the stem keeps
dropping an inch at a time, and finally the head is low enough for the

mouse to reach the seeds. Meanwhile, the mouse is positively littering the field with its little piles of cut stems into which, presumably, the author of the book is constantly stumbling.

5   If I can't see these minutiae, I still try to keep my eyes open. I'm always on the lookout for antlion traps in sandy soil, monarch pupae near milkweed, skipper larvae in locust leaves. These things are utterly common, and I've not seen one. I bang on hollow trees near water, but so far no flying squirrels have appeared. In flat country I watch every sunset in hopes of seeing the green ray. The green ray is a seldom-seen streak of light that rises from the sun like a spurting fountain at the moment of sunset; it throbs into the sky for two seconds and disappears. One more reason to keep my eyes open. A photography professor at the University of Florida just happened to see a bird die in midflight; it jerked, died, dropped, and smashed on the ground. I squint at the wind because I read Stewart Edward White: "I have always maintained that if you look closely enough you could *see* the wind—the dim, hardly-made-out, fine débris fleeing high in the air." White was an excellent observer, and devoted an entire chapter of *The Mountains* to the subject of seeing deer: "As soon as you can forget the naturally obvious and construct an artificial obvious, then you too will see deer."

6   But the artificial obvious is hard to see. My eyes account for less than one percent of the weight of my head; I'm bony and dense; I see what I expect. I once spent a full three minutes looking at a bullfrog that was so unexpectedly large I couldn't see it even though a dozen enthusiastic campers were shouting directions. Finally I asked, "What color am I looking for?" and a fellow said, "Green." When at last I picked out the frog, I saw what painters are up against: the thing wasn't green at all, but the color of wet hickory bark.

7   The lover can see, and the knowledgeable. I visited an aunt and uncle at a quarter-horse ranch in Cody, Wyoming. I couldn't do much of anything useful, but I could, I thought, draw. So, as we all sat around the kitchen table after supper, I produced a sheet of paper and drew a horse. "That's one lame horse," my aunt volunteered. The rest of the family joined in: "Only place to saddle that one is his neck"; "Looks like we better shoot the poor thing, on account of those terrible growths." Meekly, I slid the pencil and paper down the table. Everyone in that family, including my three young cousins, could draw a horse. Beautifully. When the paper came back it looked as though five shining, real quarter horses had been corraled by mistake with a papier-mâché moose; the real horses seemed to gaze at the monster with a steady, puzzled air.

I stay away from horses now, but I can do a creditable goldfish. The point is that I just don't know what the lover knows; I just can't see the artificial obvious that those in the know construct. The herpetologist asks the native, "Are there snakes in that ravine?" "Nosir." And the herpetologist comes home with, yessir, three bags full. Are there butterflies on that mountain? Are the bluets in bloom, are there arrowheads here, or fossil shells in the shale?

8   Peeping through my keyhole I see within the range of only about thirty percent of the light that comes from the sun; the rest is infrared and some little ultraviolet, perfectly apparent to many animals, but invisible to me. A nightmare network of ganglia, charged and firing without my knowledge, cuts and splices what I do see, editing it for my brain. Donald E. Carr points out that the sense impressions of one-celled animals are *not* edited for the brain: "This is philosophically interesting in a rather mournful way, since it means that only the simplest animals perceive the universe as it is."

9   A fog that won't burn away drifts and flows across my field of vision. When you see fog move against a backdrop of deep pines, you don't see the fog itself, but streaks of clearness floating across the air in dark shreds. So I see only tatters of clearness through a pervading obscurity. I can't distinguish the fog from the overcast sky; I can't be sure if the light is direct or reflected. Everywhere darkness and the presence of the unseen appalls. We estimate now that only one atom dances alone in every cubic meter of intergalactic space. I blink and squint. What planet or power yanks Halley's Comet out of orbit? We haven't seen that force yet; it's a question of distance, density, and the pallor of reflected light. We rock, cradled in the swaddling band of darkness. Even the simple darkness of night whispers suggestions to the mind. Last summer, in August, I stayed at the creek too late. . . .

10   Seeing is of course very much a matter of verbalization. Unless I call my attention to what passes before my eyes, I simply won't see it. It is, as Ruskin says, "not merely unnoticed, but in the full, clear sense of the word, unseen." My eyes alone can't solve analogy tests using figures, the ones which show, with increasing elaborations, a big square, then a small square in a big square, then a big triangle, and expect me to find a small triangle in a big triangle. I have to say the words, describe what I'm seeing. If Tinker Mountain erupted, I'd be likely to notice. But if I want to notice the lesser cataclysms of valley life, I have to maintain in my head a running description of the present. It's not that I'm

observant; it's just that I talk too much. Otherwise, especially in a strange place, I'll never know what's happening. Like a blind man at the ball game, I need a radio.

11   When I see this way I analyze and pry. I hurl over logs and roll away stones; I study the bank a square foot at a time, probing and tilting my head. Some days when a mist covers the mountains, when the muskrats won't show and the microscope's mirror shatters, I want to climb up the blank blue dome as a man would storm the inside of a circus tent, wildly, dangling, and with a steel knife claw a rent in the top, peep, and, if I must, fall.

12   But there is another kind of seeing that involves a letting go. When I see this way I sway transfixed and emptied. The difference between the two ways of seeing is the difference between walking with and without a camera. When I walk with a camera I walk from shot to shot, reading the light on a calibrated meter. When I walk without a camera, my own shutter opens, and the moment's light prints on my own silver gut. When I see this second way I am above all an unscrupulous observer.

13   It was sunny one evening last summer at Tinker Creek; the sun was low in the sky, upstream. I was sitting on the sycamore log bridge with the sunset at my back, watching the shiners the size of minnows who were feeding over the muddy sand in skittery schools. Again and again, one fish, then another, turned for a split second across the current and flash! the sun shot out from its silver side. I couldn't watch for it. It was always just happening somewhere else, and it drew my vision just as it disappeared: flash, like a sudden dazzle of the thinnest blade, a sparking over a dun and olive ground at chance intervals from every direction. Then I noticed white specks, some sort of pale petals, small, floating from under my feet on the creek's surface, very slow and steady. So I blurred my eyes and gazed towards the brim of my hat and saw a new world. I saw the pale white circles roll up, roll up, like the world's turning, mute and perfect, and I saw the linear flashes, gleaming silver, like stars being born at random down a rolling scroll of time. Something broke and something opened. I filled up like a new wineskin. I breathed an air like light; I saw a light like water. I was the lip of a fountain the creek filled forever; I was ether, the leaf in the zephyr; I was fleshflake, feather, bone.

14   When I see this way I see truly. As Thoreau says, I return to my senses. I am the man who watches the baseball game in silence in an

empty stadium. I see the game purely; I'm abstracted and dazed. When it's all over and the white-suited players lope off the green field to their shadowed dugouts, I leap to my feet; I cheer and cheer.

15   But I can't go out and try to see this way. I'll fail, I'll go mad. All I can do is try to gag the commentator, to hush the noise of useless interior babble that keeps me from seeing just as surely as a newspaper dangled before my eyes. The effort is really a discipline requiring a lifetime of dedicated struggle; it marks the literature of saints and monks of every order East and West, under every rule and no rule, discalced and shod. The world's spiritual geniuses seem to discover universally that the mind's muddy river, this ceaseless flow of trivia and trash, cannot be dammed, and that trying to dam it is a waste of effort that might lead to madness. Instead you must allow the muddy river to flow unheeded in the dim channels of consciousness; you raise your sights; you look along it, mildly, acknowledging its presence without interest and gazing beyond it into the realm of the real where subjects and objects act and rest purely, without utterance. "Launch into the deep," says Jacques Ellul, "and you shall see."

16   The secret of seeing is, then, the pearl of great price. If I thought he could teach me to find it and keep it forever I would stagger barefoot across a hundred deserts after any lunatic at all. But although the pearl may be found, it may not be sought. The literature of illumination reveals this above all: although it comes to those who wait for it, it is always, even to the most practiced and adept, a gift and a total surprise. I return from one walk knowing where the killdeer nests in the field by the creek and the hour the laurel blooms. I return from the same walk a day later scarcely knowing my own name. Litanies hum in my ears; my tongue flaps in my mouth Ailinon, alleluia! I cannot cause light; the most I can do is try to put myself in the path of its beam. It is possible, in deep space, to sail on solar wind. Light, be it particle or wave, has force: you rig a giant sail and go. The secret of seeing is to sail on solar wind. Hone and spread your spirit till you yourself are a sail, whetted, translucent, broadside to the merest puff.

QUESTIONS

1. What is Dillard's main point about seeing? Can you learn to see in the manner she describes? And in what sense is it true that "what you see is what you get"?

2. What does Dillard mean when she suggests that nature both reveals and conceals? What are the "free gifts of nature" that "catch at the throat"? Are the mockingbird, frog, and sharks of "Jest and Earnest" such gifts? Explain.

3. How is it that, as Dillard says, many wonders of nature are "utterly common," yet go unobserved and unnoticed.

4. Explain her remark: "I see what I expect." What does she expect to see as she looks for the bullfrog. Why can't she see it? In what ways does expectation influence *what* we see? How does it also influence *how* we see?

5. In paragraph 7 Dillard says that the powers of seeing are limited to the lovers and to the knowledgeable—to specialists. Do you agree? How can knowledge of and love for something or someone help you to see that person or thing better? Can love or knowledge ever be an impediment to seeing things as they are? Explain.

6. Paragraph 10 contains a remark especially significant for writing: "Seeing is of course very much a matter of verbalization." Dillard continues: "Unless I call my attention to what passes before my eyes, I simply won't see it. . . . I have to say the words, describe what I'm seeing." Explain how saying the words either by speaking them or writing them helps you to see.

7. Dillard makes a number of distinctions: between things unnoticed and things unseen; between looking for and looking; between probing and looking without a camera. Explain what you think she means by one or more of these distinctions.

Suggestions for Writing

A. Look at something you see all the time—but don't really see. Make a list of a dozen specific details concerning it.

B. Walk along a route you habitually travel. Try to notice at least ten things you've never noticed before. Jot them down as you notice them.

C. Think of something you are knowledgeable about—something that you love. You might be an expert camper, skater, sailor, dancer, athlete, guitarist, coin collector, model builder. Write an essay explaining the fine points of the activity. Try to describe, for example, what a layman might need to know to look at a rare coin, to understand a magic trick or clever con, to really see an art masterpiece. Or you might explain what to look for in a good performance—of whatever kind. Here, you would have to isolate the characteristics of a good skiing or skating performance, for example, as well as to describe and explain them in such a way that a non-skier or non-skater would know how to look at them and what to look for to appreciate the performance.

Jest and Earnest

1   A couple of summers ago I was walking along the edge of
the island to see what I could see in the water, and mainly to scare frogs.
Frogs have an inelegant way of taking off from invisible positions on the
bank just ahead of your feet, in dire panic, emitting a froggy "Yike!" and
splashing into the water. Incredibly, this amused me, and, incredibly, it
amuses me still. As I walked along the grassy edge of the island, I got
better and better at seeing frogs both in and out of the water. I learned
to recognize, slowing down, the difference in texture of the light reflected from mudbank, water, grass, or frog. Frogs were flying all around
me. At the end of the island I noticed a small green frog. He was exactly
half in and half out of the water, looking like a schematic diagram of
an amphibian, and he didn't jump.

2   He didn't jump; I crept closer. At last I knelt on the island's
winterkilled grass, lost, dumbstruck, staring at the frog in the creek just
four feet away. He was a very small frog with wide, dull eyes. And just
as I looked at him, he slowly crumpled and began to sag. The spirit
vanished from his eyes as if snuffed. His skin emptied and drooped; his
very skull seemed to collapse and settle like a kicked tent. He was
shrinking before my eyes like a deflating football. I watched the taut,
glistening skin on his shoulders ruck, and rumple, and fall. Soon, part
of his skin, formless as a pricked balloon, lay in floating folds like bright
scum on top of the water: it was a monstrous and terrifying thing. I
gaped bewildered, appalled. An oval shadow hung in the water behind
the drained frog; then the shadow glided away. The frog skin bag started
to sink.

3   I had read about the giant water bug, but never seen one. "Giant
water bug" is really the name of the creature, which is an enormous,
heavy-bodied brown beetle. It eats insects, tadpoles, fish, and frogs. Its
grasping forelegs are mighty and hooked inward. It seizes a victim with
these legs, hugs it tight, and paralyzes it with enzymes injected during
a vicious bite. That one bite is the only bite it ever takes. Through the
puncture shoot the poisons that dissolve the victim's muscles and bones
and organs—all but the skin—and through it the giant water bug sucks
out the victim's body, reduced to a juice. This event is quite common
in warm fresh water. The frog I saw was being sucked by a giant water

bug. I had been kneeling on the island grass; when the unr̶
flap of frog skin settled on the creek bottom, swaying, I stood ̶
brushed the knees of my pants. I couldn't catch my breath.

4   Of course, many carnivorous animals devour their prey alive. The
usual method seems to be to subdue the victim by downing or grasping
it so it can't flee, then eating it whole or in a series of bloody bites. Frogs
eat everything whole, stuffing prey into their mouths with their thumbs.
People have seen frogs with their wide jaws so full of live dragonflies they
couldn't close them. Ants don't even have to catch their prey: in the
spring they swarm over newly hatched, featherless birds in the nest and
eat them tiny bite by bite.

5   That it's rough out there and chancy is no surprise. Every live
thing is a survivor on a kind of extended emergency bivouac. But at the
same time we are also created. In the Koran, Allah asks, "The heaven
and the earth and all in between, thinkest thou I made them *in jest?*"
It's a good question. What do we think of the created universe, spanning
an unthinkable void with an unthinkable profusion of forms? Or what
do we think of nothingness, those sickening reaches of time in either
direction? If the giant water bug was not made in jest, was it then made
in earnest? Pascal uses a nice term to describe the notion of the creator's,
once having called forth the universe, turning his back to it: *Deus
Absconditus.* Is this what we think happened? Was the sense of it there,
and God absconded with it, ate it, like a wolf who disappears round the
edge of the house with the Thanksgiving turkey? "God is subtle,"
Einstein said, "but not malicious." Again, Einstein said that "nature
conceals her mystery by means of her essential grandeur, not by her
cunning." It could be that God has not absconded but spread, as our
vision and understanding of the universe have spread, to a fabric of spirit
and sense so grand and subtle, so powerful in a new way, that we can
only feel blindly of its hem. In making the thick darkness a swaddling
band for the sea, God "set bars and doors" and said, "Hitherto shalt
thou come, but no further." But have we come even that far? Have we
rowed out to the thick darkness, or are we all playing pinochle in the
bottom of the boat?

6   Cruelty is a mystery, and the waste of pain. But if we describe a
world to compass these things, a world that is a long, brute game, then
we bump against another mystery: the inrush of power and light, the
canary that sings on the skull. Unless all ages and races of men have been
deluded by the same mass hypnotist (who?), there seems to be such a
thing as beauty, a grace wholly gratuitous. About five years ago I saw a

mockingbird make a straight vertical descent from the roof gutter of a four-story building. It was an act as careless and spontaneous as the curl of a stem or the kindling of a star.

7   The mockingbird took a single step into the air and dropped. His wings were still folded against his sides as though he were singing from a limb and not falling, accelerating thirty-two feet per second per second, through empty air. Just a breath before he would have been dashed to the ground, he unfurled his wings with exact, deliberate care, revealing the broad bars of white, spread his elegant, white-banded tail, and so floated onto the grass. I had just rounded a corner when his insouciant step caught my eye; there was no one else in sight. The fact of his free fall was like the old philosophical conundrum about the tree that falls in the forest. The answer must be, I think, that beauty and grace are performed whether or not we will or sense them. The least we can do is try to be there.

8   Another time I saw another wonder: sharks off the Atlantic coast of Florida. There is a way a wave rises about the ocean horizon, a triangular wedge against the sky. If you stand where the ocean breaks on a shallow beach, you see the raised water in a wave is translucent, shot with lights. One late afternoon at low tide a hundred big sharks passed the beach near the mouth of a tidal river in a feeding frenzy. As each green wave rose from the churning water, it illuminated within itself the six- or eight-foot-long bodies of twisting sharks. The sharks disappeared as each wave rolled toward me; then a new wave would swell above the horizon, containing in it, like scorpions in amber, sharks that roiled and heaved. The sight held awesome wonders: power and beauty, grace tangled in a rapture with violence.

9   We don't know what's going on here. If these tremendous events are random combinations of matter run amok, the yield of millions of monkeys at millions of typewriters, then what is it in us, hammered out of those same typewriters, that they ignite? We don't know. Our life is a faint tracing on the surface of mystery, like the idle, curved tunnels of leaf miners on the face of a leaf. We must somehow take a wider view, look at the whole landscape, really see it, and describe what's going on here. Then we can at least wail the right question into the swaddling band of darkness, or, if it comes to that, choir the proper praise.

10   At the time of Lewis and Clark, setting the prairies on fire was a well-known signal that meant, "Come down to the water." It was an extravagant gesture, but we can't do less. If the landscape reveals one certainty, it is that the extravagant gesture is the very stuff of creation.

After the one extravagant gesture of creation in the first place, the universe has continued to deal exclusively in extravagances, flinging intricacies and colossi down aeons of emptiness, heaping profusions on profligacies with ever-fresh vigor. The whole show has been on fire from the word go. I come down to the water to cool my eyes. But everywhere I look I see fire; that which isn't flint is tinder, and the whole world sparks and flames.

QUESTIONS

Ideas

1. Good writing often begins with seeing, with close observation. What does Dillard look at closely and then describe for us to see?

2. Dillard's seeing does not end with literal observation. It extends outward into thought. What ideas does Dillard develop out of her seeing?

3. The first two paragraphs present a description—a shocking one. Following this comes a pair of informative paragraphs and a paragraph that offers speculation about the information and description presented up to that point. Label paragraphs 6–10 as primarily descriptive, informative, or speculative.

4. What is the connection between paragraphs 5 and 6? Look especially at the first two sentences of paragraph 6, where a link is made. If the first sentence of paragraph 6 sums up what Dillard has been saying in the preceding paragraph, what does the second sentence do? And how do the sentences following that develop the point of paragraph 6?

5. Why does Dillard separate paragraph 7 from the one before it? Why does she bother including this paragraph at all? Does she need this mockingbird section? How does it fit in with what Dillard has shown up to that point?

6. The essay can be thought of or approached in terms of the three creatures described: frog, mockingbird, shark. Why is each included, and how are the three related in the context of Dillard's idea?

7. Is the final paragraph of the essay necessary? What does it contribute to the idea of the piece? To the effect?

Sentences

8. Most of the essay consists of declarative sentences, of statements. In paragraphs 5 and 6, however, Dillard uses many questions. What is the effect of these questions and what is the tone of the paragraphs?

9. Dillard uses participles to extend sentences in paragraphs 2 and 7. Here is one example: "At last I knelt on the island's winterkilled grass, lost, dumbstruck, staring at the frog in the creek just four feet away." If you ended the sentence after "dumbstruck," beginning a new sentence after, you might get this: At last I knelt on the island's winterkilled grass, lost, dumbstruck. I stared at the frog in the creek just four feet away. What advantage—in this instance—does the participial sentence have over the two shorter sentences?

10. In paragraph 3 Dillard writes an inverted sentence: "Through the puncture shoot the poisons that dissolve the victim's bones and muscles and organs. . . ." Here is an alternate version: The poisons that dissolve the victim's bones and muscles and organs shoot through the puncture. Which version do you prefer and why?

11. Return once more to the frog description, this time for a look at Dillard's punctuation. After examining the sentences with semicolons, try to formulate a general rule for their use. What is the relationship, in each sentence, of the part before the semicolon to the part after it? Here are the important sentences: "He didn't jump; I crept closer." "His skin emptied and drooped; his very skull seemed to collapse and settle like a kicked tent." "An oval shadow hung in the water behind the drained frog; then the shadow glided away."

12. Dillard uses the colon in paragraphs 4, 6, and 8. For all three sentences, decide whether a period or comma could replace the colon. For each sentence, explain the relationship between the two parts—the part to the left of the colon and the part to the right.

Words

13. Examine the verbs in the first three sentences of paragraph 7. Compare the number and kind of verbs with the number and type of verbs in paragraph 2. What do you notice?

14. In the frog description Dillard uses a number of comparisons. What do they have in common? What is their purpose and what is their cumulative effect?

15. Imagery of light and darkness appears throughout the essay. Explain how the fire of paragraph 10 is related to the darkness of paragraphs 5, 6, and 9. What does Dillard mean when she writes: "But everywhere I look I see fire, that which isn't flint is tinder, and the whole world sparks and flames"?

16. In paragraph 5 Dillard alludes to and quotes from Einstein, Pascal, and the Koran. What is the purpose of each of these quotations and allusions? Could Dillard have made her point as well without quotation and allusion?

Suggestions for Writing

A. Write imitations of the sentences discussed in questions 9–12.

B. Write variations of some of the sentences discussed in questions 9–12. For example, you might change the punctuation or the word order of the sentences.

C. Look closely at something. Be attentive to details of shape, color, form, texture, background, line. If you like, observe a place with a considerable amount of action such as a restaurant, supermarket, or intersection. List the things you see. From your list select three or four items that stand out. Write freely, jotting down thoughts as they occur about each of the items on your list.

D. For each of the following poems explain what the speaker is looking at. Notice that in both poems a passage of explanation, generalization, or speculation accompanies the passage of description. What point does each poem make? How necessary is the descriptive, "seeing" part of each to its idea? In each poem, how is what is seen related to or connected with what is thought?

DESIGN

I found a dimpled spider, fat and white,
On a white heal-all, holding up a moth
Like a white piece of rigid satin cloth—
Assorted characters of death and blight
Mixed ready to begin the morning right,
Like the ingredients of a witches' broth—
A snow-drop spider, a flower like a froth,
And dead wings carried like a paper kite.

What had that flower to do with being white,
The wayside blue and innocent heal-all?
What brought the kindred spider to that height,
Then steered the white moth thither in the night?
What but design of darkness to appall?—
If design govern in a thing so small.

ROBERT FROST

MUSÉE DES BEAUX ARTS

About suffering they were never wrong,
The Old Masters: how well they understood
Its human position; how it takes place
While someone else is eating or opening a window or just walking dully
along;

How, when the aged are reverently, passionately waiting
For the miraculous birth, there always must be
Children who did not specially want it to happen, skating
On a pond at the edge of the wood:
They never forgot
That even the dreadful martyrdom must run its course
Anyhow in a corner, some untidy spot
Where the dogs go on with their doggy life and the torturer's horse
Scratches its innocent behind on a tree.

In Brueghel's *Icarus*, for instance: how everything turns away
Quite leisurely from the disaster; the ploughman may
Have heard the splash, the forsaken cry,
But for him it was not an important failure; the sun shone
As it had to on the white legs disappearing into the green
Water: and the expensive delicate ship that must have seen
Something amazing, a boy falling out of the sky,
Had somewhere to get to and sailed calmly on.

                                                    W. H. AUDEN

Living Like Weasels

I

1   **A** weasel is wild. Who knows what he thinks? He sleeps
in his underground den, his tail draped over his nose. Sometimes he lives
in his den for two days without leaving. Outside, he stalks rabbits, mice,
muskrats, and birds, killing more bodies than he can eat warm, and often
dragging the carcasses home. Obedient to instinct, he bites his prey at
the neck, either splitting the jugular vein at the throat or crunching the
brain at the base of the skull, and he does not let go. One naturalist
refused to kill a weasel who was socketed into his hand deeply as a
rattlesnake. The man could in no way pry the tiny weasel off, and he
had to walk half a mile to water, the weasel dangling from his palm, and
soak him off like a stubborn label.

2   And once, says Ernest Thompson Seton—once, a man shot an
eagle out of the sky. He examined the eagle and found the dry skull of
a weasel fixed by the jaws to his throat. The supposition is that the eagle

had pounced on the weasel and the weasel swiveled and bit as instinct taught him, tooth to neck, and nearly won. I would like to have seen that eagle from the air a few weeks or months before he was shot: was the whole weasel still attached to his feathered throat, a fur pendant? Or did the eagle eat what he could reach, gutting the living weasel with his talons before his breast, bending his beak, cleaning the beautiful airborne bones?

II

3   I have been reading about weasels because I saw one last week. I startled a weasel who startled me, and we exchanged a long glance.

4   Twenty minutes from my house, through the woods by the quarry and across the highway, is Hollins Pond, a remarkable piece of shallowness, where I like to go at sunset and sit on a tree trunk. Hollins Pond is also called Murray's Pond; it covers two acres of bottomland near Tinker Creek with six inches of water and six thousand lily pads. In winter, brown-and-white steers stand in the middle of it, merely dampening their hooves; from the distant shore they look like miracle itself, complete with miracle's nonchalance. Now, in summer, the steers are gone. The water lilies have blossomed and spread to a green horizontal plane that is terra firma to plodding blackbirds, and tremulous ceiling to black leeches, crayfish, and carp.

5   This is, mind you, suburbia. It is a five-minute walk in three directions to rows of houses, though none is visible here. There's a 55 mph highway at one end of the pond, and a nesting pair of wood ducks at the other. Under every bush is a muskrat hole or a beer can. The far end is an alternating series of fields and woods, fields and woods, threaded everywhere with motorcycle tracks—in whose bare clay wild turtles lay eggs.

6   So. I had crossed the highway, stepped over two low barbed-wire fences, and traced the motorcycle path in all gratitude through the wild rose and poison ivy of the pond's shoreline up into high grassy fields. Then I cut down through the woods to the mossy fallen tree where I sit. This tree is excellent. It makes a dry, upholstered bench at the upper, marshy end of the pond, a plush jetty raised from the thorny shore between a shallow blue body of water and a deep blue body of sky.

7   The sun had just set. I was relaxed on the tree trunk, ensconced in the lap of lichen, watching the lily pads at my feet tremble and part

dreamily over the thrusting path of a carp. A yellow bird appeared to
my right and flew behind me. It caught my eye; I swiveled around—and
the next instant, inexplicably, I was looking down at a weasel, who was
looking up at me.

III

8   Weasel! I'd never seen one wild before. He was ten inches long,
thin as a curve, a muscled ribbon, brown as fruitwood, soft-furred, alert.
His face was fierce, small and pointed as a lizard's; he would have made
a good arrowhead. There was just a dot of chin, maybe two brown hairs'
worth, and then the pure white fur began that spread down his underside. He had two black eyes I didn't see, any more than you see a
window.

9   The weasel was stunned into stillness as he was emerging from
beneath an enormous shaggy wild rose bush four feet away. I was
stunned into stillness twisted backward on the tree trunk. Our eyes
locked, and someone threw away the key.

10   Our look was as if two lovers, or deadly enemies, met unexpectedly
on an overgrown path when each had been thinking of something else:
a clearing blow to the gut. It was also a bright blow to the brain, or a
sudden beating of brains, with all the charge and intimate grate of
rubbed balloons. It emptied our lungs. It felled the forest, moved the
fields, and drained the pond; the world dismantled and tumbled into
that black hole of eyes. If you and I looked at each other that way, our
skulls would split and drop to our shoulders. But we don't. We keep our
skulls. So.

11   He disappeared. This was only last week, and already I don't
remember what shattered the enchantment. I think I blinked, I think
I retrieved my brain from the weasel's brain, and tried to memorize what
I was seeing, and the weasel felt the yank of separation, the careening
splashdown into real life and the urgent current of instinct. He vanished
under the wild rose. I waited motionless, my mind suddenly full of data
and my spirit with pleadings, but he didn't return.

12   Please do not tell me about "approach-avoidance conflicts." I tell
you I've been in that weasel's brain for sixty seconds, and he was in mine.
Brains are private places, muttering through unique and secret tapes—
but the weasel and I both plugged into another tape simultaneously, for
a sweet and shocking time. Can I help it if it was a blank?

13   What goes on in his brain the rest of the time? What does a weasel think about? He won't say. His journal is tracks in clay, a spray of feathers, mouse blood and bone: uncollected, unconnected, loose-leaf, and blown.

IV

14   I would like to learn, or remember, how to live. I come to Hollins Pond not so much to learn how to live as, frankly, to forget about it. That is, I don't think I can learn from a wild animal how to live in particular —shall I suck warm blood, hold my tail high, walk with my footprints precisely over the prints of my hands?—but I might learn something of mindlessness, something of the purity of living in the physical senses and the dignity of living without bias or motive. The weasel lives in necessity and we live in choice, hating necessity and dying at the last ignobly in its talons. I would like to live as I should, as the weasel lives as he should. And I suspect that for me the way is like the weasel's: open to time and death painlessly, noticing everything, remembering nothing, choosing the given with a fierce and pointed will.

V

15   I missed my chance. I should have gone for the throat. I should have lunged for that streak of white under the weasel's chin and held on, held on through mud and into the wild rose, held on for a dearer life. We could live under the wild rose wild as weasels, mute and uncomprehending. I could very calmly go wild. I could live two days in the den, curled, leaning on mouse fur, sniffing bird bones, blinking, licking, breathing musk, my hair tangled in the roots of grasses. Down is a good place to go, where the mind is single. Down is out, out of your ever-loving mind and back to your careless senses. I remember muteness as a prolonged and giddy fast, where every moment is a feast of utterance received. Time and events are merely poured, unremarked, and ingested directly, like blood pulsed into my gut through a jugular vein. Could two live that way? Could two live under the wild rose, and explore by the pond, so that the smooth mind of each is as everywhere present to the other, and as received and as unchallenged, as falling snow?

16   We could, you know. We can live any way we want. People take

vows of poverty, chastity, and obedience—even of silence—by choice. The thing is to stalk your calling in a certain skilled and supple way, to locate the most tender and live spot and plug into that pulse. This is yielding, not fighting. A weasel doesn't "attack" anything; a weasel lives as he's meant to, yielding at every moment to the perfect freedom of single necessity.

VI

17 I think it would be well, and proper, and obedient, and pure, to grasp your one necessity and not let it go, to dangle from it limp wherever it takes you. Then even death, where you're going no matter how you live, cannot you part. Seize it and let it seize you up aloft even, till your eyes burn out and drop; let your musky flesh fall off in shreds, and let your very bones unhinge and scatter, loosened over fields, over fields and woods, lightly, thoughtless, from any height at all, from as high as eagles.

QUESTIONS

Ideas

1. What does Dillard mean by suggesting we can live like the weasel? What does the weasel come to represent?

2. What is Dillard's primary purpose in this essay? To provide us with facts about weasels? To entertain us with surprising anecdotes? To convince us of something?

3. What does Dillard suggest about how men can relate to animals? How far can their communication go? Why?

Organization

4. One way of considering the structure of this essay is to divide it into four segments: paragraphs 1–2; 3–7; 8–13; and 14–17. What are the focus and concern of each section, and how are the sections related? Why do you think the author arranged the essay in six sections?

5. Consider alternative introductions—paragraphs 3–7 or paragraphs 8–13. If the essay were to begin with either of these sections, what other changes in organization would be necessitated?

Sentences

6. Many of Dillard's sentences are short, particularly those at the beginning of paragraphs. What effects do her short sentences have?

7. Dillard employs frequent questions. Why? What is her purpose in interrogating us?

Words

8. List the words in the essay that suggest violence. How many of these are verbs? What is their cumulative effect?

9. Identify and comment on the purpose and effectiveness of the comparisons Dillard employs in paragraphs 1, 8, 10, 12, and 15.

Suggestions for Writing

A. Write an essay analyzing "Living Like Weasels." Discuss the ideas and the style of the essay.

B. Discuss an experience involving nature that led you to reflect on your relationship to the natural world.

C. Write imitations of any two sentences you think especially attractive.

Transfiguration

---

1   I live on northern Puget Sound, in Washington State, alone. I have a gold cat, who sleeps on my legs, named Small. In the morning I joke to her blank face, Do you remember last night? Do you remember? I throw her out before breakfast, so I can eat.

2   There is a spider, too, in the bathroom, with whom I keep a sort of company. Her little outfit always reminds me of a certain moth I helped to kill. The spider herself is of uncertain lineage, bulbous at the abdomen and drab. Her six-inch mess of a web works, works somehow, works miraculously, to keep her alive and me amazed. The web itself is in a corner behind the toilet, connecting tile wall to tile wall and floor, in a place where there is, I would have thought, scant traffic. Yet under the web are sixteen or so corpses she has tossed to the floor.

3   The corpses appear to be mostly sow bugs, those little armadillo

creatures who live to travel flat out in houses, and die round. There is also a new shred of earwig, three old spider skins crinkled and clenched, and two moth bodies, wingless and huge and empty, moth bodies I drop to my knees to see.

4   Today the earwig shines darkly and gleams, what there is of him: a dorsal curve of thorax and abdomen, and a smooth pair of cerci by which I knew his name. Next week, if the other bodies are any indication, he will be shrunken and gray, webbed to the floor with dust. The sow bugs beside him are hollow and empty of color, fragile, a breath away from brittle fluff. The spider skins lie on their sides, translucent and ragged, their legs drying in knots. And the moths, the empty moths, stagger against each other, headless, in a confusion of arching strips of chitin like peeling varnish, like a jumble of buttresses for cathedral domes, like nothing resembling moths, so that I should hesitate to call them moths, except that I have had some experience with the figure Moth reduced to a nub.

5   Two summers ago I was camping alone in the Blue Ridge Mountains in Virginia. I had hauled myself and gear up there to read, among other things, James Ramsey Ullman's *The Day on Fire*, a novel about Rimbaud that had made me want to be a writer when I was sixteen; I was hoping it would do it again. So I read, lost, every day sitting under a tree by my tent, while warblers swung in the leaves overhead and bristle worms trailed their inches over the twiggy dirt at my feet; and I read every night by candlelight, while barred owls called in the forest and pale moths massed round my head in the clearing, where my light made a ring.

6   Moths kept flying into the candle. They would hiss and recoil, lost upside down in the shadows among my cooking pans. Or they would singe their wings and fall, and their hot wings, as if melted, would stick to the first thing they touched—a pan, a lid, a spoon—so that the snagged moths could flutter only in tiny arcs, unable to struggle free. These I could release by a quick flip with a stick; in the morning I would find my cooking stuff gilded with torn flecks of moth wings, triangles of shiny dust here and there on the aluminum. So I read, and boiled water, and replenished candles, and read on.

7   One night a moth flew into the candle, was caught, burnt dry, and held. I must have been staring at the candle, or maybe I looked up when a shadow crossed my page; at any rate, I saw it all. A golden female moth, a biggish one with a two-inch wing-span, flapped into the fire, dropped

her abdomen into the wet wax, stuck, flamed, frazzled and fried in a second. Her moving wings ignited like tissue paper, enlarging the circle of light in the clearing and creating out of the darkness the sudden blue sleeves of my sweater, the green leaves of jewelweed by my side, the ragged red trunk of a pine. At once the light contracted again and the moth's wings vanished in a fine, foul smoke. At the same time her six legs clawed, curled, blackened, and ceased, disappearing utterly. And her head jerked in spasms, making a spattering noise; her antennae crisped and burned away and her heaving mouth parts crackled like pistol fire. When it was all over, her head was, so far as I could determine, gone, gone the long way of her wings and legs. Had she been new, or old? Had she mated and laid her eggs, had she done her work? All that was left was the glowing horn shell of her abdomen and thorax—a fraying, partially collapsed gold tube jammed upright in the candle's round pool.

8   And then this moth-essence, this spectacular skeleton, began to act as a wick. She kept burning. The wax rose in the moth's body from her soaking abdomen to her thorax to the jagged hole where her head should be, and widened into flame, a saffron-yellow flame that robed her to the ground like any immolating monk. That candle had two wicks, two flames of identical height, side by side. The moth's head was fire. She burned for two hours, until I blew her out.

9   She burned for two hours without changing, without bending or leaning—only glowing within, like a building fire glimpsed through silhouetted walls, like a hollow saint, like a flame-faced virgin gone to God, while I read by her light, kindled, while Rimbaud in Paris burnt out his brains in a thousand poems, while night pooled wetly at my feet.

10   And that is why I believe those hollow crisps on the bathroom floor are moths. I think I know moths, and fragments of moths, and chips and tatters of utterly empty moths, in any state. How many of you, I asked the people in my class, which of you want to give your lives and be writers? I was trembling from coffee, or cigarettes, or the closeness of faces all around me. (Is this what we live for? I thought; is this the only final beauty: the color of any skin in any light, and living, human eyes?) All hands rose to the question. (You, Nick? Will you? Margaret? Randy? Why do I want them to mean it?) And then I tried to tell them what the choice must mean: you can't be anything else. You must go at your life with a broadax. . . . They had no idea what I was saying. (I have two hands, don't I? And all this energy, for as long as I can remember. I'll do it in the evenings, after skiing, or on the way home

from the bank, or after the children are asleep. . . .) They thought I was raving again. It's just as well.

11   I have three candles here on the table which I disentangle from the plants and light when visitors come. Small usually avoids them, although once she came too close and her tail caught fire; I rubbed it out before she noticed. The flames move light over everyone's skin, draw light to the surface of the faces of my friends. When the people leave I never blow the candles out, and after I'm asleep they flame and burn.

QUESTIONS

Ideas

1. What is the main point of this essay and where is it made most directly? Is Dillard saying something about moths? About monks? About writers? About something else? Explain.

2. Explain the central analogy that governs the essay. What connection does Dillard establish between a writer and her moth? And how is Rimbaud's life related to what she says?

Organization

3. How do paragraphs 1–4 serve to introduce the essay? What would be gained or lost if Dillard had omitted them and begun the essay with paragraph 5?

4. Dillard's essay appears above in three sections: paragraphs 1–4; 5–7; 8–11. Explain the logic of this division. Then propose another and compare its merits with the division as it now exists.

5. Consider the way Dillard organizes time in this essay. Where does she describe past and where present events?

Sentences

6. Consider the way Dillard stacks and balances details in the following sentence. It has been arranged on the page to highlight its parallelism.

> Her moving wings ignited like tissue paper,
>   enlarging the circle of light in the clearing
>   and creating out of the darkness
>   the sudden blue sleeves of my sweater,
>   the green leaves of jewelweed by my side,
>   the ragged red trunk of a pine.

7. Notice the way Dillard varies the length and type of her sentences throughout the essay. Analyze a couple of paragraphs from this standpoint, considering the effects of rhythm and sound with the varied forms and lengths of sentences.

Words

8. Consider the profusion of verbs in the third and sixth sentences of paragraph 7: *flapped, dropped, stuck, flamed, frazzled,* and *fried; clawed, curled, blackened,* and *ceased.* Which contain the most vivid pictures? Which, if any, are unfamiliar?

9. Discuss the way Dillard employs images of light and fire. Comment, especially, on the point and effect of the light image in the last sentence.

10. In paragraph 7, Dillard describes the death of the moth. What makes her description engaging and effective?

11. Identify and comment on the comparisons in paragraphs 8 and 9.

12. Look up the meanings of the following words: *transfiguration, gilded* (6), *replenished* (6), *essence* (8), *immolating* (8).

Suggestions for Writing

A. Write imitations of the sentences in questions 6 and 7. Write an imitation of paragraph 7 or 8—or both.

B. Compare and contrast Dillard's essay with White's "Death of a Pig." Consider each writer's purpose, point, tone, and style.

God's Tooth

1 Into this world falls a plane.

2 The earth is a mineral speckle planted in trees. The plane snagged its wing on a tree, fluttered in a tiny arc, and struggled down.

3 I heard it go. The cat looked up. There was no reason: the plane's engine simply stilled after takeoff, and the light plane failed to clear the firs. It fell easily; one wing snagged on a fir top; the metal fell down the air and smashed in the thin woods where cattle browse; the fuel exploded; and Julie Norwich seven years old burnt off her face.

4 Little Julie mute in some room at St. Joe's now, drugs dissolving

into the sheets. Little Julie with her eyes naked and spherical, baffled. Can you scream without lips? Yes. But do children in long pain scream? 5   It is November 19 and no wind, and no hope of heaven, and no wish for heaven, since the meanest of people show more mercy than hounding and terrorist gods.

6   The airstrip, a cleared washboard affair on the flat crest of a low hill, is a few long fields distant from my house—up the road and through the woods, or across the sheep pasture and through the woods. A flight instructor told me once that when his students get cocky, when they think they know how to fly a plane, he takes them out here and makes them land on that field. You go over the wires and down, and along the strip and up before the trees, or vice versa, vice versa, depending on the wind. But the airstrip is not unsafe. Jesse's engine failed. The FAA will cart the wreckage away, bit by bit, picking it out of the tree trunk, and try to discover just why that engine failed. In the meantime, the emergency siren has sounded, causing everyone who didn't see the plane go down to halt—Patty at her weaving, Jonathan slicing apples, Jan washing her baby's face—to halt, in pity and terror, wondering which among us got hit, by what bad accident, and why. The volunteer firemen have mustered; the fire trucks have come—stampeding Shuller's sheep—and gone, bearing burnt Julie and Jesse her father to the emergency room in town, leaving the rest of us to gossip, fight grass fires on the airstrip, and pray, or wander from window to window, fierce. 7   So she is burnt on her face and neck, Julie Norwich. The one whose teeth are short in a row, Jesse and Ann's oldest, red-kneed, green-socked, carrying cats.

8   I saw her only once. It was two weeks ago, under an English hawthorn tree, at the farm. 9   There are many farms in this neck of the woods, but only one we call "the farm"—the old Corcoran place, where Gus grows hay and raises calves: the farm, whose abandoned frame chicken coops ply the fields like longboats, like floating war canoes; whose clay driveway and grass footpaths are a tangle of orange calendula blossoms, ropes, equipment, and seeding grasses; the farm, whose canny heifers and bull calves figure the fences, run amok to the garden, and plant themselves suddenly black and white, up to their necks in green peas. 10   Between the gray farmhouse and the barn is the green grass farmyard, suitable for all projects. That day, sixteen of us were making

cider. It was cold. There were piles of apples everywhere. We had filled our trucks that morning, climbing trees and shaking their boughs, dragging tarps heavy with apples, hauling bushels and boxes and buckets of apples, and loading them all back to the farm. Jesse and Ann, who are in their thirties, with Julie and the baby, whose name I forget, had driven down from the mountains that morning with a truckload of apples, loose, to make cider with us, fill their jugs, and drive back. I had not met them before. We all drank coffee on the farmhouse porch to warm us; we hosed jugs in the yard. Now we were throwing apples into a shredder and wringing the mash through pillowcases, staining our palms and freezing our fingers, and decanting the pails into seventy one-gallon jugs. And all this long day, Julie Norwich chased my cat Small around the farmyard and played with her, manhandled her, next to the porch under the hawthorn tree.

11   She was a thin child, pointy-chinned, yellow bangs and braids. She squinted, and when you looked at her she sometimes started laughing, as if you had surprised her at using some power she wasn't yet ready to show. I kept my eye on her, wondering if she was cold with her sweater unbuttoned and bony knees bare.

12   She would hum up a little noise for half-hour stretches. In the intervals, for maybe five minutes each, she was trying, very quietly, to learn to whistle. I think. Or she was practicing a certain concentrated face. But I think she was trying to learn to whistle, because sometimes she would squeak a little falsetto note through an imitation whistle hole in her lips, as if that could fool anyone. And all day she was dressing and undressing the yellow cat, sticking it into a black dress, a black dress long and full as a nun's.

13   I was amazed at that dress. It must have been some sort of doll clothing she had dragged with her in the truck; I've never seen its kind before or since. A white collar bibbed the yoke of it like a guimpe. It had great black sleeves like wings. Julie scooped up the cat and rammed her into the cloth. I knew how she felt, exasperated, breaking her heart on a finger curl's width of skinny cat arm. I knew the many feelings she had sticking those furry arms through the sleeves. Small is not large: her limbs feel like bird bones strung in a sock. When Julie had the cat dressed in its curious habit, she would rock it like a baby doll. The cat blinked, upside down.

14   Once she whistled at it, or tried, blowing in its face; the cat poured from her arms and ran. It leapt across the driveway, lightfoot in its sleeves; its black dress pulled this way and that, dragging dust, bent up

in back by its yellow tail. I was squeezing one end of a twisted pillowcase full of apple mash and looking over my shoulder. I watched the cat hurdle the driveway and vanish under the potting shed, cringing; I watched Julie dash after it without hesitation, seize it, hit its face, and drag it back to the tree, carrying it caught fast by either forepaw, so its body hung straight from its arms.

15   She saw me watching her and we exchanged a look, a very conscious and self-conscious look—because we look a bit alike and we both knew it; because she was still short and I grown; because I was stuck kneeling before the cider pail, looking at her sidewise over my shoulder; because she was carrying the cat so oddly, so that she had to walk with her long legs parted; because it was my cat, and she'd dressed it, and it looked like a nun; and because she knew I'd been watching her, and how fondly, all along. We were laughing.

16   We *looked* a bit alike. Her face is slaughtered now, and I don't remember mine. It is the best joke there is, that we are here, and fools —that we are sown into time like so much corn, that we are souls sprinkled at random like salt into time and dissolved here, spread into matter, connected by cells right down to our feet, and those feet likely to fell us over a tree root or jam us on a stone. The joke part is that we forget it. Give the mind two seconds alone and it thinks it's Pythagoras. We wake up a hundred times a day and laugh.

17   The joke of the world is less like a banana peel than a rake, the old rake in the grass, the one you step on, foot to forehead. It all comes together. In a twinkling. You have to admire the gag for its symmetry, accomplishing all with one right angle, the same right angle which accomplishes all philosophy. One step on the rake and it's mind under matter once again. You wake up with a piece of tree in your skull. You wake up with fruit on your hands. You wake up in a clearing and see yourself, ashamed. You see your own face and it's seven years old and there's no knowing why, or where you've been since. We're tossed broadcast into time like so much grass, some ravening god's sweet hay. You wake up and a plane falls out of the sky.

18   That day was a god, too, the day we made cider and Julie played under the hawthorn tree. He must have been a heyday sort of god, a husbandman. He was spread under gardens, sleeping in time, an innocent old man scratching his head, thinking of pruning the orchard, in love with families.

19   Has he no power? Can the other gods carry time and its loves

upside down like a doll in their blundering arms? As though we the people were playing house—when we are serious and do love—and not the gods? No, that day's god has no power. No gods have power to save. There are only days. The one great god abandoned us to days, to time's tumult of occasions, abandoned us to the gods of days each brute and amok in his hugeness and idiocy.

20   Jesse her father had grabbed her clear of the plane this morning, and was hauling her off when the fuel blew. A glob of flung ignited vapor hit her face, or something flaming from the plane or fir tree hit her face. No one else was burned, or hurt in any way.

21   So this is where we are. Ashes, ashes, all fall down. How could I have forgotten? Didn't I see the heavens wiped shut just yesterday, on the road walking? Didn't I fall from the dark of the stars to these senselit and noisome days? The great ridged granite millstone of time is illusion, for only the good is real; the great ridged granite millstone of space is illusion, for God is spirit and worlds his flimsiest dreams: but the illusions are almost perfect, are apparently perfect for generations on end, and the pain is also, and undeniably, real. The pain within the millstones' pitiless turning is real, for our love for each other—for world and all the products of extension—is real, vaulting, insofar as it is love, beyond the plane of the stones' sickening churn and arcing to the realm of spirit bare. And you can get caught holding one end of a love, when your father drops, and your mother; when a land is lost, or a time, and your friend blotted out, gone, your brother's body spoiled, and cold, your infant dead, and you dying: you reel out love's long line alone, stripped like a live wire loosing its sparks to a cloud, like a live wire loosed in space to longing and grief everlasting.

22   I sit at the window. It is a fool's lot, this sitting always at windows spoiling little blowy slips of paper and myself in the process. Shall I be old? Here comes Small, old sparrow-mouth, wanting my lap. Done. Do you have any earthly idea how young I am? Where's your dress, kitty? I suppose I'll outlive this wretched cat. Get another. Leave it my silver spoons, like old ladies you hear about. I prefer dogs.

23   So I read. Angels, I read, belong to nine different orders. Seraphs are the highest; they are aflame with love for God, and stand closer to him than the others. Seraphs love God; cherubs, who are second, possess perfect knowledge of him. So love is greater than knowledge; how could I have forgotten? The seraphs are born of a stream of fire issuing from under God's throne. They are, according to Dionysius the Areopagite,

"all wings," having, as Isaiah noted, six wings apiece, two of which they fold over their eyes. Moving perpetually toward God, they perpetually praise him, crying Holy, Holy, Holy. . . . But, according to some rabbinic writings, they can sing only the first "Holy" before the intensity of their love ignites them again and dissolves them again, perpetually, into flames. "Abandon everything," Dionysius told his disciple. "God despises ideas."

24   God despises everything, apparently. If he abandoned us, slashing creation loose at its base from any roots in the real; and if we in turn abandon everything—all these illusions of time and space and lives—in order to love only the real: then where are we? Thought itself is impossible, for subject can have no guaranteed connection with object, nor any object with God. Knowledge is impossible. We are precisely nowhere, sinking on an entirely imaginary ice floe, into entirely imaginary seas themselves adrift. Then we reel out love's long line alone toward a God less lovable than a grasshead, who treats us less well than we treat our lawns.

25   Of faith I have nothing, only of truth: that this one God is a brute and traitor, abandoning us to time, to necessity and the engines of matter unhinged. This is no leap; this is evidence of things seen: one Julie, one sorrow, one sensation bewildering the heart, and enraging the mind, and causing me to look at the world stuff appalled, at the blithering rock of trees in a random wind, at my hand like some gibberish sprouted, my fist opening and closing, so that I think, Have I once turned my hand in this circus, have I ever called it home?

26   Faith would be that God is self-limited utterly by his creation—a contraction of the scope of his will; that he bound himself to time and its hazards and haps as a man would lash himself to a tree for love. That God's works are as good as we make them. That God is helpless, our baby to bear, self-abandoned on the doorstep of time, wondered at by cattle and oxen. Faith would be that God moved and moves once and for all and "down," so to speak, like a diver, like a man who eternally gathers himself for a dive and eternally is diving, and eternally splitting the spread of the water, and eternally drowned.

27   Faith would be, in short, that God has any willful connection with time whatsoever, and with us. For I know it as given that God is all good. And I take it also as given that whatever he touches has meaning, if only in his mysterious terms, the which I readily grant. The question is, then, whether God touches anything. Is anything firm, or is time on the loose? Did Christ descend once and for all to no purpose, in a kind of divine

and kenotic suicide, or ascend once and for all, pulling his cross up after him like a rope ladder home? Is there—even if Christ holds the tip of things fast and stretches eternity clear to the dim souls of men—is there no link at the base of things, some kernel or air deep in the matrix of matter from which universe furls like a ribbon twined into time?

28   Has God a hand in this? Then it is a good hand. But has he a hand at all? Or is he a holy fire burning self-contained for power's sake alone? Then he knows himself blissfully as flame unconsuming, as all brilliance and beauty and power, and the rest of us can go hang. Then the accidental universe spins mute, obedient only to its own gross terms, meaningless, out of mind, and alone. The universe is neither contingent upon nor participant in the holy, in being itself, the real, the power play of fire. The universe is illusion merely, not one speck of it real, and we are not only its victims, falling always into or smashed by a planet slung by its sun—but also its captives, bound by the mineral-made ropes of our senses.

29   But how do we know—how could we know—that the real is there? By what freak chance does the skin of illusion ever split, and reveal to us the real, which seems to know us by name, and by what freak chance and why did the capacity to prehend it evolve?

30   I sit at the window, chewing the bones in my wrist. Pray for them: for Julie, for Jesse her father, for Ann her mother, pray. Who will teach us to pray? The god of today is a glacier. We live in his shifting crevasses, unheard. The god of today is delinquent, a barn-burner, a punk with a pittance of power in a match. It is late, a late time to be living. Now it is afternoon; the sky is appallingly clear. Everything in the landscape points to sea, and the sea is nothing; it is snipped from the real as a stuff without form, rising up the sides of islands and falling, mineral to mineral, salt.

31   Everything I see—the water, the log-wrecked beach, the farm on the hill, the bluff, the white church in the trees—looks overly distinct and shining. (What is the relationship of color to this sun, of sun to anything else?) It all looks staged. It all looks brittle and unreal, a skin of colors painted on glass, which if you prodded it with a finger would powder and fall. A blank sky, perfectly blended with all other sky, has sealed over the crack in the world where the plane fell, and the air has hushed the matter up.

32   If days are gods, then gods are dead, and artists pyrotechnic fools. Time is a hurdy-gurdy, a lampoon, and death's a bawd. We're beheaded by the nick of time. We're logrolling on a falling world, on time released

from meaning and rolling loose, like one of Atalanta's golden apples, a
bauble flung and forgotten, lapsed, and the gods on the lam.

33   And now outside the window, deep on the horizon, a new thing
appears, as if we needed a new thing. It is a new land blue beyond
islands, hitherto hidden by haze and now revealed, and as dumb as the
rest. I check my chart, my amateur penciled sketch of the skyline. Yes,
this land is new, this spread blue spark beyond yesterday's new wrinkled
line, beyond the blue veil a sailor said was Salt Spring Island. How long
can this go on? But let us by all means extend the scope of our charts.
34   I draw it as I seem to see it, a blue chunk fitted just so beyond
islands, a wag of graphite rising just here above another anonymous line,
and here meeting the slope of Salt Spring: though whether this be
headland I see or heartland, or the distance-blurred bluffs of a hundred
bays, I have no way of knowing, or if it be island or main. I call it Thule,
O Julialand, Time's Bad News; I name it Terror, the Farthest Limb of
the Day, God's Tooth.

QUESTIONS

Ideas

1.   What is Dillard getting at in this essay? Does she explicitly state her point
     in a sentence or two? Where? In your own words, explain the idea of
     "God's Tooth."

2.   Does this essay affect your beliefs in any way? Is that part of Dillard's
     purpose? Is she trying to explain, to defend, to persuade—or something
     else?

3.   How do you explain the tragedy—or the kind of tragedy—that Dillard
     describes here. How do people cope with such horrors?

Organization

4.   The essay can be divided into eight sections. Provide a title for each and
     explain the point of each section. Which sections are primarily narrative
     and descriptive? Which are more speculative and expository?

5.   In section IV (paragraphs 11–17) Dillard describes the child, Julie Nor-
     wich. Where in this section does Dillard shift from direct description to
     something else? What is that something else, and what are the purpose
     and point of the non-descriptive part of section IV?

Sentences

6. Reread the opening paragraphs. What do you notice about the shape and length of Dillard's sentences? Do any of the early paragraphs rely heavily on piling up short sentences and brief, staccato phrases? Where, and to what effect?

7. Look at paragraphs 19 and 21, 28 and 29, and also paragraph 4—in that order. Why does Dillard ask so many questions in these paragraphs? Are the kinds of questions similar or different in each set of paragraphs? Explain.

8. In paragraphs 26 and 27 Dillard uses repeated words and phrases at the beginning of her sentences. What advantage is there to such a procedure?

Words

9. What is the tone of paragraphs 24 and 25? Which words in particular convey that tone? What is Dillard's attitude toward God as evidenced in these paragraphs?

10. List and explain the comparisons in paragraphs 16 and 17. What do the comparisons have in common, and what point does Dillard make in using them? What is their purpose? To describe? To amuse? To explain? To persuade?

Suggestions for Writing

A. Write an essay combining description and narration with exposition. Focus on an event that disturbed you, an event that you had (or still have) trouble understanding. Try to incorporate into your essay the process you underwent in trying to understand the experience.

B. Write an essay describing how you came to lose a belief you once held or how you came to believe (in) something you formerly didn't believe (in). Why did you hold or not hold the belief in the first place? What prompted you to give up or to adopt the belief?

C. Rewrite paragraph 2, combining the short statements into longer, smoother sentences. Compare your version with that of another student, then with Dillard's version. What differences in tone and effect do you notice?

D. Write a paragraph exclusively, or almost exclusively, of questions (like paragraphs 27, 28, or 29).

E. Write a paragraph imitating the repetition of word and phrase at the beginnings of sentences that Dillard employs in paragraphs 26 and 27.

FIVE

Loren Eiseley
(1907–1977)

Many critics bemoan the increasingly narrow focus of both scientists and humanists. Unfortunately, the age of specialization asks us to probe deep but not wide. Loren Eiseley is different. He is the rare individual who can range far, wide, and deep in both cultures. He is a renowned anthropologist and archeologist, a naturalist and a philosopher, an essayist and poet. Eiseley bridges the gulf between science and the humanities by returning to nature the wonder and mystery that reason often takes away. Although gifted with a mature and acute perception of nature's secrets, he is able in his nonfiction to maintain the child's capacity for wonder and surprise. He feels that the man of science needs balance, needs both analysis and intuition. At the end of his scientific career as a museum curator and university professor, he wrote: "When the human mind exists in the light of reason and no more than reason, we may say with absolute certainty that man and all that made him will be in that instant gone."

Eiseley did not even realize that he wanted to be a scientist until graduate school. Until then he felt he was rootless: spending his childhood on the plains of western Nebraska, attending college, riding the freight trains during the Depression, recuperating from an illness in a cabin in Colorado. For much of this time he was unhappy and lonely. In his autobiography, *All the Strange Hours* (1975), he recounts the frustration and pain of growing up in poverty in a tumultuous, neurotic family. Specifically, in "The Running Man" he tries to understand how several encounters from his childhood shaped the man he has become. He is especially obsessed with his mother and his awkward, scarring relationship with her. His description of one dramatic and public episode forms the center of this essay. It is painful and honest, haunting and lyrical.

Even though Eiseley's reputation as a scientist was firmly established through his articles in scholarly journals, it was not until his collection of popular essays, *The Immense Journey* (1957), was published that he became known to the general public.

This book marked the beginning of a new career for Eiseley as a writer of the "concealed essay," a form in which personal observations lead to thoughts of a more general, objective nature. Eiseley, like Annie Dillard, is willing to read cosmic significance into small incidents—in the flight of birds, the web of a spider, in a run-in with a neighborhood bully, and in a chance encounter with a young fox. In these essays Eiseley, as narrator, is a knowing and helpful presence, but he is also there with the reader as an observer, questioning and puzzling over the inexplicable. In "The Judgment of the Birds," for example, he comes across an improbable and transitory web, built by a spider who refuses to succumb to the weather. He observes the spider carefully, then speculates: "Maybe man himself will fight like this in the end." The everyday event reverberates in the scientist's mind until it awakens the artist. This is characteristic of Eiseley's vision: the mundane is "refracted, transmuted and clarified through the prism of his poetic imagination." In this way, the scientist looks beyond logic to beauty and mystery that defy explanation. And so wonder is returned to nature.

One of Eiseley's most persistent themes is the mystery and complexity of time—an appropriate topic for an archeologist. Eiseley treats it with the intellectual rigor and curiosity of a scientist, without neglecting eloquence and sensitivity. In "Charles Darwin" he reflects on evolution as an expert, but his style and tone are filled with poetic sensibility and an amateur's sense of wonder and reverence. Somehow he can simultaneously observe, speculate, and dream. In "The Time of Man," an early essay on evolution (1962), the following passages are characteristic of Eiseley's incantatory, lyrical prose:

A strange animal, indeed: so very quiet when one turns over the mineral-hardened skull in a gravel bed, or peers into that little dark space which has housed so much cruelty and delight. One feels that something should be there still, some indefinable essence, some jinni to be evoked out of this little space which may contain at the same time the words of Jesus and the blasphemous megatons of modern physics. They are all in there together, inextricably intermixed. . . .

Those ancient bestial stirrings which still claw at sanity are part, also, of that dark continent we long chose to forget. But we do not forget, because man in contemplation reveals something that is characteristic of no other form of life known to us: he suffers because of what he is, and wishes to become something else. The moment we cease to hunger to be otherwise, our soul is dead. Long ago we began that hunger: long ago we painted on the walls of caverns and buried the revered dead. More and more, because our brain lays hold upon and seeks to shape the future, we are conscious of what we are, and what we might be. "No man," wrote John Donne, "doth exalt Nature to the height it would beare." He saw the great discrepancy between the dream and the reality.

Loren Eiseley learned not just to study nature but to participate in it. His essays are written in the same spirit: the reader is urged to be an active voyager. Eiseley once wrote that animals understand their roles, but that man, "bereft of instinct, must search continually for meanings." These essays are a rich source for such a journey.

Charles Darwin

I

1   In the autumn of 1831 the past and the future met and dined in London—in the guise of two young men who little realized where the years ahead would take them. One, Robert Fitzroy, was a sea captain who at twenty-six had already charted the remote, sea-beaten edges of the world and now proposed another long voyage. A religious man with a strong animosity toward the new-fangled geology, Captain Fitzroy wanted a naturalist who would share his experience of wild lands and refute those who used rocks to promote heretical whisperings. The young man who faced him across the table hesitated. Charles Darwin, four years Fitzroy's junior, was a gentleman idler after hounds who had failed at medicine and whose family, in desperation, hoped he might still succeed as a country parson. His mind shifted uncertainly from fox hunting in Shropshire to the thought of shooting llamas in South Amer-

ica. Did he really want to go? While he fumbled for a decision and the future hung irresolute, Captain Fitzroy took command.

2   "Fitzroy," wrote Darwin later to his sister Susan, "says the stormy sea is exaggerated; that if I do not choose to remain with them, I can at any time get home to England; and that if I like, I shall be left in some healthy, safe and nice country; that I shall always have assistance; that he has many books, all instruments, guns, at my service. . . . There is indeed a tide in the affairs of men, and I have experienced it. Dearest Susan, Goodbye."

3   They sailed from Devonport December 27, 1831, in H.M.S. *Beagle*, a ten-gun brig. Their plan was to survey the South American coastline and to carry a string of chronometrical measurements around the world. The voyage almost ended before it began, for they at once encountered a violent storm. "The sea ran very high," young Darwin recorded in his diary, "and the vessel pitched bows under and suffered most dreadfully; such a night I never passed, on every side nothing but misery; such a whistling of the wind and roar of the sea, the hoarse screams of the officers and shouts of the men, made a concert that I shall not soon forget." Captain Fitzroy and his officers held the ship on the sea by the grace of God and the cat-o'-nine-tails. With an almost irrational stubbornness Darwin decided, in spite of his uncomfortable discovery of his susceptibility to seasickness, that "I did right to accept the offer." When the *Beagle* was buffeted back into Plymouth Harbor, Darwin did not resign. His mind was made up. "If it is desirable to see the world," he wrote in his journal, "what a rare and excellent opportunity this is. Perhaps I may have the same opportunity of drilling my mind that I threw away at Cambridge."

4   So began the journey in which a great mind untouched by an old-fashioned classical education was to feed its hunger upon rocks and broken bits of bone at the world's end, and eventually was to shape from such diverse things as bird beaks and the fused wing-cases of island beetles a theory that would shake the foundations of scientific thought in all the countries of the earth.

II

5   The intellectual climate from which Darwin set forth on his historic voyage was predominantly conservative. Insular England had been horrified by the excesses of the French Revolution and was extremely

wary of emerging new ideas which it attributed to "French atheists."
Religious dogma still held its powerful influence over natural science.
True, the seventeenth-century notion that the world had been created
in 4004 B.C. was beginning to weaken in the face of naturalists' studies
of the rocks and their succession of life forms. But the conception of a
truly ancient and evolving planet was still unformed. No one could
dream that the age of the earth was as vast as we now know it to be.
And the notion of a continuity of events—of one animal changing by
degrees into another—seemed to fly in the face not only of religious
beliefs but also of common sense. Many of the greatest biologists of the
time—men like Louis Agassiz and Richard Owen—tended to the belief
that the successive forms of life in the geological record were all separate
creations, some of which had simply been extinguished by historic accidents.

6   Yet Darwin did not compose the theory of evolution out of thin
air. Like so many great scientific generalizations, the theory with which
his name is associated had already had premonitory beginnings. All of
the elements which were to enter into the theory were in men's minds
and were being widely discussed during Darwin's college years. His own
grandfather, Erasmus Darwin, who died seven years before Charles was
born, had boldly proposed a theory of the "transmutation" of living
forms. Jean Baptiste Lamarck had glimpsed a vision of evolutionary
continuity. And Sir Charles Lyell—later to become Darwin's confidant
—had opened the way for the evolutionary point of view by demonstrating that the planet must be very old—old enough to allow extremely
slow organic change. Lyell dismissed the notion of catastrophic extinc-
tion of animal forms on a world-wide scale as impossible, and he made
plain that natural forces—the work of wind and frost and water—were
sufficient to explain most of the phenomena found in the rocks, provided
these forces were seen as operating over enormous periods. Without
Lyell's gift of time in immense quantities, Darwin would not have been
able to devise the theory of natural selection.

7   If all the essential elements of the Darwinian scheme of nature
were known prior to Darwin, why is he accorded so important a place
in biological history? The answer is simple: Almost every great scientific
generalization is a supreme act of creative synthesis. There comes a time
when an accumulation of smaller discoveries and observations can be
combined in some great and comprehensive view of nature. At this point
the need is not so much for increased numbers of facts as for a mind
of great insight capable of taking the assembled information and render-

ing it intelligible. Such a synthesis represents the scientific mind at its highest point of achievement. The stature of the discoverer is not diminished by the fact that he has slid into place the last piece of a tremendous puzzle on which many others have worked. To finish the task he must see correctly over a vast and diverse array of data.

8   Still it must be recognized that Darwin came at a fortunate time. The fact that another man, Alfred Russel Wallace, conceived the Darwinian theory independently before Darwin published it shows clearly that the principle which came to be called natural selection was in the air—was in a sense demanding to be born. Darwin himself pointed out in his autobiography that "innumerable well-observed facts were stored in the minds of naturalists ready to take their proper places as soon as any theory which would receive them was sufficiently explained."

III

9   Darwin, then, set out on his voyage with a mind both inquisitive to see and receptive to what he saw. No detail was too small to be fascinating and provocative. Sailing down the South American coast, he notes the octopus changing its color angrily in the waters of a cove. In the dry arroyos of the pampas he observes great bones and shrewdly seeks to relate them to animals of the present. The local inhabitants insist that the fossil bones grew after death, and also that certain rivers have the power of "changing small bones into large." Everywhere men wonder, but they are deceived through their thirst for easy explanations. Darwin, by contrast, is a working dreamer. He rides, climbs, spends long days on the Indian-haunted pampas in constant peril of his life. Asking at a house whether robbers are numerous, he receives the cryptic reply: "The thistles are not up yet." The huge thistles, high as a horse's back at their full growth, provide ecological cover for bandits. Darwin notes the fact and rides on. The thistles are overrunning the pampas; the whole aspect of the vegetation is altering under the impact of man. Wild dogs howl in the brakes; the common cat, run wild, has grown large and fierce. All is struggle, mutability, change. Staring into the face of an evil relative of the rattlesnake, he observes a fact "which appears to me very curious and instructive, as showing how every character, even though it may be in some degree independent of structure . . . has a tendency to vary by slow degrees."

10   He pays great attention to strange animals existing in difficult

environments. A queer little toad with a scarlet belly he whimsically nicknames *diabolicus* because it is "a fit toad to preach in the ear of Eve." He notes it lives among sand dunes under the burning sun, and unlike its brethren, cannot swim. From toads to grasshoppers, from pebbles to mountain ranges, nothing escapes his attention. The wearing away of stone, the downstream travel of rock fragments and boulders, the great crevices and upthrusts of the Andes, an earthquake—all confirm the dynamic character of the earth and its great age.

11   Captain Fitzroy by now is anxious to voyage on. The sails are set. With the towering Andes on their right flank they run north for the Galápagos Islands, lying directly on the Equator 600 miles off the west coast of South America. A one-time refuge of buccaneers, these islands are essentially chimneys of burned-out volcanoes. Darwin remarks that they remind him of huge iron foundries surrounded by piles of waste. "A little world in itself," he marvels, "with inhabitants such as are found nowhere else." Giant armored tortoises clank through the undergrowth like prehistoric monsters, feeding upon the cacti. Birds in this tiny Eden do not fear men: "One day a mocking bird alighted on the edge of a pitcher which I held in my hand. It began very quietly to sip the water, and allowed me to lift it with the vessel from the ground." Big sea lizards three feet long drowse on the beaches, and feed, fantastically, upon the seaweed. Surveying these "imps of darkness, black as the porous rocks over which they crawl," Darwin is led to comment that "there is no other quarter of the world, where this order replaces the herbivorous mammalia in so extraordinary a manner."

12   Yet only by degrees did Darwin awake to the fact that he had stumbled by chance into one of the most marvelous evolutionary laboratories on the planet. Here in the Galápagos was a wealth of variations from island to island—among the big tortoises, among plants and especially among the famous finches with remarkably diverse beaks. Dwellers on the islands, notably Vice Governor Lawson, called Darwin's attention to these strange variations, but as he confessed later, with typical Darwinian lack of pretense, "I did not for some time pay sufficient attention to this statement."

13   As one surveys the long and tangled course that led to Darwin's great discovery, one cannot but be struck by the part played in it by oceanic islands.

14   Until Darwin turned his attention to them, it appears to have been generally assumed that island plants and animals were simply marooned evidences of a past connection with the nearest continent. Darwin,

however, noted that whole classes of continental life were absent from the island; that certain plants which were herbaceous (non-woody) on the mainland had developed into trees on the islands; that island animals often differed from their counterparts on the mainland.

15   Above all, the fantastically varied finches of the Galápagos amazed and puzzled him. There were parrot-beaks, curved beaks for probing flowers, straight beaks, small beaks—beaks for every conceivable purpose. These beak variations existed nowhere but on the islands; they must have evolved there. Darwin had early observed: "One might really fancy that, from an original paucity of birds in this archipelago, one species had been taken and modified for different ends." The birds had become transformed, through the struggle for existence on their little islets, into a series of types suited to particular environmental niches where, properly adapted, they could obtain food and survive. As the ornithologist David Lack has remarked, "Darwin's finches form a little world of their own, but one which intimately reflects the world as a whole."

16   Darwin's recognition of the significance of this miniature world, where the forces operating to create new beings could be plainly seen, was indispensable to his discovery of the origin of species. The island worlds reduced the confusion of continental life to more simple proportions; one could separate the factors involved with greater success. Over and over Darwin emphasized the importance of islands in his thinking. Nothing would aid natural history more, he contended to Lyell, "than careful collecting and investigating of *all the productions* of the most isolated islands. . . . Every sea shell and insect and plant is of value from such spots."

17   Darwin was born in precisely the right age even in terms of the great scientific voyages. A little earlier, the story the islands had to tell could not have been read; a little later much of it began to be erased. Today all over the globe the populations of these little worlds are vanishing, many without ever having been seriously investigated. Man, breaking into their isolation, has brought with him cats, rats, pigs, goats, weeds and insects from the continents. In the face of these hardier, tougher, more aggressive competitors, the island faunas—the rare, the antique, the strange, the beautiful—are vanishing without a trace. The giant Galápagos tortoises are almost extinct, as is the land lizard with which Darwin played. Some of the odd little finches and rare plants have gone or will go. On the island of Madagascar our own remote relatives, the lemurs, which have radiated into many curious forms, are now being

exterminated through the destruction of the forests. Even that continental island Australia is suffering from the decimation wrought by man. The Robinson Crusoe worlds where small castaways could create existences idyllically remote from the ravening slaughter of man and his associates are about to pass away forever. Every such spot is now a potential air base where the cries of birds are drowned in the roar of jets, and the crevices once frequented by bird life are flattened into the long runways of the bombers. All this would not have surprised Darwin, one would guess.

IV

18   When Darwin reached home after the voyage of the *Beagle,* he was an ailing man, and he remained so to the end of his life. Today we know that this illness was in some degree psychosomatic, that he was anxiety-ridden, subject to mysterious headaches and nausea. Shortly after his voyage Darwin married his cousin Emma Wedgwood, granddaughter of the founder of the great pottery works, and isolated himself and his family in the little village of Down, in Kent. He avoided travel, save for brief trips to watering places for his health. For twenty-two years after the *Beagle's* return he published not one word beyond the bare journal of his trip (later titled *A Naturalist's Voyage around the World*) and technical monographs on his observations.

19   Darwin's gardener is said to have responded once to a visitor who inquired about his master's health: "Poor man, he just stands and stares at a yellow flower for minutes at a time. He would be better off with something to do." Darwin's work was of an intangible nature which eluded people around him. Much of it consisted in just such standing and staring as his gardener reported. On a visit to the Isle of Wight he watched thistle seed wafted about on offshore winds and formulated theories of plant dispersal. Sometimes he engaged in activities which his good wife must surely have struggled to keep from reaching the neighbors. When a friend sent him a half ounce of locust dung from Africa, Darwin triumphantly grew seven plants from the specimen. "There is no error," he assured Lyell, "for I dissected the seeds out of the middle of the pellets." To discover how plant seeds traveled, Darwin would go all the way down a grasshopper's gullet, or worse, without embarrassment. His eldest son Francis spoke amusedly of his father's botanical experiments: "I think he personified each seed as a small demon trying

to elude him by getting into the wrong heap, or jumping away all together; and this gave to the work the excitement of a game."

20   The point of his game Darwin kept largely to himself, waiting until it should be completely finished. He piled up vast stores of data and dreamed of presenting his evolution theory in a definitive, monumental book, so large that it would certainly have fallen dead and unreadable from the press. In the meantime, Robert Chambers, a bookseller and journalist, wrote and brought out anonymously a modified version of Lamarckian evolution, under the title *Vestiges of the Natural History of Creation*. Amateurish in some degree, the book drew savage onslaughts from the critics, including Thomas Huxley, but it caught the public fancy and was widely read. It passed through numerous editions in both England and America—evidence that *sub rosa* there was a good deal more interest on the part of the public in the "development hypothesis," as evolution was then called, than the fulminations of critics would have suggested.

21   Throughout this period Darwin remained stonily silent. Many explanations of his silence have been ventured by his biographers: that he was busy accumulating materials; that he did not wish to affront Fitzroy; that the attack on the *Vestiges* had intimidated him; that he thought it wise not to write upon so controversial a subject until he had first acquired a reputation as a professional naturalist of the first rank. A primary reason lay in his personality—a nature reluctant to face the storm that publication would bring about his ears. It was pleasanter to procrastinate, to talk of the secret to a few chosen companions such as Lyell and the great botanist Joseph Hooker.

22   The Darwin family had been well-to-do since the time of grandfather Erasmus. Charles was independent, in a position to devote all his energies to research and under no academic pressure to publish in haste.

23   "You will be anticipated," Lyell warned him. "You had better publish." That was in the spring of 1856. Darwin promised, but again delayed. We know that he left instructions for his wife to see to the publication of his notes in the event of his death. It was almost as if present fame or notoriety were more than he could bear. At all events he continued to delay, and this situation might very well have continued to the end of his life, had not Lyell's warning suddenly come true and broken his pleasant dream.

24   Alfred Russel Wallace, a comparatively unknown, youthful naturalist, had divined Darwin's great secret in a moment of fever-ridden

insight while on a collecting trip in Indonesia. He, too, had put together the pieces and gained a clear conception of the scheme of evolution. Ironically enough, it was to Darwin, in all innocence, that he sent his manuscript for criticism in June of 1858.

25   Darwin, understandably shaken, turned to his friends Lyell and Hooker, who knew the many years he had been laboring upon his *magnum opus.* The two distinguished scientists arranged for the delivery of a short summary by Darwin to accompany Wallace's paper before the Linnean Society. Thus the theory was announced by the two men simultaneously.

26   The papers drew little comment at the meeting but set in motion a mild undercurrent of excitement. Darwin, though upset by the death of his son Charles, went to work to explain his views more fully in a book. Ironically he called it *An Abstract of an Essay on the Origin of Species* and insisted it would be only a kind of preview of a much larger work. Anxiety and devotion to his great hoard of data still possessed him. He did not like to put all his hopes in this volume, which must now be written at top speed. He bolstered himself by references to the "real" book—that Utopian volume in which all that could not be made clear in his abstract would be clarified.

27   His timidity and his fears were totally groundless. When the *Origin of Species* (the title distilled by his astute publisher from Darwin's cumbersome and half-hearted one) was published in the fall of 1859, the first edition was sold in a single day. The book which Darwin had so apologetically bowed into existence was, of course, soon to be recognized as one of the great books of all time. It would not be long before its author would sigh happily and think no more of that huge, ideal volume which he had imagined would be necessary to convince the public. The public and his brother scientists would find the *Origin* quite heavy going enough. His book to end all books would never be written. It did not need to be. The world of science in the end could only agree with the sharp-minded Huxley, whose immediate reaction upon reading the *Origin* was: "How extremely stupid not to have thought of that!" And so it frequently seems in science, once the great synthesizer has done his work. The ideas were not new, but the synthesis was. Men would never again look upon the world in the same manner as before.

28   No great philosophic conception ever entered the world more fortunately. Though it is customary to emphasize the religious and scientific storm the book aroused—epitomized by the famous debate at

Oxford between Bishop Wilberforce and Thomas Huxley—the truth is
that Darwinism found relatively easy acceptance among scientists and
most of the public. The way had been prepared by the long labors of
Lyell and the wide popularity of Chambers' book, the *Vestiges.* Moreover, Darwin had won the support of Hooker and of Huxley, the most
formidable scientific debater of all time. Lyell, though more cautious,
helped to publicize Darwin and at no time attacked him. Asa Gray, one
of America's leading botanists, came to his defense. His co-discoverer,
Wallace, generously advanced the word "Darwinism" for the theory,
and minimized his own part in the elaboration of the theory as "one
week to twenty years."

29   This sturdy band of converts assumed the defense of Darwin
before the public, while Charles remained aloof. Sequestered in his
estate at Down, he calmly answered letters and listened, but not too
much, to the tumult over the horizon. "It is something unintelligible to
me how anyone can argue in public like orators do," he confessed to
Hooker. Hewett Watson, another botanist of note, wrote to him shortly
after the publication of the *Origin:* "Your leading idea will assuredly
become recognized as an established truth in science, i.e., 'Natural
Selection.' It has the characteristics of all great natural truths, clarifying
what was obscure, simplifying what was intricate, adding greatly to
previous knowledge. You are the greatest revolutionist in natural history
of this century, if not of all centuries."

30   Watson's statement was clairvoyant. Within ten years the *Origin*
and its author were known all over the globe, and evolution had become
the guiding motif in all biological studies.

QUESTIONS

Ideas

1. How does Eiseley support the topic sentence of paragraph 5: "Yet Darwin
    did not compose the theory of evolution out of thin air"?

2. What is meant by "creative synthesis"? How does this apply to Darwin?

3. What is Eiseley's attitude toward man in the last paragraph of part III?

4. Eiseley is obviously interested in Darwin as a man and a scientist. How
    would you characterize the personality of Darwin?

5. What point is Eiseley making about great scientific advances?

Organization

6. What is the purpose of each of the four parts?
7. In informational discourse, paragraphs are usually more tightly structured than in narrative or personal writing. Eiseley therefore uses several formula paragraphs. He often begins with an assertion and then supports it with reasons, examples, and details. Look, for example, at paragraphs 1, 5, 6, and 9. What is the organizational pattern of the following paragraphs: 7, 14, 16, 26?

Sentences

8. Eiseley's style here is not as lyrical or subjective as in his other pieces. It serves a different function—to inform. Compare, for example, the sentences in paragraphs 6 and 7 with the last three paragraphs of "The Running Man." What differences do you see in tone, length, syntax, and purpose?

Words

9. Make a list of a dozen scientific terms used in this essay and define them in your own words.
10. In the last paragraph what does "clairvoyant" mean? Does Eiseley mean this literally?

Suggestions for Writing

A. Based on your experiences, write an essay that focuses on Huxley's reaction: "How extremely stupid not to have thought of that!"
B. Write an extended definition of Darwin's leading idea, "Natural Selection."

The Judgment of the Birds

---

1   It is a commonplace of all religious thought, even the most primitive, that the man seeking visions and insight must go apart from his fellows and live for a time in the wilderness. If he is of the proper

sort, he will return with a message. It may not be a message from the god he set out to seek, but even if he has failed in that particular, he will have had a vision or seen a marvel, and these are always worth listening to and thinking about.

2   The world, I have come to believe, is a very queer place, but we have been part of this queerness for so long that we tend to take it for granted. We rush to and fro like Mad Hatters upon our peculiar errands, all the time imagining our surroundings to be dull and ourselves quite ordinary creatures. Actually, there is nothing in the world to encourage this idea, but such is the mind of man, and this is why he finds it necessary from time to time to send emissaries into the wilderness in the hope of learning of great events, or plans in store for him, that will resuscitate his waning taste for life. His great news services, his world-wide radio network, he knows with a last remnant of healthy distrust will be of no use to him in this matter. No miracle can withstand a radio broadcast, and it is certain that it would be no miracle if it could. One must seek, then, what only the solitary approach can give—a natural revelation.

3   Let it be understood that I am not the sort of man to whom is entrusted direct knowledge of great events or prophecies. A naturalist, however, spends much of his life alone, and my life is no exception. Even in New York City there are patches of wilderness, and a man by himself is bound to undergo certain experiences falling into the class of which I speak. I set mine down, therefore: a matter of pigeons, a flight of chemicals, and a judgment of birds, in the hope that they will come to the eye of those who have retained a true taste for the marvelous, and who are capable of discerning in the flow of ordinary events the point at which the mundane world gives way to quite another dimension.

4   New York is not, on the whole, the best place to enjoy the downright miraculous nature of the planet. There are, I do not doubt, many remarkable stories to be heard there and many strange sights to be seen, but to grasp a marvel fully it must be savored from all aspects. This cannot be done while one is being jostled and hustled along a crowded street. Nevertheless, in any city there are true wildernesses where a man can be alone. It can happen in a hotel room, or on the high roofs at dawn.

5   One night on the twentieth floor of a midtown hotel I awoke in the dark and grew restless. On an impulse I climbed upon the broad old-fashioned window sill, opened the curtains, and peered out. It was the hour just before dawn, the hour when men sigh in their sleep or,

if awake, strive to focus their wavering eyesight upon a world emerging from the shadows. I leaned out sleepily through the open window. I had expected depths, but not the sight I saw.

6   I found I was looking down from that great height into a series of curious cupolas or lofts that I could just barely make out in the darkness. As I looked, the outlines of these lofts became more distinct because the light was being reflected from the wings of pigeons who, in utter silence, were beginning to float outward upon the city. In and out through the open slits in the cupolas passed the white-winged birds on their mysterious errands. At this hour the city was theirs, and quietly, without the brush of a single wing tip against stone in that high, eerie place, they were taking over the spires of Manhattan. They were pouring upward in a light that was not yet perceptible to human eyes, while far down in the black darkness of the alleys it was still midnight.

7   As I crouched half-asleep across the sill, I had a moment's illusion that the world had changed in the night, as in some immense snowfall, and that, if I were to leave, it would have to be as these other inhabitants were doing, by the window. I should have to launch out into that great bottomless void with the simple confidence of young birds reared high up there among the familiar chimney pots and interposed horrors of the abyss.

8   I leaned farther out. To and fro went the white wings, to and fro. There were no sounds from any of them. They knew man was asleep and this light for a little while was theirs. Or perhaps I had only dreamed about man in this city of wings—which he could surely never have built. Perhaps I, myself, was one of these birds dreaming unpleasantly a moment of old dangers far below as I teetered on a window ledge.

9   Around and around went the wings. It needed only a little courage, only a little shove from the window ledge, to enter that city of light. The muscles of my hands were already making little premonitory lunges. I wanted to enter that city and go away over the roofs in the first dawn. I wanted to enter it so badly that I drew back carefully into the room and opened the hall door. I found my coat on the chair, and it slowly became clear to me that there was a way down through the floors, that I was, after all, only a man.

10   I dressed then and went back to my own kind, and I have been rather more than usually careful ever since not to look into the city of light. I had seen, just once, man's greatest creation from a strange inverted angle, and it was not really his at all. I will never forget how those wings went round and round, and how, by the merest pressure of

the fingers and a feeling for air, one might go away over the roofs. It is a knowledge, however, that is better kept to oneself. I think of it sometimes in such a way that the wings, beginning far down in the black depths of the mind, begin to rise and whirl till all the mind is lit by their spinning, and there is a sense of things passing away, but lightly, as a wing might veer over an obstacle.

11   To see from an inverted angle, however, is not a gift allotted merely to the human imagination. I have come to suspect that within their degree it is sensed by animals, though perhaps as rarely as among men. The time has to be right; one has to be, by chance or intention, upon the border of two worlds. And sometimes these two borders may shift or interpenetrate and one sees the miraculous.

12   I once saw this happen to a crow.

13   This crow lives near my house, and though I have never injured him, he takes good care to stay up in the very highest trees and, in general, to avoid humanity. His world begins at about the limit of my eyesight.

14   On the particular morning when this episode occurred, the whole countryside was buried in one of the thickest fogs in years. The ceiling was absolutely zero. All planes were grounded, and even a pedestrian could hardly see his outstretched hand before him.

15   I was groping across a field in the general direction of the railroad station, following a dimly outlined path. Suddenly out of the fog, at about the level of my eyes, and so closely that I flinched, there flashed a pair of immense black wings and a huge beak. The whole bird rushed over my head with a frantic cawing outcry of such hideous terror as I have never heard in a crow's voice before and never expect to hear again.

16   He was lost and startled, I thought, as I recovered my poise. He ought not to have flown out in this fog. He'd knock his silly brains out.

17   All afternoon that great awkward cry rang in my head. Merely being lost in a fog seemed scarcely to account for it—especially in a tough, intelligent old bandit such as I knew that particular crow to be. I even looked once in the mirror to see what it might be about me that had so revolted him that he had cried out in protest to the very stones.

18   Finally, as I worked my way homeward along the path, the solution came to me. It should have been clear before. The borders of our worlds had shifted. It was the fog that had done it. That crow, and I knew him well, never under normal circumstances flew low near men. He had been lost all right, but it was more than that. He had thought he was high up, and when he encountered me looming gigantically

through the fog, he had perceived a ghastly and, to the crow mind, unnatural sight. He had seen a man walking on air, desecrating the very heart of the crow kingdom, a harbinger of the most profound evil a crow mind could conceive of—air-walking men. The encounter, he must have thought, had taken place a hundred feet over the roofs.

19   He caws now when he sees me leaving for the station in the morning, and I fancy that in that note I catch the uncertainty of a mind that has come to know things are not always what they seem. He has seen a marvel in his heights of air and is no longer as other crows. He has experienced the human world from an unlikely perspective. He and I share a viewpoint in common: our worlds have interpenetrated, and we both have faith in the miraculous.

20   It is a faith that in my own case has been augmented by two remarkable sights. I once saw some very odd chemicals fly across a waste so dead it might have been upon the moon, and once, by an even more fantastic piece of luck, I was present when a group of birds passed a judgment upon life.

21   On the maps of the old voyageurs it is called *Mauvaises Terres*, the evil lands, and, slurred a little with the passage through many minds, it has come down to us anglicized as the badlands. The soft shuffle of moccasins has passed through its canyons on the grim business of war and flight, but the last of those slight disturbances of immemorial silences died out almost a century ago. The land, if one can call it a land, is a waste as lifeless as that valley in which lie the kings of Egypt. Like the Valley of the Kings, it is a mausoleum, a place of dry bones in what once was a place of life. Now it has silences as deep as those in the moon's airless chasms.

22   Nothing grows among its pinnacles; there is no shade except under great toadstools of sandstone whose bases have been eaten to the shape of wine glasses by the wind. Everything is flaking, cracking, disintegrating, wearing away in the long, imperceptible weather of time. The ash of ancient volcanic outbursts still sterilizes its soil, and its colors in that waste are the colors that flame in the lonely sunsets on dead planets. Men come there but rarely, and for one purpose only, the collection of bones.

23   It was a late hour on a cold, wind-bitten autumn day when I climbed a great hill spined like a dinosaur's back and tried to take my bearings. The tumbled waste fell away in waves in all directions. Blue air was darkening into purple along the bases of the hills. I shifted my knapsack, heavy with the petrified bones of long-vanished creatures, and

studied my compass. I wanted to be out of there by nightfall, and already
the sun was going sullenly down in the west.

24   It was then that I saw the flight coming on. It was moving like
a little close-knit body of black specks that danced and darted and closed
again. It was pouring from the north and heading toward me with the
undeviating relentlessness of a compass needle. It streamed through the
shadows rising out of monstrous gorges. It rushed over towering pinnacles in the red light of the sun or momentarily sank from sight within
their shade. Across that desert of eroding clay and wind-worn stone they
came with a faint wild twittering that filled all the air about me as those
tiny living bullets hurtled past into the night.

25   It may not strike you as a marvel. It would not, perhaps, unless
you stood in the middle of a dead world at sunset, but that was where
I stood. Fifty million years lay under my feet, fifty million years of
bellowing monsters moving in a green world now gone so utterly that
its very light was traveling on the farther edge of space. The chemicals
of all that vanished age lay about me in the ground. Around me still lay
the shearing molars of dead titanotheres, the delicate sabers of soft-
stepping cats, the hollow sockets that had held the eyes of many a
strange, outmoded beast. Those eyes had looked out upon a world as real
as ours; dark, savage brains had roamed and roared their challenges into
the steaming night.

26   Now they were still here, or, put it as you will, the chemicals that
made them were here about me in the ground. The carbon that had
driven them ran blackly in the eroding stone. The stain of iron was in
the clays. The iron did not remember the blood it had once moved
within, the phosphorus had forgot the savage brain. The little individual
moment had ebbed from all those strange combinations of chemicals as
it would ebb from our living bodies into the sinks and runnels of oncoming time.

27   I had lifted up a fistful of that ground. I held it while that wild
flight of south-bound warblers hurtled over me into the oncoming dark.
There went phosphorus, there went iron, there went carbon, there beat
the calcium in those hurrying wings. Alone on a dead planet I watched
that incredible miracle speeding past. It ran by some true compass over
field and waste land. It cried its individual ecstasies into the air until the
gullies rang. It swerved like a single body, it knew itself, and, lonely, it
bunched close in the racing darkness, its individual entities feeling about
them the rising night. And so, crying to each other their identity, they
passed away out of my view.

28 I dropped my fistful of earth. I heard it roll inanimate back into the gully at the base of the hill: iron, carbon, the chemicals of life. Like men from those wild tribes who had haunted these hills before me seeking visions, I made my sign to the great darkness. It was not a mocking sign, and I was not mocked. As I walked into my camp late that night, one man, rousing from his blankets beside the fire, asked sleepily, "What did you see?"

29 "I think, a miracle," I said softly, but I said it to myself. Behind me that vast waste began to glow under the rising moon.

30 I have said that I saw a judgment upon life, and that it was not passed by men. Those who stare at birds in cages or who test minds by their closeness to our own may not care for it. It comes from far away out of my past, in a place of pouring waters and green leaves. I shall never see an episode like it again if I live to be a hundred, nor do I think that one man in a million has ever seen it, because man is an intruder into such silences. The light must be right, and the observer must remain unseen. No man sets up such an experiment. What he sees, he sees by chance.

31 You may put it that I had come over a mountain, that I had slogged through fern and pine needles for half a long day, and that on the edge of a little glade with one long, crooked branch extending across it, I had sat down to rest with my back against a stump. Through accident I was concealed from the glade, although I could see into it perfectly.

32 The sun was warm there, and the murmurs of forest life blurred softly away into my sleep. When I awoke, dimly aware of some commotion and outcry in the clearing, the light was slanting down through the pines in such a way that the glade was lit like some vast cathedral. I could see the dust motes of wood pollen in the long shaft of light, and there on the extended branch sat an enormous raven with a red and squirming nestling in his beak.

33 The sound that awoke me was the outraged cries of the nestling's parents, who flew helplessly in circles about the clearing. The sleek black monster was indifferent to them. He gulped, whetted his beak on the dead branch a moment, and sat still. Up to that point the little tragedy had followed the usual pattern. But suddenly, out of all that area of woodland, a soft sound of complaint began to rise. Into the glade fluttered small birds of half a dozen varieties drawn by the anguished outcries of the tiny parents.

34   No one dared to attack the raven. But they cried there in some instinctive common misery, the bereaved and the unbereaved. The glade filled with their soft rustling and their cries. They fluttered as though to point their wings at the murderer. There was a dim intangible ethic he had violated, that they knew. He was a bird of death.

35   And he, the murderer, the black bird at the heart of life, sat on there, glistening in the common light, formidable, unmoving, unperturbed, untouchable.

36   The sighing died. It was then I saw the judgment. It was the judgment of life against death. I will never see it again so forcefully presented. I will never hear it again in notes so tragically prolonged. For in the midst of protest, they forgot the violence. There, in that clearing, the crystal note of a song sparrow lifted hesitantly in the hush. And finally, after painful fluttering, another took the song, and then another, the song passing from one bird to another, doubtfully at first, as though some evil thing were being slowly forgotten. Till suddenly they took heart and sang from many throats joyously together as birds are known to sing. They sang because life is sweet and sunlight beautiful. They sang under the brooding shadow of the raven. In simple truth they had forgotten the raven, for they were the singers of life, and not of death.

37   I was not of that airy company. My limbs were the heavy limbs of an earthbound creature who could climb mountains, even the mountains of the mind, only by a great effort of will. I knew I had seen a marvel and observed a judgment, but the mind which was my human endowment was sure to question it and to be at me day by day with its heresies until I grew to doubt the meaning of what I had seen. Eventually darkness and subtleties would ring me round once more.

38   And so it proved until, on the top of a stepladder, I made one more observation upon life. It was cold that autumn evening, and, standing under a suburban street light in a spate of leaves and beginning snow, I was suddenly conscious of some huge and hairy shadows dancing over the pavement. They seemed attached to an odd, globular shape that was magnified above me. There was no mistaking it. I was standing under the shadow of an orb-weaving spider. Gigantically projected against the street, she was about her spinning when everything was going underground. Even her cables were magnified upon the sidewalk and already I was half-entangled in their shadows.

39   "Good Lord," I thought, "she has found herself a kind of minor sun and is going to upset the course of nature."

40   I procured a ladder from my yard and climbed up to inspect the situation. There she was, the universe running down around her, warmly arranged among her guy ropes attached to the lamp supports—a great black and yellow embodiment of the life force, not giving up to either frost or stepladders. She ignored me and went on tightening and improving her web.

41   I stood over her on the ladder, a faint snow touching my cheeks, and surveyed her universe. There were a couple of iridescent green beetle cases turning slowly on a loose strand of web, a fragment of luminescent eye from a moth's wing and a large indeterminable object, perhaps a cicada, that had struggled and been wrapped in silk. There were also little bits and slivers, little red and blue flashes from the scales of anonymous wings that had crashed there.

42   Some days, I thought, they will be dull and gray and the shine will be out of them; then the dew will polish them again and drops hang on the silk until everything is gleaming and turning in the light. It is like a mind, really, where everything changes but remains, and in the end you have these eaten-out bits of experience like beetle wings.

43   I stood over her a moment longer, comprehending somewhat reluctantly that her adventure against the great blind forces of winter, her seizure of this warming globe of light, would come to nothing and was hopeless. Nevertheless it brought the birds back into my mind, and that faraway song which had traveled with growing strength around a forest clearing years ago—a kind of heroism, a world where even a spider refuses to lie down and die if a rope can still be spun on to a star. Maybe man himself will fight like this in the end, I thought, slowly realizing that the web and its threatening yellow occupant had been added to some luminous store of experience, shining for a moment in the fog-bound reaches of my brain.

44   The mind, it came to me as I slowly descended the ladder, is a very remarkable thing; it has gotten itself a kind of courage by looking at a spider in a street lamp. Here was something that ought to be passed on to those who will fight our final freezing battle with the void. I thought of setting it down carefully as a message to the future: *In the days of the frost seek a minor sun.*

45   But as I hesitated, it became plain that something was wrong. The marvel was escaping—a sense of bigness beyond man's power to grasp, the essence of life in its great dealings with the universe. It was better, I decided, for the emissaries returning from the wilderness, even if they were merely descending from a stepladder, to record their marvel, not to define its meaning. In that way it would go echoing on through the

minds of men, each grasping at that beyond out of which the miracles emerge, and which, once defined, ceases to satisfy the human need for symbols.

46   In the end I merely made a mental note: One specimen of Epeira observed building a web in a street light. Late autumn and cold for spiders. Cold for men, too. I shivered and left the lamp glowing there in my mind. The last I saw of Epeira she was hauling steadily on a cable. I stepped carefully over her shadow as I walked away.

QUESTIONS

Ideas

1. Near the end of this essay, Eiseley talks about recording events without trying to define their meaning. Does he—or can you—define the meaning of the events recorded in this essay?

2. How does the following excerpt from another Eiseley essay bear on "The Judgment of the Birds"?

    It is a funny thing what the brain will do with memories and how it will treasure them and finally bring them into odd juxtapositions with other things, as though it wanted to make a design, or get some meaning out of them, whether you want it or not, or even see it.

3. In paragraph 2 Eiseley uses the term "a natural revelation." What does he mean? (Consider the meaning of the word "reveal.")

4. In this essay and in the other Eiseley essays included in this book, Eiseley calls himself a "naturalist." What is his sense of the word?

5. In paragraphs 9 and 19, Eiseley describes a peculiar feeling that he had. What is this feeling and why is it important? (Can it be compared with his impulse to dance with the frogs? Why or why not?)

6. What does Eiseley mean by "In the days of the frost seek a minor sun"? Why does he step carefully over the spider's shadow?

Organization

7. How is the essay organized? How many parts does it have and how are they related? How does Eiseley move from one section to another? How does he link them?

8. Where does the introduction end? Where does the conclusion begin? Could paragraphs 19–28 be omitted? Why or why not?

Sentences

9. Paragraph 34 is a single sentence, as is paragraph 12. Why?

10. How does the style of Eiseley's mental note in the last paragraph differ from the syntax of the previous one?

11. In paragraphs 3 and 18 Eiseley uses the colon. What is the relationship of the right-hand part of each statement to the left-hand part? Rewrite the sentences without the colon. How are the sentences different—in tone, in rhythm, in effect?

12. Notice how dashes are used in the sentences of paragraphs 2 and 17. Rewrite the sentences without the dashes. What is different about them? Compare the sentences using dashes with those using the colon. How do they differ? Can you suggest any guidelines for using the colon or the dash?

Words

13. What words and phrases indicating attentiveness appear in the first five paragraphs? What is the effect of the language of the final sentence of paragraph 5: "I had expected depths, but not the sight I saw"?

14. Near the end of the essay (paragraph 41), Eiseley describes a spider's web, comparing the human mind to the web. How is the mind like a spider's web? What does the spider represent?

Suggestions for Writing

A. Rewrite the following sentence in normal word order: "To and fro went the white wings, to and fro." What is the difference? Do the same with this sentence: "Around and around went the wings."

B. Rewrite the following sentence: "And he, the murderer, the black bird at the heart of life, sat there, glistening in the common light, formidable, unmoving, unperturbed, untouchable."

C. Write an essay in which you examine Eiseley's ideas about nature. Consider his view of himself as a naturalist. Use at least two of his essays.

D. Compare the following passages about webs with Eiseley's comparison of the mind to a spider's web. Write an essay exploring the idea implied by one or more of the web passages—including Eiseley's.

> Experience is never limited, and it is never complete; it is an immense sensibility, a kind of huge spiderweb of the finest silken threads suspended in the chamber of consciousness, and catching every airborne particle in its tissue.
>
> —HENRY JAMES, from *"The Art of Fiction"*

The world is like an enormous spider web and if you touch it, however
lightly, at any point, the vibration ripples to the remotest perimeter and
the drowsy spider feels the tingle and is drowsy no more but springs out
to fling the gossamer coils about you who have touched the web and then
inject the black, numbing poison under your hide. It does not matter
whether or not you meant to brush the web of things.

—ROBERT PENN WARREN, from *All the King's Men*

The Dance of the Frogs

I

He was a member of the Explorers Club, and he had never
been outside the state of Pennsylvania. Some of us who were world
travelers used to smile a little about that, even though we knew his
scientific reputation had been, at one time, great. It is always the way
of youth to smile. I used to think of myself as something of an adven-
turer, but the time came when I realized that old Albert Dreyer, hud-
dling with his drink in the shadows close to the fire, had journeyed
farther into the Country of Terror than any of us would ever go, God
willing, and emerge alive.

He was a morose and aging man, without family and without
intimates. His membership in the club dated back into the decades
when he was a zoologist famous for his remarkable experiments upon
amphibians—he had recovered and actually produced the adult stage of
the Mexican axolotl, as well as achieving remarkable tissue transplants
in salamanders. The club had been flattered to have him then, travel or
no travel, but the end was not fortunate. The brilliant scientist had
become the misanthrope; the achievement lay all in the past, and Albert
Dreyer kept to his solitary room, his solitary drink, and his accustomed
spot by the fire.

The reason I came to hear his story was an odd one. I had been
north that year, and the club had asked me to give a little talk on the
religious beliefs of the Indians of the northern forest, the Naskapi of
Labrador. I had long been a student of the strange mélange of superstition and woodland wisdom that makes up the religious life of the nature

peoples. Moreover, I had come to know something of the strange similarities of the "shaking tent rite" to the phenomena of the modern medium's cabinet.

"The special tent with its entranced occupant is no different from the cabinet," I contended. "The only difference is the type of voices that emerge. Many of the physical phenomena are identical—the movement of powerful forces shaking the conical hut, objects thrown, all this is familiar to Western psychical science. What is different are the voices projected. Here they are the cries of animals, the voices from the swamp and the mountain—the solitary elementals before whom the primitive man stands in awe, and from whom he begs sustenance. Here the game lords reign supreme; man himself is voiceless."

A low, halting query reached me from the back of the room. I was startled, even in the midst of my discussion, to note that it was Dreyer.

"And the game lords, what are they?"

"Each species of animal is supposed to have gigantic leaders of more than normal size," I explained. "These beings are the immaterial controllers of that particular type of animal. Legend about them is confused. Sometimes they partake of human qualities, will and intelligence, but they are of animal shape. They control the movements of game, and thus their favor may mean life or death to man."

"Are they visible?" Again Dreyer's low, troubled voice came from the back of the room.

"Native belief has it that they can be seen on rare occasions," I answered. "In a sense they remind one of the concept of the archetypes, the originals behind the petty show of our small, transitory existence. They are the immortal renewers of substance—the force behind and above animate nature."

"Do they dance?" persisted Dreyer.

At this I grew nettled. Old Dreyer in a heckling mood was something new. "I cannot answer that question," I said acidly. "My informants failed to elaborate upon it. But they believe implicitly in these monstrous beings, talk to and propitiate them. It is their voices that emerge from the shaking tent."

"The Indians believe it," pursued old Dreyer relentlessly, "but do *you* believe it?"

"My dear fellow"—I shrugged and glanced at the smiling audience—"I have seen many strange things, many puzzling things, but I am a scientist." Dreyer made a contemptuous sound in his throat and went back to the shadow out of which he had crept in his interest. The talk was over. I headed for the bar.

II

The evening passed. Men drifted homeward or went to their rooms. I had been a year in the woods and hungered for voices and companionship. Finally, however, I sat alone with my glass, a little mellow, perhaps, enjoying the warmth of the fire and remembering the blue snowfields of the North as they should be remembered—in the comfort of warm rooms.

I think an hour must have passed. The club was silent except for the ticking of an antiquated clock on the mantel and small night noises from the street. I must have drowsed. At all events it was some time before I grew aware that a chair had been drawn up opposite me. I started.

"A damp night," I said.

"Foggy," said the man in the shadow musingly. "But not too foggy. They like it that way."

"Eh?" I said. I knew immediately it was Dreyer speaking. Maybe I had missed something; on second thought, maybe not.

"And spring," he said. "Spring. That's part of it. God knows why, of course, but we feel it, why shouldn't they? And more intensely."

"Look—" I said. "I guess—" The old man was more human than I thought. He reached out and touched my knee with the hand that he always kept a glove over—burn, we used to speculate—and smiled softly.

"You don't know what I'm talking about," he finished for me. "And, besides, I ruffled your feelings earlier in the evening. You must forgive me. You touched on an interest of mine, and I was perhaps overeager. I did not intend to give the appearance of heckling. It was only that . . ."

"Of course," I said. "Of course." Such a confession from Dreyer was astounding. The man might be ill. I rang for a drink and decided to shift the conversation to a safer topic, more appropriate to a scholar.

"Frogs," I said desperately, like any young ass in a china shop. "Always admired your experiments. Frogs. Yes."

I give the old man credit. He took the drink and held it up and looked at me across the rim. There was a faint stir of sardonic humor in his eyes.

"Frogs, no," he said, "or maybe yes. I've never been quite sure. Maybe yes. But there was no time to decide properly." The humor faded out of his eyes. "Maybe I should have let go," he said. "It was what they wanted. There's no doubting that at all, but it came too quick for me. What would you have done?"

"I don't know," I said honestly enough and pinched myself.

"You had better know," said Albert Dreyer severely, "if you're planning to become an investigator of primitive religions. Or even not. I wasn't, you know, and the things came to me just when I least suspected—But I forget, you don't believe in them."

He shrugged and half rose, and for the first time, really, I saw the black-gloved hand and the haunted face of Albert Dreyer and knew in my heart the things he had stood for in science. I got up then, as a young man in the presence of his betters should get up, and I said, and I meant it, every word: "Please, Dr. Dreyer, sit down and tell me. I'm too young to be saying what I believe or don't believe in at all. I'd be obliged if you'd tell me."

Just at that moment a strange, wonderful dignity shone out of the countenance of Albert Dreyer, and I knew the man he was. He bowed and sat down, and there were no longer the barriers of age and youthful ego between us. There were just too men under a lamp, and around them a great waiting silence. Out to the ends of the universe, I thought fleetingly, that's the way with man and his lamps. One has to huddle in, there's so little light and so much space. One—

III

"It could happen to anyone," said Albert Dreyer. "And especially in the spring. Remember that. And all I did was to skip. Just a few feet, mark you, but I skipped. Remember that, too.

"You wouldn't remember the place at all. At least not as it was then." He paused and shook the ice in his glass and spoke more easily.

"It was a road that came out finally in a marsh along the Schuylkill River. Probably all industrial now. But I had a little house out there with a laboratory thrown in. It was convenient to the marsh, and that helped me with my studies of amphibia. Moreover, it was a wild, lonely road, and I wanted solitude. It is always the demand of the naturalist. You understand that?"

"Of course," I said. I knew he had gone there, after the death of his young wife, in grief and loneliness and despair. He was not a man to mention such things. "It is best for the naturalist," I agreed.

"Exactly. My best work was done there." He held up his black-gloved hand and glanced at it meditatively. "The work on the axolotl, newt neoteny. I worked hard. I had—" he hesitated—"things to forget." There were times when I worked all night. Or diverted myself, while waiting the result of an experiment, by midnight walks. It was a strange road. Wild all right, but paved and close enough to the city that there were occasional street lamps. All uphill and downhill, with bits of forest leaning in over it, till you walked in a tunnel of trees. Then suddenly you were in the marsh, and the road ended at an old, unused wharf.

"A place to be alone. A place to walk and think. A place for shadows to stretch ahead of you from one dim lamp to another and spring back as you reached the next. I have seen them get tall, tall, but never like that night. It was like a road into space."

"Cold?" I asked.

"No. I shouldn't have said 'space.' It gives the wrong effect. Not cold. Spring. Frog time. The first warmth, and the leaves coming. A little fog in the hollows. The way they like it then in the wet leaves and bogs. No moon, though; secretive and dark, with just those street lamps wandered out from the town. I often wondered what graft had brought them there. They shone on nothing—except my walks at midnight and the journeys of toads, but still . . ."

"Yes?" I prompted, as he paused.

"I was just thinking. The web of things. A politician in town gets a rake-off for selling useless lights on a useless road. If it hadn't been for that, I might not have seen them. I might not even have skipped. Or, if I had, the effect—How can you tell about such things afterwards? Was the effect heightened? Did it magnify their power? Who is to say?"

"The skip?" I said, trying to keep things casual. "I don't under-stand. You mean, just skipping? Jumping?"

Something like a twinkle came into his eyes for a moment. "Just that," he said. "No more. You are a young man. Impulsive? You should understand."

"I'm afraid—" I began to counter.

"But of course," he cried pleasantly. "I forget. You were not there. So how could I expect you to feel or know about this skipping. Look, look at me now. A sober man, eh?"

I nodded. "Dignified," I said cautiously.

"Very well. But, young man, there is a time to skip. On country roads in the spring. It is not necessary that there be girls. You will skip without them. You will skip because something within you knows the time—frog time. Then you will skip."

"Then I will skip," I repeated, hypnotized. Mad or not, there was a force in Albert Dreyer. Even there under the club lights, the night damp of an unused road began to gather.

IV

"It was a late spring," he said. "Fog and mist in those hollows in a way I had never seen before. And frogs, of course. Thousands of them, and twenty species, trilling, gurgling, and grunting in as many keys. The beautiful keen silver piping of spring peepers arousing as the last ice leaves the ponds—if you have heard that after a long winter alone, you will never forget it." He paused and leaned forward, listening with such an intent inner ear that one could almost hear that far-off silver piping from the wet meadows of the man's forgotten years.

I rattled my glass uneasily, and his eyes came back to me.

"They come out then," he said more calmly. "All amphibia have to return to the water for mating and egg laying. Even toads will hop miles across country to streams and waterways. You don't see them unless you go out at night in the right places as I did, but that night—

"Well, it was unusual, put it that way, as an understatement. It was late, and the creatures seemed to know it. You could feel the forces of mighty and archaic life welling up from the very ground. The water was pulling them—not water as we know it, but the mother, the ancient life force, the thing that made us in the days of creation, and that lurks around us still, unnoticed in our sterile cities.

"I was no different from any other young fool coming home on a spring night, except that as a student of life, and of amphibia in particular, I was, shall we say, more aware of the creatures. I had performed experiments"—the black glove gestured before my eyes. "I was, as it proved, susceptible.

"It began on that lost stretch of roadway leading to the river, and it began simply enough. All around, under the street lamps, I saw little frogs and big frogs hopping steadily toward the river. They were going in my direction.

"At that time I had my whimsies, and I was spry enough to feel the tug of that great movement. I joined them. There was no mystery about it. I simply began to skip, to skip gaily, and enjoy the great bobbing shadow I created as I passed onward with that leaping host all headed for the river.

"Now skipping along a wet pavement in spring is infectious, particularly going downhill, as we were. The impulse to take mightier leaps, to soar farther, increases progressively. The madness worked into me. I bounded till my lungs labored, and my shadow, at first my own shadow, bounded and labored with me.

"It was only midway in my flight that I began to grow conscious that I was not alone. The feeling was not strong at first. Normally a sober pedestrian, I was ecstatically preoccupied with the discovery of latent stores of energy and agility which I had not suspected in my subdued existence.

"It was only as we passed under a street lamp that I noticed, beside my own bobbing shadow, another great, leaping grotesquerie that had an uncanny suggestion of the frog world about it. The shocking aspect of the thing lay in its size, and the fact that, judging from the shadow, it was soaring higher and more gaily than myself.

" 'Very well,' you will say"—and here Dreyer paused and looked at me tolerantly— " 'Why didn't you turn around? That would be the scientific thing to do.'

"It would be the scientific thing to do, young man, but let me tell you it is not done—not on an empty road at midnight—not when the shadow is already beside your shadow and is joined by another, and then another.

"No, you do not pause. You look neither to left nor right, for fear of what you might see there. Instead, you dance on madly, hopelessly. Plunging higher, higher, in the hope the shadows will be left behind, or prove to be only leaves dancing, when you reach the next street light. Or that whatever had joined you in this midnight bacchanal will take some other pathway and depart.

"You do not look—you cannot look—because to do so is to destroy the universe in which we move and exist and have our transient being. You dare not look, because, beside the shadows, there now comes to your ears the loose-limbed slap of giant batrachian feet, not loud, not loud at all, but there, definitely there, behind you at your shoulder, plunging with the utter madness of spring, their rhythm entering your bones until you too are hurtling upward in some gigantic ecstasy that it is not given to mere flesh and blood to long endure.

"I was part of it, part of some mad dance of the elementals behind the show of things. Perhaps in that night of archaic and elemental passion, that festival of the wetlands, my careless hopping passage under the street lights had called them, attracted their attention, brought them leaping down some fourth-dimensional roadway into the world of time.

"Do not suppose for a single moment I thought so coherently then. My lungs were bursting, my physical self exhausted, but I sprang, I hurtled, I flung myself onward in a company I could not see, that never outpaced me, but that swept me with the mighty ecstasies of a thousand springs, and that bore me onward exultantly past my own doorstep, toward the river, toward some pathway long forgotten, toward some unforgettable destination in the wetlands and the spring.

"Even as I leaped, I was changing. It was this, I think, that stirred the last remnants of human fear and human caution that I still possessed. My will was in abeyance; I could not stop. Furthermore, certain sensations, hypnotic or otherwise, suggested to me that my own physical shape was modifying, or about to change. I was leaping with a growing ease. I was—

"It was just then that the wharf lights began to show. We were approaching the end of the road, and the road, as I have said, ended in the river. It was this, I suppose, that startled me back into some semblance of human terror. Man is a land animal. He does not willingly plunge off wharfs at midnight in the monstrous company of amphibious shadows.

"Nevertheless their power held me. We pounded madly toward the wharf, and under the light that hung above it, and the beam that made a cross. Part of me struggled to stop, and part of me hurtled on. But in that final frenzy of terror before the water below engulfed me I shrieked, '*Help! In the name of God, help me! In the name of Jesus, stop!*' "

Dreyer paused and drew in his chair a little closer under the light. Then he went on steadily.

"I was not, I suppose, a particularly religious man, and the cries merely revealed the extremity of my terror. Nevertheless this is a strange thing, and whether it involves the crossed beam, or the appeal to a Christian deity, I will not attempt to answer.

"In one electric instant, however, I was free. It was like the release from demoniac possession. One moment I was leaping in an inhuman company of elder things, and the next moment I was a badly shaken human being on a wharf. Strangest of all, perhaps, was the sudden silence of that midnight hour. I looked down in the circle of the arc light, and there by my feet hopped feebly some tiny froglets of the great migration. There was nothing impressive about them, but you will understand that I drew back in revulsion. I have never been able to handle them for research since. My work is in the past."

He paused and drank, and then, seeing perhaps some lingering doubt and confusion in my eyes, held up his black-gloved hand and deliberately pinched off the glove.

A man should not do that to another man without warning, but I suppose he felt I demanded some proof. I turned my eyes away. One does not like a webbed batrachian hand on a human being.

As I rose embarrassedly, his voice came up to me from the depths of the chair.

"It is not the hand," Dreyer said. "It is the question of choice. Perhaps I was a coward, and ill prepared. Perhaps"—his voice searched uneasily among his memories—"perhaps I should have taken them and that springtime without question. Perhaps I should have trusted them and hopped onward. Who knows? They were gay enough, at least."

He sighed and set down his glass and stared so intently into empty space that, seeing I was forgotten, I tiptoed quietly away.

QUESTIONS

Ideas

1. Does Eiseley mean us to take this essay as fact or fiction? What might be the point of such a story?
2. Regardless of your belief, what are some possible explanations for what happens in this essay? Try to construct reasons along a continuum from fact to fantasy.
3. How would you describe the narrator's personality? How does his attitude toward Dreyer change?
4. What is the significance of the following line from part II: "Maybe I should have let go . . . it was what they wanted, there's no doubting that at all, but it came too quick for me"?

Organization

5. How are the two stories here, Eiseley's and Dreyer's, related?
6. What is the purpose of part I? Look especially at the exchange between Dreyer and Eiseley. What conflict of perspective, of viewpoint, is being shown here?

7. Part IV is the longest and most detailed. Why? What is its point?

8. What is the overall structure of the four parts? What is the purpose of each?

Sentences

9. Most of this essay is told in dialogue. Compare the narrator's voice in part I with Dreyer's in the last dozen paragraphs of part IV. What differences do you find in tone, diction, and sentence structure?

Words

10. In part I, the narrator refers to Dreyer as a "misanthrope." Do you think this is accurate?

11. What does "mélange" mean? How about "propitiate," "implicitly," "nettled," "whimsies," "infectious," "uncanny"?

Suggestions for Writing

A. Write down your thoughts about each of the following questions. Write quickly on each one for about five minutes:

1. What are the advantages and disadvantages of believing in events such as these?

2. What are some of the things you accept on faith?

3. Is there absolute Truth within the scientific community?

Based on your responses, write an essay that explores the idea of belief in the supernatural.

B. Compare the theme of the following poem by Eiseley to "The Dance of the Frogs."

NOCTURNE IN SILVER

Here where the barbed wire straggles in the marsh
And alkali crusts all the weeds like frost,
I have come home, I have come home to hear
The new young frogs that cry along the lost

Wild ditches where at midnight only cows
And fools with eery marsh fire in their brains
Blunder toward midnight. Silvery and clear
Cry the new frogs; the blood runs in my veins

Coldly and clearly. I am mottled, too,
And feel a silver bubble in my throat.

Lock doors, turn keys, or follow in your fear.
My eyes are green, and warily afloat

In the June darkness. I am done with fire.
Water quicksilver-like that slips through stone
Has quenched my madness—if you find me here
My lineage squat and warty will be known.

The Running Man

1   While I endured the months in the Colorado cabin, my
mother, who had been offered a safe refuge in the home of her sister,
quarreled and fought with everyone. Finally, in her own inelegant way
of putting things, she had "skipped town" to work as a seamstress,
domestic, or housekeeper upon farms. She was stone deaf. I admired her
courage, but I also knew by then that she was paranoid, neurotic and
unstable. What ensued on these various short-lived adventures I neither
know to this day, nor wish to know.

2   It comes to me now in retrospect that I never saw my mother
weep; it was her gift to make others suffer instead. She was an untutored,
talented artist and she left me, if anything, a capacity for tremendous
visual impressions just as my father, a one-time itinerant actor, had in
that silenced household of the stone age—a house of gestures, of daylong
facial contortion—produced for me the miracle of words when he came
home. My mother had once been very beautiful. It is only thus that I
can explain the fatal attraction that produced me. I have never known
how my parents chanced to meet.

3   There will be those to say, in this mother-worshipping culture,
that I am harsh, embittered. They will be quite wrong. Why should I
be embittered? It is far too late. A month ago, after a passage of many
years, I stood above her grave in a place called Wyuka. We, she and I,
were close to being one now, lying like the skeletons of last year's leaves
in a fence corner. And it was all nothing. Nothing, do you understand?
All the pain, all the anguish. Nothing. We were, both of us, merely the
debris life always leaves in its passing, like the maimed, discarded chicks
in the hatchery trays—no more than that. For a little longer I would see
and hear, but it was nothing, and to the world it would mean nothing.

4   I murmured to myself and tried to tell her this belatedly: Nothing,

mama, nothing. Rest. You could never rest. That was your burden. But now, sleep. Soon I will join you, although, forgive me, not here. Neither of us then would rest. I will go far to lie down; the time draws on; it is unlikely that I will return. Now you will understand, I said, touching the October warmth of the gravestone. It was for nothing. It has taken me all my life to grasp this one fact.

5   I am, it is true, wandering out of time and place. This narrative is faltering. To tell the story of a life one is bound to linger above gravestones where memory blurs and doors can be pushed ajar, but never opened. Listen, or do not listen, it is all the same.

6   I am every man and no man, and will be so to the end. This is why I must tell the story as I may. Not for the nameless name upon the page, not for the trails behind me that faded or led nowhere, not for the rooms at nightfall where I slept from exhaustion or did not sleep at all, not for the confusion of where I was to go, or if I had a destiny recognizable by any star. No, in retrospect it was the loneliness of not knowing, not knowing at all.

7   I was a child of the early century, American man, if the term may still be tolerated. A creature molded of plains' dust and the seed of those who came west with the wagons. The names Corey, Hollister, Appleton, McKee lie strewn in graveyards from New England to the broken sticks that rotted quickly on the Oregon trail. That ancient contingent, with a lost memory and a gene or two from the Indian, is underscored by the final German of my own name.

8   How, among all these wanderers, should I have absorbed a code by which to live? How should I have answered in turn to the restrained Puritan, and the long hatred of the beaten hunters? How should I have curbed the flaring rages of my maternal grandfather? How should—

9   But this I remember out of deepest childhood—I remember the mad Shepards as I heard the name whispered among my mother's people. I remember the pacing, the endless pacing of my parents after midnight, while I lay shivering in the cold bed and tried to understand the words that passed between my mother and my father.

10   Once, a small toddler, I climbed from bed and seized their hands, pleading wordlessly for sleep, for peace, peace. And surprisingly they relented, even my unfortunate mother. Terror, anxiety, ostracism, shame; I did not understand the words. I learned only the feelings they represent. I repeat, I am an American whose profession, even his life, is no more than a gambler's throw by the firelight of a western wagon.

11   What have I to do with the city in which I live? Why, far to the

west, does my mind still leap to great windswept vistas of grass or the eternal snows of the Cascades? Why does the sight of wolves in cages cause me to avert my eyes?

12   I will tell you only because something like this was at war in the heart of every American at the final closing of the westward trails. One of the most vivid memories I retain from my young manhood is of the wagon ruts of the Oregon trail still visible on the unplowed short-grass prairie. They stretched half a mile in width and that was only yesterday. In his young years, my own father had carried a gun and remembered the gamblers at the green tables in the cow towns. I dream inexplicably at times of a gathering of wagons, of women in sunbonnets and black-garbed, bewhiskered men. Then I wake and the scene dissolves.

13   I have strayed from the Shepards. It was a name to fear but this I did not learn for a long time. I thought they were the people pictured in the family Bible, men with white beards and long crooks with which they guided sheep.

14   In that house, when my father was away and my mother's people came to visit, the Shepards were spoken of in whispers. They were the mad Shepards, I slowly gathered, and they lay somewhere in my line of descent. When I was recalcitrant the Shepards were spoken of and linked with my name.

15   In that house there was no peace, yet we loved each other fiercely. Perhaps the adults were so far on into the midcountry that mistakes were never rectifiable, flight disreputable. We were Americans of the middle border where the East was forgotten and the one great western road no longer crawled with wagons.

16   A silence had fallen. I was one of those born into that silence. The bison had perished; the Sioux no longer rode. Only the yellow dust of the cyclonic twisters still marched across the landscape. I knew the taste of that dust in my youth. I knew it in the days of the dust bowl. No matter how far I travel it will be a fading memory upon my tongue in the hour of my death. It is the taste of one dust only, the dust of a receding ice age.

17   So much for my mother, the mad Shepards, and the land, but this is not all, certainly not. Some say a child's basic character is formed by the time he is five. I can believe it, I who begged for peace at four and was never blessed for long by its presence.

18   The late W. H. Auden once said to me over a lonely little dinner in New York before he left America, "What public event do you remember first from childhood?" I suppose the massive old lion was in his way

encouraging a shy man to speak. Being of the same age we concentrated heavily upon the subject.

19   "I think for me, the Titanic disaster," he ventured thoughtfully.

20   "Of course," I said. "That would be 1912. She was a British ship and you British have always been a sea people."

21   "And you?" he questioned, holding me with his seamed features that always gave him the aspect of a seer.

22   I dropped my gaze. Was it 1914? Was it Pancho Villa's raid into New Mexico in 1916? All westerners remembered that. We wandered momentarily among dead men and long-vanished events. Auden waited patiently.

23   "Well," I ventured, for it was a long-held personal secret, "It was an escape, just an escape from prison."

24   "Your own?" Auden asked with a trace of humor.

25   "No," I began, "it was the same year as the Titanic sinking. He blew the gates with nitroglycerin. I was five years old, like you." Then I paused, considering the time. "You are right," I admitted hesitantly. "I was already old enough to know one should flee from the universe but I did not know where to run." I identified with the man as I always had across the years. "We never made it," I added glumly, and shrugged. "You see, there was a warden, a prison, and a blizzard. Also there was an armed posse and a death." I could feel the same snow driving beside the window in New York. "We never made it," I repeated unconsciously.

26   Auden sighed and looked curiously at me. I knew he was examining the pronoun. "There are other things that constitute a child," I added hastily. "Sandpiles, for example. There was a lot of building being done then on our street. I used to spend hours turning over the gravel. Why, I wouldn't know. Finally I had a box of pretty stones and some fossils. I prospected for hours alone. It was like today in book stores, old book stores," I protested defensively.

27   Auden nodded in sympathy.

28   "I still can't tell what started it," I went on. "I was groping, I think, childishly into time, into the universe. It was to be my profession but I never understood in the least, not till much later. No other child on the block wasted his time like that. I have never understood my precise motivation, never. For actually I was retarded in the reading of clock time. Was it because, in the things found in the sand, I was already lost and wandering instinctively—amidst the debris of vanished eras?"

29   "Ah," Auden said kindly, "who knows these things?"

30   "Then there was the period of the gold crosses," I added. "Later, in another house, I had found a little bottle of liquid gilt my mother used on picture frames. I made some crosses, carefully whittled out of wood, and gilded them till they were gold. Then I placed them over an occasional dead bird I buried. Or, if I read of a tragic, heroic death like those of the war aces, I would put the clipping—I could read by then —into a little box and bury it with a gold cross to mark the spot. One day a mower in the empty lot beyond our backyard found the little cemetery and carried away all of my carefully carved crosses. I cried but I never told anyone. How could I? I had sought in my own small way to preserve the memory of what always in the end perishes: life and great deeds. I wonder what the man with the scythe did with my crosses. I wonder if they still exist."

31   "Yes, it was a child's effort against time," commented Auden. "And perhaps the archaeologist is just that child grown up."

32   It was time for Auden to go. We stood and exchanged polite amenities while he breathed in that heavy, sad way he had. "Write me at Oxford," he had said at the door. But then there was Austria and soon he was gone. Besides one does not annoy the great. Their burdens are too heavy. They listen kindly with their eyes far away.

33   After that dinner I was glumly despondent for days. Finally a rage possessed me, started unwittingly by that gentle, gifted man who was to die happily after a recitation of his magnificent verse. For nights I lay sleepless in a New York hotel room and all my memories in one gigantic catharsis were bad, spewed out of hell's mouth, invoked by that one dinner, that one question, *what do you remember first?* My God, they were all firsts. My brain was so scarred it was a miracle it had survived in any fashion.

34   For example, I remembered for the first time a ruined farmhouse that I had stumbled upon in my solitary ramblings after school. The road was one I had never taken before. Rain was falling. Leaves lay thick on the abandoned road. Hesitantly I approached and stood in the doorway. Plaster had collapsed from the ceiling; wind mourned through the empty windows. I crunched tentatively over shattered glass upon the floor. Papers lay scattered about in wild disorder. Some looked like school examination papers. I picked one up in curiosity, but this, my own mature judgment tells me, no one will believe. The name Eiseley was scrawled across the cover. I was too shocked even to read the paper. No such family had ever been mentioned by my parents. We had come from elsewhere. But here, in poverty like our own, at the edge of town, had

subsisted in this ruined house a boy with my own name. Gingerly I picked up another paper. There was the scrawled name again, not too unlike my own rough signature. The date was what might have been expected in that tottering clapboard house. It read from the last decade of the century before. They were gone, whoever they were, and another Eiseley was tiptoing through the ruined house.

35   All that remained in a room that might in those days have been called the parlor were two dice lying forlornly amidst the plaster, forgotten at the owners' last exit. I picked up the pretty cubes uncertainly in the growing sunset through the window, and on impulse cast them. I did not know how adults played, I merely cast and cast again, making up my own game as I played. Sometimes I thought I won and murmured to myself as children will. Sometimes I thought I lost, but I liked the clicking sound before I rolled the dice. For what stakes did I play, with my childish mind gravely considering? I think I was too naive for such wishes as money and fortune. I played, and here memory almost fails me. I think I played against the universe as the universe was represented by the wind, stirring papers on the plaster-strewn floor. I played against time, remembering my stolen crosses, I played for adventure and escape. Then, clutching the dice, but not the paper with my name, I fled frantically down the leaf-sodden unused road, never to return. One of the dice survives still in my desk drawer. The time is sixty years away.

36   I have said that, though almost ostracized, we loved each other fiercely there in the silent midcountry because there was nothing else to love, but was it true? Was the hour of departure nearing? My mother lavished affection upon me in her tigerish silent way, giving me cakes when I should have had bread, attempting protection when I was already learning without brothers the grimness and realities of the street.

37   There had been the time I had just encountered the neighborhood bully. His father's shoulder had been long distorted and rheumatic from the carrying of ice, and the elder son had just encountered the law and gone to prison. My antagonist had inherited his brother's status in the black Irish gang that I had heretofore succeeded in avoiding by journeying homeward from school through alleys and occasional thickets best known to me. But now brother replaced brother. We confronted each other on someone's lawn.

38   "Get down on your knees," he said contemptuously, knowing very well what was coming. He had left me no way out. At that moment I hit him most inexpertly in the face, whereupon he began very scientifi-

cally, as things go in childish circles, to cut me to ribbons. My nose went first.

39   But then came the rage, the utter fury, summoned up from a thousand home repressions, adrenalin pumped into me from my Viking grandfather, the throwback from the long ships, the berserk men who cared nothing for living when the mood came on them and they stormed the English towns. It comes to me now that the Irishman must have seen it in my eyes. By nature I was a quiet reclusive boy, but then I went utterly mad.

40   The smashed nose meant nothing, the scientific lefts and rights slicing up my features meant nothing. I went through them with body punches and my eyes. When I halted we were clear across the street and the boy was gone, running for home. Typically I, too, turned homeward but not for succor. All I wanted was access to the outside watertap to wash off the blood cascading down my face. This I proceeded to do with the stoical indifference of one who expected no help.

41   As I went about finishing my task, my mother, peering through the curtains, saw my face and promptly had hysterics. I turned away then. I always turned away. In the end, not too far distant, there would be an unbridgeable silence between us. Slowly I was leaving the world she knew and desperation marked her face.

42   I was old enough that I obeyed my father's injunction, reluctantly given out of his own pain. "Your mother is not responsible, son. Do not cross her. Do you understand?" He held me with his eyes, a man I loved, who could have taken the poor man's divorce, desertion, at any moment. The easy way out. He stayed for me. That was the simple reason. He stayed when his own closest relatives urged him to depart.

43   I cast down my eyes. "Yes, father," I promised, but I could not say for always. I think he knew it, but work and growing age were crushing him. We looked at each other in a blind despair.

44   I was like a rag doll upon whose frame skins were tightening in a distorted crippling sequence; the toddler begging for peace between his parents at midnight; the lad suppressing fury till he shook with it; the solitary with his books; the projected fugitive running desperately through the snows of 1912; the dice player in the ruined house of his own name. Who was he, really? The man, so the psychologists would say, who had to be shaped or found in five years' time. I was inarticulate but somewhere, far forward, I would meet the running man; the peace I begged for between my parents would, too often, leave me sleepless. There was another thing I could not name to Auden. The fact that I

remember it at all reveals the beginning of adulthood and a sense of sin beyond my years.

45 To grow is a gain, an enlargement of life; is not this what they tell us? Yet it is also a departure. There is something lost that will not return. We moved one fall to Aurora, Nebraska, a sleepy country town near the Platte. A few boys gathered to watch the van unload. "Want to play?" ventured one. "Sure," I said. I followed them off over a rise to a creek bed. "We're making a cave in the bank," they explained. It was a great raw gaping hole obviously worked on by more than one generation of troglodytes. They giggled. "But first you've got to swear awful words. We'll all swear."

46 I was a silent boy, who went by reading. My father did not use these words. I was, in retrospect, a very funny little boy. I was so alone I did not know how to swear, but clamoring they taught me. I wanted to belong, to enter the troglodytes' existence. I shouted and mouthed the uncouth, unfamiliar words with the rest.

47 Mother was restless in the new environment, though again my father had wisely chosen a house at the edge of town. The population was primarily Scandinavian. She exercised arbitrary judgment. She drove good-natured, friendly boys away if they seemed big, and on the other hand encouraged slighter youngsters whom I had every reason to despise.

48 Finally, because it was farmland over which children roamed at will, mother's ability to keep track of my wide-ranging absences faltered. On one memorable occasion her driving, possessive restlessness passed out of bounds. She pursued us to a nearby pasture and in the rasping voice of deafness ordered me home.

49 My comrades of the fields stood watching. I was ten years old by then. I sensed my status in this gang was at stake. I refused to come. I had refused a parental order that was arbitrary and uncalled for and, in addition, I was humiliated. My mother was behaving in the manner of a witch. She could not hear, she was violently gesticulating without dignity, and her dress was somehow appropriate to the occasion.

50 Slowly I turned and looked at my companions. Their faces could not be read. They simply waited, doubtless waited for me to break the apron strings that rested lightly and tolerably upon themselves. And so in the end I broke my father's injunction; I ran, and with me ran my childish companions, over fences, tumbling down haystacks, chuckling, with the witch, her hair flying, her clothing disarrayed, stumbling after. Escape, escape, the first stirrings of the running man. Miles of escape.

51   Of course she gave up. Of course she never caught us. Walking home alone in the twilight I was bitterly ashamed. Ashamed for the violation of my promise to my father. Ashamed at what I had done to my savage and stone-deaf mother who could not grasp the fact that I had to make my way in a world unknown to her. Ashamed for the story that would penetrate the neighborhood. Ashamed for my own weakness. Ashamed, ashamed.

52   I do not remember a single teacher from that school, a single thing I learned there. Men were then drilling in a lot close to our house. I watched them every day. Finally they marched off. It was 1917. I was ten years old. I wanted to go. Either that or back to sleeping the troglodyte existence we had created in the cave bank. But never home, not ever. Even today, as though in a far-off crystal, I can see my running, gesticulating mother and her distorted features cursing us. And they laughed, you see, my companions. Perhaps I, in anxiety to belong, did also. That is what I could not tell Auden. Only an unutterable savagery, my savagery at myself, scrawls it once and once only on this page.

QUESTIONS

Ideas

1.   Eiseley's images seem especially vivid in this remembrance. What one comes immediately to your mind? Eiseley uses narrative, anecdotes, and significant moments from his experiences, but what do these pictures convey to you? Who is this essay about? Is it about Eiseley as a child or as an adult? Or is it about his mother?

2.   What is Eiseley's purpose in writing this essay? Does he hope to do something for himself? Is he trying to learn something, discover something? Consider especially paragraphs 5 and 6.

3.   Does Eiseley himself realize that he is not "sticking to the topic" as the essay opens, that he seems to be wandering? But does he? Read the first and the last four paragraphs again. Do you see connections to the rest of the piece?

4.   What is all this business about being an "American man"? Is Eiseley trying to connect his life to yours in some way? Do you accept the notion that one life can represent the experiences of all Americans?

5.   Eiseley denies that he is "harsh, embittered" about his relationship with his mother. What do you think? In this sense, what do you make of the last paragraph? How about the first sentence of paragraph 2?

6. What exactly do you think Eiseley means by "It was for nothing"?

7. What do you make of Eiseley's comment on the writing of autobiography: "To tell the story of a life one is bound to linger about gravestones where memory blurs and doors can be pushed ajar, but never opened"? What does Eiseley seem to be implying in this paragraph about the difference between writing about one's life and living it? Look especially at the last sentence.

8. Based on paragraphs 11 and 12, what do you make of Eiseley's wagon dream?

9. Before Eiseley begins his anecdote about Auden (paragraph 18) he writes a short "introductory" paragraph about inner peace. Why does he do this, and what expectations does this raise about the subsequent narrative?

10. In the tale Eiseley tells Auden, what do you think he means by "I was already old enough to know one should flee from the universe but I did not know where to run"?

11. Why did a rage possess Eiseley after his dinner with Auden? In his attempts to remember, Eiseley narrates a series of anecdotes: about his finding dice in a ruined farmhouse, his encounter with the neighborhood bully, and, finally, his running from his "violently gesticulating" mother. What is the point of these stories? Do they make concrete and specific a generalization? Look especially at the concluding paragraph to his bully story ("As I went about . . .") and the elaborate build-up to the running-away scene (the four paragraphs preceding "Finally, because it was farm land . . .). Do you see common threads among these tales? Are they in sequence, leading somewhere?

12. Why could he not tell Auden this last episode, yet could "scrawl it once and once only on this page"?

13. What is meant by "The Running Man"? Try to suggest several different possibilities.

Organization

14. Eiseley begins and ends this essay with thoughts of his mother. Where does the introduction end? The conclusion begin?

15. List in order all the incidents in this piece. What holds them all together?

Sentences

16. Eiseley has a reputation for lyrical, evocative prose. Cite some examples. What makes them poetic?

17. Read the last three paragraphs out loud. What do you notice about Eiseley's style? How does he use repetition? Modifiers? Sentence fragments? Parallelism? Sentence length?

Words

18. Make a list of all the words Eiseley uses to describe himself. What impression do they add up to? Do the same for words describing his mother.

Suggestion for Writing

From vividly drawn episodes in his life, Eiseley tries to assemble recurring patterns to define himself, to create an image of who he is. Try to remember two or three incidents from your childhood. Just free-write for fifteen minutes on each one, until some narrative line begins to emerge.

Read over your writing, looking for possible consistent themes, key terms, gestures, beginnings, and endings. That is, can you, like Eiseley, see in that distant self beginnings of your adult self; can you see hopes, fears, likes, curiosities, needs, predictable reactions, in these brief jottings of yours? Be aware that defining yourself in a narrative is often as much a process of interpretation as of discovery.

Now try to arrange your writing in a simple pattern. Begin with a generalization, a broad theme (see Eiseley's paragraph "To grow is a gain . . .") and then get more specific about yourself. Then support that assertion with one or two brief anecdotes. Conclude with a present view of that incident (see especially Eiseley's penultimate paragraph, "Of course she gave up . . .").

SIX

Ellen Goodman

(1941–   )

Ellen Goodman, a columnist for *The Boston Globe,* has described her job as "telling people what I think." This she has been doing for many years with honesty, intelligence, and verve. Collected in two books—*Close to Home* and *At Large* —Goodman's essays range over many subjects, both public and private: family life, television, friendship, the relations between men and women (and between adults and children), anxiety, violence, the role of women, and trends, fads, and established traditions.

Her writing about these and other issues is clear, direct, and personal. Because her essays are confined to a 750-word column, she writes to the point. Because she addresses a general audience—her work is nationally syndicated—she writes clearly and simply, without pomposity or ostentation. Prizing the personal, the concrete, and the familiar, Goodman fills her essays with anecdotes, vignettes, and characters; she tells stories with real people in them. This is her way of bringing important public issues down to earth or, as she puts it, "close to home."

In "The Company Man" Goodman describes Phil, a man who "worked himself to death" at fifty-one. In a few quick strokes she sketches Phil: a man who worked six days a week, had no interests beyond his job, and "ate egg salad sandwiches at his desk." Throughout "The Company Man" Goodman works by implication rather than outright statement. She presents facts about Phil's life and work along with comments from the wife and children he rarely saw and hardly knew. She allows her readers to draw their own conclusions, with the result that her argument, inviting the reader's participation, is the more powerfully advanced by remaining implicit.

Her views in another essay are more explicitly aired. In "It's Failure, Not Success" Goodman argues against the ideas in Michael Korda's book *Success!* Countering Korda's advice to look out for Number One, to be greedy and selfish, she asserts that "it's not OK to be greedy, Machiavellian, dishonest. It's not always OK to be rich." Questioning the assumptions on which *Success!* rests, Goodman gets to the heart of the issue—an ethical one—and from her counterperspective claims that Korda's book is less about success than about failure.

In a similar way she questions some other bits of conventional wisdom in "Blame the Victim" and "Thanksgiving." "Blame the Victim" urges us to consider whether victims of illness are not themselves partly to blame for what they suffer. "Thanksgiving" uses the traditional American holiday as a spur to speculation about the relationship between the individual self and the larger social world.

Besides possessing a talent for description and a flair for argument and debate, Goodman is a shrewd and sensitive social analyst. In "The Tapestry of Friendships" she sharply contrasts the bonding styles of men and women, setting her ideas in the context of how friends are portrayed in a few recent films. Although the tone of the piece is authoritative, even judgmental, the thought is more speculative than polemical. The confident yet reasonable tone of this and many of her essays enhances their persuasiveness.

But whatever her subject and however pointedly expressed her views, Goodman is consistently witty, intelligent, and provocative. She entertains as she enlightens. Perhaps best of all, her essays reveal her as she wants to be revealed: as "a person, not a pontificator," as a writer who enjoys her work, one who communicates with intelligence and civility.

The Company Man

1   He worked himself to death, finally and precisely, at 3:00 A.M. Sunday morning.

2   The obituary didn't say that, of course. It said that he died of a coronary thrombosis—I think that was it—but everyone among his friends and acquaintances knew it instantly. He was a perfect Type A,

a workaholic, a classic, they said to each other and shook their heads—and thought for five or ten minutes about the way they lived.

3   This man who worked himself to death finally and precisely at 3:00 A.M. Sunday morning—on his day off—was fifty-one years old and a vice-president. He was, however, one of six vice-presidents, and one of three who might conceivably—if the president died or retired soon enough—have moved to the top spot. Phil knew that.

4   He worked six days a week, five of them until eight or nine at night, during a time when his own company had begun the four-day week for everyone but the executives. He worked like the Important People. He had no outside "extracurricular interests," unless, of course, you think about a monthly golf game that way. To Phil, it was work. He always ate egg salad sandwiches at his desk. He was, of course, over-weight, by 20 or 25 pounds. He thought it was okay, though, because he didn't smoke.

5   On Saturdays, Phil wore a sports jacket to the office instead of a suit, because it was the weekend.

6   He had a lot of people working for him, maybe sixty, and most of them liked him most of the time. Three of them will be seriously considered for his job. The obituary didn't mention that.

7   But it did list his "survivors" quite accurately. He is survived by his wife, Helen, forty-eight years old, a good woman of no particular marketable skills, who worked in an office before marrying and mothering. She had, according to her daughter, given up trying to compete with his work years ago, when the children were small. A company friend said, "I know how much you will miss him." And she answered, "I already have."

8   "Missing him all these years," she must have given up part of herself which had cared too much for the man. She would be "well taken care of."

9   His "dearly beloved" eldest of the "dearly beloved" children is a hard-working executive in a manufacturing firm down South. In the day and a half before the funeral, he went around the neighborhood re-searching his father, asking the neighbors what he was like. They were embarrassed.

10   His second child is a girl, who is twenty-four and newly married. She lives near her mother and they are close, but whenever she was alone with her father, in a car driving somewhere, they had nothing to say to each other.

11   The youngest is twenty, a boy, a high-school graduate who has

spent the last couple of years, like a lot of his friends, doing enough odd jobs to stay in grass and food. He was the one who tried to grab at his father, and tried to mean enough to him to keep the man at home. He was his father's favorite. Over the last two years, Phil stayed up nights worrying about the boy.

12   The boy once said, "My father and I only board here."

13   At the funeral, the sixty-year-old company president told the forty-eight-year-old widow that the fifty-one-year-old deceased had meant much to the company and would be missed and would be hard to replace. The widow didn't look him in the eye. She was afraid he would read her bitterness and, after all, she would need him to straighten out the finances—the stock options and all that.

14   Phil was overweight and nervous and worked too hard. If he wasn't at the office, he was worried about it. Phil was a Type A, a heart-attack natural. You could have picked him out in a minute from a lineup.

15   So when he finally worked himself to death, at precisely 3:00 A.M. Sunday morning, no one was really surprised.

16   By 5:00 P.M. the afternoon of the funeral, the company president had begun, discreetly of course, with care and taste, to make inquiries about his replacement. One of three men. He asked around: "Who's been working the hardest?"

QUESTIONS

Ideas

1. Goodman uses Phil as an example, a type of something. Of what is he a representative, and what is her attitude toward him and toward what he represents? What point does she make about the more general situation of which he is only a part?

2. What is implied by the boss's question at the end of the essay? Would this point have been more effective if made explicitly rather than by implication?

3. Why, in an essay about a company man, does Goodman include discussion of his family? What does this discussion contribute to her point?

Organization

4. Consider the structure of this essay. How could it be diagrammed? What figure could represent its structure—circle, square, triangle? Look at para-

graph 1 in relation to paragraph 15, and at paragraphs 2 and 3 in relation to paragraph 16.

5. Paragraphs 1, 3, and 15 repeat a particular point—the time of Phil's death. Does Goodman employ other forms of repetition? For what purpose?

Sentences

6. In paragraphs 2 and 3 Goodman includes sentences that make use of the double dash. Explain the function and tone of the information included between the dashes in each sentence. Could the "sandwiched-in" information be left out of any of these sentences? Why or why not?

7. Goodman ends a number of her paragraphs with short, emphatic sentences —paragraphs 3, 4, 6, 7, 8, 9, 14, and 15. In fact, one paragraph—14— consists of four consecutive short sentences. What tone is established with these short, almost staccato sentences?

8. Another thing to notice about Goodman's sentences in this essay is their uniformity of pattern, in this case, subject-verb-object. Almost all begin with a noun or pronoun; many begin with "Phil," "He," or "His." Is this uniformity of structure monotonous? What is the effect of such heavy use of repeated sentence forms?

Words

9. Why does Goodman repeatedly use generic terms like "the widow," "the company man," "the company president"? What is the tone of these?

10. Why are so many words and phrases in quotation marks? What tone is established through their use?

Suggestions for Writing

A. Write an essay explaining what it means to be a company man or a company woman. You might want to consider the pleasures and pressures, the liabilities and assets, the opportunities and obligations such a position accords.

B. Write an essay in which you use something that happened as an occasion to explore an idea that the event illustrates. You might consider treating the description of what happened ironically, as Goodman does in "The Company Man."

C. Imagine that you are the president of the company for which Phil worked. Write a letter to Phil's wife. Decide what you want the purpose and tone of the letter to be.

D. Imagine that you are Phil's wife. Write a letter to the company president. You might want to write the letter before Phil dies. Or you could do it after. In either case, decide what the purpose and tone of your letter should be.

It's Failure, Not Success

---

1   I knew a man who went into therapy about three years ago because, as he put it, he couldn't live with himself any longer. I didn't blame him. The guy was a bigot, a tyrant and a creep.

2   In any case, I ran into him again after he'd finished therapy. He was still a bigot, a tyrant and a creep, *but* . . . he had learned to live with himself.

3   Now, I suppose this was an accomplishment of sorts. I mean, nobody else could live with him. But it seems to me that there are an awful lot of people running around and writing around these days encouraging us to feel good about what we should feel terrible about, and to accept in ourselves what we should change.

4   The only thing they seem to disapprove of is disapproval. The only judgment they make is against being judgmental, and they assure us that we have nothing to feel guilty about except guilt itself. It seems to me that they are all intent on proving that I'm OK and You're OK, when in fact, I may be perfectly dreadful and you may be unforgivably dreary, and it may be—gasp!—*wrong*.

5   What brings on my sudden attack of judgmentitis is success, or rather, *Success!*—the latest in a series of exclamation-point books all concerned with How to Make it.

6   In this one, Michael Korda is writing a recipe book for success. Like the other authors, he leapfrogs right over the "Shoulds" and into the "Hows." He eliminates value judgments and edits out moral questions as if he were Fanny Farmer and the subject was the making of a blueberry pie.

7   It's not that I have any reason to doubt Mr. Korda's advice on the way to achieve success. It may very well be that successful men wear handkerchiefs stuffed neatly in their breast pockets, and that successful single women should carry suitcases to the office on Fridays whether or not they are going away for the weekend.

8   He may be realistic when he says that "successful people generally

have very low expectations of others." And he may be only slightly cynical when he writes: "One of the best ways to ensure success is to develop expensive tastes or marry someone who has them."

9   And he may be helpful with his handy hints on how to sit next to someone you are about to overpower.

10   But he simply finesses the issues of right and wrong—silly words, embarrassing words that have been excised like warts from the shiny surface of the new how-to books. To Korda, guilt is not a prod, but an enemy that he slays on page four. Right off the bat, he tells the would-be successful reader that:

- It's OK to be greedy.
- It's OK to look out for Number One.
- It's OK to be Machiavellian (if you can get away with it).
- It's OK to recognize that honesty is not always the best policy (provided you don't go around saying so).
- And it's always OK to be rich.

11   Well, in fact, it's not OK. It's not OK to be greedy, Machiavellian, dishonest. It's not always OK to be rich. There is a qualitative difference between succeeding by making napalm or by making penicillin. There is a difference between climbing the ladder of success, and macheteing a path to the top.

12   Only someone with the moral perspective of a mushroom could assure us that this was all OK. It seems to me that most Americans harbor ambivalence toward success, not for neurotic reasons, but out of a realistic perception of what it demands.

13   Success is expensive in terms of time and energy and altered behavior—the sort of behavior he describes in the grossest of terms: "If you can undermine your boss and replace him, fine, do so, but never express anything but respect and loyalty for him while you're doing it."

14   This author—whose *Power!* topped the best-seller list last year— is intent on helping rid us of that ambivalence which is a signal from our conscience. He is like the other "Win!" "Me First!" writers, who try to make us comfortable when we should be uncomfortable.

15   They are all Doctor Feelgoods, offering us placebo prescriptions instead of strong medicine. They give us a way to live with ourselves, perhaps, but not a way to live with each other. They teach us a whole lot more about "Failure!" than about success.

QUESTIONS

Ideas

1. How well does the title fit the essay? Where does Goodman echo the title and with what point?

2. Both near the beginning of the essay (paragraph 5) and at the end (paragraphs 14 and 15), Goodman goes beyond discussion of Korda's *Success!* Why does she do this, and what does she say about other books of this type? What is her main objection to Korda's book in particular?

Organization

3. Divide the essay into two major parts. Provide a subtitle for each and explain how they are related. Then divide the essay into three or four parts, and again provide subtitles and show how the parts are related.

4. One thing that quickly strikes the reader of this essay is the shortness of its paragraphs. Reorganize and rearrange the paragraphs, combining as many as you think can be logically connected. What differences do you detect between this new version and Goodman's present arrangement? Which do you prefer and why?

Sentences

5. Throughout the essay Goodman uses parallel sentences. She does this most noticeably in paragraphs 10, 11, and 15. Explain what is gained by use of the parallel structure.

> There is a qualitative difference between succeeding
> > by making napalm
> > or by making penicillin.

> There is a   difference between
> > climbing the ladder of success
> > or machete-ing a path to the top.

6. Examine the first four paragraphs, noting especially how Goodman varies the length of her sentences. Consider where and how she uses short sentences.

Words

7. What words and phrases are responsible for the personal, even familiar tone of the essay?

8. What point does Goodman make by comparing Korda with Fanny Farmer? How does the comparison convey her attitude toward Korda and his book?

9. Explain the function and effect of the comparisons used in paragraph 10:

> But he simply finesses the issues of right and wrong—silly words, embarrassing words that have been excised like warts from the shiny surface of the new how-to books.

> To Korda, guilt is not a prod, but an enemy that he slays on page four. . . .

Suggestions for Writing

A. Write an essay about a book you've read—perhaps a practical, how-to book or a self-help book such as Korda's. In your essay, summarize the author's views, then explain why you agree or disagree with them.

B. Write a how-to essay. Assume the role of a confident and comfortable and experienced person who knows and believes in the advice being given. If you like, you can write a humorous essay rather than a "straight" or serious one. Possible titles: "How to Annoy Your Friends"; "How to Con Your Teachers"; "How to Feel Good (or Bad) about Yourself." Try to make the essay an offering of general advice about the subject rather than a set of directions.

C. Write an essay defining and illustrating what you mean by Failure—or Success, and defending or refuting Goodman's claims.

Thanksgiving

1   *Soon they will be together again, all the people who travel* between their own lives and each other's. The package tour of the season will lure them this week to the family table.

2   By Thursday, feast day, family day, Thanksgiving day, Americans who value individualism like no other people will collect around a million tables in a ritual of belonging.

3   They will assemble their families the way they assemble dinner: each one bearing a personality as different as cranberry sauce and pumpkin pie. For one dinner they will cook for each other, fuss for each other, feed each other and argue with each other.

4   They will nod at their common heritage, the craziness and caring of other generations. They will measure their common legacy . . . the children.

5   All these complex cells, these men and women, old and young, with different dreams and disappointments will give homage again to the group they are a part of and apart from: their family.

6   Families and individuals. The "we" and the "I." As good Americans we all travel between these two ideals.

7   We take value trips from the great American notion of individualism to the great American vision of family. We wear out our tires driving back and forth, using speed to shorten the distance between these two principles.

8   There has always been some pavement between a person and a family. From the first moment we recognize that we are separate we begin to wrestle with aloneness and togetherness.

9   Here and now these conflicts are especially acute. We are, after all, raised in families . . . to be individuals. This double message follows us through life.

10   We are taught about the freedom of the "I" and the safety of the "we." The loneliness of the "I" and the intrusiveness of the "we." The selfishness of the "I" and the burdens of the "we."

11   We are taught what André Malraux said: "Without a family, man, alone in the world, trembles with the cold."

12   And taught what he said another day: "The denial of the supreme importance of the mind's development accounts for many revolts against the family."

13   In theory, the world rewards "the supreme importance" of the individual, the ego. We think alone, inside our heads. We write music and literature with an enlarged sense of self. We are graded and paid, hired and fired, on our own merit.

14   The rank individualism is both exciting and cruel. Here is where the fittest survive.

15   The family, on the other hand, at its best, works very differently. We don't have to achieve to be accepted by our families. We just have to be. Our membership is not based on credentials but on birth.

16   As Malraux put it, "A friend loves you for your intelligence, a mistress for your charm, but your family's love is unreasoning: You were born into it and of its flesh and blood."

17   The family is formed not for the survival of the fittest but for the

weakest. It is not an economic unit but an emotional one. This is not the place where people ruthlessly compete with each other but where they work for each other.

18   Its business is taking care, and when it works, it is not callous but kind.

19   There are fewer heroes, fewer stars in family life. While the world may glorify the self, the family asks us, at one time or another, to submerge it. While the world may abandon us, the family promises, at one time or another, to protect us.

20   So we commute daily, weekly, yearly between one world and another. Between a life as a family member that can be nurturing or smothering. Between life as an individual that can free us or flatten us. We vacillate between two separate sets of demands and possibilities.

21   The people who will gather around this table Thursday live in both of these worlds, a part of and apart from each other. With any luck the territory they travel from one to another can be a fertile one, rich with care and space. It can be a place where the "I" and the "we" interact.

22   On this day at least, they will bring to each other something both special and something to be shared: these separate selves.

QUESTIONS

Ideas

1. What is Goodman's main point in this essay? How much or little does it have to do with giving thanks or with the traditional meaning attributed to the holiday? What central contrast governs Goodman's thinking?

2. Do you agree with Goodman that each of us has to make an accommodation between our individual nonconforming self and our socially conforming self? How important an issue is this for you? Can you envision this balancing act as a significant feature of your future? Why or why not?

Organization

3. Divide Thanksgiving into three sections: introduction, body, and conclusion. Explain the basis of your division.

4. Goodman's paragraphs are short, sometimes only a single sentence. Suggest an alternative arrangement of paragraphs in which you reduce Goodman's 22 to from 6 to 10. What differences, if any, result?

Sentences

5. Note the parallelism of form in the following sentence from paragraph 3:

    > For one dinner, they will ask for each other,
    >   fuss for each other,
    >   feed each other,
    >   argue with each other.

    Would it make any difference if the parallel elements were rearranged?

6. Paragraphs 17 and 18 together contain four sentences, all of which establish a contrast. They include contrasts between the strong and the weak, the callous and the kind, economics and emotion, competition and cooperation. Attend to the way each sentence is constructed to highlight these contrasts. Follow up on similar contrastive sentences in paragraphs 19 and 20.

Words

7. What does Goodman mean by her contrast between to "glorify" the self and to "submerge" it? (19) What is "rank" individualism? (14)

8. Why does Goodman put quotation marks around "I" and "we"? What images does she employ in paragraphs 1, 20, and 21? What plays on words does she create in paragraphs 3 and 21? How effective is each?

Suggestions for Writing

A. Write your own essay on Thanksgiving. Speculate on the significance of the holiday as you see it. Don't worry if your thoughts lead you in a different direction from Goodman.

B. Consider the significance of another American holiday or perhaps of a day that should be set aside for celebration or commemoration. Explain what the day means to you and what it could or should mean to others, and why.

C. Discuss Goodman's quotations from Malraux in paragraph 16:

    > Your family's love is unreasoning. You were born into it and of its flesh and blood.

    Relate this remark to the following lines from Robert Frost's poem, "The Death of the Hired Man."

    > Home is the place where, when you have to go there,
    >   They have to take you in.
    >   I should have called it
    > Something you somehow haven't to deserve.

Blame the Victim

1   There is a sign I pass every day on the way to work which says in bold letters: Health Thyself. The sign is "A Friendly Message" from the Blue Cross/Blue Shield people, who have, I know, a vested interest in its meaning.

2   But the very tone of it, the sort of Eleventh Commandment, Thus Spake Blue Cross/Blue Shield attitude of it, sitting there above the highway, has slowly rubbed raw a small layer of my consciousness. I have begun to wonder whether the Self-Health movement—of which this sign is more symbol than substance—isn't another variation on our national theme song: Blame the Victim. How many measures, how many beats, how many half-notes is it from the order to Health Thyself to the attitude that blames the ill for their illness?

3   The titles on the bookshelf of my favorite store are a chorus stuck in this monotone: *Stay Out of the Hospital* instructs one; *The Anti-Cancer Diet* offers another; *You Can Stop* (smoking) cheerleads a third. They tell readers How To design their faces, control their migraines, lose weight, bear children without pain and psych themselves out of everything from back pain to heart disease.

4   Perhaps the most typical of them is one which touts *Preventing Cancer: What You Can Do to Cut Your Risks by Up to 50 Percent.* And another containing *Dr. Frank's No Aging Diet: Eat and Grow Younger.*

5   Now I am in favor—who is against it?—of proper diet and exercise. I am against—who is in favor of it?—smoking. I assume that a diet high in calories, cholesterol and cognac would eventually do me in. I think that self-consciousness about health, the desire to take responsibility for the shape of our lungs and calf muscles, is positive, and I agree that we are our own best screening system. But there is a risk. A risk that as we focus on the aspects of self-health we begin to look at all illness as self-inflicted and even regard death as a kind of personal folly.

6   There have been, among my acquaintances, the relatives of my relatives and friends of my friends, three heart attacks within the past year. One man, I was told, was, well, overweight. "He should have known better." Another woman was, her friends insist, a real "Type A." And the third man, I was assured by the most well-meaning of people, brought it on himself. "He was so out of shape."

7   Similarly, when people hear reports of cancer, how often do they inadvertently say that the victim should have stayed out of the sun, or off the pill, or away from nitrates?

8   Now maybe they are right and maybe they are wrong, but I fear that there are many who seek to know the cause of a disease not to cure it, but to judge its victims.

9   It is reassuring to hear that we can cut the risks of cancer by 50 percent. It is lovely to think that we can eat in special ways and grow younger. In a world of amorphous fears, where carcinogens are the new demons, it is very human to try to analyze illness in order to separate ourselves from it, to assure ourselves that we can be immune. There is a natural tendency to try to buy insurance packages—not of Blue Crosses and Blue Shields, but of diets and regimens and cautions.

10   But there is also something malignant about some of the extremists who make a public virtue of their health. It is the sort of self-righteousness that inspired a letter writer to suggest to me recently that we eliminate lung cancer research, because "smokers do it to themselves."

11   There is a judgmental attitude toward ill-health germinating in parts of the country and in parts of our minds that can be spread cruelly. It implies that those who do not "Health Thyself" are not only courting their own disasters, but are owed very little in the way of sympathy. It implies that illness is, at root, a punishment for foolishness.

12   This feeds into the hope, born of fear, that if we keep ourselves in shape and watch out, we can not only postpone death but prevent it. The notion that death is, in essence, suicide, and something we can avoid, is the most profound illusion of all.

QUESTIONS

Ideas

1. Is Goodman against good health? Is she against dieting, exercise, or Blue Cross/Blue Shield? Explain.

2. Is there any sense in which the ill can be blamed for their illness? Supply a few more examples of types of illnesses for which society conventionally considers the victim blameworthy.

3. What larger general idea lies behind the views Goodman begins her essay with—that victims of illness are themselves largely to blame for what they suffer.

Organization

4. Divide Goodman's essay into an introduction, body, and conclusion. Explain the reason for your groupings of paragraphs.
5. Examine Goodman's transitions between the sections—introduction, body, and conclusion—and those between paragraphs. Comment on their effectiveness.

Sentences

6. The last three sentences of the essay contain interrupters—words that slow down the movement of the sentence. Consider this example:

    It implies that illness is, at root, a punishment for foolishness.

    What would be lost if "at root" were eliminated? If it were moved to the beginning or end of the sentence?
7. Paragraphs 2 and 5 include double dashes which are used to embed information and interrupt the straightforward movement of the sentence. How would the tone of the paragraph change if the embedded details were deleted? If they were rearranged in separate sentences?
8. How effective are the questions in paragraph 2? Would you prefer to see them converted to statements? Why or why not?

Words

9. If we were to alter paragraph 6 so that there were no direct quotations would it affect the tone of the paragraph significantly? For better or worse? Why?
10. Paragraph 2 contains two images. How does each clarify Goodman's point and attitude? How is the last question in this paragraph meant to be answered?

Suggestions for Writing

A. Write imitations of paragraph 2 and 6; write imitations of the last three sentences of the essay.
B. Write a letter to Goodman agreeing or disagreeing with her and explaining why you think what you do.
C. Write an essay extending Goodman's idea from victims of illness to victims of crimes. Consider society's attitude toward victims of certain crimes such as rape. Argue for or against the idea that victims of certain crimes are partly or largely responsible for being victimized.

The Tapestry of Friendships

1   It was, in many ways, a slight movie. Nothing actually happened. There was no big-budget chase scene, no bloody shoot-out. The story ended without any cosmic conclusions.

2   Yet she found Claudia Weill's film *Girlfriends* gentle and affecting. Slowly, it panned across the tapestry of friendship—showing its fragility, its resiliency, its role as the connecting tissue between the lives of two young women.

3   When it was over, she thought about the movies she'd seen this year—*Julia, The Turning Point* and now *Girlfriends.* It seemed that the peculiar eye, the social lens of the cinema, had drastically shifted its focus. Suddenly the Male Buddy movies had been replaced by the Female Friendship flicks.

4   This wasn't just another binge of trendiness, but a kind of *cinéma vérité.* For once the movies were reflecting a shift, not just from men to women but from one definition of friendship to another.

5   Across millions of miles of celluloid, the ideal of friendship had always been male—a world of sidekicks and "pardners," of Butch Cassidys and Sundance Kids. There had been something almost atavistic about these visions of attachments—as if producers culled their plots from some pop anthropology book on male bonding. Movies portrayed the idea that only men, those direct descendants of hunters and Hemingways, inherited a primal capacity for friendship. In contrast, they portrayed women picking on each other, the way they once picked berries.

6   Well, that duality must have been mortally wounded in some shootout at the You're OK, I'm OK Corral. Now, on the screen, they were at least aware of the subtle distinction between men and women as buddies and friends.

7   About 150 years ago, Coleridge had written, "A woman's friendship borders more closely on love than man's. Men affect each other in the reflection of noble or friendly acts, whilst women ask fewer proofs and more signs and expressions of attachment."

8   Well, she thought, on the whole, men had buddies, while women had friends. Buddies bonded, but friends loved. Buddies faced adversity together, but friends faced each other. There was something palpably

different in the way they spent their time. Buddies seemed to "do" things together; friends simply "were" together.

9　　Buddies came linked, like accessories, to one activity or another. People have golf buddies and business buddies, college buddies and club buddies. Men often keep their buddies in these categories, while women keep a special category for friends.

10　　A man once told her that men weren't real buddies until they'd been "through the wars" together—corporate or athletic or military. They had to soldier together, he said. Women, on the other hand, didn't count themselves as friends until they'd shared three loathsome confidences.

11　　Buddies hang tough together; friends hang onto each other.

12　　It probably had something to do with pride. You don't show off to a friend; you show need. Buddies try to keep the worst from each other; friends confess it.

13　　A friend of hers once telephoned her lover, just to find out if he were home. She hung up without a hello when he picked up the phone. Later, wretched with embarrassment, the friend moaned, "Can you believe me? A thirty-five-year-old lawyer, making a chicken call?" Together they laughed and made it better.

14　　Buddies seek approval. But friends seek acceptance.

15　　She knew so many men who had been trained in restraint, afraid of each other's judgment or awkward with each other's affection. She wasn't sure which. Like buddies in the movies, they would die for each other, but never hug each other.

16　　She'd reread *Babbitt* recently, that extraordinary catalogue of male grievances. The only relationship that gave meaning to the claustrophobic life of George Babbitt had been with Paul Riesling. But not once in the tragedy of their lives had one been able to say to the other: You make a difference.

17　　Even now men shocked her at times with their description of friendship. Does this one have a best friend? "Why, of course, we see each other every February." Does that one call his most intimate pal long distance? "Why, certainly, whenever there's a real reason." Do those two old chums ever have dinner together? "You mean alone? Without our wives?"

18　　Yet, things were changing. The ideal of intimacy wasn't this parallel playmate, this teammate, this trenchmate. Not even in Hollywood. In the double standard of friendship, for once the female version was becoming accepted as the general ideal.

19   After all, a buddy is a fine life-companion. But one's friends, as
Santayana once wrote, "are that part of the race with which one can be
human."

QUESTIONS

Ideas

1. What does Goodman see as the main difference between male and female
    friendships? Do you agree that men "bond" and "buddy" whereas women
    "love" and "befriend" one another? Why or why not?

2. How do the movies that Goodman mentions tie in with her main point?
    Are these movie references necessary?

Organization

3. The essay falls roughly into three parts: paragraphs 1–6; paragraphs 7–17;
    paragraphs 18–19. What would have been gained and lost if Goodman had
    omitted paragraphs 1–6?

4. Two paragraphs (11 and 14) are very short, even for journalism. Should
    these short paragraphs have been attached to the paragraphs before or after
    them? Why or why not? Could they be omitted?

Sentences

5. A notable feature of Goodman's style in this essay is her use of antithetical
    sentences such as the following:

    Buddies bonded, but friends loved. (8)

    Buddies try to keep the worst from each other; friends confess it. (12)

    Buddies seek approval. But friends seek acceptance. (14)

    The basic thrust and the general idea of the three sentences are the same;
    the sentence structure is slightly different in the three instances. Find
    other sentences that make contrastive, antithetical points about buddies
    and friends—in still other, slightly different ways.

6. In the sentences that follow, Goodman uses the dash to set off part of her
    idea. For each, explain how the sentence would be different if a comma
    replaced the dash. And explain also whether the sentence could (or should)
    end where the dash occurs. (That is, imagine a period where the dash is
    with the words after the period omitted.)

Slowly, it panned across the tapestry of friendship—showing its fragility, its resiliency, its role as the connecting tissue between the lives of two young women. (2)

When it was over, she thought about the movies she'd seen this year —*Julia, The Turning Point* and now *Girlfriends.* (3)

Across millions of miles of celluloid, the ideal of friendship had always been male—a world of sidekicks and "pardners," of Butch Cassidys and Sundance Kids. (5)

A man once told her that men weren't real buddies until they'd been "through the wars" together—corporate or athletic or military. (10)

7. In paragraph 17 Goodman asks a series of questions and then provides answers in quotation marks. What is the tone and the point of these questions (and of this paragraph)?

8. Goodman twice introduces quotations into the essay—Coleridge in paragraph 7 and Santayana at the end. What is the point of each quotation, and how well does each tie in with Goodman's main idea?

Words

9. In writing of herself in this essay, Goodman uses the third person: she refers to herself as "she," rather than as the more conventional and expected "I." What is the effect of this third-person self-reference? Try reading two or three paragraphs, mentally changing the "she" to "I." How does the tone change?

10. In the first five paragraphs Goodman uses the language of film, perhaps more so than she actually needs to. What is her purpose in using film language?

11. Explain the tone and word play of each of the following sentences:

Buddies faced adversity together, but friends faced each other. (8)

Buddies hang tough together; friends hang onto each other. (11)

You don't show off to a friend; you show need. (12)

Suggestions for Writing

A. Write imitations of the sentences discussed in questions 5, 6, and 7.

B. Write your own essay on the meaning and value of friendship.

C. Attend a film—or several films—and write an essay examining the kinds of friendships portrayed.

D. Argue for or against Goodman's ideas about friendship in an essay of your own.

SEVEN

Stephen Jay Gould

(1941–   )

Most people dare not doubt the findings of modern science, thinking it an objective, dispassionate march toward truth. They assume that scientists carefully gather and analyze a multitude of facts and then come to logical conclusions. Geology and evolutionary biology, for example, are thought to be neutral inquiries, free from the social and political prejudices that distort most of our other intellectual pursuits. But not according to Stephen Jay Gould. For him, science is a creative activity, its findings deeply intertwined with the personal opinions and biases of fallible and impressionable investigators. It is this kind of iconoclastic position that lends excitement and power to Gould's science writing.

In "This View of Life," a monthly column in *Natural History,* Gould helps us understand the impact of social and political pressures on a range of supposedly objective disciplines, from paleontology and geology to zoology and evolutionary biology. Since Gould is not writing for specialists here, he switches from the technical language common in academic circles to a style that both entertains and teaches. Most first-rate scientists find this quite difficult. Only a handful have been able to popularize their specialties without also trivializing them. Along with Lewis Thomas and Loren Eiseley, Gould is able to write clearly about complicated ideas in a strong, elegant style. But even more than the intellectual content and graceful prose, the reader senses Gould's enthusiasm, his passion for ideas and rigorous thinking.

This fiery commitment began early. As a young boy in New York, Stephen's father took him to the Museum of Natural History where, like most children, his imagination and sense of wonder was electrified by the great dinosaurs. He even dedicated his first popular success, an anthology of essays, *Ever*

Since Darwin—Reflections in Natural History (1977), to his father, "who took me to see the Tyrannosaurus when I was five." Now, as a professor of geology, biology, and the history of science at Harvard, and as the winner of several prestigious book awards, Gould does a good deal more than put bones together. Besides his many professional responsibilities, his major task today is to develop and expand our understanding of how life evolves. Although his topics seem diverse, in one way or another, all his popular essays deal with Darwinian evolutionary theory: "I am a tradesman, not a polymath; what I know of planets and politics lies at their intersection with biological evolution."

In describing his own writing, Gould is equally straight-forward, claiming he uses "Darwin's evolutionary perspective as an antidote to our cosmic arrogance." In other words, Gould wants us to understand that humanity is not necessarily the ultimate goal of evolution. In fact, our presence and current domination of earth is more chance than purpose, more luck than destiny. The revolutionary ideas of Copernicus and Freud served comparable decentering and humbling functions, demonstrating that we are neither the center of the universe nor complete masters of our own actions.

Gould is a devoted scientist who reveals the power and the limitations of his profession; an insider who cares about the scientific ideas of those of us on the outside. His column demystifies science which he holds is neither magic nor religion. It is a human activity, accessible to all educated people, its findings subject to the same cultural pressures as literature and philosophy. There should really be nothing surprising about this, but science has operated in a privileged sphere for so long we easily forget that scientists can be as disturbed or myopic as anyone else. Gould's essays show us that very little that we do is free from the subjectivity of emotion and opinion. All of us reflect the values of our time, the limitations of our place. The myth of objectivity is, then, one of Gould's favorite targets, as are biological theories past and present that exploit science to justify the social superiority of one group over another.

In *Ever Since Darwin,* the strength of this opposition to biological determinism is most obvious in "Racist Arguments and IQ," the first of his four essays collected here. Gould is a master at argumentation. A study of his shrewd and vigorous method will indicate that Gould has carefully arranged his evidence while also paying attention to the psychology involved in trying to be persuasive to alert readers. "The Criminal as Nature's Mistake . . ." is also from this collection and also uses argumentation to drive home one of his favorite themes: the unmasking of famous scientists who impose their social prejudice on scientific studies passed off as the height of objectivity.

These themes are developed in more detail in two essays that explore further the connections between science and politics. In the anthologies, *Hen's Teeth and Horse's Toes* (1983), and *The Panda's Thumb* (1982), Gould is clearly angered and saddened both by the sexism of early experiments that demonstrated the innate superiority of white, middle-class males, and the distortions of "scientific creationism." In "Women's Brains," Gould does some historical research to unravel the theory and practice of the now discredited science of craniometry, an inquiry which measured intelligence by the size of the skull and the weight of the brain. It is shocking for some readers to see how an apparently meticulous science, one that seemed "particularly invulnerable to refutation," could, in fact, be heavily influenced by prevailing cultural assumptions; in this case, the common notion in the last century that women were intellectually inferior to men. Gould's talents as a writer are clear as he moves from explaining Broca's theories, to making contemporary connections, to making a plea to avoid biological labeling of disadvantaged groups.

As a writer and thinker, Gould is at his controversial best in "Evolution as Fact and Theory," a vigorous and learned rebuttal of certain religious fundamentalists, especially those on the evangelical right who challenge the theory of evolution. This is Gould's best-known piece. It appeared in *Discovery,* a magazine with a wider and more general audience than *Natural History.* Gould is not polite in his attack. He thinks the attempt to introduce "scientific creationism" into classrooms on an equal footing with modern biology is an issue of politics and power, not religion. He claims that dogmatism and distortion are more relevant motivators than religious feeling and that this issue is an ongoing replay of the Scopes trial of half a century ago. Because of his strong denunciation of the creationists and their methods, Gould has become one of the fundamentalists' major targets. Gould seems to enjoy this controversy, believing that the issues are important enough to step outside the ivory tower and fight for what he values. His strong social conscience makes him think he owes it to the integrity of science and the continuation of the separation of church and state.

There is no denying that Gould makes his readers think. He is always calling into question ideas we take for granted, ideas that form the backbone of Western thought. For example, there is a popular version of evolution that holds that we are invariably evolving into ever higher beings, that we are evolving for positive reasons, toward harmony and order, that progress is inevitable. It is hard not to believe in this optimistic account. But Gould boldly asserts that evolution has no purpose or direction or meaning. He teaches us that science provides facts, but we interpret, and that purpose and meaning are, therefore, in the eye of the beholder.

Since truth in this view is a social construct, Gould gives us not only a crucial insight, he gives us authority and responsibility. For finally that's what these essays are all about: the need for educated people to be involved, to understand that science is fallible, to be active inquiring citizens, and not to abdicate our opinions to those who claim that objectivity and truth are all theirs.

Racist Arguments and IQ

1   Louis Agassiz, the greatest biologist of mid-nineteenth-century America, argued that God had created blacks and whites as separate species. The defenders of slavery took much comfort from this assertion, for biblical prescriptions of charity and equality did not have to extend across a species boundary. What could an abolitionist say? Science had shone its cold and dispassionate light upon the subject; Christian hope and sentimentality could not refute it.

2   Similar arguments, carrying the apparent sanction of science, have been continually invoked in attempts to equate egalitarianism with sentimental hope and emotional blindness. People who are unaware of this historical pattern tend to accept each recurrence at face value: that is, they assume that each statement arises from the "data" actually presented, rather than from the social conditions that truly inspire it.

3   The racist arguments of the nineteenth century were based primarily on craniometry, the measurement of human skulls. Today, these

contentions stand totally discredited. What craniometry was to the nineteenth century, intelligence testing has been to the twentieth. The victory of the eugenics movement in the Immigration Restriction Act of 1924 signaled its first unfortunate effect—for the severe restrictions upon non-European and upon southern and eastern Europeans gained much support from results of the first extensive and uniform application of intelligence tests in America—the Army Mental Tests of World War I. These tests were engineered and administered by psychologist Robert M. Yerkes, who concluded that "education alone will not place the negro [sic] race on a par with its Caucasian competitors." It is now clear that Yerkes and his colleagues knew no way to separate genetic from environmental components in postulating causes for different performances on the tests.

4   The latest episode of this recurring drama began in 1969, when Arthur Jensen published an article entitled, "How Much Can We Boost IQ and Scholastic Achievement?" in the *Harvard Educational Review*. Again, the claim went forward that new and uncomfortable information had come to light, and that science had to speak the "truth" even if it refuted some cherished notions of a liberal philosophy. But again, I shall argue, Jensen had no new data; and what he did present was flawed beyond repair by inconsistencies and illogical claims.

5   Jensen assumes that IQ tests adequately measure something we may call "intelligence." He then attempts to tease apart the genetic and environmental factors causing differences in performance. He does this primarily by relying upon the one natural experiment we possess: identical twins reared apart—for differences in IQ between genetically identical people can only be environmental. The average difference in IQ for identical twins is less than the difference for two unrelated individuals raised in similarly varied environments. From the data on twins, Jensen obtains an estimate of environmental influence. He concludes that IQ has a heritability of about 0.8 (or 80 percent) *within* the population of American and European whites. The average difference between American whites and blacks is 15 IQ points (one standard deviation). He asserts that this difference is too large to attribute to environment, given the high heritability of IQ. Lest anyone think that Jensen writes in the tradition of abstract scholarship, I merely quote the first line of his famous work: "Compensatory education has been tried, and it apparently has failed."

6   I believe that this argument can be refuted in a "hierarchical" fashion—that is, we can discredit it at one level and then show that it

fails at a more inclusive level even if we allow Jensen's argument for the first two levels:

7   Level 1: The equation of IQ with intelligence. Who knows what IQ measures? It is a good predictor of "success" in school, but is such success a result of intelligence, apple polishing, or the assimilation of values that the leaders of society prefer? Some psychologists get around this argument by defining intelligence operationally as the scores attained on "intelligence" tests. A neat trick. But at this point, the technical definition of intelligence has strayed so far from the vernacular that we can no longer define the issue. But let me allow (although I don't believe it), for the sake of argument, that IQ measures some meaningful aspect of intelligence in its vernacular sense.

8   Level 2: The heritability of IQ. Here again, we encounter a confusion between vernacular and technical meanings of the same word. "Inherited," to a layman, means "fixed," "inexorable," or "unchangeable." To a geneticist, "inherited" refers to an estimate of similarity between related individuals based on genes held in common. It carries no implications of inevitability or of immutable entities beyond the reach of environmental influence. Eyeglasses correct a variety of inherited problems in vision; insulin can check diabetes.

9   Jensen insists that IQ is 80 percent heritable. Princeton psychologist Leon J. Kamin has done the dog-work of meticulously checking through details of the twin studies that form the basis of this estimate. He has found an astonishing number of inconsistencies and downright inaccuracies. For example, the late Sir Cyril Burt, who generated the largest body of data on identical twins reared apart, pursued his studies of intelligence for more than forty years. Although he increased his sample sizes in a variety of "improved" versions, some of his correlation coefficients remain unchanged to the third decimal place—a statistically impossible situation.* IQ depends in part upon sex and age; and other studies did not standardize properly for them. An improper correction may produce higher values between twins not because they hold genes for intelligence in common, but simply because they share the same sex and age. The data are so flawed that no valid estimate for the heritability

---

*I wrote this essay in 1974. Since then, the case against Sir Cyril has progressed from an inference of carelessness to a spectacular (and well-founded) suspicion of fraud. Reporters for the London *Times* have discovered, for example, that Sir Cyril's coauthors (for the infamous twin studies) apparently did not exist outside his imagination. In the light of Kamin's discoveries, one must suspect that the data have an equal claim to reality.

of IQ can be drawn at all. But let me assume (although no data support it), for the sake of argument, that the heritability of IQ is as high as 0.8.

10   Level 3: The confusion of within- and between-group variation. Jensen draws a causal connection between his two major assertions— that the within-group heritability of IQ is 0.8 for American whites, and that the mean difference in IQ between American blacks and whites is 15 points. He assumes that the black "deficit" is largely genetic in origin because IQ is so highly heritable. This is a *non sequitur* of the worst possible kind—for there is no necessary relationship between heritability within a group and differences in mean values of two separate groups.

11   A simple example will suffice to illustrate this flaw in Jensen's argument. Height has a much higher heritability within groups than anyone has ever claimed for IQ. Suppose that height has a mean value of five feet two inches and a heritability of 0.9 (a realistic value) within a group of nutritionally deprived Indian farmers. High heritability simply means that short farmers will tend to have short offspring, and tall farmers tall offspring. It says nothing whatever against the possibility that proper nutrition could raise the mean height to six feet (taller than average white Americans). It only means that, in this improved status, farmers shorter than average (they may now be five feet ten inches) would still tend to have shorter than average children.

12   I do not claim that intelligence, however defined, has no genetic basis—I regard it as trivially true, uninteresting, and unimportant that it does. The expression of any trait represents a complex interaction of heredity and environment. Our job is simply to provide the best environmental situation for the realization of valued potential in all individuals. I merely point out that a specific claim purporting to demonstrate a mean genetic deficiency in the intelligence of American blacks rests upon no new facts whatever and can cite no valid data in its support. It is just as likely that blacks have a genetic advantage over whites. And, either way, it doesn't matter a damn. An individual can't be judged by his group mean.

13   If current biological determinism in the study of human intelligence rests upon no new facts (actually, no facts at all), then why has it become so popular of late? The answer must be social and political. The 1960s were good years for liberalism; a fair amount of money was spent on poverty programs and relatively little happened. Enter new leaders and new priorities. Why didn't the earlier programs work? Two possibilities are open: (1) we didn't spend enough money, we didn't make sufficiently creative efforts, or (and this makes any established

leader jittery) we cannot solve these problems without a fundamental social and economic transformation of society; or (2) the programs failed because their recipients are inherently what they are—blaming the victims. Now, which alternative will be chosen by men in power in an age of retrenchment?

14   I have shown, I hope, that biological determinism is not simply an amusing matter for clever cocktail party comments about the human animal. It is a general notion with important philosophical implications and major political consequences. As John Stuart Mill wrote, in a statement that should be the motto of the opposition: "Of all the vulgar modes of escaping from the consideration of the effect of social and moral influences upon the human mind, the most vulgar is that of attributing the diversities of conduct and character to inherent natural differences."

QUESTIONS

Ideas

1. Why does Gould equate craniometry with intelligence testing? Is Gould suggesting (see paragraph 2) that certain social conditions inspire scientists to come to conclusions not necessarily supported by the data?

2. In paragraph 3, does Gould give evidence for calling nineteenth-century arguments "racist"?

3. Theorists of argument often suggest that the writer first present the opposition's side as fairly as possible before attacking it. Do you think Gould has followed this suggestion?

4. The writer of a successful argument is supposed to provide a specific refutation to the opposition's best argument. Does Gould do an adequate job here? Describe his method.

5. Why is Gould so opposed to "biological determinism"? Are you?

Organization

6. Would this essay be more or less effective if he began with the last paragraph? Can you suggest alternative ways for Gould to arrange his data?

7. One way to structure a paragraph is first to ask a question and then answer it. Evaluate the effectiveness of this method in paragraph 3. Describe one other technique Gould uses.

Sentences

8. Go through the essay and find sentences that begin with the conjunctions "and" or "but." Do you find them effective? Could they have been joined to preceding sentences?

9. Gould intends some of his questions to be answered by the reader; others are rhetorical, intended only for dramatic effect. Find examples of both. Are they effective devices?

Words

10. Much of the controversy here hinges on the meaning of "intelligence" and "inherited." What is intended by the vernacular and technical meanings of these terms? Is there a real meaning to these words?

11. Why does Gould put a "sic" after "negro" in paragraph 3? Why does he put quotes around "improved" in paragraph 9, and "data" in paragraph 2? Is Gould's use of "damn" in paragraph 12 effective?

Suggestions for Writing

A. Based on some research in the library, write an extended definition of determinism, using concrete examples.

B. Look up the issue of the *Harvard Educational Review* (1969) that Gould cites in paragraph 4, and based on your reading of Gould's attack, write a letter to the editors of this journal expressing your opinion.

The Criminal as Nature's Mistake, or the Ape in Some of Us

1   W.S. Gilbert directed his potent satire at all forms of pretension as he saw them. For the most part we continue to applaud him: pompous peers and affected poets are still legitimate targets. But Gilbert was a comfortable Victorian at heart, and much that he labeled as pretentious now strikes us as enlightened—higher education for women, in particular.

> A women's college! maddest folly going!
> What can girls learn within its walls worth knowing?

2   In *Princess Ida*, the Professor of Humanities at Castle Adamant provides a biological justification for her proposition that "man is nature's sole mistake." She tells the tale of an ape who loved a beautiful woman. To win her affection, he tried to dress and act like a gentleman, but all necessarily in vain, for

> Darwinian Man, though well-behaved,
> At best is only a monkey shaved!

3   Gilbert produced *Princess Ida* in 1884, eight years after an Italian physician, Cesare Lombroso, had initiated one of the most powerful social movements of his time with a similar claim made in all seriousness about a group of men—born criminals are essentially apes living in our midst. Later in life, Lombroso recalled his moment of revelation:

> In 1870 I was carrying on for several months researches in the prisons and asylums of Pavia upon cadavers and living persons, in order to determine upon substantial differences between the insane and criminals, without succeeding very well. Suddenly, the morning of a gloomy day in December, I found in the skull of a brigand a very long series of atavistic anomalies. . . . The problem of the nature and of the origin of the criminal seemed to me resolved; the characters of primitive men and of inferior animals must be reproduced in our times.

4   Biological theories of criminality were scarcely new, but Lombroso gave the argument a novel, evolutionary twist. Born criminals are not simply deranged or diseased; they are, literally, throwbacks to a previous evolutionary stage. The hereditary characters of our primitive and apish ancestors remain in our genetic repertoire. Some unfortunate men are born with an unusually large number of these ancestral characters. Their behavior may have been appropriate in savage societies of the past; today, we brand it as criminal. We may pity the born criminal, for he cannot help himself; but we cannot tolerate his actions. (Lombroso believed that about 40 percent of criminals fell into this category of innate biology—born criminals. Others committed misdeeds from greed, jealousy, extreme anger, and so on—criminals of occasion.)

5   I tell this tale for three reasons that combine to make it far more than an antiquarian exercise in a small corner of forgotten, late-nineteenth-century history.

6   1. A generalization about social history: It illustrates the enormous influence of evolutionary theory in fields far removed from its biological core. Even the most abstract scientists are not free agents. Major ideas have remarkably subtle and far-ranging extensions. The inhabitants of a nuclear world should know this perfectly well, but many scientists have yet to get the message.

7   2. A political point: Appeals to innate biology for the explanation of human behavior have often been advanced in the name of enlightenment. The proponents of biological determinism argue that science can cut through a web of superstition and sentimentalism to instruct us about our true nature. But their claims have usually had a different primary effect: they are used by the leaders of class-stratified societies to assert that a current social order must prevail because it is the law of nature. Of course, no view should be rejected because we dislike its implications. Truth, as we understand it, must be the primary criterion. But the claims of determinists have always turned out to be prejudiced speculation, not ascertained fact—and Lombroso's criminal anthropology is the finest example I know.

8   3. A contemporary note: Lombroso's brand of criminal anthropology is dead, but its basic postulate lives on in popular notions of criminal genes or chromosomes. These modern incarnations are worth about as much as Lombroso's original version. Their hold on our attention only illustrates the unfortunate appeal of biological determinism in our continuing attempt to exonerate a society in which so many of us flourish by blaming the victim.

9   The year 1976 marked the centenary of Lombroso's founding document—later enlarged into the famous *L'uomo delinquente (Criminal Man)*. Lombroso begins with a series of anecdotes to assert that the usual behavior of lower animals is criminal by our standards. Animals murder to suppress revolts; they eliminate sexual rivals; they kill from rage (an ant, made impatient by a recalcitrant aphid, killed and devoured it); they form criminal associations (three communal beavers shared a territory with a solitary individual; the trio visited their neighbor and were well treated; when the loner returned the visit, he was killed for his solicitude). Lombroso even brands the fly catching of insectivorous plants as an "equivalent of crime" (although I fail to see how it differs from any other form of eating).

10   In the next section, Lombroso examines the anatomy of criminals
and finds the physical signs (stigmata) of their primitive status as throwbacks to our evolutionary past. Since he has already defined the normal
behavior of animals as criminal, the actions of these living primitives
must arise from their nature. The apish features of born criminals
include relatively long arms, prehensile feet with mobile big toes, low
and narrow forehead, large ears, thick skull, large and prognathous jaw,
copious hair on the male chest, and diminished sensitivity to pain. But
the throwbacks do not stop at the primate level. Large canine teeth and
a flat palate recall a more distant mammalian past. Lombroso even
compares the heightened facial asymmetry of born criminals with the
normal condition of flatfishes (both eyes on one side of the head)!

11   But the stigmata are not only physical. The social behavior of the
born criminal also allies him with apes and living human savages. Lombroso placed special emphasis on tattooing, a common practice among
primitive tribes and European criminals. He produced voluminous statistics on the content of criminal tattoos and found them lewd, lawless,
or exculpating (although one read, he had to admit, *Vive la France et
les pommes de terres frites*—"long live France and french fried
potatoes"). In criminal slang, he found a language of its own, markedly
similar to the speech of savage tribes in such features as onomatopoeia
and personification of inanimate objects: "They speak differently because they feel differently; they speak like savages, because they are true
savages in the midst of our brilliant European civilization."

12   Lombroso's theory was no work of abstract science. He founded
and actively led an international school of "criminal anthropology" that
spearheaded one of the most influential of late-nineteenth-century social
movements. Lombroso's "positive," or "new," school campaigned vigor-
ously for changes in law enforcement and penal practices. They regarded
their improved criteria for the recognition of born criminals as a primary
contribution to law enforcement. Lombroso even suggested a preventive
criminology—society need not wait (and suffer) for the act itself, for
physical and social stigmata define the potential criminal. He can be
identified (in early childhood), watched, and whisked away at the first
manifestation of his irrevocable nature (Lombroso, a liberal, favored
exile rather than death). Enrico Ferri, Lombroso's closest colleague,
recommended that "tattooing, anthropometry, physiognomy . . . reflex
activity, vasomotor reactions [criminals, he argued, do not blush], and
the range of sight" be used as criteria of judgment by magistrates.

13   Criminal anthropologists also campaigned for a basic reform in

penal practice. An antiquated Christian ethic held that criminals should be sentenced for their deeds, but biology declares that they should be judged by their nature. Fit the punishment to the criminal, not to the crime. Criminals of occasion, lacking the stigmata and capable of reform, should be jailed for the term necessary to secure their amendment. But born criminals are condemned by their nature: "Theoretical ethics passes over the diseased brain, as oil does over marble, without penetrating it." Lombroso recommended irrevocable detention for life (in pleasant, but isolated surroundings) for any recidivist with the telltale stigmata. Some of his colleagues were less generous. An influential jurist wrote to Lombroso:

> You have shown us fierce and lubricious orang-utans with human faces. It is evident that as such they cannot act otherwise. If they ravish, steal, and kill, it is by virtue of their own nature and their past, but there is all the more reason for destroying them when it has been proved that they will always remain orang-utans.

14   And Lombroso himself did not rule out the "final solution":

> The fact that there exist such beings as born criminals, organically fitted for evil, atavistic reproductions, not simply of savage men but even of the fiercest animals, far from making us more compassionate towards them, as has been maintained, steels us against all pity.

15   One other social impact of Lombroso's school should be mentioned. If human savages, like born criminals, retained apish traits, then primitive tribes—"lesser breeds without the law"—could be regarded as essentially criminal. Thus, criminal anthropology provided a powerful argument for racism and imperialism at the height of European colonial expansion. Lombroso, in noting a reduced sensitivity to pain among criminals, wrote:

> Their physical insensibility well recalls that of savage peoples who can bear in rites of puberty, tortures that a white man could never endure. All travelers know the indifference of Negroes and American savages to pain: the former cut their hands and laugh in order to avoid work; the latter, tied to the torture post, gaily sing the praises of their tribe while they are slowly burnt. [You can't beat a racist a priori. Think of how many Western heroes died bravely in excruciating pain—Saint Joan burned, Saint Sebastian transfixed with arrows, other martyrs racked, drawn, and

quartered. But when an Indian fails to scream and beg for mercy, it can only mean that he doesn't feel the pain.]

16   If Lombroso and his colleagues had been a dedicated group of proto-Nazis, we could dismiss the whole phenomenon as a ploy of conscious demagogues. It would then convey no other message than a plea for vigilance against ideologues who misuse science. But the leaders of criminal anthropology were "enlightened" socialists and social democrats who viewed their theory as the spearhead for a rational, scientific society based on human realities. The genetic determination of criminal action, Lombroso argued, is simply the law of nature and of evolution:

> We are governed by silent laws which never cease to operate and which rule society with more authority than the laws inscribed on our statute books. Crime appears to be a natural phenomenon . . . like birth or death.

17   In retrospect, Lombroso's scientific "reality" turned out to be his social prejudice imposed before the fact upon a supposedly objective study. His notions condemned many innocent people to a prejudgment that often worked as a self-fulfilling prophecy. His attempt to understand human behavior by mapping an innate potential displayed in our anatomy served only to work against social reform by placing all blame upon a criminal's inheritance.

18   Of course, no one takes the claims of Lombroso seriously today. His statistics were faulty beyond belief; only a blind faith in inevitable conclusions could have led to his fudging and finagling. Besides, no one would look to long arms and jutting jaws today as signs of inferiority; modern determinists seek a more fundamental marker in genes and chromosomes.

19   Much has happened in the 100 years between *L'uomo delinquente* and our Bicentennial celebrations. No serious advocate of innate criminality recommends the irrevocable detention or murder of the unfortunately afflicted or even claims that a natural penchant for criminal behavior necessarily leads to criminal action. Still, the spirit of Lombroso is very much with us. When Richard Speck murdered eight nurses in Chicago, his defense argued that he couldn't help it because he bore an extra Y chromosome. (Normal females have two X chromosomes, normal males an X and a Y. A small percentage of males have an extra Y chromosome, XYY.) This revelation inspired a rash of speculation; arti-

cles on the "criminal chromosome" inundated our popular magazines. The naïvely determinist argument had little going for it beyond the following: Males tend to be more aggressive than females; this may be genetic. If genetic, it must reside on the Y chromosome; anyone possessing two Y chromosomes has a double dose of aggressiveness and might incline to violence and criminality. But the hastily collected information on XYY males in prisons seems hopelessly ambiguous, and even Speck himself turns out to be an XY male after all. Once again, biological determinism makes a splash, creates a wave of discussion and cocktail party chatter, and then dissipates for want of evidence. Why are we so intrigued by hypotheses about innate disposition? Why do we wish to fob off responsibility for our violence and sexism upon our genes? The hallmark of humanity is not only our mental capacity but also our mental flexibility. We have made our world and we can change it.

QUESTIONS

Ideas

1. Were you surprised to learn that leading scientists of the past believed in theories "no one takes . . . seriously today"? Do you think this is an historical pattern and that future scientists will find our ideas bizarre?

2. In several of his essays Gould points out examples of scientists who use supposedly objective data to "blame the victim." Explain how Gould thinks Cesare Lombroso does this. Can you think of other examples, either historical or contemporary?

3. According to Gould, what does cause criminal behavior?

4. Gould's last sentence indicates a strong belief in the power of free will. What in Lombroso's theories of criminality work against this belief? Do you think contemporary ideas about crime stress free will or determinism?

Organization

5. If the heart of this essay is an explanation of Lombroso's theories, why does Gould take eight paragraphs to get started; in other words, what is the function of Gould's introduction?

6. Describe the movement of Gould's last paragraph. Is there a connection between the first and last sentence? What is the purpose of the Speck anecdote?

Sentences

7. Describe how Gould constructs the first sentence in paragraphs 6, 7, and 8.

8. Gould's first sentence in paragraph 1 follows the common pattern of subject, verb, object. Look at the next dozen sentences. How does he vary this conventional sequence? When does he get back to it?

9. From context clues what do you think the following words or phrases mean? "comfortable Victorian" (paragraph 1); "atavistic anomalies" (paragraph 3); "genetic repertoire" (paragraph 4); "naively determinist" (paragraph 9); "prejudiced speculation" (paragraph 7); "facial asymmetry" (paragraph 10); "self-fulfilling prophecy" (paragraph 17).

10. Write synonymns for these phrases for a junior high audience.

Suggestions for Writing

A. Try to write a response to the questions Gould asks at the end of paragraph 19. Imagine a series of possible answers.

B. Imagine that you could send a letter to Lombroso through a time machine. Explain to him what scientists now think of his theories and what ideas have taken the place of *L'uomo delinquente.*

Women's Brains

1   In the prelude to *Middlemarch,* George Eliot lamented the unfulfilled lives of talented women:

> Some have felt that these blundering lives are due to the inconvenient indefiniteness with which the Supreme Power has fashioned the natures of women: if there were one level of feminine incompetence as strict as the ability to count three and no more, the social lot of women might be treated with scientific certitude.

2   Eliot goes on to discount the idea of innate limitation, but while she wrote in 1872, the leaders of European anthropometry were trying to measure "with scientific certitude" the inferiority of women. Anthropometry, or measurement of the human body, is not so fashionable a field these days, but it dominated the human sciences for much of the

nineteenth century and remained popular until intelligence testing replaced skull measurement as a favored device for making invidious comparisons among races, classes, and sexes. Craniometry, or measurement of the skull, commanded the most attention and respect. Its unquestioned leader, Paul Broca (1824–80), professor of clinical surgery at the Faculty of Medicine in Paris, gathered a school of disciples and imitators around himself. Their work, so meticulous and apparently irrefutable, exerted great influence and won high esteem as a jewel of nineteenth-century science.

3   Broca's work seemed particularly invulnerable to refutation. Had he not measured with the most scrupulous care and accuracy? (Indeed, he had. I have the greatest respect for Broca's meticulous procedure. His numbers are sound. But science is an inferential exercise, not a catalog of facts. Numbers, by themselves, specify nothing. All depends upon what you do with them.) Broca depicted himself as an apostle of objectivity, a man who bowed before facts and cast aside superstition and sentimentality. He declared that "there is no faith, however respectable, no interest, however legitimate, which must not accommodate itself to the progress of human knowledge and bend before truth." Women, like it or not, had smaller brains than men and, therefore, could not equal them in intelligence. This fact, Broca argued, may reinforce a common prejudice in male society, but it is also a scientific truth. L. Manouvrier, a black sheep in Broca's fold, rejected the inferiority of women and wrote with feeling about the burden imposed upon them by Broca's numbers:

> Women displayed their talents and their diplomas. They also invoked philosophical authorities. But they were opposed by *numbers* unknown to Condorcet or to John Stuart Mill. These numbers fell upon poor women like a sledge hammer, and they were accompanied by commentaries and sarcasms more ferocious than the most misogynist imprecations of certain church fathers. The theologians had asked if women had a soul. Several centuries later, some scientists were ready to refuse them a human intelligence.

4   Broca's argument rested upon two sets of data: the larger brains of men in modern societies, and a supposed increase in male superiority through time. His most extensive data came from autopsies performed personally in four Parisian hospitals. For 292 male brains, he calculated an average weight of 1,325 grams; 140 female brains averaged 1,144

grams for a difference of 181 grams, or 14 percent of the male weight. Broca understood, of course, that part of this difference could be attributed to the greater height of males. Yet he made no attempt to measure the effect of size alone and actually stated that it cannot account for the entire difference because we know, a priori, that women are not as intelligent as men (a premise that the data were supposed to test, not rest upon):

> We might ask if the small size of the female brain depends exclusively upon the small size of her body. Tiedemann has proposed this explanation. But we must not forget that women are, on the average, a little less intelligent than men, a difference which we should not exaggerate but which is, nonetheless, real. We are therefore permitted to suppose that the relatively small size of the female brain depends in part upon her physical inferiority and in part upon her intellectual inferiority.

5   In 1873, the year after Eliot published *Middlemarch*, Broca measured the cranial capacities of prehistoric skulls from L'Homme Mort cave. Here he found a difference of only 99.5 cubic centimeters between males and females, while modern populations range from 129.5 to 220.7. Topinard, Broca's chief disciple, explained the increasing discrepancy through time as a result of differing evolutionary pressures upon dominant men and passive women:

> The man who fights for two or more in the struggle for existence, who has all the responsibility and the cares of tomorrow, who is constantly active in combating the environment and human rivals, needs more brain than the woman whom he must protect and nourish, the sedentary woman, lacking any interior occupations, whose role is to raise children, love, and be passive.

6   In 1879, Gustave Le Bon, chief misogynist of Broca's school, used these data to publish what must be the most vicious attack upon women in modern scientific literature (no one can top Aristotle). I do not claim his views were representative of Broca's school, but they were published in France's most respected anthropological journal. Le Bon concluded:

> In the most intelligent races, as among the Parisians, there are a large number of women whose brains are closer in size to those of gorillas than to the most developed male brains. This inferiority is so obvious that no one can contest it for a moment; only its degree is worth discussion. All

psychologists who have studied the intelligence of women, as well as poets and novelists, recognize today that they represent the most inferior forms of human evolution and that they are closer to children and savages than to an adult, civilized man. They excel in fickleness, inconstancy, absence of thought and logic, and incapacity to reason. Without doubt there exist some distinguished women, very superior to the average man, but they are as exceptional as the birth of any monstrosity, as, for example, of a gorilla with two heads; consequently, we may neglect them entirely.

7   Nor did Le Bon shrink from the social implications of his views. He was horrified by the proposal of some American reformers to grant women higher education on the same basis as men:

A desire to give them the same education, and, as a consequence, to propose the same goals for them, is a dangerous chimera. . . . The day when, misunderstanding the inferior occupations which nature has given her, women leave the home and take part in our battles; on this day a social revolution will begin, and everything that maintains the sacred ties of the family will disappear.

Sound familiar?

8   I have reexamined Broca's data, the basis for all this derivative pronouncement, and I find his numbers sound but his interpretation ill-founded, to say the least. The data supporting his claim for increased difference through time can be easily dismissed. Broca based his contention on the samples from L'Homme Mort alone—only seven male and six female skulls in all. Never have so little data yielded such far ranging conclusions.

9   In 1888, Topinard published Broca's more extensive data on the Parisian hospitals. Since Broca recorded height and age as well as brain size, we may use modern statistics to remove their effect. Brain weight decreases with age, and Broca's women were, on average, considerably older than his men. Brain weight increases with height, and his average man was almost half a foot taller than his average woman. I used multiple regression, a technique that allowed me to assess simultaneously the influence of height and age upon brain size. In an analysis of the data for women, I found that, at average male height and age, a woman's brain would weigh 1,212 grams. Correction for height and age reduces Broca's measured difference of 181 grams by more than a third, to 113 grams.

10   I don't know what to make of this remaining difference because
I cannot assess other factors known to influence brain size in a major
way. Cause of death has an important effect: degenerative disease often
entails a substantial diminution of brain size. (This effect is separate
from the decrease attributed to age alone.) Eugene Schreider, also working with Broca's data, found that men killed in accidents had brains
weighing, on average, 60 grams more than men dying of infectious
diseases. The best modern data I can find (from American hospitals)
records a full 100-gram difference between death by degenerative arteri-
osclerosis and by violence or accident. Since so many of Broca's subjects
were very elderly women, we may assume that lengthy degenerative
disease was more common among them than among the men.

11   More importantly, modern students of brain size still have not
agreed on a proper measure for eliminating the powerful effect of body
size. Height is partly adequate, but men and women of the same height
do not share the same body build. Weight is even worse than height,
because most of its variation reflects nutrition rather than intrinsic size
—fat versus skinny exerts little influence upon the brain. Manouvrier
took up this subject in the 1880s and argued that muscular mass and
force should be used. He tried to measure this elusive property in various
ways and found a marked difference in favor of men, even in men and
women of the same height. When he corrected for what he called
"sexual mass," women actually came out slightly ahead in brain size.

12   Thus, the corrected 113-gram difference is surely too large; the
true figure is probably close to zero and may as well favor women as men.
And 113 grams, by the way, is exactly the average difference between
a 5 foot 4 inch and a 6 foot 4 inch male in Broca's data. We would not
(especially us short folks) want to ascribe greater intelligence to tall men.
In short, who knows what to do with Broca's data? They certainly don't
permit any confident claim that men have bigger brains than women.

13   To appreciate the social role of Broca and his school, we must
recognize that his statements about the brains of women do not reflect
an isolated prejudice toward a single disadvantaged group. They must
be weighed in the context of a general theory that supported contemporary social distinctions as biologically ordained. Women, blacks, and
poor people suffered the same disparagement, but women bore the brunt
of Broca's argument because he had easier access to data on women's
brains. Women were singularly denigrated but they also stood as surrogates for other disenfranchised groups. As one of Broca's disciples wrote
in 1881: "Men of the black races have a brain scarcely heavier than that

of white women." This juxtaposition extended into many other realms of anthropological argument, particularly to claims that, anatomically and emotionally, both women and blacks were like white children—and that white children, by the theory of recapitulation, represented an ancestral (primitive) adult stage of human evolution. I do not regard as empty rhetoric the claim that women's battles are for all of us.

14 Maria Montessori did not confine her activities to educational reform for young children. She lectured on anthropology for several years at the University of Rome, and wrote an influential book entitled *Pedagogical Anthropology* (English edition, 1913). Montessori was no egalitarian. She supported most of Broca's work and the theory of innate criminality proposed by her compatriot Cesare Lombroso. She measured the circumference of children's heads in her schools and inferred that the best prospects had bigger brains. But she had no use for Broca's conclusions about women. She discussed Manouvrier's work at length and made much of his tentative claim that women, after proper correction of the data, had slightly larger brains than men. Women, she concluded, were intellectually superior, but men had prevailed heretofore by dint of physical force. Since technology has abolished force as an instrument of power, the era of women may soon be upon us: "In such an epoch there will really be superior human beings, there will really be men strong in morality and in sentiment. Perhaps in this way the reign of women is approaching, when the enigma of her anthropological superiority will be deciphered. Woman was always the custodian of human sentiment, morality and honor."

15 This represents one possible antidote to "scientific" claims for the constitutional inferiority of certain groups. One may affirm the validity of biological distinctions but argue that the data have been misinterpreted by prejudiced men with a stake in the outcome, and that disadvantaged groups are truly superior. In recent years, Elaine Morgan has followed this strategy in her *Descent of Woman,* a speculative reconstruction of human prehistory from the woman's point of view—and as farcical as more famous tall tales by and for men.

16 I prefer another strategy. Montessori and Morgan followed Broca's philosophy to reach a more congenial conclusion. I would rather label the whole enterprise of setting a biological value upon groups for what it is: irrelevant and highly injurious. George Eliot well appreciated the special tragedy that biological labeling imposed upon members of disadvantaged groups. She expressed it for people like herself—women of extraordinary talent. I would apply it more widely—not only to those

whose dreams are flouted but also to those who never realize that they may dream—but I cannot match her prose. In conclusion, then, the rest of Eliot's prelude to *Middlemarch:*

> The limits of variation are really much wider than anyone would imagine from the sameness of women's coiffure and the favorite love stories in prose and verse. Here and there a cygnet is reared uneasily among the ducklings in the brown pond, and never finds the living stream in fellowship with its own oary-footed kind. Here and there is born a Saint Theresa, foundress of nothing, whose loving heartbeats and sobs after an unattained goodness tremble off and are dispersed among hindrances instead of centering in some long-recognizable deed.

QUESTIONS

Ideas

1. In the parenthetical sentences in paragraph 3, Gould claims that science "is an inferential exercise, not a catalog of facts." Is this what you have been taught in your science class?

2. At the end of paragraph 4, Gould places another important observation in parentheses. What do you understand by this comment about basing conclusions on *a priori* (before examination) assumptions? Do you think this happens in science today?

3. When Gould writes "Sound familiar?" at the end of paragraph 7, what do you think he has in mind?

4. How do you interpret Gould's statement in the last sentence of paragraph 13?

5. What conclusion about women's brains does Gould finally arrive at?

6. Gould assumes he is writing for an audience that shares his values. Look, for example, at the second sentence in paragraph 2. Do you think intelligence testing is a way of making harmful comparisions among races? Find other comments like this that indicate Gould's strong opinions.

Organization

7. Gould begins and ends this essay with quotes from *Middlemarch.* What point is made in each quote?

8. In arranging his argument, Gould first describes Broca's work on skull measurement. In paragraph 8 Gould begins a new phase of his attack on

craniometry. Describe what he attempts to do in this paragraph and where his argument then goes.

9. What role does Montessori play in the structure of Gould's argument?

Sentences

10. Read the two passages from George Eliot out loud. Do they sound different than the sentences of Gould in, say, paragraph 14? Try to describe why.

11. Gould uses parentheses and dashes throughout this piece. Locate examples of each. What purpose do they serve? Are there effective alternatives?

Words

12. What do the following words mean in their contexts: "invidious" (paragraph 2); "disparagement" (paragraph 13); "surrogates" (paragraph 13); "juxtaposition" (paragraph 13); "rhetoric" (paragraph 13); "scientific" (paragraph 15); "farcical" (paragraph 15).

13. Paraphrase Eliot's opening quote (paragraph 1), using words a sixth-grader would easily understand.

Suggestions for Writing

A. From your own contemporary perspective, write a letter in response to the Gustave Le Bon excerpt in paragraph 6.

B. From your own experiences, opinions, and feelings write a position paper for or against the Le Bon quote in paragraph 7.

Evolution as Fact and Theory

---

1   Kirtley Mather, who died last year at age ninety, was a pillar of both science and Christian religion in America and one of my dearest friends. The difference of a half-century in our ages evaporated before our common interests. The most curious thing we shared was a battle we each fought at the same age. For Kirtley had gone to Tennessee with Clarence Darrow to testify for evolution at the Scopes trial of 1925. When I think that we are enmeshed again in the same struggle for one of the best documented, most compelling and exciting concepts in all of science, I don't know whether to laugh or cry.

2   According to idealized principles of scientific discourse, the arousal of dormant issues should reflect fresh data that give renewed life to abandoned notions. Those outside the current debate may therefore be excused for suspecting that creationists have come up with something new, or that evolutionists have generated some serious internal trouble. But nothing has changed; the creationists have presented not a single new fact or argument. Darrow and Bryan were at least more entertaining than we lesser antagonists today. The rise of creationism is politics, pure and simple; it represents one issue (and by no means the major concern) of the resurgent evangelical right. Arguments that seemed kooky just a decade ago have reentered the mainstream.

3   The basic attack of modern creationists falls apart on two general counts before we even reach the supposed factual details of their assault against evolution. First, they play upon a vernacular misunderstanding of the word "theory" to convey the false impression that we evolutionists are covering up the rotten core of our edifice. Second, they misuse a popular philosophy of science to argue that they are behaving scientifically in attacking evolution. Yet the same philosophy demonstrates that their own belief is not science, and that "scientific creationism" is a meaningless and self-contradictory phrase, an example of what Orwell called "newspeak."

4   In the American vernacular, "theory" often means "imperfect fact"—part of a hierarchy of confidence running downhill from fact to theory to hypothesis to guess. Thus, creationists can (and do) argue: evolution is "only" a theory, and intense debate now rages about many aspects of the theory. If evolution is less than a fact, and scientists can't even make up their minds about the theory, then what confidence can we have in it? Indeed, President Reagan echoed this argument before an evangelical group in Dallas when he said (in what I devoutly hope was campaign rhetoric): "Well, it is a theory. It is a scientific theory only, and it has in recent years been challenged in the world of science —that is, not believed in the scientific community to be as infallible as it once was."

5   Well, evolution *is* a theory. It is also a fact. And facts and theories are different things, not rungs in a hierarchy of increasing certainty. Facts are the world's data. Theories are structures of ideas that explain and interpret facts. Facts do not go away while scientists debate rival theories for explaining them. Einstein's theory of gravitation replaced Newton's, but apples did not suspend themselves in mid-air pending the outcome. And human beings evolved from apelike ancestors whether

they did so by Darwin's proposed mechanism or by some other, yet to be discovered.

6   Moreover, "fact" does not mean "absolute certainty." The final proofs of logic and mathematics flow deductively from stated premises and achieve certainty only because they are *not* about the empirical world. Evolutionists make no claim for perpetual truth, though creationists often do (and then attack us for a style of argument that they themselves favor). In science, "fact" can only mean "confirmed to such a degree that it would be perverse to withhold provisional assent." I suppose that apples might start to rise tomorrow, but the possibility does not merit equal time in physics classrooms.

7   Evolutionists have been clear about this distinction between fact and theory from the very beginning, if only because we have always acknowledged how far we are from completely understanding the mechanisms (theory) by which evolution (fact) occurred. Darwin continually emphasized the difference between his two great and separate accomplishments: establishing the fact of evolution, and proposing a theory—natural selection—to explain the mechanism of evolution. He wrote in *The Descent of Man:* "I had two distinct objects in view; firstly, to show that species had not been separately created, and secondly, that natural selection had been the chief agent of change . . . Hence if I have erred in . . . having exaggerated its [natural selection's] power . . . I have at least, as I hope, done good service in aiding to overthrow the dogma of separate creations."

8   Thus Darwin acknowledged the provisional nature of natural selection while affirming the fact of evolution. The fruitful theoretical debate that Darwin initiated has never ceased. From the 1940s through the 1960s, Darwin's own theory of natural selection did achieve a temporary hegemony that it never enjoyed in his lifetime. But renewed debate characterizes our decade, and, while no biologist questions the importance of natural selection, many now doubt its ubiquity. In particular, many evolutionists argue that substantial amounts of genetic change may not be subject to natural selection and may spread through populations at random. Others are challenging Darwin's linking of natural selection with gradual, imperceptible change through all intermediary degrees; they are arguing that most evolutionary events may occur far more rapidly than Darwin envisioned.

9   Scientists regard debates on fundamental issues of theory as a sign of intellectual health and a source of excitement. Science is—and how else can I say it?—most fun when it plays with interesting ideas,

examines their implications, and recognizes that old information may
be explained in surprisingly new ways. Evolutionary theory is now enjoying this uncommon vigor. Yet amidst all this turmoil no biologist
has been led to doubt the fact that evolution occurred; we are debating *how* it happened. We are all trying to explain the same thing: the
tree of evolutionary descent linking all organisms by ties of genealogy.
Creationists pervert and caricature this debate by conveniently neglecting the common conviction that underlies it, and by falsely suggesting that we now doubt the very phenomenon we are struggling to
understand.

10   Secondly, creationists claim that "the dogma of separate creations," as Darwin characterized it a century ago, is a scientific theory
meriting equal time with evolution in high school biology curricula. But
a popular viewpoint among philosophers of science belies this creationist
argument. Philosopher Karl Popper has argued for decades that the
primary criterion of science is the falsifiability of its theories. We can
never prove absolutely, but we can falsify. A set of ideas that cannot,
in principle, be falsified is not science.

11   The entire creationist program includes little more than a rhetorical attempt to falsify evolution by presenting supposed contradictions
among its supporters. Their brand of creationism, they claim, is "scientific" because it follows the Popperian model in trying to demolish
evolution. Yet Popper's argument must apply in both directions. One
does not become a scientist by the simple act of trying to falsify a rival
and truly scientific system; one has to present an alternative system that
also meets Popper's criterion—it too must be falsifiable in principle.

12   "Scientific creationism" is a self-contradictory, nonsense phrase
precisely because it cannot be falsified. I can envision observations and
experiments that would disprove any evolutionary theory I know, but I
cannot imagine what potential data could lead creationists to abandon
their beliefs. Unbeatable systems are dogma, not science. Lest I seem
harsh or rhetorical, I quote creationism's leading intellectual, Duane
Gish, Ph.D., from his recent (1978) book, *Evolution? The Fossils Say
No!* "By creation we mean the bringing into being by a supernatural
Creator of the basic kinds of plants and animals by the process of
sudden, or fiat, creation. We do not know how the Creator created, what
processes He used, *for He used processes which are not now operating
anywhere in the natural universe* [Gish's italics]. This is why we refer to
creation as special creation. We cannot discover by scientific investigations anything about the creative processes used by the Creator." Pray

tell, Dr. Gish, in the light of your last sentence, what then is "scientific" creationism?

13　　Our confidence that evolution occurred centers upon three general arguments. First, we have abundant, direct, observational evidence of evolution in action, from both field and laboratory. This evidence ranges from countless experiments on change in nearly everything about fruit flies subjected to artificial selection in the laboratory to the famous populations of British moths that became black when industrial soot darkened the trees upon which the moths rest. (Moths gain protection from sharp-sighted bird predators by blending into the background.) Creationists do not deny these observations; how could they? Creationists have tightened their act. They now argue that God only created "basic kinds," and allowed for limited evolutionary meandering within them. Thus toy poodles and Great Danes come from the dog kind and moths can change color, but nature cannot convert a dog to a cat or a monkey to a man.

14　　The second and third arguments for evolution—the case for major changes—do not involve direct observation of evolution in action. They rest upon inference, but are no less secure for that reason. Major evolutionary change requires too much time for direct observation on the scale of recorded human history. All historical sciences rest upon inference, and evolution is no different from geology, cosmology, or human history in this respect. In principle, we cannot observe processes that operated in the past. We must infer them from results that still surround us: living and fossil organisms for evolution, documents and artifacts for human history, strata and topography for geology.

15　　The second argument—that the imperfection of nature reveals evolution—strikes many people as ironic, for they feel that evolution should be most elegantly displayed in the nearly perfect adaptation expressed by some organisms—the camber of a gull's wing, or butterflies that cannot be seen in ground litter because they mimic leaves so precisely. But perfection could be imposed by a wise creator or evolved by natural selection. Perfection covers the tracks of past history. And past history—the evidence of descent—is the mark of evolution.

16　　Evolution lies exposed in the *imperfections* that record a history of descent. Why should a rat run, a bat fly, a porpoise swim, and I type this essay with structures built of the same bones unless we all inherited them from a common ancestor? An engineer, starting from scratch, could design better limbs in each case. Why should all the large native mammals of Australia be marsupials, unless they descended from a common ancestor isolated on this island continent? Marsupials are not "better," or ideally suited for Australia; many have been wiped out by placental mammals imported by man from other continents. This principle of imperfection extends to all historical sciences. When we recognize the etymology of September, October, November, and December (seventh, eighth, ninth, and tenth), we know that the year once started in March, or that two additional months must have been added to an original calendar of ten months.

17   The third argument is more direct: transitions are often found in the fossil record. Preserved transitions are not common—and should not be, according to our understanding of evolution . . . —but they are not entirely wanting, as creationists often claim. The lower jaw of reptiles contains several bones, that of mammals only one. The non-mammalian jawbones are reduced, step by step, in mammalian ancestors until they become tiny nubbins located at the back of the jaw. The "hammer" and "anvil" bones of the mammalian ear are descendants of these nubbins. How could such a transition be accomplished? the creationists ask. Surely a bone is either entirely in the jaw or in the ear. Yet paleontologists have discovered two transitional lineages of therapsids (the so-called mammal-like reptiles) with a double jaw joint—one composed of the old quadrate and articular bones (soon to become the hammer and anvil), the other of the squamosal and dentary bones (as in modern mammals). For that matter, what better transitional form could we expect to find than the oldest human, *Australopithecus afarensis*, with its apelike palate, its human upright stance, and a cranial capacity larger than any ape's of the same body size but a full 1,000 cubic centimeters below ours? If God made each of the half-dozen human species discovered in ancient rocks, why did he create in an unbroken temporal sequence of progressively more modern features—increasing cranial capacity, reduced face and teeth, larger body size? Did he create to mimic evolution and test our faith thereby?

18   Faced with these facts of evolution and the philosophical bankruptcy of their own position, creationists rely upon distortion and innuendo to buttress their rhetorical claim. If I sound sharp or bitter, indeed I am—for I have become a major target of these practices.

19   I count myself among the evolutionists who argue for a jerky, or episodic, rather than a smoothly gradual, pace of change. In 1972 my colleague Niles Eldredge and I developed the theory of punctuated equilibrium. We argued that two outstanding facts of the fossil record —geologically "sudden" origin of new species and failure to change

thereafter (stasis)—reflect the predictions of evolutionary theory, not the imperfections of the fossil record. In most theories, small isolated populations are the source of new species, and the process of speciation takes thousands or tens of thousands of years. This amount of time, so long when measured against our lives, is a geological microsecond. It represents much less than 1 per cent of the average life-span for a fossil invertebrate species—more than ten million years. Large, widespread, and well established species, on the other hand, are not expected to change very much. We believe that the inertia of large populations explains the stasis of most fossil species over millions of years.

20   We proposed the theory of punctuated equilibrium largely to provide a different explanation for pervasive trends in the fossil record. Trends, we argued, cannot be attributed to gradual transformation within lineages, but must arise from the differential success of certain kinds of species. A trend, we argued, is more like climbing a flight of stairs (punctuations and stasis) than rolling up an inclined plane.

21   Since we proposed punctuated equilibria to explain trends, it is infuriating to be quoted again and again by creationists—whether through design or stupidity, I do not know—as admitting that the fossil record includes no transitional forms. Transitional forms are generally lacking at the species level, but they are abundant between larger groups. Yet a pamphlet entitled "Harvard Scientists Agree Evolution Is a Hoax" states: "The facts of punctuated equilibrium which Gould and Eldredge . . . are forcing Darwinists to swallow fit the picture that Bryan insisted on, and which God has revealed to us in the Bible."

22   Continuing the distortion, several creationists have equated the theory of punctuated equilibrium with a caricature of the beliefs of Richard Goldschmidt, a great early geneticist. Goldschmidt argued, in a famous book published in 1940, that new groups can arise all at once through major mutations. He referred to these suddenly transformed creatures as "hopeful monsters." (I am attracted to some aspects of the non-caricatured version, but Goldschmidt's theory still has nothing to do with punctuated equilibrium.) Creationist Luther Sunderland talks of the "punctuated equilibrium hopeful monster theory" and tells his hopeful readers that "it amounts to tacit admission that anti-evolutionists are correct in asserting there is no fossil evidence supporting the theory that all life is connected to a common ancestor." Duane Gish writes, "According to Goldschmidt, and now apparently according to Gould, a reptile laid an egg from which the first bird, feathers and all, was produced." Any evolutionist who believed such nonsense

would rightly be laughed off the intellectual stage; yet the only theory that could ever envision such a scenario for the origin of birds is creationism—with God acting in the egg.

23   I am both angry at and amused by the creationists; but mostly I am deeply sad. Sad for many reasons. Sad because so many people who respond to creationist appeals are troubled for the right reason, but venting their anger at the wrong target. It is true that scientists have often been dogmatic and elitist. It is true that we have often allowed the white-coated, advertising image to represent us—"Scientists say that Brand X cures bunions ten times faster than . . ." We have not fought it adequately because we derive benefits from appearing as a new priesthood. It is also true that faceless and bureaucratic state power intrudes more and more into our lives and removes choices that should belong to individuals and communities. I can understand that school curricula, imposed from above and without local input, might be seen as one more insult on all these grounds. But the culprit is not, and cannot be, evolution or any other fact of the natural world. Identify and fight your legitimate enemies by all means, but we are not among them.

24   I am sad because the practical result of this brouhaha will not be expanded coverage to include creationism (that would also make me sad), but the reduction or excision of evolution from high school curricula. Evolution is one of the half dozen "great ideas" developed by science. It speaks to the profound issues of genealogy that fascinate all of us—the "roots" phenomenon writ large. Where did we come from? Where did life arise? How did it develop? How are organisms related? It forces us to think, ponder, and wonder. Shall we deprive millions of this knowledge and once again teach biology as a set of dull and unconnected facts, without the thread that weaves diverse material into a supple unity?

25   But most of all I am saddened by a trend I am just beginning to discern among my colleagues. I sense that some now wish to mute the healthy debate about theory that has brought new life to evolutionary biology. It provides grist for creationist mills, they say, even if only by distortion. Perhaps we should lie low and rally around the flag of strict Darwinism, at least for the moment—a kind of old-time religion on our part.

26   But we should borrow another metaphor and recognize that we too have to tread a straight and narrow path, surrounded by roads to perdition. For if we ever begin to suppress our search to understand nature, to quench our own intellectual excitement in a misguided effort

to present a united front where it does not and should not exist, then we are truly lost.

QUESTIONS

Ideas

1. How can evolution be both a theory and a fact? What do these terms mean? What is the problem in defining them? What objection does Gould raise to President Reagan's statement, "It is a scientific theory only"?

2. How does Gould's assertion, "Unbeatable systems are dogma, not science," relate to creationism's leading theorist in paragraph 12?

3. What are the three major arguments that evolution is based on? According to Gould, what tactics do creationists rely on in the face of these arguments? How does he support his accusations?

4. In writing an argument support for one's own ideas is important, as is the careful refutation of the opposition. But equally important is the writer's persona, or voice—how the writer sounds to you. Do you trust Gould's persona here? Does he sound credible? Is he too harsh on the opposition? If you were his editor, would you advise him to change his tone in any way?

5. Do you find Gould's personal response in the last three paragraphs effective? Were you impressed by his aggressive stance in the last paragraph? Do you think presenting a "united front" more important than an individual's search for understanding?

Organization

6. Most theories of argument suggest that the writer first spend some time refuting the opposition's position before presenting evidence. How does Gould pay attention to this?

7. If you were to divide this essay into sections, how would you describe the purpose of each? Write a brief sentence outline of the major divisions.

8. Look at how Gould organizes paragraphs 23, 24, and 25. He begins with a focus ("but mostly I am deeply sad"). Describe how he develops this idea in the next three paragraphs.

Sentences

9. Compare the sentence patterns in paragraphs 3 and 23. Do they seem different, similar? What is Gould's purpose in each paragraph?

10. Note how Gould's sentence length varies; see for example, paragraphs 5, 6, and 7. Does he vary them enough? Is there a purpose in writing long sentences or short sentences?

Words

11. Go through this essay as if you were editing it for a junior high school class. Choose a dozen words you think you would have to explain in a glossary, then write brief definitions.

12. In the last sentence of paragraph 18, Gould admits he is sharp and bitter. Underline words or phrases that could be used to support this.

Suggestions for Writing

A. In paragraph 24 Gould says evolution is one of six "great ideas." Write an essay in which you explain, in layman's terms, other great ideas that might be included.

B. Write a 150-word summary of this essay by first going through the piece underlining key sentences. Then focus on just those sentences, changing them into your own words. Revise and edit this draft, paying attention to economy and transition between sentences.

EIGHT

Lillian Hellman

(1906–1984)

Lillian Hellman has the reputation for being a tough-minded woman, a kind of "super-literate female Humphrey Bogart." Her friend Dorothy Parker once remarked, "When Lillian gets mad, I regret to say she screams." It is no accident that her writing reflects this vigor and intensity. Her style is not poetic; instead it is rather stark and abrupt. In *Scoundrel Time*, for example, she writes about Richard Nixon and Joseph McCarthy searching in the State Department for Communists and left-wing subversives: "I do not think they believed much, if anything, of what they said: the time was ripe for a new wave in America, and they seized their political chance to lead it along each day's opportunity, spitballing whatever and with whoever came into view."

Her style has been called "laconic, reserved, unfooled." Hellman manages to blend slang and polish, the sassy and the graceful. She uses the combination to create a conversational yet serious voice. Although she wants to be lucid and cogent, *Scoundrel Time* is not an attempt at objective history. So her casual tone is appropriate: it signals the personal nature of her memoirs. Her "moral history" of the investigations by the House Un-American Activities Committee (HUAC) is, then, flinty and stylish. She writes:

It was not the first time in history that the confusions of honest people were picked up in space by cheap baddies who, hearing a few bars of popular notes, made them into an opera of public disorder, staged and sung, as much of the congressional testimony shows, in the wards of an insane asylum.

Her voice here is angry, but under control—what Hellman later called "pretend cool." And the natural rhythms of

American speech together with her extended metaphor are typical of the ironic, point-blank bluntness of her style. This ironic bluntness also corresponds nicely to her sense of moral outrage at injustice and arrogance.

Although she was born and raised in New Orleans, a good deal of her childhood was spent on Riverside Drive in New York City. She tells us that she felt slightly out of place in both locations. She went to high school in New York and for a couple of years attended New York University and Columbia. For a while she worked as a manuscript reader for a prestigious publishing house, as a book reviewer for the *New York Herald-Tribune,* and as a scenario reader in Hollywood. Then, in 1934, *The Children's Hour,* Hellman's drama about the effects of lies and sexual prejudice, opened to sensational reviews. She was an immediate success. She went on to write other hits, including *The Little Foxes,* an indictment of selfishness and hypocrisy in Southern families, and *Watch on the Rhine,* about an anti-Nazi and his sacrifice of personal happiness for freedom.

Although never overtly political, Hellman has always been interested in left-wing causes, especially the Loyalists' struggle against Franco during the Spanish Civil War. Her friendship with some socialists and communists in Hollywood during the 1930s eventually aroused the suspicions of HUAC, and in 1952 she was subpoenaed to testify. She refused to do so and for years afterward was blacklisted from working in Hollywood. Columnist Murray Kempton wrote about her sense of ethics and honor when she refused to give the committee the names of acquaintances who had attended left-wing political meetings: "The most important thing is never to forget that here is someone who knew how to act when there was nothing harder on earth than knowing how to act."

Although she is still considered one of America's leading dramatists, Lillian Hellman is best known for her nonfiction. In 1969, *An Unfinished Woman,* the first memoir in her autobiographical trilogy, won the National Book Award. Two of the selections taken from that book, "In the Fig Tree" and "Wasting Time," are self-portraits. She freely admits, however, that some of the details are part memory, part imagination.

In these sketches she introduces themes that recur throughout her memoirs: her rebellious bent, her groping toward self-knowledge through rites of initiation, and her interweaving of the past and the present as a way to clarify and understand. The character portrayed in these pieces is, of course, Lillian Hellman in her youth, but we should separate that portrait from the narrator, since the voice or persona a writer creates is not meant as a literal replica of the writer.

"A Lost Passion" was written around 1978, after she reread *An Unfinished Woman;* in it, she reaffirms her rebel spirit and her frustration with the limitations of writing. "Giants" is a typical selection from that memoir, especially in its use of irony and metaphor. Her third memoir, *Scoundrel Time* (1976), recounts Hellman's "own history" of the McCarthy era (the late 1940s, and early 1950s). One critic noted the book's "understated fury." In fact, in the short coda printed here, Hellman tells us that she is still angry at the scoundrels (most intellectuals) who let McCarthyism happen. Also included here is a famous letter to John S. Wood, Chairman of HUAC, containing her much quoted line: "I cannot and will not cut my conscience to fit this year's fashions. . . ." The final selection (reprinted in the Questions section) was written some years after the publication of *Scoundrel Time* and represents Hellman's reaction to rereading this very controversial memoir. She is, as you can see, still convinced that she had told the truth.

Her rereading seems to have rekindled the emotional turmoil of those years: "But I am angrier now than I hope I will ever be again; more disturbed now than when it all took place." After rereading all three books, Hellman is still unsparing in her attempts to be honest with herself; she shows us how writing can be a process of searching for personal meaning. We sense in the following paragraph that she comes to know what she thinks as she is writing about it. It is the kind of moral and intellectual toughness that is characteristic of a woman who risked smuggling $50,000 into Nazi Germany to save the lives of hundreds of Jews. For Hellman, style is character.

What a word is truth. Slippery, tricky, unreliable. I tried in these books to tell the truth. I did not fool with facts. But, of course, that is a shallow definition of the truth. I see now, in rereading, that I kept much from myself, not always, but sometimes. And so sometimes in this edition I have tried to correct that. But I can be sure I still do not see it and never will. That is a common experience for all writers, I think, and I wonder, therefore, whether what I, or they, have to say about past work is worth very much. Judge for yourself, is the only answer.

In the Fig Tree

There was a heavy fig tree on the lawn where the house turned the corner into the side street, and to the front and sides of the fig tree were three live oaks that hid the fig from my aunts' boarding-house. I suppose I was eight or nine before I discovered the pleasures of the fig tree, and although I have lived in many houses since then, including a few I made for myself, I still think of it as my first and most beloved home.

I learned early, in our strange life of living half in New York and half in New Orleans, that I made my New Orleans teachers uncomfortable because I was too far ahead of my schoolmates, and my New York teachers irritable because I was too far behind. But in New Orleans, I found a solution: I skipped school at least once a week and often twice, knowing that nobody cared or would report my absence. On those days I would set out for school done up in polished strapped shoes and a prim hat against what was known as "the climate," carrying my books and a little basket filled with delicious stuff my Aunt Jenny and Carrie, the cook, had made for my school lunch. I would round the corner of the side street, move on toward St. Charles Avenue, and sit on a bench as if I were waiting for a streetcar until the boarders and the neighbors had gone to work or settled down for the post-breakfast rest that all Southern ladies thought necessary. Then I would run back to the fig tree, dodging in and out of bushes to make sure the house had no dangers for me. The fig tree was heavy, solid, comfortable, and I had, through time, convinced myself that it wanted me, missed me when I was absent, and approved all the rigging I had done for the happy days I spent in its arms: I had made a sling to hold the school books, a pulley rope for my lunch basket, a hole for the bottle of afternoon cream-soda pop, a fishing pole and a smelly little bag of elderly bait, a pillow embroidered with a picture of Henry Clay on a horse that I had stolen from Mrs. Stillman, one of my aunts' boarders, and a proper nail to hold my dress and shoes to keep them neat for the return to the house.

It was in that tree that I learned to read, filled with the passions that can only come to the bookish, grasping, very young, bewildered by almost all of what I read, sweating in the attempt to understand a world of adults I fled from in real life but desperately wanted to join in books. (I did not connect the grown men and women in literature with the grown men and women I saw around me. They were, to me, another species.)

It was in the fig tree that I learned that anything alive in water was of enormous excitement to me. True, the water was gutter water and the fishing could hardly be called that: sometimes the things that swam in New Orleans gutters were not pretty, but I didn't know what was pretty and I liked them all. After lunch—the men boarders returned for a large lunch and a siesta—the street would be safe again, with only the noise from Carrie and her helpers in the kitchen, and they could be counted on never to move past the back porch, or the chicken coop. Then I would come down from my tree to sit on the side street gutter with my pole and bait. Often I would catch a crab that had wandered in from the Gulf, more often I would catch my favorite, the crayfish, and sometimes I would, in that safe hour, have at least six of them for my basket. Then, about 2:30, when house and street would stir again, I would go back to my tree for another few hours of reading or dozing or having what I called the ill hour. It is too long ago for me to know why I thought the hour "ill," but certainly I did not mean sick. I think I meant an intimation of sadness, a first recognition that there was so much to understand that one might never find one's way and the first signs, perhaps, that for a nature like mine, the way would not be easy. I cannot be sure that I felt all that then, although I can be sure that it was in the fig tree, a few years later, that I was first puzzled by the conflict which would haunt me, harm me, and benefit me the rest of my life: simply, the stubborn, relentless, driving desire to be alone as it came into conflict with the desire not to be alone when I wanted not to be. I already guessed that other people wouldn't allow that, although, as an only child, I pretended for the rest of my life that they would and must allow it to me.

QUESTIONS

Ideas

1. Hellman seems to be building toward a theme. The momentum picks up as she remembers the "ill" hour. How does this word lead her into a larger meaning? How would you paraphrase the last two sentences?

2. What do you make of Hellman's belief that the fig tree missed her? Does this fantasy seem unusual? Is it connected to her central concern about being alone?

3. This essay is part description, part narrative, and part exposition. Hellman mixes these modes to discover something about herself from her childhood. What does she learn? Is this consistent with her thoughts about herself in the first two paragraphs?

Organization

4. There are only four paragraphs in this selection. Briefly state the purpose of each.

5. Does each paragraph have an explicit or implicit topic sentence?

6. The last paragraph seems rather long. Is the first sentence related to the last? How does this paragraph develop? Is there a clear and logical sequence from one thought to the next?

7. An inductive pattern moves from details to a general observation. A deductive arrangement starts with a thesis and then supports it with particulars. Which pattern does Hellman use here? Would it matter if she worked the other way?

Sentences

8. What kind of voice do you hear in the second paragraph? Do you think it is true that "nobody cared"? Could this be an indication that she felt abandoned? Might that explain her behavior here?

9. Look at the last sentence in the second paragraph: Why does she choose to write such a long sentence? Should she have? Would a sentence as long as this one work in informational or scientific prose? Why?

10. Compare this sentence with the penultimate sentence in the last paragraph. What is the purpose of each? Why does she use the colon in both of these sentences?

Words

11. What does the phrase "intimation of sadness" mean to you?

12. Hellman doesn't seem to use polysyllabic words. Why do you think this is?

Suggestions for Writing

A. Think of a place from your childhood that has significance for you. Using specific details, try to recapture that time and place, describing what you did and what it means to you now.

B. Can you see continuity in your life? Write an essay that traces some characteristic of your personality from childhood to the present. Blend narration and exposition in either an inductive or deductive pattern.

C. Rewrite the last two sentences using polysyllabic or Latinate words. Which version do you prefer?

D. Rewrite the last sentence in the second paragraph using a series of short sentences.

Wasting Time

1   My mother had gone to Sophie Newcomb College in New Orleans, and although the experience had left little on the memory except a fire in her dormitory, she felt it was the right place for me. (My aunts Jenny and Hannah could keep an eye on me.) But I had had enough of Southern education and wanted to go to Smith. A few months before the autumn entrance term, when I thought the matter had been settled, my mother and father held out for Goucher on the strange ground that it was closer to New York. But a month before I was to leave for Goucher, my mother became ill and it was obvious that I was meant to stay at home. I do not remember any sharp words about these changes and that in itself is odd, because sharp words came often in those years, but I do remember a feeling of what difference did it make. I knew, without rancor, that my parents were worried about a wild and head-strong girl; and then, too, a defeat for an only child can always be turned into a later victory.

2   New York University had started its Washington Square branch only a few years before, with an excellent small faculty and high requirements for the students it could put into one unattractive building. I was, of course, not where I wanted to be and I envied those of my friends who were. And yet I knew that in another place I might have been lost, because the old story was still true: I was sometimes more advanced but often less educated than other students and I had little desire to be shown up. And by seventeen, I was openly rebellious against almost everything. I knew that the seeds of the rebellion were scattered and aimless in a nature that was wild to be finished with something-or-other and to find something-else-or-other, and I had sense enough to know that I was overproud, oversensitive, overdaring because I was shy and

frightened. Ah, what a case can be made for vanity in the shy. (And what a losing game is self-description in the long ago.)

3   It was thus in the cards that college would mean very little to me, although one professor opened up a slit into another kind of literature: I began an exciting period of Kant and Hegel, a little, very little, of Karl Marx and Engels. In a time when students didn't leave classes or even skip them very often, I would slip away from a class conducted by a famous editor, annoyed at the glimpses of his well-bred life, and would slam my seat as I left in the middle of a lecture by the famous Alexander Woollcott whenever he paraded the gibe-wit and shabby literary taste of his world. (My bad manners interested Woollcott. He went out of his way, on several occasions, to find me after class and to offer a ride uptown. But the kindness or interest made me resentful and guilty, and I remember a tart exchange about a novel written by a friend of his. Years later, because Woollcott admired Hammett, who did not admire him, I was to meet him again. And after that, when I wrote plays, he was pleasant to me—if saying that I looked like a prow head on a whaling ship is pleasant.)

4   A good deal of the college day I spent in a Greenwich Village restaurant called Lee Chumley's curled up on a dark bench with a book, or arguing with a brilliant girl called Marie-Louise and her extraordinary, foppish brother, up very often from Princeton, carrying a Paris copy of *Ulysses* when he wasn't carrying Verlaine. (Hal was a handsome, strange young man and we all hoped to be noticed by him. A few years later he married one of our group and a few years after that he killed himself and a male companion in a Zurich hotel room.)

5   In my junior year, I knew I was wasting time. My mother took me on a long tour to the Midwest and the South, almost as a reward for leaving college. We returned to New York for my nineteenth birthday and the day after I began what was then called an "affair." It was an accident: the young man pressed me into it partly because it satisfied the tinkering malice that has gone through the rest of his life, mostly because it pained his best friend. The few months it lasted did not mean much to me, but I have often asked myself whether I underestimated the damage that so loveless an arrangement made on my future. But my generation did not often deal with the idea of love—we were ashamed of the word, and scornful of the misuse that had been made of it—and I suppose that the cool currency of the time carried me past the pain of finding nastiness in what I had hoped would be a moving adventure.

QUESTIONS

Ideas

1. In an attempt to define who she is, Hellman narrates events from her youth. Do you find the young woman pictured here "rebellious" and "headstrong"?

2. Even though Lillian Hellman is a writer from an earlier generation, is there evidence that "Wasting Time" applies to college students of today?

3. If you ever read the whole of Hellman's autobiography, you will notice many sentences like the one in parentheses at the end of paragraph 2. What do you think she means by this?

4. What do you make of the "thus" in the first sentence of paragraph 3? What connection between "overproud, oversensitive, overdaring" and college is she making? Do you agree?

5. Does Hellman's attitude toward her affair fit into your image of her?

6. Does your generation have a different view of love than that expressed in the last sentence?

Organization

7. Of the five paragraphs in this piece, which ones are narrative, which expository?

8. Although "Wasting Time" is excerpted from one chapter of a book, it reads like a unified piece. What holds it together?

9. Does the first sentence of the last paragraph "cover" the details of this piece?

Sentences

10. Find the sentences that begin with "and" or "but." What relation does each have to the sentence before?

11. What is the purpose of the sentences in parentheses? Can you generalize about Hellman's use of parentheses?

Words

12. Although Hellman tries to avoid "big" words, she does like to use phrases like "tinkering malice," "cool currency," and "gibe-wit." Do you think her blend of strong basic words and literary phrases works well?

Suggestions for Writing

A.   What were your parents' reactions to your college choice? Write a list of
     their reasons for approving or disapproving your choice and then a list of
     your own reasons for your choice. In a paragraph or two, compare the lists.
B.   Hellman offers some complicated reasons for her affair. From your experi-
     ences and observations, write a short essay that tries to develop reasons why
     students have affairs.

A Lost Passion

---

1   World War I, for many intelligent people, ended in a
revulsion against the high-toned rhetoric that could not hide a dislocated
world and a dangerous future. World War II was, in the first years,
fought in Europe in a bewildered, half-crazed confusion of inefficient
defense, and then, too late, in patriotic protection of homeland. The
strength of the patriotism came only after the Germans had started their
long, terrible and triumphant march toward the north, south and east.
2   Many people here who were neither callous nor cowards remembered the palaver of Woodrow Wilson, and while they were revolted by
Hitler and Mussolini, they fought the war in good-natured consent only
because they had been conscripted, and you fought for your country
when your country said it needed you. We forget that it took us a long
time to believe in the German death camps for Jews and political
dissenters because it took us a long time to stop the dismissive talk about
the little Austrian house painter and the Italian clown with the frown.
3   There wasn't much to say about the Korean War and almost
nobody said it. There is much to say about the dirty Vietnam War and
some good stuff has been said, but it remains a puzzling time out, and
one still wants to turn one's face away from the memory of American
kids doing murder, being murdered, and from those of them who remain
in our hospitals, crippled forever by the Washington loonies and the
boys who tell the loonies how to think.
4   But among these wars, tucked away, there was a so-called little war
in Spain, a minute of history that caught the imagination not only of
the generation that is old enough to remember it, but of the present
young who, in every college where I have ever taught, know more of the

Spanish Civil War and ask more questions than they do about World War II or even Vietnam, about which they are surprisingly ignorant. (Where are history departments now and what do they teach?)

5   The Spanish Republicans, politically denouncing each other every minute of the way, managed to fight with extraordinary force for nothing more radical than the right to continue free elections. We approved of that, and so did the French, but approval did not mean guns or planes. Only the Russians supplied those and then not enough, and under such accusations from the squabbling political parties of the Left that even that amount driveled down to almost nothing towards the end.

6   But the Spanish were fighting for their country, as we all would, given an enemy of danger. The International Brigades, however, were made up of strangers to Spain, men from all over Europe and America who came to fight against Fascism: middle-aged Germans; Yugoslavs, including Tito; young Englishmen from Oxford and Cambridge. And us. And us was something of a sight. Young men came from the Middle West who had been auto mechanics and were sudden geniuses with planes and tanks. And boys like Jim Lardner just out of Harvard. (I will remember all my life the night before Lardner left Paris, only a short time before he was killed in Spain, when I tried all during dinner to persuade him not to go. He listened politely and then asked me if I wanted to see a puzzle he had just invented.) And slum kids who had never been out of their own neighborhoods in the giant cities of their birth. They were an extraordinary bunch: strangers in a country with an unattractive history, often wounded and sent to inadequate hospitals, many of them dying without recognition or honors or enough pain-killers to make death anything but weeks of agony.

7   In the Abraham Lincoln Brigade, the American section of the International Brigades, there were a large number of Jewish kids. Ernest Hemingway said three or four times to me and to other people, "God damn it, these little Jews fight fine." I do not believe he meant anything anti-Semitic. I think he never could understand that lower middle class kids could fight as well as his sporting types raised on fine guns and rods. A basic conviction of Hemingway's life was shaken, but not so shaken as to alter the nature of his war heroes or his personal taste ever.

8   Any form of the word "ideal" has suspect meanings, but the foreigners in the Brigades were more than idealists. You become more, I think, when you lay yourself on the line. That must, has to be, a very pure state of being and I think the cleanness and clarity of it is what the present generation recognizes, envies, or wants for itself.

9   And yet and yet. My pieces here about Spain do not say all or even
much of what I wanted to say. I knew it when I first wrote them, I knew
it when I included them in this book, and I knew it last week when I
read them again. I wish I understood why. Somehow they do not include
the passion that I felt, my absolute conviction that when the Spanish
War was lost, we were all going to be caught in a storm of murder and
destruction in another, larger war. It does not console me that almost
nothing that has been written about Spain includes what I missed.
Certainly not "For Whom the Bell Tolls," nor the brilliant but limited
political stuff of Orwell's. Certainly some of Malraux, but not enough,
and on and on. Maybe passion, passion on paper, takes more than most
of us have.

QUESTIONS

Ideas

1. This piece blends Hellman's very personal historical view of several wars
    with anecdotes and rememberances, all as a context for her main concern,
    the Spanish Civil War. Why do you think this war was so important for her?

2. How does she characterize the men of the Abraham Lincoln Brigade?

3. How do you respond to the Hemingway quote in paragraph 7? What do
    you think Hellman's last sentence means here? What is she implying about
    Hemingway's biases?

4. What do you think she means by "You become more . . . when you lay
    yourself on the line"?

5. What is the meaning of "And yet and yet"?

6. What do you think she means by the last sentence? Is she referring to the
    inadequacies of memory, language, or skill?

7. What does paragraph 3 tell you about her political views?

Organization

8. How would you group the nine paragraphs in this piece? Why do certain
    ones belong together?

9. What is the relationship between paragraphs 5 and 6? Between 7 and 8?

10. Several sentences in paragraph 6 begin with conjunctions. Do you think
    this is an effective device?

Sentences

11. Hellman often connects a series of independent clauses by using "and" or "but." Look especially at paragraphs 3 and 4. Is this better than writing them as separate sentences? How do you decide to do either?

12. Are there any irregular sentences in paragraphs 3 and 4? What is their purpose?

Words

13. Why did Hellman choose the word "palaver"? What is the meaning of this term? What might have been some alternatives?

14. Connotation is the emotional association a word carries. "Die" has such unpleasant connotations that we often substitute other, less harsh words such as "passed away" or "deceased." What connotation do these words have (from paragraph 3): "loonies," "boys," "stuff," "dirty." Why do you think Hellman chose them?

Suggestions for Writing

A. Read the first sentence of paragraph 4. What do you think of its structure and its length? Rewrite it into several shorter sentences and compare yours with hers. Which is easier to read?

B. Write a sketch of your remembrances of some public event that you have some feeling about.

C. Do you agree with Hellman's idea that your generation "recognizes, envies, or wants for itself" the "cleanness and clarity" of laying yourselves on the line? Write an essay in which you discuss what you think your generation's "commitments" are.

Scoundrel Time

---

1   I have tried twice before to write about what has come to be known as the McCarthy period but I didn't much like what I wrote. My reasons for not being able to write about my part in this sad, comic, miserable time of our history were simple to me, although some people thought I had avoided it for mysterious reasons. There was no mystery.

I had strange hangups and they are always hard to explain. Now I tell myself that if I face them, maybe I can manage.

2   The prevailing eccentricity was and is my inability to feel much against the leading figures of the period, the men who punished me. Senators McCarthy and McCarran, Representatives Nixon, Walter and Wood, all of them, were what they were: men who invented when necessary, maligned even when it wasn't necessary. I do not think they believed much, if anything, of what they said: the time was ripe for a new wave in America, and they seized their political chance to lead it along each day's opportunity, spitballing whatever and with whoever came into view.

3   But the new wave was not so new. It began with the Russian Revolution of 1917. The victory of the revolution, and thus its menace, had haunted us through the years that followed, then twisted the tail of history when Russia was our ally in the Second World War and, just because that had been such an unnatural connection, the fears came back in fuller force after the war when it looked to many people as if Russia would overrun Western Europe. Then the revolution in China caused an enormous convulsion in capitalist societies and somewhere along the line gave us the conviction that we could have prevented it if only. If only was never explained with any sense, but the times had very little need of sense.

4   The fear of Communism did not begin that year, but the new China, allied in those days with Russia, had a more substantial base and there were many honest men and women who were, understandably, frightened that their pleasant way of life could end in a day.

5   It was not the first time in history that the confusions of honest people were picked up in space by cheap baddies who, hearing a few bars of popular notes, made them into an opera of public disorder, staged and sung, as much of the congressional testimony shows, in the wards of an insane asylum.

6   A theme is always necessary, a plain, simple, unadorned theme to confuse the ignorant. The anti-Red theme was easily chosen from the grab bag, not alone because we were frightened of socialism, but chiefly, I think, to destroy the remains of Roosevelt and his sometimes advanced work. The McCarthy group—a loose term for all the boys, lobbyists, Congressmen, State Department bureaucrats, CIA operators—chose the anti-Red scare with perhaps more cynicism than Hitler picked anti-Semitism. He, history can no longer deny, deeply believed in the im-purity of the Jew. But it is impossible to remember the drunken face of

McCarthy, merry often with a kind of worldly malice, as if he were mocking those who took him seriously, and believe that he himself could take seriously anything but his boozed-up nightmares. And if all the rumors were true the nightmares could have concerned more than the fear of a Red tank on Pennsylvania Avenue, although it is possible that in his case a tank could have turned him on. Mr. Nixon's beliefs, if indeed they ever existed, are best left to jolly quarter-historians like Theodore White. But one has a right to believe that if Whittaker Chambers* was capable of thinking up a pumpkin, and he was, Mr. Nixon seized upon this strange hiding place with the eagerness of a man who already felt deep contempt for public intelligence. And he was right.

7   But none of them, even on the bad morning of my hearing before the House Un-American Activities Committee, interested me or disturbed me at a serious level. They didn't and they don't. They are what they are, or were, and are no relation to me by blood or background. (My own family held more interesting villains of another, wittier nature.)

8   I have written before that my shock and my anger came against what I thought had been the people of my world, although in many cases, of course, I did not know the men and women of that world except by name. I had, up to the late 1940's, believed that the educated, the intellectual, lived by what they claimed to believe: freedom of thought and speech, the right of each man to his own convictions, a more than implied promise, therefore, of aid to those who might be persecuted. But only a very few raised a finger when McCarthy and the boys appeared. Almost all, either by what they did or did not do, contributed to McCarthyism, running after a bandwagon which hadn't bothered to stop to pick them up.

9   Simply, then and now, I feel betrayed by the nonsense I had believed. I had no right to think that American intellectuals were peo-

---

*In August 1948 Whittaker Chambers appeared before the House Un-American Activities Committee. Chambers, a senior editor of *Time* magazine, told the Committee that he had once been a Communist and an underground courier. He named ten men as his former associates, the best known being Alger Hiss, formerly a high official of the State Department. Chambers accused Hiss of giving him secret government material, which Chambers preserved by placing it in a pumpkin at his farm in Maryland. Hiss was indicted, tried twice, and sent to jail for almost four years. In 1975 the secret pumpkin papers were found to contain nothing secret, nothing confidential. They were, in fact, nonclassified, which is Washington's way of saying anybody who says please can have them.

ple who would fight for anything if doing so would injure them; they
have very little history that would lead to that conclusion. Many of
them found in the sins of Stalin Communism—and there were plenty
of sins and plenty that for a long time I mistakenly denied—the excuse to join those who should have been their hereditary enemies.
Perhaps that, in part, was the penalty of nineteenth-century immigration. The children of timid immigrants are often remarkable people:
energetic, intelligent, hardworking; and often they make it so good
that they are determined to keep it at any cost. The native grandees,
of course, were glad to have them as companions on the conservative
ship: they wrote better English, had read more books, talked louder
and with greater fluency.

10   But I don't want to write about my historical conclusions—it isn't
my game. I tell myself that this third time out, if I stick to what I know,
what happened to me, and a few others, I have a chance to write my
own history of the time.

QUESTIONS

Ideas

1. What do you think of Hellman's reason for waiting over twenty years to
    write about this critical period in her life?

2. Although Hellman makes no pretense at objectivity, she does try to under-
    stand what motivated "the men who punished me." What do you think
    of her explanation?

3. How does Hellman's tone change from paragraph 4 to paragraph 5?

4. Objectivity and subjectivity are rarely absolute, rather are they points on
    a continuum. What sentences seem most obviously subjective, personal?
    Which ones seem closer to our traditional notions of "facts"?

5. What is the effect of the last paragraph? Is she trying to soften her previous
    accusations?

6. How would you characterize Hellman's attitude here? Is she bitter? Do you
    think she is trying to control herself? Should she?

7. Who are the scoundrels? Why? Do you agree with Hellman?

8. The following two paragraphs conclude *Scoundrel Time.* How would you
    compare her attitude here toward the McCarthy followers and the intellec-
    tuals with her opening ten paragraphs?

Epilogue

I have written here that I have recovered. I mean it only in a worldly sense because I do not believe in recovery. The past, with its pleasures, its rewards, its foolishness, its punishments, is there for each of us forever, and it should be.

As I finish writing about this unpleasant part of my life, I tell myself that was then, and there is now, and the years between then and now, and the then and now are one.

9. The following piece was written five or six years after Hellman wrote *Scoundrel Time*. Has the meaning of the McCarthy era changed for her? In what ways? Be specific about attitude, tone, and persona.

It is six thirty on a bright August morning. I finished reading "Scoundrel Time" again an hour ago. I made myself a cup of coffee, carried it to the beach, and watched some minnows moving about. I do not now see as well as I once did and so, leaning over to look at them more closely, I couldn't find them again. I spilled the coffee and thought, O.K., watch yourself, sit down, be still. I don't know how long I stayed, but when I got up the memory of a small dinner party last year in San Francisco had come back and with it the reason for my occasional discomfort during last night's reading of this book.

The dinner was with a few old friends, most pleasant and easy until the host, a distinguished scientist, announced that one of my critics who also happened to be in town from New York—the crankiest, in fact —would join us. I believe that the host had really forgotten this man's strangely based, oddly personal case against the book and me. (Who can be expected to remember other people's book fights?) We were polite to each other, the new arrival and I, and I said nothing throughout his almost manic long speeches. The speeches were, in any case, not meant for me, but for a famous French visitor. When my critic left early, not because of me, but because the Frenchman was not responding with proper admiration or interest, the hostess, for her own reasons, was annoyed with me.

She said, "You must really learn to be more tolerant and forgiving."

Many people have more than a distaste for certain words. My great-uncle, who was a corrupt man, would cover his face and make a sound at the use of the word "toilet." My hostess could not be expected to know that I feel strongly about "tolerance." It is, to me, an arrogant conception. Who am I to forgive? To forget, not to punish, is one thing, but forgiveness is for God if you believe in him and maybe even if you don't. I wanted to tell my hostess that, couldn't, couldn't even say that it is not pleasant to correct people for what they haven't done.

So I said, "Yes, and that's a long story."

"No," she said, "I mean it. You do not forgive people. You must learn to forgive. The time has come in your life when you must learn to be tolerant and forgive."

Wine makes for repetition, and the fourth time she said it I was in the elevator. But I was not thinking of her, the evening or my critic. I was thinking of something else and the something else only came clear this morning on the beach.

For years before "Scoundrel Time" was written I had many offers to publish such a book. But I believed I had to wait until I could reach a view, make a "tone" that was not a jumble, not chaotic with judgments and weary storms that were meaningless to anybody but me. I was waiting for a period of what my hostess would have called "tolerance," what I called "calm." It came, I thought; I wrote the book and I misrepresented myself in the book. I am, of course, sorry for that. I am not cool about those days, I am not tolerant about them and I never wish to be.

This book seemed to me last night too restrained. All those years I had waited for a view that came only because of time and recovery from pain and disorder. Or maybe I didn't have the final nerve—an accusation made by Tolstoi against Chekhov in another context, but coming out the same place here—to say that my mistakes and the political commitments of other more radical people were no excuse for the disgraceful conduct of intellectuals no matter how much they disagreed.

I believe that I am telling the truth, not the survivors' consolation, when I say that the disasters of the McCarthy period were, in many ways, good for me: I learned things, I got rid of much I didn't need. But I am angrier now than I hope I will ever be again; more disturbed now than when it all took place. I tried to avoid, when I wrote this book, what is called a moral stand. I'd like to take that stand now. I never want to live again to watch people turn into liars and cowards and others into frightened, silent collaborators. And to hell with the fancy reasons they give for what they did.

Organization

10. What is the function of the first and last paragraphs of this piece?

11. What is the function of the first sentence of paragraph 3? Is that sentence supported?

12. Some theorists believe that paragraphs cluster together, to form a stadium of discourse. What paragraphs would you group together? Why?

13. How is the first sentence of paragraph 6 supported?

Sentences

14. Compare the voice and imagery of paragraphs 4 and 5. Is there a reason for this difference?

15. In paragraph 9, how are the sentences related to one another: with words? ideas? Can you explain Hellman's use of the dash, the colon, the comma, and the semicolon in this paragraph?

Words

16. What is the effect of the following words and phrases: "spitballing" (2); "cheap buddies" (5); "boozed-up nightmares" and "quarter-historians" (6)?
17. What do the following phrases mean in context: "prevailing eccentricity" (2); "pleasant way of life" (4); "opera of public disorder" (5)?

Suggestions for Writing

A. Do you agree with Hellman's last sentence in paragraph 6? Begin an essay with a sentence that agrees or disagrees with her assessment of the public's intelligence. Use reasons and examples to support your thesis.
B. Do you think that educated intellectuals have a responsibility to aid those who are persecuted? Take a position on this issue and write an editorial for the college newspaper. Use a current controversial topic as your focus.

Letter to John S. Wood

May 19, 1952

Honorable John S. Wood
Chairman
House Committee on Un-American Activities
Room 226 Old House Office Building
Washington 25, D.C.

Dear Mr. Wood:

As you know, I am under subpoena to appear before your Committee on May 21, 1952.

I am most willing to answer all questions about myself. I have nothing to hide from your Committee and there is nothing in my life of which I am ashamed. I have been advised by counsel that under the

Fifth Amendment I have a constitutional privilege to decline to answer any questions about my political opinions, activities and associations, on the grounds of self-incrimination. I do not wish to claim this privilege. I am ready and willing to testify before the representatives of our Government as to my own opinions and my own actions, regardless of any risks or consequences to myself.

But I am advised by counsel that if I answer the Committee's questions about myself, I must also answer questions about other people and that if I refuse to do so, I can be cited for contempt. My counsel tells me that if I answer questions about myself, I will have waived my rights under the Fifth Amendment and could be forced legally to answer questions about others. This is very difficult for a layman to understand. But there is one principle that I do understand: I am not willing, now or in the future, to bring bad trouble to people who, in my past association with them, were completely innocent of any talk or any action that was disloyal or subversive. I do not like subversion or disloyalty in any form and if I had ever seen any I would have considered it my duty to have reported it to the proper authorities. But to hurt innocent people whom I knew many years ago in order to save myself is, to me, inhuman and indecent and dishonorable. I cannot and will not cut my conscience to fit this year's fashions, even though I long ago came to the conclusion that I was not a political person and could have no comfortable place in any political group.

I was raised in an old-fashioned American tradition and there were certain homely things that were taught to me: to try to tell the truth, not to bear false witness, not to harm my neighbor, to be loyal to my country, and so on. In general, I respected these ideals of Christian honor and did as well with them as I knew how. It is my belief that you will agree with these simple rules of human decency and will not expect me to violate the good American tradition from which they spring. I would, therefore, like to come before you and speak of myself.

I am prepared to waive the privilege against self-incrimination and to tell you anything you wish to know about my views or actions if your Committee will agree to refrain from asking me to name other people. If the Committee is unwilling to give me this assurance, I will be forced to plead the privilege of the Fifth Amendment at the hearing.

A reply to this letter would be appreciated.

Sincerely yours,
Lillian Hellman

QUESTIONS

Ideas

1. Hellman knows that millions of people will read this letter. What, then, are her purposes? In analyzing the needs of her audience, what techniques of persuasion does she assume will work?

2. What traditional American values does she imply the committee is violating?

Organization

3. Why does Hellman begin with a cooperative statement? What do you think Hellman's best argument is? Is it effectively placed?

4. What is the purpose of each paragraph?

Sentences/Words

5. How would you compare the tone of this letter to that of the selection from *Scoundrel Time?* How does Hellman's sentence structure contribute to her tone?

6. What words and phrases does Hellman hope will have a salubrious effect? Notice especially words that have strong emotional overtones—"decency," for example.

Suggestions for Writing

A. Write a letter to Hellman agreeing or disagreeing with the principle of her defense.

B. Write an analysis of this letter as a piece of persuasion. Include audience, persona, arguments, and organization.

Giants

Moscow was always an ugly city except for the Kremlin Red Square and a few rich merchant sections, but now it is much uglier, as if Los Angeles had no sun and no grass. The city sprawls around, is

inconvenient and haphazard with brash new buildings pushing against
the old, as if bright mail order teeth were fitted next to yellowed fangs.
There is a brutality about modern architecture in America, but in
Moscow the brutality is mixed with something idiot-minded, as if their
architects could loll about, giggling, poking at each other at a tipsy party
given in honor of nothing.

There are still some fine nineteenth-century houses in Moscow
—it has very few from the eighteenth century—and while they never
could have compared to the great houses of London or Paris, now they
seem lovely and soft, often in pinks and fading yellows, next to the
new shabbiness on the next block. More churches are open, more have
been restored since I was last here during the war, and St. Basil's,
opposite my window at the hotel, is a wonderful building, as if wild
bands of children had painted the brilliant onion domes and put the
cheerful blocks into rounded shape. The light comes up late in Moscow in November, but there is never a morning that I don't want to
walk across Red Square to look at St. Basil's. But you can't walk across
Red Square anymore: I guess it was smart to allow no dangerous foot
traffic in the giant spaces of the Square, but it is a tiring nuisance to
go down the subway steps through the long corridors, up again and
down, pushed and shoved, simply to find yourself across the street.
True, it is very nice when you get there: nice to see the crowds all day,
every day, waiting to look in religious reverence at Lenin's body, nice
that the grounds of the Kremlin are now open to the public, wonderful to be able to go inside the exquisite small churches. Greek Catholicism, Russian form, has a warmth and coziness unlike other
architectural church forms, as if God needed only brilliance of color
and carving to feel praised.

The Palace of Congresses, the new building inside the walls of the
Kremlin, is less bad than most, but it was vanity to put it so close to the
wonderful old Kremlin buildings and ask it to compete. The new apartment buildings, spread out in all directions in the flat, ugly land, have
no color and no form. The new hotels are imitations, I guess, of Abramo-
vitz, or maybe men of the same time share the same vulgarities. The
Danes and the Swedes have done some decent modern design, but the
Russians have ignored their close neighbors and seem to be intent on
imitating the mess we have made of our cities. But then everybody who
has been in the Soviet Union for any length of time has noticed their
concern with the United States: we may be the enemy, but we are the
admired enemy, and the so-called good life for us is the to-be-good life
for them. During the war, the Russian combination of dislike and

grudging admiration for us, and ours for them, seemed to me like the innocent rivalry of two men proud of being large, handsome and successful. But I was wrong. They have chosen to imitate and compete with the most vulgar aspects of American life, and we have chosen, as in the revelations of the CIA bribery of intellectuals and scholars, to say, "But the Russians do the same thing," as if honor were a mask that you put on and took off at a costume ball. They condemn Vietnam, we condemn Hungary. But the moral tone of giants with swollen heads, fat fingers pressed over the atom bomb, staring at each other across the forests of the world, is monstrously comic.

QUESTIONS

Ideas

1. What impact does this essay have on you? Are you shocked, annoyed, sympathetic?

2. Hellman starts off talking about architecture in Moscow. In her judgment, what is wrong with Moscow's buildings?

3. Somewhere in that long third paragraph Hellman gradually shifts her analysis from the Kremlin's buildings to the Soviet Union and the United States. Have we been prepared for this?

4. About what was she wrong? How does her tone change after this sentence? Can nations be monstrously comic? How?

5. Now that you have read the last four or five sentences, does this piece seem more or less focused?

Organization

6. Assume that this piece is all one paragraph; where would you break it for new paragraphs?

7. Can you defend the organization of Hellman's last paragraph? Try to see reasons why all these sentences belong together.

8. Explain how the three paragraphs of the essay cohere, i.e., stick together, one sentence with the next.

Sentences

9. Notice how many times Hellman uses the phrase "as if." It appears, in fact, in the first sentence and links Los Angeles and Moscow. What is her purpose in doing this and what effect does it have on you?

10. Why do you think Hellman decided to use so much coordination ("and" and "but") in the last section of the essay?

Words

11. Each sentence in the first paragraph is structured similarly. What is the pattern? Is it effective?
12. After using similes throughout this piece, Hellman abandons them for the directness of metaphor in the last sentence. Why?

Suggestions for Writing

A. Compare and contrast the USSR and the USA around one specific focus. Hellman suggests architecture and morality, but you might want to try others, for example, sports, culture, foreign affairs, or space exploration. Try to come to some conclusions as a result of your comparison.
B. Write a letter to Lillian Hellman agreeing or disagreeing with those last half dozen sentences.
C. Describe in some detail a particularly ugly scene. What makes it so? Can you see how others might see it differently? Notice the details and Hellman's personal reaction in the second paragraph and see if you can use this approach.

NINE

Norman Mailer

(1923–   )

As a writer and a public personality, Norman Mailer wants to affect the consciousness of his time; he wants to alter history. Since these are hardly modest goals, Mailer is often thought of as an outrageous character: egocentric, posturing, quixotic. He probably is. But he is also a generous, inspired scholar and a gifted writer of a remarkably rich and varied body of nonfiction. He is many people, sometimes in the same book. He simply refuses to conform to traditional notions of what is normal. He resists harmony and balance. And he abhors consistency, which he suspects is another name for inertia.

Mailer's writing and life-style are restless, robust, and intellectually awesome. He is challenging. He does not talk or write simply. He wants you to think—he demands that you do. If you want to keep up with his fertile and energetic mind, you must concentrate. His thought is often filled with idiosyncratic digression, foolish posturing, and brilliant flashes of insight. His prose is a record of an intricate and complex mind at work. He has written books about the first journey to the moon, boxing, women's liberation, the antiwar movement, film stars, other writers, and politics. And, of course, he has also written novels —among them, *The Naked and the Dead, An American Dream, The Deer Park,* and *Why Are We in Vietnam?*—plays, movies, and short stories. He has punched strangers and friends in bars and at society parties; he stabbed one of his four wives with a penknife; he has been abrasive and obscene to talk-show hosts; he boxed with José Torres on television; he ran for mayor of New York City; he has been arrested, praised, condemned, and honored.

Because Mailer is dedicated to avoiding the easy answer and typical response, his writing is often unpredictable. For Mailer, composing is a quest for truth, not merely a record of it. Because he knows he is searching, his writing does appear to wander at times. Some critics, in fact, are upset by his taste for long sentences and "associative rambling." But Mailer has made a conscious artistic choice to do just that. He wants to let his writing be exploratory, to look this way and that for possible answers. He doesn't want to give the impression that truth can be just simply stated and defended. So his style and content mirror truth's complexity.

In *The Armies of the Night*, for example, he jumps from one thought to the next, in a dizzying array of allusions to history, politics, sex, drugs, and technology. He uses this stylistic technique to suggest his own uncertainty about what is going on. He is trying to explore the confusion of the march on the Pentagon from as many angles as he can. So the "tributary contributions to the main direction" that perplex the critics are really attempts to be accurate and honest. Style becomes a way to understand.

Closely related to style are Mailer's innovative ideas on persona. He is often a character in his own books. In *Of a Fire on the Moon*, he calls himself Aquarius and writes about his observation of the moon shot in the third person. In *The Armies of the Night*, he is "Mailer" or the "novelist" or sometimes just "he." In an extreme form of New Journalism, Mailer actually participates in the event he has come to write about. His presence at the Pentagon is, in fact, a good deal of the story. Still, Norman Mailer the writer is not identical with this participant. In an attempt to go beyond the conventional "objective" accounts of this massive protest, Mailer the writer describes Mailer the participant's perceptions of what is going on; hence, the reader gets a double vision, from both the inside and the outside. For Mailer, the multiplex nature of such an enormous event demands an innovative perspective.

In "A Confrontation by the River," the reader is invited to join "Mailer" as he runs past MPs to be arrested. But later on, in "Why Are We in Vietnam?" (also from *The Armies of the Night*), the writer changes this almost adolescent persona into a voice that seems quite reasonable, balanced, and credible. Mailer has many personalities, and he is not afraid to switch, midstream if need be. And he is even willing to disappear altogether. In the opening pages of *The Fight* ("Carnal Indifference"), he is obviously watching Ali at his training camp, but he refrains from participating. He reports. He adapts his style to the occasion, using energetic, snappy sentences laced with fight jargon and expertise.

Norman Mailer graduated from Boys High in Brooklyn,

New York, and entered Harvard in 1939, where he majored in aeronautical engineering. In his freshman year he discovered the modern American novel. This discovery so reshaped his mind and heart that he decided then to become a major American writer. After graduation he fought in World War II, mostly in the Philippines. *The Naked and the Dead,* a spectacularly successful novel of this war, was published in 1947. Later he helped to found *The Village Voice,* an avant-garde newspaper on the arts and politics.

During the 1950s he lived in Greenwich Village. For Mailer this was a time of turbulent experimentation in his personal life. His reputation as a reckless drinker and ruffian became widely known. He seemed to be obsessed with overturning the foundations of traditional American values. But this rebellion against convention did not improve his declining reputation as a novelist. When *The Deer Park* (1955), an ironic and complex novel about a Hollywood resort, received mixed reviews, Mailer became frustrated with his fictional failures and wrote *Advertisements for Myself,* a collection of nonfiction exploring his own character.

Although racy and sensational copy still followed him, Mailer's critical reputation as a journalist began to increase. In fact, his aggressive public performances seem to have helped him clarify and understands his complex personality. *The Presidential Papers* (1963) and *Cannibals and Christians* (1966) established Mailer as one of America's leading social and political critics. His more recent nonfiction, *The Prisoner of Sex* (1971), *Marilyn* (1973), *Genius and Lust* (1976), and *The Faith of Graffiti* (1974), have solidified his stature as a writer of prodigious range and talent. His imagination, intelligence, and "extraordinary powers of expressiveness" have widened the artistic and intellectual possibilities of nonfiction. Through his innovative use of style and persona to reinforce meaning, he has demonstrated that skilled writers create their own rules, by working against the obvious and the trite.

Carnal Indifference

There is always a shock in seeing him again. Not *live* as in television but standing before you, looking his best. Then the World's

Greatest Athlete is in danger of being our most beautiful man, and the vocabulary of Camp is doomed to appear. Women draw an *audible* breath. Men look *down.* They are reminded again of their lack of worth. If Ali never opened his mouth to quiver the jellies of public opinion, he would still inspire love and hate. For he is the Prince of Heaven—so says the silence around his body when he is luminous.

When he is depressed, however, his pale skin turns the color of coffee with milky water, no cream. There is the sickly green of a depressed morning in the muddy washes of the flesh. He looks not quite well. That may be a fair description of how he appeared at his training camp in Deer Lake, Pennsylvania, on a September afternoon seven weeks before his fight in Kinshasa with George Foreman.

His sparring was spiritless. Worse. He kept getting hit with stupid punches, shots he would normally avoid, and that was not like Ali! There was an art to watching him train and you acquired it over the years. Other champions picked sparring partners who could imitate the style of their next opponent and, when they could afford it, added a fighter who was congenial: someone they could hit at will, someone fun to box. Ali did this also, but reversed the order. For the second fight with Sonny Liston, his favorite had been Jimmy Ellis, an intricate artist who had nothing in common with Sonny. As boxers, Ellis and Liston had such different moves one could not pass a bowl of soup to the other without spilling it. Of course, Ali had other sparring partners for that fight. Shotgun Sheldon comes to mind. Ali would lie on the ropes while Sheldon hit him a hundred punches to the belly—that was Ali conditioning stomach and ribs to take Liston's pounding. In that direction lay his duty, but his pleasure was by way of sparring with Ellis as if Ali had no need to study Sonny's style when he could elaborate the wit and dazzle of his own.

Fighters generally use a training period to build confidence in their reflexes, even as an average skier, after a week of work on his parallel, can begin to think he will yet look like an expert. In later years, however, Ali would concentrate less on building his own speed and more on how to take punches. Now, part of his art was to reduce the force of each blow he received to the head and then fraction it further. Every fighter does that, indeed a young boxer will not last long if his neck fails to swivel at the instant he is hit, but it was as if Ali were teaching his nervous system to transmit shock faster than other men could.

Maybe all illness results from a failure of communication between mind and body. It is certainly true of such quick disease as a knockout.

The mind can no longer send a word to the limbs. The extreme of this theory, laid down by Cus D'Amato when managing Floyd Patterson and José Torres, is that a pugilist with an authentic desire to win cannot be knocked out if he sees the punch coming, for then he suffers no dramatic lack of communication. The blow may hurt but cannot wipe him out. In contrast, a five-punch combination in which every shot lands is certain to stampede any opponent into unconsciousness. No matter how light the blows, a jackpot has been struck. The sudden overloading of the victim's message center is bound to produce that inrush of confusion known as coma.

Now it was as if Ali carried the idea to some advanced place where he could assimilate punches faster than other fighters, could literally transmit the shock through more parts of his body, or direct it to the best path, as if ideally he were working toward the ability to receive that five-punch combination (or six or seven!) yet be so ready to ship the impact out to each arm, each organ and each leg, that the punishment might be digested, and the mind remain clear. It was a study to watch Ali take punches. He would lie on the ropes and paw at his sparring partner like a mother cat goading her kitten to belt away. Then Ali would flip up his glove and let the other's punch bounce from that glove off his head, repeating the move from other angles, as if the second half of the art of getting hit was to learn the trajectories with which punches glanced off your gloves and still hit you; Ali was always studying how to deaden such shots or punish the gloves that threw the punch, forever elaborating his inner comprehension of how to trap, damp, modify, mock, curve, cock, warp, distort, deflect, tip, and turn the bombs that came toward him, and do this with a minimum of movement, back against the ropes, languid hands up. He invariably trained by a scenario that cast him as a fighter in deep fatigue, too tired to raise his arms in the twelfth round of a fifteen-round fight. Such training may have saved him from being knocked out by Frazier in their first fight, such training had been explored by him in every fight since. His corner would scream "Stop playing!," the judges would score against him for lying on the ropes, the fight writers would report that he did not look like the old Ali and all the while he was refining methods.

This afternoon, however, in Deer Lake it looked as if he were learning very little. He was getting hit by stupid punches and they seemed to take him by surprise. He was not languid but sluggish. He looked bored. He showed, as he worked, all the sudden ardor of a husband obliging himself to make love to his wife in the thick of carnal indifference.

QUESTIONS

Ideas

1. How did you respond to the first paragraph? Do "men look down," literally? What do you think Mailer means by calling Ali "the Prince of Heaven"?

2. This little snapshot of Ali is punctuated by ideas from boxing theory. What are some of the skills Mailer most admires in Ali? What principles is Ali violating as Mailer watches?

3. Mailer clearly sees Ali as more than a mere fighter. Why do you think this is? Is it something in Ali or a need in Mailer for a hero larger than life? Is the concluding analogy meant to be amusing? Shocking? Thought-provoking?

Organization

4. Which paragraphs are about what is actually taking place in Deer Lake and which are not?

5. What is the topic sentence (implied or direct) in the penultimate paragraph? Do all the sentences here relate directly to this general idea? Is there a beginning, middle, and end to this paragraph? What term does Mailer use in the first sentence that he returns to in the last?

Sentences

6. Why does Mailer decide to begin the last four sentences with "He"? Is this effective?

7. Why does Mailer write, "He looks not quite well"? Does this sound natural?

Words

8. What is the function of "however" in the second and last paragraphs?

9. What purpose does "Now" serve in the penultimate paragraph?

10. What does "luminous" mean? Is there any boxing jargon or argot here? What function do these terms serve?

Suggestions for Writing

A. Rewrite the sentence in the penultimate paragraph that begins, "Then Ali would flip . . ." Try for four or five varied sentences.

B. Can you remember meeting an impressive person? Write a short piece describing the person and your response to the meeting.

C. Write an editorial supporting or opposing boxing.

The Siege of Chicago

---

1   Meanwhile, a mass meeting was taking place about the bandshell in Grant Park, perhaps a quarter of a mile east of Michigan Avenue and the Conrad Hilton. The meeting was under the auspices of the Mobilization, and a crowd of ten or fifteen thousand appeared. The Mayor had granted a permit to assemble, but had refused to allow a march. Since the Mobilization had announced that it would attempt, no matter how, the march to the Amphitheatre that was the first purpose of their visit to Chicago, the police were out in force to surround the meeting.

2   An episode occurred during the speeches. Three demonstrators climbed a flag pole to cut down the American flag and put up a rebel flag. A squad of police charged to beat them up, but got into trouble themselves, for when they threw tear gas, the demonstrators lobbed the canisters back, and the police, choking on their own gas, had to fight their way clear through a barrage of rocks. Then came a much larger force of police charging the area, overturning benches, busting up members of the audience, then heading for Rennie Davis at the bullhorn. He was one of the coordinators of the Mobilization, his face was known, he had been fingered and fingered again by plainclothesmen. Now urging the crowd to sit down and be calm, he was attacked from behind by the police, his head laid open in a three-inch cut, and he was unconscious for a period. Furious at the attack, Tom Hayden, who had been in disguise these last two days to avoid any more arrests for himself, spoke to the crowd, said he was leaving to perform certain special tasks, and suggested that others break up into small groups and go out into the

streets of the Loop "to do what they have to do." A few left with him; the majority remained. While it was a People's Army and therefore utterly unorganized by uniform or unity, it had a variety of special troops and regular troops; everything from a few qualified Kamikaze who were ready to charge police lines in a Japanese snake dance and dare on the consequence, some vicious beatings, to various kinds of small saboteurs, rock-throwers, gauntlet-runners—some of the speediest of the kids were adept at taunting cops while keeping barely out of range of their clubs —not altogether aline to running the bulls at Pamplona. Many of those who remained, however, were still nominally pacifists, protesters, Gandhians—they believed in non-violence, in the mystical interposition of their body to the attack, as if the violence of the enemy might be drained by the spiritual act of passive resistance over the years, over the thousands, tens of thousands, hundreds of thousands of beatings over the years. So Allen Ginsberg was speaking now to them.

3   The police looking through the plexiglass face shields they had flipped down from their helmets were then obliged to watch the poet with his bald head, soft eyes magnified by horn-rimmed eyeglasses, and massive dark beard, utter his words in a croaking speech. He had been gassed Monday night and Tuesday night, and had gone to the beach at dawn to read Hindu Tantras to some of the Yippies, the combination of the chants and the gassings had all but burned out his voice, his beautiful speaking voice, one of the most powerful and hypnotic instruments of the Western world was down to the scrapings of the throat now, raw as flesh after a curettage.

4   "The best strategy for you," said Ginsberg, "in cases of hysteria, overexcitement or fear, is still to chant 'OM' together. It helps to quell flutterings of butterflies in the belly. Join me now as I try to lead you."

5   The crowd chanted with Ginsberg. They were of a generation which would try every idea, every drug, every action—it was even possible a few of them had made out with freaky kicks on tear gas these last few days—so they would chant OM. There were Hindu fanatics in the crowd, children who loved India and scorned everything in the West; there were cynics who thought the best thing to be said for a country which allowed its excess population to die by the millions in famine-ridden fields was that it would not be ready soon to try to dominate the rest of the world. There were also militants who were ready to march. And the police there to prevent them, busy now in communication with other detachments of police, by way of radios whose aerials were attached to their helmets, thereby giving them the look of giant insects.

6   A confused hour began. Lincoln Park was irregular in shape with curving foot walks; but Grant Park was indeed not so much a park as a set of belts of greenery cut into files by major parallel avenues between Michigan Avenue and Lake Michigan half a mile away. Since there were also cross streets cutting the belts of green perpendicularly, a variety of bridges and pedestrian overpasses gave egress to the city. The park was in this sense an alternation of lawn with superhighways. So the police were able to pen the crowd. But not completely. There were too many bridges, too many choices, in effect, for the police to anticipate. To this confusion was added the fact that every confrontation of demonstrators with police, now buttressed by the National Guard, attracted hundreds of newsmen, and hence began a set of attempted negotiations between spokesmen for the demonstrators and troops, the demonstrators finally tried to force a bridge and get back to the city. Repelled by tear gas, they went to other bridges, still other bridges, finally found a bridge lightly guarded, broke through a passage and were loose in the city at six-thirty in the evening. They milled about in the Loop for a few minutes, only to encounter the mules and three wagons of the Poor People's Campaign. City officials, afraid of provoking the Negroes on the South Side, had given a permit to the Reverend Abernathy, and he was going to march the mules and wagons down Michigan Avenue and over to the convention. An impromptu march of the demonstrators formed behind the wagons immediately on encountering them and ranks of marchers, sixty, eighty, a hundred in line across the width of Michigan Avenue began to move forward in the gray early twilight of 7 P.M.; Michigan Avenue was now suddenly jammed with people in the march, perhaps so many as four or five thousand people, including onlookers on the sidewalk who jumped in. The streets of the Loop were also reeking with tear gas—the wind had blown some of the gas west over Michigan Avenue from the drops on the bridges, some gas still was penetrated into the clothing of the marchers. In broken ranks, half a march, half a happy mob, eyes red from gas, faces excited by the tension of the afternoon, and the excitement of the escape from Grant Park, now pushing down Michigan Avenue toward the Hilton Hotel with dreams of a march on to the Amphitheatre four miles beyond, and in the full pleasure of being led by the wagons of the Poor People's March, the demonstrators shouted to everyone on the sidewalk, "Join us, join us, join us," and the sidewalk kept disgorging more people ready to march.

7   But at Balbo Avenue, just before Michigan Avenue reached the

Hilton, the marchers were halted by the police. It was a long halt.
Perhaps thirty minutes. Time for people who had been walking on the
sidewalk to join the march, proceed for a few steps, halt with the others,
wait, get bored, and leave. It was time for someone in command of the
hundreds of police in the neighborhood to communicate with his headquarters, explain the problem, time for the dilemma to be relayed,
alternatives examined, and orders conceivably sent back to attack and
disperse the crowd. If so, a trap was first set. The mules were allowed
to cross Balbo Avenue, then were separated by a line of police from the
marchers, who now, several thousand compressed in this one place, filled
the intersection of Michigan Avenue and Balbo. There, dammed by
police on three sides, and cut off from the wagons of the Poor People's
March, there, right beneath the windows of the Hilton which looked
down on Grant Park and Michigan Avenue, the stationary march was
abruptly attacked. The police attacked with tear gas, with mace, and
with clubs, they attacked like a chain saw cutting into wood, the teeth
of the saw the edge of their clubs, they attacked like a scythe through
grass, lines of twenty and thirty policemen striking out in an arc, their
clubs beating, demonstrators fleeing. Seen from overhead, from the
nineteenth floor, it was like a wind blowing dust, or the edge of waves
riding foam on the shore.

8   The police cut through the crowd one way, then cut through them
another. They chased people into the park, ran them down, beat them
up; they cut through the intersection at Michigan and Balbo like a razor
cutting a channel through a head of hair, and then drove columns of new
police into the channel who in turn pushed out, clubs flailing, on each
side, to cut new channels, and new ones again. As demonstrators ran,
they reformed in new groups only to be chased by the police again. The
action went on for ten minutes, fifteen minutes, with the absolute
ferocity of a tropical storm, and watching it from a window on the
nineteenth floor, there was something of the detachment of studying a
storm at evening through a glass, the light was a lovely gray-blue, the
police had uniforms of sky-blue, even the ferocity had an abstract elemental play of forces of nature at battle with other forces, as if sheets
of tropical rain were driving across the street in patterns, in curving
patterns which curved upon each other again. Police cars rolled up,
prisoners were beaten, shoved into wagons, driven away. The rain of
police, maddened by the uncoiling of their own storm, pushed against
their own barricades of tourists pressed on the street against the Hilton

Hotel, then pressed them so hard—but here is a quotation from
J. Anthony Lukas in *The New York Times:*

> Even elderly bystanders were caught in the police onslaught. At one
> point, the police turned on several dozen persons standing quietly behind
> police barriers in front of the Conrad Hilton Hotel watching the demon-
> strators across the street.
>   For no reason that could be immediately determined, the blue-
> helmeted policemen charged the barriers, crushing the spectators against
> the windows of the Haymarket Inn, a restaurant in the hotel. Finally the
> window gave way, sending screaming middle-aged women and children
> backward through the broken shards of glass.
>   The police then ran into the restaurant and beat some of the
> victims who had fallen through the windows and arrested them.

9   Now another quote from Steve Lerner in *The Village Voice:*

> When the charge came, there was a stampede toward the sidelines.
> People piled into each other, humped over each other's bodies like cou-
> pling dogs. To fall down in the crush was just as terrifying as facing the
> police. Suddenly I realized my feet weren't touching the ground as the
> crowd pushed up onto the sidewalk. I was grabbing at the army jacket of
> the boy in front of me; the girl behind me had a stranglehold on my neck
> and was screaming incoherently in my ear.

10   Now, a longer quotation from Jack Newfield in *The Village Voice.*
(The accounts in *The Voice* of September 5 were superior to any others
encountered that week.)

> At the southwest entrance to the Hilton, a skinny, long-haired kid of
> about seventeen skidded down on the sidewalk, and four overweight cops
> leaped on him, chopping strokes on his head. His hair flew from the force
> of the blows. A dozen small rivulets of blood began to cascade down the
> kid's temple and onto the sidewalk. He was not crying or screaming, but
> crawling in a stupor toward the gutter. When he saw a photographer take
> a picture, he made a V sign with his fingers.
>   A doctor in a white uniform and Red Cross arm band began to run
> toward the kid, but two other cops caught him from behind and knocked
> him down. One of them jammed his knee into the doctor's throat and
> began clubbing his rib cage. The doctor squirmed away, but the cops
> followed him, swinging hard, sometimes missing.
>   A few feet away a phalanx of police charged into a group of women,

reporters, and young McCarthy activists standing idly against the window of the Hilton Hotel's Haymarket Inn. The terrified people began to go down under the unexpected police charge when the plate glass window shattered, and the people tumbled backward through the glass. The police then climbed through the broken window and began to beat people, some of whom had been drinking quietly in the hotel bar.

At the side entrance of the Hilton Hotel four cops were chasing one frightened kid of about seventeen. Suddenly, Fred Dutton, a former aide to Robert Kennedy, moved out from under the marquee and interposed his body between the kid and the police.

"He's my guest in this hotel," Dutton told the cops.

The police started to club the kid.

Dutton screamed for the first cop's name and badge number. The cop grabbed Dutton and began to arrest him, until a Washington *Post* reporter identified Dutton as a former RFK aide.

Demonstrators, reporters, McCarthy workers, doctors, all began to stagger into the Hilton lobby, blood streaming from face and head wounds. The lobby smelled from tear gas, and stink bombs dropped by the Yippies. A few people began to direct the wounded to a makeshift hospital on the fifteenth floor, the McCarthy staff headquarters.

Fred Dutton was screaming at the police, and at the journalists to report all the "sadism and brutality." Richard Goodwin, the ashen nub of a cigar sticking out of his fatigued face, mumbled, "This is just the beginning. There'll be four years of this."

The defiant kids began a slow, orderly retreat back up Michigan Avenue. They did not run. They did not panic. They did not fight back. As they fell back they helped pick up fallen comrades who were beaten or gassed. Suddenly, a plainclothesman dressed as a soldier moved out of the shadows and knocked one kid down with an overhand punch. The kid squatted on the pavement of Michigan Avenue, trying to cover his face, while the Chicago plainclothesman punched him with savage accuracy. Thud, thud, thud. Blotches of blood spread over the kid's face. Two photographers moved in. Several police formed a closed circle around the beating to prevent pictures. One of the policemen then squirted Chemical Mace at the photographers, who dispersed. The plainclothesman melted into the line of police.

11   Let us escape to the street. The reporter, watching in safety from the nineteenth floor, could understand now how Mussolini's son-in-law had once been able to find the bombs he dropped from his airplane beautiful as they burst, yes, children, and youths, and middle-aged men and women were being pounded and clubbed and gassed and beaten, hunted and driven, sent scattering in all directions by teams of police-

men who had exploded out of their restraints like the bursting of a boil, and nonetheless he felt a sense of calm and beauty, void even of the desire to be down there, as if in years to come there would be beatings enough, some chosen, some from nowhere, but it was as if the war had finally begun, and this was therefore a great and solemn moment, as if indeed even the gods of history had come together from each side to choose the very front of the Hilton Hotel before the television cameras of the world and the eyes of the campaign workers and the delegates' wives, yes, there before the eyes of half the principals at the convention was this drama played, as if the military spine of a great liberal party had finally separated itself from the skin, as if, no metaphor large enough to suffice, the Democratic Party had here broken in two before the eyes of a nation like Melville's whale charging right out of the sea.

12   A great stillness rose up from the street through all the small noise of clubbing and cries, small sirens, sigh of loaded arrest vans as off they pulled, shouts of police as they wheeled in larger circles, the intersection clearing further, then further, a stillness rose through the steel and stone of the hotel, congregating in the shocked centers of every room where delegates and wives and Press and campaign workers innocent until now of the intimate working of social force, looked down now into the murderous paradigm of Vietnam there beneath them at this huge intersection of this great city. Look—a boy was running through the park, and a cop was chasing. There he caught him on the back of the neck with his club! There! The cop is returning to his own! And the boy stumbling to his feet is helped off the ground by a girl who has come running up.

13   Yes, it could only have happened in a meeting of the Gods, that history for once should take place not on some back street, or some inaccessible grand room, not in some laboratory indistinguishable from others, or in the sly undiscoverable hypocrisies of a committee of experts, but rather on the center of the stage, as if each side had said, "Here we will have our battle. Here we will win."

14   The demonstrators were afterward delighted to have been manhandled before the public eye, delighted to have pushed and prodded, antagonized and provoked the cops over these days with rocks and bottles and cries of "Pig" to the point where police had charged in a blind rage and made a stage at the one place in the city (besides the Amphitheatre) where audience, actors, and cameras could all convene, yes, the rebels thought they had had a great victory, and perhaps they did; but the reporter wondered, even as he saw it, if the police in that

half hour of waiting had not had time to receive instructions from the power of the city, perhaps the power of the land, and the power had decided, "No, do not let them march another ten blocks and there disperse them on some quiet street, no, let it happen before all the land, let everybody see that their dissent will soon be equal to their own blood; let them realize that the power is implacable, and will beat and crush and imprison and yet kill before it will ever relinquish the power. So let them see before their own eyes what it will cost to continue to mock us, defy us, and resist. There are more millions behind us than behind them, more millions who wish to weed out, poison, gas, and obliterate every flower whose power they do not comprehend than heroes for their side who will view our brute determination and still be ready to resist. There are more cowards alive than the brave. Otherwise we would not be where we are," said the Prince of Greed.

15   Who knew. One could thank the city of Chicago where drama was still a property of the open stage. It was quiet now, there was nothing to stare down on but the mules, and the police guarding them. The mules had not moved through the entire fray. Isolated from the battle, they had stood there in harness waiting to be told to go on. Only once in a while did they turn their heads. Their role as actors in the Poor People's March was to wait and to serve. Finally they moved on. The night had come. It was dark. The intersection was now empty. Shoes, ladies' handbags, and pieces of clothing lay on the street outside the hotel.

QUESTIONS

Ideas

1. What is Mailer's purpose in this piece? To report? To entertain? To persuade?

2. Do you think the persona Mailer has adopted here is effective? Is he stating the facts or interpreting them? Is there a difference?

3. Examine the descriptions of the police and of the demonstrators in paragraphs 2, 3, and 5. How does Mailer reveal his attitude toward each?

4. In his descriptions of the demonstrators, Mailer is careful to show their heterogeneity, their differences from one another. Why? Does he do the same thing in the descriptions of the police?

5. Since there is no explicit conclusion, Mailer invites the reader to decide who won and who lost. In the next-to-last paragraph, who do you think is right?

Organization

6. How is the essay organized? Divide it into sections and give each section a title. Explain the purpose of each section and explain how the parts are related.

7. Why does Mailer include news accounts of the incident and print them intact within his own account? How do the accounts compare with one another and with Mailer's own version? Do you think these reports are a representative cross section of the reporting that went on? How could you verify this?

8. Where is Mailer as he reports on the scene? Where is his vantage point, and how does this affect his perspective on the scene he witnesses?

Sentences

9. Throughout the essay, Mailer employs short sentences. Explain how the short sentences at the beginning of the following paragraphs work: 2, 5, 6, 9, 11, 15. What is the effect of the series of short sentences at the end of the essay?

10. The final sentence of paragraph 6 is a long periodic sentence in which a series of modifiers precedes the main clause. State the main clause and give your reaction to the way the sentence is constructed. What is the effect of accumulating many details and of putting them at the beginning?

11. A loose sentence, on the other hand, begins with the main clause and then add modifiers. Look, for example, at the second sentence in paragraph 8. Find other examples of loose and periodic sentences. Why does Mailer choose each?

12. The next-to-last sentence of paragraph 7 runs together a number of actions and details. Would these have been better separated into discrete, simple sentences? Explain.

13. Paragraph 11 consists of two sentences, one very short and one very long. Examine the long sentence and explain how Mailer keeps it going, how he extends it, adds on to it, without losing control of either his idea or his language, without losing us along the way, as he attempts to understand his feelings about what he has seen, as he tries to explain its meaning to us and to himself.

14. Explain how the series of short sentences in the final paragraph affects the tone of the entire paragraph.

Words

15. In paragraph 2 Mailer describes the protesters as a People's Army. He also compares some of them to Kamikaze pilots and to the people who run the bulls at Pamplona. How do these comparisons help characterize the

demonstrators? What do they reveal of Mailer's attitude toward the protesters? Look also at paragraph 5.

16. At the end of paragraph 7 Mailer describes the police attack on the crowd.
What do the comparisons in this account have in common, and what is
their cumulative effect?

17. The description of the attack is continued in paragraph 8, with more
comparisons. How do these relate to, extend, and develop those used in
the previous paragraph?

18. Examine the verbs in the last two sentences of paragraph 7 and throughout
paragraph 8. Which are repeated? Why? To what effect?

19. What are the tone and effect of the speech Mailer imagines given by the
"Prince of Greed"? (paragraph 14).

20. In the final three paragraphs Mailer introduces and sustains the imagery
of drama and theater. What point does he make by means of this extended
comparison?

Suggestions for Writing

A. Write sentences imitating Mailer's use of the dash and double dash in
paragraph 2; the front-loaded sentence from paragraph 6; the run-together
sentence of paragraph 7; the long sentence of paragraph 11.

B. Write an imitation of paragraph 15 using all short sentences.

C. Write a paragraph imitating Mailer's technique of using one short and one
long sentence (as in paragraph 11).

D. Write an essay analyzing Mailer's use of metaphor in this essay. Explain
how he uses metaphor, where and why he uses it, and what he achieves
through its repeated use.

E. Write an essay challenging Mailer's description of the scene. You might
consider writing a letter to Mailer asking him why he wrote the piece and
what he hoped to accomplish with it. You might explain why you like or
dislike the piece, what you think about the political viewpoint expressed
in it, perhaps even including some of your own ideas about politics, protest,
and police.

Into Orbit

1   Just as the Greeks could be confident they had discovered
the secret of beauty because the aesthetic of their sculptors permitted

no blemish to the skin, because their sculptors said in fact that the surface of marble was equal to the surface of skin, so classical physics remained simple because it did not try to deal with anything less than ideal form. Later, Western aesthetics was sufficiently ambitious to wish to discover the laws of beauty in skins with blemish and bodies with twisted limbs (and indeed would never quite succeed), just indeed as engineering could never prove simple and comprehensible to amateurs. At its best engineering was a judicious mixture of physics and a man's life-experience with machines: one insignificant dial on one bank of instruments was often the product of the acquired wisdom of a good engineer who had put in years of work reducing the deviations of an imperfect instrument of measure.

2   Any attempt to explain the mechanics of the flight of Apollo II in engineering terms is then near to impossible for one would be obliged to rewrite a set of extracts from technical manuals, and each manual would finally prove nothing but an extract from other more detailed manuals, which in turn would be summaries of the verbally transmittable and therefore less instinctive experience of veteran engineers. Yet, the pure physics of the flight was still simple, so simple and pleased with itself as a Greek statue.

3   The rocket rose because the forces which were pushing it up were larger than the forces which held it down. The thrust of its motor was greater than the heft of its bulk. So it rose upward, even as we can jump in the air for a moment because for just a moment the push of our legs up against our body is greater than our weight. Speak of potency!—the force of our legs immediately ceases; almost immediately we descend. While the rocket had no legs to propel it upward, it had rather a burning gas expelled from its rear, and this force did not cease. So the rocket continued to rise. In the beginning it did not rise very quickly. Seven million seven hundred thousand pounds pushed upward against six million five hundred thousand pounds of weight which pressed downward. The difference was therefore to be calculated at one million two hundred thousand. That was the same as saying that if the rocket had been mounted on wheels in order to travel down a level road (and so did not have to be lifted), one million two hundred thousand pounds would be pushing the same six million five hundred thousand pounds of rocket. It can be remarked in anticipation that as this force continued to push, the rocket would begin to go faster. Its velocity would increase at an even rate if the push remained the same and the weight remained the same. If at the end of a second, its measured speed was about what it should be—five feet a second—it would reach fifty feet a second after ten

seconds, and one hundred feet a second after twenty. The reason was not complex. The push did not diminish. Therefore the rocket would go five feet faster every second than the second just before. After two seconds it would be going at ten feet a second because five feet a second would have been added in that second interval of measure to the first five feet a second. After three seconds, fifteen feet a second would be its speed. The velocity would increase five feet a second, every second, so long as the push remained steady on that rocket rolling on wheels down that level road. At the end of seventeen and a half minutes the rocket we have used for an imaginary model would be moving at an imaginary speed of a mile every second.

4   Yet that hypothetical rocket is still traveling at a much slower rate than Apollo-Saturn. When Apollo-Saturn went into orbit one hundred miles up and fifteen hundred miles out, not twelve minutes were gone, yet it was traveling at five miles a second or eighteen thousand miles an hour.

5   The explanation is agreeable to a liberal mentality, for it suggests that expenditure is power. The greatest weight in the rocket is fuel, and the fuel is being consumed. The rocket loses weight at a rate as immense as thirty-five hundred gallons of fuel each second. Somewhere about thirty-five thousand pounds of weight vanish in the same interval, which comes out by calculation as close to two million pounds a minute. At the end of a minute, seven million seven hundred thousand pounds are pushing not six and a half million pounds but four and a half million. Thus, the ship is accelerating more rapidly each instant. Its speed of increase now would be not five feet a second but more than twenty. Since the engines, however, also increase their effectiveness as the rocket takes on high altitude and the near-vacuum of the thinning atmosphere offers less resistance to the fires of the exhaust, so at the end of two minutes and fifteen seconds of flight the thrust has actually reached over nine million pounds and is then pushing only a little more than two and a half million pounds. Now the rocket is being propelled by a force almost four times as great as itself: so its acceleration would be not five feet a second as at lift-off nor twenty feet a second at the end of a minute, but more like ninety feet a second.

6   Apollo-Saturn however does not travel that fast for long. It takes two minutes and fifteen seconds to reach such acceleration, and then the center motor is shut down. The thrust reduces to seven million two hundred thousand pounds from the four continuing engines. Twenty-five seconds later the outboard motors are cut off. A few more seconds,

and the first stage is released. The rocket begins to travel on the motors of the second stage, and these next five engines are not nearly so powerful. Never again will Apollo-Saturn pick up speed so quickly.

7   It hardly matters. The more modest acceleration of the second stage is added onto the high velocities already attained by the first stage. Apollo-Saturn will increase its speed to four and a half miles a second, and will be altogether out of sight when the second stage is discarded after nine minutes and twelve seconds of flight. Stripped of its first stage and its second stage, powered now by but a single motor which develops hardly one part in forty of the force the first engines developed to get off the ground, the ship now weighs only four hundred thousand pounds, or a sixteenth of its original weight. Drastically reduced, it is still in need of a little more speed, and the third stage will give it that, the third stage will take it up to something near five miles a second, or eighteen thousand miles an hour. To reach the moon it will yet have to go faster, it will have to reach twenty-five thousand miles an hour to escape the force of the earth's gravity. But that is a subsequent step. Now the ship is wheeling through the near-heavens. A little bit more than one hundred miles overhead, it proceeds to circumnavigate the earth every hour and twenty-eight minutes. Its weight, fuel of the third stage partially consumed, is now down to three hundred thousand pounds and it is in that magical condition of defiance to gravity which is known as orbit.

QUESTIONS

Ideas

1. What is the point of Mailer's opening comparison? Why doesn't Mailer explain Apollo's trip in engineering terms? What terms does he use?

2. What does Mailer mean by "pleased with itself as a Greek statue"?

3. Describe in your own words the process Apollo uses to get into orbit.

Organization

4. Describe the function of paragraphs 1 and 2. How about paragraph 4?

5. The bulk of the orbital process is described in paragraphs 5 and 7. How does Mailer organize these two chunks of discourse?

6. Which paragraphs have first sentences that refer to ideas in the preceding paragraph? Why does he do this?

Sentences

7. Try to write the first sentence three or four different ways.
8. If you were Mailer's editor, what might you suggest as a revision of the last sentence?

Words

9. Rewrite the first sentence of paragraph 5 using a primer vocabulary.
10. From the context, what does Mailer mean by "aesthetic"?

Suggestion for Writing

Using Mailer's discursive style as a model, describe a complicated process you know well, for example, driving a truck, developing film, playing a guitar, surfing, or skiing. Try to begin with an analogy.

Why Are We in Vietnam?

He knew the arguments for the war, and against the war —finally they bored him. The arguments in support of the war were founded on basic assumptions which had not been examined and were endlessly repeated—the arguments to withdraw never pursued the consequences.

He thought we were in the war as the culmination to a long sequence of events which had begun in some unrecorded fashion toward the end of World War II. A consensus of the most powerful middle-aged and elderly Wasps in America—statesmen, corporation executives, generals, admirals, newspaper editors, and legislators—had pledged an intellectual troth: they had sworn with a faith worthy of medieval knights that Communism was the deadly foe of Christian culture. If it were not resisted in the postwar world, Christianity itself would perish. So had begun a Cold War with intervals of overt war, mixed with periods of modest collaboration. As Communist China grew in strength, and her antagonisms with the Soviet Union quickened their pace, the old troth of the Wasp knights had grown sophisticated and abstract. It was now a part of the technology of foreign affairs, a thesis to be called upon when needed. The latest focus of this thesis was of course to be found in Vietnam. The arguments presented by the parties of war suggested that if Vietnam fell to the Communists, soon then would Southeast Asia, Indonesia, the Philippines, Australia, Japan, and India fall also to the Chinese Communists. Since these Chinese Communists were in the act of developing a nuclear striking force, America would face eventually a united Asia (and Africa?) ready to engage America (and Russia?) in a suicidal atomic war which might level the earth, a condition to the advantage of the Chinese Communists, since their low level of subsistence would make it easier for them to recover from the near to unendurable privations of the postatomic world.

Like most simple political theses, this fear of a total nuclear war was not uttered aloud by American statesmen, for the intimations of such a thesis are invariably more powerful than the thesis itself. It was sufficient that a paralysis of thought occurred in the average American at the covert question: should we therefore bomb the nuclear installations of the Chinese now? Obviously, public discussion preferred to move over to the intricate complexities of Vietnam. Of course, that was an ugly unattractive sometimes disgraceful war, murmured the superior apologists for the Hawks, perhaps the unhappiest war America had ever fought, but it was one of the most necessary, for (1) it demonstrated to China that she could not advance her guerrilla activities into Asia without paying a severe price; (2) it rallied the small Asian powers to confidence in America; (3) it underlined the depth of our promise to defend small nations; (4) it was an inexpensive means of containing a great power, far more inexpensive than fighting the power itself; and (5) it was probably superior to starting a nuclear war on China.

In answer, the debaters best armed for the Doves would reply that it was certainly an ugly disgraceful unattractive war but not necessary to our defense. If South Vietnam fell to the Vietcong, Communism would be then not 12,000 miles from our shores, but 11,000 miles. Moreover, we had not necessarily succeeded in demonstrating to China that guerrilla wars exacted too severe a price from the Communists. On the contrary, a few more guerrilla wars could certainly bankrupt America, since we now had 500,000 troops in South Vietnam to the 50,000 of the North Vietnamese, and our costs for this one small war had mounted to a figure between $25,000,000,000 and $30,000,000,000 a year, not so small an amount if one is reminded that the Second World War cost a total of $300,000,000,000 over four years, or less than three times as much on an average year as Vietnam! (Of course, there has been inflation since, but still! What incredible expense for so small a war—what scandals of procurement yet to be uncovered. How many more such inexpensive wars could the economy take?)

The Doves picked at the seed of each argument. Yes, they said, by fulfilling our commitments to South Vietnam, we have certainly inspired confidence in the other small Asian powers. But who has this confidence? Why the most reactionary profiteers of the small Asian nations now have the confidence; so the small Asian nations are polarized, for the best of their patriots, foreseeing a future plunder of Asia by Asian Capitalists under America's protection, are forced over to the Communists.

Yes, the Doves would answer, it is better to have a war in Vietnam than to bomb China, but then the war in Vietnam may serve as the only possible pretext to attack China. Besides the question of Chinese aggression has been begged. China is not, by its record, an aggressive nation, but a timid one, and suffers from internal contradictions which will leave her incapable for years of even conceiving of a major war.

This was not the least of the arguments of the Doves: they could go on to point out that North Vietnam had been occupied for centuries by China, and therefore was as hostile to China as Ireland was to England—our intervention had succeeded therefore in bringing North Vietnam and China closer together. This must eventually weaken the resistance of other small Asian powers to China.

Besides, said the Doves, part of the real damage of Vietnam takes place in America where civil rights have deteriorated into city riots, and an extraordinary number of the best and most talented students in America are exploring the frontiers of nihilism and drugs.

The Doves seemed to have arguments more powerful than the Hawks. So the majority of people in America, while formidably patriotic were also undecided and tended to shift in their opinion like the weather. Yet the Hawks seemed never too concerned. They held every power securely but one, a dependable consensus of public opinion. Still this weakness left them unperturbed—their most powerful argument remained inviolate. There, the Doves never approached. The most powerful argument remained: what if we leave Vietnam, and all Asia eventually goes Communist? all of Southeast Asia, Indonesia, the Philippines, Australia, Japan, and India?

Well, one could laugh at the thought of Australia going Communist. The Hawks were nothing if not humorless. If Communist China had not been able to build a navy to cross the Straits of Formosa and capture Taiwan, one did not see them invading Australia in the next century. No, any decent Asian Communist would probably shudder at the thought of engaging the Anzacs, descendants of the men who fought at Gallipoli. Yes, the Hawks were humorless, and Lyndon Johnson was shameless. He even invoked the defense of Australia.

But could the Dove give bona fides that our withdrawal from Vietnam would produce no wave of Communism through Asia? Well, the Dove was resourceful in answers, and gave many. The Dove talked of the specific character of each nation, and the liberal alternatives of supporting the most advanced liberal elements in these nations, the Dove returned again and again to the profound weaknesses of China, the extraordinary timidity of Chinese foreign policy since the Korean war, spoke of the possibility of enclaves, and the resources of adroit, well-managed economic war in Asia.

Yet the Doves, finally, had no answer to the Hawks. For the Doves were divided. Some of them, a firm minority, secretly desired Asia to go Communist, their sympathies were indeed with Asian peasants, not American corporations, they wanted what was good for the peasant, and in private they believed Communism was probably better suited than Capitalism to introduce the technological society to the peasant. But they did not consider it expedient to grant this point, so they talked around it. The others, the majority of the Doves, simply refused to face the possibility. They were liberals. To explore the dimensions of the question, might have exploded the foundation of their liberalism, for they would have had to admit they were willing to advocate policies which could conceivably end in major advances of Asian Communism, and this admission might oblige them to move over to the Hawks.

Mailer was bored with such arguments. The Hawks were smug and self-righteous, the Doves were evasive of the real question.

Mailer was a Left Conservative. So he had his own point of view. To himself he would suggest that he tried to think in the style of Marx in order to attain certain values suggested by Edmund Burke. Since he was a conservative, he would begin at the root. He did not see all wars as bad. He could conceive of wars which might be noble. But the war in Vietnam was bad for America because it was a bad war, as all wars are bad if they consist of rich boys fighting poor boys when the rich boys have an advantage in the weapons. He recollected a statistic: it was droll if it was not obscene. Next to every pound of supplies the North Vietnamese brought into South Vietnam for their soldiers, the Americans

brought in one thousand pounds. Yes, he would begin at the root. All
wars were bad which undertook daily operations which burned and
bombed large numbers of women and children; all wars were bad which
relocated populations (for the root of a rich peasant lore was then
destroyed) all wars were bad which had no line of battle or discernible
climax (an advanced notion which supposes that wars may be in part
good because they are sometimes the only way to define critical conditions rather than blur them) certainly all wars were bad which took some
of the bravest young men of a nation and sent them into combat with
outrageous superiority and outrageous arguments: such conditions of
combat had to excite a secret passion for hunting other humans. Certainly any war was a bad war which required an inability to reason as the
price of retaining one's patriotism; finally any war which offered no
prospect of improving itself as a war—so complex and compromised
were its roots—was a bad war. A good war, like anything else which is
good, offers the possibility that further effort will produce a determin-
able effect upon chaos, evil, or waste. By every conservative measure
(reserving to Conservatism, the right to approve of wars) the war in
Vietnam was an extraordinarily bad war.

Since he was also a *Left* Conservative, he believed that radical
measures were sometimes necessary to save the root. The root in this
case was the welfare of the nation, not the welfare of the war. So he had
an answer to the Hawks. It was: pull out of Vietnam completely. Leave
Asia to the Asians. What then would happen?

He did not know. Asia might go to the Communists, or it might
not. He was certain no one alive knew the answer to so huge a question
as that. It was only in the twentieth century, in the upper chambers of
technology land (both Capitalist *and* Communist) that men began to
believe there must be concrete answers to every large question. No! So
far as he had an opinion (before the vastness of this question) his opinion
existed on the same order of magnitude of undiscovered ignorance as the
opinion of any Far Eastern expert. While he thought it was probable
most of Asia would turn to Communism in the decade after any American withdrawal from that continent, he did not know that it really
mattered. In those extraordinary World War II years when the Wasp
admirals, generals, statesmen, legislators, editors and corporation presi-
dents had whispered to each other that the next war was going to be
Christianity versus Communism, the one striking omission in their
Herculean crusade was the injunction to read Marx. They had studied
his ideas, of course; in single-spaced extracts on a typewritten page! but
because they had not read his words, but merely mouthed the extracts,

they had not had the experience of encountering a mind which taught one to reason, even to reason away from his own mind; so the old Wasps and the young Wasps in the power elite could not comprehend that Communists who read their Marx might come to reason away from the particular monoliths of Marxism which had struck the first spark of their faith. It seemed never to occur to the most powerful Wasps that one could count quite neatly on good Communists and bad Communists just as one would naturally expect good Christians and bad. In fact, just as Christianity seemed to create the most unexpected saints, artists, geniuses, and great warriors out of its profound contradictions, so Communism seemed to create great heretics and innovators and converts (Sartre and Picasso for two) out of the irreducible majesty of Marx's mind (perhaps the greatest single tool for celebration Western man had ever produced). Or at least—and here was the kernel of Mailer's sleeping thesis—Communism would continue to produce heretics and great innovators just so long as it expanded. Whenever it ceased to expand, it would become monolithic again, mediocre, and malign. An ogre.

An explanation? A submersion of Asia in Communism was going to explode a shock into Marxism which might take a half century to digest. Between Poland and India, Prague and Bangkok, was a diversity of primitive lore which would jam every fine gear of the Marxist. There were no quick meals in Asia. Only indigestion. The real difficulty might be then to decide who would do more harm to Asia, Capitalism or Communism. In either case, the conquest would be technological, and so primitive Asian societies would be uprooted. Probably, the uprooting would be savage, the psychic carnage unspeakable. He did not like to contemplate the compensating damage to America if it chose to dominate a dozen Asian nations with its technologies and its armies while having to face their guerrilla wars.

No, Asia was best left to the Asians. If the Communists absorbed those countries, and succeeded in building splendid nations who made the transition to technological culture without undue agony, one would be forced to applaud; it seemed evident on the face of the evidence in Vietnam, that America could not bring technology land to Asia without bankrupting itself in operations ill-conceived, poorly comprehended, and executed in waste. But the greater likelihood was that if the Communists prevailed in Asia they would suffer in much the same fashion. Divisions, schisms, and sects would appear. An endless number of collisions between primitive custom and Marxist dogma, a thousand daily pullulations of intrigue, a heritage of cruelty, atrocity, and betrayal would fall upon the Communists. It was not difficult to envision a time when one Communist nation in Asia might look for American aid against another Communist nation. Certainly Russia and China would be engaged in a cold war with each other for decades. Therefore, to leave Asia would be precisely to gain the balance of power. The answer then was to get out, to get out any way one could. Get out. There was nothing to fear—perhaps there never had been. For the more Communism expanded, the more monumental would become its problems, the more flaccid its preoccupations with world conquest. In the expansion of Communism, was its own containment. The only force which could ever defeat Communism, was Communism itself.

QUESTIONS

Ideas

1. Although Mailer is again writing about himself in the third person ("he"), his stance seems more serious than usual, more objective. Do you think he is objective, or is he only giving the appearance of giving both sides a fair chance?

2. In the second paragraph Mailer gives an explanation of the Vietnam war. Does it make sense to you? Does he offer any evidence for the intellectual pledge? Does he have to?

3. Does Mailer allow the Hawks' solid arguments for their side? Do the Doves' answers to the five defenses for the war seem fair? Does he seem to favor one side?

4. How does he deal with the "arguments to withdraw"?

5. From the evidence given, what do you think Mailer's definition of a "Left Conservative" is?

6. Does Mailer think all communists are bad?

7. What are some of the elements of a bad war? Do you agree with him that there could be a good war?

8. What does Mailer think will happen if Asia goes communist? Do you agree with this speculative idea?

9. What is his final position in the last paragraph? Does it take into consideration the arguments of the Doves and the Hawks?

Organization

10. Mailer uses comparison and contrast here as a way to persuade. He is trying to convince you to change your mind. To do this he adopts a certain

persona. Do you think he chose an appropriate one? What if he had used his persona from "A Confrontation by the River"?

11. What is the sequence of Mailer's argument? Notice that he says in the first paragraph that he is bored by the arguments of the Hawks and the Doves. Does he support that statement? Where is this feeling repeated?

12. Does Mailer use the metaphor of the medieval knights developed in the second paragraph in other places in the essay? What is the purpose of this technique?

13. Writers sometimes use a short transitional paragraph to build a bridge between one section of a long essay and another. Find an example of this device here.

14. Some writers think it is wise to hold your best argument for last. Does Mailer? What would have been another possible organization strategy for this piece?

Sentences

15. Compare Mailer's sentences in "A Confrontation by the River" with those in "Why Are We in Vietnam?" Consider sentence forms, length, and tone.

16. What do you think are Mailer's most effective sentences here, i.e., which ones did you respond to most favorably? Was it the conversational ones —"No, Asia was best left to the Asians"—or the clear, assertive ones— "The only force which could ever defeat Communism, was Communism itself"? Or did you prefer the ones with imagery and literary diction—"A consensus of the most powerful . . ."?

Words

17. What does "truth" mean? Why did Mailer choose this word instead of "pledge"?

18. In the third paragraph from the end, Mailer writes, ". . . it would become monolithic again, mediocre, and malign. An ogre." What do these words mean? Did he choose them for meaning, for sound? Why "ogre" and not "monster" or "beast"?

Suggestions for Writing

A. Write a persuasive essay about a controversial subject in which you carefully analyze the position of both sides before developing your own argument. Be sure to state the opposing points of view as objectively as you can

before you explain their flaws. Try to imitate the "searching-for-the-truth"
persona Mailer adopts.

B.   Write a paragraph in which you adopt a biased, extremist position about
      a controversial issue. Cast the opposing side's argument in the worst possi-
      ble light. All right is on your side. Now do the same thing taking the
      completely opposite side.

A Confrontation by the River

It was not much of a situation to study. The MPs stood in
two widely spaced ranks. The first rank was ten yards behind the rope,
and each MP in that row was close to twenty feet from the next man.
The second rank, similarly spaced, was ten yards behind the first rank
and perhaps thirty yards behind them a cluster appeared, every fifty
yards or so, of two or three U. S. Marshals in white helmets and dark
blue suits. They were out there waiting. Two moods confronted one
another, two separate senses of a private silence.

It was not unlike being a boy about to jump from one garage roof
to an adjoining garage roof. The one thing not to do was wait. Mailer
looked at Macdonald and Lowell. "Let's go," he said. Not looking again
at them, not pausing to gather or dissipate resolve, he made a point of
stepping neatly and decisively over the low rope. Then he headed across
the grass to the nearest MP he saw.

It was as if the air had changed, or light had altered; he felt
immediately much more alive—yes, bathed in air—and yet disembodied
from himself, as if indeed he were watching himself in a film where this
action was taking place. He could feel the eyes of the people behind the
rope watching him, could feel the intensity of their existence as spectators. And as he walked forward, he and the MP looked at one another
with the naked stricken lucidity which comes when absolute strangers
are for the moment absolutely locked together.

The MP lifted his club to his chest as if to bar all passage. To
Mailer's great surprise—he had secretly expected the enemy to be calm
and strong, why should they not? they had every power, all the guns—
to his great surprise, the MP was trembling. He was a young Negro, part

white, who looked to have come from some small town where perhaps there were not many other Negroes; he had at any rate no Harlem smoke, no devil swish, no black, no black power for him, just a simple boy in an Army suit with a look of horror in his eye, "Why, why did it have to happen to me?" was the message of the petrified marbles in his face.

"Go back," he said hoarsely to Mailer.

"If you don't arrest me, I'm going to the Pentagon."

"No. Go back."

The thought of a return—"since they won't arrest me, what can I do?"—over these same ten yards was not at all suitable.

As the MP spoke, the raised club quivered. He did not know if it quivered from the desire of the MP to strike him, or secret military wonder was he now possessed of a moral force which implanted terror in the arms of young soldiers? Some unfamiliar current, now gyroscopic, now a sluggish whirlpool, was evolving from that quiver of the club, and the MP seemed to turn slowly away from his position confronting the rope, and the novelist turned with him, each still facing the other until the axis of their shoulders was now perpendicular to the rope, and still they kept turning in this psychic field, not touching, the club quivering, and then Mailer was behind the MP, he was free of him, and he wheeled around and kept going in a half run to the next line of MPs and then on the push of a sudden instinct, sprinted suddenly around the nearest MP in the second line, much as if he were a back cutting around the nearest man in the secondary to break free—that was actually his precise thought—and had a passing perception of how simple it was to get past these MPs. They looked petrified. Stricken faces as he went by. They did not know what to do. It was his dark pinstripe suit, his vest, the maroon and blue regimental tie, the part in his hair, the barrel chest, the early paunch—he must have looked like a banker himself, a banker gone ape! And then he saw the Pentagon to his right across the field, not a hundred yards away, and a little to his left, the marshals, and he ran on a jog toward them, and came up, and they glared at him and shouted, "Go back."

He had a quick impression of hard-faced men with gray eyes burning some transparent fuel for flame, and said, "I won't go back. If you don't arrest me, I'm going on to the Pentagon," and knew he meant it, some absolute certainty had come to him, and then two of them leaped on him at once in the cold clammy murderous fury of all cops at the existential moment of making their bust—all cops who secretly expect to be struck at that instant for their sins—and a surprising force came to his voice, and he roared, to his own distant pleasure in new achievement and new authority—"Take your hands off me, can't you see? I'm not resisting arrest," and one then let go of him, and the other stopped trying to pry his arm into a lock, and contented himself with a hard hand under his armpit, and they set off walking across the field at a rapid intent quick rate, walking parallel to the wall of the Pentagon, fully visible on his right at last, and he was arrested, he had succeeded in that, and without a club on his head, the mountain air in his lungs as thin and fierce as smoke, yes, the livid air of tension on this livid side promised a few events of more interest than the routine wait to be free, yes he was more than a visitor, he was in the land of the enemy now, he would get to see their face.

QUESTIONS

Ideas

1. Do you think Mailer has, as he speculates, "gone ape"? Are you surprised that a famous writer would act in such a way?

2. When Mailer finally decides to go, what new feelings does he experience? Does this seem like a normal reaction?

3. Why do you think the MPs allow him to get as far as he does? What do you think of Mailer's characterization of the "murderous fury of all cops"?

4. Based on the last sentence, what do you think Mailer's motives are?

5. Do you think that this passage is more like fiction than history? Why? Is Mailer the writer trying to create a sense of objectivity by writing about himself in the third person as Mailer the participant?

Organization

6. Although this essay is essentially a narrative, it also has description, dialogue, speculation, and analysis. Does the narrative conform to the traditional structure of beginning, middle, and end?

7. In what ways does Mailer create unity in this piece? Are phrases, words, or ideas repeated in various places? Look, for example, at the first two words of the first three paragraphs.

Sentences

8. Most readers assume that Mailer writes mostly complex sentences with lots of subordinate clauses. Is this true? Look carefully at the sentence structure of the first paragraph.

9. What is Mailer's point in making the last sentence so long, so involved?

Words

10. What does Mailer mean by "no Harlem smoke, no devil swish"?

11. What does "existential moment" mean? What do "gyroscopic" and "sluggish whirlpool" mean?

Suggestions for Writing

A. Rewrite the last sentence in two different ways. Try first to use a series of short sentences, then your own preference.

B. Rewrite the sentence that begins, "Some unfamiliar current, now gyroscopic . . .".

C. Write a narrative paragraph about an event you recently participated in using Mailer's technique of writing in the third person. Now rewrite the paragraph using "I." Is there a difference? Do you simply change the pronoun reference or do other elements also have to change? Under what circumstances would each technique be more effective?

TEN

John McPhee

(1931–   )

John McPhee is a master of detail, a poet of information, an artist of the factual. His passion for getting it right is almost obsessive. If he were a painter, he would probably be a photo-realist; if a filmmaker, he would broaden the artistic possibilities of the documentary. In fact, according to one critic, he has already "stretched the artistic dimensions of reportage." His book *Oranges* (1967) is typical of his literary nonfiction. Although we learn an enormous amount about citrus botany and history, about international customs and economic realities, we are also aesthetically entertained by the craft and photographic precision of his prose—by the clarity of his accurate and authentic details.

Unlike Tom Wolfe and Joan Didion, John McPhee is not a New Journalist: his presence is barely noticeable in the events he is describing, and he almost never tells the reader what he is thinking. He is self-effacing. The persona he adopts as a narrator reveals little; instead he usually lets his carefully arranged details convey his feelings. In a traditional sense, he tries for objectivity. However, because writing is a process of selecting, rejecting, and arranging information, a writer cannot possibly be completely objective. McPhee has to leave some material out; he has to put other material in. All writers have to choose. In McPhee's case it is easy enough to infer his attitude. He leaves many traces.

McPhee is interested in the values that people live by, and he usually writes about people he likes. They can be basketball players, scientists, headmasters, or canoe makers. He clearly admires the finesse and dedication of the basketball player Bill Bradley and likes the independence and pluck of Fred Brown, a piney backwoodsman. Very often his heroes possess competence, self-assurance, modesty, and self-discipline. Many critics attribute these same qualities to McPhee.

But he is more interested in giving the reader a precisely rendered account of the people he writes about than in extolling them. When we encounter the people of the Pine Barrens, we find out about their lives and the codes they live by through details that have been meticulously researched and verified. McPhee gains authority through fact and layers of details. We trust his persona because he has mastered his material. He has done his homework. His scholarly attention to creating a particular atmosphere makes his nonfiction as complex as a novel. His refined, economically controlled portraits make his characters breathe. McPhee once said that "factual characters can live as much on the page as any fictional character . . . writing is more than just the delivery of information per se."

None of this comes easy, of course. In fact, McPhee says that writing "gets harder and harder the older you get. Not easier." He claims that as a young writer he "would thread my bathrobe sash through the spokes of the chair and tie myself in." Even today McPhee finds the life of a writer difficult. Although he is a staff writer for *The New Yorker* and has an office there, he does all his writing in a study on Main Street in Princeton, New Jersey. He arrives at 8:30 in the morning and doesn't leave until 8:30 at night. He maintains, however, that he gets only two or three hours of good writing done. "The rest of the time I wander around in here going nuts—trying to bring it all into focus."

To make the process of composing easier, McPhee tries to follow a pattern that he feels comfortable with, one that fits his personality. He does not use a tape recorder, preferring instead to fill up notebooks in longhand with the results of interviews, observations, and library research. After reading and rereading these notes, he looks for gaps that will need future research. Then he jots down possible structures, later trying possible opening paragraphs. He then arranges his notes according to a tentative structure.

Unlike many writers, McPhee does most of his planning in his head instead of on paper. He decides whether to use a prearranged pattern or to let the material suggest an organic pattern. Generally he prefers a logical, simple form. Then he writes his first draft. A critic described his composing processes: "Some authors overwrite and later boil down; he culls before ever typing a phrase."

McPhee's first draft is for him the most difficult. After that he edits, pruning and polishing his sentences. Because of the "laborious planning and composing" that McPhee goes through in the early stages of his writing, he can concentrate on style in the closing stages.

Although he doesn't begin to write until the end of his planning stage, his overall composing sequence is comparable to that of many other experienced writers who spend up to 80 percent of their composing effort in preparation for the first good draft. For most writers, revising that draft involves a good deal of rearranging, refocusing, and reseeing. However, McPhee feels he has already laid a solid foundation and so makes few changes in the original structure. His purpose in choosing an organization is to create an unobtrusive design, one so logical and simple that the reader's attention will be drawn only to meaning, to content; not to the window, but to the scene beyond.

His style is as unaffected as his organization. His prose is strong, direct, and economical. His most characteristic sentence pattern is the straightforward assertion: "Bradley is not an innovator" or "Bradley's graceful hook shot is a masterpiece of eclecticism." These sentences are often placed first in a paragraph so that he can follow them with supporting details. And these specifics are concrete and knowledgeable. He achieves some of his authority by absorbing the vocabulary, the "sound" of whatever he is writing about. If it is pinballs, he will use the right jargon: "Ballys" and "Gottliebs," "reinforcing" and "death channels." If it is oranges, we will hear about "Maltese Ovals" and "Lue Gim Gongs," "zygotic seedlings" and "pomologists." His use of the concrete suggests a writer deeply involved in his subject, a person totally in touch with his surroundings. Readers trust a writer who sounds as if he knows what he is talking about.

John McPhee uses disciplined hard work to let readers see, to make us understand. With *The Pine Barrens* (1968), *Coming Into the Country* (1979), and *Basin and Range* (1981), he earned a reputation as one of the most versatile and literate journalists in America, a reporter who creates living art out of inert information. Through a patient and textured prose filled with carefully selected details, he shows us how it was to be there. By standing back and letting his sentences evoke special people and special places, McPhee invites the reader to activate his prose. In his recent *La Place de la Concorde Suisse* (1985), he has perfected his persona as the "invisible interlocutor," in prose so clean and controlled it almost seems too effortless, too simple. But that is just the illusion a skilled artisan like McPhee wants to achieve. Lucid prose does not come easily. McPhee works all day, every day on his writing, constantly revising. It is this dedication to the writing process that makes McPhee's prose so readable.

Bradley

Bradley is one of the few basketball players who have ever been appreciatively cheered by a disinterested away-from-home crowd while warming up. This curious event occurred last March, just before Princeton eliminated the Virginia Military Institute, the year's Southern Conference champion, from the N.C.A.A. championships. The game was played in Philadelphia and was the last of a tripleheader. The people there were worn out, because most of them were emotionally committed to either Villanova or Temple—two local teams that had just been involved in enervating battles with Providence and Connecticut, respectively, scrambling for a chance at the rest of the country. A group of Princeton boys shooting basketballs miscellaneously in preparation for still another game hardly promised to be a high point of the evening, but Bradley, whose routine in the warmup time is a gradual crescendo of activity, is more interesting to watch before a game than most players are in play. In Philadelphia that night, what he did was, for him, anything but unusual. As he does before all games, he began by shooting set shots close to the basket, gradually moving back until he was shooting long sets from twenty feet out, and nearly all of them dropped into the net with an almost mechanical rhythm of accuracy. Then he began a series of expandingly difficult jump shots, and one jumper after another went cleanly through the basket with so few exceptions that the crowd began to murmur. Then he started to perform whirling reverse moves before another cadence of almost steadily accurate jump shots, and the murmur increased. Then he began to sweep hook shots into the air. He moved in a semicircle around the court. First with his right hand, then with his left, he tried seven of these long, graceful shots—the most difficult ones in the orthodoxy of basketball—and ambidextrously made them all. The game had not even begun, but the presumably unimpressible Philadelphians were applauding like an audience at an opera.

QUESTIONS

Ideas

1. Why do the crowds react to Bradley so enthusiastically?
2. What kind of person does Bradley seem to be? Would Magic Johnson warm up like this? How about Michael Jordan?
3. Although McPhee is reporting objectively, we somehow get a clear sense of his attitude toward Bradley. What is McPhee's reaction and how do we know it?

Organization

4. If you were going to divide this paragraph into a beginning, middle, and end, how would you defend your partitioning?
5. In what way is the first sentence related to what follows?
6. How is the last sentence connected to the first?

Sentences

7. Some critics have praised McPhee's style as "unaffected and strong." Read this paragraph aloud; does it sound that way to you? Why?
8. Probably the most basic sentence structure is the simple declaration, e.g., McPhee's first sentence. Are there other examples here? What is the effect of stringing these assertions together?

Words

9. Why does McPhee say "like an audience at an opera"? Why not at another sporting event? Has McPhee prepared us for this simile?

Suggestions for Writing

10. Sit someplace on campus and observe people interacting. Write a brief sketch that follows McPhee's tight organization of supporting a simple assertion with concrete detail.
11. Write a brief portrait of someone you admire, but don't tell the reader why directly: let the details of his or her actions convey your admiration.

Oranges

1   The custom of drinking orange juice with breakfast is not very widespread, taking the world as a whole, and it is thought by many peoples to be a distinctly American habit. But many Danes drink it regularly with breakfast, and so do Hondurans, Filipinos, Jamaicans, and the wealthier citizens of Trinidad and Tobago. The day is started with orange juice in the Colombian Andes, and, to some extent, in Kuwait. Bolivians don't touch it at breakfast time, but they drink it steadily for the rest of the day. The "play lunch," or morning tea, that Australian children carry with them to school is usually an orange, peeled spirally halfway down, with the peel replaced around the fruit. The child unwinds the peel and holds the orange as if it were an ice-cream cone. People in Nepal almost never peel oranges, preferring to eat them in cut quarters, the way American athletes do. The sour oranges of Afghanistan customarily appear as seasoning agents on Afghan dinner tables. Squeezed over Afghan food, they cut the grease. The Shamouti Orange, of Israel, is seedless and sweet, has a thick skin, and grows in Hadera, Gaza, Tiberias, Jericho, the Jordan Valley, and Jaffa; it is exported from Jaffa, and for that reason is known universally beyond Israel as the Jaffa Orange. The Jaffa Orange is the variety that British people consider superior to all others, possibly because Richard the Lionhearted spent the winter of 1191–92 in the citrus groves of Jaffa. Citrus trees are spread across the North African coast from Alexandria to Tangier, the city whose name was given to tangerines. Oranges tend to become less tart the closer they are grown to the equator, and in Brazil there is one kind of orange that has virtually no acid in it at all. In the principal towns of Trinidad and Tobago, oranges are sold on street corners. The vendor cuts them in half and sprinkles salt on them. In Jamaica, people halve oranges, get down on their hands and knees and clean floors with one half in each hand. Jamaican mechanics use oranges to clear away grease and oil. The blood orange of Spain, its flesh streaked with red, is prized throughout Europe. Blood oranges grow well in Florida, but they frighten American women. Spain has about thirty-five million orange trees, grows six billion oranges a year, and exports more oranges than any other country, including the United States. In the Campania region of Italy, land is scarce; on a typical small patch, set on a steep slope, orange

trees are interspersed with olive and walnut trees, grapes are trained to cover trellises overhead, and as many as five different vegetables are grown on the ground below. The over-all effect is that a greengrocer's shop is springing out of the hillside. Italy produces more than four billion oranges a year, but most of its citrus industry is scattered in gardens of one or two acres. A Frenchman sits at the dinner table, and, as the finishing flourish of the meal, slowly and gently disrobes an orange. In France, peeling the fruit is not yet considered an inconvenience. French preferences run to the blood oranges and the Thomson Navels of Spain, and to the thick-skinned, bland *Maltaises,* which the French import not from Malta but from Tunisia. France itself only grows about four hundred thousand oranges each year, almost wholly in the Department of the *Alpes Maritimes.* Sometimes, Europeans eat oranges with knives and forks. On occasion, they serve a dessert orange that has previously been peeled with such extraordinary care that strips of the peel arc outward like the petals of a flower from the separated and reassembled segments in the center. The Swiss sometimes serve oranges under a smothering of sugar and whipped cream; on a hot day in a Swiss garden, orange juice with ice is a luxurious drink. Norwegian children like to remove the top of an orange, make a little hole, push a lump of sugar into it, and then suck out the juice. English children make orange-peel teeth and wedge them over their gums on Halloween. Irish children take oranges to the movies, where they eat them while they watch the show, tossing the peels at each other and at the people on the screen. In Reykjavik, Iceland, in greenhouses that are heated by volcanic springs, orange trees yearly bear fruit. In the New York Botanical Garden, six mature orange trees are growing in the soil of the Bronx. Their trunks are six inches in diameter, and they bear well every year. The oranges are for viewing and are not supposed to be picked. When people walk past them, however, they sometimes find them irresistible.

. . .

2   Oranges and orange blossoms have long been symbols of love. Boccaccio's *Decameron,* written in the fourteenth century, is redolent with the scent of oranges and orange blossoms, with lovers who wash in orange-flower water, a courtesan who sprinkles her sheets with orange perfume, and the mournful Isabella, who cuts off the head of her dead lover, buries it in an ample pot, plants sweet basil above it, and irrigates the herbs exclusively with rosewater, orange-flower water, and tears. In

the fifteenth century, the Countess Mathilda of Württemberg received from her impassioned admirer, Dr. Heinrich Steinbowel, a declaration of love in the form of a gift of two dozen oranges. Before long, titled German girls were throwing oranges down from their balconies in the way that girls in Italy or Spain were dropping handkerchiefs. After Francis I dramatically saved Marseilles from a Spanish siege, a great feast was held for him at the city's harborside, and Marseillaise ladies, in token of their love and gratitude, pelted him with oranges. Even Nostradamus was sufficiently impressed with the sensual power of oranges to publish, in 1556, a book on how to prepare various cosmetics from oranges and orange blossoms. Limes were also used cosmetically, by ladies of the French court in the seventeenth century, who kept them on their persons and bit into them from time to time in order to redden their lips. In the nineteenth century, orange blossoms were regularly shipped to Paris in salted barrels from Provence, for no French bride wanted to be married without wearing or holding them.

. . .

3   The color of an orange has no absolute correlation with the maturity of the flesh and juice inside. An orange can be as sweet and ripe as it will ever be and still glisten like an emerald in the tree. Cold—coolness, rather—is what makes an orange orange. In some parts of the world, the weather never gets cold enough to change the color; in Thailand, for example, an orange is a green fruit, and traveling Thais often blink with wonder at the sight of oranges the color of flame. The ideal nighttime temperature in an orange grove is forty degrees. Some of the most beautiful oranges in the world are grown in Bermuda, where the temperature, night after night, falls consistently to that level. Andrew Marvell's poem wherein the "remote Bermudas ride in the ocean's bosom unespied" was written in the sixteen-fifties, and contains a description, from hearsay, of Bermuda's remarkable oranges, set against their dark foliage like "golden lamps in a green night." Cool air comes down every night into the San Joaquin Valley in California, which is formed by the Coast Range to the west and the Sierra Nevadas to the east. The tops of the Sierras are usually covered with snow, and before dawn the temperature in the valley edges down to the frost point. In such cosmetic surroundings, it is no wonder that growers have heavily implanted the San Joaquin Valley with the Washington Navel Orange, which is the most beautiful orange grown in any quantity in the United

States, and is certainly as attractive to the eye as any orange grown in the world. Its color will go to a deep, flaring cadmium orange, and its surface has a suggestion of coarseness, which complements its perfect ellipsoid shape.

QUESTIONS

Ideas

1. Can you think of a generalization that would cover all the facts in paragraph 1; on what basis do they all hang together? Look carefully at the first two sentences.

2. Even though the last sentences in paragraph 1 refer specifically to the trees in the Bronx, could they serve as indirect topic sentences?

3. How would you describe the persona McPhee is using in all three paragraphs (which appear at the beginning of his book)?

4. For his opening, McPhee has decided to jump right into the uses of oranges around the world. How does this technique affect you?

5. Can you explain why oranges were used as symbols of love?

Organization

6. Should McPhee have used a more traditional introduction, stating explicitly what he intends to do?

7. After reading the first paragraph—and after catching your breath—what is your impression of how McPhee ordered his notes?

8. Is McPhee breaking the rules of paragraphing here? Are there hard-and-fast rules for professional writers or do you think they make up their own?

9. If you turned paragraph 1 in to one of your high school English teachers, what might have been the response?

10. Paragraphs 2 and 3 seem more traditional than paragraph 1. How are they organized and developed? What is the relation between the first sentence and those that follow?

Sentences

11. Typically, paragraphs cohere, that is, sentences are connected to preceding and succeeding sentences. Sometimes a writer will use explicit connecting chains, such as repeated words, synonyms, and transitional terms ("however," "but," "next," "this"). Sometimes the connections are less direct:

an extension of a previous idea, a more specific example of a general notion. Pick any six consecutive sentences in "Oranges" and explain how they are bound together.

Words

12. McPhee occasionally uses metaphors and similes (direct and indirect comparisons). Find as many of these devices as you can. What is their effect? Why do writers decide to make these comparisons?

Suggestions for Writing

A. Using the information in these three paragraphs, rewrite the piece, using a conventional beginning, middle, and end. Use an explicit topic sentence and arrange your details to support this generalization.
B. Pick another fruit, or a vegetable, and after doing library research, write an essay that develops in some details an aspect (use, history, etc.) of this food.

The Pineys

While isolation in the woods was bringing out self-reliance, it was also contributing to other developments that eventually attracted more attention. After the pine towns lost touch, to a large extent, with the outside world, some of the people slid into illiteracy, and a number slid further than that. Marriages were pretty casual in the pines late in the nineteenth century and early in the twentieth. For lawful weddings, people had to travel beyond the woods, to a place like Mt. Holly. Many went to native "squires," who performed weddings for a fee of one dollar. No questions were asked, even if the squires recognized the brides and the grooms as people they had married to other people a week or a month before. Given the small population of the pines, the extreme rarity of new people coming in, and the long span of time that most families had been there, some relationships were extraordinarily complicated and a few were simply incestuous. To varying degrees, there was a relatively high incidence in the pines of what in the terms of the era was called degeneracy, feeblemindedness, or mental deficiency.

In 1913, startling publicity was given to the most unfortunate stratum of the pine society, and the effects have not yet faded. In that year, Elizabeth Kite, a psychological researcher, published a report called "The Pineys," which had resulted from two years of visits to cabins in the pines. Miss Kite worked for the Vineland Training School, on the southern edge of the Pine Barrens, where important early work was being done with people of subnormal intelligence, and she was a fearless young woman who wore spotless white dresses as she rode in a horse-drawn wagon through the woods. Her concern for the people there became obvious to the people themselves, who grew fond of her, and even dependent upon her, and a colony for the care of the "fee-bleminded" was founded in the northern part of the Pine Barrens as a result of her work. Her report told of children who shared their bedrooms with pigs, of men who could not count beyond three, of a mother who walked nine miles with her children almost every day to get whiskey, of a couple who took a wheelbarrow with them when they went out drinking, so that one could wheel the other home. "In the heart of the region, scattered in widely separated huts over miles of territory, exists today a group of human beings as distinct in morals and manners as to excite curiosity and wonder in the mind of any outsider brought into contact with them," Miss Kite wrote. "They are recognized as a distinct people by the normal communities living on the borders of their forests." The report included some extremely gnarled family trees, such as one headed by Sam Bender, who conceived a child with his daughter, Mollie Bender Brooks, whose husband, Billie Brooks, sometimes said the child had been fathered by his wife's brother rather than her father, both possibilities being strong ones. When a district nurse was sent around to help clean up Mollie's house, chickens and a pig were found in the kitchen, and the first implement used in cleaning the house was a hoe. Mollie, according to Miss Kite, was "good-looking and sprightly, which fact, coupled with an utter lack of sense of decency, made her attractive even to men of otherwise normal intelligence." When Billie and all of their children were killed in a fire, Mollie said cheerfully, "Well, they was all insured. I'm still young and can easy start another family." Miss Kite reported some relationships that are almost impossible to follow. Of the occupants of another cabin, she wrote, "That May should call John 'Uncle' could be accounted for on the basis of a childish acceptance of 'no-matter-what' conditions, for the connection was that her mother was married to the brother of John's other woman's second man, and her mother's sister had had children by John. This bond of kinship did not, however, keep the families long together." Miss Kite also told of a woman who came to ask for food at a state almshouse on a bitter winter day. The people at the almshouse gave her a large burlap sack containing a basket of potatoes, a basket of turnips, three cabbages, four pounds of pork, five pounds of rye flour, two pounds of sugar, and some tea. The woman shouldered the sack and walked home cross-country through snow. Thirty minutes after she reached her home, she had a baby. No one helped her deliver it, nor had anyone helped her with the delivery of her nine other children.

Miss Kite's report was made public. Newspapers printed excerpts from it. All over the state, people became alarmed about conditions in the Pine Barrens—a region most of them had never heard of. James T. Fielder, the governor of New Jersey, travelled to the pines, returned to Trenton, and sought to increase his political momentum by recommending to the legislature that the Pine Barrens be somehow segregated from the rest of New Jersey in the interest of the health and safety of the people of the state at large. "I have been shocked at the conditions I have found," he said. "Evidently these people are a serious menace to the State of New Jersey because they produce so many persons that inevitably become public charges. They have inbred, and led lawless and scandalous lives, till they have become a race of imbeciles, criminals, and defectives." Meanwhile, H. H. Goddard, director of the research laboratory at the Vineland Training School and Miss Kite's immediate superior, had taken the genealogical charts that Miss Kite had painstakingly assembled, pondered them, extrapolated a bit, and published what became a celebrated treatise on a family called Kallikak—a name that Goddard said he had invented to avoid doing harm to real people. According to the theory set forth in the treatise, nearly all pineys were descended from one man. This man, Martin Kallikak, conceived an illegitimate son with an imbecile barmaid. Martin's bastard was said to be the forebear of generations of imbeciles, prostitutes, epileptics, and drunks. Martin himself, however, married a normal girl, and among their progeny were generations of normal and intelligent people, including doctors, lawyers, politicians, and a president of Princeton University. Goddard coined the name Kallikak from the Greek *kalós* and *kakós*— "good" and "bad." Goddard's work has been discredited, but its impact, like that of Governor Fielder's proposal to segregate the Pine Barrens, was powerful in its time. Even Miss Kite seemed to believe that there was some common flaw in the blood of all the people of the pines. Of one pinelands woman, Miss Kite wrote, "Strangely enough, this woman belonged originally to good stock. No piney blood flowed in her veins."

The result of all this was a stigma that has never worn off. A surprising number of people in New Jersey today seem to think that the Pine Barrens are dark backlands inhabited by hostile and semiliterate people who would as soon shoot an outsider as look at him. A policeman in Trenton who had never been to the pines—"only driven through on the way downa shore," as people usually say—once told me, in an anxious tone, that if I intended to spend a lot of time in the Pine Barrens I was asking for trouble. Some of the gentlest of people—botanists, canoemen, campers—spent a great deal of time in the pines, but their influence has not been sufficient to correct an impression, vivid in some parts of the state for fifty years, that the pineys are weird and sometimes dangerous barefoot people who live in caves, marry their sisters, and eat snakes. Pineys are, for the most part, mild and shy, but their resentment is deep, and they will readily and forcefully express it. The unfortunate people that Miss Kite described in her report were a minor fraction of the total population of the Pine Barrens, and the larger number suffered from it, and are still suffering from it. This appalled Elizabeth Kite, who said to an interviewer in 1940, some years before her death, "Nothing would give me greater pleasure than to correct the idea that has unfortunately been given by the newspapers regarding the pines. Anybody who lived in the pines was a piney. I think it a most terrible calamity that the newspapers publicly took the term and gave it the degenerate sting. Those families who were not potential state cases did not interest me as far as my study was concerned. I have no language in which I can express my admiration for the pines and the people who live there."

The people of the Pine Barrens turn cold when they hear the word "piney" spoken by anyone who is not a native. Over the years since 1913, in many places outside the pines, the stigma of degeneracy has been concentrated in that word. A part of what hurts them is that they themselves are fond of the word. They refer to one another freely, and frequently, as pineys. They have a strong regional pride, and, in a way that is not at all unflattering to them, they *are* different from the run of the people of the state. A visitor who stays awhile in the Pine Barrens soon feels that he is in another country, where attitudes and ambitions are at variance with the American norm. People who drive around in the pines and see houses like Fred Brown's, with tarpaper peeling from the walls, and automobiles overturned in the front yard, often decide, as they drive on, that they have just looked destitution in the face. I wouldn't call it that. I have yet to meet anyone living in the Pine Barrens who has in any way indicated envy of people who live elsewhere. One reason there are so many unpainted houses in the Pine Barrens is that the pineys believe, correctly, that their real-estate assessments would be higher if their houses were painted. Some pineys who make good money in blueberries or cranberries or in jobs on the outside would never think of painting their houses. People from other parts of New Jersey will say of Pine Barrens people, "They don't like to work. They can't seem to hold jobs." This, too, is a judgment based on outside values. What the piney usually says is "I hate to be tied down long to any one job." That remark is made so often in the pines that it is almost a local slogan. It expresses an attitude born of the old pines cycle—sphagnum in the spring, berries in the summer, coaling when the weather is cold. With the plenitude of the woodland around them—and, historically, behind them—pineys are bored with the idea of doing the same thing all year long, in every weather. Many of them have to, of course. Many work at regular jobs outside the woods. But many try that and give it up, preferring part-time labor—always at rest in the knowledge that no one who knows the woods and is willing to do a little work on his own is ever going to go hungry. The people have no difficulty articulating what it is that gives them a special feeling about the landscape they live in; they know that their environment is unusual and they know why they value it. Some, of course, put it with more finesse than others do. "I'm just a woods boy," a fellow named Jim Leek said to me one day. "There ain't nobody bothers you here. You can be alone. I'm just a woods boy. I wouldn't want to live in a town." When he said "town," he meant one of the small communities in the pines; he preferred living in the woods to living in a Pine Barrens town. When pineys talk about going to "the city," they usually mean Mt. Holly or the Moorestown Mall or the Two Guys from Harrison store on Route 206. When Jim Leek said "nobody bothers you" and "you can be alone," he was sounding two primary themes of the pines. Bill Wasovwich said one day, "The woods just look nice and it's more quieter. It's quiet anywhere in the pines. That's why I like it here." Another man, Scorchy Jones, who works for the state Fish and Game Division, said this to an interviewer from a small New Jersey radio station: "A sense of security is high among us. We were from pioneers. We know how to survive in the woods. Here in these woods areas, you have a reputation. A dishonest person can't survive in the community. You have to maintain your reputation, or you would have to jump from place to place. A man lives by his reputation and by his honesty and by his ambition to work. If he doesn't have it, he would be an outcast. These people have the reputations of their parents and grandparents ahead of them—and they are proud of them, and they want to maintain that same standard. They don't worship gold. All they want is necessities. They would rather live than make a lot of money. They live by this code. They're the best citizens in this country." Later in the interview, Jones said, "Unless these wild areas are preserved, we're going to get to the point where dense population is going to work on the nervous systems of the people, and the more that takes place, the poorer neighbors they become. Eventually, like birds or animals confined to too small an area, they will fight among themselves. Man is an animal as well." People known in the pines as "the old-time pineys"—those who lived wholly by the cycle, and seldom, if ever, saw an outsider—are gone now. When the United States Army built Camp Dix on the northwestern edge of the Pine Barrens during the First World War, civilian jobs were created, and many people of the pines first got to know what money was and how to use it. Paved roads first crossed the pines in the nineteen-twenties. Electrical lines, the Second World War, and television successively brought an end to the utter isolation of the pineys. But so far all this has not materially changed their attitudes. They are apparently a tolerant people, with an attractive spirit of live and let live. They seem to like hard work, if not steady work, and they like to brag about working hard. When they say they will do something, they do it. They seem shy, like the people who went before them, but when they get to know an outsider they are not shy and will generously share their tables, which often include new-potato stews and cranberry potpies. I have met Pine Barrens people who have, at one time or another, moved to other parts of the country. Most of them tried other lives for a while, only to return unreluctantly to the pines. One of them explained to me, "It's a privilege to live in these woods."

QUESTIONS

Ideas

1. How do you explain the behavior of the pineys?
2. What function does Miss Kite serve in this piece?
3. Do you think Mollie is amoral? What principles do the pineys operate on? Do they have a morality or a code that they follow?
4. Do you think it was unusual for the newspapers to have given the pineys such negative publicity?

5. What do you think McPhee thinks about the pineys? How can you tell? Look especially at the extended quotes he uses.

6. If you regarded this piece as a research essay (which, of course, it is), you might find it profitable to examine McPhee's way of integrating facts, details, quotes, dialogue, narration, and commentary into a seamless whole. At the end of this piece the reader knows a good deal. Jot down in phrases what you remember from a first reading, then go back and read the piece again, noting the amount of information McPhee is able to blend almost unnoticed into his account.

Organization

7. As Aristotle perceptively noted, effective pieces of writing tend to have a beginning, a middle, and an end. Composition textbooks often say an introduction, a body, and a conclusion. What kind of pattern is being used here?

8. Can you point to a thematic sentence that suggests the focus of this piece?

9. Look at the first sentence in each paragraph. What function does it serve?

Sentences

10. Is the first sentence in each paragraph shorter than the others, on the average? What might be a reason for this?

11. Notice how McPhee weaves quotes into his sentences to give them authority and force. Based on the second paragraph, write some general rules for using quotes. Include the use of commas, capital letters, and quote marks, and note especially McPhee's technique of using a quote as part of his sentence.

Words

12. What emotional association do you have to these words: "feeblemindedness," "mental deficiency," "imbeciles," and "degenerate." Can such connotations be changed?

Suggestions for Writing

A. Interview someone in class on a specific topic (favorite guitar player, sports hero, whatever). Copy down exact quotes and indirect quotes (exact meaning but not the specific words used). Now write up the interview using the quotes. Blend as many of the quotes as you can into your own sentences.

B. Do some focused research on a group that typically gets bad publicity. In writing your brief research essay arrange your facts and quotes so as to convey your attitude toward the group. (It can, of course, be positive or negative.)

The Swiss at War

1   It seems likely that the two most widely circulated remarks ever made about Switzerland's military prowess were made by Napoleon Bonaparte and Orson Welles.

2   Welles said, "In Italy for thirty years under the Borgias, they had warfare, terror, murder, bloodshed—but they produced Michelangelo, Leonardo da Vinci, and the Renaissance. In Switzerland, they have brotherly love, five hundred years of democracy and peace, and what did that produce? The cuckoo clock."

3   Napoleon said, "The best troops—those in whom you can have the most confidence—are the Swiss."

4   Welles spoke his lines in "The Third Man," a motion picture that deservedly attracted an extensive worldwide audience. The screenplay was written by Graham Greene, who later published the preliminary treatment in book form, but Greene was not the author of the lines about the Borgias and Switzerland. They were interpolated by the ingenious Welles, who may have chosen to suppress in his memory the fact that when Italy was enjoying the Borgias, Switzerland was enjoying a reputation as—to quote Douglas Miller's "The Swiss at War"—"the most powerful and feared military force in Europe." Switzerland was about as neutral in those days as had been Mongolia under Genghis Khan. Not only were the Swiss ready to fight. They fought. They had a militia system that could mobilize fifty-four thousand soldiers. They knew enough warfare and bloodshed to sicken a Borgia. They were so chillingly belligerent that even if they were destroyed in battle they had been known in the same moment to win a war. One afternoon in mid-Renaissance, a few hundred Swiss who were outnumbered fifteen to one elected not to run away but to wade across a river and break into the center of the opposition, where all of them died, but not before they had slaughtered three thousand of their French enemies. The French Army was so unnerved that it struck its tents and fled.

5   It was the Swiss who unhorsed the mounted knight, and in a sense

their confederation—their Everlasting League—was formed with that in mind. The peasants of the forest cantons made their pact of mutual defense because they wished not to be the vassals of alien equestrian lords. They waited twenty-four years for the first big test of their ability to resist—ample time to be prepared, to rehearse what they would do. Then, in 1315, two thousand Austrian knights appeared, leading a considerable army, and fatally attempted to make use of Morgarten pass. The knights were aristocrats, accustomed to tournament warfare and not to peasants attacking them from higher ground. The peasants came down on them with tree trunks, halberds, axes, and plummeting rock. The pass was blocked. The horses and riders became compressed and hopelessly jammed. The peasants rushed among them and hacked them down. Few knights survived. ("In the mountains, mechanization doesn't help you any. You are almost lost with armored cars.")

6   Also in the Renaissance, Swiss soldiers began sewing white crosses on their doublets, so they would recognize one another in the confusion of infantry battle. When mounted knights attacked them in open country, the Swiss formed squares—ten thousand soldiers in a square, bristling with twenty-one-foot pikes: the Porcupine Principle. In the course of time, they developed some interesting equipment. They developed the Lucerne hammer, fundamentally a poleaxe with a brass fist on its head and spikes protruding between the fingers. They developed the Morgenstern, an eight-foot cudgel with a sixteen-spike pineapple head. And they developed the Swiss Army knife.

7   Its precursor was a simple fifteenth-century dagger that every warrior carried. Over a hundred years, it acquired so many additions and complications that only officers and rich citizens could afford it, and it fell into disuse. It was an infantry weapon, but in its advanced stages it acquired built-in forks and other utensils. Competition waxed in the decorating of sheaths with scroll ornaments in gold and silver, and expensive foreign artists—such as the Hans Holbeins—were employed to do the work. The knife every soldier is issued today is jacketed with quilted gray aluminum, has one blade, a can opener, a bottle opener, a hole punch, two screwdrivers, and no corkscrew. On one side is a small red shield bearing the white cross. The knife is made identically by two companies—Victorinox and Wenger—that also make the red knives that in commercial display cases are all stuck apart like swastikas and include fish disgorgers, ski-wax scrapers, international wrenches, magnifying glasses, tweezers, toothpicks, scissors, and saws. The gray army knife resembles the simpler of the commercial offerings, minus the red plastic. Officers included, everyone in the Swiss Army carries a Swiss

Army knife. Once, at the end of a long session in driving snow with machine guns firing and grenades exploding—up on the high ground where such practice can be conducted with live ammunition—I walked down with the Fifth Regiment's Colonel Marc-Henri Chaudet, and when he reached the roadhead he discovered that his automobile would not start. It was a gray Mercedes-Benz, and—with its hood up—its engine looked even grayer, there in the wind and stinging snow, many miles from the nearest garage and almost as many from the nearest warm room. After six hours of storm weather and steep inclines, the Colonel might have been forgiven if he had displayed exasperation. This, after all, was Switzerland, where everything works; Switzerland, where trains run like clocks, and clocks run like watches, and watches are synchronous with the pulse of the universe; Switzerland, where electric eyes watch underground parking spaces and turn on green lights when they are free; Switzerland, where electric eyes watch urinals and flush not only the one under address but the one next to it as well; Switzerland, where switches in mattresses cause rooms to go dark as people get into bed; and now, in Switzerland, the Colonel was inconvenienced by this weather-whipped, tuned-down, one-jewel German car, which wheezed but would not cough. Colonel Chaudet—a Vevey lawyer—gave it a cool glance, sighting along his nose. Tall, slim, handsome—his trousers taut and neatly creased and disappearing inside his boots like a downhill skier's —the Colonel had a certain downplay in the corners of his mouth, suggesting, among other things, detached amusement. Besides, he had complete confidence in his soldiers and their equipment. Observing the difficulty, a corporal stepped forward, removed from a pocket his Swiss Army knife, used a fingernail to expose the can opener, and leaned into the Mercedes. Within ten minutes, the engine was running.

8   The Swiss infantry, six hundred years ago, knew not only how to form a square but also how to break through almost anything. At Sempach—a name of resonance in Switzerland—a soldier named Arnold Winkelried gathered to his body the pike points of many foemen, thus opening on either side of him holes in the Austrian line, through which the Swiss backfield poured, swinging six-foot halberds, while Winkelried died. For each Swiss who died at Sempach, nine Austrians died as well, many of them dismounted knights. Machiavelli called the Swiss "the new Romans." In the Quattrocento, exactly three hundred years before the United States declared its independence, the Swiss won a great victory at a small town called Morat, defeating Burgundian invaders who were threatening the city of Fribourg. Among the Swiss ordnance were mortars that shot chunks of limestone and granite. Four hundred and

ten Swiss died at Morat—and twelve thousand Burgundians. A durable legend sprang from this battle. To wit: a Swiss courier-soldier, carrying a linden branch, ran with the glorious news to Fribourg; all but breathless, he at last approached the ramparts and the towers of the town, and passed through the main gate and into the central square, where anxious Fribourgeois had formed a human circle—magistrates, priests, women on their knees—in the center of which the courier gathered his last three breaths, shouted "Victoire! Victoire! Victoire!" and fell dead, as later recorded, "la face contre terre." It has been suggested that this story is not without companionship in a genre! However that may be, there is an old sick linden in Fribourg that is thought to have grown from the branch the runner carried. Each year, in October, a footrace is run from Morat to Fribourg, and it now attracts about a hundred thousand spectators and eleven thousand runners. The race has been held for fifty years, with runners sometimes preparing for the ordeal by stretching their minds as well as their muscles—chanting in the streets, "Morat! Morat! Morat!" It doesn't matter that the distance is four-tenths of a marathon.

9   Swiss neutrality began in 1515, when the Swiss were thoroughly beaten by a French Army under François I at Marignano, in what is now Italy. "I have conquered those whom only Caesar managed to conquer before me," said the French king, and his words were struck in coin. The confederated cantons, by then thirteen, decided to fight thereafter only as mercenaries in other people's wars. They were a small nation, rustic, poor—nothing at all like the service-industry and manufacturing society we know today—and to embellish their economy they leased their incomparable soldiers. The cantons have always been importantly autonomous, and never more so than in the sixteenth century, when the political bond between Catholics and Protestants was under so much strain. It is unlikely that during the heaviest reverberations of the Reformation a cooperating army could have been assembled from the Protestant and Catholic cantons, and so, regardless of Marignano, neutrality was now less a matter of policy than a de-facto condition of Swiss life. The militia was then, as it has generally remained, cantonal in character. The cantons did the selling of soldiers. The French bought heavily for three hundred years—now twelve thousand Swiss, now seventy thousand Swiss, now a hundred and sixty-three thousand Swiss, depending on the intensity of the problems of France. For all that time, the Compagnie des Cent-Suisses were the personal bodyguards of the French kings. Scarcely had the Swiss soldiers appeared in the French court when the Pope decided that he wanted some, too; and the Pope,

of course, still has them, ninety in all—the only vestige of the Swiss mercenaries.

10   Switzerland is so conscious—not to say proud—of the service of its mercenaries in foreign armies that a château outside Geneva has been refurbished as a Musée des Suisses à l'Étranger. The most eminent mercenary of all was Colonel Louis Pfyffer, Roi des Suisses, who became a Swiss hero by serving four French kings. Jérôme d'Erlach, of Bern, became a Swiss hero as an Austrian field marshal. François Lefort, of Geneva, became a Swiss hero as a Russian general under Peter the Great, as Viceroy of the Grand Duchy of Novgorod, as President of all the Councils of Russia, and as the creator and Grand Admiral of the Russian Navy. Swiss mercenaries fought for the Scandinavian kingdoms, the Holy Roman Empire, the Netherlands, Prussia, Poland, Lorraine, Saxony, Savoy, Spain. In various battles, they fought on both sides. They served the Doge of Genoa, the King of Naples, the Elector of Brandenburg. For a large unnegotiable discount, they served Napoleon. Later, they became one of the perennially toughest components of the French Foreign Legion. In the Château de Penthes—the Musée des Suisses à l'Étranger—hangs a British Union Jack with a prominently inset Swiss white cross.

11   Contracts always specified that if Switzerland was attacked the soldiers would go back to Switzerland. All such contracts have been illegal for something over a hundred years. Meanwhile, by 1830 or so, in places like Bière, the militias of the various cantons were getting together to march, to exercise, to perform military legerdemain before people with parasols and uncorked wine, men in top hats chatting with soldiers in uniform attending the beginning of the federal army. Upward of a hundred thousand people will turn out today to watch the army parade and perform. A retired soldier will visit his unit's refresher course like an old college football player returning to watch a practice. Quite voluntarily, several thousand civilian soldiers annually collect for a thirty-kilometre footrace in which they carry packs and rifles. Beneath the long neutrality, there lies what the Swiss describe as "an aptitude for war." It appears to be an appetite as well-sublimited and under close control. The Landesmuseum in Zurich is the Louvre of the toy soldier. In glass cases there, toy soldiers by the ten thousand engage in replica battles. There are eight military museums in La Suisse Romande alone. In Morges, there are displays not only of Swiss military exploits but also of Aztec sacrifices, the Siege of Alesia (52 B.C.), and the Battle of Zama, with elephants. In the rooms the women come and go talking of Saint-Lô.

QUESTIONS

Ideas

1. Even though it is McPhee's style to efface himself, letting his facts do the work, can you still sense his attitude toward the Swiss military exploits? Point to specifics that suggest his opinions.

2. What seem to you to be the best examples of the Swiss "aptitude for war."

3. What was your response to the incident at the end of paragraph 4?

4. What impression of modern Switzerland is created? Do you think it is accurate?

5. McPhee often tries to make a point by stacking detail upon detail, gaining momentum through specifics. What, then, seems to be the purpose of paragraph 7?

Organization

6. If you were to use conventional structural designations such as beginning, middle, and end—or introduction, body, and conclusion—how would this piece be divided?

7. To some readers McPhee's paragraphs seem too long and dense. Might you break up paragraph 7 or does it hold together? How about paragraph 8?

Sentences

8. Look carefully at the sentence in paragraph 7 that begins, "this, after all, was Switzerland . . ." Imitate this pattern by writing one of your own, substituting "the United States" for the repeated "Switzerland."

9. Find other ways McPhee uses repetition in either his sentence beginnings or in their structure. Do you find it an effective technique?

Words

10. Look up the weapons McPhee mentions in a dictionary until you locate definitions for all of them. Explain the etymology of one. You might try the *Oxford English Dictionary*.

Suggestions for Writing

A. Write an essay in which you try to describe the American attitude toward war. You should try to take a broad historical perspective.

B. Is the American "aptitude for war . . . sublimated and under close control"? Write an essay using this question as a focus.

ELEVEN

Richard Selzer
(1928–   )

Richard Selzer is both a doctor and a writer. Like the American poet and pediatrician, William Carlos Williams, Selzer combines practicing medicine with writing about it. His books include one collection of stories, *Rituals of Surgery* (1974), and three collections of essays—*Mortal Lessons* (1977), *Confessions of a Knife* (1979), and *Letters to a Young Doctor* (1982). Throughout his work, Selzer explores the role and image of the physician, the relations between doctor and patient, and the workings of the diseased and healthy body in all its splendor.

Born in Troy, New York, in 1928, Selzer was educated at Union College, Albany Medical College, and Yale University. Since 1960 he has lived in New Haven, where he writes, teaches at the Yale Medical School, and conducts a private practice in surgery, his father's medical specialty.

Selzer did not begin his writing career until he was nearly forty, when he experienced a restless urgency to do something besides practice medicine. When he realized that he possessed the talent and the desire to be a writer, Selzer dedicated himself to learning the craft of writing as he had earlier devoted himself to the art of surgery. He began, as he put it, "suturing words together," a suturing he had to teach himself. His major preparation for this writerly work was reading. Among the writers Selzer cites as formative influences were the English essayists, particularly Chesterton, Lamb, and Hazlitt. Important also were the fiction writers, Poe and Patrick White, and the Catholic mystics, especially Saint Catherine of Siena and Saint John of the Cross. To these Selzer adds the French symbolist poets, Rimbaud, Verlaine, Baudelaire, and Mallarmé. From these writers Selzer derived a sense of linguistic precision and artistic passion. His own writing combines these elements in striking ways.

Selzer has spoken in an interview with Charles Shuster about the process of writing, which for him is a solitary one. He writes in longhand, which he says possesses "a special kind of magic" in which "the manual work of fashioning the words . . . flows out of your hand as though it were a secretion from your own body." The energy of writing carries Selzer along as he goes on line by line "to get it down as the burst comes." Following this "initial fever" of writing comes what Selzer describes as the work of the "sly fox" who calculates and manipulates the draft, tinkering with it, reconstructing and polishing it. And Selzer enjoys both these stages—the impetuous commitment to paper of words recording thoughts and feelings and the disciplined reining in of revision and editing.

Selzer has calculated that he writes sixty to seventy polished, publishable pages a year—and hundreds more from which he distills those. In his published prose he aims to accomplish a number of things: to evoke experience, to amuse, to inform. Amid his lyric outpourings of language, his sometimes sensational subjects and details, Selzer aims to establish, as he points out, "a kinship with the reader," as if to say, "we're both in this together." (And by "this" Selzer means both this life about which the writing centers and also the writing itself.)

Beneath these purposes lie two others: to come to terms with his vocation and identity as doctor and writer; to make out of his experience as surgeon works of literary art. Selzer himself put it clearly and forcefully: "I am writing," he says, "to make art. That's the whole thing. To write the best I can." And when he is writing to this high standard, Selzer's words perform a double function: they teach and they heal. They heal the writer, who makes himself whole in finding language to express his sense of self and the world; and they heal the reader, who experiences the power and pleasure of art. In the act of writing, Selzer the surgeon of the body becomes a doctor of the soul.

Love Sick

---

1   Love is an illness, and has its own set of obsessive thoughts. Behold the poor wretch afflicted with love: one moment strewn upon a sofa, scarcely breathing save for an occasional sigh upsucked from the

deep well of his despair; the next, pacing *agitato,* his cheek alternately pale and flushed. Is he pricked? What barb, what gnat stings him thus?

2　At noon he waves away his plate of food. Unloved, he loathes his own body, and refuses it the smallest nourishment. At half-past twelve, he receives a letter. She loves him! And soon he is snout-deep in his dish, voracious as any wolf at entrails. Greeted by a friend, a brother, he makes no discernible reply, but gazes to and fro, unable to recall who it is that salutes him. Distraught, he picks up a magazine, only to stand wondering what it is he is holding. Was he once clever at the guitar? He can no longer play at all. And so it goes.

3　Ah, Cupid, thou wanton boy. How cruel thy sport!

4　See how the man of sorrows leans against a wall, one hand shielding his eyes from vertigo, the other gripping his chest to muffle the palpitations there. Let some stray image of his beloved flit across his mind, her toe perhaps, or scarf, and all at once, his chin and brow gleam with idiotic rapture. But wait! Now some trivial slight is recalled, and once again, his face is a mask of anguish, empurpled and carved with deep lines.

5　Such, such are the joys of love. May Heaven protect us, one and all, from this happiness. One marvels at the single-celled paramecium, who, without the least utterance of distemper, procreates by splitting in two. One can but envy the paramecium his solitary fission.

6　Love is an illness and, not unlike its sister maladies, hysteria, hypochondriasis, and melancholia, has its own set of obsessive thoughts. In love, the *idée fixe* that harries the patient every waking hour is not remorse, nor the fear of cancer, nor the dread of death, but that single other *person.* Every disease has its domain, its *locus operandi.* If, in madness, it is the brain, in cirrhosis, the liver, and lumbago, the spine, in love it is that web of knobs and filaments known as the autonomic nervous system. How ironic that here, in this all but invisible network, should lie hidden the ultimate carnal mystery. Mischievous Nature, having arranged to incite copulation by assigning opposite hormones to half the human race, and sculpted the curves of the flesh to accommodate the process, now throws over the primitive rite a magic veil, a web of difficulty that is the autonomic nervous system. It is the malfunction, the deficiency of this system that produces the disease of love. Here it fulminates, driving its luckless victims to madness or suicide. How many the lovers that have taken that final tragic step, and were found swinging from the limb of some lonely tree, airing their pathetic rags? The autonomic nervous system! Why not the massive liver? The solid spleen?

Or the skin, from which the poison might be drawn with knife or poultice?

7   Lying upon the front of each of the vertebrae, from the base of the skull to the tip of the coccyx, is a paired chain of tiny nodes, each of which is connected to the spinal cord and to each other. From these nodes, bundles of nerves extend to meet at relay stations scattered in profusion throughout the body. These ganglia are in anatomical touch with their fellows by a system of circuitry complex and various enough to confound into self-destruction a whole race of computers. Here all is chemical rush and wave-to-wave ripple. Here is fear translated for the flesh, and pride and jealousy. Here dwell zeal and ardor. And love is contracted. By microscopic nervelets, the impulses are carried to all the capillaries, hair follicles and sweat glands of the body. The smooth muscle of the intestine, the lachrymal glands, the bladder, and the genitalia are all subject to the bombardment that issues from this vibrating harp of knobs and strings. Innumerable are the orders delivered: Constrict! Dilate! Secrete! Stand erect! It is all very busy, effervescent.

8   In defense of the autonomic nervous system, it must be said that it is uncrippled by the intellect or the force of the will. Intuition governs here. Here is one's flesh wholly trustworthy, for it speaks with honesty all the attractions and repulsions of our lives. Consciousness here would be an intruder, justly driven away from the realm of the transcendent. One *feels;* therefore one *is.* No opinion but spontaneous feeling prevails. Is tomorrow's love expected? Yesterday's recalled? Instantly, the thought is captured by the autonomic nervous system. And alchemy turns wish and dream to ruddy reality. The billion capillaries of the face dilate and fill with blood. You blush. You are prettier. Is love spurned? Again the rippling, the dance of energy, and the bed of capillaries constricts, squeezing the blood from the surface to some more central pool. Now you blanch. The pallor of death is upon you. Icy are your own fingertips. It is the flesh responding to the death of love with its own facsimile.

9   Imagine that you are in the painful state of unrequited love. You are seated at a restaurant table with your beloved. You reach for the salt; at the same moment, she for the pepper goes. Your fingers accidentally touch cellar-side. There is a sudden instantaneous discharge of the autonomic nervous system, and your hand recoils. It is singed by fire. Now, the capillaries of your cheeks are commanded to dilate. They fill with blood. Its color is visible in your skin. You go from salmon pink to

fiery red. "Why, you are blushing," she says, and smiles cruelly. Even as she speaks, your sweat glands have opened their gates, and you are coated with wetness. You sop. She sees, and raises one eyebrow. Now the sounds of your intestine, those gurgles and gaseous pops called borborygmi, come distinctly to your ears. You press your abdomen to still them. But, she hears! The people at the neighboring tables do, too. All at once, she turns her face to the door. She rises. Suddenly, it is time for her to go. Unhappy lover, you are in the grip of your autonomic nervous system, and by its betrayal you are thus undone.

10   Despite that love is an incurable disease, yet is there reason for hope. Should the victim survive the acute stages, he may then expect that love will lose much of its virulence, that it will burn itself out, like other self-limiting maladies. In fact, this is becoming more and more the natural history of love, and a good thing at that. Lucky is he in whom love dies, and lust lives on. For he who is tormented by the protracted fevers of chronic undying love awaits but a premature and exhausted death. While lust, which engages not the spirit, serves but to restore the vigor and stimulate the circulation.

11   Still, one dreams of bringing about a cure. For the discoverer of such, a thousand Nobels would be too paltry a reward. Thus I have engaged the initial hypothesis (call it a hunch) that there is somewhere in the body, under the kneecap perhaps, or between the fourth and fifth toes . . . somewhere . . . a single, as yet unnoticed master gland, the removal of which would render the person so operated upon immune to love. Daily, in my surgery, I hunt this *glans amoris,* turning over membranes, reaching into dim tunnels, straining all the warm extrusions of the body for some residue that will point the way.

12   Perhaps I shall not find it in my lifetime. But never, I vow it, shall I cease from these labors, and shall charge those who come after me to carry on the search. Until then, I would agree with my Uncle Frank, who recommends a cold shower and three laps around the block for the immediate relief of the discomforts of love.

QUESTIONS

Ideas

1. What view of love emerges from this essay? What image of the lover is presented and what is Selzer's attitude toward him?

2. Do you agree with Selzer that love is an illness like hypochondria or melancholia? Do you see any problems with a definition of love that explains a state of mind and feeling in terms of the autonomic nervous system?

Organization

3. Divide "Love Sick" into sections. Title the sections and explain the basis of your division.

4. Reorder Selzer's paragraphs. Consider, for example, using paragraph 9 as the opening of the essay, followed by paragraphs 7 and 8. Where might the essay go from there?

Sentences

5. Consider the frequency, manner, and purpose of Selzer's interrogative sentences, which appear in paragraphs 1, 6, and 8. What is their effect? How would the tone of the essay change if you were to rewrite the questions as declarative statements?

6. Consider also the frequency of the exclamatory sentences in paragraphs 3, 4, and 7. What effect do these exclamations create?

7. Notice the use of repeated sentence forms in paragraph 8: "Here all is . . ." "Here is fear . . ." "Here dwell zeal . . ." What is the effect of this repetition in form. Notice, too, how throughout the essay Selzer varies the lengths of his sentences. Look, for example, at paragraphs 5 and 8.

Words

8. Identify the foreign words Selzer uses. Substitute for each an English equivalent and explain any difference in tone you detect.

9. What effect does Selzer's inclusion of technical language have? Check on the meanings of the following words: "autonomic," "coccyx," "nodes," "ganglia," "capillaries," "virulence," "borborygmi."

Suggestions for Writing

A. Write imitations of the following sentences.

One *feels;* therefore one *is.*

No opinion but spontaneous feeling prevails.

Such, such are the joys of love.

B. Write an imitation of any paragraphs (5 or 6 perhaps) attending particularly to its mixture of long and short sentences.

C. Argue for or against Selzer's view that love is an illness.
D. Compare and contrast the image of the lover in "Love Sick" with that in the following poem.

SYMPTOMS OF LOVE

Love is a universal migraine,
A bright stain on the vision
Blotting out reason.

Symptoms of true love
Are leanness, jealousy,
Laggard dawns;

Are omens and nightmares—
Listening for a knock,
Waiting for a sign:

For a touch of her fingers
In a darkened room,
For a searching look.

Take courage, lover!
Could you endure such pain
At any hand but hers?

—ROBERT GRAVES

The Knife

1   One holds the knife as one holds the bow of a cello or a tulip—by the stem. Not palmed nor gripped nor grasped, but lightly, with the tips of the fingers. The knife is not for pressing. It is for drawing across the field of skin. Like a slender fish, it waits, at the ready, then, go! It darts, followed by a fine wake of red. The flesh parts, falling away to yellow globules of fat. Even now, after so many times, I still marvel at its power—cold, gleaming, silent. More, I am still struck with a kind of dread that it is I in whose hand the blade travels, that my hand is its vehicle, that yet again this terrible steel-bellied thing and I have conspired for a most unnatural purpose, the laying open of the body of a human being.

2   A stillness settles in my heart and is carried to my hand. It is the quietude of resolve layered over fear. And it is this resolve that lowers

us, my knife and me, deeper and deeper into the person beneath. It is an entry into the body that is nothing like a caress; still, it is among the gentlest of acts. Then stroke and stroke again, and we are joined by other instruments, hemostats and forceps, until the wound blooms with strange flowers whose looped handles fall to the sides in steely array.

3   There is sound, the tight click of clamps fixing teeth into severed blood vessels, the snuffle and gargle of the suction machine clearing the field of blood for the next stroke, the litany of monosyllables with which one prays his way down and in: *clamp, sponge, suture, tie, cut.* And there is color. The green of the cloth, the white of the sponges, the red and yellow of the body. Beneath the fat lies the fascia, the tough fibrous sheet encasing the muscles. It must be sliced and the red beef of the muscles separated. Now there are retractors to hold apart the wound. Hands move together, part, weave. We are fully engaged, like children absorbed in a game or the craftsmen of some place like Damascus.

4   Deeper still. The peritoneum, pink and gleaming and membranous, bulges into the wound. It is grasped with forceps, and opened. For the first time we can see into the cavity of the abdomen. Such a primitive place. One expects to find drawings of buffalo on the walls. The sense of trespassing is keener now, heightened by the world's light illuminating the organs, their secret colors revealed—maroon and salmon and yellow. The vista is sweetly vulnerable at this moment, a kind of welcoming. An arc of the liver shines high and on the right, like a dark sun. It laps over the pink sweep of the stomach, from whose lower border the gauzy omentum is draped, and through which veil one sees, sinuous, slow as just-fed snakes, the indolent coils of the intestine.

5   You turn aside to wash your gloves. It is a ritual cleansing. One enters this temple doubly washed. Here is man as microcosm, representing in all his parts the earth, perhaps the universe.

6   I must confess that the priestliness of my profession has ever been impressed on me. In the beginning there are vows, taken with all solemnity. Then there is the endless harsh novitiate of training, much fatigue, much sacrifice. At last one emerges as celebrant, standing close to the truth lying curtained in the Ark of the body. Not surplice and cassock but mask and gown are your regalia. You hold no chalice, but a knife. There is no wine, no wafer. There are only the facts of blood and flesh.

7   In the room the instruments lie on trays and tables. They are arranged precisely by the scrub nurse, in an order that never changes, so that you can reach blindly for a forceps or hemostat without looking away from the operating field. The instruments lie *thus!* Even at the beginning, when all is clean and tidy and no blood has been spilled, it

is the scalpel that dominates. It has a figure the others do not have, the retractors and the scissors. The scalpel is all grace and line, a fierceness. It grins. It is like a cat—to be respected, deferred to, but which returns no amiability. To hold it above a belly is to know the knife's force—as though were you to give it slightest rein, it would pursue an intent of its own, driving into the flesh, a wild energy.

8   In a story by Borges, a deadly knife fight between two rivals is depicted. It is not, however, the men who are fighting. It is the knives themselves that are settling their own old score. The men who hold the knives are mere adjuncts to the weapons. The unguarded knife is like the unbridled war-horse that not only carries its helpless rider to his death, but tramples all beneath its hooves. The hand of the surgeon must tame this savage thing. He is a rider reining to capture a pace.

9   So close is the joining of knife and surgeon that they are like the Centaur—the knife, below, all equine energy, the surgeon, above, with his delicate art. One holds the knife back as much as advances it to purpose. One is master of the scissors. One is partner, sometimes rival, to the knife. In a moment it is like the long red fingernail of the Dragon Lady. Thus does the surgeon curb in order to create, restraining the scalpel, governing it shrewdly, setting the action of the operation into a pattern, giving it form and purpose.

10   It is the nature of creatures to live within a tight cuirass that is both their constriction and their protection. The carapace of the turtle is his fortress and retreat, yet keeps him writhing on his back in the sand. So is the surgeon rendered impotent by his own empathy and compassion. The surgeon cannot weep. When he cuts the flesh, his own must not bleed. Here it is all work. Like an asthmatic hungering for air, longing to take just one deep breath, the surgeon struggles not to feel. It is suffocating to press the feeling out. It would be easier to weep or mourn—for you know that the lovely precise world of proportion contains, just beneath, *there*, all disaster, all disorder. In a surgical operation, a risk may flash into reality: the patient dies . . . of *complication.* The patient knows this too, in a more direct and personal way, and he is afraid.

11   And what of that *other,* the patient, you, who are brought to the operating room on a stretcher, having been washed and purged and dressed in a white gown? Fluid drips from a bottle into your arm, diluting you, leaching your body of its personal brine. As you wait in the corridor, you hear from behind the closed door the angry clang of steel upon steel, as though a battle were being waged. There is the odor of antiseptic and ether, and masked women hurry up and down the halls,

in and out of rooms. There is the watery sound of strange machinery, the tinny beeping that is the transmitted heartbeat of yet another *human being*. And all the while the dreadful knowledge that soon you will be taken, laid beneath great lamps that will reveal the secret linings of your body. In the very act of lying down, you have made a declaration of surrender. One lies down gladly for sleep or for love. But to give over one's body and will for surgery, to *lie down* for it, is a yielding of more than we can bear.

12   Soon a man will stand over you, gowned and hooded. In time the man will take up a knife and crack open your flesh like a ripe melon. Fingers will rummage among your viscera. Parts of you will be cut out. Blood will run free. Your blood. All the night before you have turned with the presentiment of death upon you. You have attended your funeral, wept with your mourners. You think, "I should never have had surgery in the springtime." It is too cruel. Or on a Thursday. It is an unlucky day.

13   Now it is time. You are wheeled in and moved to the table. An injection is given. "Let yourself go," I say. "It's a pleasant sensation," I say. "Give in," I say.

14   Let go? Give in? When you know that you are being tricked into the hereafter, that you will end when consciousness ends? As the monstrous silence of anesthesia falls discourteously across your brain, you watch your soul drift off.

15   Later, in the recovery room, you awaken and gaze through the thickness of drugs at the world returning, and you guess, at first dimly, then surely, that you have not died. In pain and nausea you will know the exultation of death averted, of life restored.

16   What is it, then, this thing, the knife, whose shape is virtually the same as it was three thousand years ago, but now with its head grown detachable? Before steel, it was bronze. Before bronze, stone—then back into unremembered time. Did man invent it or did the knife precede him here, hidden under ages of vegetation and hoofprints, lying in wait to be discovered, picked up, used?

17   The scalpel is in two parts, the handle and the blade. Joined, it is six inches from tip to tip. At one end of the handle is a narrow notched prong upon which the blade is slid, then snapped into place. Without the blade, the handle has a blind, decapitated look. It is helpless as a trussed maniac. But slide on the blade, click it home, and the knife springs instantly to life. It is headed now, edgy, leaping to mount the fingers for the gallop to its feast.

18 Now is the moment from which you have turned aside, from which you have averted your gaze, yet toward which you have been hastened. Now the scalpel sings along the flesh again, its brute run unimpeded by germs or other frictions. It is a slick slide home, a barracuda spurt, a rip of embedded talon. One listens, and almost hears the whine—nasal, high, delivered through that gleaming metallic snout. The flesh splits with its own kind of moan. It is like the penetration of rape.

19 The breasts of women are cut off, arms and legs sliced to the bone to make ready for the saw, eyes freed from sockets, intestines lopped. The hand of the surgeon rebels. Tension boils through his pores, like sweat. The flesh of the patient retaliates with hemorrhage, and the blood chases the knife wherever it is withdrawn.

20 Within the belly a tumor squats, toadish, fungoid. A gray mother and her brood. The only thing it does not do is croak. It too is hacked from its bed as the carnivore knife lips the blood, turning in it in a kind of ecstasy of plenty, a gluttony after the long fast. It is just for this that the knife was created, tempered, heated, its violence beaten into paper-thin force.

21 At last a little thread is passed into the wound and tied. The monstrous booming fury is stilled by a tiny thread. The tempest is silenced. The operation is over. On the table, the knife lies spent, on its side, the bloody meal smear-dried upon its flanks. The knife rests.

22 And waits.

QUESTIONS

Ideas

1. What does Selzer suggest about the surgeon's knife, the scalpel? What images of the instrument does he present?

2. What impression of the surgeon emerges in this essay? What attitude toward the body does the writer take?

Organization

3. Map out the structure of the essay. What are its major divisions? Provide titles for the sections you identify.

4. In paragraph 8 Selzer alludes to a story by the Argentinian writer, Jorge Luis Borges. How is this allusion relevant to Selzer's discussion? What would be gained or lost if this paragraph were omitted? Why?

Sentences

5. Notice the balanced phrasing of the following sentence, and comment on the effect of its repetitions.

> More, I am still struck with a kind of dread
> that it is I in whose hand the blade travels,
> that my hand is its vehicle,
> that yet again I have conspired for a most unnatural purpose,
> the laying open of the body of a human being.

6. Consider the effect of the following sentences, all of which include dashes. Substitute commas for the dashes and comment on the differences in tone you detect.

> One holds the knife as one holds the bow of a cello or a tulip—by the stem.

> Even now, after so many times, I still marvel at its power—cold, gleaming, silent.

7. Throughout the essay Selzer switches from the informal pronoun, "I," to the formal "one," with an occasional use of the second-person pronoun, "you." Look, for example, at paragraphs 1, 5, and 6. Try making all the pronouns the same. What happens? What are the advantages or disadvantages of mixing pronouns as Selzer does here?

8. What effects does Selzer achieve with his use of questions in paragraphs 11, 12, and 16?

9. Identify and comment on the effectiveness of the sentence fragments in paragraphs 1, 3, 4, 12, 20, and 22.

Words

10. Identify and comment on the effectiveness of the comparisons in the first two paragraphs.

11. Consider the use of onomatopoeia—the use of words to imitate the sounds they describe—in paragraph 3: "click," "snuffle," "gargle."

12. Identify the medical terms Selzer employs. Substitute a less technical word for each and explain what is gained or lost with the alterations.

Suggestions for Writing

A. Describe an object that is important in your work or play: a musical instrument, a tool, a vehicle, a piece of equipment—some item you are thoroughly familiar with. Try to see it as possessing a life and set of intentions. Try to see it in different ways. In the process, explain what it does and why it's important.

B. If you've undergone surgery, write an essay describing your perception of the event. Try to remember what the experience was like for you so you can recreate it for your readers.

The Masked Marvel's Last Toehold

MORNING ROUNDS.

On the fifth floor of the hospital, in the west wing, I know that a man is sitting up in his bed, waiting for me. Elihu Koontz is seventy-five, and he is diabetic. It is two weeks since I amputated his left leg just below the knee. I walk down the corridor, but I do not go straight into his room. Instead, I pause in the doorway. He is not yet aware of my presence, but gazes down at the place in the bed where his leg used to be, and where now there is the collapsed leg of his pajamas. He is totally absorbed, like an athlete appraising the details of his body. What is he thinking, I wonder. Is he dreaming the outline of his toes? Does he see there his foot's incandescent ghost? Could he be angry? Feel that I have taken from him something for which he yearns now with all his heart? Has he forgotten so soon the pain? It was a pain so great as to set him apart from all other men, in a red-hot place where he had no kith or kin. What of those black gorilla toes and the soupy mess that was his heel? I watch him from the doorway. It is a kind of spying, I know.

2   Save for a white fringe open at the front, Elihu Koontz is bald. The hair has grown too long and is wilted. He wears it as one would wear a day-old laurel wreath. He is naked to the waist, so that I can see his breasts. They are the breasts of Buddha, inverted triangles from which the nipples swing, dark as garnets.

3   I have seen enough. I step into the room, and he sees that I am there.

4   "How did the night go, Elihu?"

5   He looks at me for a long moment. "Shut the door," he says.

6   I do, and move to the side of the bed. He takes my left hand in both of his, gazes at it, turns it over, then back, fondling, at last holding it up to his cheek. I do not withdraw from this loving. After a while he relinquishes my hand, and looks up at me.

7   "How is the pain?" I ask.

8   He does not answer, but continues to look at me in silence. I know at once that he has made a decision.

9   "Ever hear of The Masked Marvel?" He says this in a low voice, almost a whisper.

10   "What?"

11   "The Masked Marvel," he says. "You never heard of him?"

12   "No."

13   He clucks his tongue. He is exasperated.

14   All at once there is a recollection. It is dim, distant, but coming near.

15   "Do you mean the wrestler?"

16   Eagerly, he nods, and the breasts bob. How gnomish he looks, oval as the huge helpless egg of some outlandish lizard. He has very long arms, which, now and then, he unfurls to reach for things—a carafe of water, a get-well card. He gazes up at me, urging. He *wants* me to remember.

17   "Well . . . yes," I say. I am straining backward in time. "I saw him wrestle in Toronto long ago."

18   "Ha!" He smiles. "You saw *me*. And his index finger, held rigid and upright, bounces in the air."

19   The man has said something shocking, unacceptable. It must be challenged.

20   "You?" I am trying to smile.

21   Again that jab of the finger. "You saw *me*."

22   "No," I say. But even then, something about Elihu Koontz, those prolonged arms, the shape of his head, the sudden agility with which he leans from his bed to get a large brown envelope from his nightstand, something is forcing me toward a memory. He rummages through his papers, old newspaper clippings, photographs, and I remember . . .

23   It is almost forty years ago. I am ten years old. I have been sent to Toronto to spend the summer with relatives. Uncle Max has bought two tickets to the wrestling match. He is taking me that night.

24   "He isn't allowed," says Aunt Sarah to me. Uncle Max has angina.

25   "He gets too excited," she says.

26   "I wish you wouldn't go, Max," she says.

27   "You mind your own business," he says.

28   And we go. Out into the warm Canadian evening. I am not only abroad, I am abroad in the *evening!* I have never been taken out in the evening. I am terribly excited. The trolleys, the lights, the horns. It is a bazaar. At the Maple Leaf Gardens, we sit high and near the center. The vast arena is dark except for the brilliance of the ring at the bottom.

29   It begins.

30   The wrestlers circle. They grapple. They are all haunch and paunch. I am shocked by their ugliness, but I do not show it. Uncle Max is exhilarated. He leans forward, his eyes unblinking, on his face a look of enormous happiness. One after the other, a pair of wrestlers enter the ring. The two men join, twist, jerk, tug, bend, yank, and throw. Then they leave and are replaced by another pair. At last it is the main event. "The Angel vs. The Masked Marvel."

31   On the cover of the program notes, there is a picture of The Angel hanging from the limb of a tree, a noose of thick rope around his neck. The Angel hangs just so for an hour every day, it is explained, to strengthen his neck. The Masked Marvel's trademark is a black stocking cap with holes for the eyes and mouth. He is never seen without it, states the program. No one knows who The Masked Marvel really is!

32   "Good," says Uncle Max. "Now you'll see something." He is fidgeting, waiting for them to appear. They come down separate aisles, climb into the ring from opposite sides. I have never seen anything like them. It is The Angel's neck that first captures the eye. The shaved nape rises in twin columns to puff into the white hood of a sloped and bosselated skull that is too small. As though, strangled by the sinews of that neck, the skull had long since withered and shrunk. The thing about The Angel is the absence of any mystery in his body. It is simply *there.* A monosyllabic announcement. A grunt. One looks and knows everything at once, the fat thighs, the gigantic buttocks, the great spine from which hang knotted ropes and pale aprons of beef. And that prehistoric head. He is all of a single hideous piece, The Angel is. No detachables.

33   The Masked Marvel seems dwarfish. His fingers dangle kneeward. His short legs are slightly bowed as if under the weight of the cask they are forced to heft about. He has breasts that swing when he moves! I have never seen such breasts on a man before.

34   There is a sudden ungraceful movement, and they close upon one another. The Angel stoops and hugs The Marvel about the waist, lock-

ing his hands behind The Marvel's back. Now he straightens and lifts
The Marvel as though he were uprooting a tree. Thus he holds him, then
stoops again, thrusts one hand through The Marvel's crotch, and with
the other grabs him by the neck. He rears and . . . The Marvel is aloft!
For a long moment, The Angel stands as though deciding where to make
the toss. Then throws. Was that board or bone that splintered there?
Again and again, The Angel hurls himself upon the body of The Masked
Marvel.

35   Now The Angel rises over the fallen Marvel, picks up one foot in
both of his hands, and twists the toes downward. It is far beyond the
tensile strength of mere ligament, mere cartilage. The Masked Marvel
does not hide his agony, but pounds and slaps the floor with his hand,
now and then reaching up toward The Angel in an attitude of supplica-
tion. I have never seen such suffering. And all the while his black mask
rolls from side to side, the mouth pulled to a tight slit through which
issues an endless hiss that I can hear from where I sit. All at once, I hear
a shouting close by.

36   "Break it off! Tear off a leg and throw it up here!"

37   It is Uncle Max. Even in the darkness I can see that he is gray.
A band of sweat stands upon his upper lip. He is on his feet now,
panting, one fist pressed at his chest, the other raised warlike toward the
ring. For the first time I begin to think that something terrible might
happen here. Aunt Sarah was right.

38   "Sit down, Uncle Max," I say. "Take a pill, please."

39   He reaches for the pillbox, gropes, and swallows without taking his
gaze from the wrestlers. I wait for him to sit down.

40   "That's not fair," I say, "twisting his toes like that."

41   "It's the toehold," he explains.

42   "But it's not *fair*," I say again. The whole of the evil is laid open
for me to perceive. I am trembling.

43   And now The Angel does something unspeakable. Holding the
foot of The Marvel at full twist with one hand, he bends and grasps the
mask where it clings to the back of The Marvel's head. And he pulls.
He is going to strip it off! Lay bare an ultimate carnal mystery! Suddenly
it is beyond mere physical violence. Now I am on my feet, shouting into
the Maple Leaf Gardens.

44   "Watch out," I scream. "Stop him. Please, somebody, stop him."

45   Next to me, Uncle Max is chuckling.

46   Yet The Masked Marvel hears me, I know it. And rallies from his

bed of pain. Thrusting with his free heel, he strikes The Angel at the back of the knee. The Angel falls. The Masked Marvel is on top of him, pinning his shoulders to the mat. One! Two! Three! And it is over. Uncle Max is strangely still. I am grasping for breath. All this I remember as I stand at the bedside of Elihu Koontz.

47   Once again, I am in the operating room. It is two years since I amputated the left leg of Elihu Koontz. Now it is his right leg which is gangrenous. I have already scrubbed. I stand to one side wearing my gown and gloves. And . . . *I am masked.* Upon the table lies Elihu Koontz, pinned in a fierce white light. Spinal anesthesia has been administered. One of his arms is taped to a board placed at a right angle to his body. Into this arm, a needle has been placed. Fluid drips here from a bottle overhead. With his other hand, Elihu Koontz beats feebly at the side of the operating table. His head rolls from side to side. His mouth is pulled into weeping. It seems to me that I have never seen such misery.

48   An orderly stands at the foot of the table, holding Elihu Koontz's leg aloft by the toes so that the intern can scrub the limb with antiseptic solutions. The intern paints the foot, ankle, leg, and thigh, both front and back, three times. From a corner of the room where I wait, I look down as from an amphitheater. Then I think of Uncle Max yelling, "Tear off a leg. Throw it up here." And I think that forty years later I am making the catch.

49   "It's not fair," I say aloud. But no one hears me. I step forward to break The Masked Marvel's last toehold.

QUESTIONS

Ideas

1. What are the point and purpose of this essay? What do you think Selzer tries to accomplish here? Does the essay have a single main point or thesis? If so, what do you think it is?

2. In what way(s) does the surgeon break The Masked Marvel's toehold? Consider the various meanings of "break."

3. Compare the reactions of the boy and his uncle as they watch the wrestling match. How do you respond and evaluate the reactions of each? Why?

Organization

4. Selzer arranges his essay in three parts. Explain the relationship among the three sections. Consider how time is shaped—how chronology is broken—and with what effects.

5. What details from the second section parallel those of the first? What parallels exist between parts II and III? (Consider especially the opening paragraph of part III.)

Sentences

6. What are the purpose and effect of the interrogative sentences in the opening paragraph? How would the tone of the paragraph change if these questions were converted to declarative sentences?

7. On occasion Selzer employs sentence fragments, especially in paragraphs 21, 32, and 46. Identify the fragments and consider whether they would be more or less effective if revised into complete sentences.

Words

8. Identify and consider the effectiveness of the similes and metaphors in paragraphs 1 and 32. Explain the purposes and bases of each of the comparisons.

9. Note the profusion and precision of verbs at specific points in the essay —in paragraphs 30 and 34, for example. Account for the accuracy of each verb in these paragraphs. Substitute a few alternative verbs and consider their effectiveness.

Suggestions for Writing

A. Using the questions above, write an essay analyzing "The Masked Marvel's Last Toehold." Interpret the essay, considering not only what Selzer says, but how he says it as well.

B. Describe a climactic moment of an athletic event—or of any kind of performance or contest. Try to recapture your experience of the event and provide the reader with a sense of being there.

C. Write an essay comparing or classifying different kinds of sports fans. You might compare two kinds of wrestling or baseball fans. Or you might identify characteristics that distinguish baseball fans from football fans. As another possibility, consider defining the word *fan* in an essay that highlights and explains the qualities that make a fan what he or she is.

Imelda

I

1   I heard the other day that Hugh Franciscus had died. I knew him once. He was the Chief of Plastic Surgery when I was a medical student at Albany Medical College. Dr. Franciscus was the archetype of the professor of surgery—tall, vigorous, muscular, as precise in his technique as he was impeccable in his dress. Each day a clean lab coat monkishly starched, that sort of thing. I doubt that he ever read books. One book only, that of the human body, took the place of all others. He never raised his eyes from it. He read it like a printed page as though he knew that in the calligraphy there just beneath the skin were all the secrets of the world. Long before it became visible to anyone else, he could detect the first sign of granulation at the base of a wound, the first blue line of new epithelium at the periphery that would tell him that a wound would heal, or the barest hint of necrosis that presaged failure. This gave him the appearance of a prophet. "This skin graft will take," he would say, and you must believe beyond all cyanosis, exudation and inflammation that it would.

2   He had enemies, of course, who said he was arrogant, that he exalted activity for its own sake. Perhaps. But perhaps it was no more than the honesty of one who knows his own worth. Just look at a scalpel, after all. What a feeling of sovereignty, megalomania even, when you know that it is you and you alone who will make certain use of it. It was said, too, that he was a ladies' man. I don't know about that. It was all rumor. Besides, I think he had other things in mind than mere living. Hugh Franciscus was a zealous hunter. Every fall during the season he drove upstate to hunt deer. There was a glass-front case in his office where he showed his guns. How could he shoot a deer? we asked. But he knew better. To us medical students he was someone heroic, someone made up of several gods, beheld at a distance, and always from a lesser height. If he had grown accustomed to his miracles, we had not. He had no close friends on the staff. There was something a little sad in that. As though once long ago he had been flayed by friendship and now the

slightest breeze would hurt. Confidences resulted in dishonor. Perhaps
the person in whom one confided would scorn him, betray. Even though
he spent his days among those less fortunate, weaker than he—the sick,
after all—Franciscus seemed aware of an air of personal harshness in his
environment to which he reacted by keeping his own counsel, by a
certain remoteness. It was what gave him the appearance of being
haughty. With the patients he was forthright. All the facts laid out,
every question anticipated and answered with specific information. He
delivered good news and bad with the same dispassion.

3   I was a third-year student, just turned onto the wards for the first
time, and clerking on Surgery. Everything—the operating room, the
morgue, the emergency room, the patients, professors, even the nurses
—was terrifying. One picked one's way among the mines and booby
traps of the hospital, hoping only to avoid the hemorrhage and perfora-
tion of disgrace. The opportunity for humiliation was everywhere.

4   It all began on Ward Rounds. Dr. Franciscus was demonstrating
a cross-leg flap graft he had constructed to cover a large fleshy defect
in the leg of a merchant seaman who had injured himself in a fall. The
man was from Spain and spoke no English. There had been a com-
minuted fracture of the femur, much soft tissue damage, necrosis. After
weeks of débridement and dressings, the wound had been made ready
for grafting. Now the patient was in his fifth postoperative day. What
we saw was a thick web of pale blue flesh arising from the man's left
thigh, and which had been sutured to the open wound on the right
thigh. When the surgeon pressed the pedicle with his finger, it
blanched; when he let up, there was a slow return of the violaceous color.

5   "The circulation is good," Franciscus announced. "It will get
better." In several weeks, we were told, he would divide the tube of flesh
at its site of origin, and tailor it to fit the defect to which, by then, it
would have grown more solidly. All at once, the webbed man in the bed
reached out, and gripping Franciscus by the arm, began to speak rapidly,
pointing to his groin and hip. Franciscus stepped back at once to disengage his arm from the patient's grasp.

6   "Anyone here know Spanish? I didn't get a word of that."

7   "The cast is digging into him up above," I said. "The edges of the
plaster are rough. When he moves, they hurt."

8   Without acknowledging my assistance, Dr. Franciscus took a plaster shears from the dressing cart and with several large snips cut away
the rough edges of the cast.

9   "*Gracias, gracias.*" The man in the bed smiled. But Franciscus

had already moved on to the next bed. He seemed to me a man of immense strength and ability, yet without affection for the patients. He did not want to be touched by them. It was less kindness that he showed them than a reassurance that he would never give up, that he would bend every effort. If anyone could, he would solve the problems of their flesh.

10   Ward Rounds had disbanded and I was halfway down the corridor when I heard Dr. Franciscus' voice behind me.

11   "You speak Spanish." It seemed a command.

12   "I lived in Spain for two years," I told him.

13   "I'm taking a surgical team to Honduras next week to operate on the natives down there. I do it every year for three weeks, somewhere. This year, Honduras. I can arrange the time away from your duties here if you'd like to come along. You will act as interpreter. I'll show you how to use the clinical camera. What you'd see would make it worthwhile."

14   So it was that, a week later, the envy of my classmates, I joined the mobile surgical unit—surgeons, anesthetists, nurses and equipment —aboard a Military Air Transport plane to spend three weeks performing plastic surgery on people who had been previously selected by an advance team. Honduras. I don't suppose I shall ever see it again. Nor do I especially want to. From the plane it seemed a country made of clay —burnt umber, raw sienna, dry. It had a deadweight quality, as though the ground had no buoyancy, no air sacs through which a breeze might wander. Our destination was Comayagua, a town in the Central Highlands. The town itself was situated on the edge of one of the flatlands that were linked in a network between the granite mountains. Above, all was brown, with only an occasional Spanish cedar tree; below, patches of luxuriant tropical growth. It was a day's bus ride from the airport. For hours, the town kept appearing and disappearing with the convolutions of the road. At last, there it lay before us, panting and exhausted at the bottom of the mountain.

15   That was all I was to see of the countryside. From then on, there was only the derelict hospital of Comayagua, with the smell of spoiling bananas and the accumulated odors of everyone who had been sick there for the last hundred years. Of the two, I much preferred the frank smell of the sick. The heat of the place was incendiary. So hot that, as we stepped from the bus, our own words did not carry through the air, but hung limply at our lips and chins. Just in front of the hospital was a thirsty courtyard where mobs of waiting people squatted or lay in the meager shade, and where, on dry days, a fine dust rose through which

untethered goats shouldered. Against the walls of this courtyard, gaunt, dejected men stood, their faces, like their country, preternaturally solemn, leaden. Here no one looked up at the sky. Every head was bent beneath a wide-brimmed straw hat. In the days that followed, from the doorway of the dispensary, I would watch the brown mountains sliding about, drinking the hospital into their shadow as the afternoon grew later and later, flattening us by their very altitude.

16   The people were mestizos, of mixed Spanish and Indian blood. They had flat, broad, dumb museum feet. At first they seemed to me indistinguishable the one from the other, without animation. All the vitality, the hidden sexuality, was in their black hair. Soon I was to know them by the fissures with which each face was graven. But, even so, compared to us, they were masked, shut away. My job was to follow Dr. Franciscus around, photograph the patients before and after surgery, interpret and generally act as aide-de-camp. It was exhilarating. Within days I had decided that I was not just useful, but essential. Despite that we spent all day in each other's company, there were no overtures of friendship from Dr. Franciscus. He knew my place, and I knew it, too. In the afternoon he examined the patients scheduled for the next day's surgery. I would call out a name from the doorway to the examining room. In the courtyard someone would rise. I would usher the patient in, and nudge him to the examining table where Franciscus stood, always, I thought, on the verge of irritability. I would read aloud the case history, then wait while he carried out his examination. While I took the "before" photographs, Dr. Franciscus would dictate into a tape recorder:

17   "Ulcerating basal cell carcinoma of the right orbit—six by eight centimeters—involving the right eye and extending into the floor of the orbit. Operative plan: wide excision with enucleation of the eye. Later, bone and skin grafting." The next morning we would be in the operating room where the procedure would be carried out.

18   We were more than two weeks into our tour of duty—a few days to go—when it happened. Earlier in the day I had caught sight of her through the window of the dispensary. A thin, dark Indian girl about fourteen years old. A figurine, orange-brown, terra-cotta, and still attached to the unshaped clay from which she had been carved. An older, sun-weathered woman stood behind and somewhat to the left of the girl. The mother was short and dumpy. She wore a broad-brimmed hat with a high crown, and a shapeless dress like a cassock. The girl had long, loose black hair. There were tiny gold hoops in her ears. The dress she wore

could have been her mother's. Far too big, it hung from her thin shoulders at some risk of slipping down her arms. Even with her in it, the dress was empty, something hanging on the back of a door. Her breasts made only the smallest imprint in the cloth, her hips none at all. All the while, she pressed to her mouth a filthy, pink, balled-up rag as though to stanch a flow or buttress against pain. I knew that what she had come to show us, what we were there to see, was hidden beneath that pink cloth. As I watched, the woman handed down to her a gourd from which the girl drank, lapping like a dog. She was the last patient of the day. They had been waiting in the courtyard for hours.

19   "Imelda Valdez," I called out. Slowly she rose to her feet, the cloth never leaving her mouth, and followed her mother to the examining-room door. I shooed them in.

20   "You sit up there on the table," I told her. "Mother, you stand over there, please." I read from the chart:

21   "This is a fourteen-year-old girl with a complete, unilateral, left-sided cleft lip and cleft palate. No other diseases or congenital defects. Laboratory tests, chest X ray—negative."

22   "Tell her to take the rag away," said Dr. Franciscus. I did, and the girl shrank back, pressing the cloth all the more firmly.

23   "Listen, this is silly," said Franciscus. "Tell her I've got to see it. Either she behaves, or send her away."

24   "Please give me the cloth," I said to the girl as gently as possible. She did not. She could not. Just then, Franciscus reached up and, taking the hand that held the rag, pulled it away with a hard jerk. For an instant the girl's head followed the cloth as it left her face, one arm still upflung against showing. Against all hope, she would hide herself. A moment later, she relaxed and sat still. She seemed to me then like an animal that looks outward at the infinite, at death, without fear, with recognition only.

25   Set as it was in the center of the girl's face, the defect was utterly hideous—a nude rubbery insect that had fastened there. The upper lip was widely split all the way to the nose. One white tooth perched upon the protruding upper jaw projected through the hole. Some of the bone seemed to have been gnawed away as well. Above the thing, clear almond eyes and long black hair reflected the light. Below, a slender neck where the pulse trilled visibly. Under our gaze the girl's eyes fell to her lap where her hands lay palms upward, half open. She was a beautiful bird with a crushed beak. And tense with the expectation of more shame.

26   "Open your mouth," said the surgeon. I translated. She did so, and the surgeon tipped back her head to see inside.

27   "The palate, too. Complete," he said. There was a long silence. At last he spoke.

28   "What is your name?" The margins of the wound melted until she herself was being sucked into it.

29   "Imelda." The syllables leaked through the hole with a slosh and a whistle.

30   "Tomorrow," said the surgeon, "I will fix your lip. *Mañana.*"

31   It seemed to me that Hugh Franciscus, in spite of his years of experience, in spite of all the dreadful things he had seen, must have been awed by the sight of this girl. I could see it flit across his face for an instant. Perhaps it was her small act of concealment, that he had had to demand that she show him the lip, that he had had to force her to show it to him. Perhaps it was her resistance that intensified the disfigurement. Had she brought her mouth to him willingly, without shame, she would have been for him neither more nor less than any other patient.

32   He measured the defect with calipers, studied it from different angles, turning her head with a finger at her chin.

33   "How can it ever be put back together?" I asked.

34   "Take her picture," he said. And to her, "Look straight ahead." Through the eye of the camera she seemed more pitiful than ever, her humiliation more complete.

35   "Wait!" The surgeon stopped me. I lowered the camera. A strand of her hair had fallen across her face and found its way to her mouth, becoming stuck there by saliva. He removed the hair and secured it behind her ear.

36   "Go ahead," he ordered. There was the click of the camera. The girl winced.

37   "Take three more, just in case."

38   When the girl and her mother had left, he took paper and pen and with a few lines drew a remarkable likeness of the girl's face.

39   "Look," he said. "If this dot is A, and this one B, this, C and this, D, the incisions are made A to B, then C to D. CD must equal AB. It is all equilateral triangles." All well and good, but then came X and Y and rotation flaps and the rest.

40   "Do you see?" he asked.

41   "It is confusing," I told him.

42   "It is simply a matter of dropping the upper lip into a normal

position, then crossing the gap with two triangular flaps. It is geometry," he said.

43   "Yes," I said. "Geometry." And relinquished all hope of becoming a plastic surgeon.

II

44   In the operating room the next morning the anesthesia had already been administered when we arrived from Ward Rounds. The tube emerging from the girl's mouth was pressed against her lower lip to be kept out of the field of surgery. Already, a nurse was scrubbing the face which swam in a reddish-brown lather. The tiny gold earrings were included in the scrub. Now and then, one of them gave a brave flash. The face was washed for the last time, and dried. Green towels were placed over the face to hide everything but the mouth and nose. The drapes were applied.

45   "Calipers!" The surgeon measured, locating the peak of the distorted Cupid's bow.

46   "Marking pen!" He placed the first blue dot at the apex of the bow. The nasal sills were dotted; next, the inferior philtral dimple, the vermilion line. The *A* flap and the *B* flap were outlined. On he worked, peppering the lip and nose, making sense out of chaos, realizing the lip that lay waiting in that deep essential pink, that only he could see. The last dot and line were placed. He was ready.

47   "Scalpel!" He held the knife above the girl's mouth.

48   "O.K. to go ahead?" he asked the anesthetist.

49   "Yes."

50   He lowered the knife.

51   "No! Wait!" The anesthetist's voice was tense, staccato. "Hold it!"

52   The surgeon's hand was motionless.

53   "What's the matter?"

54   "Something's wrong. I'm not sure. God, she's hot as a pistol. Blood pressure is way up. Pulse one eighty. Get a rectal temperature." A nurse fumbled beneath the drapes. We waited. The nurse retrieved the thermometer.

55   "One hundred seven . . . no . . . eight." There was disbelief in her voice.

56   "Malignant hyperthermia," said the anesthetist. "Ice! Ice! Get lots of ice!" I raced out the door, accosted the first nurse I saw.

57   "Ice!" I shouted. *"Hielo!* Quickly! *Hielo!"* The woman's expression was blank. I ran to another. *"Hielo! Hielo!* For the love of God, ice."

58   *"Hielo?"* She shrugged. *"Nada."* I ran back to the operating room.

59   "There isn't any ice," I reported. Dr. Franciscus had ripped off his rubber gloves and was feeling the skin of the girl's abdomen. Above the mask his eyes were the eyes of a horse in battle.

60   "The EKG is wild . . ."

61   "I can't get a pulse . . ."

62   "What the hell . . ."

63   The surgeon reached for the girl's groin. No femoral pulse.

64   "EKG flat. My God! She's dead!"

65   "She can't be."

66   "She is."

67   The surgeon's fingers pressed the groin where there was no pulse to be felt, only his own pulse hammering at the girl's flesh to be let in.

III

68   It was noon, four hours later, when we left the operating room. It was a day so hot and humid I felt steamed open like an envelope. The woman was sitting on a bench in the courtyard in her dress like a cassock. In one hand she held the piece of cloth the girl had used to conceal her mouth. As we watched, she folded it once neatly, and then again, smoothing it, cleaning the cloth which might have been the head of the girl in her lap that she stroked and consoled.

69   "I'll do the talking here," he said. He would tell her himself, in whatever Spanish he could find. Only if she did not understand was I to speak for him. I watched him brace himself, set his shoulders. How could he tell her? I wondered. What? But I knew he would tell her everything, exactly as it had happened. As much for himself as for her, he needed to explain. But suppose she screamed, fell to the ground, attacked him, even? All that hope of love . . . gone. Even in his discomfort I knew that he was teaching me. The way to do it was professionally. Now he was standing above her. When the woman saw that he did not speak, she lifted her eyes and saw what he held crammed in his mouth to tell her. She knew, and rose to her feet.

70 "*Señora,*" he began, "I am sorry." All at once he seemed to me shorter than he was, scarcely taller than she. There was a place at the crown of his head where the hair had grown thin. His lips were stones. He could hardly move them. The voice dry, dusty.

71 "No one could have known. Some bad reaction to the medicine for sleeping. It poisoned her. High fever. She did not wake up." The last, a whisper. The woman studied his lips as though she were deaf. He tried, but could not control a twitching at the corner of his mouth. He raised a thumb and forefinger to press something back into his eyes.

72 "*Muerte,*" the woman announced to herself. Her eyes were human, deadly.

73 "*Si, muerte.*" At that moment he was like someone cast, still alive, as an effigy for his own tomb. He closed his eyes. Nor did he open them until he felt the touch of the woman's hand on his arm, a touch from which he did not withdraw. Then he looked and saw the grief corroding her face, breaking it down, melting the features so that eyes, nose, mouth ran together in a distortion, like the girl's. For a long time they stood in silence. It seemed to me that minutes passed. At last her face cleared, the features rearranged themselves. She spoke, the words coming slowly to make certain that he understood her. She would go home now. The next day her sons would come for the girl, to take her home for burial. The doctor must not be sad. God has decided. And she was happy now that the harelip had been fixed so that her daughter might go to Heaven without it. Her bare feet retreating were the felted pads of a great bereft animal.

IV

74 The next morning I did not go to the wards, but stood at the gate leading from the courtyard to the road outside. Two young men in striped ponchos lifted the girl's body wrapped in a straw mat onto the back of a wooden cart. A donkey waited. I had been drawn to this place as one is drawn, inexplicably, to certain scenes of desolation—executions, battlefields. All at once, the woman looked up and saw me. She had taken off her hat. The heavy-hanging coil of her hair made her head seem larger, darker, noble. I pressed some money into her hand.

75 "For flowers," I said. "A priest." Her cheeks shook as though minutes ago a stone had been dropped into her naval and the ripples were just now reaching her head. I regretted having come to that place.

76 "*Si, si,*" the woman said. Her own face was stitched with flies.

"The doctor is one of the angels. He has finished the work of God. My daughter is beautiful."

77   What could she mean! The lip had not been fixed. The girl had died before he would have done it.

78   "Only a fine line that God will erase in time," she said.

79   I reached into the cart and lifted a corner of the mat in which the girl had been rolled. Where the cleft had been there was now a fresh line of tiny sutures. The Cupid's bow was delicately shaped, the vermilion border aligned. The flattened nostril had now the same rounded shape as the other one. I let the mat fall over the face of the dead girl, but not before I had seen the touching place where the finest black hairs sprang from the temple.

80   *"Adiós, adiós . . ."* And the cart creaked away to the sound of hooves, a tinkling bell.

V

81   There are events in a doctor's life that seem to mark the boundary between youth and age, seeing and perceiving. Like certain dreams, they illuminate a whole lifetime of past behavior. After such an event, a doctor is not the same as he was before. It had seemed to me then to have been the act of someone demented, or at least insanely arrogant. An attempt to reorder events. Her death had come to him out of order. It should have come after the lip had been repaired, not before. He could have told the mother that, no, the lip had not been fixed. But he did not. He said nothing. It had been an act of omission, one of those strange lapses to which all of us are subject and which we live to regret. It must have been then, at that moment, that the knowledge of what he would do appeared to him. The words of the mother had not consoled him; they had hunted him down. He had not done it for her. The dire necessity was his. He would not accept that Imelda had died before he could repair her lip. People who do such things break free from society. They follow their own lonely path. They have a secret which they can never reveal. I must never let on that I knew.

VI

82   How often I have imagined it. Ten o'clock at night. The hospital of Comayagua is all but dark. Here and there lanterns tilt and skitter

up and down the corridors. One of these lamps breaks free from the others and descends the stone steps to the underground room that is the morgue of the hospital. This room wears the expression as if it had waited all night for someone to come. No silence so deep as this place with its cargo of newly dead. Only the slow drip of water over stone. The door closes gassily and clicks shut. The lock is turned. There are four tables, each with a body encased in a paper shroud. There is no mistaking her. She is the smallest. The surgeon takes a knife from his pocket and slits open the paper shroud, that part in which the girl's head is enclosed. The wound seems to be living on long after she has died. Waves of heat emanate from it, blurring his vision. All at once, he turns to peer over his shoulder. He sees nothing, only a wooden crucifix on the wall.

83   He removes a package of instruments from a satchel and arranges them on a tray. Scalpel, scissors, forceps, needle holder. Sutures and gauze sponges are produced. Stealthy, hunched, engaged, he begins. The dots of blue dye are still there upon her mouth. He raises the scalpel, pauses. A second glance into the darkness. From the wall a small lizard watches and accepts. The first cut is made. A sluggish flow of dark blood appears. He wipes it away with a sponge. No new blood comes to take its place. Again and again he cuts, connecting each of the blue dots until the whole of the zigzag slice is made, first on one side of the cleft, then on the other. Now the edges of the cleft are lined with fresh tissue. He sets down the scalpel and takes up scissors and forceps, undermining the little flaps until each triangle is attached only at one side. He rotates each flap into its new position. He must be certain that they can be swung without tension. They can. He is ready to suture. He fits the tiny curved needle into the jaws of the needle holder. Each suture is placed precisely the same number of millimeters from the cut edge, and the same distance apart. He ties each knot down until the edges are apposed. Not too tightly. These are the most meticulous sutures of his life. He cuts each thread close to the knot. It goes well. The vermilion border with its white skin roll is exactly aligned. One more stitch and the Cupid's bow appears as if by magic. The man's face shines with moisture. Now the nostril is incised around the margin, released, and sutured into a round shape to match its mate. He wipes the blood from the face of the girl with gauze that he has dipped in water. Crumbs of light are scattered on the girl's face. The shroud is folded once more about her. The instruments are handed into the satchel. In a moment the morgue is dark and a lone lantern ascends the stairs and is extinguished.

VII

84   Six weeks later I was in the darkened amphitheater of the Medical School. Tiers of seats rose in a semicircle above the small stage where Hugh Franciscus stood presenting the case material he had encountered in Honduras. It was the highlight of the year. The hall was filled. The night before he had arranged the slides in the order in which they were to be shown. I was at the controls of the slide projector.

85   "Next slide!" he would order from time to time in that military voice which had called forth blind obedience from generations of medical students, interns, residents and patients.

86   "This is a fifty-seven-year-old man with a severe burn contracture of the neck. You will notice the rigid webbing that has fused the chin to the presternal tissues. No motion of the head on the torso is possible. . . . Next slide!"

87   "Click," went the projector.

88   "Here he is after the excision of the scar tissue and with the head in full extension for the first time. The defect was then covered. . . . Next slide!"

89   "Click."

90   ". . . with full-thickness drums of skin taken from the abdomen with the Padgett dermatome. Next slide!"

91   "Click."

92   And suddenly there she was, extracted from the shadows, suspended above and beyond all of us like a resurrection. There was the oval face, the long black hair unbraided, the tiny gold hoops in her ears. And that luminous gnawed mouth. The whole of her life seemed to have been summed up in this photograph. A long silence followed that was the surgeon's alone to break. Almost at once, like the anesthetist in the operating room in Comayagua, I knew that something was wrong. It was not that the man would not speak as that he could not. The audience of doctors, nurses and students seemed to have been infected by the black, limitless silence. My own pulse doubled. It was hard to breathe. Why did he not call out for the next slide? Why did he not save himself? Why had he not removed this slide from the ones to be shown? All at once I knew that he had used his camera on her again. I could see the long black shadows of her hair flowing into the darker shadows of the morgue. The sudden blinding flash . . . The next slide would be the one taken in the morgue. He would be exposed.

93   In the dim light reflected from the slide, I saw him gazing up at her, seeing not the colored photograph, I thought, but the negative of

it where the ghost of the girl was. For me, the amphitheater had become Honduras. I saw again that courtyard littered with patients. I could see the dust in the beam of light from the projector. It was then that I knew that she was his measure of perfection and pain—the one lost, the other gained. He, too, had heard the click of the camera, had seen her wince and felt his mercy enlarge. At last he spoke.

94   "Imelda." It was the one word he had heard her say. At the sound of his voice I removed the next slide from the projector. "Click" . . . and she was gone. "Click" again, and in her place the man with the orbital cancer. For a long moment Franciscus looked up in my direction, on his face an expression that I have given up trying to interpret. Gratitude? Sorrow? It made me think of the gaze of the girl when at last she understood that she must hand over to him the evidence of her body.

95   "This is a sixty-two-year-old man with a basal cell carcinoma of the temple eroding into the bony orbit . . ." he began as though nothing had happened.

96   At the end of the hour, even before the lights went on, there was loud applause. I hurried to find him among the departing crowd. I could not. Some weeks went by before I caught sight of him. He seemed vaguely convalescent, as though a fever had taken its toll before burning out.

97   Hugh Franciscus continued to teach for fifteen years, although he operated a good deal less, then gave it up entirely. It was as though he had grown tired of blood, of always having to be involved with blood, of having to draw it, spill it, wipe it away, stanch it. He was a quieter, softer man, I heard, the ferocity diminished. There were no more expeditions to Honduras or anywhere else.

98   I, too, have not been entirely free of her. Now and then, in the years that have passed, I see that donkey-cart cortège, or his face bent over hers in the morgue. I would like to have told him what I now know, that his unrealistic act was one of goodness, one of those small, persevering acts done, perhaps, to ward off madness. Like lighting a lamp, boiling water for tea, washing a shirt. But, of course, it's too late now.

QUESTIONS

Ideas

1. Identify three ideas that emerge in the essay. Comment briefly on each.
2. Explain the purpose of the essay. How do you think Selzer wants us to respond to Imelda, to Dr. Franciscus, and to himself as a medical student?

Organization

3. "Imelda" is arranged in seven sections. Provide a title and explain the purpose of each.

4. Provide another way of thinking about the organization of the essay, one that comprises fewer than the seven sections Selzer has established. Can any of the short sections be grouped? On what basis?

Sentences

5. Notice the way each of the following sentences employs units of three:

> There was the oval face, the long black hair unbraided, the tiny gold hoops in her ears. (92)
>
> Like lighting a lamp, boiling water for tea, washing a shirt. (98)
> It was as though he had grown tired of blood, of always having to be involved with blood, of having to draw it, spill it, wipe it away, stanch it. (97)
> The heavy coil of her hair made her head seem larger, darker, noble.
> Then he looked and saw the grief corroding her face, breaking it down, melting the features so that eyes, nose, mouth ran together in a distortion, like the girl's. (73)
> Stealthy, hunched, engaged, he begins. (83)

6. Notice how in the following sentences Selzer preserves a balance of word against word, phrase against phrase, clause against clause.

> There are events in a doctor's life that seem to mark the boundary between youth and age, seeing and perceiving. (81)
> It seemed to me then to have been the act of someone demented, or at least insanely arrogant. (81)
> The words of the mother had not consoled him; they had hunted him down. (81)
> The door closes gassily and clicks shut. (82)
> It was then that I knew that she was his measure of perfection and pain, the one lost, the other gained. (93)

Words

7. Consider carefully the diction (word choices) and images of comparison in section III. Comment on their tone, their effect, their descriptive power, their precision, and their emotional weight.

8. What is the effect of using Spanish words throughout the essay rather than English equivalents? Substitute English for the Spanish and consider the differences.

Suggestions for Writing

A. Write an essay in which you describe your feelings as you were reading "Imelda." Try to account for your state of mind and feeling as you read. Include also your response upon finishing it and after having had some time to think about it.

B. Discuss what you take to be an important idea that emerges in the essay: perhaps something Selzer states in one of the more reflective moments in the piece; perhaps something you discover in its dialogue or action.

C. Write imitations of the sentences referred to in questions 5 and 6.

TWELVE

Lewis Thomas
(1913–   )

Lewis Thomas uses science to tell us something important about the human predicament. But unlike many similar commentators, he does not tell a pessimistic tale. The cosmic melancholy of Loren Eiseley, another acclaimed science writer, is perhaps more typical of the modern outlook. Thomas, instead, celebrates life, seeing "possibilities where others see only doom." Recently, however, even Thomas's optimism has been diminished by thoughts of nuclear war. In "Night Thoughts," he is so upset by the grotesque calm of a defense analyst that he permits his readers to see a rare event: Lewis Thomas in a dark frame of mind.

In "To Err Is Human," he turns our typically negative reaction to error completely around, finding in mistakes progress and growth. He sees hope everywhere. For example, in an essay not included in this collection, "On Natural Death," instead of wincing at the spectacle of a dying field mouse in "the jaws of an amiable household cat," he uses the incident to speculate that, instead of being an abomination, nature is wise and kind. Since there are scientific reasons for thinking that fear releases peptide hormones that have the "pharmacologic properties of opium," it is plausible to think that the mouse does not feel pain. He goes on to cite a passage from Montaigne that suggests that nature will teach us all how to die, "take you no care for it."

This is typical Lewis Thomas: after something in nature is encountered, he lets it reverberate in his mind until he comes to a tentative hypothesis. He then tests it and invariably arrives at an encouraging vision of both man and nature. It is a traditional and logical thought process and one that is made more plausible because of its simplicity.

Although he doesn't share Eiseley's mood, Thomas has

a similar purpose in writing about scientific matters: "to communicate truths too mysterious for old-fashioned common sense." Ironically, even though Eiseley and Thomas have both contributed significantly to scientific understanding, they both stress how much we *don't* know about the workings of nature.

This is not to say that there is not a great deal of scientific information in Thomas's essays. His three collections of essays, *The Lives of a Cell: Notes of a Biology Watcher* (1974), *The Medusa and the Snail: More Notes of a Biology Watcher* (1979), *Late Night Thoughts on Listening to Mahler's Ninth Symphony* (1983), and his memoir *The Youngest Science: Notes of a Medicine Watcher* (1983), explore a wide range of complex scientific topics, from pheromones and embryology to cloning and germs. He is also not afraid to deal with such diverse subjects as linguistics, music, computers, and literature. In exploring these complex issues, he is never dogmatic, even when he is clearly the expert. He always invites the reader to join in, to share with him the joy of "being dumbfounded."

Indeed, it is refreshing to be told we are better than we think. In "The Iks," for example, he strongly disagrees with a famous anthropologist's depressing idea that a repellent mountain tribe from Uganda is an appropriate symbol for mankind. Thomas argues that it is society that corrupts man, not the opposite. At heart, he believes, we are all good. In his characteristically plain and exact style, Thomas rejects the view that man is inherently evil with "He's all right."

In "The Lives of a Cell," he develops another of his central concerns—our connection to nature. Symbiosis, in fact, is one of his favorite notions. He seems quite upset by our nineteenth-century view that man is superior to and independent from nature. In his graceful, gently persuasive prose, he argues instead that "man is embedded in nature." We can, he believes, no longer see ourselves as separate and detached entities. In fact, it is an illusion to see ourselves as autonomous. In this regard he echoes Annie Dillard's almost mystic urge toward the total unity of all life.

Even though Chekhov, William Carlos Williams, and other creative writers have been medical doctors, it still seems unusual for a famous pathologist to write about scientific matters with such grace, clarity, and eloquence. For the president of a world-famous cancer center to have the reputation of being one of America's best essayists is a tribute to Thomas's diversity as a scientist and humanist.

The Iks

1   The small tribe of Iks, formerly nomadic hunters and gath-erers in the mountain valleys of northern Uganda, have become celebri-ties, literary symbols for the ultimate fate of disheartened, heartless mankind at large. Two disastrously conclusive things happened to them: the government decided to have a national park, so they were compelled by law to give up hunting in the valleys and become farmers on poor hillside soil, and then they were visited for two years by an anthropolo-gist who detested them and wrote a book about them.

2   The message of the book is that the Iks have transformed them-selves into an irreversibly disagreeable collection of unattached, brutish creatures, totally selfish and loveless, in response to the dismantling of their traditional culture. Moreover, this is what the rest of us are like in our inner selves, and we will all turn into Iks when the structure of our society comes all unhinged.

3   The argument rests, of course, on certain assumptions about the core of human beings, and is necessarily speculative. You have to agree in advance that man is fundamentally a bad lot, out for himself alone, displaying such graces as affection and compassion only as learned hab-its. If you take this view, the story of the Iks can be used to confirm it. These people seem to be living together, clustered in small, dense villages, but they are really solitary, unrelated individuals with no evident use for each other. They talk, but only to make ill-tempered demands and cold refusals. They share nothing. They never sing. They turn the children out to forage as soon as they can walk, and desert the elders to starve whenever they can, and the foraging children snatch food from the mouths of the helpless elders. It is a mean society.

4   They breed without love or even casual regard. They defecate on each other's doorsteps. They watch their neighbors for signs of misfor-tune, and only then do they laugh. In the book they do a lot of laughing, having so much bad luck. Several times they even laughed at the an-thropologist, who found this especially repellent (one senses, between the lines, that the scholar is not himself the world's luckiest man). Worse, they took him into the family, snatched his food, defecated on his doorstep, and hooted dislike at him. They gave him two bad years.

5   It is a depressing book. If, as he suggests, there is only Ikness at the center of each of us, our sole hope for hanging on to the name of

humanity will be in endlessly mending the structure of our society, and it is changing so quickly and completely that we may never find the threads in time. Meanwhile, left to ourselves alone, solitary, we will become the same joyless, zestless, untouching lone animals.

6   But this may be too narrow a view. For one thing, the Iks are extraordinary. They are absolutely astonishing, in fact. The anthropologist has never seen people like them anywhere, nor have I. You'd think, if they were simply examples of the common essence of mankind, they'd seem more recognizable. Instead, they are bizarre, anomalous. I have known my share of peculiar, difficult, nervous, grabby people, but I've never encountered any genuinely, consistently detestable human beings in all my life. The Iks sound more like abnormalities, maladies.

7   I cannot accept it. I do not believe that the Iks are representative of isolated, revealed man, unobscured by social habits. I believe their behavior is something extra, something laid on. This unremitting, compulsive repellence is a kind of complicated ritual. They must have learned to act this way; they copied it, somehow.

8   I have a theory, then. The Iks have gone crazy.

9   The solitary Ik, isolated in the ruins of an exploded culture, has built a new defense for himself. If you live in an unworkable society you can make up one of your own, and this is what the Iks have done. Each Ik has become a group, a one-man tribe on its own, a constituency.

10   Now everything falls into place. This is why they do seem, after all, vaguely familiar to all of us. We've seen them before. This is precisely the way groups of one size or another, ranging from committees to nations, behave. It is, of course, this aspect of humanity that has lagged behind the rest of evolution, and this is why the Ik seems so primitive. In his absolute selfishness, his incapacity to give anything away, no matter what, he is a successful committee. When he stands at the door of his hut, shouting insults at his neighbors in a loud harangue, he is city addressing another city.

11   Cities have all the Ik characteristics. They defecate on doorsteps, in rivers and lakes, their own or anyone else's. They leave rubbish. They detest all neighboring cities, give nothing away. They even build institutions for deserting elders out of sight.

12   Nations are the most Iklike of all. No wonder the Iks seem familiar. For total greed, rapacity, heartlessness, and irresponsibility there is nothing to match a nation. Nations, by law, are solitary, self-centered, withdrawn into themselves. There is no such thing as affection between nations, and certainly no nation ever loved another. They bawl insults

from their doorsteps, defecate into whole oceans, snatch all the food, survive by detestation, take joy in the bad luck of others, celebrate the death of others, live for the death of others.

13   That's it, and I shall stop worrying about the book. It does not signify that man is a sparse, inhuman thing at his center. He's all right. It only says what we've always known and never had enough time to worry about, that we haven't yet learned how to stay human when assembled in masses. The Ik, in his despair, is acting out this failure, and perhaps we should pay closer attention. Nations have themselves become too frightening to think about, but we might learn some things by watching these people.

QUESTIONS

Ideas

1. How does Thomas react to the Iks? To the book about them? The anthropologist, in his book, does indeed suggest "that man is a sparse, inhuman thing at his center?" Does Thomas think so? Do you think so? What is Thomas's position in paragraph 3? Does he think man is basically good at heart? Does his view seem reasonable? Fair? Flexible? Why or why not?

2. Thomas lets us follow his train of thought as he comes to terms with the nature of the Iks and finally with the nature of man. After he sketches the necessary background, he asserts, in paragraph 5, that this "is a depressing book." Try to outline, in brief sentences, his reasoning from this point on. How does he counter the anthropologist's thesis?

3. What is the effect of "That's it," in the last paragraph? Has he convinced you that "he's all right"? Who is this "he"?

Organization

4. Go back through this essay, reading only the first and last sentences in each paragraph. What does this tell you about Thomas's view of the paragraph's opening sentence? Notice paragraphs 11 and 12. After the opening sentence, what do the rest of the sentences try to do?

5. What do you make of the one-sentence paragraph 8? Is this effective?

6. How is the last sentence of paragraph 3 related to and connected with the five sentences before it?

7. Where does the essay seem to change direction? To shift in ideas?

8. Do you think the organization represents Thomas's actual thinking process? Would the essay have been more effective if he had begun with a thesis and then set out to defend it? What organization would you have chosen?

9. As part of his organization and thematic plan Thomas compares the Iks first to cities, then to nations. How does he do this? What aspects of each does he compare?

Sentences

10. Is the repetition of "they" effective in paragraph 4?

11. When Thomas wants to be emphatic he usually writes short, assertive sentences. Can you point to some that seem especially effective? (Read paragraphs 3 and 4 aloud.)

12. There don't seem to be many compound sentences here. There's one in paragraph 10; can you find others? What is the effect of making sentences simple?

13. Take a close look at Thomas's use of commas in the first sentence. Why does he use the first two? Could he have used a colon instead of the third comma? Can you explain the function of these commas?

Words

14. What words and specific details does Thomas repeat in the essay? To what effect?

15. What words, in paragraphs 5 and 6, carry negative connotations? Which describe or define "Ikness"?

Suggestion for Writing

Write an essay that supports either the anthropologist's or Thomas's position on the Iks. Try to use personal experience to support your stand.

The Lives of a Cell

1   We are told that the trouble with Modern Man is that he has been trying to detach himself from nature. He sits in the topmost tiers of polymer, glass, and steel, dangling his pulsing legs, surveying at

a distance the writhing life of the planet. In this scenario, Man comes on as a stupendous lethal force, and the earth is pictured as something delicate, like rising bubbles at the surface of a country pond, or flights of fragile birds.

2   But it is illusion to think that there is anything fragile about the life of the earth; surely this is the toughest membrane imaginable in the universe, opaque to probability, impermeable to death. We are the delicate part, transient and vulnerable as cilia. Nor is it a new thing for man to invent an existence that he imagines to be above the rest of life; this has been his most consistent intellectual exertion down the millennia. As illusion, it has never worked out to his satisfaction in the past, any more than it does today. Man is embedded in nature.

3   The biologic science of recent years has been making this a more urgent fact of life. The new, hard problem will be to cope with the dawning, intensifying realization of just how interlocked we are. The old, clung-to notions most of us have held about our special lordship are being deeply undermined.

4   *Item.* A good case can be made for our nonexistence as entities. We are not made up, as we had always supposed, of successively enriched packets of our own parts. We are shared, rented, occupied. At the interior of our cells, driving them, providing the oxidative energy that sends us out for the improvement of each shining day, are the mitochondria, and in a strict sense they are not ours. They turn out to be little separate creatures, the colonial posterity of migrant prokaryocytes, probably primitive bacteria that swam into ancestral precursors of our eukaryotic cells and stayed here. Ever since, they have maintained themselves and their ways, replicating in their own fashion, privately, with their own DNA and RNA quite different from ours. They are as much symbionts as the rhizobial bacteria in the roots of beans. Without them, we would not move a muscle, drum a finger, think a thought.

5   Mitochondria are stable and responsible lodgers, and I choose to trust them. But what of the other little animals, similarly established in my cells, sorting and balancing me, clustering me together? My centrioles, basal bodies, and probably a good many other more obscure tiny beings at work inside my cells, each with its own special genome, are as foreign, and as essential, as aphids in anthills. My cells are no longer the pure line entities I was raised with; they are ecosystems more complex than Jamaica Bay.

6   I like to think that they work in my interest, that each breath they

draw for me, but perhaps it is they who walk through the local park in the early morning, sensing my senses, listening to my music, thinking my thoughts.

7   I am consoled, somewhat, by the thought that the green plants are in the same fix. They could not be plants, or green, without their chloroplasts, which run the photosynthetic enterprise and generate oxygen for the rest of us. As it turns out, chloroplasts are also separate creatures with their own genomes, speaking their own language.

8   We carry stores of DNA in our nuclei that may have come in, at one time or another, from the fusion of ancestral cells and the linking of ancestral organisms in symbiosis. Our genomes are catalogues of instructions from all kinds of sources in nature, filed for all kinds of contingencies. As for me, I am grateful for differentiation and speciation, but I cannot feel as separate an entity as I did a few years ago, before I was told these things, nor, I should think, can anyone else.

9   *Item.* The uniformity of the earth's life, more astonishing than its diversity, is accountable by the high probability that we derived, originally, from some single cell, fertilized in a bolt of lightning as the earth cooled. It is from the progeny of this parent cell that we take our looks; we still share genes around, and the resemblance of the enzymes of grasses to those of whales is a family resemblance.

10   The viruses, instead of being single-minded agents of disease and death, now begin to look more like mobile genes. Evolution is still an infinitely long and tedious biologic game, with only the winners staying at the table, but the rules are beginning to look more flexible. We live in a dancing matrix of viruses; they dart, rather like bees, from organism to organism, from plant to insect to mammal to me and back again, and into the sea, tugging along pieces of this genome, strings of genes from that, transplanting grafts of DNA, passing around heredity as though at a great party. They may be a mechanism for keeping new, mutant kinds of DNA in the widest circulation among us. If this is true, the odd virus disease, on which we must focus so much of our attention in medicine, may be looked on as an accident, something dropped.

11   *Item.* I have been trying to think of the earth as a kind of organism, but it is no go. I cannot think of it this way. It is too big, too complex, with too many working parts lacking visible connections. The other night, driving through a hilly, wooded part of southern New England, I wondered about this. If not like an organism, what is it like, what is it *most* like? Then, satisfactorily for that moment, it came to me: it is *most* like a single cell.

QUESTIONS

Ideas

1. From your experience, do you think Thomas's image in the first paragraph is correct? Have we been trying to detach ourselves from nature?

2. Does his "correction" of this scenario seem more or less optimistic? Does it worry you that he claims "we are the delicate part"?

3. In the last paragraph, what difference does it make whether we accept Thomas's analogy that the earth is an organism or a single cell?

Organization

4. Thomas chooses to put a traditional topic sentence (the assertion of an opinion) at the end of the second paragraph. What does he try to do in the succeeding paragraphs? Is this exposition (explanation), or is he trying to persuade you of something? Look especially at the last sentence in paragraph 8.

5. Thomas appears to be trying to alter our misconceptions about our "special lordship." In this regard, do you think he arranges his essay effectively?

6. Where does his introduction end? Where does his conclusion begin?

7. How does Thomas support his opening sentence in paragraph 4?

8. How does Thomas get us from paragraph 1 to 2 and on to 3? Underline all the connections; include the syntactic and semantic ways the paragraphs are linked.

9. Look at the ways Thomas begins his sentences in the first two paragraphs. How many follow the normal subject, verb, object (S–V–O) pattern?

10. Look at the first sentence of the second paragraph. The two three-word phrases at the end are free modifiers, meaning they can be moved to other positions in the sentence. Where else might they go?

11. Count the words in each sentence in the second paragraph. Is there a reason for this pattern?

12. In paragraph 9, why did Thomas decide to use a semicolon in the last sentence? Are there other options?

Words

13. Unlike much of "scientific writing," Thomas opens this piece on a technical subject with an attention-getting image. Does this "popular technique" make his argument seem less serious?

14. Do you find Thomas mixing levels of diction, for example, using scientific jargon and informational speech? Where does he do it and for what effect? Does it work?

15. What kind of voice (or persona) do you hear in this essay? Try reading the last two paragraphs out loud. Is this a voice of authority? Is he trying to be down to earth? What voice might you take in handling this subject? Does it depend on your purpose? What do you think Thomas's purpose is?

Suggestions for Writing

A. Throughout the essay, Thomas frequently uses triplets—three words in parallel form, three phrases in parallel structure, three sentences in parallel motion. Paragraph 3 contains two examples, paragraph 5, one. Rewrite these sentences, destroying the parallelism or adding connecting words (like "and") to join the three elements. What is lost in these revisions?

B. Even more frequently than triplets, Thomas uses doublets of words and phrases, of sentences and paragraphs. What kinds of "pairs" can you find in the essay? How effective are they? Consider especially the balances and parallels of paragraphs 6, 7, and 11. Write a short paragraph describing a familiar scene using doublets.

C. Think of a scientific or technical subject that concerns you, say, pollution and protecting (or not protecting) the environment, or cloning, or chemical additives in our food. Try to write about it using the Thomas structure of beginning with a misconception our society shares and then demonstrating why the illusion is false. In writing your piece keep in mind how Thomas combines anecdote, comparison and contrast, exposition, persuasion, and description.

The Tucson Zoo

1   Science gets most of its information by the process of reductionism, exploring the details, then the details of the details, until all the smallest bits of the structure, or the smallest parts of the mechanism, are laid out for counting and scrutiny. Only when this is done can the investigation be extended to encompass the whole organism or the entire system. So we say.

2   Sometimes it seems that we take a loss, working this way. Much

of today's public anxiety about science is the apprehension that we may forever be overlooking the whole by an endless, obsessive preoccupation with the parts. I had a brief, personal experience of this misgiving one afternoon in Tucson, where I had time on my hands and visited the zoo, just outside the city. The designers there have cut a deep pathway between two small artificial ponds, walled by clear glass, so when you stand in the center of the path you can look into the depths of each pool, and at the same time you can regard the surface. In one pool, on the right side of the path, is a family of otters; on the other side, a family of beavers. Within just a few feet from your face, on either side, beavers and otters are at play, underwater and on the surface, swimming toward your face and then away, more filled with life than any creatures I have ever seen before, in all my days. Except for the glass, you could reach across and touch them.

3   I was transfixed. As I now recall it, there was only one sensation in my head: pure elation mixed with amazement at such perfection. Swept off my feet, I floated from one side to the other, swiveling my brain, staring astounded at the beavers, then at the otters. I could hear shouts across my corpus callosum, from one hemisphere to the other. I remember thinking, with what was left in charge of my consciousness, that I wanted no part of the science of beavers and otters; I wanted never to know how they performed their marvels; I wished for no news about the physiology of their breathing, the coordination of their muscles, their vision, their endocrine systems, their digestive tracts. I hoped never to have to think of them as collections of cells. All I asked for was the full hairy complexity, then in front of my eyes, of whole, intact beavers and otters in motion.

4   It lasted, I regret to say, for only a few minutes, and then I was back in the late twentieth century, reductionist as ever, wondering about the details by force of habit, but not, this time, the details of otters and beavers. Instead, me. Something worth remembering had happened in my mind, I was certain of that; I would have put it somewhere in the brain stem; maybe this was my limbic system at work. I became a behavioral scientist, an experimental psychologist, an ethologist, and in the instant I lost all the wonder and the sense of being overwhelmed. I was flattened.

5   But I came away from the zoo with something, a piece of news about myself: I am coded, somehow, for otters and beavers. I exhibit instinctive behavior in their presence, when they are displayed close at hand behind glass, simultaneously below water and at the surface. I have

receptors for this display. Beavers and otters possess a "releaser" for me, in the terminology of ethology, and the releasing was my experience. What was released? Behavior. What behavior? Standing, swiveling flabbergasted, feeling exultation and a rush of friendship. I could not, as the result of the transaction, tell you anything more about beavers and otters than you already know. I learned nothing new about them. Only about me, and I suspect also about you, maybe about human beings at large: we are endowed with genes which code out our reaction to beavers and otters, maybe our reaction to each other as well. We are stamped with stereotyped, unalterable patterns of response, ready to be released. And the behavior released in us, by such confrontations, is, essentially, a surprised affection. It is compulsory behavior and we can avoid it only by straining with the full power of our conscious minds, making up conscious excuses all the way. Left to ourselves, mechanistic and autonomic, we hanker for friends.

6   Everyone says, stay away from ants. They have no lessons for us; they are crazy little instruments, inhuman, incapable of controlling themselves, lacking manners, lacking souls. When they are massed together, all touching, exchanging bits of information held in their jaws like memoranda, they become a single animal. Look out for that. It is a debasement, a loss of individuality, a violation of human nature, an unnatural act.

7   Sometimes people argue this point of view seriously and with deep thought. Be individuals, solitary and selfish, is the message. Altruism, a jargon word for what used to be called love, is worse than weakness, it is sin, a violation of nature. Be separate. Do not be a social animal. But this is a hard argument to make convincingly when you have to depend on language to make it. You have to print up leaflets or publish books and get them bought and sent around, you have to turn up on television and catch the attention of millions of other human beings all at once, and then you have to say to all of them, all at once, all collected and paying attention: be solitary; do not depend on each other. You can't do this and keep a straight face.

8   Maybe altruism is our most primitive attribute, out of reach, beyond our control. Or perhaps it is immediately at hand, waiting to be released, disguised now, in our kind of civilization, as affection or friendship or attachment. I don't see why it should be unreasonable for all human beings to have strands of DNA coiled up in chromosomes, coding out instincts for usefulness and helpfulness. Usefulness may turn out to be the hardest test of fitness for survival, more important than aggression, more effective, in the long run, than grabbiness. If this is the

sort of information biological science holds for the future, applying to us as well as to ants, then I am all for science.

9   One thing I'd like to know most of all: when those ants have made the Hill, and are all there, touching and exchanging, and the whole mass begins to behave like a single huge creature, and *thinks,* what on earth is that thought? And while you're at it, I'd like to know a second thing: when it happens, does any single ant know about it? Does his hair stand on end?

QUESTIONS

Ideas

1. Think of this essay as a counterpart to "The Iks." Do they have a common theme? What does Thomas hope is bound up in our DNA? What does this have to do with the Iks' problem? Look especially at the first two sentences in paragraph 8.

2. Like many writers, including Eiseley and Dillard, Thomas uses his response to an experience as a jumping-off place to further thinking. Try to outline the chain of reasoning that the beavers and otters of the Tucson Zoo set off in Thomas's mind.

3. What do you think Thomas means by "full hairy complexity" in paragraph 3? Why does he "want no part of the science of beavers and otters"?

4. What did Thomas learn about himself from his zoo experience? What does he mean by saying he is "coded for beavers"? (Consider paragraph 5 carefully.)

5. Do you agree that our conscious minds fight against the loss of individuality? What is Thomas's rejoinder to those who urge us "not to be a social animal"?

6. Even though Thomas is using the questions in the last paragraph for effect, how might you answer them?

Organization

7. What is the function of the first paragraph? What do you think Thomas intended in the last sentence by, "So we say"?

8. Does Thomas come back to that opening paragraph to summarize or strengthen? Does he do so explicitly, implicitly, or not at all?

9. Why does Thomas begin paragraph 5 with "But"? Is this an effective device?

10. Read the first sentence of paragraphs 2 and 7. How does Thomas connect them to the previous paragraphs?

11. In paragraph 6, what is the relation between the first and the remaining sentences? How are the sentences in this paragraph connected to each other?

12. If you split the essay into two parts, where would you break it and why?

Sentences

13. Thomas is trying to make his prose seem effortless, but we know that prose that is easy to read is hard to write. Thomas's prose did not spontaneously flow from his typewriter. He worked at it, long and hard. All writers do. For example, read paragraph 3 out loud several times. Can you describe some of the techniques Thomas uses here to achieve fluency? Some hints: Do all the sentences begin the same way? How does he vary the S–V–O pattern? How many words are in each sentence?

14. How is the fifth sentence constructed? Why the specific detail (endocrine systems, etc.) and the repetition? Does this paragraph have a beginning, a middle, and an end? How would you partition it?

15. Thomas occasionally uses short sentences, sometimes only two or three words long. Look through paragraphs 1–4, noting those. What is the effect of each?

Words

16. Thomas uses some scientific words in this essay. Do they confuse you? Did you get lost while reading them?

17. Why does Thomas use personal pronouns? See paragraphs 2 (you), 3 and 4(I), and 5(we).

Suggestion for Writing

Write a letter to Lewis Thomas agreeing or disagreeing with paragraphs 6, 7, or 8—or with the whole essay.

To Err Is Human

---

1   Everyone must have had at least one personal experience with a computer error by this time. Bank balances are suddenly reported

to have jumped from $379 into the millions, appeals for charitable contributions are mailed over and over to people with crazy-sounding names at your address, department stores send the wrong bills, utility companies write that they're turning everything off, that sort of thing. If you manage to get in touch with someone and complain, you then get instantaneously typed, guilty letters from the same computer, saying, "Our computer was in error, and an adjustment is being made in your account."

2   These are supposed to be the sheerest, blindest accidents. Mistakes are not believed to be part of the normal behavior of a good machine. If things go wrong, it must be a personal, human error, the result of fingering, tampering, a button getting stuck, someone hitting the wrong key. The computer, at its normal best, is infallible.

3   I wonder whether this can be true. After all, the whole point of computers is that they represent an extension of the human brain, vastly improved upon but nonetheless human, superhuman maybe. A good computer can think clearly and quickly enough to beat you at chess, and some of them have even been programmed to write obscure verse. They can do anything we can do, and more besides.

4   It is not yet known whether a computer has its own consciousness, and it would be hard to find out about this. When you walk into one of those great halls now built for the huge machines, and stand listening, it is easy to imagine that the faint, distant noises are the sound of thinking, and the turning of the spools gives them the look of wild creatures rolling their eyes in the effort to concentrate, choking with information. But real thinking, and dreaming, are other matters.

5   On the other hand, the evidences of something like an *unconscious*, equivalent to ours, are all around, in every mail. As extensions of the human brain, they have been constructed with the same property of error, spontaneous, uncontrolled, and rich in possibilities.

6.   Mistakes are at the very base of human thought, embedded there, feeding the structure like root nodules. If we were not provided with the knack of being wrong, we could never get anything useful done. We think our way along by choosing between right and wrong alternatives, and the wrong choices have to be made as frequently as the right ones. We get along in life this way. We are built to make mistakes, coded for error.

7   We learn, as we say, by "trial and error." Why do we always say that? Why not "trial and rightness" or "trial and triumph"? The old phrase puts it that way because that is, in real life, the way it is done.

8   A good laboratory, like a good bank or a corporation or government, has to run like a computer. Almost everything is done flawlessly,

by the book, and all the numbers add up to the predicted sums. The days go by. And then, if it is a lucky day, and a lucky laboratory, somebody makes a mistake: the wrong buffer, something in one of the blanks, a decimal misplaced in reading counts, the warm room off by a degree and a half, a mouse out of his box, or just a misreading of the day's protocol. Whatever, when the results come in, something is obviously screwed up, and then the action can begin.

9.   The misreading is not the important error; it opens the way. The next step is the crucial one. If the investigator can bring himself to say, "But even so, look at that!" then the new finding, whatever it is, is ready for snatching. What is needed, for progress to be made, is the move based on the error.

10   Whenever new kinds of thinking are about to be accomplished, or new varieties of music, there has to be an argument beforehand. With two sides debating in the same mind, haranguing, there is an amiable understanding that one is right and the other wrong. Sooner or later the thing is settled, but there can be no action at all if there are not the two sides, and the argument. The hope is in the faculty of wrongness, the tendency toward error. The capacity to leap across mountains of information to land lightly on the wrong side represents the highest of human endowments.

11   It may be that this is a uniquely human gift, perhaps even stipulated in our genetic instructions. Other creatures do not seem to have DNA sequences for making mistakes as a routine part of daily living, certainly not for programmed error as a guide for action.

12   We are at our human finest, dancing with our minds, when there are more choices than two. Sometimes there are ten, even twenty different ways to go, all but one bound to be wrong, and the richness of selection in such situations can lift us onto totally new ground. This process is called exploration and is based on human fallibility. If we had only a single center in our brains, capable of responding only when a correct decision was to be made, instead of the jumble of different, credulous, easily conned clusters of neurones that provide for being flung off into blind alleys, up trees, down dead ends, out into blue sky, along wrong turnings, around bends, we could only stay the way we are today, stuck fast.

13   The lower animals do not have this splendid freedom. They are limited, most of them, to absolute infallibility. Cats, for all their good side, never make mistakes. I have never seen a maladroit, clumsy, or blundering cat. Dogs are sometimes fallible, occasionally able to make

charming minor mistakes, but they get this way by trying to mimic their masters. Fish are flawless in everything they do. Individual cells in a tissue are mindless machines, perfect in their performance, as absolutely inhuman as bees.

14   We should have this in mind as we become dependent on more complex computers for the arrangement of our affairs. Give the computers their heads, I say; let them go their way. If we can learn to do this, turning our heads to one side and wincing while the work proceeds, the possibilities for the future of mankind, and computerkind, are limitless. Your average good computer can make calculations in an instant which would take a lifetime of slide rules for any of us. Think of what we could gain from the near infinity of precise, machine-made miscomputation which is now so easily within our grasp. We could begin the solving of some of our hardest problems. How, for instance, should we go about organizing ourselves for social living on a planetary scale, now that we have become, as a plain fact of life, a single community? We can assume, as a working hypothesis, that all the right ways of doing this are unworkable. What we need, then, for moving ahead, is a set of wrong alternatives much longer and more interesting than the short list of mistaken courses that any of us can think up right now. We need, in fact, an infinite list, and when it is printed out we need the computer to turn on itself and select, at random, the next way to go. If it is a big enough mistake, we could find ourselves on a new level, stunned, out in the clear, ready to move again.

QUESTIONS

Ideas

1. How is the title of this piece relevant? What does it have to do with Thomas's theme? Where is that theme expressed? Underline at least three sentences you think are related to this theme.

2. Do you agree that our ability to make mistakes is a "splendid freedom"? Does our society agree? Does your university, your instructor?

3. Again, Thomas takes an apparently negative topic and makes it seem optimistic. Do you see hope in our "faculty of wrongness, the tendency toward error"?

4. In paragraph 8 Thomas discusses "error." And he makes what at first might seem the rather strange remark ". . . if it's a lucky day, and a lucky

laboratory, somebody makes a mistake: . . . when the results come in, something is obviously screwed up, and then the action can begin." Can you explain this paradoxical idea? (Look ahead to paragraph 9 for help.)

5. Why does Thomas celebrate choice and alternative, especially multiple alternatives most of which will be "wrong"? Explain his idea that exploration is based on human fallibility (paragraph 12).

6. Suppose Thomas is "wrong" about what he says in this essay. Does that invalidate his view entirely? Does it make what he says here useless? Why or why not?

7. To err means, of course, to be mistaken. But the original meaning of the word carries the idea of wandering (L. *errare*, to wander). How do Thomas's ideas about error reflect this aspect of the word's meaning?

8. Does what Thomas says about error have any bearing on learning? On writing?

Organization

9. What is the purpose of Thomas's opening two paragraphs? How do they compare to the introductions in "The Iks" and "The Lives of a Cell"?

10. In the overall scheme of these fourteen paragraphs, what is the function of paragraph 6?

11. Where does Thomas support his notion that we are "coded for error"?

12. The last paragraph is rather long for Thomas. What holds it together? Is there an implicit or explicit topic sentence?

13. How many paragraphs have a "this" in the first sentence? Why do you think he does this?

14. Experienced writers try to move between the abstract and the concrete, often supporting general statements with specific details. How does Thomas do this in paragraphs 8, 12, and 13?

Sentences

15. Thomas sometimes adds words, phrases, and clauses to sentences, clarifying an idea, making a general point more specific. See the last sentence, for example. Locate several similar examples.

Words

16. How would you distinguish among "error," "mistake," and "accident"?

17. What does "maladroit" mean? "Haranguing"? "Protocol"?

Suggestion for Writing

Now that Thomas has alerted the reader to the paradox of error, can you see mistakes you made in the past or are continuing to make as enabling you to be "in the clear, ready to move again"? Write an essay involving personal experience to support this optimistic view of error.

Late Night Thoughts on Listening to Mahler's Ninth Symphony

1   **I** cannot listen to Mahler's Ninth Symphony with anything like the old melancholy mixed with the high pleasure I used to take from this music. There was a time, not long ago, when what I heard, especially in the final movement, was an open acknowledgment of death and at the same time a quiet celebration of the tranquillity connected to the process. I took this music as a metaphor for reassurance, confirming my own strong hunch that the dying of every living creature, the most natural of all experiences, has to be a peaceful experience. I rely on nature. The long passages on all the strings at the end, as close as music can come to expressing silence itself, I used to hear as Mahler's idea of leave-taking at its best. But always, I have heard this music as a solitary, private listener, thinking about death.

2   Now I hear it differently. I cannot listen to the last movement of the Mahler Ninth without the door-smashing intrusion of a huge new thought: death everywhere, the dying of everything, the end of humanity. The easy sadness expressed with such gentleness and delicacy by that repeated phrase on faded strings, over and over again, no longer comes to me as old, familiar news of the cycle of living and dying. All through the last notes my mind swarms with images of a world in which the thermonuclear bombs have begun to explode, in New York and San Francisco, in Moscow and Leningrad, in Paris, in Paris, in Paris. In Oxford and Cambridge, in Edinburgh. I cannot push away the thought of a cloud of radioactivity drifting along the Engadin, from the Moloja

Pass to Ftan, killing off the part of the earth I love more than any other part.

3   I am old enough by this time to be used to the notion of dying, saddened by the glimpse when it has occurred but only transiently knocked down, able to regain my feet quickly at the thought of continuity, any day. I have acquired and held in affection until very recently another sideline of an idea which serves me well at dark times: the life of the earth is the same as the life of an organism: the great round being possesses a mind: the mind contains an infinite number of thoughts and memories: when I reach my time I may find myself still hanging around in some sort of midair, one of those small thoughts, drawn back into the memory of the earth: in that peculiar sense I will be alive.

4   Now all that has changed. I cannot think that way anymore. Not while those things are still in place, aimed everywhere, ready for launching.

5   This is a bad enough thing for the people in my generation. We can put up with it, I suppose, since we must. We are moving along anyway, like it or not. I can even set aside my private fancy about hanging around, in midair.

6   What I cannot imagine, what I cannot put up with, the thought that keeps grinding its way into my mind, making the Mahler into a hideous noise close to killing me, is what it would be like to be young. How do the young stand it? How can they keep their sanity? If I were very young, sixteen or seventeen years old, I think I would begin, perhaps very slowly and imperceptibly, to go crazy.

7   There is a short passage near the very end of the Mahler in which the almost vanishing violins, all engaged in a sustained backward glance, are edged aside for a few bars by the cellos. Those lower notes pick up fragments from the first movement, as though prepared to begin everything all over again, and then the cellos subside and disappear, like an exhalation. I used to hear this as a wonderful few seconds of encouragement: we'll be back, we're still here, keep going, keep going.

8   Now, with a pamphlet in front of me on a corner of my desk, published by the Congressional Office of Technology Assessment, entitled *MX Basing,* an analysis of all the alternative strategies for placement and protection of hundreds of these missiles, each capable of creating artificial suns to vaporize a hundred Hiroshimas, collectively capable of destroying the life of any continent, I cannot hear the same Mahler. Now, those cellos sound in my mind like the opening of all the hatches and the instant before ignition.

9   If I were sixteen or seventeen years old, I would not feel the cracking of my own brain, but I would know for sure that the whole world was coming unhinged. I can remember with some clarity what it was like to be sixteen. I had discovered the Brahms symphonies. I knew that there was something going on in the late Beethoven quarters that I would have to figure out, and I knew that there was plenty of time ahead for all the figuring I would ever have to do. I had never heard of Mahler. I was in no hurry. I was a college sophomore and had decided that Wallace Stevens and I possessed a comprehensive understanding of everything needed for a life. The years stretched away forever ahead, forever. My great-great grandfather had come from Wales, leaving his signature in the family Bible on the same page that carried, a century later, my father's signature. It never crossed my mind to wonder about the twenty-first century; it was just there, given, somewhere in the sure distance.

10   The man on television, Sunday midday, middle-aged and solid, nice-looking chap, all the facts at his fingertips, more dependable looking than most high-school principals, is talking about civilian defense, his responsibility in Washington. It can make an enormous difference, he is saying. Instead of the outright death of eighty million American citizens in twenty minutes, he says, we can, by careful planning and practice, get that number down to only forty million, maybe even twenty. The thing to do, he says, is to evacuate the cities quickly and have everyone get under shelter in the countryside. That way we can recover, and meanwhile we will have retaliated, incinerating all of Soviet society, he says. What about radioactive fallout? he is asked. Well, he says. Anyway, he says, if the Russians know they can only destroy forty million of us instead of eighty million, this will deter them. Of course, he adds, they have the capacity to kill all two hundred and twenty million of us if they were to try real hard, but they know we can do the same to them. If the figure is only forty million this will deter them, not worth the trouble, not worth the risk. Eighty million would be another matter, we should guard ourselves against losing that many all at once, he says.

11   If I were sixteen or seventeen years old and had to listen to that, or read things like that, I would want to give up listening and reading. I would begin thinking up new kinds of sounds, different from any music heard before, and I would be twisting and turning to rid myself of human language.

QUESTIONS

Ideas

1. Thomas's notions of death have obviously been upset. What were they? Specifically, what are the ways Thomas used to deal with death?

2. What does Thomas now hear when he listens to Mahler's Ninth Symphony?

3. What about the man on television who angers Thomas? Does he anger you? How do you keep your sanity in the face of nuclear war? Do you have a defense?

4. What does Thomas mean to suggest about his present pessimism with the phrase "there was plenty of time ahead" in paragraph 9?

5. Do you think it is unusual for something like the MX missile to color someone's perception about music?

Organization

6. Much of this essay is structured on a then-and-now pattern. Point out how Thomas integrates these shifts between the past and the present.

7. In paragraph 6, Thomas makes his point about the difficulty of being young in the last sentence. How does that thought control the remaining five paragraphs?

Sentences

8. Read carefully the second sentence in paragraph 3. Explain how Thomas uses this rarely seen colon sequence. Is it effective? What are some alternatives?

9. Look at the many "if" clauses and sentences in this essay. Are there special rules for them; for example, are the verb tenses different than in normal declarative sentences?

Words

10. Why does Thomas repeat "in Paris" in paragraph 2?

11. What is the effect of calling missiles "those things" in paragraph 4?

Suggestions for Writing

A. Write a paragraph in response to Thomas's last paragraph. Do you agree with him? Is he exaggerating?

B. Write a brief paper using "denial of death" as your initial focus.

THIRTEEN

Barbara Tuchman

(1912–)

Barbara Tuchman is not a typical academic historian: she has no graduate degrees, does not teach in a university, and is more interested in telling a story readers feel compelled to follow than in historical objectivity. She is, in other words, a popular historian, and after winning two Pulitzer Prizes and numerous honorary degrees, probably the most eminent in America.

She writes to inform and enthrall an audience of average readers, not to impress history professors. Because she knows her chosen audience will not automatically be interested in her subject, she adopts a lively, colorful style that will keep the reader turning pages. She tries to win the reader over by ordering her writing as if she were writing fiction. She builds suspense by selecting and arranging dramatic details from her copious research notes, discarding the irrelevant, and maintaining a strong story line. The following passage from *The Proud Tower* is typical of her approach. She is writing about the reaction to the assassination of Jaurès, a popular French socialist before World War I.

The news licked through Paris like a flame. Crowds gathered so quickly in the street outside the restaurant that it took the police fifteen minutes to open a passage for the ambulance. When the body was carried out a great silence fell. As the ambulance clanged away, escorted by policemen on bicycles, a sudden clamor arose, as if to deny the fact of death, "Jaurès! Jaurès! Vive Jaurès!" Elsewhere people were stupefied, numb with sorrow. Many wept in the streets. "My heart is breaking," said Anatole France when he heard. Informed at its night session by a white-faced aide, the Cabinet was stunned and fearful. Visions rose of working-class riots and civil strife on the eve of war. The Premier issued a public appeal for unity and calm. Troops were alerted but next morning, in the national peril, there was only deep grief and deep quiet. At Carmaux the miners stopped work. "They have cut down a mighty oak," said one. In Leipzig a Spanish Socialist student at the University wandered blindly through the streets for hours; "everything took on the color of blood."

These techniques have sometimes drawn criticism from more traditional historians who say that she sacrifices depth and intellectual content for the immediacy and literary flavor of dramatic narrative. Barbara Tuchman insists, however, that although her subject matter is historical, she is a writer first, and her loyalty is primarily to her craft, to the drama, coherence, and color of good writing. She does not, however, avoid ideas. But even here she goes her own way, sometimes preferring bold opinion to scholarly detachment. The "Afterword" to her book on Europe before World War I, *The Proud Tower,* provides a good example of her engaging mix of stylistic flair and intelligent insight:

The four years that followed were, as Graham Wallas wrote, "four years of the most intense and heroic effort the human race has ever made." When the effort was over, illusions and enthusiasms possible up to 1914 slowly sank beneath a sea of massive disillusionment. For the price it had paid, humanity's major gain was a painful view of its own limitations.

The proud tower built up through the great age of European civilization was an edifice of grandeur and passion, of riches and beauty and dark cellars. Its inhabitants lived, as compared to a later time, with more self-reliance, more confidence, more hope, greater magnificence, extravagance and elegance; more careless ease, more gaiety, more pleasure in each other's company and conversation, more injustice and hypocrisy, more misery and want, more sentiment including false sentiment, less sufferance of mediocrity, more dignity in work, more delight in nature, more zest. The Old World had much that has since been lost, whatever may have been gained. Looking back on it from 1915, Emile Verhaeren, the Belgian Socialist poet, dedicated his pages, "With emotion, to the man I used to be."

Since Tuchman is not limited by the usual narrow specializations, her topics spring from her present interests. Her subjects have been diverse. Her first success, *The Guns of August* (1962), dealt with the failures of the early military strategy of World War I. She followed that in 1966 with *The Proud Tower: A Portrait of the World before the War—1890–1914,* filled with thickly described, selective narratives of socialists, patricians, anarchists, and statesmen. Five years later she turned her attention to relations between China and America in *Stilwell and the American Experience in China, 1911–1945*, winning praise from specialists for not sacrificing complexity and for "an admirably structured work that is excellent as narrative and fascinating as history." Her most popular book, the best-selling *A Distant Mirror: The Calamitous Fourteenth Century* (1978), was seen by many critics as Tuchman's greatest achievement. In it she weaves a gripping drama of social, political, and historical events around themes that recur in her work: the complexity of life, the hopes and upheavals of people and nations, and the persistent folly of governments. This last concern dominates her most recent book, *The March of Folly: From Troy to Vietnam* (1984), an indictment of governments that consistently make unwise decisions. In a related essay on political wooden-headedness, Tuchman blames the poor performance of leaders on the passions and the emotions: "greed, fear, facesaving, the instinct to dominate, the needs of the ego, the whole bundle of personal vanities and anxieties."

Herein lies the motivating power and moral power of Tuchman's career as a writer. She has a message, a warning that she hopes her readers will assimilate from her work. She believes that the modern world can no longer afford to repeat the mistakes of the past: "Today there are no more cushions." She hopes for reason, for intellect, and is outraged when powerful men seem to follow their baser instincts. She is unsparing, for example, with President Johnson, who seemed to her to have a shaky self-image. "Johnson's showed in his deliberate coarseness and compulsion to humiliate others in crude physical ways. No self-confident man would have needed to do that." Idealistically she hopes instead for the "truest wisdom" of magnanimity, rationality, and fitness of character. She writes history in the hope that an informed electorate might choose leaders with these virtues.

In Search of History

1   One learns to write, I have since discovered, in the practice thereof. After seven years' apprenticeship in journalism I discovered that an essential element for good writing is a good ear. One must *listen* to

the sound of one's own prose. This, I think, is one of the failings of much American writing. Too many writers do not listen to the sound of their own words. For example, listen to this sentence from the organ of my own discipline, the *American Historical Review:* "His presentation is not vitiated historically by efforts at expository simplicity." In one short sentence five long Latin words of four or five syllables each. One has to read it three times over and take time out to think, before one can even make out what it means.

2   In my opinion, short words are always preferable to long ones; the fewer syllables the better, and monosyllables, beautiful and pure like "bread" and "sun" and "grass," are the best of all. Emerson, using almost entirely one-syllable words, wrote what I believe are among the finest lines in English:

> By the rude bridge that arched the flood,
> Their flag to April's breeze unfurled,
>   Here once the embattled farmers stood
> And fired the shot heard round the world.

Out of twenty-eight words, twenty-four are monosyllables. It is English at its purest, though hardly characteristic of its author.

3   Or take this:

> On desperate seas long wont to roam,
>   Thy hyacinth hair, thy classic face,
> Thy Naiad airs have brought me home
>   To the glory that was Greece
>   And the grandeur that was Rome.

Imagine how it must feel to have composed those lines! Though coming from a writer satisfied with the easy rhythms of "The Raven" and "Annabel Lee," they represent, I fear, a fluke. To quote poetry, you will say, is not a fair comparison. True, but what a lesson those stanzas are in the sound of words! What superb use of that magnificent instrument that lies at the command of all of us—the English language. Quite by chance both practitioners in these samples happen to be Americans, and both, curiously enough, writing about history.

4   To write history so as to enthrall the reader and make the subject as captivating and exciting to him as it is to me has been my goal since

that initial failure with my thesis. A prerequisite, as I have said, is to be enthralled one's self and to feel a compulsion to communicate the magic. Communicate to whom? We arrive now at the reader, a person whom I keep constantly in mind. Catherine Drinker Bowen has said that she writes her books with a sign pinned up over her desk asking, "Will the reader turn the page?"

5   The writer of history, I believe, has a number of duties *vis-à-vis* the reader, if he wants to keep him reading. The first is to distill. He must do the preliminary work for the reader, assemble the information, make sense of it, select the essential, discard the irrelevant—above all, discard the irrelevant—and put the rest together so that it forms a developing dramatic narrative. Narrative, it has been said, is the life-blood of history. To offer a mass of undigested facts, of names not identified and places not located, is of no use to the reader and is simple laziness on the part of the author, or pedantry to show how much he has read. To discard the unnecessary requires courage and also extra work, as exemplified by Pascal's effort to explain an idea to a friend in a letter which rambled on for pages and ended, "I am sorry to have wearied you with so long a letter but I did not have time to write you a short one." The historian is continually being beguiled down fascinating byways and sidetracks. But the art of writing—the test of the artist—is to resist the beguilement and cleave to the subject.

6   Should the historian be an artist? Certainly a conscious art should be part of his equipment. Macaulay describes him as half poet, half philosopher. I do not aspire to either of these heights. I think of myself as a storyteller, a narrator, who deals in true stories, not fiction. The distinction is not one of relative values; it is simply that history interests me more than fiction. I agree with Leopold von Ranke, the great nineteenth-century German historian, who said that when he compared the portrait of Louis XI in Scott's *Quentin Durward* with the portrait of the same king in the memoirs of Philippe de Comines, Louis' minister, he found "the truth more interesting and beautiful than the romance."

7   It was Ranke, too, who set the historian's task: to find out *wie es eigentlich gewesen ist,* what really happened, or, literally, how it really was. His goal is one that will remain forever just beyond our grasp for reasons I explained in a "Note on Sources" in *The Guns of August* (a paragraph that no one ever reads but *I* think is the best thing in the book). Summarized, the reasons are that we who write about the past were not there. We can never be certain that we have recaptured it as it really was. But the least we can do is to stay within the evidence.

8   I do not invent anything, even the weather. One of my readers
told me he particularly liked a passage in *The Guns* which tells how the
British Army landed in France and how on that afternoon there was a
sound of summer thunder in the air and the sun went down in a
blood-red glow. He thought it an artistic touch of doom, but the fact
is it was true. I found it in the memoirs of a British officer who landed
on that day and heard the thunder and saw the blood-red sunset. The
art, if any, consisted only in selecting it and ultimately using it in the
right place.

9   Selection is what determines the ultimate product, and that is why
I use material from primary sources only. My feeling about secondary
sources is that they are helpful but pernicious. I use them as guides at
the start of a project to find out the general scheme of what happened,
but I do not take notes from them because I do not want to end up
simply rewriting someone else's book. Furthermore, the facts in a secondary source have already been pre-selected, so that in using them one
misses the opportunity of selecting one's own.

10   I plunge as soon as I can into the primary sources: the memoirs
and the letters, the generals' own accounts of their campaigns, however
tendentious, not to say mendacious, they may be. Even an untrustworthy source is valuable for what it reveals about the personality of the
author, especially if he is an actor in the events, as in the case of Sir John
French, for example. Bias in a primary source is to be expected. One
allows for it and corrects it by reading another version. I try always to
read two or more for every episode. Even if an event is not controversial,
it will have been seen and remembered from different angles of view by
different observers. If the event *is* in dispute, one has extra obligation
to examine both sides. As the lion in Aesop said to the Man, "There
are many statues of men slaying lions, but if only the lions were sculptors
there might be quite a different set of statues."

11   The most primary source of all is unpublished material: private
letters and diaries or the reports, orders, and messages in government
archives. There is an immediacy and intimacy about them that reveals
character and makes circumstances come alive. I remember Secretary of
State Robert Lansing's desk diary, which I used when I was working on
The Zimmermann Telegram. The man himself seemed to step right out
from his tiny neat handwriting and his precise notations of every visitor
and each subject discussed. Each day's record opened and closed with
the Secretary's time of arrival and departure from the office. He even
entered the time of his lunch hour, which invariably lasted sixty minutes:
"Left at 1:10; returned at 2:10." Once, when he was forced to record

his morning arrival at 10:15, he added, with a worried eye on posterity, "Car broke down."

12   Inside the National Archives even the memory of Widener paled. Nothing can compare with the fascination of examining material in the very paper and ink of its original issue. A report from a field agent with marginal comments by the Secretary of War, his routing directions to State and Commerce, and the scribbled initials of subsequent readers can be a little history in itself. In the Archives I found the original decode of the Zimmermann Telegram, which I was able to have declassified and photostated for the cover of my book.

13   Even more immediate is research on the spot. Before writing *The Guns* I rented a little Renault and in another August drove over the battle areas of August 1914, following the track of the German invasion through Luxembourg, Belgium, and northern France. Besides obtaining a feeling of the geography, distances, and terrain involved in military movements, I saw the fields ripe with grain which the cavalry would have trampled, measured the grain which the cavalry would have trampled, measured the great width of the Meuse at Liège, and saw how the lost territory of Alsace looked to the French soldiers who gazed down upon it from the heights of the Vosges. I learned the discomfort of the Belgian *pavé* and discovered, in the course of losing my way almost permanently in a tangle of country roads in a hunt for the house that had been British Headquarters, why a British motorcycle dispatch rider in 1914 had taken three hours to cover twenty-five miles. Clearly, owing to the British officers' preference for country houses, he had not been able to find Headquarters either. French army commanders, I noticed, located themselves in *towns*, with railroad stations and telegraph offices.

14   As to the mechanics of research, I take notes on four-by-six index cards, reminding myself about once an hour of a rule I read long ago in a research manual, "Never write on the back of anything." Since copying is a chore and a bore, use of the cards, the smaller the better, forces one to extract the strictly relevant, to distill from the very beginning, to pass the material through the grinder of one's own mind, so to speak. Eventually, as the cards fall into groups according to subject or person or chronological sequence, the pattern of my story will emerge. Besides, they are convenient, as they can be filed in a shoebox and carried around in a pocketbook. When ready to write I need only take along a packet of them, representing a chapter, and I am equipped to work anywhere; whereas if one writes surrounded by a pile of books, one is tied to a single place, and furthermore likely to be too much influenced by other authors.

15   The most important thing about research is to know when to stop. How does one recognize the moment? When I was eighteen or thereabouts, my mother told me that when out with a young man I should always leave a half-hour before I wanted to. Although I was not sure how this might be accomplished, I recognized the advice as sound, and exactly the same rule applies to research. One must stop *before* one has finished; otherwise, one will never stop and never finish. I had an object lesson in this once in Washington at the Archives. I was looking for documents in the case of Perdicaris, an American—or supposed American—who was captured by Moroccan brigands in 1904. The Archives people introduced me to a lady professor who had been doing research in United States relations with Morocco all her life. She had written her Ph.D. thesis on the subject back in, I think, 1936, and was still coming for six months each year to work in the Archives. She was in her seventies and, they told me, had recently suffered a heart attack. When I asked her what year was her cut-off point, she looked at me in surprise and said she kept a file of newspaper clippings right up to the moment. I am sure she knew more about United States–Moroccan relations than anyone alive, but would she ever leave off her research in time to write that definitive history and tell the world what she knew? I feared the answer. Yet I know how she felt. I too feel compelled to follow every lead and learn everything about a subject, but fortunately I have an even more overwhelming compulsion to see my work in print. That is the only thing that saves me.

16   Research is endlessly seductive; writing is hard work. One has to sit down on that chair and think and transform thought into readable, conservative, interesting sentences that both make sense and make the reader turn the page. It is laborious, slow, often painful, sometimes agony. It means rearrangement, revision, adding, cutting, rewriting. But it brings a sense of excitement, almost of rapture; a moment on Olympus. In short, it is an act of creation.

QUESTIONS

Ideas

1. What does Tuchman mean by her opening question in paragraph 6? How does she answer her own question? How would you?

2. Tuchman's goal is to find out "how it really was." To do that she tries to stay "within the evidence." What is evidence, how do you think a historian

finds it, judges it, and decides what to use? How do the historian's own values and experiences influence choices?

3. In reference to paragraph 5, how do you know "when to stop" researching or writing? How does Tuchman describe her composing process in writing history? What seems most important to her? What does it mean to enthrall the reader?

4. What writing techniques that Tuchman describes might be most useful to your own writing?

5. Below is the selection from *The Guns of August* that Tuchman mentions in paragraph 7. Do you agree with her definition of "truth"? Are there absolute facts we could all agree on?

SOURCES

A full bibliography of the subject would fill a book. No other episode in history has been more fully documented by its participants. They seem to have known, while they lived it, that like the French Revolution, the First World War was one of the great convulsions of history, and each felt the hand of history heavily on his own shoulder. When it was over, despite courage, skill, and sacrifice, the war they had fought proved to have been, on the whole, a monument of failure, tragedy, and disillusion. It had not led to a better world. Men who had taken part at the command level, political and military, felt driven to explain their decisions and actions. Men who had fallen from high command, whether for cause or as scapegoats—and these included most of the commanders of August—wrote their private justifications. As each account appeared, inevitably shifting responsibility or blame to someone else, another was provoked. Private feuds became public; public controversies expanded. Men who would otherwise have remained mute were stung to publish, as Sir Horace Smith-Dorrien by Sir John French. Books proliferated. Whole schools of partisans, like those of Gallieni and Joffre, produced libraries of controversy.

Through this forest of special pleading the historian gropes his way, trying to recapture the truth of past events and find out "what really happened." He discovers that truth is subjective and separate, made up of little bits seen, experienced, and recorded by different people. It is like a design seen through a kaleidoscope; when the cylinder is shaken the countless colored fragments form a new picture. Yet they are the same fragments that made a different picture a moment earlier. This is the problem inherent in the records left by actors in past events. That famous goal, *"wie es wirklich war,"* is never wholly within our grasp.

Organization

6. In describing her writing philosophy Tuchman arranges her ideas in a particular way. Why does she choose this sequence, does she put the most important ideas first or last? Try to find an explanation, a pattern.

7. Look at the organization of paragraph 5: describe the relationship between her sentences. Is there one umbrella sentence under which the others might fit?

Sentences

8. Take a look at the last sentence in each paragraph and then the first sentences in the following paragraph. Are they connected?
9. Does Tuchman try to vary her sentence length? Count the number of words in each sentence in paragraphs 4 and 16, for example.

Words

10. Does Tuchman follow the advice she gives in paragraph 2?
11. Throughout this and other essays Tuchman consistently uses "he" or "him" even when she is talking about herself (e.g., in paragraph 5). Do you think she should have used "her" or some other alternative?

Suggestions for Writing

A. Look again at the second paragraph in "Sources." Based on this notion of truth, how might a historian tell what really happened in your life; in the semester you are in; in the specific class you are sitting in?
B. Think of some famous historical event and write about it from a perspective that would surprise or shock us and alter our usual expectations.

The Idea and the Deed

---

1   So enchanting was the vision of a stateless society, without government, without law, without ownership of property, in which, corrupt institutions having been swept away, man would be free to be good as God intended him, that six heads of state were assassinated for its sake in the twenty years before 1914. They were President Carnot of France in 1894, Premier Canovas of Spain in 1897, Empress Elizabeth of Austria in 1898, King Humbert of Italy in 1900, President McKinley of the United States in 1901, and another Premier of Spain, Canalejas, in 1912. Not one could qualify as a tyrant. Their deaths were the gestures of desperate or deluded men to call attention to the Anarchist idea.

2   No single individual was the hero of the movement that swallowed up these lives. The Idea was its hero. It was, as a historian of revolt has called it, "a daydream of desperate romantics." It had its theorists and thinkers, men of intellect, sincere and earnest, who loved humanity. It also had its tools, the little men whom misfortune or despair or the anger, degradation and hopelessness of poverty made susceptible to the Idea until they became possessed by it and were driven to act. These became the assassins. Between the two groups there was no contact. The thinkers in press and pamphlet constructed marvelous paper models of the Anarchist millennium; poured out tirades of hate and invective upon the ruling class and its despised ally, the bourgeoisie; issued trumpet calls for action, for a "propaganda of the deed" to accomplish the enemy's overthrow. Whom were they calling? What deed were they asking for? They did not say precisely. Unknown to them, down in the lower depths of society lonely men were listening. They heard echoes of the tirades and the trumpets and caught a glimpse of the shining millennium that promised a life without hunger and without a boss. Suddenly one of them, with a sense of injury or a sense of mission, would rise up, go out and kill—and sacrifice his own life on the altar of the Idea.

3   They came from the warrens of the poor, where hunger and dirt were king, where consumptives coughed and the air was thick with the smell of latrines, boiling cabbage and stale beer, where babies wailed and couples screamed in sudden quarrels, where roofs leaked and unmended windows let in the cold blasts of winter, where privacy was unimaginable, where men, women, grandparents and children lived together, eating, sleeping, fornicating, defecating, sickening and dying in one room, where a teakettle served as a wash boiler between meals, old boxes served as chairs, heaps of foul straw as beds, and boards propped across two crates as tables, where sometimes not all the children in a family could go out at one time because there were not enough clothes to go round, where decent families lived among drunkards, wife-beaters, thieves and prostitutes, where life was a seesaw of unemployment and endless toil, where a cigar-maker and his wife earning 13 cents an hour worked seventeen hours a day seven days a week to support themselves and three children, where death was the only exit and the only extravagance and the scraped savings of a lifetime would be squandered on a funeral coach with flowers and a parade of mourners to ensure against the anonymity and last ignominy of Potter's Field.

4   The Anarchists believed that with Property, the monarch of all evil, eliminated, no man could again live off the labour of another and human nature would be released to seek its natural level of justice among

men. The role of State would be replaced by voluntary cooperation among individuals and the role of the law by the supreme law of the general welfare. To this end no reform of existing social evils through vote or persuasion was of any use, for the ruling class would never give up its property or the powers and laws which protected ownership of property. Therefore, the necessity of violence. Only revolutionary over-turn of the entire malignant existing system would accomplish the desired result. Once the old structure was in rubble, a new social order of utter equality and no authority, with enough of everything for every-body, would settle smilingly upon the earth. So reasonable seemed the proposition that once apprised of it the oppressed classes could not fail to respond. The Anarchist task was to awaken them to the Idea by propaganda of the word and of the Deed, and one day, one such deed would flash the signal for revolt.

5   During the first and formulative period of Anarchism, beginning around the time of the revolutionary year 1848, its two major prophets were Pierre Proudhon of France and his disciple, Michael Bakunin, a Russian exile who became the active leader of the movement.

6   "Whoever lays his hand on me to govern me," Proudhon pro-claimed, "is a usurper and a tyrant; I declare him to be my ene-my. . . . Government of man by man is slavery" and its laws are "cobwebs for the rich and chains of steel for the poor." The "highest perfection" for free society is no government, to which Proudhon was the first to give the name "An-archy." He excoriated government in a passion of contempt. "To be governed is to be watched, inspected, spied on, regulated, indoctrinated, preached at, controlled, ruled, censored, by persons who have neither wisdom nor virtue. It is every action and transaction to be registered, stamped, taxed, patented, licensed, as-sessed, measured, reprimanded, corrected, frustrated. Under pretext of the public good it is to be exploited, monopolized, embezzled, robbed and then, at the least protest or word of complaint, to be fined, harassed, vilified, beaten up, bludgeoned, disarmed, judged, condemned, impris-oned, shot, garroted, deported, sold, betrayed, swindled, deceived, out-raged, dishonored. That's government, that's its justice, that's its morality! And imagine that among us there are democrats who believe government to be good, socialists who in the name of liberty, equality and fraternity support this ignominy, proletarians who offer themselves candidates for President of the Republic! What hypocrisy!"

7   Proudhon believed that the "abstract idea of right" would obviate the need of revolution and man would be persuaded to adopt the

stateless society through reason. What Bakunin added, learning from Russia under Nicholas I, was the necessity of violent revolution. As opposed to his rival, Karl Marx, who maintained that revolution would come only from an industrial proletariat, organized and trained for the task, Bakunin believed that immediate revolution could explode in one of the more economically backward countries—Italy, Spain or Russia—where the workers, though untrained, unorganized and illiterate, with no understanding of their own wants, would be ready to rise because they had nothing to lose. The task of the conscientious revolutionist was to popularize the Idea among the masses, hitherto bound in ignorance and prejudice by the ruling class. It was necessary to make them conscious of their own wants and "evoke" from them thoughts to match their impulses, thoughts of revolt. When this happened the workers would know their own will and then "their power will be irresistible." Bakunin, however, lost control of the First International to Marx, who believed in organization.

8   There was an inherent paradox within the body of Anarchism that frustrated progress. Anarchism rejected the political party, which Proudhon had called a mere "variety of absolutism"; yet to bring about a revolution it was necessary to submit to authority, organization and discipline. Whenever Anarchists met to prepare a program, this terrible necessity rose up to face them. Loyal to their Idea, they rejected it. Revolution would burst from the masses spontaneously. All that was needed was the Idea—and a spark.

9   Each strike or bread riot or local uprising the Anarchist hoped—and the capitalist feared—might be the spark. Mme Hennebau, the manager's wife in Zola's *Germinal,* watching the march of the striking miners under the bloody gleam of the setting sun, saw "the red vision of revolution that on some sombre evening at the end of the century would carry everything away. Yes, on that evening the people, unbridled at last, would make the blood of the middle class flow, . . . in a thunder of boots the same terrible troop, with their dirty skins and tainted breath, would sweep away the old world. . . . Fires would flame, there would be nothing left, not a *sou* of the great fortunes, not a title deed of acquired properties."

10   Yet each time, as when Zola's miners faced the guns of the gendarmerie, the spark was stamped out. The magic moment when the masses would awaken to their wants and their power did not come. The Paris Commune flared and died in 1871 and failed to signal a general

insurrection. "We reckoned without the masses who did not want to be roused to passion for their own freedom," wrote Bakunin, disillusioned, to his wife. "The passion being absent what good did it do us to have been right theoretically? We were powerless." He despaired of saving the world and died, disillusioned, in 1876, a Columbus, as Alexander Herzen said, without America.

11   Meanwhile in his native land his ideas took root in the Narodniki, or Populists, otherwise the Party of the People's Will, founded in 1879. Because of communal use of land peculiar to the Russian peasant, reformers worshipped the peasant as a natural Socialist who needed only the appearance of a Messiah to be awakened from his lethargy and impelled upon the march to revolution. The bomb was to be the Messiah. "Terrorist activity," stated the Narodniki program, "consisting in destroying the most harmful person in government, aims to undermine the prestige of the government and arouse in this manner the revolutionary spirit of the people and their confidence in the success of the cause."

12   In 1881 the Narodniki struck a blow that startled the world: they assassinated the Czar, Alexander II. It was a triumphant coup, equal, they imagined, to the battering down of the Bastille. It would shout aloud their protest, summon the oppressed and terrorize the oppressors. Instead it ushered in reaction. The dead Czar, whose crown may have been the symbol of autocracy but who in person was the "Liberator" of the serfs, was mourned by the peasants, who believed "the gentry had murdered the Czar to get back the land." His ministers opened a campaign of savage repression, the public, abandoning all thoughts of reform, acquiesced, and the revolutionary movement, "broken and demoralized, withdrew into the conspirators' cellar." There Anarchism's first period came to an end.

13   Before the movement burst into renewed bloom in the nineties, a single terrible event which enlarged the stature of Anarchism took place, not in Europe, but in America, in the city of Chicago. There in August, 1886, eight Anarchists were sentenced by Judge Joseph Gary to be hanged for the murder of seven police killed on the previous May 4 by a bomb hurled into the midst of an armed police force who were about to break up a strikers' meeting in Haymarket Square.

14   The occasion was the climax of a campaign for the eight-hour day, which in itself was the climax of a decade of industrial war centering on Chicago. In every clash the employers fought with the forces of law—police, militia and courts—as their allies. The workers' demands were

met with live ammunition and lockouts and with strikebreakers protected by Pinkertons who were armed and sworn in as deputy sheriffs. In the war between the classes, the State was not neutral. Driven by misery and injustice, the workers' anger grew and with it the employers' fear, their sense of a rising menace and their determination to stamp it out. Even a man as remote as Henry James sensed a "sinister anarchic underworld heaving in its pain, its power and its hate."

15   Anarchism was not a labour movement and was no more than one element in the general upheaval of the lower class. But Anarchists saw in the struggles of labour the hot coals of revolution and hoped to blow them into flame. "A pound of dynamite is worth a bushel of bullets," cried August Spies, editor of Chicago's German-language Anarchist daily, *Die Arbeiter-Zeitung.* "Police and militia, the bloodhounds of capitalism, are ready to murder!" In this he was right, for in the course of a clash between workers and strikebreakers, the police fired, killing two. "Revenge! Revenge! Workingmen to arms!" shrieked handbills printed and distributed by Spies that night. He called for a protest meeting the next day. It took place in Haymarket Square, the police marched to break it up, the bomb was thrown. Who threw it has never been discovered.

16   The defendants' speeches to the court after sentence, firm in Anarchist principle and throbbing with consciousness of martyrdom, resounded throughout Europe and America and provided the best propaganda Anarchism ever had. In the absence of direct evidence establishing their guilt, they knew and loudly stated that they were being tried and sentenced for the crime, not of murder, but of Anarchism. "Let the world know," cried August Spies, "that in 1886 in the state of Illinois eight men were sentenced to death because they believed in a better future!" Their belief had included the use of dynamite, and society's revenge matched its fright. In the end the sentences of three of the condemned were commuted to prison terms. One, Louis Lingg, the youngest, handsomest and most fervent, who was shown by evidence at the trial to have made bombs, blew himself up with a capsule of fulminate of mercury on the night before the execution and wrote in his blood before he died, "Long live anarchy!" His suicide was regarded by many as a confession of guilt. The remaining four, including Spies, were hanged on November 11, 1887.

17   For years afterward the silhouette of the gallows and its four hanging bodies decorated Anarchist literature, and the anniversary of November 11 was celebrated by Anarchists in Europe and America as

a revolutionary memorial. The public conscience, too, was made aware
by the gallow's fruit of the misery, protest and upheaval in the working
class.

18   Men who were Anarchists without knowing it stood on every
street corner. Jacob Riis, the New York police reporter who described
in 1890 *How the Other Half Lives,* saw one on the corner of Fifth
Avenue and Fourteenth Street. The man suddenly leaped at a carriage
carrying two fashionable ladies on an afternoon's shopping and slashed
at the sleek and shining horses with a knife. When arrested and locked
up, he said, "They don't have to think of tomorrow. They spend in an
hour what would keep me and my little ones for a year." He was the
kind from which Anarchists of the Deed were made.

19   Most of them were voiceless or could speak their protest only in
the wail of a dispossessed Irish peasant spading his field for the last time,
who was asked by a visitor what he wanted. "What is it I am wantin'?"
cried the old man, shaking his fist at the sky. "I want the Day av
Judgment!"

20   The poor lived in a society in which power, wealth and magnificent spending were never more opulent, in which the rich dined on fish,
fowl and red meat at one meal, lived in houses of marble floors and
damask walls and of thirty or forty or fifty rooms, wrapped themselves
in furs in winter and were cared for by a retinue of servants who blacked
their boots, arranged their hair, drew their baths and lit their fires. In
this world, at a luncheon for Mme Nellie Melba at the Savoy, when
perfect peaches, a delicacy of the season, were served up "fragrant and
delicious in their cotton wool," the surfeited guests made a game of
throwing them at passers-by beneath the windows.

21   These were the rulers and men of property whose immense posses-
sions could, it seemed, only be explained as having been accumulated
out of the pockets of the exploited masses. "What is Property?" asked
Proudhon in a famous question and answered, "Property is theft." "Do
you not know," cried Enrico Malatesta in his *Talk Between Two Workers,* an Anarchist classic of the nineties, "that every bit of bread they
eat is taken from your children, every fine present they give to their wives
means the poverty, hunger, cold, even perhaps prostitution of yours?"

22   If in their economics the Anarchists were hazy, their hatred of the
ruling class was strong and vibrant. They hated "all mankind's tormen-
tors," as Bakunin called them, "priests, monarchs, statesmen, soldiers,
officials, financiers, capitalists, moneylenders, lawyers." To the workers

themselves it was not the faraway rich but their visible representatives, the landlord, the factory owner, the boss, the policeman, who were the Enemy.

23   They could hate but only a few were rebels. Most existed in apathy, stupefied by poverty. Some gave up. A woman with four children who made match boxes at 4½ cents a gross, and by working fourteen hours could make seven gross a day for a total of 31½ cents, threw herself out of the window one day and was carried from the street dead. She was "discouraged," a neighbor said. A young man who had a sick mother and had lost his job was charged in magistrate's court with attempted suicide. The lockkeeper's wife who pulled him out of the river testified how "as fast as I pulled to get him out, he crawled back" until some workmen came to assist her. When the magistrate congratulated the woman on her muscular powers, the courtroom laughed, but an observer named Jack London wrote, "All I could see was a boy on the threshold of life passionately crawling to a muddy death."

24   The failure of practical attempts at Anarchism in Bakunin's period caused Anarchist theory and practice to veer off in a direction not toward the earth but toward the clouds. In the new period beginning in the nineties, its aims, always idyllic, became even more utopian and its deeds less than ever connected with reality. It became impatient. It despised the puny efforts of Socialists and trade unionists to achieve the eight-hour day. "Eight hours of work for the boss is eight hours too much," proclaimed the Anarchist paper, *La Révolte.* "We know that what is wrong with our society is not that the worker works ten, twelve or fourteen hours, but that the boss exists."

QUESTIONS

Ideas

1. How would you define the Anarchist idea? Do you think it has value as a political theory? Could you imagine a situation in which you could become an Anarchist?

2. At times Tuchman seems sympathetic to the Anarchists, at other times, critical. Where do these feelings seem most obvious?

3. Some political thinkers say that human nature is basically corrupt and needs strong controls if we are to have an orderly society. Others say we

are basically good; it is our institutions that are flawed. Which position do the Anarchists favor? Which do you?

4. Where does Tuchman believe the Anarchists went wrong? Was it a tactical or a conceptual error? In retrospect, could they have succeeded? How?

5. Based on the evidence Tuchman gives in paragraphs 13–16, do you think Spies should have been hanged?

6. How do you respond to paragraphs 20–23? What might be the solution to the condition described?

Organization

7. History is a story. How that narrative is arranged by the historian is crucial to the reader's understanding. Tuchman, for example, could have given us heart-rendering sketches of the families of the policemen who were blown up. She didn't. Does that suggest she is unsympathetic? Is her organizational scheme fair-minded?

8. This essay might be seen as an attempt at cause and effect. How does Tuchman set this up? Where does she narrate the causes of anarchism, where the effects?

9. Paragraph 13 begins the second part of this essay. How does Tuchman arrange this section? Write a brief one-sentence description of all twelve paragraphs. How would you describe the movement of her thinking here?

Sentences

10. The third paragraph is one long cumulative sentence. The first eight words form the base clause. Tuchman just adds adverbial clauses on to that foundation. Why do you think she decided to use such a dramatic sentence? Read it out loud. What effect does it have on you?

11. Now read paragraph 23. Tuchman's purpose here might be the same as in paragraph 3, but her sentence strategy is different. What kinds of sentences does she use here? Try to change these sentences into the pattern she used in the third paragraph: base clause plus additions (such as phrases or clauses).

Words

12. Describe the words used by Proudhon in the sixth paragraph. Do they differ from Tuchman's?

13. Make a list of the words (nouns, adjectives, adverbs) Tuchman uses to describe the Anarchists. Make another list for the rich and the establishment. Is she balanced, fair?

Suggestions for Writing

A. The anecdotes in paragraphs 20 and 23 seem effective. Try to reverse the effect Tuchman is after by substituting positive incidents for the rich and negative ones for the poor.

B. Write an extended definition of "the Anarchist idea" that Bakunin would agree is fair and accurate.

C. Imagine that you are either the lawyer prosecuting or defending the Haymarket Square Anarchists. Write a summation speech to the jury trying to get the Anarchists freed or hanged.

The Black Death

In October 1347, two months after the fall of Calais, Genoese trading ships put into the harbor of Messina in Sicily with dead and dying men at the oars. The ships had come from the Black Sea port of Caffa (now Feodosīya) in the Crimea, where the Genoese maintained a trading post. The diseased sailors showed strange black swellings about the size of an egg or an apple in the armpits and groin. The swellings oozed blood and pus and were followed by spreading boils and black blotches on the skin from internal bleeding. The sick suffered severe pain and died quickly within five days of the first symptoms. As the disease spread, other symptoms of continuous fever and spitting of blood appeared instead of the swellings or buboes. These victims coughed and sweated heavily and died even more quickly, within three days or less, sometimes in 24 hours. In both types everything that issued from the body—breath, sweat, blood from the buboes and lungs, bloody urine, and blood-blackened excrement—smelled foul. Depression and despair accompanied the physical symptoms, and before the end "death is seen seated on the face."

2   The disease was bubonic plague, present in two forms: one that infected the bloodstream, causing the buboes and internal bleeding, and was spread by contact; and a second, more virulent pneumonic type that infected the lungs and was spread by respiratory infection. The presence of both at once caused the high mortality and speed of contagion. So lethal was the disease that cases were known of persons going to bed well and dying before they woke, of doctors catching the illness at a

bedside and dying before the patient. So rapidly did it spread from one to another that to a French physician, Simon de Covino, it seemed as if one sick person "could infect the whole world." The malignity of the pestilence appeared more terrible because its victims knew no prevention and no remedy.

3   The physical suffering of the disease and its aspect of evil mystery were expressed in a strange Welsh lament which saw "death coming into our midst like black smoke, a plague which cuts off the young, a rootless phantom which has no mercy for fair countenance. Woe is me of the shilling in the armpit! It is seething, terrible . . . a head that gives pain and causes a loud cry . . . a painful angry knob . . . Great is its seething like a burning cinder . . . a grievous thing of ashy color." Its eruption is ugly like the "seeds of black peas, broken fragments of brittle sea-coal . . . the early ornaments of black death, cinders of the peelings of the cockle weed, a mixed multitude, a black plague like halfpence, like berries. . . ."

4   Rumors of a terrible plague supposedly arising in China and spreading through Tartary (Central Asia) to India and Persia, Mesopotamia, Syria, Egypt, and all of Asia Minor had reached Europe in 1346. They told of a death toll so devastating that all of India was said to be depopulated, whole territories covered by dead bodies, other areas with no one left alive. As added up by Pope Clement VI at Avignon, the total of reported dead reached 23,840,000. In the absence of a concept of contagion, no serious alarm was felt in Europe until the trading ships brought their black burden of pestilence into Messina while other infected ships from the Levant carried it to Genoa and Venice.

5   By January 1348 it penetrated France via Marseille, and North Africa via Tunis. Shipborne along coasts and navigable rivers, it spread westward from Marseille through the ports of Languedoc to Spain and northward up the Rhône to Avignon, where it arrived in March. It reached Narbonne, Montpellier, Carcassonne, and Toulouse between February and May, and at the same time in Italy spread to Rome and Florence by their hinterlands. Between June and August it reached Bordeaux, Lyon, and Paris, spread to Burgundy and Normandy, and crossed the Channel from Normandy into southern England. From Italy during the same summer it crossed the Alps into Switzerland and reached eastward to Hungary.

6   In a given area the plague accomplished its kill within four to six months and then faded, except in the larger cities, where, rooting into the close-quartered population, it abated during the winter, only to reappear in spring and rage for another six months.

7   In 1349 it resumed in Paris, spread to Picardy, Flanders, and the Low Countries, and from England to Scotland and Ireland as well as to Norway, where a ghost ship with a cargo of wool and a dead crew drifted offshore until it ran aground near Bergen. From there the plague passed into Sweden, Denmark, Prussia, Iceland, and as far as Greenland. Leaving a strange pocket of immunity in Bohemia, and Russia unattacked until 1351, it had passed from most of Europe by mid-1350. Although the mortality rate was erratic, ranging from one fifth in some places to nine tenths or almost total elimination in others, the overall estimate of modern demographers has settled—for the area extending from India to Iceland—around the same figure expressed in Froissart's casual words: "a third of the world died." His estimate, the common one at the time, was not an inspired guess but a borrowing of St. John's figure for mortality from plague in Revelation, the favorite guide to human affairs of the Middle Ages.

8   A third of Europe would have meant about 20 million deaths. No one knows in truth how many died. Contemporary reports were an awed impression, not an accurate count. In crowded Avignon, it was said, 400 died daily; 7,000 houses emptied by death were shut up; a single graveyard received 11,000 corpses in six weeks; half the city's inhabitants reportedly died, including 9 cardinals or one third of the total, and 70 lesser prelates. Watching the endlessly passing death carts, chroniclers let normal exaggeration take wings and put the Avignon death toll at 62,000 and even at 120,000, although the city's total population was probably less than 50,000.

9   When graveyards filled up, bodies at Avignon were thrown into the Rhône until mass burial pits were dug for dumping the corpses. In London in such pits corpses piled up in layers until they overflowed. Everywhere reports speak of the sick dying too fast for the living to bury. Corpses were dragged out of homes and left in front of doorways. Morning light revealed new piles of bodies. In Florence the dead were gathered up by the Compagnia della Misericordia—founded in 1244 to care for the sick—whose members wore red robes and hoods masking the face except for the eyes. When their efforts failed, the dead lay putrid in the streets for days at a time. When no coffins were to be had, the bodies were laid on boards, two or three at once, to be carried to graveyards or common pits. Families dumped their own relatives into the pits, or buried them so hastily and thinly "that dogs dragged them forth and devoured their bodies."

10   Amid accumulating death and fear of contagion, people died without last rites and were buried without prayers, a prospect that

terrified the last hours of the stricken. A bishop in England gave permission to laymen to make confession to each other as was done by the Apostles, "or if no man is present then even to a woman," and if no priest could be found to administer extreme unction, "then faith must suffice." Clement VI found it necessary to grant remissions of sin to all who died of the plague because so many were unattended by priests. "And no bells tolled," wrote a chronicler of Siena, "and nobody wept no matter what his loss because almost everyone expected death.... And people said and believed, 'This is the end of the world.' "

11   In Paris, where the plague lasted through 1349, the reported death rate was 800 a day, in Pisa 500, in Vienna 500 to 600. The total dead in Paris numbered 50,000 or half the population. Florence, weakened by the famine of 1347, lost three to four fifths of its citizens, Venice two thirds, Hamburg and Bremen, though smaller in size, about the same proportion. Cities, as centers of transportation, were more likely to be affected than villages, although once a village was infected, its death rate was equally high. At Givry, a prosperous village in Burgundy of 1,200 to 1,500 people, the parish register records 615 deaths in the space of fourteen weeks, compared to an average of thirty deaths a year in the previous decade. In three villages of Cambridgeshire, manorial records show a death rate of 47 percent, 57 percent, and in one case 70 percent. When the last survivors, too few to carry on, moved away, a deserted village sank back into the wilderness and disappeared from the map altogether, leaving only a grass-covered ghostly outline to show where mortals once had lived.

12   In enclosed places such as monasteries and prisons, the infection of one person usually meant that of all, as happened in the Franciscan convents of Carcassonne and Marseille, where every inmate without exception died. Of the 140 Dominicans at Montpellier only seven survived. Petrarch's brother Gherardo, member of a Carthusian monastery, buried the prior and 34 fellow monks one by one, sometimes three a day, until he was left alone with his dog and fled to look for a place that would take him in. Watching every comrade die, men in such places could not but wonder whether the strange peril that filled the air had not been sent to exterminate the human race. In Kilkenny, Ireland, Brother John Clyn of the Friars Minor, another monk left alone among dead men, kept a record of what had happened lest "things which should be remembered perish with time and vanish from the memory of those who come after us." Sensing "the whole world, as it were, placed within the grasp of the Evil One," and waiting for death to visit him too, he wrote, "I leave

parchment to continue this work, if perchance any man survive and any of the race of Adam escape this pestilence and carry on the work which I have begun." Brother John, as noted by another hand, died of the pestilence, but he foiled oblivion.

13   The largest cities of Europe, with populations of about 100,000, were Paris and Florence, Venice and Genoa. At the next level, with more than 50,000, were Ghent and Bruges in Flanders, Milan, Bologna, Rome, Naples, and Palermo, and Cologne. London hovered below 50,000, the only city in England except York with more than 10,000. At the level of 20,000 to 50,000 were Bordeaux, Toulouse, Montpellier, Marseille, and Lyon in France, Barcelona, Seville, and Toledo in Spain, Siena, Pisa, and other secondary cities in Italy, and the Hanseatic trading cities of the Empire. The plague raged through them all, killing anywhere from one third to two thirds of their inhabitants. Italy, with a total population of 10 to 11 million, probably suffered the heaviest toll. Following the Florentine bankruptcies, the crop failures and workers' riots of 1346–47, the revolt of Cola di Rienzi that plunged Rome into anarchy, the plague came as the peak of successive calamities. As if the world were indeed in the grasp of the Evil One, its first appearance on the European mainland in January 1348 coincided with a fearsome earthquake that carved a path of wreckage from Naples up to Venice. Houses collapsed, church towers toppled, villages were crushed, and the destruction reached as far as Germany and Greece. Emotional response, dulled by horrors, underwent a kind of atrophy epitomized by the chronicler who wrote, "And in these days was burying without sorrowe and wedding without friendschippe."

14   In Siena, where more than half the inhabitants died of the plague, work was abandoned on the great cathedral, planned to be the largest in the world, and never resumed, owing to loss of workers and master masons and "the melancholy and grief" of the survivors. The cathedral's truncated transept still stands in permanent witness to the sweep of death's scythe. Agnolo di Tura, a chronicler of Siena, recorded the fear of contagion that froze every other instinct. "Father abandoned child, wife husband, one brother another," he wrote, "for this plague seemed to strike through the breath and sight. And so they died. And no one could be found to bury the dead for money or friendship. . . . And I, Agnolo di Tura, called the Fat, buried my five children with my own hands, and so did many others likewise."

15   There were many to echo his account of inhumanity and few to balance it, for the plague was not the kind of calamity that inspired

mutual help. Its loathsomeness and deadliness did not herd people together in mutual distress, but only prompted their desire to escape each other. "Magistrates and notaries refused to come and make the wills of the dying," reported a Franciscan friar of Piazza in Sicily; what was worse, "even the priests did not come to hear their confessions." A clerk of the Archbishop of Canterbury reported the same of English priests who "turned away from the care of their benefices from fear of death." Cases of parents deserting children and children their parents were reported across Europe from Scotland to Russia. The calamity chilled the hearts of men, wrote Boccaccio in his famous account of the plague in Florence that serves as introduction to the *Decameron*. "One man shunned another . . . kinsfolk held aloof, brother was forsaken by brother, oftentimes husband by wife; nay, what is more, and scarcely to be believed, fathers and mothers were found to abandon their own children to their fate, untended, unvisited as if they had been strangers." Exaggeration and literary pessimism were common in the 14th century, but the Pope's physician, Guy de Chauliac, was a sober, careful observer who reported the same phenomenon: "A father did not visit his son, nor the son his father. Charity was dead."

16   Yet not entirely. In Paris, according to the chronicler Jean de Venette, the nuns of the Hôtel Dieu or municipal hospital, "having no fear of death, tended the sick with all sweetness and humility." New nuns repeatedly took the places of those who died, until the majority "many times renewed by death now rest in peace with Christ as we may piously believe."

17   When the plague entered northern France in July 1348, it settled first in Normandy and, checked by winter, gave Picardy a deceptive interim until the next summer. Either in mourning or warning, black flags were flown from church towers of the worst-stricken villages of Normandy. "And in that time," wrote a monk of the abbey of Fourcarment, "the mortality was so great among the people of Normandy that those of Picardy mocked them." The same unneighborly reaction was reported of the Scots, separated by a winter's immunity from the English. Delighted to hear of the disease that was scourging the "southrons," they gathered forces for an invasion, "laughing at their enemies." Before they could move, the savage mortality fell upon them too, scattering some in death and the rest in panic to spread the infection as they fled.

18   In Picardy in the summer of 1349 the pestilence penetrated the castle of Coucy to kill Enguerrand's mother, Catherine, and her new

husband. Whether her nine-year-old son escaped by chance or was perhaps living elsewhere with one of his guardians is unrecorded. In nearby Amiens, tannery workers, responding quickly to losses in the labor force, combined to bargain for higher wages. In another place villagers were seen dancing to drums and trumpets, and on being asked the reason, answered that, seeing their neighbors die day by day while their village remained immune, they believed they could keep the plague from entering "by the jollity that is in us. That is why we dance." Further north in Tournai on the border of Flanders, Gilles li Muisis, Abbot of St. Martin's, kept one of the epidemic's most vivid accounts. The passing bells rang all day and night, he recorded, because sextons were anxious to obtain their fees while they could. Filled with the sound of mourning, the city became oppressed by fear, so that the authorities forbade the tolling of bells and the wearing of black and restricted funeral services to two mourners. The silencing of funeral bells and of criers' announcements of deaths was ordained by most cities. Siena imposed a fine on the wearing of mourning clothes by all except widows.

19 Flight was the chief recourse of those who could afford it or arrange it. The rich fled to their country places like Boccaccio's young patricians of Florence, who settled in a pastoral palace "removed on every side from the roads" with "wells of cool water and vaults of rare wines." The urban poor died in their burrows, "and only the stench of their bodies informed neighbors of their death." That the poor were more heavily afflicted than the rich was clearly remarked at the time, in the north as in the south. A Scottish chronicler, John of Fordun, stated flatly the the pest "attacked especially the meaner sort and common people—seldom the magnates." Simon de Covino of Montpellier made the same observation. He ascribed it to the misery and want and hard lives that made the poor more susceptible, which was half the truth. Close contact and lack of sanitation was the unrecognized other half. It was noticed too that the young died in greater proportion than the old; Simon de Covino compared the disappearance of youth to the withering of flowers in the fields.

20 In the countryside peasants dropped dead on the roads, in the fields, in their houses. Survivors in growing helplessness fell into apathy, leaving ripe wheat uncut and livestock untended. Oxen and asses, sheep and goats, pigs and chickens ran wild and they too, according to local reports, succumbed to the pest. English sheep, bearers of the precious wool, died throughout the country. The chronicler Henry Knighton, canon of Leicester Abbey, reported 5,000 dead in one field alone, "their

bodies so corrupted by the plague that neither beast nor bird would touch them," and spreading an appalling stench. In the Austrian Alps wolves came down to prey upon sheep and then, "as if alarmed by some invisible warning, turned and fled back into the wilderness." In remote Dalmatia bolder wolves descended upon a plague-stricken city and attacked human survivors. For want of herdsmen, cattle strayed from place to place and died in hedgerows and ditches. Dogs and cats fell like the rest.

21   The dearth of labor held a fearful prospect because the 14th century lived close to the annual harvest both for food and for next year's seed. "So few servants and laborers were left," wrote Knighton, "that no one knew where to turn for help." The sense of a vanishing future created a kind of dementia of despair. A Bavarian chronicler of Neuberg on the Danube recorded that "Men and women . . . wandered around as if mad" and let their cattle stray "because no one had any inclination to concern themselves about the future." Fields went uncultivated, spring seed unsown. Second growth with nature's awful energy crept back over cleared land, dikes crumbled, salt water reinvaded and soured the lowlands. With so few hands remaining to restore the work of centuries, people felt, in Walsingham's words, that "the world could never again regain its former prosperity."

22   Ignorance of the cause augmented the sense of horror. Of the real carriers, rats and fleas, the 14th century had no suspicion, perhaps because they were so familiar. Fleas, though a common household nuisance, are not once mentioned in contemporary plague writings, and rats only incidentally, although folklore commonly associated them with pestilence. The legend of the Pied Piper arose from an outbreak of 1284. The actual plague bacillus, *Pasturella pestis*, remained undiscovered for another 500 years. Living alternately in the stomach of the flea and the bloodstream of the rat who was the flea's host, the bacillus in its bubonic form was transferred to humans and animals by the bite of either rat or flea. It traveled by virtue of *Rattus rattus*, the small medieval black rat that lived on ships, as well as by the heavier brown or sewer rat. What precipitated the turn of the bacillus from innocuous to virulent form is unknown, but the occurrence is now believed to have taken place not in China but somewhere in central Asia and to have spread along the caravan routes. Chinese origin was a mistaken notion of the 14th century based on real but belated reports of huge death tolls in China from drought, famine, and pestilence which have since been traced to the

1330s, too soon to be responsible for the plague that appeared in India in 1346.

23 The phantom enemy had no name. Called the Black Death only in later recurrences, it was known during the first epidemic simply as the Pestilence or Great Mortality. Reports from the East, swollen by fearful imaginings, told of strange tempests and "sheets of fire" mingled with huge hailstones that "slew almost all," or a "vast rain of fire" that burned up men, beasts, stones, trees, villages, and cities. In another version, "foul blasts of wind" from the fires carried the infection to Europe "and now as some suspect it cometh round the seacoast." Accurate observation in this case could not make the mental jump to ships and rats because no idea of animal- or insect-borne contagion existed.

24 The earthquake was blamed for releasing sulfurous and foul fumes from the earth's interior, or as evidence of a titanic struggle of planets and oceans causing waters to rise and vaporize until fish died in masses and corrupted the air. All these explanations had in common a factor of poisoned air, of miasmas and thick, stinking mists traced to every kind of natural or imagined agency from stagnant lakes to malign conjunction of the planets, from the hand of the Evil One to the wrath of God. Medical thinking, trapped in the theory of astral influences, stressed air as the communicator of disease, ignoring sanitation or visible carriers. The existence of two carriers confused the trail, the more so because the flea could live and travel independently of the rat for as long as a month and, if infected by the particularly virulent septicemic form of the bacillus, could infect humans without reinfecting itself from the rat. The simultaneous presence of the pneumonic form of the disease, which was indeed communicated through the air, blurred the problem further.

25 The mystery of the contagion was "the most terrible of all the terrors," as an anonymous Flemish cleric in Avignon wrote to a correspondent in Bruges. Plagues had been known before, from the plague of Athens (believed to have been typhus) to the prolonged epidemic of the 6th century A.D., to the recurrence of sporadic outbreaks in the 12th and 13th centuries, but they had left no accumulated store of understanding. That the infection came from contact with the sick or with their houses, clothes, or corpses was quickly observed but not comprehended. Gentile da Foligno, renowned physician of Perugia and doctor of medicine at the universities of Bologna and Padua, came close to respiratory infection when he surmised that poisonous material was "communicated by means of air breathed out and in." Having no idea of microscopic carriers, he had to assume that the air was corrupted by

planetary influences. Planets, however, could not explain the ongoing contagion. The agonized search for an answer gave rise to such theories as transference by sight. People fell ill, wrote Guy de Chauliac, not only by remaining with the sick but "even by looking at them." Three hundred years later Joshua Barnes, the 17th century biographer of Edward III, could write that the power of infection had entered into beams of light and "darted death from the eyes."

26   Doctors struggling with the evidence could not break away from the terms of astrology, to which they believed all human physiology was subject. Medicine was the one aspect of medieval life, perhaps because of its links with the Arabs, not shaped by Christian doctrine. Clerics detested astrology, but could not dislodge its influence. Guy de Chauliac, physician to three popes in succession, practiced in obedience to the zodiac. While his *Cirurgia* was the major treatise on surgery of its time, while he understood the use of anesthesia made from the juice of opium, mandrake, or hemlock, he nevertheless prescribed bleeding and purgatives by the planets and divided chronic from acute diseases on the basis of one being under the rule of the sun and the other of the moon.

27   In October 1348 Philip VI asked the medical faculty of the University of Paris for a report on the affliction that seemed to threaten human survival. With careful thesis, antithesis, and proofs, the doctors ascribed it to a triple conjunction of Saturn, Jupiter, and Mars in the 40th degree of Aquarius said to have occurred on March 20, 1345. They acknowledged, however, effects "whose cause is hidden from even the most highly trained intellects." The verdict of the masters of Paris became the official version. Borrowed, copied by scribes, carried abroad, translated from Latin into various vernaculars, it was everywhere accepted, even by the Arab physicians of Cordova and Granada, as the scientific if not the popular answer. Because of the terrible interest of the subject, the translations of the plague tracts stimulated use of national languages. In that one respect, life came from death.

QUESTIONS

Ideas

1. Are you surprised by the reported decline of social concern during the plague? Take, for example, paragraphs 14 and 15.

2. Do you think events like this are a thing of the past and that comparable events are not likely to occur again?

3. List the causes given for the plague. Do any still sound plausible? Is it clear that we are better able to cope with the unknown than our ancestors?

4. What do you think your community's reaction would be to such an event? What should it be?

Organization

5. Tuchman often develops paragraphs by combining explicit topic sentences —general ideas—with concrete examples and facts. Sometimes she puts her general ideas first, sometimes last. Find examples of both.

6. In what order and in what ways does Tuchman answer the journalist's questions: who, what, when, where, why, and how?

Sentences

7. Throughout this essay Tuchman uses many quotes, for example, paragraphs 10 and 19. Describe the ways she does this. Are they effective?

8. The most common sentence pattern in English is subject, verb, object. Study a paragraph and see how many times and in what ways Tuchman varies this pattern.

Words

9. What is the meaning of the following phrases Tuchman uses or quotes: "virulent pneumonic" (paragraph 2); "fair countenance" (paragraph 3); "foiled oblivion" (paragraph 12); "truncated transept" (paragraph 14); "dementia of despair" (paragraph 21); "thesis, antithesis, and proofs" (paragraph 27).

10. Do you find any contradictions here to Tuchman's position in paragraph 2 or in "In Search of History"?

Suggestions for Writing

A. Write a brief explanation of this disease that you think might convince a fourteenth-century audience.

B. Imagine that you have been transported to 1348, to a house in the middle of London. What would you do, how would you try to survive? Assuming you could communicate with your neighbors, what would you advise them to do, if anything?

C. Are there lessons to be learned from this event? Write a brief response to this question.

Is History a Guide to the Future?

1   The commonest question asked of historians by laymen is whether history serves a purpose. Is it useful? Can we learn from the lessons of history?

2   When people want history to be utilitarian and teach us lessons, that means they also want to be sure that it meets scientific standards. This, in my opinion, it cannot do, for reasons which I will come to in a moment. To practice history as a science is sociology, an altogether different discipline which I personally find antipathetic—although I suppose the sociologists would consider that my deficiency rather than theirs. The sociologists plod along with their noses to the ground assembling masses of statistics in order to arrive at some obvious conclusion which a reasonably perceptive historian, not to mention a large part of the general public, knows anyway, simply from observation—that social mobility is increasing, for instance, or that women have different problems from men. One wishes they would just cut loose someday, lift up their heads, and look at the world around them.

3   If history were a science, we should be able to get a grip on her, learn her ways, establish her patterns, know what will happen tomorrow. Why is it that we cannot? The answer lies in what I call the Unknowable Variable—namely, man. Human beings are always and finally the subject of history. History is the record of human behavior, the most fascinating subject of all, but illogical and so crammed with an unlimited number of variables that it is not susceptible of the scientific method nor of systematizing.

4   I say this bravely, even in the midst of the electronic age when computers are already chewing at the skirts of history in the process called Quantification. Applied to history, quantification, I believe, has its limits. It depends on a method called "data manipulation," which means that the facts, or data, of the historical past—that is, of human behavior—are manipulated into named categories so that they can be programmed into computers. Out comes—hopefully—a pattern. I can only tell you that for history "data manipulation" is a built-in invalidator, because to the degree that you manipulate your data to suit some

extraneous requirement, in this case the requirements of the machine, to that degree your results will be suspect—and run the risk of being invalid. Everything depends on the naming of the categories and the assigning of facts to them, and this depends on the quantifier's individual judgment at the very base of the process. The categories are not revealed doctrine nor are the results scientific truth.

5   The hope for quantification, presumably, is that by processing a vast quantity of material far beyond the capacity of the individual to encompass, it can bring to light and establish reliable patterns. That remains to be seen, but I am not optimistic. History has a way of escaping attempts to imprison it in patterns. Moreover, one of its basic data is the human soul. The conventional historian, at least the one concerned with truth, not propaganda, will try honestly to let his "data" speak for themselves, but data which are shut up in prearranged boxes are helpless. Their nuances have no voice. They must carry one fixed meaning or another and weight the result accordingly. For instance, in a quantification study of the origins of World War I which I have seen, the operators have divided all the diplomatic documents, messages, and utterances of the July crisis into categories labeled "hostility," "friendship," "frustration," "satisfaction," and so on, with each statement rated for intensity on a scale from one to nine, including fractions. But no pre-established categories could match all the private character traits and public pressures variously operating on the nervous monarchs and ministers who were involved. The massive effort that went into this study brought forth a mouse—the less than startling conclusion that the likelihood of war increased in proportion to the rise in hostility of the messages.

6   Quantification is really only a new approach to the old persistent effort to make history fit a pattern, but *reliable* patterns, or what are otherwise called the lessons of history, remain elusive.

7   For instance, suppose Woodrow Wilson' had not been President of the United States in 1914 but instead Theodore Roosevelt, who had been his opponent in the election of 1912. Had that been the case, America might have entered the war much earlier, perhaps at the time of the *Lusitania* in 1915, with possible shortening of the war and incalculable effects on history. Well, it happens that among the Anarchists in my book *The Proud Tower* is an obscure Italian named Miguel Angiolillo, whom nobody remembers but who shot dead Premier Canovas of Spain in 1897. Canovas was a strong man who was just about to succeed in quelling the rebels in Cuba when he was assassinated. Had

he lived, there might have been no extended Cuban insurrection for Americans to get excited about, no Spanish-American War, no San Juan Hill, no Rough Riders, no Vice-Presidency for Theodore Roosevelt to enable him to succeed when another accident, another Anarchist, another unpredictable human being, killed McKinley. If Theodore had never been President, there would have been no third party in 1912 to split the Republicans, and Woodrow Wilson would not have been elected. The speculations from that point on are limitless. To me it is comforting rather than otherwise to feel that history is determined by the illogical human record and not by large immutable scientific laws beyond our power to deflect.

8   I know very little (a euphemism for "nothing") about laboratory science, but I have the impression that conclusions are supposed to be logical; that is, from a given set of circumstances a predictable result should follow. The trouble is that in human behavior and history it is impossible to isolate or repeat a given set of circumstances. Complex human acts cannot be either reproduced or deliberately initiated—or counted upon like the phenomena of nature. The sun comes up every day. Tides are so obedient to schedule that a timetable for them can be printed like that for trains, though more reliable. In fact, tides and trains sharply illustrate my point: One depends on the moon and is certain; the other depends on man and is uncertain.

9   In the absence of dependable recurring circumstance, too much confidence cannot be placed on the lessons of history.

10   There *are* lessons, of course, and when people speak of learning from them, they have in mind, I think, two ways of applying past experience: One is to enable us to avoid past mistakes and to manage better in similar circumstances next time; the other is to enable us to anticipate a future course of events. (History could tell us something about Vietnam, I think, if we would only listen.) To manage better next time is within our means; to anticipate does not seem to be.

11   World War II, for example, with the experience of the previous war as an awful lesson, was certainly conducted, once we got into it, more intelligently than World War I. Getting into it was another matter. When it was important to anticipate the course of events, Americans somehow failed to apply the right lesson. Pearl Harbor is the classic example of failure to learn from history. From hindsight we now know that what we should have anticipated was a surprise attack by Japan in the midst of negotiations. Merely because this was dishonorable, did that make it unthinkable? Hardly. It was exactly the procedure

Japan had adopted in 1904 when she opened the Russo–Japanese War by surprise attack on the Russian fleet at Port Arthur.

12   In addition we had every possible physical indication. We had broken the Japanese code, we had warnings on radar, we had a constant flow of accurate intelligence. What failed? Not information but *judgment.* We had all the evidence and refused to interpret it correctly, just as the Germans in 1944 refused to believe the evidence of a landing in Normandy. Men will not believe what does not fit in with their plans or suit their prearrangements. The flaw in all military intelligence, whether twenty or fifty or one hundred percent accurate, is that it is no better than the judgment of its interpreters, and this judgment is the product of a mass of individual, social, and political biases, prejudgments, and wishful thinkings; in short, it is human and therefore fallible. If man can break the Japanese code and yet not believe what it tells him, how can he be expected to learn from the lessons of history?

13   Would a computer do better? In the case of Pearl Harbor, probably yes. If one could have fed all the pieces of intelligence available in November 1941 into a computer, it could have hardly failed to reply promptly, "Air attack, Hawaii, Philippines" and probably even "December 7." But will this work every time? Can we trust the lessons of history to computers? I think not, because history will fool them. They may make the right deductions and draw the right conclusions, but a twist occurs, someone sneezes, history swerves and takes another path. Had Cleopatra's nose been shorter, said Pascal, the whole aspect of the world would have been changed. Can a computer account for Cleopatra?

14   Once long ago when the eternal verities seemed clear—that is, during the Spanish Civil War—I thought the lessons of history were unmistakable. It appeared obvious beyond dispute that if fascism under Franco won, Spain in the foreshadowed European war would become a base for Hitler and Mussolini, the Mediterranean would become an Italian lake, Britain would lose Gibraltar and be cut off from her empire east of Suez. The peril was plain, the logic of the thing implacable, every sensible person saw it, and I, just out of college, wrote a small book published in England to point it up, all drawn from the analogy of history. The book showed how, throughout the eighteenth and nineteenth centuries, Britain had consistently interposed herself against the gaining of undue influence over Spain by whatever power dominated the continent. The affair of the Spanish marriages, the campaigns of Wellington, the policies of Castlereagh, Canning, and Palmerston all were directed toward the same objective: The strongest continental power

must be prevented from controlling Spain. My treatise was, I thought, very artful and very telling. It did not refer to the then current struggle, but let the past speak for itself and make the argument. It was an irrefutable one—until history refuted it. Franco, assisted by Hitler and Mussolini, *did* win, European war *did* follow, yet unaccountably Spain remained neutral—at least nominally. Gibraltar did not fall, the portals of the Mediterranean did *not* close. I, not to mention all the other "premature" anti-fascists, as we were called, while morally right about the general danger of fascism, had been wrong about a particular outcome. The lessons of history I had so carefully set forth simply did not operate. History misbehaved.

15   Pearl Harbor and Spain demonstrate two things: One, that man fails to profit from the lessons of history because his prejudgments prevent him from drawing the indicated conclusions; and, two, that history will often capriciously take a different direction from that in which her lessons point. Herein lies the flaw in systems of history.

16   When it comes to systems, history played her greatest betrayal on Karl Marx. Never was a prophet so sure of his premises, never were believers so absolutely convinced of a predicted outcome, never was there an interpretation of history that seemed so foolproof. Analyzing the effects of the Industrial Revolution, Marx exposed the terrible riddle of the nineteenth century: that the greater the material progress, the wider and deeper the resulting poverty, a process which could only end, he decided, in the violent collapse of the existing order brought on by revolution. From this he formulated the doctrine of *Verelendung* (progressive impoverishment) and *Zusammenbruch* (collapse) and decreed that since working-class self-consciousness increased in proportion to industrialization, revolution would come first in the most industrialized country.

17   Marx's analysis was so compelling that it seemed impossible history could follow any other course. His postulates were accepted by followers of his own and later generations as if they had been graven on the tablets of Sinai. Marxism as the revealed truth of history was probably the most convincing dogma ever enunciated. Its influence was tremendous, incalculable, continuing. The founder's facts were correct, his thinking logical and profound; he was right in everything but his conclusions. Developing events did not bear him out. The working class grew progressively better, not worse, off. Capitalism did not collapse. Revolution came in the least, not the most, industrialized country. Under collectivism the state did not wither but extended itself in power and

function and in its grip on society. History, ignoring Marx, followed her own mysterious logic, and went on her own way.

18   When it developed that Marx was wrong, men in search of determinism rushed off to submit history to a new authority—Freud. His hand is now upon us. The Unconscious is king. At least it was. There are new voices, I believe, claiming that the Unconscious is a fraud—iconoclasm has reached even Freud. Nevertheless, in his effect on the modern outlook, Freud, I believe, unquestionably was the greatest influence for change between the nineteenth and twentieth centuries. It may well be that our time may one day be named for him and the Freudian Era said to have succeeded the Victorian Era. Our understanding of human motivation has taken on a whole new dimension since his ideas took hold. Yet it does not seem to me that unconscious sexual and psychological drives are as relevant in all circumstances as they are said to be by the Freudians, who have become as fixed in their system as were the orthodox Marxists. They can supply historians with insights but not with guidance to the future because man *en masse* cannot be relied upon to behave according to pattern. All salmon swim back to spawn in the headwaters of their birth; that is universal for salmon. But man lives in a more complicated world than a fish. Too many influences are at work on him to make it applicable that every man is driven by an unconscious desire to swim back to the womb.

19   It has always seemed to me unfortunate, for instance, that Freud chose the experiences of two royal families to exemplify his concept of the Oedipus and Elektra complexes. Royalty lives under special circumstances, particularly as regards the issue of power between the sovereign and his heir, which are not valid as universal experience. The legend of Oedipus killing his father may have derived from the observed phenomenon that every royal heir has always hated his father, not because he wants to sleep with his mother but because he wants to ascend the throne. If the parental sovereign happens to be his mother, he hates her just as much. She will dislike him equally from birth because she knows he is destined to take her place, as in the case of Queen Victoria and her eldest son, who became Edward VII. That is not Freudian, it is simply dynastic.

20   As for Elektra, it is hard to know what to make of that tale. The House of Atreus was a very odd family indeed. More was going on there than just Elektra being in love with her father. How about Orestes, who helped her to kill their mother, or killed her himself, according to another version? Was not that the wrong parent? How come he did not

kill his father? How about Iphigenia, the sister, whom Agememnon killed as a sacrifice? What is the Freudian explanation for that? They do not say, which is not being historical. A historian cannot pick and choose his facts; he must deal with all the evidence.

21   Or take Martin Luther. As you know, Professor Erik Erikson of Harvard has discovered that Luther was constipated from childhood and upon this interesting physiological item he has erected a system which explains everything about his man. This is definitely the most camp thing that has happened to history in years. It even made Broadway. Nevertheless I do not think Luther pinned the 95 Theses on the church door at Wittenberg solely or even mainly because of the activity, or inactivity rather, of his anal muscle. His personal motive for protest may have had an anal basis for all I know, but what is important historically is the form the protest took, and this had to do with old and deep social grievances concerned with the worldliness of the church, the sale of indulgences, corruption of the clergy, and so on. If it had not been Luther who protested, it would have been someone else; Protestantism would have come with or without him, and its causes had nothing whatever to do with his private physiological impediment. Professor Erikson, I am sure, was attempting to explain Luther, not Protestantism, but his book has started a fad for psycho-history among those without the adequate knowledge or training to use it.

22   Following Freud there flourished briefly a minor prophet, Oswald Spengler, who proclaimed the Decline of the West, based on an elaborate study of the lessons of history. Off and on since then people have been returning to his theme, especially since World War II and the end of colonialism. The rise of China and the rash of independence movements in Asia and Africa have inspired many nervous second looks at Spengler. Europe is finished, say the knowing ones; the future belongs to the colored races and all that.

23   People have been burying Europe for quite some time. I remember a political thinker for whom I had great respect telling me in the thirties that Europe's reign was over; the future belonged to America, Russia, and China. It was a new and awful thought to me then and I was immensely impressed. As I see it now, his grouping has not been justified. I do not think Russia and America can be disassociated from Europe; rather, we are extensions of Europe. I hesitate to be dogmatic about Russia, but I am certain about the United States. American culture stems from Europe, our fortunes are linked with hers, in the long run we are aligned. My impression is that Europe, and by exten-

sion the white race, is far from finished. Europe's vitality keeps reviving; as a source of ideas she is inexhaustible. Nuclear fission, the most recent, if unwanted, advance, came from the work of a whole series of Europeans: Max Planck, the Curies, Einstein, Rutherford, Fermi, Nils Bohr, Szilard. Previously the three great makers of the modern mind, Darwin, Marx, and Freud, were Europeans. I do not know of an original idea to have importantly affected the *modern* world which has come from Asia or Africa (except perhaps for Gandhi's concept of non-violent resistance or civil disobedience, and, after all, Thoreau had the same idea earlier).

24   It does not seem to me a passing phenomenon or an accident that the West, in ideas and temporal power, has been dominant for so long. Far from falling behind, it seems to be extending its lead, except in the fearful matter of mere numbers and I like to think the inventiveness of the West will somehow eventually cope with that. What is called the emergence of the peoples of Asia and Africa is taking place in Western terms and is measured by the degree to which they take on Western forms, political, industrial, and otherwise. That they are losing their own cultures is sad, I think, but I suppose it cannot be helped. The new realm is space, and that too is being explored by the West. So much for Spengler.

25   Theories of history go in vogues which, as is the nature of vogues, soon fade and give place to new ones. Yet this fails to discourage the systematizers. They believe as firmly in this year's as last year's, for, as Isaiah Berlin says, the "obstinate craving for unity and symmetry at the expense of experience" is always with us. When I grew up, the economic interpretation of history, as formulated with stunning impact by Charles Beard, was the new gospel—as incontrovertible as if it had been revealed to Beard in a burning bush. Even to question that financial interests motivated our Founding Fathers in the separation from Britain, or that equally mercenary considerations decided our entrance into the First World War, was to convict oneself of the utmost naïveté. Yet lately the fashionable—indeed, what appears to be the required—exercise among historians has been jumping on Beard with both feet. He and the considerable body of his followers who added to his system and built it up into a dogma capable of covering any historical situation have been knocked about, analyzed, dissected, and thoroughly disposed of. Presently the historical establishment has moved on to dispose of Frederick Jackson Turner and his theory of the Frontier. I do not know what the new explanation is, but I am sure there must be some thesis, for, as one

academic historian recently ruled, the writing of history requires a "large organizing idea."

26   I visualize the "large organizing idea" as one of those iron chain mats pulled behind by a tractor to smooth over a plowed field. I see the professor climbing up on the tractor seat and away he goes, pulling behind his large organizing idea over the bumps and furrows of history until he has smoothed it out to a nice, neat, organized surface—in other words, into a system.

27   The human being—you, I, or Napoleon—is unreliable as a scientific factor. In combination of personality, circumstance, and historical moment, each man is a package of variables impossible to duplicate. His birth, his parents, his siblings, his food, his home, his school, his economic and social status, his first job, his first girl, and the variables inherent in all of these, make up that mysterious compendium, personality—which then combines with another set of variables: country, climate, time, and historical circumstance. Is it likely, then, that all these elements will meet again in their exact proportions to reproduce a Moses, or Hitler, or De Gaulle, or for that matter Lee Harvey Oswald, the man who killed Kennedy?

28   So long as man remains the Unknowable Variable—and I see no immediate prospect of his ever being pinned down in every facet of his infinite variety—I do not see how his actions can be usefully programmed and quantified. The eager electronic optimists will go on chopping up man's past behavior into the thousands of little definable segments which they call Input, and the machine will whirr and buzz and flash its lights and in no time at all give back Output. But will Output be dependable? I would lay ten to one that history will pay no more attention to Output than it did to Karl Marx. It will still need historians. Electronics will have its uses, but it will not, I am confident, transform historians into button-pushers or history into a system.

QUESTIONS

Ideas

1.   Are there historical events in your memory that could illustrate Tuchman's point that "history misbehaves"? For example, can you narrate events that would illustrate the "illogical human record" Tuchman refers to in paragraph 7?

2. In the last paragraph Tuchman says there will always be a need for historians. Why does she feel a need to say this? Is she answering an opposing view?

3. Why do you think Tuchman is opposed to the "large organizing idea" she mentions in the last line of paragraph 25? What are examples of these master theories?

4. Is Tuchman saying that Freud's theories should not be used to interpret the behavior of historical figures? Is she implying that Marx's influence on history was insignificant? How do you think students at the University of Moscow would respond to that question?

5. Do you think Tuchman's discussion of the non-Decline of the West in paragraphs 22 through 24 is fair? Do you think university students in, say, Japan or Kenya would agree with Tuchman's last sentence in paragraph 23?

6. Based on your reading this essay, how do you think Tuchman would describe human nature?

7. In your opinion, what purposes does the study of history serve? Who should write history? Should there be a women's history? Should minorities like Blacks and Indians be encouraged to write a separate history or should they be assimilated into a larger perspective? Are historical events open to interpretation like poems?

Organization

8. What is the function of paragraphs 6, 9, and 15?

9. An essay with 28 paragraphs is usually divided into parts, with maybe four or five paragraphs used to develop an idea in some detail. Find examples of these "discourse blocks" in the last half of the essay.

10. Divide this essay into five parts. What might be an appropriate title for each?

Sentences

11. Paragraph 13 contains a number of questions. In fact, there are a large number of questions throughout. Do you think this is an effective device? Might the fact that this is a talk have something to do with her choice?

12. Look again at paragraph 18, reading it out loud. Are the sentences varied in type, length, and beginning?

13. Tuchman often uses the colon (e.g., the first sentence in paragraph 15). Find other examples, then write some of your own sentences in imitation of this pattern.

Words

14. Why do you think Tuchman uses German words in paragraph 16?
15. A euphemism is a polite word or phrase used to cover up an unpleasant fact (e.g., *departed* for *dead, strategic backward movement* for *retreat*). Can you find some examples in paragraph 21?

Suggestions for Writing

A. Write a brief letter to Barbara Tuchman disagreeing with one of the ideas she presents.
B. Try to write a paragraph in Tuchman's style that would fit into this essay and go unnoticed by a reader.
C. Write an essay that argues that we can learn from history. Give examples.

FOURTEEN

Alice Walker
(1944–   )

Born in Georgia in 1944, Alice Walker is the youngest of eight children of black sharecroppers. She attended Spellman College and Sarah Lawrence, from which she graduated with a B.A. During her college years she became deeply involved in the civil rights movement and worked with a variety of social programs, including voter registration, welfare rights, and Head Start. She has also taught at a number of colleges including Jackson State, Wellesley, Brandeis, and the University of California at Berkeley.

Alice Walker's prose has been highly acclaimed for its passion, its honesty, and its beauty. Walker is perhaps best known for her fiction, which includes two collections of short stories and three novels, the most recent of which, *The Color Purple*, won both the Pulitzer Prize and the American Book Award. Her essays, from which the selections that follow were taken, are collected in her 1983 volume, *In Search of Our Mothers' Gardens*.

Throughout her nonfictional prose, Walker ranges over subjects such as family relations, race relations, and the relations between the sexes. In "Brothers and Sisters" she explores family relationships, which, in another context, she has described as "sacred." Walker believes that "love, cohesion, and support" are crucial for the survival of the family, especially the black family. In "Choice" she pays tribute to Martin Luther King, Jr., explaining how his courage and devotion to freedom inspired her. In an essay not included in this volume, Walker pays similar tribute to Zora Neale Hurston, a black woman writer whose work and life provided her with a model of independence and integrity. In the title essay of her book, *In Search of Our Mothers' Gardens*, she raises questions about artistic creativity, inviting us to consider how, despite prejudice and oppression, poor black women such as Walker's own mother found outlets for their considerable artistic talent. And, finally, in "Beauty: When the Other Dancer Is the Self," Walker writes movingly of how she came to terms with a physical disfigurement.

Walker's writing is consistently polemical: she has a position to argue from and a case to advance. Writing as a black feminist, Walker reveals the tremendous suffering, frustration, and waste in the lives of the poor black women she considers to be "among America's greatest heroes." Yet, while she makes the lives of such women her most frequent subject, she occasionally transcends this subject, enlarging it to explore questions about our common humanity. On such occasions the impact of her writing is felt across boundaries of race, sex, and social class, largely because Walker offers us a vision of survival, suggesting, as one of her reviewers has written, that her work exemplifies the capacity of human beings "to live in spiritual health and beauty" in such a way that "their inner selves can blossom."

One additional quality of her character and writing remains to be noted: her gratitude. Walker gives thanks, throughout her essays, for her past, for her rich Southern experience, and especially for her family. She is grateful for her skill as a writer and for the dedicated support she has had in the forms of both public grants and of private encouragement. And she is grateful, finally, for the strong and inspiring models she memorializes so lovingly in her work.

Brothers and Sisters

---

1   We lived on a farm in the South in the fifties, and my brothers, the four of them I knew (the fifth had left home when I was three years old), were allowed to watch animals being mated. This was not unusual; nor was it considered unusual that my older sister and I were frowned upon if we even asked, innocently, what was going on. One of my brothers explained the mating one day, using words my father had given him: "The bull is getting a little something on his stick," he said. And he laughed. "What stick?" I wanted to know.

"Where did he get it? How did he pick it up? Where did he put it?" All my brothers laughed.

2   I believe my mother's theory about raising a large family of five boys and three girls was that the father should teach the boys and the mother teach the girls the facts, as one says, of life. So my father went around talking about bulls getting something on their sticks and she went around saying girls did not need to know about such things. They were "womanish" (a very bad way to be in those days) if they asked.

3   The thing was, watching the matings filled my brothers with an aimless sort of lust, as dangerous as it was unintentional. They knew enough to know that cows, months after mating, produced calves, but they were not bright enough to make the same connection between women and their offspring.

4   Sometimes, when I think of my childhood, it seems to me a particularly hard one. But in reality, everything awful that happened to me didn't seem to happen to *me* at all, but to my older sister. Through some incredible power to negate my presence around people I did not like, which produced invisibility (as well as an ability to appear mentally vacant when I was nothing of the kind), I was spared the humiliation she was subjected to, though at the same time, I felt every bit of it. It was as if she suffered for my benefit, and I vowed early in my life that none of the things that made existence so miserable for her would happen to me.

5   The fact that she was not allowed at official matings did not mean she never saw any. While my brothers followed my father to the mating pens on the other side of the road near the barn, she stationed herself near the pigpen, or followed our many dogs until they were in a mating mood, or, failing to witness something there, she watched the chickens. On a farm it is impossible *not* to be conscious of sex, to wonder about it, to dream . . . but to whom was she to speak of her feelings? Not to my father, who thought all young women perverse. Not to my mother, who pretended all her children grew out of stumps she magically found in the forest. Not to me, who never found anything wrong with this lie.

6   When my sister menstruated she wore a thick packet of clean rags between her legs. It stuck out in front like a penis. The boys laughed at her as she served them at the table. Not knowing any better, and because our parents did not dream of actually *discussing* what was going on, she would giggle nervously at herself. I hated her for giggling, and it was at those times I would think of her as dim-witted. She never

complained, but she began to have strange fainting fits whenever she had her period. Her head felt as if it were splitting, she said, and everything she ate came up again. And her cramps were so severe she could not stand. She was forced to spend several days of each month in bed.

7   My father expected all of his sons to have sex with women. "Like bulls," he said, "a man *needs* to get a little something on his stick." And so, on Saturday nights, into town they went, chasing the girls. My sister was rarely allowed into town alone, and if the dress she wore fit too snugly at the waist, or if her cleavage dipped too far below her collarbone, she was made to stay home.

8   "But why can't I go too," she would cry, her face screwed up with the effort not to wail.

9   "They're boys, your brothers, *that's* why they can go."

10   Naturally, when she got the chance, she responded eagerly to boys. But when this was discovered she was whipped and locked up in her room.

11   I would go in to visit her.

12   "Straight Pine," she would say, "you don't know what it *feels* like to want to be loved by a man."

13   "And if this is what you get for feeling like it I never will," I said, with—I hoped—the right combination of sympathy and disgust.

14   "Men smell so good," she would whisper ecstatically. "And when they look into your eyes, you just melt."

15   Since they were so hard to catch, naturally she thought almost any of them terrific.

16   "Oh, that Alfred!" she would moon over some mediocre, square-headed boy, "he's so *sweet!*" And she would take his ugly picture out of her bosom and kiss it.

17   My father was always warning her not to come home if she ever found herself pregnant. My mother constantly reminded her that abortion was a sin. Later, although she never became pregnant, her period would not come for months at a time. The painful symptoms, however, never varied or ceased. She fell for the first man who loved her enough to beat her for looking at someone else, and when I was still in high school, she married him.

18   My fifth brother, the one I never knew, was said to be different from the rest. He had not liked matings. He would not watch them. He thought the cows should be given a choice. My father had disliked him because he was soft. My mother took up for him. "Jason is just tender-

hearted," she would say in a way that made me know he was her favorite; "he takes after me." It was true that my mother cried about almost anything.

19   Who was the oldest brother? I wondered.

20   "Well," said my mother, "he was someone who always loved you. Of course he was a great big boy when you were born and out working on his own. He worked on a road gang building roads. Every morning before he left he would come in the room where you were and pick you up and give you the biggest kisses. He used to look at you and just smile. It's a pity you don't remember him."

21   I agreed.

22   At my father's funeral I finally "met" my oldest brother. He is tall and black with thick gray hair above a young-looking face. I watched my sister cry over my father until she blacked out from grief. I saw my brothers sobbing, reminding each other of what a great father he had been. My oldest brother and I did not shed a tear between us. When I left my father's grave he came up and introduced himself. "You don't ever have to walk alone," he said, and put his arms around me.

23   One out of five ain't *too* bad, I thought, snuggling up.

24   But I didn't discover until recently his true uniqueness: He is the only one of my brothers who assumes responsibility for all his children. The other four all fathered children during those Saturday-night chases of twenty years ago. Children—my nieces and nephews whom I will probably never know—they neither acknowledge as their own, provide for, or even see.

25   It was not until I became a student of women's liberation ideology that I could understand and forgive my father. I needed an ideology that would define his behavior in context. The black movement had given me an ideology that helped explain his colorism (he *did* fall in love with my mother partly because she was so light; he never denied it). Feminism helped explain his sexism. I was relieved to know his sexist behavior was not something uniquely his own, but, rather, an imitation of the behavior of the society around us.

26   All partisan movements add to the fullness of our understanding of society as a whole. They never detract; or, in any case, one must not allow them to do so. Experience adds to experience. "The more things the better," as O'Connor and Welty both have said, speaking, one of marriage, the other of Catholicism.

27   I desperately needed my father and brothers to give me male models I could respect, because white men (for example; being par-

ticularly handy in this sort of comparison)—whether in films or in
person—offered man as dominator, as killer, and always as hypocrite.
28   My father failed because he copied the hypocrisy. And my brothers—except for one—never understood they must represent half the
world to me, as I must represent the other half to them.

QUESTIONS

Ideas

1. What ideas about family life emerge in this essay? What sexual stereotypes
    appear?

2. What is Walker's attitude toward her brothers and sisters? Where is her
    feeling about them most directly expressed?

Organization

3. Divide the essay into two, three, or four parts. Provide titles for each part
    and explain the relationship of one part to another.

4. Explain how the last paragraphs return the essay to concerns voiced earlier.
    What do these paragraphs add to those concerns?

Sentences

5. Explain the purpose and effect of the parenthetical interpolations in sent-
    ences from paragraphs 1, 2, 4, 25, and 27.

6. Paragraphs 4 and 5 include a variety of moderately long, well-controlled
    sentences. Consider carefully the structure of the last two sentences of
    paragraph 4 and the second sentence of paragraph 5. Notice also the
    parallelism Walker establishes at the end of paragraph 5 by repeating with
    variations the following sentence opening:

    Not to my father . . . Not to my mother . . . Not to me . . .

Words

7. Characterize and explain the language of the following bits of dialogue:

    The bull is getting a little something on his stick.
    Oh that Alfred, he's so *sweet!*
    You don't ever have to walk alone.

8. What do you think Walker means by the following words: *colorism,*
    feminism, sexism, movement, and *ideology*—all from paragraph 25.

Suggestions for Writing

A. Agree or disagree with Walker's contention that "all partisan movements add to the fullness of our understanding of our society as a whole." In what sense do you think this statement may be true or not, whether you think of women's liberation or of any other movement or ideology?

B. Write an essay explaining and responding to the idea you think Walker advances in paragraph 27 or 28.

C. Reflect on your own relations with your brothers and sisters. Write an essay exploring some aspect of sibling relationship.

D. Write an imitation of paragraph 4 or 5. Attend particularly to the punctuation, length, and rhythms of Walker's sentences.

Choice: A Tribute to Dr. Martin Luther King, Jr.

---

1 My great-great-great-grandmother walked as a slave from Virginia to Eatonton, Georgia—which passes for the Walker ancestral home—with two babies on her hips. She lived to be a hundred and twenty-five years old and my own father knew her as a boy. (It is in memory of this walk that I choose to keep and to embrace my "maiden" name, Walker.)

2 There is a cemetery near our family church where she is buried; but because her marker was made of wood and rotted years ago, it is impossible to tell exactly where her body lies. In the same cemetery are most of my mother's people, who have lived in Georgia for so long nobody even remembers when they came. And all of my great-aunts and -uncles are there, and my grandfather and grandmother, and, very recently, my own father.

3 If it is true that land does not belong to anyone until they have buried a body in it, then the land of my birthplace belongs to me, dozens of times over. Yet the history of my family, like that of all black Southerners, is a history of dispossession. We loved the land and worked the land, but we never owned it; and even if we bought land, as my great-grandfather did after the Civil War, it was always in danger of being taken away, as his was, during the period following Reconstruction.

4   My father inherited nothing of material value from his father, and when I came of age in the early sixties I awoke to the bitter knowledge that in order just to continue to love the land of my birth, I was expected to leave it. For black people—including my parents—had learned a long time ago that to stay willingly in a beloved but brutal place is to risk losing the love and being forced to acknowledge only the brutality.

5   It is a part of the black Southern sensibility that we treasure memories; for such a long time, that is all of our homeland those of us who at one time or another were forced away from it have been allowed to have.

6   I watched my brothers, one by one, leave our home and leave the South. I watched my sisters do the same. This was not unusual; abandonment, except for memories, was the common thing, except for those who "could not do any better," or those whose strength or stubbornness was so colossal they took the risk that others could not bear.

7   In 1960, my mother bought a television set, and each day after school I watched Hamilton Holmes and Charlayne Hunter as they struggled to integrate—fair-skinned as they were—the University of Georgia. And then, one day, there appeared the face of Dr. Martin Luther King, Jr. What a funny name, I thought. At the moment I first saw him, he was being handcuffed and shoved into a police truck. He had dared to claim his rights as a native son, and had been arrested. He displayed no fear, but seemed calm and serene, unaware of his own extraordinary courage. His whole body, like his conscience, was at peace.

8   At the moment I saw his resistance I knew I would never be able to live in this country without resisting everything that sought to disinherit me, and I would never be forced away from the land of my birth without a fight.

9   He was The One, The Hero, The One Fearless Person for whom we had waited. I hadn't even realized before that we *had* been waiting for Martin Luther King, Jr., but we had. And I knew it for sure when my mother added his name to the list of people she prayed for every night.

10   I sometimes think that it was literally the prayers of people like my mother and father, who had bowed down in the struggle for such a long time, that kept Dr. King alive until five years ago. For years we went to bed praying for his life, and awoke with the question "Is the 'Lord' still here?"

11   The public acts of Dr. King you know. They are visible all around

you. His voice you would recognize sooner than any other voice you have heard in this century—this in spite of the fact that certain municipal libraries, like the one in downtown Jackson, do not carry recordings of his speeches, and the librarians chuckle cruelly when asked why they do not.

12   You know, if you have read his books, that his is a complex and revolutionary philosophy that few people are capable of understanding fully or have the patience to embody in themselves. Which is our weakness, which is our loss.

13   And if you know anything about good Baptist preaching, you can imagine what you missed if you never had a chance to hear Martin Luther King, Jr., preach at Ebeneezer Baptist Church.

14   You know of the prizes and awards that he tended to think very little of. And you know of his concern for the disinherited: the American Indian, the Mexican-American, and the poor American white—for whom he cared much.

15   You know that this very room, in this very restaurant, was closed to people of color not more than five years ago. And that we eat here together tonight largely through his efforts and his blood. We accept the common pleasures of life, assuredly, in his name.

16   But add to all of these things the one thing that seems to me second to none in importance: He gave us back our heritage. He gave us back our homeland; the bones and dust of our ancestors, who may now sleep within our caring *and* our hearing. He gave us the blueness of the Georgia sky in autumn as in summer; the colors of the Southern winter as well as glimpses of the green of vacation-time spring. Those of our relatives we used to invite for a visit we now can ask to stay. . . . He gave us full-time use of our own woods, and restored our memories to those of us who were forced to run away, as realities we might each day enjoy and leave for our children.

17   He gave us continuity of place, without which community is ephemeral. He gave us home.

QUESTIONS

Ideas

1. There's no question that Walker thinks highly of King. Why does she value him and how does she characterize him?

2. Before referring specifically to King, Walker talks about the South—her home. What does she say about the South and about her relation to it?

Organization

3. "Choice" can be divided into two parts: paragraphs 1–7 and paragraphs 8–17. Explain how the two final paragraphs can be related to the concerns of the first seven. Comment on the effectiveness of returning at the end of the essay to its opening.
4. Consider paragraph 3 or 5 as an alternative introductory paragraph for the essay. Which makes a better lead? How would you reorganize the first seven paragraphs to accommodate either 5 or 3 as a new introduction?

Sentences

5. How effective is the sentence fragment in paragraph 12?

   Which is our weakness, which is our loss.

   Would it be better in this alternative version?

   This has been both our weakness and our loss.

   How effective is the fragment in paragraph 15?
6. What is the rhetorical purpose of the colon in the opening sentence of paragraph 16? Explain the relationship of the information on the two sides of the colon.
7. Explain the effect in paragraphs 14–17 of Walker's use of similar patterns of sentence opening:

   You know of . . . And you know of . . . You know that . . . And that . . .
   He gave us back . . . He gave us back . . . He gave us . . . He gave us . . .

Words

8. Notice how Walker repeats key words in paragraph 4: love–beloved–love; knowledge–acknowledge; brutal–brutality. What is the effect of such repetition and variation? Locate and comment on another example from another paragraph.
9. In paragraphs 11–15 Walker addresses her readers directly as "you." What is the effect of this choice of pronoun on the tone of the piece? Why does Walker shift from *you* to *we* in the concluding paragraphs (16–17) and how effective is this shift?

Suggestions for Writing

A. Write an essay or a speech in which you extol the virtues of a public figure you value. Consider imitating Walker's style in the last four paragraphs of "Choice."

B. Write imitations of the dash sentences in paragraphs 1, 4, 7, 11, and 14.

Beauty: When the Other Dancer Is the Self

---

1   It is a bright summer day in 1947. My father, a fat, funny man with beautiful eyes and a subversive wit, is trying to decide which of his eight children he will take with him to the county fair. My mother, of course, will not go. She is knocked out from getting most of us ready: I hold my neck stiff against the pressure of her knuckles as she hastily completes the braiding and then beribboning of my hair.

2   My father is the driver for the rich old white lady up the road. Her name is Miss Mey. She owns all the land for miles around, as well as the house in which we live. All I remember about her is that she once offered to pay my mother thirty-five cents for cleaning her house, raking up piles of her magnolia leaves, and washing her family's clothes, and that my mother—she of no money, eight children, and a chronic earache—refused it. But I do not think of this in 1947. I am two and a half years old. I want to go everywhere my daddy goes. I am excited at the prospect of riding in a car. Someone has told me fairs are fun. That there is room in the car for only three of us doesn't faze me at all. Whirling happily in my starchy frock, showing off my biscuit-polished patent-leather shoes and lavender socks, tossing my head in a way that makes my ribbons bounce, I stand, hands on hips, before my father. "Take me, Daddy," I say with assurance; "I'm the prettiest!"

3   Later, it does not surprise me to find myself in Miss Mey's shiny black car, sharing the back seat with the other lucky ones. Does not surprise me that I thoroughly enjoy the fair. At home that night I tell the unlucky ones all I can remember about the merry-go-round, the man

who eats live chickens, and the teddy bears, until they say: that's enough, baby Alice. Shut up now, and go to sleep.

4   It is Easter Sunday, 1950. I am dressed in a green, flocked, scal-loped-hem dress (handmade by my adoring sister, Ruth) that has its own smooth satin petticoat and tiny hot-pink roses tucked into each scallop. My shoes, new T-strap patent leather, again highly biscuit-polished. I am six years old and have learned one of the longest Easter speeches to be heard that day, totally unlike the speech I said when I was two: "Easter lilies/pure and white/blossom in/the morning light." When I rise to give my speech I do so on a great wave of love and pride and expectation. People in the church stop rustling their new crinolines. They seem to hold their breath. I can tell they admire my dress, but it is my spirit, bordering on sassiness (womanishness), they secretly ap-plaud.

5   "That girl's a little *mess*," they whisper to each other, pleased.

6   Naturally I say my speech without stammer or pause, unlike those who stutter, stammer, or, worst of all, forget. This is before the word "beautiful" exists in people's vocabulary, but "Oh, isn't she the *cutest* thing!" frequently floats my way. "And got so much sense!" they grate-fully add . . . for which thoughtful addition I thank them to this day.

7   *It was great fun being cute. But then, one day, it ended.*

8   I am eight years old and a tomboy. I have a cowboy hat, cowboy boots, checkered shirt and pants, all red. My playmates are my brothers, two and four years older than I. Their colors are black and green, the only difference in the way we are dressed. On Saturday nights we all go to the picture show, even my mother; Westerns are her favorite kind of movie. Back home, "on the ranch," we pretend we are Tom Mix, Hopalong Cassidy, Lash LaRue (we've even named one of our dogs Lash LaRue); we chase each other for hours rustling cattle, being outlaws, delivering damsels from distress. Then my parents decide to buy my brothers guns. These are not "real" guns. They shoot "BBs," copper pellets my brothers say will kill birds. Because I am a girl, I do not get a gun. Instantly I am relegated to the position of Indian. Now there appears a great distance between us. They shoot and shoot at everything with their new guns. I try to keep up with my bow and arrows.

9   One day while I am standing on top of our makeshift "garage"— pieces of tin nailed across some poles—holding my bow and arrow and

looking out toward the fields, I feel an incredible blow in my right eye. I look down just in time to see my brother lower his gun.

10   Both brothers rush to my side. My eye stings, and I cover it with my hand. "If you tell," they say, "we will get a whipping. You don't want that to happen, do you?" I do not. "Here is a piece of wire," says the older brother, picking it up from the roof; "say you stepped on one end of it and the other flew up and hit you." The pain is beginning to start. "Yes," I say. "Yes, I will say that is what happened." If I do not say this is what happened, I know my brothers will find ways to make me wish I had. But now I will say anything that gets me to my mother.

11   Confronted by our parents we stick to the lie agreed upon. They place me on a bench on the porch and I close my left eye while they examine the right. There is a tree growing from underneath the porch that climbs past the railing to the roof. It is the last thing my right eye sees. I watch as its trunk, its branches, and then its leaves are blotted out by the rising blood.

12   I am in shock. First there is intense fever, which my father tries to break using lily leaves bound around my head. Then there are chills: my mother tries to get me to eat soup. Eventually, I do not know how, my parents learn what has happened. A week after the "accident" they take me to see a doctor. "Why did you wait so long to come?" he asks, looking into my eye and shaking his head. "Eyes are sympathetic," he says. "If one is blind, the other will likely become blind too."

13   This comment of the doctor's terrifies me. But it is really how I look that bothers me most. Where the BB pellet struck there is a glob of whitish scar tissue, a hideous cataract, on my eye. Now when I stare at people—a favorite pastime, up to now—they will stare back. Not at the "cute" little girl, but at her scar. For six years I do not stare at anyone, because I do not raise my head.

14   Years later, in the throes of a mid-life crisis, I ask my mother and sister whether I changed after the "accident." "No," they say, puzzled. "What do you mean?"

15   *What do I mean?*

16   I am eight, and, for the first time, doing poorly in school, where I have been something of a whiz since I was four. We have just moved to the place where the "accident" occurred. We do not know any of the people around us because this is a different county. The only time I see the friends I knew is when we go back to our old church. The new school is the former state penitentiary. It is a large stone building, cold and

drafty, crammed to overflowing with boisterous, ill-disciplined children. On the third floor there is a huge circular imprint of some partition that has been torn out.

17   "What used to be here?" I ask a sullen girl next to me on our way past it to lunch.

18   "The electric chair," says she.

19   At night I have nightmares about the electric chair, and about all the people reputedly "fried" in it. I am afraid of the school, where all the students seem to be budding criminals.

20   "What's the matter with your eye?" they ask, critically.

21   When I don't answer (I cannot decide whether it was an "accident" or not), they shove me, insist on a fight.

22   My brother, the one who created the story about the wire, comes to my rescue. But then brags so much about "protecting" me, I become sick.

23   After months of torture at the school, my parents decide to send me back to our old community, to my old school. I live with my grandparents and the teacher they board. But there is no room for Phoebe, my cat. By the time my grandparents decide there *is* room, and I ask for my cat, she cannot be found. Miss Yarborough, the boarding teacher, takes me under her wing, and begins to teach me to play the piano. But soon she marries an African—a "prince," she says—and is whisked away to his continent.

24   At my old school there is at least one teacher who loves me. She is the teacher who "knew me before I was born" and bought my first baby clothes. It is she who makes life bearable. It is her presence that finally helps me turn on the one child at the school who continually calls me "one-eyed bitch." One day I simply grab him by his coat and beat him until I am satisfied. It is my teacher who tells me my mother is ill.

25   My mother is lying in bed in the middle of the day, something I have never seen. She is in too much pain to speak. She has an abscess in her ear. I stand looking down on her, knowing that if she dies, I cannot live. She is being treated with warm oils and hot bricks held against her cheek. Finally a doctor comes. But I must go back to my grandparents' house. The weeks pass but I am hardly aware of it. All I know is that my mother might die, my father is not so jolly, my brothers still have their guns, and I am the one sent away from home.

26   "You did not change," they say.

27   *Did I imagine the anguish of never looking up?*

28 I am twelve. When relatives come to visit I hide in my room. My cousin Brenda, just my age, whose father works in the post office and whose mother is a nurse, comes to find me. "Hello," she says. And then she asks, looking at my recent school picture, which I did not want taken, and on which the "glob," as I think of it, is clearly visible, "You still can't see out of that eye?"

29 "No," I say, and flop back on the bed over my book.

30 That night, as I do almost every night, I abuse my eye. I rant and rave at it, in front of the mirror. I plead with it to clear up before morning. I tell it I hate and despise it. I do not pray for sight. I pray for beauty.

31 "You did not change," they say.

32 I am fourteen and baby-sitting for my brother Bill, who lives in Boston. He is my favorite brother and there is a strong bond between us. Understanding my feelings of shame and ugliness he and his wife take me to a local hospital, where the "glob" is removed by a doctor named O. Henry. There is still a small bluish crater where the scar tissue was, but the ugly white stuff is gone. Almost immediately I become a different person from the girl who does not raise her head. Or so I think. Now that I've raised my head I win the boyfriend of my dreams. Now that I've raised my head I have plenty of friends. Now that I've raised my head classwork comes from my lips as faultlessly as Easter speeches did, and I leave high school as valedictorian, most popular student, and *queen*, hardly believing my luck. Ironically, the girl who was voted most beautiful in our class (and was) was later shot twice through the chest by a male companion, using a "real" gun, while she was pregnant. But that's another story in itself. Or is it?

33 "You did not change," they say.

34 It is now thirty years since the "accident." A beautiful journalist comes to visit and to interview me. She is going to write a cover story for her magazine that focuses on my latest book. "Decide how you want to look on the cover," she says. "Glamorous, or whatever."

35 Never mind "glamorous," it is the "whatever" that I hear. Suddenly all I can think of is whether I will get enough sleep the night before the photography session: if I don't, my eye will be tired and wander, as blind eyes will.

36 At night in bed with my lover I think up reasons why I should not appear on the cover of a magazine. "My meanest critics will say

I've sold out," I say. "My family will now realize I write scandalous books."

37 "But what's the real reason you don't want to do this?" he asks.

38 "Because in all probability," I say in a rush, "my eye won't be straight."

39 "It will be straight enough," he says. Then, "Besides, I thought you'd made your peace with that."

40 And I suddenly remember that I have.

41 *I remember:*

42 I am talking to my brother Jimmy, asking if he remembers anything unusual about the day I was shot. He does not know I consider that day the last time my father, with his sweet home remedy of cool lily leaves, chose me, and that I suffered and raged inside because of this. "Well," he says, "all I remember is standing by the side of the highway with Daddy, trying to flag down a car. A white man stopped, but when Daddy said he needed somebody to take his little girl to the doctor, he drove off."

43 *I remember:*

44 I am in the desert for the first time. I fall totally in love with it. I am so overwhelmed by its beauty, I confront for the first time, consciously, the meaning of the doctor's words years ago: "Eyes are sympathetic. If one is blind, the other will likely become blind too." I realize I have dashed about the world madly, looking at this, looking at that, storing up images against the fading of the light. *But I might have missed seeing the desert!* The shock of that possibility—and gratitude for over twenty-five years of sight—sends me literally to my knees. Poem after poem comes—which is perhaps how poets pray.

ON SIGHT

I am so thankful I have seen
The Desert
And the creatures in the desert
And the desert Itself.

The desert has its own moon
Which I have seen
With my own eye.

There is no flag on it.

Trees of the desert have arms
All of which are always up
That is because the moon is up
The sun is up
Also the sky
The stars
Clouds
None with flags.

If there *were* flags, I doubt
the trees would point.
Would you?

45   *But mostly, I remember this:*

46   I am twenty-seven, and my baby daughter is almost three. Since her birth I have worried about her discovery that her mother's eyes are different from other people's. Will she be embarrassed? I think. What will she say? Every day she watches a television program called "Big Blue Marble." It begins with a picture of the earth as it appears from the moon. It is bluish, a little battered-looking, but full of light, with whitish clouds swirling around it. Every time I see it I weep with love, as if it is a picture of Grandma's house. One day when I am putting Rebecca down for her nap, she suddenly focuses on my eye. Something inside me cringes, gets ready to try to protect myself. All children are cruel about physical differences, I know from experience, and that they don't always mean to be is another matter. I assume Rebecca will be the same.

47   But no-o-o-o. She studies my face intently as we stand, her inside and me outside her crib. She even holds my face maternally between her dimpled little hands. Then, looking every bit as serious and lawyerlike as her father, she says, as if it may just possibly have slipped my attention: "Mommy, there's a *world* in your eye." (As in, "Don't be alarmed, or do anything crazy.") And then, gently, but with great interest: "Mommy, where did you *get* that world in your eye?"

48   For the most part, the pain left then. (So what, if my brothers grew up to buy even more powerful pellet guns for their sons and to carry real guns themselves. So what, if a young "Morehouse man" once nearly fell off the steps of Trevor Arnett Library because he thought my eyes were blue.) Crying and laughing I ran to the bathroom, while Rebecca mumbled and sang herself off to sleep. Yes indeed, I realized, looking into the mirror. There *was* a world in my eye. And I saw that it was

possible to love it: that in fact, for all it had taught me of shame and anger and inner vision, I *did* love it. Even to see it drifting out of orbit in boredom, or rolling up out of fatigue, not to mention floating back at attention in excitement (bearing witness, a friend has called it), deeply suitable to my personality, and even characteristic of me.

49   That night I dream I am dancing to Stevie Wonder's song "Always" (the name of the song is really "As," but I hear it as "Always"). As I dance, whirling and joyous, happier than I've ever been in my life, another bright-faced dancer joins me. We dance and kiss each other and hold each other through the night. The other dancer has obviously come through all right, as I have done. She is beautiful, whole and free. And she is also me.

QUESTIONS

Ideas

1. In what ways does the young Alice Walker change after the injury to her eye? What effect has the injury had on her as an adult?

2. Discuss whether Walker has overreacted to her injury. Consider how an injury can alter our perception of ourselves or our sense of how others perceive and respond to us.

Organization

3. How is the essay organized? How does Walker signal her changes of focus and emphasis? What ties the various sections of the essay together?

4. Cite at least one example of a repeated sentence and comment on Walker's purpose in using it.

Sentences

5. Consider the effect in paragraph 32 of the use of a repeated sentence pattern: "Now that I've . . ." In the same paragraph comment on the effect of these two short sentences: "Or so I think." "Or is it?"

6. Explain the effect of the double dashes in the following sentence:

> But soon she marries an African—a "prince," she says—and is whisked away to his continent. (23)

> The shock of that possibility—and gratitude for over twenty-five years of sight—sends me literally to my knees. (44)

Consider the differences in tone that would result if the dashes were replaced either with parentheses or with commas.

Words

7. Cite three uses of dialogue you think effective and explain what makes them so.
8. At the end of the essay Walker invokes the image of a dancer—another dancer who joins her in a dance. She also makes reference to a world in her eye. What do you think is the point and purpose of each of these images?

Suggestions for Writing

A. Describe a time when an accident or other turn of events damaged your self-image, made you feel insecure or unhappy with yourself. Explain how you came to terms with your situation and what the consequences for your later life have been or might be.
B. Compare Walker's discussion of her injury and its effects with Richard Selzer's essay "Love Sick."

In Search of Our Mothers' Gardens

MOTHEROOT

Creation often
needs two hearts
one to root
and one to flower
One to sustain
in time of drouth
and hold fast
against winds of pain
the fragile bloom
that in the glory
of its hour

affirms a heart
unsung, unseen.

—MARILOU AWIAKTA,
ABIDING APPALACHIA

I described her own nature and temperament. Told how they needed a
larger life for their expression. . . . I pointed out that in lieu of proper
channels, her emotions had overflowed into paths that dissipated them.
I talked, beautifully I thought, about an art that would be born, an art
that would open the way for women the likes of her. I asked her to hope,
and build up an inner life against the coming of that day. . . . I sang, with
a strange quiver in my voice, a promise song.

—JEAN TOOMER, "AVEY,"
CANE

1   The poet speaking to a prostitute who falls asleep while he's
talking—

2   When the poet Jean Toomer walked through the South in the
early twenties, he discovered a curious thing: black women whose spirituality was so intense, so deep, so *unconscious,* that they were themselves
unaware of the richness they held. They stumbled blindly through their
lives: creatures so abused and mutilated in body, so dimmed and confused by pain, that they considered themselves unworthy even of hope.
In the selfless abstractions their bodies became to the men who used
them, they became more than "sexual objects," more even than mere
women: they became "Saints." Instead of being perceived as whole
persons, their bodies became shrines: what was thought to be their
minds became temples suitable for worship. These crazy Saints stared
out at the world, wildly, like lunatics—or quietly, like suicides; and the
"God" that was in their gaze was as mute as a great stone.

3   Who were these Saints? These crazy, loony, pitiful women?

4   Some of them, without a doubt, were our mothers and grandmothers.

5   In the still heat of the post-Reconstruction South, this is how they
seemed to Jean Toomer: exquisite butterflies trapped in an evil honey,
toiling away their lives in an era, a century, that did not acknowledge
them, except as "the *mule* of the world." They dreamed dreams that
no one knew—not even themselves, in any coherent fashion—and saw
visions no one could understand. They wandered or sat about the coun-

tryside crooning lullabies to ghosts, and drawing the mother of Christ in charcoal on courthouse walls.

6   They forced their minds to desert their bodies and their striving spirits sought to rise, like frail whirlwinds from the hard red clay. And when those frail whirlwinds fell, in scattered particles, upon the ground, no one mourned. Instead, men lit candles to celebrate the emptiness that remained, as people do who enter a beautiful but vacant space to resurrect a God.

7   Our mothers and grandmothers, some of them: moving to music not yet written. And they waited.

8   They waited for a day when the unknown thing that was in them would be made known; but guessed, somehow in their darkness, that on the day of their revelation they would be long dead. Therefore to Toomer they walked, and even ran, in slow motion. For they were going nowhere immediate, and the future was not yet within their grasp. And men took our mothers and grandmothers, "but got no pleasure from it." So complex was their passion and their calm.

9   To Toomer, they lay vacant and fallow as autumn fields, with harvest time never in sight: and he saw them enter loveless marriages, without joy; and become prostitutes, without resistance; and become mothers of children, without fulfillment.

10   For these grandmothers and mothers of ours were not Saints, but Artists; driven to a numb and bleeding madness by the springs of creativity in them for which there was no release. They were Creators, who lived lives of spiritual waste, because they were so rich in spirituality —which is the basis of Art—that the strain of enduring their unused and unwanted talent drove them insane. Throwing away this spirituality was their pathetic attempt to lighten the soul to a weight their work-worn, sexually abused bodies could bear.

11   What did it mean for a black woman to be an artist in our grandmothers' time? In our great-grandmothers' day? It is a question with an answer cruel enough to stop the blood.

12   Did you have a genius of a great-great-grandmother who died under some ignorant and depraved white overseer's lash? Or was she required to bake biscuits for a lazy backwater tramp, when she cried out in her soul to paint watercolors of sunsets, or the rain falling on the green and peaceful pasturelands? Or was her body broken and forced to bear children (who were more often than not sold away from her)—eight, ten, fifteen, twenty children—when her one joy was the thought of modeling heroic figures of rebellion, in stone or clay?

13   How was the creativity of the black woman kept alive, year after year and century after century, when for most of the years black people have been in America, it was a punishable crime for a black person to read or write? And the freedom to paint, to sculpt, to expand the mind with action did not exist. Consider, if you can bear to imagine it, what might have been the result if singing, too, had been forbidden by law. Listen to the voices of Bessie Smith, Billie Holiday, Nina Simone, Roberta Flack, and Aretha Franklin, among others, and imagine those voices muzzled for life. Then you may begin to comprehend the lives of our "crazy," "Sainted" mothers and grandmothers. The agony of the lives of women who might have been Poets, Novelists, Essayists, and Short-Story Writers (over a period of centuries), who died with their real gifts stifled within them.

14   And, if this were the end of the story, we would have cause to cry out in my paraphrase of Okot p'Bitek's great poem:

> O, my clanswomen
> Let us all cry together!
> Come,
> Let us mourn the death of our mother,
> The death of a Queen
> The ash that was produced
> By a great fire!
> O, this homestead is utterly dead
> Close the gates
> With *lacari* thorns,
> For our mother
> The creator of the Stool is lost!
> And all the young women
> Have perished in the wilderness!

15   But this is not the end of the story, for all the young women— our mothers and grandmothers, *ourselves*—have not perished in the wilderness. And if we ask ourselves why, and search for and find the answer, we will know beyond all efforts to erase it from our minds, just exactly who, and of what, we black American women are.

16   One example, perhaps the most pathetic, most misunderstood one, can provide a backdrop for our mothers' work: Phillis Wheatley, a slave in the 1700s.

17   Virginia Woolf, in her book *A Room of One's Own*, wrote that

in order for a woman to write fiction she must have two things, certainly: a room of her own (with key and lock) and enough money to support herself.

18   What then are we to make of Phillis Wheatley, a slave, who owned not even herself? This sickly, frail black girl who required a servant of her own at times—her health was so precarious—and who, had she been white, would have been easily considered the intellectual superior of all the women and most of the men in the society of her day.

19   Virginia Woolf wrote further, speaking of course not of our Phillis, that "any woman born with a great gift in the sixteenth century [insert "eighteenth century," insert "black woman," insert "born or made a slave"] would certainly have gone crazed, shot herself, or ended her days in some lonely cottage outside the village, half witch, half wizard [insert "Saint"], feared and mocked at. For it needs little skill and psychology to be sure that a highly gifted girl who had tried to use her gift for poetry would have been so thwarted and hindered by contrary instincts [add "chains, guns, the lash, the ownership of one's body by someone else, submission to an alien religion"], that she must have lost her health and sanity to a certainty."

20   The key words, as they relate to Phillis, are "contrary instincts." For when we read the poetry of Phillis Wheatley—as when we read the novels of Nella Larsen or the oddly false-sounding autobiography of that freest of all black women writers, Zora Hurston—evidence of "contrary instincts" is everywhere. Her loyalties were completely divided, as was, without question, her mind.

21   But how could this be otherwise? Captured at seven, a slave of wealthy, doting whites who instilled in her the "savagery" of the Africa they "rescued" her from . . . one wonders if she was even able to remember her homeland as she had known it, or as it really was.

22   Yet, because she did try to use her gift for poetry in a world that made her a slave, she was "so thwarted and hindered by . . . contrary instincts, that she . . . lost her health. . . ." In the last years of her brief life, burdened not only with the need to express her gift but also with a penniless, friendless "freedom" and several small children for whom she was forced to do strenuous work to feed, she lost her health, certainly. Suffering from malnutrition and neglect and who knows what mental agonies, Phillis Wheatley died.

23   So torn by "contrary instincts" was black, kidnapped, enslaved Phillis that her description of "the Goddess"—as she poetically called the Liberty she did not have—is ironically, cruelly humorous. And, in

fact, has held Phillis up to ridicule for more than a century. It is usually read prior to hanging Phillis's memory as that of a fool. She wrote:

> The Goddess comes, she moves divinely fair,
> Olive and laurel binds her *golden* hair.
> Wherever shines this native of the skies,
> Unnumber'd charms and recent graces rise. [My italics]

24   It is obvious that Phillis, the slave, combed the "Goddess's" hair every morning; prior, perhaps, to bringing in the milk, or fixing her mistress's lunch. She took her imagery from the one thing she saw elevated above all others.

25   With the benefit of hindsight we ask, "How could she?"

26   But at last, Phillis, we understand. No more snickering when your stiff, struggling, ambivalent lines are forced on us. We know now that you were not an idiot or a traitor; only a sickly little black girl, snatched from your home and country and made a slave; a woman who still struggled to sing the song that was your gift, although in a land of barbarians who praised you for your bewildered tongue. It is not so much what you sang, as that you kept alive, in so many of our ancestors, *the notion of song.*

27   Black women are called, in the folklore that so aptly identifies one's status in society, "the *mule* of the world," because we have been handed the burdens that everyone else—*everyone* else—refused to carry. We have also been called "Matriarchs," "Superwomen," and "Mean and Evil Bitches." Not to mention "Castraters" and "Sapphire's Mama." When we have pleaded for understanding, our character has been distorted; when we have asked for simple caring, we have been handed empty inspirational appellations, then stuck in the farthest corner. When we have asked for love, we have been given children. In short, even our plainer gifts, our labors of fidelity and love, have been knocked down our throats. To be an artist and a black woman, even today, lowers our status in many respects, rather than raises it: and yet, artists we will be.

28   Therefore we must fearlessly pull out of ourselves and look at and identify with our lives the living creativity some of our great-grandmothers were not allowed to know. I stress *some* of them because it is well known that the majority of our great-grandmothers knew, even without

"knowing" it, the reality of their spirituality, even if they didn't recognize it beyond what happened in the singing at church—and they never had any intention of giving it up.

29   How they did it—those millions of black women who were not Phillis Wheatley, or Lucy Terry or Frances Harper or Zora Hurston or Nella Larsen or Bessie Smith; or Elizabeth Catlett, or Katherine Dunham, either—brings me to the title of this essay, "In Search of Our Mothers' Gardens," which is a personal account that is yet shared, in its theme and its meaning, by all of us. I found, while thinking about the far-reaching world of the creative black woman, that often the truest answer to a question that really matters can be found very close.

30   In the late 1920s my mother ran away from home to marry my father. Marriage, if not running away, was expected of seventeen-year-old girls. By the time she was twenty, she had two children and was pregnant with a third. Five children later, I was born. And this is how I came to know my mother: she seemed a large, soft, loving-eyed woman who was rarely impatient in our home. Her quick, violent temper was on view only a few times a year, when she battled with the white landlord who had the misfortune to suggest to her that her children did not need to go to school.

31   She made all the clothes we wore, even my brothers' overalls. She made all the towels and sheets we used. She spent the summers canning vegetables and fruits. She spent the winter evenings making quilts enough to cover all our beds.

32   During the "working" day, she labored beside—not behind—my father in the fields. Her day began before sunup, and did not end until late at night. There was never a moment for her to sit down, undisturbed, to unravel her own private thoughts; never a time free from interruption—by work or the noisy inquiries of her many children. And yet, it is to my mother—and all our mothers who were not famous—that I went in search of the secret of what has fed that muzzled and often mutilated, but vibrant, creative spirit that the black woman has inherited, and that pops out in wild and unlikely places to this day.

33   But when, you will ask, did my overworked mother have time to know or care about feeding the creative spirit?

34   The answer is so simple that many of us have spent years discovering it. We have constantly looked high, when we should have looked high—and low.

35   For example: in the Smithsonian Institution in Washington,
D.C., there hangs a quilt unlike any other in the world. In fanciful,
inspired, and yet simple and identifiable figures, it portrays the story of
the Crucifixion. It is considered rare, beyond price. Though it follows
no known pattern of quilt-making, and though it is made of bits and
pieces of worthless rags, it is obviously the work of a person of powerful
imagination and deep spiritual feeling. Below this quilt I saw a note that
says it was made by "an anonymous Black woman in Alabama, a hundred
years ago."

36   If we could locate this "anonymous" black woman from Alabama,
she would turn out to be one of our grandmothers—an artist who left
her mark in the only materials she could afford, and in the only medium
her position in society allowed her to use.

37   As Virginia Woolf wrote further, in *A Room of One's Own:*

Yet genius of a sort must have existed among women as it must have
existed among the working class. [Change this to "slaves" and "the wives and
daughters of sharecroppers."] Now and again an Emily Brontë or a Robert Burns
[change this to "a Zora Hurston or a Richard Wright"] blazes out and proves
its presence. But certainly it never got itself on to paper. When, however, one
reads of a witch being ducked, of a woman possessed by devils [or "Sainthood"],
of a wise woman selling herbs [our root workers], or even a very remarkable man
who had a mother, then I think we are on the track of a lost novelist, a
suppressed poet, of some mute and inglorious Jane Austen. . . . Indeed, I would
venture to guess that Anon, who wrote so many poems without signing them,
was often a woman. . . .

38   And so our mothers and grandmothers have, more often than not
anonymously, handed on the creative spark, the seed of the flower they
themselves never hoped to see: or like a sealed letter they could not
plainly read.

39   And so it is, certainly, with my own mother. Unlike "Ma"
Rainey's songs, which retained their creator's name even while blasting
forth from Bessie Smith's mouth, no song or poem will bear my mother's
name. Yet so many of the stories that I write, that we all write, are my
mother's stories. Only recently did I fully realize this: that through years
of listening to my mother's stories of her life, I have absorbed not only
the stories themselves, but something of the manner in which she spoke,
something of the urgency that involves the knowledge that her stories
—like her life—must be recorded. It is probably for this reason that so

much of what I have written is about characters whose counterparts in real life are so much older than I am.

40   But the telling of these stories, which came from my mother's lips as naturally as breathing, was not the only way my mother showed herself as an artist. For stories, too, were subject to being distracted, to dying without conclusion. Dinners must be started, and cotton must be gathered before the big rains. The artist that was and is my mother showed itself to me only after many years. This is what I finally noticed:

41   Like Mem, a character in *The Third Life of Grange Copeland*, my mother adorned with flowers whatever shabby house we were forced to live in. And not just your typical straggly country stand of zinnias, either. She planted ambitious gardens—and still does—with over fifty different varieties of plants that bloom profusely from early March until late November. Before she left home for the fields, she watered her flowers, chopped up the grass, and laid out new beds. When she returned from the fields she might divide clumps of bulbs, dig a cold pit, uproot and replant roses, or prune branches from her taller bushes or trees—until night came and it was too dark to see.

42   Whatever she planted grew as if by magic, and her fame as a grower of flowers spread over three counties. Because of her creativity with her flowers, even my memories of poverty are seen through a screen of blooms—sunflowers, petunias, roses, dahlias, forsythia, spirea, delphiniums, verbena . . . and on and on.

43   And I remember people coming to my mother's yard to be given cuttings from her flowers; I hear again the praise showered on her because whatever rocky soil she landed on, she turned into a garden. A garden so brilliant with colors, so original in its design, so magnificent with life and creativity, that to this day people drive by our house in Georgia—perfect strangers and imperfect strangers—and ask to stand or walk among my mother's art.

44   I notice that it is only when my mother is working in her flowers that she is radiant, almost to the point of being invisible—except as Creator: hand and eye. She is involved in work her soul must have. Ordering the universe in the image of her personal conception of Beauty.

45   Her face, as she prepares the Art that is her gift, is a legacy of respect she leaves to me, for all that illuminates and cherishes life. She has handed down respect for the possibilities—and the will to grasp them.

46   For her, so hindered and intruded upon in so many ways, being an artist has still been a daily part of her life. This ability to hold on, even in very simple ways, is work black women have done for a very long time.

47   This poem is not enough, but it is something, for the woman who literally covered the holes in our walls with sunflowers:

> They were women then
> My mama's generation
> Husky of voice—Stout of
> Step
> With fists as well as
> Hands
> How they battered down
> Doors
> And ironed
> Starched white
> Shirts
> How they led
> Armies
> Headragged Generals
> Across mined
> Fields
> Booby-trapped
> Kitchens
> To discover books
> Desks
> A place for us
> How they knew what we
> *Must* know
> Without knowing a page
> Of it
> Themselves.

48   Guided by my heritage of a love of beauty and a respect for strength—in search of my mother's garden, I found my own.

49   And perhaps in Africa over two hundred years ago, there was just such a mother; perhaps she painted vivid and daring decorations in oranges and yellows and greens on the walls of her hut; perhaps she sang —in a voice like Roberta Flack's—*sweetly* over the compounds of her village; perhaps she wove the most stunning mats or told the most

ingenious stories of all the village storytellers. Perhaps she was herself a poet—though only her daughter's name is signed to the poems that we know.

50   Perhaps Phillis Wheatley's mother was also an artist.

51   Perhaps in more than Phillis Wheatley's biological life is her mother's signature made clear.

QUESTIONS

Ideas

1. What does Walker propose as an answer to the question she asks in paragraph 11: "What did it mean for a black woman to be an artist in our grandmother's time?" How about the question she asks in paragraph 13: "How was the creativity of the black woman kept alive . . . century after century?"

2. Explain the relationships Walker postulates between sainthood, madness, and artistic creation.

3. Define in your own words the main point and purpose of this piece.

Organization

4. If the introductory portion of this essay comprises paragraphs 1–14, what constitutes its body and its conclusion?

5. What function do the paragraphs about Phillis Wheatley serve: What would be lost if they were to be omitted? Would anything be gained?

Sentences

6. Single out for analysis and study two sentences that strike you as arresting or beautiful. Account for their power.

7. What are the function and effect of the interrogative sentences in paragraphs 11, 12, 13, and 18?

Words

8. What is the point of the description in the opening of the essay of southern black women as saints?

9. What are the force and effect of the comparisons Walker alludes to in paragraph 9?

10. Explain the function and effect of the garden and flower images in paragraphs 41–45.

Suggestions for Writing

A. Write an essay recording your debt to someone or something in your past. Explain how the person or event has helped you become who and what you are. If a tribute seems in order, pay tribute—as Walker does.

B. Write an essay analyzing Walker's piece. Consider its main ideas; its structure, purpose, and tone; its language and imagery.

C. Compare this essay with Walker's tribute to Martin Luther King, Jr. in her essay, "Choice."

FIFTEEN

E. B. White

(1899–1985)

E. B. White is generally recognized as one of America's finest writers. Long associated with *The New Yorker,* for which he wrote stories, sketches, essays, and editorials, White has also contributed to another prominent magazine, *Harper's,* writing a monthly column, "One Man's Meat," from 1938 to 1943. These columns were collected and published with a few additional pieces from *The New Yorker* as *One Man's Meat* (1944). This book was followed by two other collections of miscellany, *The Second Tree from the Corner* (1954) and *The Points of My Compass* (1962). Besides these collections, White published, over a slightly longer span of years, three children's books: *Stuart Little* (1945), *Charlotte's Web* (1952), and *The Trumpet of the Swan* (1970). In 1976, White published a selection of his best essays, those, as he says, which had "an odor of durability clinging to them." *The Essays of E. B. White* were followed a year later by a selection of White's letters, entitled simply enough, *Letters of E. B. White. Poems and Sketches of E. B. White* appeared in 1981.

Though not a complete bibliography of White's published work, this list does suggest something of White's range and versatility, as well as something about the way writing has been for him steady work over a long stretch of time. And the steadiest of White's work, in both senses of the word, has been his essays. In fact, it is as an essayist that White is best known and most highly acclaimed. And it is as an essayist that he identifies himself, defining an essayist as "a self-liberated man sustained by the childish belief that everything he thinks about, everything that happens to him, is of general interest." And again, as one who is "content with living a free life and enjoying the satisfactions of a somewhat undisciplined existence."

Edward Hoagland has recently noted that White's name

has become almost synonymous with "essay." And for good reason, we might add, since it is the form most congenial to his temperament, a form that allows him the latitude he needs to roam freely in thought, a form that he has been able to stamp with his own imprint. This imprint is reflected in the following elements: a scrupulous respect for his readers; an uncanny accuracy in the use of language; and an uncommon delight in common, everyday things. White sees the extraordinary in the ordinary, noticing and valuing what most of us either overlook or take for granted. And from his repeated and respectful acts of attention flow reminiscences, speculations, explorations, and questions about our common humanity, about our relationships with one another, with the past, with the worlds of technology and nature.

White is a writer whose insights derive directly from his literal observations, from what he sees. Thoreau, one of White's favorite writers—and one with whom White has much in common—once remarked that "you can't say more than you can see." White's writing bears this out. The relationship between sight and insight, between observation and speculation, is evident in essays such as "The Ring of Time," which begins with a description of a circus act and ends with speculations about time and change, and "Once More to the Lake," in which White reminisces about his boyhood summer holidays in Maine, both describing the place with startling vividness and offering unsettling speculations about the meaning of his memories. In these and in other essays, White's writing is rooted in the crucial act of vision, a vision which sees into and beyond the surface of his subjects.

White's best writing, however, is more than a record of what he has seen and thought. It is also art, literature. His best work is crafted, shaped, formed with the same attention to details of structure, texture, image, and tone that a poet or painter, sculptor or novelist gives his work. In "The Ring of Time" and "Once More to the Lake," matters of fact, details of time, place, and circumstance give way to larger concerns. The circus is more than a circus ring: it becomes an emblem of time and change; the lake is more than a summer vacation place: it becomes an image of serenity and a reminder of time, change, even death. The images of light and water, the symbolism of circus ring and lake, along with a concern for understanding the present in relation to the past and the future— these lift their respective essays beyond the merely personal and reminiscent, beyond the ordinary and the everyday into the extraordinary universality of art.

About writing itself White has said a good deal, and said it well. In the chapter he contributed to the now famous *Elements of Style*, White notes that when we speak of a writer's style we mean "the sound his words make on paper." The voice that we hear is what distinguishes one writer from another; and it is one good reason why, to get a good sense of a writer's style, we should read his work aloud. Beyond this concern for hearing what language can do, White notes that a writer's style "reveals something of his spirit, his habits, his capacities, his bias . . . it is the Self escaping into the open." And, as White suggests, this Self cannot be hidden, for a writer's style "reveals his identity as surely as would his fingerprints."

Recognizing that writing is hard work requiring endurance, thought, and revision ("revising is part of writing"), White advises that the beginning writer let his ear be his guide, that he avoid all tricks and mannerisms, that he see writing as "one way to go about thinking," and, finally, that he achieve style both by affecting none and by believing "in the truth and worth of the scrawl."

Throughout his years as a writing man, White has often been asked for advice about writing. To one seeker he wrote: "Remember that writing is translation, and the opus to be translated is yourself." On another occasion he responded to a seventeen-year-old girl this way:

You asked me about writing—how I did it. There is no trick to it. If you like to write and want to write, you write, no matter where you are or what else you are doing or whether anyone pays any heed. . . . If you want to write about feelings, about the end of summer, about growing, write about it. A great deal of writing is not "plotted" —most of my essays have no plot structure, they are a ramble in the woods, or a ramble in the basement of my mind.

There is a naturalness, an ease about White's writing, both in these offhand remarks from his letters and in his more elaborately plotted essays. It is an ease that derives in part from a refusal to be either pompous or pedantic; it is an ease that derives also from a consistent attempt to be honest, to achieve the candor he admires in Montaigne; and it is a naturalness that is reflected in his style, a style that mingles the high subject and the low, the big word and the small, without flamboyance or

ostentation. White's style, in short, is a badge of his character
—intelligent, honest, witty, exact, and fundamentally endear-
ing.

The Essayist

---

1   The essayist is a self-liberated man, sustained by the childish belief that everything he thinks about, everything that happens to
him, is of general interest. He is a fellow who thoroughly enjoys his work,
just as people who take bird walks enjoy theirs. Each new excursion of
the essayist, each new "attempt," differs from the last and takes him into
new country. This delights him. Only a person who is congenitally
self-centered has the effrontery and the stamina to write essays.

2   There are as many kinds of essays as there are human attitudes or
poses, as many essay flavors as there are Howard Johnson ice creams. The
essayist arises in the morning and, if he has work to do, selects his garb
from an unusually extensive wardrobe: he can pull on any sort of shirt,
be any sort of person, according to his mood or his subject matter—
philosopher, scold, jester, raconteur, confidant, pundit, devil's advocate,
enthusiast. I like the essay, have always liked it, and even as a child was
at work, attempting to inflict my young thoughts and experiences on
others by putting them on paper. I early broke into print in the pages
of *St. Nicholas.* I tend still to fall back on the essay form (or lack of form)
when an idea strikes me, but I am not fooled about the place of the essay
in twentieth-century American letters—it stands a short distance down
the line. The essayist, unlike the novelist, the poet, and the playwright,
must be content in his self-imposed role of second-class citizen. A writer
who has his sights trained on the Nobel Prize or other earthly triumphs
had best write a novel, a poem, or a play, and leave the essayist to ramble
about, content with living a free life and enjoying the satisfactions of
a somewhat undisciplined existence. (Dr. Johnson called the essay "an
irregular, undigested piece"; this happy practitioner has no wish to
quarrel with the good doctor's characterization.)

3   There is one thing the essayist cannot do, though—he cannot
indulge himself in deceit or in concealment, for he will be found out in
no time. Desmond MacCarthy, in his introductory remarks to the 1928

E. P. Dutton & Company edition of Montaigne, observes that Montaigne "had the gift of natural candour. . . ." It is the basic ingredient. And even the essayist's escape from discipline is only a partial escape: the essay, although a relaxed form, imposes its own disciplines, raises its own problems, and these disciplines and problems soon become apparent and (we all hope) act as a deterrent to anyone wielding a pen merely because he entertains random thoughts or is in a happy or wandering mood.

4   I think some people find the essay the last resort of the egoist, a much too self-conscious and self-serving form for their taste; they feel that it is presumptuous of a writer to assume that his little excursions or his small observations will interest the reader. There is some justice in their complaint. I have always been aware that I am by nature self-absorbed and egoistical; to write of myself to the extent I have done indicates a too great attention to my own life, not enough to the lives of others. I have worn many shirts, and not all of them have been a good fit. But when I am discouraged or downcast I need only fling open the door of my closet, and there, hidden behind everything else, hangs the mantle of Michel de Montaigne, smelling slightly of camphor.

5   The essays in this collection cover a long expanse of time, a wide variety of subjects. I have chosen the ones that have amused me in the rereading, along with a few that seemed to have the odor of durability clinging to them. Some, like "Here is New York," have been seriously affected by the passage of time and now stand as period pieces. I wrote about New York in the summer of 1948, during a hot spell. The city I described has disappeared, and another city has emerged in its place —one that I'm not familiar with. But I remember the former one, with longing and with love. David McCord, in his book *About Boston* tells of a journalist from abroad visiting this country and seeing New York for the first time. He reported that it was "inspiring but temporary in appearance." I know what he means. The last time I visited New York, it seemed to have suffered a personality change, as though it had a brain tumor as yet undetected.

6   Two of the Florida pieces have likewise experienced a sea change. My remarks about the condition of the black race in the South have happily been nullified, and the pieces are merely prophetic, not definitive.

7   To assemble these essays I have rifled my other books and have added a number of pieces that are appearing for the first time between covers. Except for extracting three chapters, I have let "One Man's

Meat" alone, since it is a sustained report of about five years of country living—a report I prefer not to tamper with. The arrangement of the book is by subject matter or by mood or by place, not by chronology. Some of the pieces in the book carry a dateline, some do not. Chronology enters into the scheme, but neither the book nor its sections are perfectly chronological. Sometimes the reader will find me in the city when he thinks I am in the country, and the other way round. This may cause a mild confusion; it is unavoidable and easily explained. I spent a large part of the first half of my life as a city dweller, a large part of the second half as a countryman. In between, there were periods when nobody, including myself, quite knew (or cared) where I was: I thrashed back and forth between Maine and New York for reasons that seemed compelling at the time. Money entered into it, affection for *The New Yorker* magazine entered in. And affection for the city.

8   I have finally come to rest.

QUESTIONS

1. Why does White write? What image of the writer does he present? Why do you write, and more generally, why does anybody write?

2. What does White enjoy about being an essayist? What does he mean when he says that the essayist is "self-liberated"? Liberated from what and for what?

3. White defines an essay as an "attempt" and an "excursion." An attempt at what and an excursion where? And for what purpose?

4. What, according to White, distinguishes the essay from the novel, the story, and the poem? Do you agree with White's (and Dr. Johnson's) characterization of the essay as "an irregular undigested piece"? Why or why not?

5. At more than one point in this essay, White suggests that essayists are egoists. Is White an egocentric writer? Are you? Explain.

6. Explain the point of White's comparisons in paragraph 2, the comparisons between essays and ice cream, and between essays and clothes.

7. "The Essayist" can be divided into two parts: paragraphs 1–4 and paragraphs 5–8. What are the purpose and the point of each part?

Suggestions for Writing

A. White mentions that the essential characteristic of any essayist must be "candor." Discuss why you think this is or is not an essential quality of good writing. Include some discussion of other qualities you think a good essayist ought to possess, and why.

B. Examine the writing of one of the authors in this book for one or more of the following qualities: candor, humor, wit, subtlety, charm, egotism, arrogance, irony, satire, mystery, power.

C. White identifies himself as an essayist, a writer of essays. This is an important aspect of his self-image. Think of some aspect of your identity, or think of something you do that is important to your sense of who and what you are. Write an essay on the meaning and value of this—whatever it is.

The Sea and the Wind that Blows

1   Waking or sleeping, I dream of boats—usually of rather small boats under a slight press of sail. When I think how great a part of my life has been spent dreaming the hours away and how much of this total dream life has concerned small craft, I wonder about the state of my health, for I am told that it is not a good sign to be always voyaging into unreality, driven by imaginary breezes.

2   I have noticed that most men, when they enter a barber shop and must wait their turn, drop into a chair and pick up a magazine. I simply sit down and pick up the thread of my sea wandering, which began more than fifty years ago and is not quite ended. There is hardly a waiting room in the East that has not served as my cockpit, whether I was waiting to board a train or to see a dentist. And I am usually still trimming sheets when the train starts or the drill begins to whine.

3   If a man must be obsessed by something, I suppose a boat is as good as anything, perhaps a bit better than most. A small sailing craft is not only beautiful, it is seductive and full of strange promise and the hint of trouble. If it happens to be an auxiliary cruising boat, it is without question the most compact and ingenious arrangement for living ever devised by the restless mind of man—a home that is stable without being stationary, shaped less like a box than like a fish or a bird or a girl, and in which the homeowner can remove his daily affairs as far from shore as he has the nerve to take them, close-hauled or running free— parlor, bedroom, and bath, suspended and alive.

4   Men who ache all over for tidiness and compactness in their lives

often find relief for their pain in the cabin of a thirty-foot sailboat at anchor in a sheltered cove. Here the sprawling panoply of The Home is compressed in orderly miniature and liquid delirium, suspended between the bottom of the sea and the top of the sky, ready to move on in the morning by the miracle of canvas and the witchcraft of rope. It is small wonder that men hold boats in the secret place of their mind, almost from the cradle to the grave.

5   Along with my dream of boats has gone the ownership of boats, a long succession of them upon the surface of the sea, many of them makeshift and crank. Since childhood I have managed to have some sort of sailing craft and to raise a sail in fear. Now, in my seventies, I still own a boat, still raise my sail in fear in answer to the summons of the unforgiving sea. Why does the sea attract me in the way it does? Whence comes this compulsion to hoist a sail, actually or in dream? My first encounter with the sea was a case of hate at first sight. I was taken, at the age of four, to a bathing beach in New Rochelle. Everything about the experience frightened and repelled me: the taste of salt in my mouth, the foul chill of the wooden bathhouse, the littered sand, the stench of the tide flats. I came away hating and fearing the sea. Later, I found that what I had feared and hated, I now feared and loved.

6   I returned to the sea of necessity, because it would support a boat; and although I knew little of boats, I could not get them out of my thoughts. I became a pelagic boy. The sea became my unspoken challenge: the wind, the tide, the fog, the ledge, the bell, the gull that cried help, the never-ending threat and bluff of weather. Once having permitted the wind to enter the belly of my sail, I was not able to quit the helm; it was as though I had seized hold of a high-tension wire and could not let go.

7   I liked to sail alone. The sea was the same as a girl to me—I did not want anyone else along. Lacking instruction, I invented ways of getting things done, and usually ended by doing them in a rather queer fashion, and so did not learn to sail properly, and still cannot sail well, although I have been at it all my life. I was twenty before I discovered that charts existed; all my navigating up to that time was done with the wariness and the ignorance of the early explorers. I was thirty before I learned to hang a coiled halyard on its cleat as it should be done. Until then I simply coiled it down on deck and dumped the coil. I was always in trouble and always returned, seeking more trouble. Sailing became a compulsion: there lay the boat, swinging to her mooring, there blew the wind; I had no choice but to go. My earliest boats were so small that

when the wind failed, or when I failed, I could switch to manual control
—I could paddle or row home. But then I graduated to boats that only
the wind was strong enough to move. When I first dropped off my
mooring in such a boat, I was an hour getting up the nerve to cast off
the pennant. Even now, with a thousand little voyages notched in my
belt, I still feel a memorial chill on casting off, as the gulls jeer and the
empty mainsail claps.

8   Of late years, I have noticed that my sailing has increasingly
become a compulsive activity rather than a simple source of pleasure.
There lies the boat, there blows the morning breeze—it is a point of
honor, now, to go. I am like an alcoholic who cannot put his bottle out
of his life. With me, I cannot not sail. Yet I know well enough that I
have lost touch with the wind and, in fact, do not like the wind anymore.
It jiggles me up, the wind does, and what I really love are windless days,
when all is peace. There is a great question in my mind whether a man
who is against wind should longer try to sail a boat. But this is an
intellectual response—the old yearning is still in me, belonging to the
past, to youth, and so I am torn between past and present, a common
disease of later life.

9   When does a man quit the sea? How dizzy, how bumbling must he
be? Does he quit while he's ahead, or wait till he makes some major
mistake, like falling overboard or being flattened by an accidental jibe?
This past winter I spent hours arguing the question with myself. Finally,
deciding that I had come to the end of the road, I wrote a note to the
boatyard, putting my boat up for sale. I said I was "coming off the water."
But as I typed the sentence, I doubted that I meant a word of it.

10   If no buyer turns up, I know what will happen: I will instruct the
yard to put her in again—"just till somebody comes along." And then
there will be the old uneasiness, the old uncertainty, as the mild southeast breeze ruffles the cove, a gentle, steady, morning breeze, bringing
the taint of the distant wet world, the smell that takes a man back to
the very beginning of time, linking him to all that has gone before.
There will lie the sloop, there will blow the wind, once more I will get
under way. And as I reach across to the red nun off the Torry Islands,
dodging the trap buoys and toggles, the shags gathered on the ledge will
note my passage. "There goes the old boy again," they will say. "One
more rounding of his little Horn, one more conquest of his Roaring
Forties." And with the tiller in my hand, I'll feel again the wind impart-
ing life to a boat, will smell again the old menace, the one that imparts
life to me: the cruel beauty of the salt world, the barnacle's tiny knives,

the sharp spine of the urchin, the stinger of the sun jelly, the claw of the crab.

QUESTIONS

Ideas

1. How does White suggest the strength of his attraction to sailing? What, specifically, attracts him?
2. There is evidence that White is writing of more than his love of sailing. What else is his subject? Where do you find hints of deeper meanings?

Organization

3. White begins by writing that he often dreams of sailing. Where does he go from there? Chart the course of White's thought by identifying how he gets from one aspect of his subject to another.
4. The essay can be divided into three sections: paragraphs 1–4, 5–7, and 8–10. What are the concerns of each section and how are the sections related?

Sentences

5. In paragraphs 5 and 6 White stacks details, piling them up behind a colon. Examine the following examples:

> (a) Everything about the experience frightened and repelled me:
>   the taste of salt in my mouth,
>   the foul chill of the wooden bathhouse,
>   the littered sand,
>   the stench of the tide flats.

Should White have put the word "and" between the last two details?

> (b) The sea became my unspoken challenge:
>   the wind,
>   the tide,
>   the fog,
>   the ledge,
>   the gull that cried help,
>   the never ending threat and bluff of weather.

Would it make much difference if the details were reordered? Try moving the items around. Compare your versions with those of other students and with White's original. Which version do you prefer and why?

(c) And with the tiller in my hand
> I'll feel again the wind imparting life to a boat,
> will smell again the old menace,
>> the one that imparts life to me:
>>> the cruel beauty of the salt world,
>>> the barnacles' tiny knives,
>>> the sharp spine of the urchin,
>>> the stinger of the sun jelly,
>>> the claw of the crab.

In this last example you can see the balance of phrasing White achieves in the second and third lines and in the third and fourth, and of course in the stacked details of lines 5–9.

6. Twice in the essay, in paragraphs 5 and 9, White strings questions together. Why? What do these questions accomplish? Would a conversion to statements alter the meaning or change the effect of either paragraphs? Why or why not?

7. As the final sentence of paragraph 4 White wrote:

> It is small wonder that men hold boats in the secret place of their mind, almost from the cradle to the grave.

How do these revisions compare with White's original?

(a) It is small wonder that boats are so important to men.
(b) It is small wonder that men hold boats in such high regard.

Reread this sentence in context (paragraph 4). What unusual words and phrases provide a contrasting backdrop to its easy familiarity? What other conversational phrases occur in the paragraph?

8. In paragraph 8 White writes a brief striking sentence:

> With me, I cannot not sail.

If we eliminate the double negative we get: With me, I can sail. What is the difference?

Words

9. White uses many specific details and much concrete language. Select one passage in which precise, specific language enables you to envision or imagine what White describes.

10. Throughout the essay, White uses comparisons—for different reasons and with different effects. Explain the meaning and the feeling behind each of the following comparisons:

a) the miracle of canvas and the witchcraft of rope. (4)
b) I am like an alcoholic who cannot put his bottle out of his life. (8)

c) it was as though I had seized hold of a high-tension wire and could not let go. (6)

What comparison is developed in paragraph 3? What does it imply about White's attitude toward boats and the sea?

11. In the final paragraph, you will notice quotation marks around some phrases and sentences. Why are they there? Can they be omitted?

Suggestions for Writing

A. In the beginning and at the end of paragraph 5 White repeats words and phrases. Rewrite the paragraph without the repetitions. Compare your version with those of other students and with White's paragraph.

B. Write imitations of the sentences in questions 5, 6, 7, and 8.

C. Write an imitation of either paragraph 5 or paragraph 9.

D. Most of us are strongly attracted to some special activity or hobby. In an essay, discuss one of your favorite activities, explaining what draws you to it. Try to explain why it attracts you as powerfully as it does.

Good-bye to Forty-eighth Street

Turtle Bay, November 12, 1957

1   For some weeks now I have been engaged in dispersing the contents of this apartment, trying to persuade hundreds of inanimate objects to scatter and leave me alone. It is not a simple matter. I am impressed by the reluctance of one's worldly goods to go out again into the world. During September I kept hoping that some morning, as by magic, all books, pictures, records, chairs, beds, curtains, lamps, china, glass, utensils, keepsakes would drain away from around my feet, like the outgoing tide, leaving me standing silent on a bare beach. But this did not happen. My wife and I diligently sorted and discarded things from day to day, and packed other objects for the movers, but a six-room apartment holds as much paraphernalia as an aircraft carrier. You can whittle away at it, but to empty the place completely takes real ingenuity and great staying power. On one of the mornings of disposal, a man from

a secondhand bookstore visited us, bought several hundred books, and told us of the death of his brother, the word "cancer" exploding in the living room like a time bomb detonated by his grief. Even after he had departed with his heavy load, there seemed to be almost as many books as before, and twice as much sorrow.

2   Every morning, when I left for work, I would take something in my hand and walk off with it, for deposit in the big municipal wire trash basket at the corner of Third, on the theory that the physical act of disposal was the real key to the problem. My wife, a strategist, knew better and began quietly mobilizing the forces that would eventually put our goods to rout. A man could walk away for a thousand mornings carrying something with him to the corner and there would still be a home full of stuff. It is not possible to keep abreast of the normal tides of acquisition. A home is like a reservoir equipped with a check valve: the valve permits influx but prevents outflow. Acquisition goes on night and day—smoothly, subtly, imperceptibly. I have no sharp taste for acquiring things, but it is not necessary to desire things in order to acquire them. Goods and chattels seek a man out; they find him even though his guard is up. Books and oddities arrive in the mail. Gifts arrive on anniversaries and fête days. Veterans send ballpoint pens. Banks send memo books. If you happen to be a writer, readers send whatever may be cluttering up their own lives; I had a man once send me a chip of wood that showed the marks of a beaver's teeth. Someone dies, and a little trickle of indestructible keepsakes appears, to swell the flood. This steady influx is not counterbalanced by any comparable outgo. Under ordinary circumstances, the only stuff that leaves a home is paper trash and garbage; everything else stays on and digs in.

3   Lately we haven't spent our nights in the apartment; we are bivouacked in a hotel and just come here mornings to continue the work. Each of us has a costume. My wife steps into a cotton dress while I shift into midnight-blue tropical pants and bowling shoes. Then we buckle down again to the unending task.

4   All sorts of special problems arise during the days of disposal. Anyone who is willing to put his mind to it can get rid of a chair, say, but what about a trophy? Trophies are like leeches. The ones made of paper, such as a diploma from a school or a college, can be burned if you have the guts to light the match, but the ones made of bronze not only are indestructible but are almost impossible to throw away, because they usually carry your name, and a man doesn't like to throw away his good name, or even his bad one. Some busybody might find it. People

differ in their approach to trophies, of course. In watching Edward R. Murrow's "Person to Person" program on television, I have seen several homes that contained a "trophy room," in which the celebrated pack rat of the house had assembled all his awards, so that they could give out the concentrated aroma of achievement whenever he wished to loiter in such an atmosphere. This is all very well if you enjoy the stale smell of success, but if a man doesn't care for that air he is in a real fix when disposal time comes up. One day a couple of weeks ago, I sat for a while staring moodily at a plaque that had entered my life largely as a result of some company's zest for promotion. It was bronze on walnut, heavy enough to make an anchor for a rowboat, but I didn't need a rowboat anchor, and this thing had my name on it. By deft work with a screwdriver, I finally succeeded in prying the nameplate off; I pocketed this, and carried the mutilated remains to the corner, where the wire basket waited. The work exhausted me more than did the labor for which the award was presented.

5   Another day, I found myself on a sofa between the chip of wood gnawed by the beaver and an honorary hood I had once worn in an academic procession. What I really needed at the moment was the beaver himself, to eat the hood. I shall never wear the hood again, but I have too weak a character to throw it away, and I do not doubt that it will tag along with me to the end of my days, not keeping me either warm or happy but occupying a bit of my attic space.

6   Right in the middle of the dispersal, while the mournful rooms were still loaded with loot, I had a wonderful idea: we would shut the apartment, leave everything to soak for a while, and go to the Fryeburg Fair, in Maine, where we could sit under a tent at a cattle auction and watch somebody else trying to dispose of something. A fair, of course, is a dangerous spot if a man is hoping to avoid acquisition, and the truth is I came close to acquiring a very pretty whiteface heifer, safe in calf —which would have proved easily as burdensome as a chip of wood gnawed by a beaver. But Fryeburg is where some of my wife's ancestors lived, and is in the valley of the Saco, looking west to the mountains, and the weather promised to be perfect, and the premium list of the Agricultural Society said, "Should Any Day Be Stormy, the Exercises for That Day Will Be Postponed to the First Fair Day," and I would rather have a ringside seat at a cattle sale than a box at the opera, so we picked up and left town, deliberately overshooting Fryeburg by 175 miles in order to sleep one night at home.

7   The day we spent at the Fryeburg Fair was the day the first little

moon was launched by the new race of moon-makers. Had I known in advance that a satellite was about to be added to my world, in this age of additives, I might have stayed in New York and sulked instead of going to the Fair, but in my innocence I was able to enjoy a day watching the orbiting of trotting horses—an ancient terrestrial phenomenon that has given pleasure to unnumbered thousands. We attended the calf scramble, the pig scramble, and the baby-beef auction; we ate lunch in the back seat of our flashy old 1949 automobile, parked in the infield; and then I found myself a ringside seat with my feet in the shavings at the Hereford sale, under the rattling tongue and inexorable hammer of auctioneer Dick Murray, enjoying the wild look in the whites of a cow's eyes.

8   The day had begun under the gray blanket of a fall overcast, but the sky soon cleared. Nobody had heard of the Russian moon. The wheels wheeled, the chairs spun, the cotton candy tinted the faces of children, the bright leaves tinted the woods and hills. A cluster of amplifiers spread the theme of love over everything and everybody; the mild breeze spread the dust over everything and everybody. Next morning, in the Lafayette Hotel in Portland, I went down to breakfast and found May Craig looking solemn at one of the tables and Mr. Murray, the auctioneer, looking cheerful at another. The newspaper headlines told of the moon. At that hour of the morning, I could not take in the exact significance, if any, of a national heavenly body. But I was glad I had spent the last day of the natural firmament at the One Hundred and Seventh Annual Exhibition of the West Oxford Agricultural Society. I see nothing in space as promising as the view from a Ferris wheel.

9   But that was weeks ago. As I sit here this afternoon in this disheveled room, surrounded by the boxes and bales that hold my undisposable treasure, I feel the onset of melancholy. I look out onto Forty-eighth Street; one out of every ten passers-by is familiar to me. After a dozen years of gazing idly at the passing show, I have assembled, quite unbeknownst to them, a cast of characters that I depend on. They are the nameless actors who have a daily walk-on part in my play—the greatest of dramas. I shall miss them all, them and their dogs. Even more, I think, I shall miss the garden out back—the wolf whistle of the starling, the summer-night murmur of the fountain; the cat, the vine, the sky, the willow. And the visiting birds of spring and fall—the small, shy birds that drop in for one drink and stay two weeks. Over a period of thirty years, I have occupied eight caves in New York, eight digs—four in the Village, one on Murray Hill, three in Turtle Bay. In New York, a citizen

is likely to keep on the move, shopping for the perfect arrangement of rooms and vistas, changing his habitation according to fortune, whim, and need. And in every place he abandons he leaves something vital, it seems to me, and starts his new life somewhat less encrusted, like a lobster that has shed its skin and is for a time soft and vulnerable.

QUESTIONS

Ideas

1. What is White's purpose in this essay? Is he trying to convince us of something? Is he concerned with amusing us? With something else?
2. Why does White find it so hard to throw things away? Why does he find it so difficult to leave? Are you convinced of these difficulties? Why or why not?
3. What does White mean by saying that when a person moves he leaves something vital behind?

Organization

4. How is this essay organized? And how does White help us keep our bearings as we read?
5. Paragraphs 6, 7, and 8 form a digression from the main business of the essay. Are these paragraphs necessary? How would the essay read if you cut them out, connecting paragraph 5 directly with paragraph 9?
6. Reread paragraph 4 carefully. The first sentence is the controlling sentence: it contains the main point and provides a center of gravity. Explain how the rest of the paragraph opens out of and develops the opening sentence.

Sentences

7. Throughout "Good-bye to Forty-eighth Street," White writes sentences with balanced phrasing. In paragraph 2, for example, he writes:

> The valve permits influx
>   but prevents outflow.

and

> It is not necessary to desire things
>   in order to acquire them.

What advantage does such balanced phrasing provide? (Note also the parallels of sound in each example.)

8. Paragraph 2 is noteworthy for another kind of balance—the balance of long and short sentences. The first three sentences are loose and expansive; the next three are shorter, more cryptic. What is the tone of each set of sentences? Is there any advantage in using the two kinds of sentences together?

9. In the following sentences White splits the information he wants to convey, using a colon. What is the effect of the colon in these sentences, and what is the relationship of the right-hand part of each sentence to the left-hand side?

> A home is like a reservoir equipped with a check valve: the valve permits influx but prevents outflow.

> Right in the middle of the dispersal, while the mournful rooms were still loaded with loot, I had a wonderful idea: we would shut the apartment, leave everything to soak for a while, and go to the Fryeburg Fair, in Maine, where we could sit under a tent at a cattle auction and watch somebody else trying to dispose of something.

10. In paragraph 2 White uses a sentence that contains a dash:

> Acquisition goes on night and day—smoothly, subtly, imperceptibly.

If we make one small change in the sentence—substitute a comma for the dash—there is a difference.

> Acquisition goes on night and day, smoothly, subtly, imperceptibly.

And if we take the comma out we get this:

> Acquisition goes on night and day smoothly, subtly, imperceptibly.

Which version do you prefer and why?

11. Examine in paragraphs 6 and 9 sentences that contain a dash. What generalizations can you make about the use of the dash based on the ways White uses it?

Words

12. In the first sentence of the essay, White remarks that he tries to "persuade" the objects to leave him alone. Isn't that rather strange language for talking about the contents of an apartment? How is that kind of animating and personifying language carried through and modified in the remainder of the essay? Look, for example, at paragraph 2, where White says that his wife, a "strategist," began "mobilizing the forces that would

eventually put our goods to rout." What other imagery is used to describe the various items to be discarded and the way they remain undiscarded?

13. White's diction in "Good-bye to Forty-eighth Street" is a mix of the everyday with the occasional, the common with the recondite. Big words jostle small; words of Latin derivation sit alongside native, Saxon words. In paragraph 1, for example, "dispersing," "inanimate," and "reluctance" exist beside "leave me alone," "go out again into the world," and "It is not a simple matter." Later (paragraphs 2 and 4) "home full of stuff" occurs alongside "tides of acquisition," and "if you have the guts" is followed a bit later by "the concentrated aroma of achievement." What effect is achieved by balancing and combining the two kinds of language in this way?

14. Throughout the essay White repeats varied forms of two words that establish the focus and center of gravity of the piece. These words, "acquisition" and "disposal," reappear as "acquire" and "acquiring"; "dispose," "undisposable," "dispersal," and "dispersing." Would White have been better off substituting different words—synonyms—for disposal and acquisition? Or is there an advantage to repeating related forms of a word?

15. In paragraph 4 White uses the following phrases:

> the concentrated aroma of achievement
> the stale smell of success

What is the difference between them? What would be gained or lost if you switched the final word of each?

> the concentrated aroma of success
> the stale smell of achievement

Suggestions for Writing

A. Discuss the idea White mentions in his final paragraph: that you leave a part of yourself when you move from a place you love.

B. Describe something that has been hard for you to give up, to let go of. Explain why this separation was difficult for you, how it affected you.

C. Describe a time when you had to move from a place where you felt at home. Try to give the reader a sense of how you felt and why. Explain what you were leaving and what you thought you were heading for. You might compare what you left to what you found.

D. Write imitations of the sentences discussed in questions 7, 9, and 10.

E. Compare this essay with Joan Didion's "Goodbye to All That," pp. 97–105. Consider what the essays have in common and how they differ. Attend to the writers' styles, voices, structures, language, attitudes, and ideas.

Death of a Pig

Autumn 1947

1   I spent several days and nights in mid-September with an ailing pig and I feel driven to account for this stretch of time, more particularly since the pig died at last, and I lived, and things might easily have gone the other way round and none left to do the accounting. Even now, so close to the event, I cannot recall the hours sharply and am not ready to say whether death came on the third night or the fourth night. This uncertainty afflicts me with a sense of personal deterioration; if I were in decent health I would know how many nights I had sat up with a pig.

2   The scheme of buying a spring pig in blossomtime, feeding it through summer and fall, and butchering it when the solid cold weather arrives, is a familiar scheme to me and follows an antique pattern. It is a tragedy enacted on most farms with perfect fidelity to the original script. The murder, being premeditated, is in the first degree but is quick and skillful, and the smoked bacon and ham provide a ceremonial ending whose fitness is seldom questioned.

3   Once in a while something slips—one of the actors goes up in his lines and the whole performance stumbles and halts. My pig simply failed to show up for a meal. The alarm spread rapidly. The classic outline of the tragedy was lost. I found myself cast suddenly in the role of pig's friend and physician—a farcical character with an enema bag for a prop. I had a presentiment, the very first afternoon, that the play would never regain its balance and that my sympathies were now wholly with the pig. This was slapstick—the sort of dramatic treatment that instantly appealed to my old dachshund, Fred, who joined the vigil, held the bag, and, when all was over, presided at the interment. When we slid the body into the grave, we both were shaken to the core. The loss we felt was not the loss of ham but the loss of pig. He had evidently become precious to me, not that he represented a distant nourishment in a hungry time, but that he had suffered in a suffering world. But I'm running ahead of my story and shall have to go back.

4   My pigpen is at the bottom of an old orchard below the house. The pigs I have raised have lived in a faded building that once was an ice-house. There is a pleasant yard to move about in, shaded by an apple

tree that overhangs the low rail fence. A pig couldn't ask for anything better—or none has, at any rate. The sawdust in the icehouse makes a comfortable bottom in which to root, and a warm bed. This sawdust, however, came under suspicion when the pig took sick. One of my neighbors said he thought the pig would have done better on new ground—the same principle that applies in planting potatoes. He said there might be something unhealthy about that sawdust, that he never thought well of sawdust.

5   It was about four o'clock in the afternoon when I first noticed that there was something wrong with the pig. He failed to appear at the trough for his supper, and when a pig (or a child) refuses supper a chill wave of fear runs through any household, or ice-household. After examining my pig, who was stretched out in the sawdust inside the building, I went to the phone and cranked it four times. Mr. Dameron answered. "What's good for a sick pig?" I asked. (There is never any identification needed on a country phone; the person on the other end knows who is talking by the sound of the voice and by the character of the question.)

6   "I don't know, I never had a sick pig," said Mr. Dameron, "but I can find out quick enough. You hang up and I'll call Henry."

7   Mr. Dameron was back on the line again in five minutes. "Henry says roll him over on his back and give him two ounces of castor oil or sweet oil, and if that doesn't do the trick give him an injection of soapy water. He says he's almost sure the pig's plugged up, and even if he's wrong, it can't do any harm."

8   I thanked Mr. Dameron. I didn't go right down to the pig, though. I sank into a chair and sat still for a few minutes to think about my troubles, and then I got up and went to the barn, catching up on some odds and ends that needed tending to. Unconsciously I held off, for an hour, the deed by which I would officially recognize the collapse of the performance of raising a pig; I wanted no interruption in the regularity of feeding, the steadiness of growth, the even succession of days. I wanted no interruption, wanted no oil, no deviation. I just wanted to keep on raising a pig, full meal after full meal, spring into summer into fall. I didn't even know whether there were two ounces of castor oil on the place.

9   Shortly after five o'clock I remembered that we had been invited out to dinner that night and realized that if I were to dose a pig there was no time to lose. The dinner date seemed a familiar conflict: I move in a desultory society and often a week or two will roll by without my going to anybody's house to dinner or anyone's coming to mine, but

when an occasion does arise, and I am summoned, something usually turns up (an hour or two in advance) to make all human intercourse seem vastly inappropriate. I have come to believe that there is in hostesses a special power of divination, and that they deliberately arrange dinners to coincide with pig failure or some other sort of failure. At any rate, it was after five o'clock and I knew I could put off no longer the evil hour.

10   When my son and I arrived at the pigyard, armed with a small bottle of castor oil and a length of clothesline, the pig had emerged from his house and was standing in the middle of his yard, listlessly. He gave us a slim greeting. I could see that he felt uncomfortable and uncertain. I had brought the clothesline thinking I'd have to tie him (the pig weighed more than a hundred pounds) but we never used it. My son reached down, grabbed both front legs, upset him quickly, and when he opened his mouth to scream I turned the oil into his throat—a pink, corrugated area I had never seen before. I had just time to read the label while the neck of the bottle was in his mouth. It said Puretest. The screams, slightly muffled by oil, were pitched in the hysterically high range of pig-sound, as though torture were being carried out, but they didn't last long: it was all over rather suddenly, and, his legs released, the pig righted himself.

11   In the upset position the corners of his mouth had been turned down, giving him a frowning expression. Back on his feet again, he regained the set smile that a pig wears even in sickness. He stood his ground, sucking slightly at the residue of oil; a few drops leaked out of his lips while his wicked eyes, shaded by their coy little lashes, turned on me in disgust and hatred. I scratched him gently with oily fingers and he remained quiet, as though trying to recall the satisfaction of being scratched when in health, and seeming to rehearse in his mind the indignity to which he had just been subjected. I noticed, as I stood there, four or five small dark spots on his back near the tail end, reddish brown in color, each about the size of a housefly. I could not make out what they were. They did not look troublesome but at the same time they did not look like mere surface bruises or chafe marks. Rather they seemed blemishes of internal origin. His stiff white bristles almost completely hid them and I had to part the bristles with my fingers to get a good look.

12   Several hours later, a few minutes before midnight, having dined well and at someone else's expense, I returned to the pighouse with a flashlight. The patient was asleep. Kneeling, I felt his ears (as you might

put your hand on the forehead of a child) and they seemed cool, and then with the light made a careful examination of the yard and the house for sign that the oil had worked. I found none and went to bed.

13   We had been having an unseasonable spell of weather—hot, close days, with the fog shutting in every night, scaling for a few hours in midday, then creeping back again at dark, drifting in first over the trees on the point, then suddenly blowing across the fields, blotting out the world and taking possession of houses, men, and animals. Everyone kept hoping for a break, but the break failed to come. Next day was another hot one. I visited the pig before breakfast and tried to tempt him with a little milk in his trough. He just stared at it, while I made a sucking sound through my teeth to remind him of past pleasures of the feast. With very small, timid pigs, weanlings, this ruse is often quite successful and will encourage them to eat; but with a large, sick pig the ruse is senseless and the sound I made must have made him feel, if anything, more miserable. He not only did not crave food, he felt a positive revulsion to it. I found a place under the apple tree where he had vomited in the night.

14   At this point, although a depression had settled over me, I didn't suppose that I was going to lose my pig. From the lustiness of a healthy pig a man derives a feeling of personal lustiness; the stuff that goes into the trough and is received with such enthusiasm is an earnest of some later feast of his own, and when this suddenly comes to an end and the food lies stale and untouched, souring in the sun, the pig's imbalance becomes the man's, vicariously, and life seems insecure, displaced, transitory.

15   As my own spirits declined, along with the pig's, the spirits of my vile old dachshund rose. The frequency of our trips down the footpath through the orchard to the pigyard delighted him, although he suffers greatly from arthritis, moves with difficulty, and would be bedridden if he could find anyone willing to serve him meals on a tray.

16   He never missed a chance to visit the pig with me, and he made many professional calls on his own. You could see him down there at all hours, his white face parting the grass along the fence as he wobbled and stumbled about, his stethoscope dangling—a happy quack, writing his villainous prescriptions and grinning his corrosive grin. When the enema bag appeared, and the bucket of warm suds, his happiness was complete, and he managed to squeeze his enormous body between the two lowest rails of the yard and then assumed full charge of the irriga-

tion. Once, when I lowered the bag to check the flow, he reached in and hurriedly drank a few mouthfuls of the suds to test their potency. I have noticed that Fred will feverishly consume any substance that is associated with trouble—the bitter flavor is to his liking. When the bag was above reach, he concentrated on the pig and was everywhere at once, a tower of strength and inconvenience. The pig, curiously enough, stood rather quietly through this colonic carnival, and the enema, though ineffective, was not as difficult as I had anticipated.

17 I discovered, though, that once having given a pig an enema there is no turning back, no chance of resuming one of life's more stereotyped roles. The pig's lot and mine were inextricably bound now, as though the rubber tube were the silver cord. From then until the time of his death I held the pig steadily in the bowl of my mind; the task of trying to deliver him from his misery became a strong obsession. His suffering soon became the embodiment of all earthly wretchedness. Along toward the end of the afternoon, defeated in physicking, I phoned the veterinary twenty miles away and placed the case formally in his hands. He was full of questions, and when I casually mentioned the dark spots on the pig's back, his voice changed its tone.

18 "I don't want to scare you," he said, "but when there are spots, erysipelas has to be considered."

19 Together we considered erysipelas, with frequent interruptions from the telephone operator, who wasn't sure the connection had been established.

20 "If a pig has erysipelas can he give it to a person?" I asked.

21 "Yes, he can," replied the vet.

22 "Have they answered?" asked the operator.

23 "Yes, they have," I said. Then I addressed the vet again. "You better come over here and examine this pig right away."

24 "I can't come myself," said the vet, "but McFarland can come this evening if that's all right. Mac knows more about pigs than I do anyway. You needn't worry too much about the spots. To indicate erysipelas they would have to be deep hemorrhagic infarcts."

25 "Deep hemorrhagic what?" I asked.

26 "Infarcts," said the vet.

27 "Have they answered?" asked the operator.

28 "Well," I said, "I don't know what you'd call these spots, except they're about the size of a housefly. If the pig has erysipelas I guess I have it, too, by this time, because we've been very close lately."

29 "McFarland will be over," said the vet.

30   I hung up. My throat felt dry and I went to the cupboard and got a bottle of whiskey. Deep hemorrhagic infarcts—the phrase began fastening its hooks in my head. I had assumed that there could be nothing much wrong with a pig during the months it was being groomed for murder; my confidence in the essential health and endurance of pigs had been strong and deep, particularly in the health of pigs that belonged to me and that were part of my proud scheme. The awakening had been violent and I minded it all the more because I knew that what could be true of my pig could be true also of the rest of my tidy world. I tried to put this distasteful idea from me, but it kept recurring. I took a short drink of the whiskey and then, although I wanted to go down to the yard and look for fresh signs, I was scared to. I was certain I had erysipelas.

31   It was long after dark and the supper dishes had been put away when a car drove in and McFarland got out. He had a girl with him. I could just make her out in the darkness—she seemed young and pretty. "This is Miss Owen," he said. "We've been having a picnic supper on the shore, that's why I'm late."

32   McFarland stood in the driveway and stripped off his jacket, then his shirt. His stocky arms and capable hands showed up in my flashlight's gleam as I helped him find his coverall and get zipped up. The rear seat of his car contained an astonishing amount of paraphernalia, which he soon overhauled, selecting a chain, a syringe, a bottle of oil, a rubber tube, and some other things I couldn't identify. Miss Owen said she'd go along with us and see the pig. I led the way down the warm slope of the orchard, my light picking out the path for them, and we all three climbed the fence, entered the pighouse, and squatted by the pig while McFarland took a rectal reading. My flashlight picked up the glitter of an engagement ring on the girl's hand.

33   "No elevation," said McFarland, twisting the thermometer in the light. "You needn't worry about erysipelas." He ran his hand slowly over the pig's stomach and at one point the pig cried out in pain.

34   "Poor piggledy-wiggledy!" said Miss Owen.

35   The treatment I had been giving the pig for two days was then repeated, somewhat more expertly, by the doctor, Miss Owen and I handing him things as he needed them—holding the chain that he had looped around the pig's upper jaw, holding the syringe, holding the bottle stopper, the end of the tube, all of us working in darkness and in comfort, working with the instinctive teamwork induced by emergency conditions, the pig unprotesting, the house shadowy, protecting, intimate. I went to bed tired but with a feeling of relief that I had turned

over part of the responsibility of the case to a licensed doctor. I was beginning to think, though, that the pig was not going to live.

36   He died twenty-four hours later, or it might have been forty-eight —there is a blur in time here, and I may have lost or picked up a day in the telling and the pig one in the dying. At intervals during the last day I took cool fresh water down to him and at such times as he found the strength to get to his feet he would stand with head in the pail and snuffle his snout around. He drank a few sips but no more; yet it seemed to comfort him to dip his nose in water and bobble it about, sucking in and blowing out through his teeth. Much of the time, now, he lay indoors half buried in sawdust. Once, near the last, while I was attending him I saw him try to make a bed for himself but he lacked the strength, and when he set his snout into the dust he was unable to plow even the little furrow he needed to lie down in.

37   He came out of the house to die. When I went down, before going to bed, he lay stretched in the yard a few feet from the door. I knelt, saw that he was dead, and left him there: his face had a mild look, expressive neither of deep peace nor of deep suffering, although I think he had suffered a good deal. I went back up to the house and to bed, and cried internally—deep hemorrhagic intears. I didn't wake till nearly eight the next morning, and when I looked out the open window the grave was already being dug, down beyond the dump under a wild apple. I could hear the spade strike against the small rocks that blocked the way. Never send to know for whom the grave is dug, I said to myself, it's dug for thee. Fred, I well knew, was supervising the work of digging, so I ate breakfast slowly.

38   It was a Saturday morning. The thicket in which I found the gravediggers at work was dark and warm, the sky overcast. Here, among alders and young hackmatacks, at the foot of the apple tree, Lennie had dug a beautiful hole, five feet long, three feet wide, three feet deep. He was standing in it, removing the last spadefuls of earth while Fred patrolled the brink in simple but impressive circles, disturbing the loose earth of the mound so that it trickled back in. There had been no rain in weeks and the soil, even three feet down, was dry and powdery. As I stood and stared, an enormous earthworm which had been partially exposed by the spade at the bottom dug itself deeper and made a slow withdrawal, seeking even remoter moistures at even lonelier depths. And just as Lennie stepped out and rested his spade against the tree and lit a cigarette, a small green apple separated itself from a branch overhead and fell into the hole. Everything about this last scene seemed overwritten—

the dismal sky, the shabby woods, the imminence of rain, the worm (legendary bedfellow of the dead), the apple (conventional garnish of a pig).

39   But even so, there was a directness and dispatch about animal burial, I thought, that made it a more decent affair than human burial: there was no stopover in the undertaker's foul parlor, no wreath nor spray; and when we hitched a line to the pig's hind legs and dragged him swiftly from his yard, throwing our weight into the harness and leaving a wake of crushed grass and smoothed rubble over the dump, ours was a businesslike procession, with Fred, the dishonorable pall-bearer, staggering along in the rear, his perverse bereavement showing in every seam in his face; and the post-mortem performed handily and swiftly right at the edge of the grave, so that the inwards that had caused the pig's death preceded him into the ground and he lay at last resting squarely on the cause of his own undoing.

40   I threw in the first shovelful, and then we worked rapidly and without talk, until the job was complete. I picked up the rope, made it fast to Fred's collar (he is a notorious ghoul), and we all three filed back up the path to the house, Fred bringing up the rear and holding back every inch of the way, feigning unusual stiffness. I noticed that although he weighed far less than the pig, he was harder to drag, being possessed of the vital spark.

41   The news of the death of my pig traveled fast and far, and I received many expressions of sympathy from friends and neighbors, for no one took the event lightly and the premature expiration of a pig is, I soon discovered, a departure which the community marks solemnly on its calendar, a sorrow in which it feels fully involved. I have written this account in penitence and in grief, as a man who failed to raise his pig, and to explain my deviation from the classic course of so many raised pigs. The grave in the woods is unmarked, but Fred can direct the mourner to it unerringly and with immense good will, and I know he and I shall often revisit it, singly and together, in seasons of reflection and despair, on flagless memorial days of our own choosing.

QUESTIONS

Ideas

1. What is the tone of the opening paragraph? Of the second paragraph? How far is this tone sustained throughout the essay? In what ways is it modified?

2. What is the main point of White's essay? What is the essayist's purpose?
3. What connections does White make between pigs and men? Why do the pig's illness and death matter to him?

Organization

4. The essay could easily begin with paragraph 2. Why? Could it begin as readily with paragraph 3 or 4? Why or why not?
5. How is the essay organized? How important is chronology to the essay?

Sentences

6. As the final sentence of paragraph 7 White has written:

> At any rate, it was after five o'clock and I knew I could put off no longer the evil hour.

Consider this alternative:

> At any rate it was after five o'clock and I knew I could put off the evil hour no longer.

7. Analyze the following sentence, paying attention particularly to its use of present participles (*ing* verbs):

> We had been having an unseasonable spell of weather—hot,
> close days, with the fog shutting in every night,
>   scaling for a few hours in midday,
>   then creeping back again at dark,
>   drifting in first over the trees on the point,
>   then suddenly blowing across the fields,
>   blotting out the world
>   and taking possession of houses,
>   men,
>   and animals.

Words

8. What is the effect of White's comparing the pig to a child in paragraphs 5 and 12? What other comparisons with the pig does White make? What is their point and how effective are they?
9. Comment on the underlined words in the following phrases:

> [Fred] was everywhere at once, a tower of strength and <u>inconvenience</u>. (16)
> I held the pig steadily in the <u>bowl</u> of my mind. (17)
> The pig's imbalance becomes the man's <u>vicariously</u>. (14)
> He would stand with his head in the pail and <u>snuffle</u> his snout around. (36)

I went back up to the house and cried <u>internally</u>—deep hemorrhagic <u>intears</u>. (24)

Suggestions for Writing

A. Write imitations of any two of White's sentences.
B. Write an essay recounting the death of an animal.
C. Compare White's treatment of the death of a pig with Dillard's of the death of a moth. Consider the writers' purposes, tones, ideas, and styles.

The Ring of Time

Fiddler Bayou, March 22, 1956

1   After the lions had returned to their cages, creeping angrily through the chutes, a little bunch of us drifted away and into an open doorway nearby, where we stood for a while in semidarkness, watching a big brown circus horse go harumphing around the practice ring. His trainer was a woman of about forty, and the two of them, horse and woman, seemed caught up in one of those desultory treadmills of afternoon from which there is no apparent escape. The day was hot, and we kibitzers were grateful to be briefly out of the sun's glare. The long rein, or tape, by which the woman guided her charge counterclockwise in his dull career formed the radius of their private circle, of which she was the revolving center; and she, too, stepped a tiny circumference of her own, in order to accommodate the horse and allow him his maximum scope. She had on a short-skirted costume and a conical straw hat. Her legs were bare and she wore high heels, which probed deep into the loose tanbark and kept her ankles in a state of constant turmoil. The great size and meekness of the horse, the repetitious exercise, the heat of the afternoon, all exerted a hypnotic charm that invited boredom; we spectators were experiencing a languor—we neither expected relief nor felt entitled to any. We had paid a dollar to get into the grounds, to be sure, but we had got our dollar's worth a few minutes before, when the lion tamer's whiplash had got caught around a toe of one of the lions. What more did we want for a dollar?

2   Behind me I heard someone say, "Excuse me, please," in a low

voice. She was halfway into the building when I turned and saw her—
a girl of sixteen or seventeen, politely threading her way through us
onlookers who blocked the entrance. As she emerged in front of us, I
saw that she was barefoot, her dirty little feet fighting the uneven
ground. In most respects she was like any of two or three dozen showgirls
you encounter if you wander about the winter quarters of Mr. John
Ringling North's circus, in Sarasota—cleverly proportioned, deeply
browned by the sun, dusty, eager, and almost naked. But her grave face
and the naturalness of her manner gave her a sort of quick distinction
and brought a new note into the gloomy octagonal building where we
had all cast our lot for a few moments. As soon as she had squeezed
through the crowd, she spoke a word or two to the older woman, whom
I took to be her mother, stepped to the ring, and waited while the horse
coasted to a stop in front of her. She gave the animal a couple of
affectionate swipes on his enormous neck and then swung herself
aboard. The horse immediately resumed his rocking canter, the woman
goading him on, chanting something that sounded like "Hop! Hop!"

3   In attempting to recapture this mild spectacle, I am merely acting
as recording secretary for one of the oldest of societies—the society of
those who, at one time or another, have surrendered, without even a
show of resistance, to the bedazzlement of a circus rider. As a writing
man, or secretary, I have always felt charged with the safekeeping of all
unexpected items of worldly or unworldly enchantment, as though I
might be held personally responsible if even a small one were to be lost.
But it is not easy to communicate anything of this nature. The circus
comes as close to being the world in microcosm as anything I know; in
a way, it puts all the rest of show business in the shade. Its magic is
universal and complex. Out of its wild disorder comes order; from its
rank smell rises the good aroma of courage and daring; out of its preliminary shabbiness comes the final splendor. And buried in the familiar
boasts of its advance agents lies the modesty of most of its people. For
me the circus is at its best before it has been put together. It is at its
best at certain moments when it comes to a point, as though a burning
glass, in the activity and destiny of a single performer out of so many.
One ring is always bigger than three. One rider, one aerialist, is always
greater than six. In short, a man has to catch the circus unawares to
experience its full impact and share its gaudy dream.

4   The ten-minute ride the girl took achieved—as far as I was concerned, who wasn't looking for it, and quite unbeknownst to her, who
wasn't even striving for it—the thing that is sought by performers

everywhere, on whatever stage, whether struggling in the tidal currents of Shakespeare or bucking the difficult motion of a horse. I somehow got the idea she was just cadging a ride, improving a shining ten minutes in the diligent way all serious artists seize free moments to hone the blade of their talent and keep themselves in trim. Her brief tour included only elementary postures and tricks, perhaps because they were all she was capable of, perhaps because her warmup at this hour was unscheduled and the ring was not rigged for a real practice session. She swung herself off and on the horse several times, gripping his mane. She did a few knee-stands—or whatever they are called—dropping to her knees and quickly bouncing back up on her feet again. Most of the time she simply rode in a standing position, well aft on the beast, her hands hanging easily at her sides, her head erect, her straw-colored ponytail lightly brushing her shoulders, the blood of exertion showing faintly through the tan of her skin. Twice she managed a one-foot stance—a sort of ballet pose, with arms outstretched. At one point the neck strap of her bathing suit broke and she went twice around the ring in the classic attitude of a woman making minor repairs to a garment. The fact that she was standing on the back of a moving horse while doing this invested the matter with a clownish significance that perfectly fitted the spirit of the circus—jocund, yet charming. She just rolled the strap into a neat ball and stowed it inside her bodice while the horse rocked and rolled beneath her in dutiful innocence. The bathing suit proved as self-reliant as its owner and stood up well enough without benefit of strap.

5   The richness of the scene was in its plainness, its natural condition —of horse, of ring, of girl, even to the girl's bare feet that gripped the bare back of her proud and ridiculous mount. The enchantment grew not out of anything that happened or was performed but out of something that seemed to go round and around and around with the girl, attending her, a steady gleam in the shape of a circle—a ring of ambition, of happiness, of youth. (And the positive pleasures of equilibrium under difficulties.) In a week or two, all would be changed, all (or almost all) lost: the girl would wear makeup, the horse would wear gold, the ring would be painted, the bark would be clean for the feet of the horse, the girl's feet would be clean for the slippers that she'd wear. All, all would be lost.

6   As I watched with the others, our jaws adroop, our eyes alight, I became painfully conscious of the element of time. Everything in the

hideous old building seemed to take the shape of a circle, conforming to the course of the horse. The rider's gaze, as she peered straight ahead, seemed to be circular, as though bent by force of circumstance; then time itself began running in circles, and so the beginning was where the end was, and the two were the same, and one thing ran into the next and time went round and around and got nowhere. The girl wasn't so young that she did not know the delicious satisfaction of having a perfectly behaved body and the fun of using it to do a trick most people can't do, but she was too young to know that time does not really move in a circle at all. I thought: "She will never be as beautiful as this again" —a thought that made me acutely unhappy—and in a flash my mind (which is too much of a busybody to suit me) had projected her twenty-five years ahead, and she was now in the center of the ring, on foot, wearing a conical hat and high-heeled shoes, the image of the older woman, holding the long rein, caught in the treadmill of an afternoon long in the future. "She is at that enviable moment in life [I thought] when she believes she can go once around the ring, make one complete circuit, and at the end be exactly the same age as at the start." Everything in her movements, her expression, told you that for her the ring of time was perfectly formed, changeless, predictable, without beginning or end, like the ring in which she was traveling at this moment with the horse that wallowed under her. And then I slipped back into my trance, and time was circular again—time, pausing quietly with the rest of us, so as not to disturb the balance of a performer.

7   Her ride ended as casually as it had begun. The older woman stopped the horse, and the girl slid to the ground. As she walked toward us to leave, there was a quick, small burst of applause. She smiled broadly, in surprise and pleasure; then her face suddenly regained its gravity and she disappeared through the door.

8   It has been ambitious and plucky of me to attempt to describe what is indescribable, and I have failed, as I knew I would. But I have discharged my duty to my society; and besides, a writer, like an acrobat, must occasionally try a stunt that is too much for him. At any rate, it is worth reporting that long before the circus comes to town, its most notable performances have already been given. Under the bright lights of the finished show, a performer need only reflect the electric candle power that is directed upon him; but in the dark and dirty old training rings and in the makeshift cages, whatever light is generated, whatever excitement, whatever beauty, must come from original sources—from

internal fires of professional hunger and delight, from the exuberance and gravity of youth. It is the difference between planetary light and the combustion of stars.

QUESTIONS

Ideas

1. What does White mean by his suggestion in paragraph 3 that the circus is "the world in microcosm"?
2. In what sense is this an essay about the circus, about performance, about time?
3. Has White failed to accomplish what he set out to do (paragraph 8)? What seems to be his purpose in "The Ring of Time"?
4. Twice in the essay White refers to his task and responsibility as a writer. What is his point?

Organization

5. In the opening paragraph White locates and describes the scene. Later, he moves from that initial description to speculation about what he has seen. As you read, or reread, the essay, note which sections are descriptive and which speculative. Explain how the essay as a whole is structured.
6. Try reorganizing the essay by ordering its paragraphs another way: 1, 2, 4, 7, 3, 5, 6, 8. Is there any advantage to reading (and writing) the essay this way? Any disadvantage?
7. What connections exist between the end of the essay and the beginning? Explain why paragraph 8 does or does not sound like a conclusion, an ending.

Sentences

8. The following sentence appears in paragraph 3:

   (1) Out of its wild disorder comes order;
   (2) from its rank smell rises the good aroma of courage and daring;
   (3) out of its preliminary shabbiness comes the final splendor.

Read the sentence aloud as it is written. Then read it aloud as you reorder its three parts. Try a few different combinations (2, 3, 1; 2, 1, 3; 1, 3, 2; 3, 2, 1; 3, 1, 2). Which version(s) do you prefer and why? Besides experimenting with different arrangements of the three major parts of the sentence, you might consider different kinds of word order within each part. The first clause, for example, might be rewritten like this: "Order comes out of its wild disorder"; and the second: "the good aroma of courage and daring rises from its rank smell." How would the third section be rewritten? Which versions of each do you prefer and why?

9. The following sentence, like the sentence discussed in question 8, inverts the regular word order of the English sentence—subject, verb, object. How does the following alteration compare with the sentence as White wrote it?

   White: And buried in the familiar boasts of its advance agents lies the modesty of most of its people.

   Revised: The modesty of most of its people lies buried in the familiar boasts of its advance agents.

   Look at each version in the context in which White's original sentence appears (paragraph 3). Notice what kinds of sentences precede and follow. Then explain which version you prefer.

10. Read paragraph 5 aloud. Mark off the repeated sounds at the level of syllable, phrase, and sentence.

Words

11. Reread the opening paragraph and underline, circle, or list all the words suggesting circularity—all the "circle" words. Why does White include so many of them? And how is the notion of circularity relevant to the ideas and title of the essay?

12. Look through paragraph 6 for echoes and repetitions of the details of the opening paragraph. What is the effect of the repetitions? How are these repetitions of word and phrase related to what White is suggesting about the girl and about time?

13. If paragraph 1 is heavily saturated with "circle" words, primarily nouns, paragraph 2 is noteworthy for its use of precise, vivid verbs. Before you reread the paragraph fill in the blanks in the verb-deleted version below. Compare your choices with White's and with the choices of other students. Discuss the different effects of the various verbs used.

   Behind me I _____ someone _____, "Excuse me, please," in a low voice. She _____ halfway into the building when I turned and _____ her—a girl of sixteen or seventeen, politely _____ her way through us onlookers who _____ the entrance. As she _____ in front of us, I _____ that she _____ barefoot, her dirty little feet

_____ the uneven ground. In most respects she _____ like any of two or three dozen showgirls you _____ if you _____ about the winter quarters of Mr. John Ringling North's circus in Sarasota—cleverly proportioned, deeply browned by the sun, dusty, eager, and almost naked. But her grave face and the naturalness of her manner _____ her a sort of quick distinction and _____ a new note into the gloomy octagonal building where we had all _____ our lot for a few moments. As soon as she had _____ through the crowd, she _____ a word or two to the older woman, whom I _____ to be her mother, _____ to the ring, and _____ while the horse _____ to a stop in front of her. She _____ the animal a couple of affectionate swipes on his enormous neck and then _____ herself aboard. The horse immediately _____ his rocking canter, the woman _____ him on, _____ something that sounded like "Hop! Hop!"

14. Paragraph 3 introduces the language of light, which burns so brilliantly in the essay's final sentences. List all the "light" (and "dark") words you can find in this paragraph. Explain what each of the images means, especially this one: "out of its preliminary shabbiness comes the final splendor."

15. Paragraph 8 contains a number of "light" words. Explain which are literal and which metaphorical. Explain the point of each metaphorical word, especially the following: "whatever light is generated, whatever excitement, whatever beauty, must come from original sources—from internal fires of professional hunger and delight, from the exuberance and gravity of youth. It is the difference between planetary light and the combustion of stars."

Suggestions for Writing

A. Recall an incident in your life which made you feel old, perhaps when something had passed you by, when someone else was moving into the place you once held. You might think, for example, of periods of transition or graduation—from elementary school, from high school, from Little League, Girl Scouts, or something similar. Recreate the scene from your past, its time, place, and tone with concrete details. Weave into your description your insights and speculations on time, change, and age.

B. Write imitations of the sentences discussed in questions 8 and 9.

C. Write an imitation of paragraph 5.

D. Write an analysis of "The Ring of Time." Explain what White is saying in the essay. Discuss his strategy of organization and his use of language. Summarize his main points and paraphrase the essay's most important paragraphs.

Once More to the Lake

August 1941

1   One summer, along about 1904, my father rented a camp on a lake in Maine and took us all there for the month of August. We all got ringworm from some kittens and had to rub Pond's Extract on our arms and legs night and morning, and my father rolled over in a canoe with all his clothes on; but outside of that the vacation was a success and from then on none of us ever thought there was any place in the world like that lake in Maine. We returned summer after summer —always on August 1 for one month. I have since become a salt-water man, but sometimes in summer there are days when the restlessness of the tides and the fearful cold of the sea water and the incessant wind that blows across the afternoon and into the evening make me wish for the placidity of a lake in the woods. A few weeks ago this feeling got so strong I bought myself a couple of bass hooks and a spinner and returned to the lake where we used to go, for a week's fishing and to revisit old haunts.

2   I took along my son, who had never had any fresh water up his nose and who had seen lily pads only from train windows. On the journey over to the lake I began to wonder what it would be like. I wondered how time would have marred this unique, this holy spot—the coves and streams, the hills that the sun set behind, the camps and the paths behind the camps. I was sure that the tarred road would have found it out, and I wondered in what other ways it would be desolated. It is strange how much you can remember about places like that once you allow your mind to return into the grooves that lead back. You remember one thing, and that suddenly reminds you of another thing. I guess I remembered clearest of all the early mornings, when the lake was cool and motionless, remembered how the bedroom smelled of the lumber it was made of and of the wet woods whose scent entered through the screen. The partitions in the camp were thin and did not extend clear to the top of the rooms, and as I was always the first up I would dress softly so as not to wake the others, and sneak out into the sweet outdoors and start out in the canoe, keeping close along the shore in the long shadows of the pines. I remembered being very careful never to rub my

paddle against the gunwale for fear of disturbing the stillness of the cathedral.

3   The lake had never been what you would call a wild lake. There were cottages sprinkled around the shores, and it was in farming country although the shores of the lake were quite heavily wooded. Some of the cottages were owned by nearby farmers, and you would live at the shore and eat your meals at the farmhouse. That's what our family did. But although it wasn't wild, it was a fairly large and undisturbed lake and there were places in it that, to a child at least, seemed infinitely remote and primeval.

4   I was right about the tar: it led to within half a mile of the shore. But when I got back there, with my boy, and we settled into a camp near a farmhouse and into the kind of summertime I had known, I could tell that it was going to be pretty much the same as it had been before —I knew it, lying in bed the first morning, smelling the bedroom and hearing the boy sneak quietly out and go off along the shore in a boat. I began to sustain the illusion that he was I, and therefore, by simple transposition, that I was my father. This sensation persisted, kept cropping up all the time we were there. It was not an entirely new feeling, but in this setting it grew much stronger. I seemed to be living a dual existence. I would be in the middle of some simple act, I would be picking up a bait box or laying down a table fork, or I would be saying something, and suddenly it would be not I but my father who was saying the words or making the gesture. It gave me a creepy sensation.

5   We went fishing the first morning. I felt the same damp moss covering the worms in the bait can, and saw the dragonfly alight on the tip of my rod as it hovered a few inches from the surface of the water. It was the arrival of this fly that convinced me beyond any doubt that everything was as it always had been, that the years were a mirage and that there had been no years. The small waves were the same, chucking the rowboat under the chin as we fished at anchor, and the boat was the same boat, the same color green and the ribs broken in the same places, and under the floorboards the same fresh-water leavings and débris—the dead helgramite, the wisps of moss, the rusty discarded fishhook, the dried blood from yesterday's catch. We stared silently at the tips of our rods, at the dragonflies that came and went. I lowered the tip of mine into the water, tentatively, pensively dislodging the fly, which darted two feet away, poised, darted two feet back, and came to rest again a little farther up the rod. There had been no years between the ducking of this dragonfly and the other one—the one that was part of memory. I looked

at the boy, who was silently watching his fly, and it was my hands that held his rod, my eyes watching. I felt dizzy and didn't know which rod I was at the end of.

6   We caught two bass, hauling them in briskly as though they were mackerel, pulling them over the side of the boat in a businesslike manner without any landing net, and stunning them with a blow on the back of the head. When we got back for a swim before lunch, the lake was exactly where we had left it, the same number of inches from the dock, and there was only the merest suggestion of a breeze. This seemed an utterly enchanted sea, this lake you could leave to its own devices for a few hours and come back to, and find that it had not stirred, this constant and trustworthy body of water. In the shallows, the dark, water-soaked sticks and twigs, smooth and old, were undulating in clusters on the bottom against the clean ribbed sand, and the track of the mussel was plain. A school of minnows swam by, each minnow with its small individual shadow, doubling the attendance, so clear and sharp in the sunlight. Some of the other campers were in swimming, along the shore, one of them with a cake of soap, and the water felt thin and clear and unsubstantial. Over the years there had been this person with the cake of soap, this cultist, and here he was. There had been no years.

7   Up to the farmhouse to dinner through the teeming, dusty field, the road under our sneakers was only a two-track road. The middle track was missing, the one with the marks of the hooves and the splotches of dried, flaky manure. There had always been three tracks to choose from in choosing which track to walk in; now the choice was narrowed down to two. For a moment I missed terribly the middle alternative. But the way led past the tennis court, and something about the way it lay there in the sun reassured me; the tape had loosened along the backline, the alleys were green with plantains and other weeds, and the net (installed in June and removed in September) sagged in the dry noon, and the whole place steamed with midday heat and hunger and emptiness. There was a choice of pie for dessert, and one was blueberry and one was apple, and the waitresses were the same country girls, there having been no passage of time, only the illusion of it as in a dropped curtain —the waitresses were still fifteen; their hair had been washed, that was the only difference—they had been to the movies and seen the pretty girls with the clean hair.

8   Summertime, oh, summertime, pattern of life indelible, the fade-proof lake, the woods unshatterable, the pasture with the sweetfern and the juniper forever and ever, summer without end; this was the back-

ground, and the life along the shore was the design, the cottagers with their innocent and tranquil design, their tiny docks with the flagpole and the American flag floating against the white clouds in the blue sky, the little paths over the roots of the trees leading from camp to camp and the paths leading back to the outhouses and the can of lime for sprinkling, and at the souvenir counters at the store the miniature birchbark canoes and the postcards that showed things looking a little better than they looked. This was the American family at play, escaping the city heat, wondering whether the newcomers in the camp at the head of the cove were "common" or "nice," wondering whether it was true that the people who drove up for Sunday dinner at the farmhouse were turned away because there wasn't enough chicken.

9   It seemed to me, as I kept remembering all this, that those times and those summers had been infinitely precious and worth saving. There had been jollity and peace and goodness. The arriving (at the beginning of August) had been so big a business in itself, at the railway station the farm wagon drawn up, the first smell of the pine-laden air, the first glimpse of the smiling farmer, and the great importance of the trunks and your father's enormous authority in such matters, and the feel of the wagon under you for the long ten-mile haul, and at the top of the last long hill catching the first view of the lake after eleven months of not seeing this cherished body of water. The shouts and cries of the other campers when they saw you, and the trunks to be unpacked, to give up their rich burden. (Arriving was less exciting nowadays, when you sneaked up in your car and parked it under a tree near the camp and took out the bags and in five minutes it was all over, no fuss, no loud wonderful fuss about trunks.)

10   Peace and goodness and jollity. The only thing that was wrong now, really, was the sound of the place, an unfamiliar nervous sound of the outboard motors. This was the note that jarred, the one thing that would sometimes break the illusion and set the years moving. In those other summertimes all motors were inboard; and when they were at a little distance, the noise they made was a sedative, an ingredient of summer sleep. They were one-cylinder and two-cylinder engines, and some were make-and-break and some were jump-spark, but they all made a sleepy sound across the lake. The one-lungers throbbed and fluttered, and the twin-cylinder ones purred and purred, and that was a quiet sound, too. But now the campers all had outboards. In the daytime, in the hot mornings, these motors made a petulant, irritable sound; at night, in the still evening when the afterglow lit the water, they whined

about one's ears like mosquitoes. My boy loved our rented outboard, and his great desire was to achieve single-handed mastery over it, and authority, and he soon learned the trick of choking it a little (but not too much), and the adjustment of the needle valve. Watching him I would remember the things you could do with the old one-cylinder engine with the heavy flywheel, how you could have it eating out of your hand if you got really close to it spiritually. Motorboats in those days didn't have clutches, and you would make a landing by shutting off the motor at the proper time and coasting in with a dead rudder. But there was a way of reversing them, if you learned the trick, by cutting the switch and putting it on again exactly on the final dying revolution of the flywheel, so that it would kick back against compression and begin reversing. Approaching a dock in a strong following breeze, it was difficult to slow up sufficiently by the ordinary coasting method, and if a boy felt he had complete mastery over his motor, he was tempted to keep it running beyond its time and then reverse it a few feet from the dock. It took a cool nerve, because if you threw the switch a twentieth of a second too soon you would catch the flywheel when it still had speed enough to go up past center, and the boat would leap ahead, charging bull-fashion at the dock.

11   We had a good week at the camp. The bass were biting well and the sun shone endlessly, day after day. We would be tired at night and lie down in the accumulated heat of the little bedrooms after the long hot day and the breeze would stir almost imperceptibly outside and the smell of the swamp drift in through the rusty screens. Sleep would come easily and in the morning the red squirrel would be on the roof, tapping out his gay routine. I kept remembering everything, lying in bed in the mornings —the small steamboat that had a long rounded stern like the lip of a Ubangi, and how quietly she ran on the moonlight sails, when the older boys played their mandolins and the girls sang and we ate doughnuts dipped in sugar, and how sweet the music was on the water in the shining night, and what it had felt like to think about girls then. After breakfast we would go up to the store and the things were in the same place—the minnows in a bottle, the plugs and spinners disarranged and pawed over by the youngsters from the boys' camp, the Fig Newtons and the Beeman's gum. Outside, the road was tarred and cars stood in front of the store. Inside, all was just as it had always been, except there was more Coca-Cola and not so much Moxie and root beer and birch beer and sarsaparilla. We would walk out with the bottle of pop apiece and sometimes the pop would backfire up our noses and hurt. We explored

the streams, quietly, where the turtles slid off the sunny logs and dug their way into the soft bottom; and we lay on the town wharf and fed worms to the tame bass. Everywhere we went I had trouble making out which was I, the one walking at my side, the one walking in my pants.

12   One afternoon while we were there at that lake a thunderstorm came up. It was like the revival of an old melodrama that I had seen long ago with childish awe. The second-act climax of the drama of the electrical disturbance over a lake in America had not changed in any important respect. This was the big scene, still the big scene. The whole thing was so familiar, the first feeling of oppression and heat and a general air around camp of not wanting to go very far away. In midafternoon (it was all the same) a curious darkening of the sky, and a lull in everything that had made life tick; and then the way the boats suddenly swung the other way at their moorings with the coming of a breeze out of the new quarter, and the premonitory rumble. Then the kettle drum, then the snare, then the bass drum and cymbals, then crackling light against the dark, and the gods grinning and licking their chops in the hills. Afterward the calm, the rain steadily rustling in the calm lake, the return of light and hope and spirits, and the campers running out in joy and relief to go swimming in the rain, their bright cries perpetuating the deathless joke about how they were getting simply drenched, and the children screaming with delight at the new sensation of bathing in the rain, and the joke about getting drenched linking the generations in a strong indestructible chain. And the comedian who waded in carrying an umbrella.

13   When the others went swimming, my son said he was going in, too. He pulled his dripping trunks from the line where they had hung all through the shower and wrung them out. Languidly, and with no thought of going in, I watched him, his hard little body, skinny and bare, saw him wince slightly as he pulled up around his vitals the small, soggy, icy garment. As he buckled the swollen belt, suddenly my groin felt the chill of death.

QUESTIONS

Ideas

1. Like "The Ring of Time," "Once More to the Lake" is a lyrical and speculative essay. It is, of course, a reminiscence of a memorable summer.

But it is something more: a meditation on time. What ideas about time does White suggest? Consider especially what he says in paragraphs 4, 5, and 6.

2. Explain what you think White means by the following statements:

I seemed to be living a dual existence. (4)

I felt dizzy and didn't know which rod I was at the end of. (5)

I began to sustain the illusion that he was I, and therefore, by simple transposition, that I was my father. (4)

3. Besides time and change, what is this essay about?

Organization

4. Divide the essay into sections and provide titles for each part. In deciding upon your sections and titles, consider which paragraphs are primarily descriptive and which are speculative.

5. White gains emphasis by positioning his key ideas at the ends of paragraphs. Reread paragraphs 4, 5, and 6, attending to the final sentence of each paragraph. All three build toward the concluding sentence, which completes the idea in a forceful statement or embodies it in a striking image. Find at least one other example of a final effective sentence in a paragraph. Explain how it completes the paragraph.

6. Examine paragraphs 9 and 10 to see how White uses comparison and contrast to elaborate his point about the place. Note all the words and phrases that set up and emphasize the comparisons White makes between the lake in the past and the present.

Sentences

7. A number of White's sentences resonate and reverberate with repeated words and phrases. Read the following sentence aloud, noting its repetitions:

The small waves were the same, chucking the rowboat under the chin as we fished at anchor, and the boat was the same boat, the same color green and the ribs broken in the same places, and under the floorboards the same fresh-water leavings and débris—the dead helgramite, the wisps of moss, the rusty discarded fishhook, the dried blood from yesterday's catch.

8. Another way White uses repetition in the essay is to employ the same words in different sentences. For example, the following sentences occur in different paragraphs:

There had been jollity and peace and goodness. (9)

Peace and goodness and jollity. (10)

Reread these two sentences in their context. Does the reordering of words affect the meaning? Why might White have altered the word order when he came to repeat the words?

9. In the sentences that follow, White expands his thought and accumulates details toward the end—after a brief direct statement of idea. You might think of the sentence formed this way as a string or a stack of details laid out in a series of parallel clauses or phrases.

> It was the arrival of this fly that convinced me beyond any doubt
>   that everything was as it always had been,
>   that the years were a mirage
> and that there had been no years.

> We caught two bass,
>   hauling them in briskly as though they were mackerel,
>   pulling them in over the side of the boat in a businesslike
>   manner without any landing net,
> and stunning them with a blow on the back of the head.

10. Compare the following sentence by White with the alternate form for sound and rhythm.

> *White:* I wondered how time would have marred this unique, this holy spot—the coves and streams, the hills that the sun set behind, the camps and the paths behind the camps.

> *Alternate:* I wondered how time would have marred this unique, holy spot—the coves, streams, hills, camps and paths.

Words

11. What words in paragraphs 1 and 2 describe the lake? What connotations does each possess? What overall impression of the lake is created by the accumulation of these words? How do the final words of paragraph 3 reinforce this impression?

12. "Once More to the Lake" is rich in sensuous detail—in images of sight, sound, smell, taste, and touch. List the visual details of paragraph 7 and the sound and sense details of paragraphs 10, 11, and 12. What is the overall effect of each paragraph?

13. White's diction in this essay and in others combines the high and the low, the common and the unusual, the formally elegant and the colloquially casual. Compare the tone, sound, and rhythm of the following remarks: (1) "the restlessness of the tides"; "the incessant wind that blows across

the afternoon"; "the placidity of a lake in the woods." (2) "A few weeks ago this feeling got so strong I bought myself a couple of bass hooks and a spinner and returned to the lake where we used to go, for a week's fishing and to revisit old haunts." What is different about the second voice? Which words in particular are responsible for its feeling and tone?

14. In this essay and in others White combines factual with emotional details. He extends a literal fact into a metaphoric detail, which carries a charge of meaning and a spark of feeling. Here is an example: "the whole place steamed with midday heat and hunger and emptiness" (7). To obtain the full force of how this literal fact (the heat) is extended to a human fact of feeling (hunger and emptiness) you'll need to read the sentence in context. Try to find another example of White's shading a fact into a metaphor and explain how the literal and metaphorical meanings intersect.

Suggestions for Writing

A. Write an essay about a place you have revisited after a long absence. Try to account for what the place meant to you after the first visit and after the later visit. Give some sense of what you expected and hoped for on the later visit. Try to suggest how the place had changed and how it remained the way you remembered it.

B. Explain, in a short essay, the sources of White's appeal as a writer. Does it have something to do with his subjects? With his ideas? His attitude and tone? His style?

C. In a paragraph or short essay, explain the idea of the following poem. Consider especially the imagery of stanzas 3 and 4. Compare the ideas about time in the poem with the ideas about time in White's essay. (Note especially the last stanza of the poem and the last paragraph of the essay.)

MEN AT FORTY

Men at forty
Learn to close softly
The doors to rooms they will not be
Coming back to.

At rest on a stair landing,
They feel it moving
Beneath them now like the deck of a ship,
Though the swell is gentle.

And deep in mirrors
They rediscover
The face of the boy as he practices tying

His father's tie there in secret

And the face of that father,
Still warm with the mystery of lather.
They are more fathers than sons themselves now.
Something is filling them, something

That is like the twilight sound
Of the crickets, immense,
Filling the woods at the foot of the slope
Behind their mortgaged houses.

—DONALD JUSTICE

D. Write an essay explaining White's ideas in two of his essays. You might
    compare and contrast his treatment of a similar subject or discuss his
    treatment of a similar theme using two different subjects.

E. Write imitations of the sentences discussed in questions 7, 9, and 10.

SIXTEEN

Tom Wolfe
(1931–   )

Tom Wolfe is one of the most famous of the New Journalists, a group of writers who imported the techniques of fiction into journalism. Wolfe's account of how he wrote his essay on custom cars, "The Kandy-Kolored Tangerine-Flake Streamline Baby," provides an insight into both his working habits and the new style he was unwittingly developing.

With an abundance of material about his subject and with too little time to organize, write, revise, and edit in the conventional manner, Wolfe began typing his notes in a letter to his editor at *Esquire,* where the piece was to be published. His letter took the form of a long memorandum, Wolfe supposing that somebody at the magazine would be responsible for shaping his rambling notes and writing the story. Wolfe describes the experience of writing the piece this way: "I just recorded it all, and inside a couple of hours, typing along like a madman, I could tell that something was beginning to happen. By midnight this memorandum was . . . twenty pages long and I was still typing like a maniac. . . . about 6:15 A.M. . . . it was 49 pages long." *Esquire* published it as written, inaugurating thereby an alternate writing style that was later named the "New Journalism."

In an introduction to an anthology of new-journalistic essays entitled, appropriately enough, *The New Journalism,* Wolfe singles out four techniques as being especially important for this new style. The basic device, he notes, is "scene-by-scene construction, telling the story by moving from scene to scene and resorting as little as possible to sheer historical narrative." Another technique is to rely heavily on dialogue since, as Wolfe has pointed out, "realistic dialogue involves the reader more completely than any other single device. It also establishes and defines character more quickly than any other single device."

The third device involves manipulating the point of view, the angle of vision, the perspective from which a scene is presented. New Journalists will interview someone at the center of a scene, then import into their write-ups the thoughts and emotions of those interviewed. The purpose of this strategy, as Wolfe notes, is to "give the reader the feeling of being inside the character's mind and experiencing the emotional reality of the scene as he experiences it." The fourth technique concerns what Wolfe describes as "the recording of everyday gestures, habits, manners, customs . . . looks, glances, poses, styles of walking and other symbolic details. . . ."

To these can be added what Winston Weathers in his fine book *An Alternate Style* calls the *crot*—an obsolete word meaning "bit" or "fragment": "an autonomous unit, characterized by the absence of any transitional devices . . . in its most intense form . . . by a certain abruptness in its termination." Crots are something like snapshots, something like vignettes. Putting them together without transitions can make for effects of montage, collage, surprise—and sometimes confusion. They challenge readers and involve them by inviting them to figure out how the fragments are related to one another. Besides the crot, about which Wolfe has said, "it will have you making crazy leaps of logic, leaps you never dreamed of before," Weathers singles out other devices frequently used by Wolfe and his new-journalistic colleagues: the labyrinthine sentence, the fragment, and the use of repetitions, lists, and refrains.

Wolfe began his career as an academic, earning a doctorate in American Studies at Yale. But his inclination was more journalistic than academic, and he worked for *The Washington Post* as a reporter and then as a magazine writer for *The New York Herald-Tribune.* Since 1968 he has been a contributing editor to *New York Magazine.* He has written articles on trends in American popular culture, primarily essays that have been published first in magazines and later in books. Following his first collection, *The Kandy-Kolored Tangerine-Flake Streamline Baby* (1965), came a series of books with such zany titles as *The Electric Kool-Aid Acid Test* (1968)—on pot; *The Pump House Gang* (1968)—on California surfers (among other things); *Radical Chic and Mau-Mauing the Flak Catchers* (1970)—on rich New Yorkers vis-à-vis the Black Panthers; *Mauve Gloves and Madmen, Clutter and Vine* (1976)—on miscellaneous subjects; *The Right Stuff* (1979)—on the astronauts; *In Our Time* (1980), a collection of satirical pictorial sketches with brief notes and comments; and *From Bauhaus to Our House* (1981), a critique of modern architecture. His most recent book, *The Purple Decade* (1982), is a selection from his earlier books.

Wolfe takes great risks in his writing: his style is daring, flamboyant, energetic, humorous, and satirical. Reading him is like listening to a talented raconteur who reenacts the scenes and situations he describes, who comments on them in a free-wheeling style filled with digressions and associative ramblings, with less concern to instruct and moralize than to entertain and delight. His essays tend to be long and steeped in detail. He seems to need room to present the various facets of his subjects, time to amass details, and space to allow his characters to reveal, even display themselves. The masses of detail, the loose structure, the transcriptions of dialogue, the crots, lists, repetitions, and refrains cumulatively create a sense of immediacy and authenticity which suggests the reality of "This is how it is; this is what it's like."

The Right Stuff, Wolfe's longest and most ambitious work, has drawn wide critical acclaim, as well as becoming a best seller. Early in the book Wolfe describes just what the right stuff is that men need to become successful test pilots and astronauts. His comments relate as much to his own style and performance as a writer as they do to the astronauts. The right stuff, Wolfe explains, is "an amalgam of stamina, guts, fast neural synapses and old-fashioned hell raising." These elements, along with nerve, exhilaration, and a satirically edged humor, suggest something of Wolfe's tone and voice.

The five essays included here span Wolfe's new-journalistic career. "Clean Fun at Riverhead," taken from *The Kandy-Kolored Tangerine-Flake Streamline Baby*, is about a demolition derby. In this piece Wolfe reflects on the importance of the automobile in American culture, especially on its symbolic value. "Las Vegas," from the same book, offers a series of impressions about one of America's most famous places. "Only One Life" is excerpted from a long essay, "The Me Decade and the Third Great Awakening," which appeared in *Mauve Gloves and Madmen, Clutter and Vine*. The essay satirizes the self-centered manias of people looking out for and looking into themselves. "The Lab Rat" and "The Right Stuff" are both taken from *The Right Stuff*. "The Lab Rat" depicts in comic terms the intensive and extensive physical examinations the astronauts and test pilots are put through; "The Right

Stuff" shows what it takes to make it as a test pilot, defining the ineffable quality through illustration and description, anecdote and analysis.

Wolfe has been interviewed frequently and has commented extensively on writing. On one occasion he noted that "writing, unlike painting or drawing, is a process in which you *can't* tell right away whether it's successful or not. Some nights you go to bed thinking you've written some brilliant stuff, and you wake up the next morning and you realize it *is* just pure bullshit." And in response to a question about why he writes, Wolfe noted that he doesn't have a ready answer, but that if pressed he thinks that he writes out of a concern for his own glory, with more concern for *how* he handles the materials of his craft than for the issues he writes about. The challenge in writing, thus, for Wolfe, seems to reside in the compositional problem that confronts him. Aesthetic and linguistic challenges excite him more than the subjects he writes about. But this subjective priority of form over content hasn't prevented Wolfe from offering acutely intelligent analyses of contemporary fads, fashions, and mores. He is one of our best cultural critics and one of our most innovative and entertaining writers.

Las Vegas (What?) Las Vegas (Can't hear you! Too noisy) Las Vegas!!!!

1   Hernia, hernia, hernia, hernia, hernia, hernia, hernia, hernia, hernia, hernia, hernia, hernia, hernia, HERNia; hernia, HERNia, hernia, hernia, hernia, hernia, HERNia, HERNia, HERNia, hernia, hernia, hernia, hernia, hernia, hernia, hernia, eight is the point, the point is eight; hernia, hernia, HERNia; hernia, hernia, hernia, hernia, all right, hernia, hernia, hernia, hernia, hard eight, hernia, hernia, hernia, HERNia, hernia, hernia, hernia, HERNia, hernia, hernia, hernia, HERNia, hernia, hernia, hernia, hernia.

2   "What is all this *hernia hernia* stuff?"

3   This was Raymond talking to the wavy-haired fellow with the

stick, the dealer, at the craps table about 3:45 Sunday morning. The stickman had no idea what this big wiseacre was talking about, but he resented the tone. He gave Raymond that patient arch of the eyebrows known as a Red Hook brush-off, which is supposed to convey some such thought as, I am a very tough but cool guy, as you can tell by the way I carry my eyeballs low in the pouches, and if this wasn't such a high-class joint we would take wiseacres like you out back and beat you into jellied madrilene.

4   At this point, however, Raymond was immune to subtle looks.

5   The stickman tried to get the game going again, but every time he would start up his singsong, by easing the words out through the nose, which seems to be the style among craps dealers in Las Vegas—"All right, a new shooter . . . eight is the point, the point is eight" and so on—Raymond would start droning along with him in exactly the same tone of voice, "Hernia, hernia, hernia; hernia, HERNia, HERNia, hernia; hernia, hernia, hernia."

6   Everybody at the craps table was staring in consternation to think that anybody would try to needle a tough, hip, elite *soldat* like a Las Vegas craps dealer. The gold-lamé odalisques of Los Angeles were staring. The Western sports, fifty-eight-year-old men who wear Texas string ties, were staring. The old babes at the slot machines, holding Dixie Cups full of nickels, were staring at the craps tables, but cranking away the whole time.

7   Raymond, who is thirty-four years old and works as an engineer in Phoenix, is big but not terrifying. He has the sort of thatchwork hair that grows so low all along the forehead there is no logical place to part it, but he tries anyway. He has a huge, prognathous jaw, but it is as smooth, soft and round as a melon, so that Raymond's total effect is that of an Episcopal divinity student.

8   The guards were wonderful. They were dressed in cowboy uniforms like Bruce Cabot in *Sundown* and they wore sheriff's stars.

9   "Mister, is there something we can do for you?"

10   "The expression is 'Sir,' " said Raymond. "You said 'Mister.' The expression is 'Sir.' How's your old Cosa Nostra?"

11   Amazingly, the casino guards were easing Raymond out peaceably, without putting a hand on him. I had never seen the fellow before, but possibly because I had been following his progress for the last five minutes, he turned to me and said, "Hey, do you have a car? This wild stuff is starting again."

12   The gist of it was that he had left his car somewhere and he

wanted to ride up the Strip to the Stardust, one of the big hotel-casinos. I am describing this big goof Raymond not because he is a typical Las Vegas tourist, although he has some typical symptoms, but because he is a good example of the marvelous impact Las Vegas has on the senses. Raymond's senses were at a high pitch of excitation, the only trouble being that he was going off his nut. He had been up since Thursday afternoon, and it was now about 3:45 A.M. Sunday. He had an envelope full of pep pills—amphetamine—in his left coat pocket and an envelope full of Equanils—meprobamate—in his right pocket, or were the Equanils in the left and the pep pills in the right? He could tell by looking, but he wasn't going to look anymore. He didn't care to see how many were left.

13   He had been rolling up and down the incredible electric-sign gauntlet of Las Vegas' Strip, U.S. Route 91, where the neon and the par lamps—bubbling, spiraling, rocketing, and exploding in sunbursts ten stories high out in the middle of the desert—celebrate one-story casinos. He had been gambling and drinking and eating now and again at the buffet tables the casinos keep heaped with food day and night, but mostly hopping himself up with good old amphetamine, cooling himself down with meprobamate, then hooking down more alcohol, until now, after sixty hours, he was slipping into the symptoms of toxic schizophrenia.

14   He was also enjoying what the prophets of hallucinogen call "consciousness expansion." The man was psychedelic. He was beginning to isolate the components of Las Vegas' unique bombardment of the senses. He was quite right about this *hernia hernia* stuff. Every casino in Las Vegas is, among the other things, a room full of craps tables with dealers who keep up a running singsong that sounds as though they are saying "hernia, hernia, hernia, hernia, hernia" and so on. There they are day and night, easing a running commentary through their nostrils. What they have to say contains next to no useful instruction. Its underlying message is, We are the initiates, riding the crest of chance. That the accumulated sound comes out "hernia" is merely an unfortunate phonetic coincidence. Actually, it is part of something rare and rather grand: a combination of baroque stimuli that brings to mind the bronze gongs, no larger than a blue plate, that Louis XIV, his ruff collars larded with the lint of the foul Old City of Byzantium, personally hunted out in the bazaars of Asia Minor to provide exotic acoustics for his new palace outside Paris.

15   The sounds of the craps dealer will be in, let's say, the middle

register. In the lower register will be the sound of the old babes at the slot machines. Men play the slots too, of course, but one of the indelible images of Las Vegas is that of the old babes at the row upon row of slot machines. There they are at six o'clock Sunday morning no less than at three o'clock Tuesday afternoon. Some of them pack their old hummocky shanks into Capri pants, but many of them just put on the old print dress, the same one day after day, and the old hob-heeled shoes, looking like they might be going out to buy eggs in Tupelo, Mississippi. They have a Dixie Cup full of nickels or dimes in the left hand and an Iron Boy work glove on the right hand to keep the calluses from getting sore. Every time they pull the handle, the machine makes a sound much like the sound a cash register makes before the bell rings, then the slot pictures start clattering up from left to right, the oranges, lemons, plums, cherries, bells, bars, buckaroos—the figure of a cowboy riding a bucking bronco. The whole sound keeps churning up over and over again in eccentric series all over the place, like one of those random-sound radio symphonies by John Cage. You can hear it at any hour of the day or night all over Las Vegas. You can walk down Fremont Street at dawn and hear it without even walking in a door, that and the spins of the wheels of fortune, a boring and not very popular sort of simplified roulette, as the tabs flap to a stop. As an overtone, or at times simply as a loud sound, comes the babble of the casino crowds, with an occasional shriek from the craps tables, or, anywhere from 4 P.M. to 6 A.M., the sound of brass instruments or electrified string instruments from the cocktail-lounge shows.

16   The crowd and band sounds are not very extraordinary, of course. But Las Vegas' Muzak is. Muzak pervades Las Vegas from the time you walk into the airport upon landing to the last time you leave the casinos. It is piped out to the swimming pool. It is in the drugstores. It is as if there were a communal fear that someone, somewhere in Las Vegas, was going to be left with a totally vacant minute on his hands.

17   Las Vegas has succeeded in wiring an entire city with this electronic stimulation, day and night, out in the middle of the desert. In the automobile I rented, the radio could not be turned off, no matter which dial you went after. I drove for days in a happy burble of Action Checkpoint News, "Monkey No. 9," "Donna, Donna, the Prima Donna," and picking-and-singing jingles for the Frontier Bank and the Fremont Hotel.

18   One can see the magnitude of the achievement. Las Vegas takes what in other American towns is but a quixotic inflammation of the

senses for some poor salary mule in the brief interval between the flagstone rambler and the automatic elevator downtown and magnifies it, foliates it, embellishes it into an institution.

19   For example, Las Vegas is the only town in the world whose skyline is made up neither of buildings, like New York, nor of trees, like Wilbraham, Massachusetts, but signs. One can look at Las Vegas from a mile away on Route 91 and see no buildings, no trees, only signs. But such signs! They tower. They revolve, they oscillate, they soar in shapes before which the existing vocabulary of art history is helpless. I can only attempt to supply names—Boomerang Modern, Palette Curvilinear, Flash Gordon Ming-Alert Spiral, McDonald's Hamburger Parabola, Mint Casino Elliptical, Miami Beach Kidney. Las Vegas' sign makers work so far out beyond the frontiers of conventional studio art that they have no names themselves for the forms they create. Vaughan Cannon, one of those tall, blond Westerners, the builders of places like Las Vegas and Los Angeles, whose eyes seem to have been bleached by the sun, is in the back shop of the Young Electric Sign Company out on East Charleston Boulevard with Herman Boernge, one of his designers, looking at the model they have prepared for the Lucky Strike Casino sign, and Cannon points to where the sign's two great curving faces meet to form a narrow vertical face and says:

20   "Well, here we are again—what do we call that?"

21   "I don't know," says Boernge. "It's sort of a nose effect. Call it a nose."

22   Okay, a nose, but it rises sixteen stories high above a two-story building. In Las Vegas no farseeing entrepreneur buys a sign to fit a building he owns. He rebuilds the building to support the biggest sign he can get up the money for and, if necessary, changes the name. The Lucky Strike Casino today is the Lucky Casino, which fits better when recorded in sixteen stories of flaming peach and incandescent yellow in the middle of the Mojave Desert. In the Young Electric Sign Co. era signs have become the architecture of Las Vegas, and the most whimsical, Yale-seminar-frenzied devices of the two late geniuses of Baroque Modern, Frank Lloyd Wright and Eero Saarinen, seem rather stuffy business, like a jest at a faculty meeting, compared to it. Men like Boernge, Kermit Wayne, Ben Mitchem and Jack Larsen, formerly an artist for Walt Disney, are the designer-sculptor geniuses of Las Vegas, but their motifs have been carried faithfully throughout the town by lesser men, for gasoline stations, motels, funeral parlors, churches, public buildings, flophouses and sauna baths.

23   Then there is a stimulus that is both visual and sexual—the Las

Vegas buttocks décolletage. This is a form of sexually provocative dress seen more and more in the United States, but avoided like Broadway message-embroidered ("Kiss Me, I'm Cold") underwear in the fashion pages, so that the euphemisms have not been established and I have no choice but clinical terms. To achieve buttocks décolletage a woman wears bikini-style shorts that cut across the round fatty masses of the buttocks rather than cupping them from below, so that the outer-lower edges of these fatty masses, or "cheeks," are exposed. I am in the cocktail lounge of the Hacienda Hotel, talking to managing director Dick Taylor about the great success his place has had in attracting family and tour groups, and all around me the waitresses are bobbing on their high heels, bare legs and décolletage-bare backsides, set off by pelvis-length lingerie of an uncertain denomination. I stare, but I am new here. At the White Cross Rexall drugstore on the Strip a pregnant brunette walks in off the street wearing black shorts with buttocks décolletage aft and illusion-of-cloth nylon lingerie hanging fore, and not even the old mom's-pie pensioners up near the door are staring. They just crank away at the slot machines. On the streets of Las Vegas, not only the show girls, of which the town has about two hundred fifty, bona fide, in residence, but girls of every sort, including, especially, Las Vegas' little high-school buds, who adorn what locals seeking roots in the sand call "our city of churches and schools," have taken up the chic of wearing buttocks décolletage step-ins under flesh-tight slacks, with the outline of the undergarment showing through fashionably. Others go them one better. They achieve the effect of having been dipped once, briefly, in Helenca stretch nylon. More and more they look like those wonderful old girls out of Flash Gordon who were wrapped just once over in Baghdad pantaloons of clear polyethylene with only Flash Gordon between them and the insane red-eyed assaults of the minions of Ming. It is as if all the hip young suburban gals of America named Lana, Deborah and Sandra, who gather wherever the arc lights shine and the studs steady their coiffures in the plate-glass reflection, have convened in Las Vegas with their bouffant hair above and anatomically stretch-pant-swathed little bottoms below, here on the new American frontier. But exactly!

24   The allure is most irresistible not to the young but the old. No one in Las Vegas will admit it—it is not the modern, glamorous notion—but Las Vegas is a resort for old people. In those last years, before the tissue deteriorates and the wires of the cerebral cortex hang in the skull like a clump of dried seaweed, they are seeking liberation.

25   At eight o'clock Sunday morning it is another almost boringly sunny day in the desert, and Clara and Abby, both about sixty, and their

husbands, Earl, sixty-three, and Ernest, sixty-four, come squinting out of the Mint Casino onto Fremont Street.

26   "I don't know what's wrong with me," Abby says. "Those last three drinks, I couldn't even feel them. It was just like drinking fizz. You know what I mean?"

27   "Hey," says Ernest, "how about that place back 'ere? We ain't been back 'ere. Come on."

28   The others are standing there on the corner, squinting and looking doubtful. Abby and Clara have both entered old babehood. They have that fleshy, humped-over shape across the back of the shoulders. Their torsos are hunched up into fat little loaves supported by bony, atrophied leg stems sticking up into their hummocky hips. Their hair has been fried and dyed into improbable designs.

29   "You know what I mean? After a while it just gives me gas," says Abby. "I don't even feel it."

30   "Did you see me over there?" says Earl. "I was just going along, nice and easy, not too much, just riding along real nice. You know? And then, boy, I don't know what happened to me. First thing I know I'm laying down fifty dollars. . . ."

31   Abby lets out a great belch. Clara giggles.

32   "Gives me gas," Abby says mechanically.

33   "Hey, how about that place back 'ere?" says Ernest.

34   ". . . Just nice and easy as you please. . . ."

35   ". . . get me all fizzed up. . . ."

36   "Aw, come on. . . ."

37   And there at eight o'clock Sunday morning stand four old parties from Albuquerque, New Mexico, up all night, squinting at the sun, belching from a surfeit of tall drinks at eight o'clock Sunday morning, and—marvelous!—there is no one around to snigger at what an old babe with decaying haunches looks like in Capri pants with her heels jacked up on decorated wedgies.

38   "Where do we *come* from?" Clara said to me, speaking for the first time since I approached them on Fremont Street. "He wants to know where we come from. I think it's past your bedtime, sweets."

39   "Climb the stairs and go to bed," said Abby.

40   Laughter all around.

41   "Climb the stairs" was Abby's finest line. At present there are almost no stairs to climb in Las Vegas. Avalon homes are soon to go up, advertising "Two-Story Homes!" as though this were an incredibly lavish and exotic concept. As I talked to Clara, Abby, Earl and Ernest, it came out that "climb the stairs" was a phrase they brought along to

Albuquerque with them from Marshalltown, Iowa, those many years ago, along with a lot of other baggage, such as the entire cupboard of Protestant taboos against drinking, lusting, gambling, staying out late, getting up late, loafing, idling, lollygagging around the streets and wearing Capri pants—all designed to deny a person short-term pleasures so he will center his energies on bigger, long-term goals.

42   "We was in 'ere"—the Mint—"a couple of hours ago, and that old boy was playing the guitar, you know. 'Walk right in, set right down,' and I kept hearing an old song I haven't heard for twenty years. It has this little boy and his folks keep telling him it's late and he has to go to bed. He keeps saying, 'Don't make me go to bed and I'll be good.' Am I *good*, Earl? Am I *good?*"

43   The liberated cortex in all its glory is none other than the old babes at the slot machines. Some of them are tourists whose husbands said, *Here is fifty bucks, go play the slot machines,* while they themselves went off to more complex pleasures. But most of these old babes are part of the permanent landscape of Las Vegas. In they go to the Golden Nugget or the Mint, with their Social Security check or their pension check from the Ohio telephone company, cash it at the casino cashier's, pull out the Dixie Cup and the Iron Boy work glove, disappear down a row of slots and get on with it. I remember particularly talking to another Abby— a widow, sixty-two years old, built short and up from the bottom like a fire hydrant. After living alone for twelve years in Canton, Ohio, she had moved out to Las Vegas to live with her daughter and her husband, who worked for the Army.

44   "They were wonderful about it," she said. "Perfect hypocrites. She kept saying, you know, 'Mother, we'd be delighted to have you, only we don't think you'll *like* it. It's practically a fron*tier* town,' she says. 'It's so *gar*ish,' she says. So I said, I told her, 'Well, if you'd rather I didn't come. . . .' 'Oh, no!' she says. I wish I could have heard what her husband was saying. He calls me 'Mother.' *'Mother,'* he says. Well, once I was here, they figured, well, I *might* make a good baby-sitter and dishwasher and duster and mopper. The children are nasty little things. So one day I was in town for something or other and I just played a slot machine. It's fun—I can't describe it to you. I suppose I lose. I lose a little. And *they* have fits about it. 'For God's sake, Grandmother,' and so forth. They always say *'Grand*mother' when I am supposed to 'act my age' or crawl through a crack in the floor. Well, I'll tell you, the slot machines are a *whole lot* better than sitting in that little house all day. They kind of get you; I can't explain it."

45   The childlike megalomania of gambling is, of course, from the

same cloth as the megalomania of the town. And, as the children of the liberated cortex, the old guys and babes are running up and down the Strip around the clock like everybody else. It is not by chance that much of the entertainment in Las Vegas, especially the second-stringers who perform in the cocktail lounges, will recall for an aging man what was glamorous twenty-five years ago when he had neither the money nor the freedom of spirit to indulge himself in it. In the big theatre-dining room at the Desert Inn, The Painted Desert Room, Eddie Fisher's act is on and he is saying cozily to a florid guy at a table right next to the stage, "Manny, you know you shouldn'a sat this close —you know you're in for it now, Manny, baby," while Manny beams with fright. But in the cocktail lounge, where the idea is chiefly just to keep the razzle-dazzle going, there is Hugh Farr, one of the stars of another era in the West, composer of two of the five Western songs the Library of Congress has taped for posterity, "Cool Water" and "Tumbling Tumbleweed," when he played the violin for the Sons of the Pioneers. And now around the eyes he looks like an aging Chinese savant, but he is wearing a white tuxedo and powder-blue leather boots and playing his sad old Western violin with an electric cord plugged in it for a group called The Country Gentlemen. And there is Ben Blue, looking like a waxwork exhibit of vaudeville, doffing his straw skimmer to reveal the sculptural qualities of his skull. And down at the Flamingo cocktail lounge—Ella Fitzgerald is in the main room—there is Harry James, looking old and pudgy in one of those toy Italian-style show-biz suits. And the Ink Spots are at the New Frontier and Louis Prima is at the Sahara, and the old parties are seeing it all, roaring through the dawn into the next day, until the sun seems like a par lamp fading in and out. The casinos, the bars, the liquor stores are open every minute of every day, like a sempiternal wading pool for the childhood ego. ". . . Don't make me go to bed. . . ."

QUESTIONS

Ideas

1. What image of Las Vegas does Wolfe convey? What is his attitude toward what he describes?

2. In what ways can Las Vegas be considered a "frontier," whether new or old? What American cultural values are illustrated in Wolfe's piece?

Organization

3. How is the essay organized? Describe the structure of the selection by dividing it into sections, characterizing them and pointing out their relation to one another.

4. How does Wolfe move from one aspect of his description of Las Vegas to another? What transitions does he use?

Sentences

5. Examine one of Wolfe's long sentences—such as the second sentence of paragraph 16. Explain how Wolfe keeps it going, how he structures it grammatically. Consider the effect of breaking it into three or four shorter sentences.

6. Three of Wolfe's short sentences are worth noting—the second of paragraph 17, the first of paragraph 19, and the final sentence of paragraph 26. What effects does Wolfe achieve with these sentences?

Words

7. Identify three comparisons, whether similes, metaphors, images, or symbols, and explain their purpose and point. Comment on the effectiveness of each.

8. Explain the following underlined words:

   a *quixotic inflammation* of the senses (21)
   buttocks *decolletage* (26)
   baroque stimuli (17)

Suggestions for Writing

A. Imitate the sentences described in questions 5 and 6.
B. Compare Wolfe's portrayal of Las Vegas with Joan Didion's in "Marrying Absurd."
C. Argue with Wolfe by offering a counterview of Las Vegas.
D. Imitate Wolfe by satirically describing a place you know.

Clean Fun at Riverhead

---

1   The inspiration for the demolition derby came to Lawrence Mendelsohn one night in 1958 when he was nothing but a spare-ribbed

twenty-eight-year-old stock-car driver halfway through his 10th lap around the Islip, L.I., Speedway and taking a curve too wide. A lubberly young man with a Chicago boxcar haircut came up on the inside in a 1949 Ford and caromed him 12 rows up into the grandstand, but Lawrence Mendelsohn and his entire car did not hit once spectator.

2   "That was what got me," he said, "I remember I was hanging upside down from my seat belt like a side of Jersey bacon and wondering why no one was sitting where I hit. 'Lousy promotion,' I said to myself.

3   "Not only that, but everybody who *was* in the stands forgot about the race and came running over to look at me gift-wrapped upside down in a fresh pile of junk."

4   At that moment occurred the transformation of Lawrence Mendelsohn, racing driver, into Lawrence Mendelsohn, promoter, and, a few transactions later, owner of the Islip Speedway, where he kept seeing more of this same underside of stock car racing that everyone in the industry avoids putting into words. Namely, that for every purist who comes to see the fine points of the race, such as who is going to win, there are probably five waiting for the wrecks to which stock car racing is so gloriously prone.

5   The pack will be going into a curve when suddenly two cars, three cars, four cars tangle, spinning and splattering all over each other and the retaining walls, upside down, right side up, inside out and in pieces, with the seams bursting open and discs, rods, wires and gasoline spewing out and yards of sheet metal shearing off like Reynolds Wrap and crumpling into the most baroque shapes, after which an ash-blue smoke starts seeping up from the ruins and a thrill begins to spread over the stands like Newburg sauce.

6   So why put up with the monotony between crashes?

7   Such, in brief, is the early history of what is culturally the most important sport ever originated in the United States, a sport that ranks with the gladiatorial games of Rome as a piece of national symbolism. Lawrence Mendelsohn had a vision of an automobile sport that would be all crashes. Not two cars, not three cars, not four cars, but 100 cars would be out in an arena doing nothing but smashing each other into shrapnel. The car that outrammed and outdodged all the rest, the last car that could still move amid the smoking heap, would take the prize money.

8   So at 8:15 at night at the Riverhead Raceway, just west of Riverhead, L.I., on Route 25, amid the quaint tranquility of the duck and turkey farm flatlands of eastern Long Island, Lawrence Mendelsohn

stood up on the back of a flat truck in his red neon warmup jacket and lectured his 100 drivers on the rules and niceties of the new game, the "demolition derby." And so at 8:30 the first 25 cars moved out onto the raceway's quarter-mile stock car track. There was not enough room for 100 cars to mangle each other. Lawrence Mendelsohn's dream would require four heats. Now the 25 cars were placed at intervals all about the circumference of the track, making flatulent revving noises, all headed not around the track but toward a point in the center of the infield.

9   Then the entire crowd, about 4,000, started chanting a countdown, "Ten, nine, eight, seven, six, five, four, three, two," but it was impossible to hear the rest, because right after "two" half the crowd went into a strange whinnying wail. The starter's flag went up, and the 25 cars took off, roaring into second gear with no mufflers, all headed toward that same point in the center of the infield, converging nose on nose.

10   The effect was exactly what one expects that many simultaneous crashes to produce: the unmistakable tympany of automobiles colliding and cheap-gauge sheet metal buckling; front ends folding together at the same cockeyed angles police photographs of night-time wreck scenes capture so well on grainy paper; smoke pouring from under the hoods and hanging over the infield like a howitzer cloud; a few of the surviving cars lurching eccentrically on bent axles. At last, after four heats, there were only two cars moving through the junk, a 1953 Chrysler and a 1958 Cadillac. In the Chrysler a small fascia of muscles named Spider Ligon, who smoked a cigar while he drove, had the Cadillac cornered up against a guard rail in front of the main grandstand. He dispatched it by swinging around and backing full throttle through the left side of its grille and radiator.

11   By now the crowd was quite beside itself. Spectators broke through a gate in the retaining screen. Some rushed to Spider Ligon's car, hoisted him to their shoulders and marched off the field, howling. Others clambered over the stricken cars of the defeated, enjoying the details of their ruin, and howling. The good, full cry of triumph and annihilation rose from Riverhead Raceway, and the demolition derby was over.

12   That was the 154th demolition derby in two years. Since Lawrence Mendelsohn staged the first one at Islip Speedway in 1961, they have been held throughout the United States at the rate of one every five days, resulting in the destruction of about 15,000 cars. The figures

alone indicate a gluttonous appetite for the sport. Sports writers, of course, have managed to ignore demolition derbies even more successfully than they have ignored stock car racing and drag racing. All in all, the new automobile sports have shown that the sports pages, which on the surface appear to hum with life and earthiness, are at bottom pillars of gentility. This drag racing and demolition derbies and things, well, there are too many kids in it with sideburns, tight Levis and winkle-picker boots.

13   Yet the demolition derbies keep growing on word-of-mouth publicity. The "nationals" were held last month at Langhorne, Pa., with 50 cars in the finals, and demolition derby fans everywhere know that Don McTavish, of Dover, Mass., is the new world's champion. About 1,250,000 spectators have come to the 154 contests held so far. More than 75 per cent of the derbies have drawn full houses.

14   The nature of their appeal is clear enough. Since the onset of the Christian era, i.e., since about 500 A.D., no game has come along to fill the gap left by the abolition of the purest of all sports, gladiatorial combat. As late as 300 A.D. these bloody duels, usually between men but sometimes between women and dwarfs, were enormously popular not only in Rome but throughout the Roman Empire. Since then no game, not even boxing, has successfully acted out the underlying motifs of most sport, that is, aggression and destruction.

15   Boxing, of course, is an aggressive sport, but one contestant has actually destroyed the other in a relatively small percentage of matches. Other games are progressively more sublimated forms of sport. Often, as in the case of football, they are encrusted with oddments of passive theology and metaphysics to the effect that the real purpose of the game is to foster character, teamwork, stamina, physical fitness and the ability to "give-and-take."

16   But not even those wonderful clergymen who pray in behalf of Congress, expressway ribbon-cuttings, urban renewal projects and testimonial dinners for ethnic aldermen would pray for a demolition derby. The demolition derby is, pure and simple, a form of gladiatorial combat for our times.

17   As hand-to-hand combat has gradually disappeared from our civilization, even in wartime, and competition has become more and more sophisticated and abstract, Americans have turned to the automobile to satisfy their love of direct aggression. The mild-mannered man who turns into a bear behind the wheel of a car—i.e., who finds in the power of the automobile a vehicle for the release of his inhibitions—is part of

American folklore. Among teen-agers the automobile has become the symbol, and in part the physical means, of triumph over family and community restrictions. Seventy-five per cent of all car thefts in the United States are by teen-agers out for "joy rides."

18 The symbolic meaning of the automobile tones down but by no means vanishes in adulthood. Police traffic investigators have long been convinced that far more accidents are purposeful crashes by belligerent drivers than they could ever prove. One of the heroes of the era was the Middle Eastern diplomat who rammed a magazine writer's car from behind in the Kalorama embassy district of Washington two years ago. When the American bellowed out the window at him, he backed up and smashed his car again. When the fellow leaped out of his car to pick a fight, he backed up and smashed his car a third time, then drove off. He was recalled home for having "gone native."

19 The unabashed, undisguised, quite purposeful sense of destruction of the demolition derby is its unique contribution. The aggression, the battering, the ruination are there to be enjoyed. The crowd at a demolition derby seldom gasps and often laughs. It enjoys the same full-throated participation as Romans at the Colosseum. After each trial or heat at a demolition derby, two drivers go into the finals. One is the driver whose car was still going at the end. The other is the driver the crowd selects from among the 24 vanquished on the basis of his courage, showmanship or simply the awesomeness of his crashes. The numbers of the cars are read over loudspeakers, and the crowd chooses one with its cheers. By the same token, the crowd may force a driver out of competition if he appears cowardly or merely cunning. This is the sort of driver who drifts around the edge of the battle avoiding crashes with the hope that the other cars will eliminate one another. The umpire waves a yellow flag at him and he must crash into someone within 30 seconds or run the risk of being booed off the field in dishonor and disgrace.

20 The frank relish of the crowd is nothing, however, compared to the kick the contestants get out of the game. It costs a man an average of $50 to retrieve a car from a junk yard and get it running for a derby. He will only get his money back—$50—for winning a heat. The chance of being smashed up in the madhouse first 30 seconds of a round are so great, even the best of drivers faces long odds in his shot at the $500 first prize. None of that matters to them.

21 Tommy Fox, who is nineteen, said he entered the demolition derby because, "You know, it's fun. I like it. You know what I mean?"

What was fun about it? Tommy Fox had a way of speaking that was much like the early Marlon Brando. Much of what he had to say came from the trapezii, which he rolled quite a bit, and the forehead, which he cocked, and the eyebrows, which he could bring together expressively from time to time. "Well," he said, "you know, like when you hit 'em, and all that. It's fun."

22   Tommy Fox had a lot of fun in the first heat. Nobody was bashing around quite like he was in his old green Hudson. He did not win, chiefly because he took too many chances, but the crowd voted him into the finals as the best showman.

23   "I got my brother," said Tommy. "I came in from the side and he didn't even see me."

24   His brother is Don Fox, thirty-two, who owns the junk yard where they both got their cars. Don likes to hit them, too, only he likes it almost too much. Don drives with such abandon, smashing into the first car he can get a shot at and leaving himself wide open, he does not stand much chance of finishing the first three minutes.

25   For years now sociologists have been calling upon one another to undertake a serious study of America's "car culture." No small part of it is the way the automobile has, for one very large segment of the population, become the focus of the same sort of quasi-religious dedication as art is currently for another large segment of a higher social order. Tommy Fox is unemployed, Don Fox runs a junk yard, Spider Ligon is a maintenance man for Brookhaven Naval Laboratory, but to categorize them as such is getting no closer to the truth than to have categorized William Faulkner in 1926 as a clerk at Lord & Taylor, although he was.

26   Tommy Fox, Don Fox and Spider Ligon are acolytes of the car culture, an often esoteric world of arts and sciences that came into its own after World War II and now has believers of two generations. Charlie Turbush, thirty-five, and his son, Buddy, seventeen, were two more contestants, and by no stretch of the imagination can they be characterized as bizarre figures or cultists of the death wish. As for the dangers of driving in a demolition derby, they are quite real by all physical laws. The drivers are protected only by crash helmets, seat belts and the fact that all glass, interior handles, knobs and fixtures have been removed. Yet Lawrence Mendelsohn claims that there have been no serious injuries in 154 demolition derbies and now gets his insurance at a rate below that of stock car racing.

27   The sport's future may depend in part on word getting around about its relative safety. Already it is beginning to draw contestants here

and there from social levels that could give the demolition derby the cachet of respectability. In eastern derbies so far two doctors and three young men of more than passable connections in eastern society have entered under whimsical *noms de combat* and emerged neither scarred nor victorious. Bull fighting had to win the same social combat.

28   All of which brings to mind that fine afternoon when some high-born Roman women were out in Nero's box at the Colosseum watching this sexy Thracian carve an ugly little Samnite up into prime cuts, and one said, darling, she had an inspiration, and Nero, needless to say, was all for it. Thus began the new vogue of Roman socialites fighting as gladiators themselves, for kicks. By the second century A.D. even the Emperor Commodus was out there with a tiger's head as a helmet hacking away at some poor dazed fall guy. He did a lot for the sport. Arenas sprang up all over the empire like shopping center bowling alleys.

29   The future of the demolition derby, then, stretches out over the face of America. The sport draws no lines of gender, and post-debs may reach Lawrence Mendelsohn at his office in Deer Park.

QUESTIONS

Ideas

1. Why does Wolfe say that the demolition derby is "culturally the most important sport ever originated in the United States"? (7) What does the sport symbolize for Wolfe?

2. What is Wolfe's attitude toward the demolition drivers themselves? Where is it most clearly expressed? How is Wolfe's attitude revealed?

3. What is the point of the opening anecdote? What sense is given of the fans of car racing? Can the same point be made about fans of other sports —hockey or boxing or football, for instance? Why or why not?

Organization

4. Wolfe alternates between description of the races and explanation of his ideas about them. Trace this pattern through the essay, labeling each paragraph as either descriptive or explanatory. Where does Wolfe rely most heavily and thoroughly on explanation? Is there an advantage to this alternating method of organizing, or would a simple two-part form have worked just as well (with the description first and the explanation afterward)?

5. Paragraphs 1–11 describe a typical demolition derby and also explain how
    the sport began. What is the function of paragraphs 12 and 13? Of
    paragraphs 14–19?

6. Can this essay be divided into the conventional three-part format—intro-
    duction, body, and conclusion? Why or why not?

Sentences

7. Why do sentences in paragraphs 5 and 6 exist as independent paragraphs?
    Would the sentence in paragraph 5 be better as three or four short
    sentences? Why or why not?

8. What is the function of the colon and the semicolons in the opening
    sentence of paragraph 10? How do they help you to organize and process
    the information in the sentence?

Words

9. In paragraphs 2 and 3, and later in paragraph 21, Wolfe quotes directly
    the words of Lawrence Mendelsohn and Tommy Fox. Why are their
    comments quoted directly instead of reported indirectly? What does each
    man's comment reveal about him?

10. In his descriptive paragraphs Wolfe makes occasional use of simile. Exam-
    ine the similes in paragraphs 5 and 10. What is the point of each?

11. Examine the verbs in paragraphs 5, 10, and 11. Why are there so many?
    What common feature of form do the verbs of paragraphs 5 and 10 share?
    What is the cumulative effect of these verbs?

Suggestions for Writing

A. Write an essay arguing that demolition driving is or is not a sport. Consider
    Wolfe's notion that it is the "purest" modern sport, the closest to the
    purest of all sports ever—gladiatorial combat.

B. Write an essay explaining the appeal of the automobile. You may want to
    develop the ideas Wolfe mentions in paragraphs 17–18 and 25–26. Or you
    may want to develop some other idea about cars, perhaps their connection
    with status, sex, self-image.

C. Look through a few issues of a popular car magazine like *Car and Driver*
    or *Road and Track*. On the basis of the articles, advertisements, editorials,
    letters to the editor, write an essay explaining why such a magazine exists,
    who it appeals to and why.

D. Look through any popular magazine that contains automobile ads. Select
    one ad and analyze its purpose, audience, appeals, strategies of persuasion,
    and language.

E. Write an essay about one kind of sports fan—or about the fans of one sport. Or compare the fans of two sports—football fans and baseball fans, for instance.

Only One Life

---

1   In 1961 a copy writer named Shirley Polykoff was working for the Foote, Cone & Belding advertising agency on the Clairol hair-dye account when she came up with the line: "If I've only one life, let me live it as a blonde!" In a single slogan she had summed up what might be described as the secular side of the Me Decade. "If I've only one life, let me live it as a _____ !" (You have only to fill in the blank.)

2   This formula accounts for much of the popularity of the women's liberation or feminist movement. "What does a woman want?" said Freud. Perhaps there are women who want to humble men or reduce their power or achieve equality or even superiority for themselves and their sisters. But for every one such woman, there are nine who simply want to *fill in the blank* as they see fit. "If I've only one life, let me live it as . . . a free spirit!" (Instead of . . . a house slave: a cleaning woman, a cook, a nursemaid, a station-wagon hacker, and an occasional household sex aid.) But even that may be overstating it, because often the unconscious desire is nothing more than: *Let's talk about Me.* The great unexpected dividend of the feminist movement has been to elevate an ordinary status—woman, housewife—to the level of drama. One's very existence as *a woman* . . . as *Me* . . . becomes something all the world analyzes, agonizes over, draws cosmic conclusions from, or, in any event, takes seriously. Every woman becomes Emma Bovary, Cousin Bette, or Nora . . . or Erica Jong or Consuelo Saah Baehr.

3   Among men the formula becomes: "If I've only one life, let me live it as a . . . Casanova or a Henry VIII!" (instead of a humdrum workadaddy, eternally faithful, except perhaps for a mean little skulking episode here and there, to a woman who now looks old enough to be your aunt and needs a shave or else has electrolysis lines above her upper lip, as well as atrophied calves, and is an embarrassment to be seen with when you take her on trips). The right to shuck overripe wives and take on fresh ones was once seen as the prerogative of kings only, and even then it was scandalous. In the 1950's and 1960's it began to be seen as

the prerogative of the rich, the powerful, and the celebrated (Nelson Rockefeller, Henry Ford, and Show Business figures), although it retained the odor of scandal. Wife-shucking damaged Adlai Stevenson's chances of becoming President in 1952 and 1956 and Rockefeller's chances of becoming the Republican nominee in 1964 and 1968. Until the 1970's wife-shucking made it impossible for an astronaut to be chosen to go into space. Today, in the Me Decade, it becomes *normal behavior*, one of the factors that has pushed the divorce rate above 50 percent.

4   When Eugene McCarthy filled in the blank in 1972 and shucked his wife, it was hardly noticed. Likewise in the case of several astronauts. When Wayne Hays filled in the blank in 1976 and shucked his wife of thirty-eight years, it did not hurt his career in the slightest. Copulating with the girl in the office, however, was still regarded as scandalous. (Elizabeth Ray filled in the blank in another popular fashion: If I've only one life, let me live it as a . . . Celebrity!" As did Arthur Bremer, who kept a diary during his stalking of Nixon and, later, George Wallace . . . with an eye toward a book contract. Which he got.) Some wiseacre has remarked, supposedly with levity, that the federal government may in time have to create reservations for women over thirty-five, to take care of the swarms of shucked wives and widows. In fact, women in precisely those categories have begun setting up communes or "extended families" to provide one another support and companionship in a world without workadaddies. ("If I've only one life, why live it as an anachronism?")

5   Much of what is now known as the "sexual revolution" has consisted of both women and men filling in the blank this way: "If I've only one life, let me live it as . . . a Swinger!" (Instead of a frustrated, bored monogamist.) In "swinging," a husband and wife give each other license to copulate with other people. There are no statistics on the subject that mean anything, but I do know that it pops up in conversation today in the most unexpected corners of the country. It is an odd experience to be in De Kalb, Illinois, in the very corncrib of America, and have some conventional-looking housewife (not *housewife*, damn it!) come up to you and ask: "Is there much tripling going on in New York?"

6   *"Tripling?"*

7   Tripling turns out to be a practice, in De Kalb, anyway, in which a husband and wife invite a third party—male or female, but more often female—over for an evening of whatever, including polymorphous perversity, even the practices written of in the one-hand magazines, such

as *Hustler,* all the things involving tubes and hoses and tourniquets and cups and double-jointed sailors.

8   One of the satisfactions of this sort of life, quite in addition to the groin spasms, is talk: *Let's talk about Me.* Sexual adventurers are given to the most relentless and deadly serious talk . . . about Me. They quickly succeed in placing themselves onstage in the sexual drama whose outlines were sketched by Freud and then elaborated by Wilhelm Reich. Men and women of all sorts, not merely swingers, are given just now to the most earnest sort of talk about the Sexual Me. A key drama of our own day is Ingmar Bergman's movie *Scenes from a Marriage.* In it we see a husband and wife who have good jobs and a well-furnished home but who are unable to "communicate"—to cite one of the signature words of the Me Decade. Then they begin to communicate, and thereupon their marriage breaks up and they start divorce proceedings. For the rest of the picture they communicate endlessly, with great candor, but the "relationship"—another signature word—remains doomed. Ironically, the lesson that people seem to draw from this movie has to do with . . . "the need to communicate."

9   *Scenes from a Marriage* is one of those rare works of art, like *The Sun Also Rises,* that not only succeed in capturing a certain mental atmosphere in fictional form . . . but also turn around and help radiate it throughout real life. I personally know of two instances in which couples, after years of marriage, went to see *Scenes from a Marriage* and came home convinced of the "need to communicate." The discussions began with one of the two saying, Let's try to be completely candid for once. You tell me exactly what you don't like about me, and I'll do the same for you. At this, the starting point, the whole notion is exciting. We're going to talk about *Me!* (And I can take it.) I'm going to find out what he (or she) really thinks about me! (Of course, I have my faults, but they're minor . . . or else exciting.)

10   She says, "Go ahead. What don't you like about me?"

11   They're both under the Bergman spell. Nevertheless, a certain sixth sense tells him that they're on dangerous ground. So he decides to pick something that doesn't seem too terrible.

12   "Well," he says, "one thing that bothers me is that when we meet people for the first time, you never know what to say. Or else you get nervous and start chattering away, and it's all so banal, it makes me look bad."

13   Consciously she's still telling herself, "I can take it." But what he has just said begins to seep through her brain like scalding water. What's

he talking about?—makes *him* look bad? *He's saying I'm unsophis-
ticated, a social liability and an embarrassment. All those times we've
gone out, he's been ashamed of me!* (And what makes it worse—it's the
sort of disease for which there's no cure!) She always knew she was
awkward. His crime is: he *noticed!* He's known it, too, all along. He's
had *contempt* for me.

14   Out loud she says, "Well, I'm afraid there's nothing I can do about
that."

15   He detects the petulant note. "Look," he says, "you're the one
who said to be candid."

16   She says, "I know. I *want* you to be."

17   He says, "Well, it's your turn."

18   "Well," she says, "I'll tell *you* something about when we meet
people and when we go places. You never clean yourself properly—you
don't know how to wipe yourself. Sometimes we're standing there talking to people, and there's . . . a smell. And I'll tell you something else:
People can tell it's you."

19   And he's still telling *him*self, "I can take it"—but what inna
namea Christ is *this?*

20   He says, "But you've never said anything—about anything like
that."

21   She says, "But I *tried* to. How many times have I told you about
your dirty drawers when you were taking them off at night?"

22   Somehow this really makes him angry . . . All those times . . .
and his mind immediately fastens on Harley Thatcher and his wife,
whom he has always wanted to impress . . . *From underneath my $350
suits I smelled of shit!* What infuriates him is that this is a humiliation
from which there's no recovery. *How often have they sniggered about
it later?—or not invited me places? Is it something people say every
time my name comes up?* And all at once he is intensely annoyed with
his wife, not because she never told him all these years, but simply
because she *knows* about his disgrace—and she was the one who
brought him the bad news!

23   From that moment on they're ready to get the skewers in. It's only
a few minutes before they've begun trying to sting each other with
confessions about their little affairs, their little slipping around, their
little coitus on the sly—"Remember that time I told you my flight from
Buffalo was canceled?"—and at that juncture the ranks of those *who can
take it* become very thin indeed. So they communicate with great

candor! and break up! and keep on communicating! and they find the relationship hopelessly doomed.

24   One couple went into group therapy. The other went to a marriage counselor. Both types of therapy are very popular forms, currently, of *Let's talk about Me.* This phase of the breakup always provides a rush of exhilaration—for what more exhilarating topic is there than . . . *Me?* Through group therapy, marriage counseling, and other forms of "psychological consultation" they can enjoy that same *Me* euphoria that the very rich have enjoyed for years in psychoanalysis. The cost of the new Me sessions is only $10 to $30 an hour, whereas psychoanalysis runs from $50 to $125. The woman's exhilaration, however, is soon complicated by the fact that she is (in the typical case) near or beyond the cutoff age of thirty-five and will have to retire to the reservation.

25   Well, my dear Mature Moderns . . . Ingmar never promised you a rose garden!

QUESTIONS

Ideas

1. What is Wolfe's subject here? Women's Liberation? Talk Therapy? Selfishness? Something else? And what is the predominant tone of the essay? How does this tone reveal and carry Wolfe's attitude toward his subject?

2. What is Wolfe's purpose, and who is his implied audience? Consider the literary allusions in paragraph 2, the historical and political allusions in paragraph 3, and the contemporary allusions in paragraph 4.

Organization

3. "Only One Life" falls into two major parts: paragraphs 1–8 and paragraphs 9–23—with paragraphs 24 and 25 as a wrap-up. Identify the subject and point of the two main parts and explain how Wolfe moves, in paragraphs 8 and 9, from the subject of the first part to the subject of the second.

4. Paragraphs 1 and 2 are about women, 3 and 4 about men, and 5–8 about both. What ties all eight paragraphs together?

5. Examine the transitions Wolfe uses to link his first eight paragraphs. How does the first sentence of each paragraph tie it to the preceding paragraph?

What specific words and phrases form the links? And why are transitions sparse in paragraphs 9–25?

Sentences

6. Wolfe uses a slogan, which he repeats throughout the first part of the essay: "If I've only one life, let me live it as a *blonde!*" Examine the variations he works on this slogan. What is the point of the variations?

7. He uses another repeated sentence as well, this one without variation: "Let's talk about Me" (paragraphs 2, 8, and 24). What tone is established with this repeated sentence?

8. What are the function and the effect of the parenthetical sentences in paragraphs 1, 2, 4, 9, and 13? Of the ellipses in sentences in paragraphs 2, 3, 4, 5, 8, 9, and 24?

Words

9. Reread the dialogue in paragraphs 9–23. Explain why some words are italicized. What is the effect of this?

10. Wolfe's diction ranges from the colloquial and the familiar to the unusual and the recondite. Find examples of different kinds of words and phrases showing evidence of Wolfe's range and diversity of language.

Suggestions for Writing

A. Write an essay responding to the comments from paragraph 2 that follow:

1. "The great unexpected dividend of the feminist movement has been to elevate an ordinary status—woman, housewife—to the level of drama."

2. "One's very existence as a *woman* . . . as *Me* . . . becomes something all the world analyzes, agonizes over, draws conclusions from, or, in any event, takes seriously."

B. Imitate the second part of this essay by writing a dialogue that includes not only what the speakers say, but also what they think. You will have, then, an inner-outer dialogue, which gains effect by the discrepancy between what is said and what is thought. You may include, as Wolfe does, a narrator to explain the conversation, perhaps to comment on it.

C. Take a popular slogan from advertising or from a contemporary issue. Write an essay examining its implications and ramifications. Explain how the slogan sums up and epitomizes important attitudes, ideals, and values of whoever uses it, believes in it, or lives by it.

The Lab Rat

1   Albuquerque, home of the Lovelace Clinic, was a dirty red sod-hut tortilla highway desert city that was remarkably short on charm, despite the Mexican touch here and there. But career officers were used to dreary real estate. That was what they inhabited in America, especially if they were fliers. No, it was Lovelace itself that began to get everybody's back up. Lovelace was a fairly new private diagnostic clinic, somewhat like the Mayo Clinic, doing "aerospace-medical" work for the government, among other things. Lovelace had been founded by Randy Lovelace—W. Randolph Lovelace II—who had served along with Crossfield and Flickinger on the committee on "human factors" in space flight. The chief of the medical staff at Lovelace was a recently retired general of the Air Force medical corps, Dr. A. H. Schwichtenberg. He was General Schwichtenberg to everybody at Lovelace. The operation took itself very seriously. The candidates for astronaut would be given their physical testing here. Then they would go to Wright-Patterson Air Force Base in Dayton for psychological and stress testing. It was all very hush-hush. Conrad went to Lovelace in a group of only six men, once more in their ill-fitting mufti and terrific watches, apparently so that they would blend in with the clinic's civilian patients. They had been warned that the tests at Lovelace and Wright-Patterson would be more exacting and strenuous than any they had ever taken. It was not the tests *per se,* however, that made every self-respecting fighter jock, early in the game, begin to hate Lovelace.

2   Military pilots were veterans of physical examinations, but in addition to all the usual components of "the complete physical," the Lovelace doctors had devised a series of novel tests involving straps, tubes, hoses, and needles. They would put a strap around your head, clamp some sort of instrument over your eyes—and then stick a hose in your ear and pump cold water into your ear canal. It would make your eyeballs flutter. It was an unpleasant, disorienting sensation, although not painful. If you wanted to know what it was all about, the Lovelace doctors and technicians, in their uncompromising white smocks, indicated that you really didn't need to know, and that was that.

3   What really made Conrad feel that something *eccentric* was going on here, however, was the business of the electrode in the

thumb muscle. They brought him into a room and strapped his hand
down to a table, palm up. Then they brought out an ugly-looking
needle attached to an electrical wire. Conrad didn't like needles in the
first place, and this one looked like a monster. *Hannh?*—they drove
the needle into the big muscle at the base of his thumb. It hurt like
a bastard. Conrad looked up as if to say, "What the hell's going on?"
But they weren't even looking at him. They were looking—at the
meter. The wire from the needle led to what looked like a doorbell.
They pushed the buzzer. Conrad looked down, and his hand—his own
goddamned hand!—was balling up into a fist and springing open and
balling up into a fist and springing open and balling up into a fist and
springing open and balling up into a fist and springing open at an
absolutely furious rate, faster than he could have ever made it do so on
its own, and there seemed to be nothing that he, with his own mind
and his own central nervous system, could do to stop his own hand or
even slow it down. The Lovelace doctors in their white smocks, with
their reflectors on their heads, were having a hell of a time for themselves . . . with *his* hand . . . They were reading the meter and scrib-
bling away on their clipboards at a jolly rate.

4   Afterward Conrad said, "What was that for?"

5   A doctor looked up, distractedly, as if Conrad were interrupting
an important train of thought.

6   "I'm afraid there's no simple way to explain it to you," he said.
"There's nothing for you to worry about."

7   It was then that it began to dawn on Conrad, first as a feeling
rather than as a fully formed thought: "Lab rats."

8   It went on like that. The White Smocks gave each of them a test
tube and said they wanted a sperm count. *What do you mean?* Place
your sperm in the tube. *How?* Through ejaculation. *Just like that?*
Masturbation is the customary procedure. *What!* The best results seem
to be obtained through fantasization, accompanied by masturbation,
followed by ejaculation. *Where, f'r chrissake?* Use the bathroom. A
couple of the boys said things such as, "Well, okay, I'll do it if you'll
send a nurse in with me—to help me along if I get stuck." The White
Smocks looked at them as if they were schoolboys making obscene
noises. This got the pilots' back up, and a couple of them refused, flat
out. But by and by they gave in, and so now you had the ennobling
prospect of half a dozen test pilots padding off one by one to the head
in their skivvies to jack off for the Lovelace Clinic, Project Mercury, and
America's battle for the heavens. Sperm counts were supposed to deter-

mine the density and motility of the sperm. What this had to do with a man's fitness to fly on top of a rocket or anywhere else was incomprehensible. Conrad began to get the feeling that it wasn't just him and his brother lab rats who didn't know what was going on. He now had the suspicion that the Reflector Heads didn't know, either. They had somehow gotten *carte blanche* to try out any goddamned thing they could think up—and that was what they were doing, whether there was any logic to it or not.

9   Each candidate was to deliver two stool specimens to the Lovelace laboratory in Dixie cups, and days were going by and Conrad had been unable to egest even one, and the staff kept getting after him about it. Finally he managed to produce a single bolus, a mean hard little ball no more than an inch in diameter and shot through with some kind of seeds, whole seeds, undigested. Then he remembered. The first night in Albuquerque he had gone to a Mexican restaurant and eaten a lot of jalapeño peppers. They were jalapeño seeds. Even in the turd world this was a pretty miserable-looking *objet*. So Conrad tied a red ribbon around the goddamned thing, with a bow and all, and put it in the Dixie cup and delivered it to the lab. Curious about the ribbons that flopped out over the lip of the cup, the technicians all peered in. Conrad broke into his full cackle of mirth, much the way Wally might have. No one was swept up in the joke, however. The Lovelace staffers looked at the beribboned bolus, and then they looked at Conrad . . . as if he were a bug on the windshield of the pace car of medical progress.

10   One of the tests at Lovelace was an examination of the prostate gland. There was nothing exotic about this, of course; it was a standard part of the complete physical for men. The doctor puts a rubber sleeve on a finger and slips the finger up the subject's rectum and presses the prostate, looking for signs of swelling, infection, and so on. But several men in Conrad's group had come back from the prostate examination gasping with pain and calling the doctor a sadistic little pervert and worse. He had prodded the prostate with such force a couple of them had passed blood.

11   Conrad goes into the room, and sure enough, the man reams him so hard the pain brings him to his knees.

12   "What the hell!—"

13   Conrad comes up swinging, but an orderly, a huge monster, immediately grabs him, and Conrad can't move. The doctor looks at him blankly, as if he's a vet and Conrad's a barking dog.

14   The probings of the bowels seemed to be endless, full proctosig-

moidoscope examinations, the works. These things were never pleasant; in fact, they were a bit humiliating, involving, as they did, various
things being shoved up your tail. The Lovelace Clinic specialty seemed
to be the exacting of maximum indignity from each procedure. The
pilots had never run into anything like this before. Not only that,
before each ream-out you had to report to the clinic at seven o'clock
in the morning and give yourself an enema. *Up yours!* seemed to be
the motto of the Lovelace Clinic—and they even made you do it to
yourself. So Conrad reports at seven one morning and gives himself
the enema. He's supposed to undergo a lower gastrointestinal tract
examination that morning. In the so-called lower G.I. examination,
barium is pumped into the subject's bowels; then a little hose with a
balloon on the end of it is inserted in the rectum, and the balloon is
inflated, blocking the canal to keep the barium from forcing its way
out before the radiologist can complete his examination. After the
examination, like everyone who has ever been through the procedure,
Conrad now feels as if there are eighty-five pounds of barium in his
intestines and they are about to explode. The Smocks inform him that
there is no john on this floor. He's supposed to pick up the tube that
is coming out of his rectum and follow an orderly, who will lead him
to a john two floors below. On the tube there is a clamp, and he can
release the clamp, deflating the balloon, at the proper time. *It's unbelievable!* To try to walk, with this explosive load sloshing about in your
pelvic saddle, is agony. Nevertheless, Conrad picks up the tube and
follows the orderly. Conrad has on only the standard bed patient's
tunic, the angel robes, open up the back. The tube leading out of his
tail to the balloon gizmo is so short that he has to hunch over to about
two feet off the floor to carry it in front of him. His tail is now, as the
saying goes, flapping in the breeze, with a tube coming out of it. The
orderly has on red cowboy boots. Conrad is intensely aware of that
fact, because he is now hunched over so far that his eyes hit the orderly at about calf level. He's hunched over, with his tail in the breeze,
scuttling like a crab after a pair of red cowboy boots. Out into the
corridor they go, an ordinary public corridor, the full-moon hunchback
and the red cowboy boots, amid men, women, children, nurses, nuns,
the lot. The red cowboy boots are beginning to trot along like mad.
The orderly is no fool. He's been through this before. He's been
through the whole disaster. He's seen the explosions. Time is of the
essence. There's a hunchback stick of dynamite behind him. To Conrad it becomes more incredible every step of the way. They actually

have to go down an elevator—full of sane people—and do their crazy tango through another public hallway—agog with normal human beings—before finally reaching the goddamned john.

15   Later that day Conrad received, once more, instructions to report to the clinic at seven the next morning to give himself an enema. The next thing the people in the administrative office of the clinic knew, a small but enraged young man was storming into the office of General Schwichtenberg himself, waving a great flaccid flamingo-pink enema bag and hose like some sort of obese whip. As he waved it, it gurgled.

16   The enema bag came slamming down on the general's desk. It landed with a tremendous *plop* and then began gurgling and sighing.

17   "General Schwichtenberg," said Conrad, "you're looking at a man who has given himself his last enema. If you want enemas from me, from now on you can come get 'em yourself. You can take this bag and give it to a nurse and send her over—"

18   Just you—

19   "—and let her do the honors. I've given myself my last enema. Either things shape up around here, or I ship out."

20   The general stared at the great flamingo bag, which lay there heaving and wheezing on his desk, and then he stared at Conrad. The general seemed appalled . . . All the same it wouldn't do anybody any good, least of all the Lovelace Clinic, if one of the candidates pulled out, firing broadsides at the operation. The general started trying to mollify this vision of enema rage.

21   "Now, Lieutenant," he said, "I know this hasn't been pleasant. This is probably the toughest examination you'll ever have to go through in your life, but as you know, it's for a project of utmost importance. The project needs men like yourself. You have a compact build, and every pound saved in Project Mercury can be critical."

22   And so forth and so on. He kept spraying Conrad's fire.

23   "All the same, General, I've given myself my last enema."

24   Word of the Enema Bag Showdown spread rapidly among the other candidates, and they were delighted to hear about it. Practically all of them had wanted to do something of the sort. It wasn't just that the testing procedures were unpleasant; the entire atmosphere of the testing constituted an affront. There was something . . . decidedly *out of joint* about it. Pilots and doctors were natural enemies, of course, at least as pilots saw it. The flight surgeon was pretty much kept *in his place* in the service. His only real purpose was to tend to pilots and keep 'em

flying. He was an attendant to the pilots' vital stuff. In fact, flight surgeons were encouraged to fly backseat with fighter pilots from time to time, so as to understand what stresses and righteous stuff the job entailed. Regardless of how much he thought of himself, no flight surgeon dared position himself *above* the pilots in his squadron in the way he conducted himself before them: i.e., it was hard for him to be a consummate panjandrum, the way the typical civilian doctor was.

25   But at Lovelace, in the testing for Project Mercury, the natural order was turned upside down. These people not only did not treat them as righteous pilots, they did not treat them as pilots of any sort. They never even alluded to the fact that they were pilots. An irksome thought was beginning to intrude. In the competition for *astronaut* the kind of stuff you were made of as a *pilot* didn't count for a goddamned thing. They were looking for a certain type of animal who registered bingo on the meter. You wouldn't win this competition in the air. If you won it, it would be right here on the examination table in the land of the rubber tubes.

26   Yes, the boys were delighted when Conrad finally told off General Schwichtenberg. Attaboy, Pete! At the same time, they were quite content to let the credit for the Lab Rat Revolt fall to Conrad and to him alone.

QUESTIONS

Ideas

1. What is Wolfe's purpose in presenting the details of the physical examinations? What point does he make about the relationship between pilots and doctors?

2. What is the dominant tone of the piece? Does the tone shift at any point?

Organization

3. "Lab Rat" breaks into three main sections: paragraphs 1–14 (1, 2–13, 14), paragraphs 15–23, and paragraphs 24–25. Explain what Wolfe is showing in each section and how the sections are related. In which section is Wolfe's writing primarily explanatory? Primarily descriptive? Primarily narrative-dramatic?

4. Could paragraphs 15–23 be omitted? What does Wolfe gain by including them?

Sentences

5. In paragraph 3 Wolfe includes a long sentence that contains repeated elements. Could or should this long sentence have been condensed and its repeated words excised? It begins: "Conrad looked down . . ."

6. About two-thirds of the way through paragraph 14, the sentences become shorter. In addition, the final sentence of paragraph 14 is interrupted twice by pairs of dashes. What is the effect of each of these changes of sentence style, and why are these changes appropriate?

Words

7. Wolfe employs colloquial language in a number of places in "Lab Rat": "jack off" (8), "get everybody's back up" (1), "shoved up your tail" (14), "with his tail between his legs" (14). What are the tone and effect of such language? Why do you think Wolfe uses it?

8. Compare the language of the pilots with the language of the doctors. See especially paragraphs 8 and 10. What is the point of the different kinds of talk?

9. The major image of this essay, is, of course, the pilot as test animal—as laboratory rat. How does Wolfe initiate, sustain, and develop this analogy? Where is it most emphatic?

10. Discuss the effectiveness of the comparisons in paragraphs 9, 13, and 14.

11. In paragraphs 10–14 Wolfe uses present-tense verbs. Would it make any difference if these verbs were in the past tense? Why or why not?

Suggestions for Writing

A. Describe an experience in which you were put through a series of tests without knowing what was happening or what the tests were for. Try to give the reader a sense of what it was like to have this happen to you.

B. Write imitations of Wolfe's long sentence in paragraph 3 and of the entire final paragraph.

C. Write a paragraph in which you focus on, sustain, and develop an analogy.

The Right Stuff

---

1   A young man might go into military flight training believing that he was entering some sort of technical school in which he was

simply going to acquire a certain set of skills. Instead, he found himself all at once enclosed in a fraternity. And in this fraternity, even though it was military, men were not rated by their outward rank as ensigns, lieutenants, commanders, or whatever. No, herein the world was divided into those who had it and those who did not. This quality, this *it*, was never named, however, nor was it talked about in any way.

2   As to just what this ineffable quality was . . . well, it obviously involved bravery. But it was not bravery in the simple sense of being willing to risk your life. The idea seemed to be that any fool could do that, if that was all that was required, just as any fool could throw away his life in the process. No, the idea here (in the all-enclosing fraternity) seemed to be that a man should have the ability to go up in a hurtling piece of machinery and put his hide on the line and then have the moxie, the reflexes, the experience, the coolness, to pull it back in the last yawning moment—and then to go up again *the next day,* and the next day, and every next day, even if the series should prove infinite—and, ultimately, in its best expression, do so in a cause that means something to thousands, to a people, a nation, to humanity, to God. Nor was there *a test* to show whether or not a pilot had this righteous quality. There was, instead, a seemingly infinite series of tests. A career in flying was like climbing one of those ancient Babylonian pyramids made up of a dizzy progression of steps and ledges, a ziggurat, a pyramid extraordinarily high and steep; and the idea was to prove at every foot of the way up that pyramid that you were one of the elected and anointed ones who had *the right stuff* and could move higher and higher and even— ultimately, God willing, one day—that you might be able to join that special few at the very top, that elite who had the capacity to bring tears to men's eyes, the very Brotherhood of the Right Stuff itself.

3   None of this was to be mentioned, and yet it was acted out in a way that a young man could not fail to understand. When a new flight (i.e., a class) of trainees arrived at Pensacola, they were brought into an auditorium for a little lecture. An officer would tell them: "Take a look at the man on either side of you." Quite a few actually swiveled their heads this way and that, in the interest of appearing diligent. Then the officer would say: "One of the three of you is not going to make it!"— meaning, not get his wings. That was the opening theme, the *motif* of primary training. We already know that one-third of you do not have the right stuff—it only remains to find out who.

4   Furthermore, that was the way it turned out. At every level in one's progress up that staggeringly high pyramid, the world was once

more divided into those men who had the right stuff to continue the climb and those who had to be *left behind* in the most obvious way. Some were eliminated in the course of the opening classroom work, as either not smart enough or not hardworking enough, and were left behind. Then came the basic flight instruction, in single-engine, propeller-driven trainers, and a few more—even though the military tried to make this stage easy—were washed out and left behind. Then came more demanding levels, one after the other, formation flying, instrument flying, jet training, all-weather flying, gunnery, and at each level more were washed out and left behind. By this point easily a third of the original candidates had been, indeed, eliminated . . . from the ranks of those who might prove to have the right stuff.

5   In the Navy, in addition to the stages that Air Force trainees went through, the neophyte always had waiting for him, out in the ocean, a certain grim gray slab; namely, the deck of an aircraft carrier; and with it perhaps the most difficult routine in military flying, carrier landings. He was shown films about it, he heard lectures about it, and he knew that carrier landings were hazardous. He first practiced touching down on the shape of a flight deck painted on an airfield. He was instructed to touch down and gun right off. This was safe enough—the shape didn't move, at least—but it could do terrible things to, let us say, the gyroscope of the soul. *That shape!—it's so damned small!* And more candidates were washed out and left behind. Then came the day, without warning, when those who remained were sent out over the ocean for the first of many days of reckoning with the slab. The first day was always a clear day with little wind and a calm sea. The carrier was so steady that it seemed, from up there in the air, to be resting on pilings, and the candidate usually made his first carrier landing successfully, with relief and even *élan*. Many young candidates looked like terrific aviators up to that very point—and it was not until they were actually standing on the carrier deck that they first began to wonder if they had the proper stuff, after all. In the training film the flight deck was a grand piece of gray geometry, perilous, to be sure, but an amazing abstract shape as one looks down upon it on the screen. And yet once the newcomer's two feet were on it . . . *Geometry*—my God, man, this is a . . . skillet! It *heaved*, it moved up and down underneath his feet, it pitched up, it pitched down, it rolled to port (this great beast *rolled!*) and it rolled to starboard, as the ship moved into the wind and, therefore, into the waves, and the wind kept sweeping across, sixty feet up in the air out in the open sea, and there were no railings whatsoever. This was a *skillet!*—a frying pan!

—a short-order grill!—not gray but black, smeared with skid marks from one end to the other and glistening with pools of hydraulic fluid and the occasional jet-fuel slick, all of it still hot, sticky, greasy, runny, virulent from God knows what traumas—still ablaze!—consumed in detonations, explosions, flames, combustion, roars, shrieks, whines, blasts, horrible shudders, fracturing impacts, as little men in screaming red and yellow and purple and green shirts with black Mickey Mouse helmets over their ears skittered about on the surface as if for their very lives (you've said it now!), hooking fighter planes onto the catapult shuttles so that they can explode their afterburners and be slung off the deck in a red-mad fury with a *kaboom!* that pounds through the entire deck— a procedure that seems absolutely controlled, orderly, sublime, however, compared to what he is about to watch as aircraft return to the ship for what is known in the engineering stoicisms of the military as "recovery and arrest." To say that an F-4 was coming back onto this heaving barbecue from out of the sky at a speed of 135 knots . . . that might have been the truth in the training lecture, but it did not begin to get across the idea of what the newcomer saw from the deck itself, because it created the notion that perhaps the plane was gliding in. On the deck one knew differently! As the aircraft came closer and the carrier heaved on into the waves and the plane's speed did not diminish and the deck did not grow steady—indeed, it pitched up and down five or ten feet per greasy heave—one experienced a neural alarm that no lecture could have prepared him for: This is not an *airplane* coming toward me, it is a brick with some poor sonofabitch riding it *(someone much like myself!)*, and it is not *gliding,* it is *falling,* a fifty-thousand-pound brick, headed not for a stripe on the deck but for *me*—and with a horrible *smash!* it hits the skillet, and with a blur of momentum as big as a freight train's it hurtles toward the far end of the deck—another blinding storm!—another roar as the pilot pushes the throttle up to full military power and another smear of rubber screams out over the skillet—and this is nominal!—quite okay!—for a wire stretched across the deck has grabbed the hook on the end of the plane as it hit the deck tail down, and the smash was the rest of the fifteen-ton brute slamming onto the deck, as it tripped up, so that it is now straining against the wire at full throttle, in case it hadn't held and the plane had "boltered" off the end of the deck and had to struggle up into the air again. And already the Mickey Mouse helmets are running toward the fiery monster . . .

6   And the candidate, looking on, begins to *feel* that great heaving sun-blazing deathboard of a deck wallowing in his own vestibular system

—and suddenly he finds himself backed up against his own limits. He ends up going to the flight surgeon with so-called conversion symptoms. Overnight he develops blurred vision or numbness in his hands and feet or sinusitis so severe that he cannot tolerate changes in altitude. On one level the symptom is real. He really cannot see too well or use his fingers or stand the pain. But somewhere in his subconscious he knows it is a plea and a beg-off; he shows not the slightest concern (the flight surgeon notes) that the condition might be permanent and affect him in whatever life awaits him outside the arena of the right stuff.

7   Those who remained, those who qualified for carrier duty—and even more so those who later on qualified for *night* carrier duty—began to feel a bit like Gideon's warriors. *So many have been left behind!* The young warriors were now treated to a deathly sweet and quite unmentionable sight. They could gaze at length upon the crushed and wilted pariahs who had washed out. They could inspect those who did not have that righteous stuff.

8   The military did not have very merciful instincts. Rather than packing up these poor souls and sending them home, the Navy, like the Air Force and the Marines, would try to make use of them in some other role, such as flight controller. So the washout has to keep taking classes with the rest of his group, even though he can no longer touch an airplane. He sits there in the classes staring at sheets of paper with cataracts of sheer human mortification over his eyes while the rest steal looks at him . . . this man reduced to an ant, this untouchable, this poor sonofabitch. And in what test had he been found wanting? Why, it seemed to be nothing less than *manhood* itself. Naturally, this was never mentioned, either. Yet there it was. *Manliness, manhood, manly courage* . . . there was something ancient, primordial, irresistible about the challenge of this stuff, no matter what a sophisticated and rational age one might think he lived in.

9   Perhaps because it could not be talked about, the subject began to take on superstitious and even mystical outlines. A man either had it or he didn't! There was no such thing as having *most* of it. Moreover, it could blow at any seam. One day a man would be ascending the pyramid at a terrific clip, and the next—bingo!—he would reach his own limits in the most unexpected way. Conrad and Schirra met an Air Force pilot who had had a great pal at Tyndall Air Force Base in Florida. This man had been the budding ace of the training class; he had flown the hottest fighter-style trainer, the T-38, like a dream; and then he began the routine step of being checked out in the T-33. The T-33 was not

nearly as hot an aircraft as the T-38; it was essentially the old P-80 jet fighter. It had an exceedingly small cockpit. The pilot could barely move his shoulders. It was the sort of airplane of which everybody said, "You don't get into it, you *wear* it." Once inside a T-33 cockpit this man, this budding ace, developed claustrophobia of the most paralyzing sort. He tried everything to overcome it. He even went to a psychiatrist, which was a serious mistake for a military officer if his superiors learned of it. But nothing worked. He was shifted over to flying jet transports, such as the C-135. Very demanding and necessary aircraft they were, too, and he was still spoken of as an excellent pilot. But as everyone knew—and, again, it was never explained in so many words—only those who were assigned to fighter squadrons, the "fighter jocks," as they called each other with a self-satisfied irony, remained in the true fraternity. Those assigned to transports were not humiliated like washouts—*somebody* had to fly those planes—nevertheless, they, too, had been *left behind* for lack of the right stuff.

10   Or a man could go for a routine physical one fine day, feeling like a million dollars, and be grounded for *fallen arches.* It happened!—just like that! (And try raising them.) Or for breaking his wrist and losing only *part* of its mobility. Or for a minor deterioration of eyesight, or for any of hundreds of reasons that would make no difference to a man in an ordinary occupation. As a result all fighter jocks began looking upon doctors as their natural enemies. Going to see a flight surgeon was a no-gain proposition; a pilot could only hold his own or lose in the doctor's office. To be grounded for a medical reason was no humiliation, looked at objectively. But it was a humiliation, nonetheless!—for it meant you no longer had that indefinable, unutterable, integral stuff. (It could blow at *any* seam.)

11   All the hot young fighter jocks began trying to test the limits themselves in a superstitious way. They were like believing Presbyterians of a century before who used to probe their own experience to see if they were truly among *the elect.* When a fighter pilot was in training, whether in the Navy or the Air Force, his superiors were continually spelling out strict rules for him, about the use of the aircraft and conduct in the sky. They repeatedly forbade so-called hot-dog stunts, such as outside loops, buzzing, flat-hatting, hedgehopping and flying under bridges. But somehow one got the message that the man who truly *had* it could ignore those rules—not that he should make a point of it, but that he *could*—and that after all there was only one way to find out— and that in some strange unofficial way, peeking through his fingers, his

instructor halfway expected him to challenge all the limits. They would give a lecture about how a pilot should never fly without a good solid breakfast—eggs, bacon, toast, and so forth—because if he tried to fly with his blood-sugar level too low, it could impair his alertness. Naturally, the next day every hot dog in the unit would get up and have a breakfast consisting of one cup of black coffee and take off and go up into a vertical climb until the weight of the ship exactly canceled out the upward pull of the engine and his air speed was zero, and he would hang there for one thick adrenal instant—and then fall like a rock, until one of three things happened: he keeled over nose first and regained his aerodynamics and all was well, he went into a spin and fought his way out of it, or he went into a spin and had to eject or crunch it, which was always supremely possible.

12   Likewise, "hassling"—mock dogfighting—was strictly forbidden, and so naturally young fighter jocks could hardly wait to go up in, say, a pair of F-100s and start the duel by making a pass at each other at 800 miles an hour, the winner being the pilot who could slip in behind the other one and get locked in on his tail ("wax his tail"), and it was not uncommon for some eager jock to try too tight an outside turn and have his engine flame out, whereupon, unable to restart it, he has to eject . . . and he shakes his fist at the victor as he floats down by parachute and his half-a-million-dollar aircraft goes *kaboom!* on the palmetto grass or the desert floor, and he starts thinking about how he can get together with the other guy back at the base in time for the two of them to get their stories straight before the investigation: "I don't know what happened, sir. I was pulling up after a target run, and it just flamed out on me." Hassling was forbidden, and hassling that led to the destruction of an aircraft was a serious court-martial offense, and the man's superiors knew that the engine hadn't *just flamed out,* but every unofficial impulse on the base seemed to be saying: "Hell, we wouldn't give you a nickel for a pilot who hasn't done some crazy rat-racing like that. It's all part of the right stuff."

13   The other side of this impulse showed up in the reluctance of the young jocks to admit it when they had maneuvered themselves into a bad corner they couldn't get out of. There were two reasons why a fighter pilot hated to declare an emergency. First, it triggered a complex and very public chain of events at the field: all other incoming flights were held up, including many of one's comrades who were probably low on fuel; the fire trucks came trundling out to the runway like yellow toys (as seen from way up there), the better to illustrate one's hapless state;

and the bureaucracy began to crank up the paper monster for the investigation that always followed. And second, to declare an emergency, one first had to reach that conclusion in his own mind, which to the young pilot was the same as saying: "A minute ago I still *had* it—now I need your help!" To have a bunch of young fighter pilots up in the air thinking this way used to drive flight controllers crazy. They would see a ship beginning to drift off the radar, and they couldn't rouse the pilot on the microphone for anything other than a few meaningless mumbles, and they would know he was probably out there with engine failure at a low altitude, trying to reignite by lowering his auxiliary generator rig, which had a little propeller that was supposed to spin in the slipstream like a child's pinwheel.

14   "Whiskey Kilo Two Eight, do you want to declare an emergency?"

15   *This* would rouse him!—to say: "Negative, negative, Whiskey Kilo Two Eight is not declaring an emergency."

16   Kaboom. Believers in the right stuff would rather crash and burn.

17   One fine day, after he had joined a fighter squadron, it would dawn on the young pilot exactly how the losers in the great fraternal competition were now being left behind. Which is to say, not by instructors or other superiors or by failures at prescribed levels of competence, but by death. At this point the essence of the enterprise would begin to dawn on him. Slowly, step by step, the ante had been raised until he was now involved in what was surely the grimmest and grandest gamble of manhood. Being a fighter pilot—for that matter, simply taking off in a single-engine jet fighter of the Century series, such as an F-102, or any of the military's other marvelous bricks with fins on them—presented a man, on a perfectly sunny day, with more ways to get himself killed than his wife and children could imagine in their wildest fears. If he was barreling down the runway at two hundred miles an hour, completing the takeoff run, and the board started lighting up red, should he (a) abort the takeoff (and try to wrestle with the monster, which was gorged with jet fuel, out in the sand beyond the end of the runway) or (b) eject (and hope that the goddamned human cannonball trick works at zero altitude and he doesn't shatter an elbow or a kneecap on the way out) or (c) continue the takeoff and deal with the problem aloft (knowing full well that the ship may be on fire and therefore seconds away from exploding)? He would have one second to sort out the options and act, and this kind of little workaday decision came up all the time. Occasionally a man would look coldly at the binary problem he was now confronting every

day—Right Stuff/Death—and decide it wasn't worth it and voluntarily shift over to transports or reconnaissance or whatever. And his comrades would wonder, for a day or so, what evil virus had invaded his soul . . . as they left him behind. More often, however, the reverse would happen. Some college graduate would enter Navy aviation through the Reserves, simply as an alternative to the Army draft, fully intending to return to civilian life, to some waiting profession or family business; would become involved in the obsessive business of ascending the ziggurat pyramid of flying; and, at the end of his enlistment, would astound everyone back home and very likely himself as well by signing up for another one. What on earth got into him? He couldn't explain it. After all, the very words for it had been amputated. A Navy study showed that two-thirds of the fighter pilots who were rated in the top rungs of their groups—i.e., the hottest young pilots—reenlisted when the time came, and practically all were college graduates. By this point, a young fighter jock was like the preacher in *Moby Dick* who climbs up into the pulpit on a rope ladder and then pulls the ladder up behind him; except the pilot could not use the words necessary to express the vital lessons. Civilian life, and even home and hearth, now seemed not only far away but far *below*, back down many levels of the pyramid of the right stuff.

18   A fighter pilot soon found he wanted to associate only with other fighter pilots. Who else could understand the nature of the little proposition (right stuff/death) they were all dealing with? And what other subject could compare with it? It was riveting! To talk about it in so many words was forbidden, of course. The very words *death, danger, bravery, fear* were not to be uttered except in the occasional specific instance or for ironic effect. Nevertheless, the subject could be adumbrated in *code* or *by example*. Hence the endless evenings of pilots huddled together talking about flying. On these long and drunken evenings (the bane of their family life) certain theorems would be propounded and demonstrated—and all by *code* and *example*. One theorem was: There are no *accidents* and no fatal flaws in the machines; there are only pilots with the wrong stuff. (I.e., blind Fate can't kill me.) When Bud Jennings crashed and burned in the swamps at Jacksonville, the other pilots in Peter Conrad's squadron said: *How could he have been so stupid?* It turned out that Jennings had gone up in the SNJ with his cockpit canopy opened in a way that was expressly forbidden in the manual, and carbon monoxide had been sucked in from the exhaust, and he passed out and crashed. All agreed that Bud Jennings was a good guy and a good pilot, but his epitaph on the ziggurat was: *How could he have*

been so stupid? This seemed shocking at first, but by the time Conrad
had reached the end of that bad string at Pax River, he was capable of
his own corollary to the theorem: viz., no single factor ever killed a pilot;
there was always a chain of mistakes. But what about Ted Whelan, who
fell like a rock from 8,100 feet when his parachute failed? Well, the
parachute was merely part of the chain: first, someone should have
caught the structural defect that resulted in the hydraulic leak that
triggered the emergency; second, Whelan did not check out his seat-
parachute rig, and the drogue failed to separate the main parachute from
the seat; but even after those two mistakes, Whelan had fifteen or
twenty seconds, as he fell, to disengage himself from the seat and open
the parachute manually. Why just stare at the scenery coming up to
smack you in the face! And everyone nodded. (He failed—but I
wouldn't have!) Once the theorem and the corollary were understood,
the Navy's statistics about one in every four Navy aviators dying meant
nothing. The figures were averages, and averages applied to those with
average stuff.

19   A riveting subject, especially if it were one's own hide that was on
the line. Every evening at bases all over America, there were military
pilots huddled in officers clubs eagerly cutting the right stuff up in coded
slices so they could talk about it. What more compelling topic of conversation was there in the world? In the Air Force there were even pilots
who would ask the tower for priority landing clearance so that they could
make the beer call on time, at 4 P.M. sharp, at the Officers Club. They
would come right out and state the reason. The drunken rambles began
at four and sometimes went on for ten or twelve hours. Such conversations! They diced that righteous stuff up into little bits, bowed ironically
to it, stumbled blindfolded around it, groped, lurched, belched, stag-
gered, bawled, sang, roared, and feinted at it with self-deprecating
humor. Nevertheless!—they never mentioned it by name. No, they used
the approved codes, such as: "Like a jerk I got myself into a hell of a
corner today." They told of how they "lucked out of it." To get across
the extreme peril of his exploit, one would use certain oblique cues. He
would say, "I looked over at Robinson"—who would be known to the
listeners as a non-com who sometimes rode backseat to read radar—"and
he wasn't talking any more, he was just staring at the radar, like this,
giving it that *zombie* look. Then I *knew* I was in trouble!" Beautiful!
Just right! For it would also be known to the listeners that the non-coms
advised one another: *"Never* fly with a lieutenant. *Avoid* captains and
majors. Hell, man, do yourself a favor: don't fly with anybody below

colonel." Which in turn said: "Those young bucks shoot dice with death!" And yet once in the air the non-com had his own standards. He was determined to remain as outwardly cool as the pilot, so that when the pilot did something that truly petrified him, he would say nothing; instead, he would turn silent, catatonic, like a zombie. Perfect! *Zombie.* There you had it, compressed into a single word all of the foregoing. I'm a hell of a pilot! I shoot dice with death! And now all you fellows know it! And I haven't spoken of that unspoken stuff even once!

20   The talking and drinking began at the beer call, and then the boys would break for dinner and come back afterward and get more wasted and more garrulous or else more quietly fried, drinking good cheap PX booze until 2 a.m. The night was young! Why not get the cars and go out for a little proficiency run? It seemed that every fighter jock thought himself an ace driver, and he would do anything to obtain a hot car, especially a sports car, and the drunker he was, the more convinced he would be about his driving skills, as if the right stuff, being indivisible, carried over into any enterprise whatsoever, under any conditions. A little proficiency run, boys! (There's only one way to find out!) And they would roar off in close formation from, say, Nellis Air Force Base, down Route 15, into Las Vegas, barreling down the highway, rat-racing, sometimes four abreast, jockeying for position, piling into the most listless curve in the desert flats as if they were trying to root each other out of the groove at the Rebel 500—and then bursting into downtown Las Vegas with a rude fraternal roar like the Hell's Angels—and the natives chalked it up to youth and drink and the bad element that the Air Force attracted. They knew nothing about the right stuff, of course.

21   More fighter pilots died in automobiles than in airplanes. Fortunately, there was always some kindly soul up the chain to certify the papers "line of duty," so that the widow could get a better break on the insurance. That was okay and only proper because somehow the system itself had long ago said *Skol!* and *Quite right!* to the military cycle of Flying & Drinking and Drinking & Driving, as if there were no other way. Every young fighter jock knew the feeling of getting two or three hours' sleep and then waking up at 5:30 a.m. and having a few cups of coffee, a few cigarettes, and then carting his poor quivering liver out to the field for another day of flying. There were those who arrived not merely hungover but still drunk, slapping oxygen tank cones over their faces and trying to burn the alcohol out of their systems, and then going up, remarking later: "I don't *advise* it, you understand, but it *can* be done." (Provided you have the right stuff, you miserable pudknocker.)

22   Air Force and Navy airfields were usually on barren or marginal stretches of land and would have looked especially bleak and Low Rent to an ordinary individual in the chilly light of dawn. But to a young pilot there was an inexplicable bliss to coming out to the flight line while the sun was just beginning to cook up behind the rim of the horizon, so that the whole field was still in shadow and the ridges in the distance were in silhouette and the flight line was a monochrome of Exhaust Fume Blue, and every little red light on top of the water towers or power stanchions looked dull, shriveled, congealed, and the runway lights, which were still on, looked faded, and even the landing lights on a fighter that had just landed and was taxiing in were no longer dazzling, as they would be at night, and looked instead like shriveled gobs of candlepower out there—and yet it was beautiful, exhilarating!—for he was revved up with adrenalin, anxious to take off before the day broke, to burst up into the sunlight over the ridges before all those thousands of comatose souls down there, still dead to the world, snug in home and hearth, even came to their senses. To take off in an F-100F at dawn and cut on the afterburner and hurtle twenty-five thousand feet up into the sky in thirty seconds, so suddenly that you felt not like a bird but like a trajectory, yet with full control, full control of *four tons* of thrust, all of which flowed from your will and through your fingertips, with the huge engine right beneath you, so close that it was as if you were riding it bareback, until all at once you were supersonic, an event registered on earth by a tremendous cracking boom that shook windows, but up here only by the fact that you now felt utterly free of the earth—to describe it, even to wife, child, near ones and dear ones, seemed impossible. So the pilot kept it to himself, along with an even more indescribable . . . an even more sinfully inconfessable . . . feeling of superiority, appropriate to him and to his kind, lone bearers of the right stuff.

23   From *up here* at dawn the pilot looked down upon poor hopeless Las Vegas (or Yuma, Corpus Christi, Meridian, San Bernardino, or Dayton) and began to wonder: How can all of them down there, those poor souls who will soon be waking up and trudging out of their minute rectangles and inching along their little noodle highways toward whatever slots and grooves make up their everyday lives—how could they live like that, with such earnestness, if they had the faintest idea of what it was like up here in this righteous zone?

24   But of course! Not only the washed-out, grounded, and dead pilots had been left behind—but also all of those millions of sleepwalking souls who never even attempted the great gamble. The entire world below

. . . left behind. Only at this point can one begin to understand just how big, how titanic, the ego of the military pilot could be. The world was used to enormous egos in artists, actors, entertainers of all sorts, in politicians, sports figures, and even journalists, because they had such familiar and convenient ways to show them off. But that slim young man over there in uniform, with the enormous watch on his wrist and the withdrawn look on his face, that young officer who is so shy that he can't even open his mouth unless the subject is flying—that young pilot— well, my friends, his ego is even *bigger!*—so big, it's *breathtaking!* Even in the 1950's it was difficult for civilians to comprehend such a thing, but *all* military officers and many enlisted men tended to feel superior to civilians. It was really quite ironic, given the fact that for a good thirty years the rising business classes in the cities had been steering their sons away from the military, as if from a bad smell, and the officer corps had never been held in lower esteem. Well, career officers returned the contempt in trumps. They looked upon themselves as men who lived by higher standards of behavior than civilians, as men who were the bearers and protectors of the most important values of American life, who maintained a sense of discipline while civilians abandoned themselves to hedonism, who maintained a sense of honor while civilians lived by opportunism and greed. Opportunism and greed: there you had your much-vaunted corporate business world. Khrushchev was right about one thing: when it came time to hang the capitalist West, an American businessman would sell him the rope. When the showdown came—and the showdowns always came—not all the wealth in the world or all the sophisticated nuclear weapons and radar and missile systems it could buy would take the place of those who had the uncritical willingness to face danger, those who, in short, had the right stuff.

25   In fact, the feeling was so righteous, so exalted, it could become religious. Civilians seldom understood this, either. There was no one to teach them. It was no longer the fashion for serious writers to de- scribe the glories of war. Instead, they dwelt upon its horrors, often with cynicism or disgust. It was left to the occasional pilot with a literary flair to provide a glimpse of the pilot's self-conception in its heavenly or spiritual aspect. When a pilot named Robert Scott flew his P-43 over Mount Everest, quite a feat at the time, he brought his hand up and snapped a salute to his fallen adversary. He thought he had *defeated* the mountain, surmounting all the forces of nature that had made it formidable. And why not? "God is my co-pilot," he said —that became the title of his book—and he meant it. So did the most

gifted of all the pilot authors, the Frenchman Antoine de Saint-Exu-péry. As he gazed down upon the world . . . from up there . . . during transcontinental flights, the good Saint-Ex saw civilization as a series of tiny fragile patches clinging to the otherwise barren rock of Earth. He felt like a lonely sentinel, a protector of those vulnerable little oases, ready to lay down his life in their behalf, if necessary; a saint, in short, true to his name, flying up here at the right hand of God. The good Saint-Ex! And he was not the only one. He was merely the one who put it into words most beautifully and anointed himself before the altar of the right stuff.

QUESTIONS

Ideas

1. While recognizing and allowing for differences among individuals, Wolfe presents a generalized profile of a military test pilot. He suggests that to succeed, a test pilot needs "the right stuff." What is "the right stuff"? What qualities and attributes are necessary for success as a military test pilot?

2. What does Wolfe mean when he says that the men were in "an enclosing fraternity"? How does that fact affect their view of themselves and their behavior? Is such isolation necessary?

3. In paragraphs 11 and 12, Wolfe presents two sides of the test pilots—the official and the unofficial. Why is it important for us to see both sides? What effect does Wolfe create with these contrasted views?

4. Paragraphs 22 and 23 are written from the point of view of the pilot. We are taken up with him into the sky, and we enter into and read his thoughts. Can Wolfe legitimately include such details even though he himself never piloted a jet?

5. What point is made at the end of paragraph 21? In paragraphs 24–25? In paragraph 9?

Organization

6. The overall structure of this selection breaks down into something like this: paragraphs 1–4; 5; 6–10; 11–16; 17–25. Explain what unifies the paragraphs in each grouping. And explain how each section is related to the one before. (Why is paragraph 5 a self-contained unit?)

7. Paragraph 5—the odd one in the structure of the whole—is extremely long. Is there a reason for this? What would be the effect of breaking it

into two or three or even more parts? What is the purpose of this paragraph?

8. Read the first two paragraphs for coherence. Note how within each paragraph Wolfe joins one sentence to another, and also how he links one paragraph to another.

9. Wolfe doesn't bother with interparagraph transitions in paragraphs 14–17. Why not?

10. What do you notice about the final sentence of each paragraph? Are there any differences among the various repetitions and variations? Consider, for example, the final words of paragraphs 6 and 7.

11. In paragraphs 17 and 18 Wolfe makes different points at the beginning and at the end. Explain how, in each paragraph, Wolfe gets from his opening idea to his concluding one.

Sentences

12. In paragraph 5 Wolfe uses an extraordinarily long sentence beginning "This was a skillet. . . ." What would be lost or gained if this sentence were divided into three or four parts?

13. What is the effect of the two long sentences of paragraph 22? Should these two sentences be converted to a series of shorter ones? Why or why not?

14. In the last sentence of paragraph 2 Wolfe stacks a series of parallel phrases:

> a dizzy progression of steps
> a ziggurat
> a pyramid

and again:

> that special few
> that elite
> the very Brotherhood

What would be lost if in each of these series there were not three items, but only two? (Or only one?)

15. Explain which version of the following sentence you prefer.

> *Wolfe:* In the Navy, in addition to the stages that Air Force trainees went through, the neophyte always had waiting for him, out in the ocean, a certain grim gray slab! (5)

> *Revision:* In addition to the stages that Air Force trainees went through, in the Navy the neophyte always had a grim gray slab waiting for him out in the ocean.

16. Wolfe mixes the lengths of his sentences effectively throughout "The Right Stuff." Look closely at paragraph 2, attending both to the variety

of sentence lengths and to the long sentence with its series of parallel
pieces:

the moxie, the reflexes, the experience, the coolness:

and later:

to go up, to go up again the next day
and the next day
and every next day
in a cause that means something to thousands,
to a people,
a nation,
to humanity,
to God.

What is the effect of this elaboration and repetition? Why does Wolfe mix
in some short sentences as well?

Words

17. Throughout "The Right Stuff" Wolfe mixes idiomatic, colloquial language
with formal, technical diction. Find passages where one or the other
predominates.

18. In paragraph 5 Wolfe compares the slab, the aircraft carrier, to a skillet,
a frying pan, a short-order grill. Does that comparison in its three variations
seem appropriate? Farfetched? What is Wolfe's point in making it? What
details does he use to elaborate and extend the analogy?

19. How do the quoted remarks in paragraph 19 help us understand what
Wolfe means by "the right stuff"? Why don't the pilots use the words
Wolfe uses in paragraph 18: "death," "danger," "bravery," "fear"?

20. Wolfe makes frequent use of triplets—groups of three words, phrases or
details. He often uses them at the ends of paragraphs, as in the following
examples:

ancient, primordial, irresistible (8)

manliness, manhood, manly courage (8)

indefinable, unutterable, integral (10)

Find two more examples. Try mentally eliminating one of the three terms
from each set, as in this revised version of the triplet from paragraph 8:
"ancient and primordial" or "ancient and irresistible." What is different
about the triplet?

21. What is the effect of the direct speech, the dialogue, that Wolfe uses in
paragraphs 12–15?

22. What is the effect of Wolfe's repetitions and variations of the term "the right stuff"? Why is the term capitalized at the end of paragraph 2?

23. Wolfe frequently italicizes words and phrases. Explain the effect of each of the following:

    it (1)
    the next day; the right stuff; a test (2)
    left behind (4)
    that shape—it's so damned small; heaved; rolled (5)

Suggestions for Writing

A. Write an essay explaining what field you will go into—what kind of work you expect to do, and why. Explain what "the right stuff" is that you think necessary for success in whatever you expect to do.

B. Interview three or four athletes, teachers, musicians, scholars, students, who have what you think of as "the right stuff." Write an essay presenting a composite picture of a _____ with the right stuff.

C. Write imitations of the sentences discussed in questions 13–16.

Acknowledgments

1982 by Annie Dillard. Reprinted by permission of Harper & Row, Publishers, Inc.

"Transfiguration" (pp. 13–19) from *Holy The Firm* by Annie Dillard. Copyright © 1977 by Annie Dillard. Reprinted by permission of Harper & Row, Publishers, Inc.

"God's Tooth" (pp. 35–51) from *Holy The Firm* by Annie Dillard. Copyright © 1977 by Annie Dillard. Reprinted by permission of Harper & Row, Publishers, Inc.

"Charles Darwin," Loren C. Eiseley, *Scientific American* (February 1956, pp. 62–72). Copyright © 1956 by Scientific American, Inc. Reprinted with permission. All rights reserved.

"The Judgment of the Birds" from *The Immense Journey* by Loren Eiseley. Copyright © 1956 by Loren Eiseley. Reprinted by permission of Random House, Inc.

"The Dance of the Frogs" (pp. 106–115) from *The Star Thrower* by Loren Eiseley. Copyright © 1978 by the Estate of Loren C. Eiseley, Mabel L. Eiseley, Executrix. Reprinted by permission of Times Books, a division of Random House, Inc.

"The Running Man" from *All the Strange Hours: The Excavation of a Life* by Loren Eiseley. Copyright © 1965 by Loren Eiseley. Reprinted with the permission of Charles Scribner's Sons.

"The Company Man" (pp. 18–19) from *Close to Home* by Ellen Goodman. Copyright © 1979 by The Washington Post Company. Reprinted by permission of Simon & Schuster, Inc.

"It's Failure, Not Success" (pp. 32–33) from *Close to Home* by Ellen Goodman. Copyright © 1979 by The Washington Post Company. Reprinted by permission of Simon & Schuster, Inc.

About the Editors

John Clifford is presently an Associate Professor of English at the University of North Carolina at Wilmington where he also directs the writing program. He has taught literature and writing at Queens College, CUNY, and the University of Pennsylvania. During 1980–81 he was an NEH Fellow-in-Residence in Literature and Literacy at the University of Southern California. He has published articles in *Research in the Teaching of English, College Composition and Communication,* and *Freshman English News.* He received his Ph.D. from New York University.

His current interests include writing theory, the rhetorical criticism of nonfiction, and reader-response theory. Two recent essays were included in *The Territory of Language* (Southern Illinois University Press, 1986) and *Perspectives on Research and Scholarship in Composition* (MLA, 1985). He has also published a rhetoric with Richard Veit, *Writing, Reading, and Research* (Macmillan, 1985), and is now working on a text on the teaching of literature.

Robert DiYanni is an Associate Professor of English at Pace University, Pleasantville, where he directs the writing program and teaches British and American Literature and Composition. He received his B.A. from Rutgers and his Ph.D. from the City University of New York. His publications include articles and reviews on various aspects of English and American literature and on rhetoric and composition. Included also are a number of textbooks: *Connections: Reading, Writing, and Thinking* (Boynton/Cook, 1985); *Literature: Reading Fiction, Poetry, Drama, and the Essay* (Random House, 1986); and a pair of collaborations with Eric Gould and Bill Smith, *The Art of Reading* and *The Craft of Writing,* both forthcoming from Random House. He is currently writing a book on George Orwell.